Pelican Books
Philosophy Through Its Past

Ted Honderich is Professor of Philosophy at University College London. He has been Reader and Lecturer there, Lecturer at the University of Sussex, and Visiting Professor at Yale and the City University of New York. He is the author of *Punishment: The Supposed Justifications* (1969) and *Violence for Equality: Inquiries in Political Philosophy* (Pelican, 1980), and of many articles in philosophical journals. He is the editor of *Essays on Freedom of Action* (1973), *Social Ends and Political Means* (1976) and, with Myles Burnyeat, of *Philosophy As It Is* (Pelican, 1979), the companion volume to this one. He is the general editor of three series of books, including The International Library of Philosophy and Scientific Methods, The Arguments of the Philosophers, and The Problems of Philosophy: Their Past and Present.

PHILOSOPHY THROUGH ITS PAST

Edited and introduced by Ted Honderich

Penguin Books

Penguin Books Ltd, Harmondsworth, Middlesex, England
Penguin Books, 40 West 23rd Street, New York, New York 10010, U.S.A.
Penguin Books Australia Ltd, Ringwood, Victoria, Australia
Penguin Books Canada Ltd, 2801 John Street, Markham, Ontario, Canada L3R 1B4
Penguin Books (N.Z.) Ltd, 182–190 Wairau Road, Auckland 10, New Zealand

Published in Pelican Books 1984
Copyright © Ted Honderich, 1984

The Acknowledgements on pages 9–10
constitute an extension of the copyright
notice

Made and printed in Great Britain by
Cox & Wyman Ltd, Reading
Set in Bembo 9/11 (Linotron 202)

FOR MY SISTER MARY TREGENZA
WITH LOVE AND ADMIRATION

Contents

Contents

Acknowledgements

'Plato: The Individual as an Object of Love' by Gregory Vlastos, reprinted from his *Platonic Studies* by permission of the author and Princeton University Press. Copyright © 1973 by Gregory Vlastos.
'Aristotle: On Learning to be Good' by M. F. Burnyeat, reprinted from *Essays on Aristotle's Ethics*, ed. Amélie Rorty, by permission of the author, the editor and the University of California Press. Copyright © The Regents of the University of California.
'Aquinas: Intentionality' by Anthony Kenny, published here for the first time. Copyright © Anthony Kenny, 1984.
'Hobbes: His Concept of Obligation' by Thomas Nagel, reprinted from *The Philosophical Review*, Vol. LXVIII, No. 1 (January 1959), pp. 68–83, by permission of Thomas Nagel and *The Philosophical Review*.
'Descartes: Cogito and Sum' by Bernard Williams, reprinted from his *Descartes: The Project of Pure Inquiry* (Harmondsworth: Penguin Books, 1978) with the permission of the author and publisher. Copyright © Bernard Williams, 1978.
'Spinoza: His Indentity Theory' by Timothy L. S. Sprigge, reprinted from *Inquiry*, Vol. 20, 1977, pp. 419–45, with the permission of the author, editor and publisher (Universitets Forlaget, Oslo).
'Locke: Primary and Secondary Qualities' by J. L. Mackie, reprinted from his *Problems from Locke* (Oxford: Clarendon Press, 1976) with the permission of Joan Mackie and the Oxford University Press. Copyright © J. L. Mackie, 1976.
'Leibniz and Descartes: Proof and Eternal Truths' by Ian Hacking, Dawes Hicks Lecture on Philosophy to the British Academy, 1973. Reprinted from *Proceedings of the British Academy*, Vol. LIX (1973), with the permission of the author and the Academy, from whom offprints are available.
'Berkeley: His Immaterialism and Kant's Transcendental Idealism' by M. R. Ayers, reprinted from *Idealism Past and Present*, Royal Institute of Philosophy Lectures, 1981, ed. Godfrey Vesey, with the permission of the author, editor and the Cambridge University Press.

'Hume: Action, Reason and Passion' by Barry Stroud, reprinted from his *Hume* (London: Routledge & Kegan Paul, 1977). Reprinted with the permission of the author and publisher. Copyright © Barry Stroud, 1977.

'Kant: The Critique of Pure Reason' by P. F. Strawson, reprinted from his *The Bounds of Sense: An Essay on Kant's Critique of Pure Reason* (London: Methuen, 1960) with the permission of the author and publisher.

'Hegel: On Faces and Skulls' by Alasdair MacIntyre, reprinted from *Hegel: A Collection of Critical Essays* (Garden City, N.Y.: Doubleday, 1972), ed. Alasdair MacIntyre, with the permission of the author and the University of Notre Dame Press, Notre Dame, Ind.

'Mill: The Ends of Life and the Preliminaries of Morality' by Richard Wollheim, reprinted from *The Idea of Freedom: Essays in Honour of Isaiah Berlin* (Oxford: Oxford University Press, 1979), ed. Alan Ryan, with the permission of the author and publisher.

'Marx: The Critique of Justice' by Alan Wood, reprinted from *Philosophy and Public Affairs*, Vol. 1, no. 3 (Spring 1972), with the permission of the author and Princeton University Press. Copyright © 1972 by Princeton University Press.

'Nietzsche: Art and Artists' by Richard Schacht, reprinted from his *Nietzsche* (London: Routledge & Kegan Paul, 1983) with the permission of author and publisher. Copyright © Richard Schacht, 1983.

'Frege: Sense and Reference' by Michael Dummett, reprinted from his *Frege: Philosophy of Language*, 2nd edn (London: Duckworth, 1981), with the permission of the author and publisher.

'Russell: The Theory of Descriptions, Names, and Reality' by A. J. Ayer, reprinted from his *Russell and Moore: The Analytic Heritage* (London: Macmillan, 1971; Cambridge, Mass.: Harvard University Press, 1971) with the permission of author and publisher. Copyright © A. J. Ayer, 1971.

'Wittgenstein: His Treatment of the Will' by Peter Winch, reprinted from *Ratio*, 1968, and his *Ethics and Action* (London: Routledge & Kegan Paul, 1972) with the permission of the author, editor and publisher.

'Sartre: Shame, or, The Problem of Other Minds' by Arthur Danto, reprinted from his *Jean-Paul Sartre* (New York, Viking Press, 1975; London, Fontana Paperbacks, Fontana Modern Masters Series, 1975) with the permission of the author and Fontana Paperbacks.

Introduction

This volume is brother to one called *Philosophy As It Is*, and has the same principal aim. That aim derives from the strong feeling that introductions to philosophy, descriptions of its nature and parts, overviews of its history and certainly potted accounts of the great philosophers do not give much sense of the subject and in fact are no true introduction to it. The largest reason for this is that Western philosophy in its principal tradition is among what might be called the *rigorous* inquiries into the physical and the human world. Despite the fact that philosophy, although bounded by empirical fact, is not itself empirical, it stands closer than is often supposed to the sciences generally, including mathematics, which is also not empirical. It stands closer, certainly, than appears to be supposed by those occasional public librarians who cause a *frisson* of dismay to the browsing philosopher, and increase his sense of professional insecurity, by shelving Hume's *Treatise* or Hegel's *Phenomenology* or Ayer's *Language, Truth and Logic* or Strawson's *Individuals* in with volumes on the occult, the way to the emancipation of the self, the wisdom of the East, and the transcending of schism within psychoanalysis. The rigorousness of philosophy, a matter of clarity, explicitness, distinctions, precision, order, close argument, logical sequence, persistence, completeness and the like – this rigorousness of philosophy does not survive dilution into introductions to it. Indeed, since most of these qualities do not make for easy reading, it is the business of introductions to eschew them. Almost all introductions stand to philosophy itself as impressionistic talk of a proof in mathematics stands to the proof itself.

Philosophy As It Is collected together writings of contemporary philosophers on subjects and problems: John Rawls on justice, Donald Davidson on mental events, Stuart Hampshire on knowledge, Derek Parfit on personal identity, Saul Kripke on identity and necessity, and so on. To look at almost any issue of a philosophical journal, say the *Journal of Philosophy* or *Mind*, is to be aware that contemporary philosophers include very many who are much concerned with the past of philosophy, its history over two millennia. Often enough, they are those same contemporary philosophers who write elsewhere of subjects and problems. The present volume is given over to what was left out of *Philosophy As It Is*, writings by contemporary philosophers which have to do with the past of the subject, the great philosophers.

It would have been a small pleasure to have entitled the present volume 'Philosophy As It Was', but mistaken. It is not an anthology of philosophy as it was. It is not history, although on some pages it moves in that direction. Contemporary philosophers who write about the great philosophers of the past fairly rarely take themselves to be reporting on what was once important or engaging, but no longer is. The purpose of philosophy, one must dare to say, is truth, truth with respect to fundamental and general questions, typically questions whose answering has not yet been made a matter of settled method. The intention of a philosopher who writes about Locke – as certainly it was the intention of John Mackie, a contributor here – is almost always the intention to shed light, by way of a classic text, on what has remained obscure and continues to be compelling. It is the intention to make clear and to answer questions that are *alive*.

If this is the shared intention of the contributors to this volume, it is none the less true that they go about acting on it in different ways. Their contributions are in a sense very diverse. It has sometimes been supposed recently, or so it seems, that there are but two kinds of writing which have to do with the past of the subject. One, in the view of its critics, amounts to the enterprise of no more than recovery of the past. It *does* consist in history, the history of ideas, which, whatever its virtues, is not philosophy. Its intention, in the view of its critics, and by way of examples, is not the truth about love, or the aboutness of language, or the foundations of knowledge, or justice, or the sense and reference of descriptions, or the will, but the doctrines and judgements on these subjects of Plato, Aquinas, Descartes, Marx, Frege or Wittgenstein. The other kind of writing which has to do with the past of the subject, in the view of *its* critics, consists in a kind of philosophical pilferage, or perhaps vandalism. Aristotle, Spinoza, Kant, Nietzsche and even Russell are hunted through or more likely glanced at for those of their ideas which measure up to the ephemeral standard of contemporary philosophical enthusiasm. The rest is discarded. This, say the critics, is no pursuit of truth about the past, certainly, but neither is it the pursuit of truth. The problems of philosophy are such that they have their candidate-solutions within settings, the settings of the thought of particular men. To wrench a candidate-solution out of that setting is to give it no chance of displaying the truth it may contain.

The present volume pretty well destroys that supposed division into two parts of writings having to do with the past of the subject. It goes a good way, I think, to divesting both lots of critics of their stock in trade. The true view, it must be said, is less stark. In place of two parties of philosophers, what we unastonishingly find is a spectrum. Towards one end of the spectrum, in terms of contributors to this book, are Ian Hacking, Michael Ayers, Richard Schacht and Timothy Sprigge. That is not to say they are identical in their use of the past, more particularly in their attitudes to Leibniz, Berkeley, Nietzsche and Spinoza. Towards the other end of the spectrum are P. F. Strawson, Bernard Williams and John Mackie. Again, they are not identical in their outlooks on the past. The first group are more inclined wholly to enter into the thought of, and hope in a resolute way for truth in, the great philosophers about whom they write. The second group are more inclined to suppose that philosophy advances, and that its attention to its past must be selective and certainly judgemental. Between these two groups are the other contributors included in this volume. The spectrum as a whole consists in many different degrees and kinds of inclination.

Each of the pieces in the book is preceded by my introductory précis. The principal recommendation of each précis, perhaps, is simply to make clear what is the primary content of the following piece, and what is secondary. Teachers of philosophy, I think, would be in some considerable agreement that those approaching the subject for the first time, understandably enough, are commonly diverted by this or that secondary consideration. The introductions do not make what follows them simple, and they cannot explain all the conceptions and ideas that are used or mentioned. Help can be had from such good sources, to name two, as A. R. Lacey's *A Dictionary of Philosophy* (London: Routledge & Kegan Paul, 1976) and Paul Edwards' eight-volume *Encyclopedia of Philosophy* (London: Macmillan, 1967).

It is bravely said in the introduction to *Philosophy As It Is* that it comes about as close as a single book can to recording the achievement at this time of ongoing philosophical reflection in English on subjects and problems. It was impossible to include consideration in the present book of all past philosophers who continue to get serious attention. I am sad that Bentham, Kierkegaard and Schopenhauer in particular have not made it, and would like to have included another Greek or two, as well as Augustine, Bergson, Bradley, Brentano, Dewey, Fichte,

Heidegger, Husserl, Meinong, Peirce, Reid and Santayana. I hope, none the less, that the present book has something like the recommendation of its predecessor.

Gregory Vlastos

Plato: The Individual as an Object of Love

Philosophy did not start with Plato, and there is not much more than monumental piety in the idea, expressed often enough, that its subsequent history has consisted in footnotes to his work. Philosophy did come to a first great fruition in his dialogues, and it is as large a truth that they continue to be among the various means whereby the subject is advanced. This is so, perhaps, for the reason that it is one of the many roles of philosophy to provide visions of our existence and its possibilities, and to do so in a way that satisfies reflective demands of a kind that have not often been satisfied, and perhaps cannot truly be satisfied, by the relevant one of philosophy's several competitors, which is religion. Such visions are not victims of a new century's facts, as the theories and speculations of science may be, and, if they are visions which are true to commitments and aspirations which form a true part of human life, they are not victims either of a new century's taste or inclination. The given role of philosophy, certainly, is not one that is valued or even much tolerated by all philosophers. *None* of the endeavours carried forward under the name of philosophy has the esteem of *all* its practitioners, which is no embarrassment. Philosophy consists more in subjects than a subject.

Conceptions of love, one above all, are essential to Plato's dialogues, entering into his propositions, argument and doctrine. They are fundamental to his vision of our existence and in particular to the nature or character of the life whose contemplation he urges upon us. They are among the several things that give the whole of that contemplated life the cast of feeling which it has.

In the following chapter from his admirable book, *Platonic Studies*, Gregory Vlastos comes to a clear and succinct view of Plato on love,

Plato, 428–348 B.C. Pupil of Socrates and the founder of the Academy in Athens, describable as the first university. The earliest European philosopher whose works substantially survive. Attempted without success to found his utopia, in Sicily.

or a most significant part of Plato on love, and he subjects what he finds to judgement. It is a judgement which is generous, but of a resolute independence. If his central concern is with what is of greater importance, he does not at all eschew questions which, if smaller, are engaging. Was the love which Plato idealized what we now call 'Platonic love', which is to say purely spiritual love for one of the opposite sex? What touch of justice is there in the description of his dialogue, the *Symposium*, as 'a sort of lurid devotional book – the sulphurous breviary of the pederast'?

Vlastos begins, as he says, by setting out a standard by which to judge Plato's conception of love. It is a standard got from the other of the greatest Greek philosophers, Aristotle. To get this ground of comparison, what is necessary is a kind of inquiry which is fundamental to 'Greek philosophy' – that is, contemporary philosophy whose subject-matter is the Greek philosophers, or a subject-matter pursued by way of study of the Greek philosophers. This kind of inquiry combines classical scholarship and a philosophical intention, sometimes an intention having to do with philosophy as visionary, often an intention having to do with the circumscribed questions of moral philosophy, say, or epistemology. For the whole enterprise to count as *philosophy*, necessarily, the questions of classical scholarship which are opened must be the right ones, and, it needs to be said, the place given to classical scholarship must be limited. Vlastos satisfies these demands. Principally through an examination of the Greek which is transliterated into *philein*, *philos* and *philia*, we come to Aristotle's idea that to love another person is to wish for that person's good for that person's sake, and to try to secure it. This is modified by him, however, by the cool addition that perfect or complete love also has benefits for the loving as distinct from the loved person, benefits of a certain kind. The modification has an unhappy consequence.

The second section of the chapter is concerned with the conception of love in one of Plato's early dialogues, the *Lysis*. Here, when Plato was more subject to the influence of Socrates than later, what is advanced is a picture of love as no less than profitable. Love is taken to be utility-love, a response to the producing of goods for the loving person by the person loved. '. . . if one were in want of nothing, one would feel no affection . . .' There are yet more disagreeable consequences of this conception, such as to falsify it as a true general account of love. It is in fact not an account which meets the standard derived from Aristotle. It is not so adequate as the Aristotelian conception. It is an account, however, which involves the idea of what will be important, the final or ultimate thing or end – *prōton philon* – to which all things are or ought to be taken as means, or for which all things are or ought to be loved as means.

A conception of love is part and parcel of Plato's political philosophy in his middle dialogues, above all the *Republic*. The ideal community which he envisions, the *polis*, is a community to be based on love for the *polis*. There is the result that an individual is to be an object of love in so far as he contributes to the well-being of the *polis*, whether in his role as philosopher–ruler or in his other appointed place. Here the person loved is also loved for his producing of good, but not good merely for the loving person. In setting out this part of Plato's philosophy in the third section of the chapter, Vlastos corrects the view of Karl Popper and others to the effect that Plato's celebration of the *polis* is a celebration of something related to the totalitarian state. His principal point is that the *polis* is not an end in itself, not what ought to be the ultimate end. To defend Plato in this way, however, is not at all to accept his political philosophy, or the part played in it by love of the given kind. There are reasons against.

The fourth section of the chapter takes us into consideration of that one thing which is to be the ultimate object of love, *prōton philon*. It is the chief one of the Forms or Ideas, the ideal entities which are the great constituents of Plato's philosophical vision. The Idea of Beauty is to be the true object of love. Platonic love, of the fundamental kind, is not a love of persons. It is a love whose conception involves the great problems of the doctrine of the Ideas or Forms, and which is bound up with creativity. A lesser kind of Platonic love, a love of persons, has a cardinal flaw which is owed to its root in the fundamental kind of Platonic love. The appendix to the chapter clarifies further this lesser Platonic love, and the place in it of sexuality and homosexuality.

The footnotes are copious, indeed plenteous, but they are not such as to tempt an editor to cavil or to ask their value. They complement and are a means to the momentum and the economy of this examination into one part of the first great foundation of philosophy.

Full details of the works referred to in the excerpt by the name of the author and the date of publication are given in the note on further reading at the end of the excerpt.

Gregory Vlastos

Plato: The Individual as an Object of Love

I

'Let *philein* be defined,' writes Aristotle in the *Rhetoric*, 'as wishing for someone what you believe to be good things – wishing this not for your own sake but for his – and acting so far as you can to bring them about.'[1] The same thing is said about *philos* in the essay on friendship in the *Nicomachean Ethics*: 'They define a *philos* as one who wishes and acts for the good, or the apparent good, of one's *philos*, for the sake of one's *philos*; or as one who wishes for the existence and life of one's *philos* for that man's sake.'[2] In the standard translations of these passages *philos* comes through as 'friend', *philein* as 'friendly feeling', and *philia* as 'friendship'. This blunts the force of Aristotle's Greek, as should be clear from one of his illustrations: maternal affection is one of his star examples of *philein* and *philia*;[3] would 'friendly feeling' do justice to what we normally have in view when we speak of a mother's love for her child? Or again, consider the compounds: *philargyros*, *philotimos*, *philonikos*, and so forth: twenty-two columns of them in Liddell and Scott. *Philargyros* is Greek for 'miser'. A man would need to have something considerably stronger than 'friendly feeling' for money to live up (or down) to that name. Much the same would be true in the case of the vast majority of the other compounds. 'Money-lover', 'honour-lover', etc. would be the best that we could do to approach the natural sense of the Greek words. 'Love' is the only English word that is robust and versatile enough to cover *philein* and *philia*.[4] Nor is there any difficulty in seeing why Aristotle should undertake to define 'love' in order to elucidate the meaning of 'friendship': he thinks of friendship as a special case of inter-personal love.

Gregory Vlastos, 'The Individual as an Object of Love', reprinted from *Platonic Studies* (Princeton, 1973; new edition 1982). Except for the elimination of untransliterated Greek, the only changes of any consequence are the added material within square brackets in notes 14 and 21; the abbreviation of notes 45 and 76; and the dropping of the Appendix entitled 'Is the *Lysis* a Vehicle of Platonic Doctrine?'

So what Aristotle is telling us is that to love another person is to wish for that person's good for that person's sake, doing whatever you can to make that wish come true. This is not meant to be a run-of-the-mill definition. Its purpose is not to explain all uses of *philein* but only those that answer to what Aristotle takes to be its 'focal meaning'[5] – to capture the kind of love we can have only for persons and could not possibly have for things, since in their case it would make no sense to speak of wishing for their own good *for their own sake*: 'It would be absurd, no doubt,' says Aristotle, 'to wish good for wine; if one wishes it at all, it is that the wine may keep, so that we may have it for ourselves.'[6] He says this, knowing quite well that love for persons *could* be just like love for inanimates in this crucial respect. This is how Swann loves Odette in *Swann's Way*. At the height of his infatuation he is so far from wishing for her good for her own sake, that he is scarcely capable of thinking of her at all except as an adjunct to his own existence. A chance remark about her from someone who had seen her in an outfit she had never worn for him comes as a shock: 'It upset him because it made him realize all of a sudden that Odette had a life which was not wholly his.'[7] Aristotle recognizes two varieties of this kind of love, admitting them as *philia* of an incomplete, imperfect kind: 'pleasure-love', 'utility-love',[8] affective bonds with men or women whose good we want because they serve our need, or interest, or pleasure, and for no other reason.

But suppose we do wish for someone's good for his own sake. Must we then forfeit utility and pleasure? Not necessarily, Aristotle would insist, and not at all when the relation is 'complete' or perfect *philia*. In friendships with good and noble men one who is himself good and noble will find both profit and delight;[9] so he will love his friends for his own sake as well as for theirs. This is the only kind of love that gets a high rating in Aristotle's design of life. What then of that mother, in one of his examples, whose children, separated from her, do not know her, while she loves them, wishes for their good and works for it, yet gets nothing from them in return, and expects nothing (1159A27–33)? Though he cites this as evidence (*sēmeion*) that 'love is thought to consist more in loving than in being loved',[10] it will not fit his concept of 'perfect' *philia*. So what could he have made of it? He does not say. Either he fails to see that his concept of *philia* makes no provision for this and other hard cases or, if he does, the discrepancy does not disturb him. The only love of persons as persons that really interests him is that between the members of a social élite, each of whom can afford disinterested affection for his peers, assured in advance that he will normally have theirs in return, so that 'in loving the friend each will love what is good for himself'.[11] That Aristotle's notion of 'perfect' love should be so limited is disappointing.[12] But this does not spoil it for my purposes in this essay. All I need here is to find a standard against which to measure Plato's concept of love – a standard from his own time and place, so that I would not have to risk gross anachronism by going with Anders Nygren[13] so far afield as the New Testament. This standard Aristotle does supply. That to love a person we must wish for that person's good for that person's sake, not for ours – so much Aristotle understands. Does Plato?

II

I start with the *Lysis* – one of those earlier dialogues where Plato's thought still moves within the ambit of his Socratic heritage. What does Socrates here make of *philia*. Consider this exchange:[14]

And shall we be dear [*philoi*] to anyone, and will anyone love us [*philēsei*], in those respects in which we are unprofitable?
Of course not, he said.
So your father does not love [*philei*] you now, nor do others love anyone so far as he is useless?
Evidently not, he said.
So if you become wise [*sophos*], my boy, everyone will love you and all will be your *oikeioi*[15] – for you will be useful and good – otherwise no one will love you[16]: Neither your father nor your mother nor your *oikeioi*. (210CD)

'Useful' and 'profitable' in Plato – as in Greek usage generally – must not be given the narrow sense these adjectives ordinarily have in English. Plato uses them to cover any attribute – physical, economic, aesthetic, intellectual, or moral – that makes the one who has it a valuable asset. It is as broad as 'good-producing', with no strings on the kind of good produced; and with Socrates as the speaker we can count on a bias in favour of moral and spiritual good. Socrates then is saying that a person will be loved if, and only if, he produces good. Produces it *for whom*? Jowett translated as though our text had said that A will love B only if B produces good *for A*.[17] If that were right, what Socrates calls 'love' would coincide with Aristotle's utility-love: the Socratic lover would look on those he loves simply as sources of benefits to him. But the text does not say this. For all that is said there to the contrary, A might love B because B produces benefits for a third person or for a group or groups of persons or, for that matter, for B himself. So far, then, Socrates has said nothing which could fairly be said to endorse the egocentricity of utility-love. Yet neither has he made a place, even marginally, for what we found at dead centre in Aristotle's conception of love: wishing another person's good *for that person's sake*. Nothing of this is said or even hinted at in our passage. There is not a word here to imply that Lysis' father and mother love him when he is 'wise' because they see how beneficial it would be *for Lysis* if he were wise, and that they wish this for him just because their loving him *means* wishing for his own good for his own sake. What Socrates says of their love for the boy would have been perfectly true even if they had happened to be arrant egoists who wanted their son to be sensible and well-behaved only because of the trouble this would spare them and the credit it would bring on them. So egoistic love is not excluded though, so far, neither is it implied.

But as we go on reading in the dialogue we find that it is implied, in effect, after all.[18] This happens when Socrates goes on to argue (213E ff.) that if A loves B, he does so because of some benefit *he* needs from B and for the sake of just that benefit: The sick man loves his[19] doctor for the sake of health (218E); the poor love the affluent and the weak the strong for the sake of aid (215D); 'and everyone who is ignorant has affection and love for the one who has knowledge' (loc. cit.). This is straightforward utility-love: the doctor, the rich, the wise are loved by one who needs them for what *he* can get out of them, and no reason is offered why we love anyone except for what we get out of him. The egoistic perspective of 'love' so conceived becomes unmistakable when Socrates, generalizing, argues that 'if one were in want of nothing, one would feel no affection, . . . and he who felt no affection would not love'.[20] The lover Socrates has in view seems positively incapable of loving others for their own sake,[21] else why must he feel no affection for anyone whose good-producing qualities *he* did not happen to need?[22]

Socrates then goes on to argue that just as we love the doctor for the sake of health, so we love health for the sake of something else; hence, short of an infinite regress, there must be a 'first [i.e., terminal] object of love, for whose sake, we say, all other objects are loved' (219D), this being the only thing that is 'truly' or 'really' loved – or, more precisely that *should be* so loved. There is danger, Socrates warns, that 'those other objects, of which we said that they are loved for *its* sake, should deceive us, like so many images[23] of it' (219D2–4). So unless a man we loved actually *was* this *prōton philon*, it would be a mistake to love him 'for his own sake', to treat him, in Kant's phrase, as 'an end in himself'.[24] We would then stand in need of a philosopher, like Socrates, to cure us by his dialectic, to break the illusion, and make us see that what we 'really' love is something else.[25] What is it then, this sovereign *prōton philon*? All Socrates seems to be prepared to say is that it is 'the good';[26] and 'the good for any given person' Socrates understands to mean: what makes that person happy.[27] For something more definite we must go to the dialogues of Plato's middle period. Only there do we find the new theory of love which we can call distinctively Plato's.

III

The ideal society of the *Republic* is a political community held together by bonds of fraternal love.[28] The Allegory of the Metals which epitomizes its ethos pictures all citizens as children of the same mother, the Earth (= the polis). They are told: 'You are all brothers in the *polis* . . ., all akin . . .'[29] They are expected to have the same solicitude for the welfare of the polis which men ordinarily feel for that of their own family. Those appointed to govern must excel not only in intelligence and all-around ability but also in their concern for the welfare of the polis, which is said to be a function of their love for it: 'One is most concerned for what one loves' (412D). Radical institutional innovations are to insure that this affection will be wholehearted, undistracted by economic self-interest, on the one hand, by special attachments to kith and kin, on the other. The whole of the ruling class now becomes a single communal family, where no one is an 'outsider'[30] and everyone is 'a brother or sister or son or daughter' or other kin 'to everyone he meets'.[31] The maxim of this extended family is that '*philoi* have all things in common, so far as possible'.[32] The last four words explain why the same institutions are not laid down for the producers in spite of the fact that, as the Allegory of the Metals so clearly implies, all of the members of the polis are expected to be *philoi*: if the communistic property and family arrangements do not apply to them, this must be due only to the fact that Plato does not think these institutions would be practicable in their case, however desirable ideally for all.[33] But there can be no doubt of his confidence that they too will feel love for their motherland and for their rulers, who are their 'saviours and helpers' (463B) and think of them as '*philoi* and sustainers' (547C). In a postscript which gives in a nutshell the rationale of the beneficent subjection of the producers to the philosophers we are told that those who are 'naturally weak in the principle of the best' (i.e., of reason) ought to be governed by those who are strong in this principle 'so that we may all be alike and *philoi* so far as possible, all governed by the same principle'.[34] Subjection[35] to another's will is justified on the assumption that it may not only coexist with, but also promote, *philia*.

Since we are given no formal definition of *philia* and *philos* in the *Republic*, let us try out what we heard from Socrates in the *Lysis*. 'You will be loved,' Socrates had told Lysis there, 'if and only if you are useful.' Does this fit the *Republic*? It fits perfectly. The institutions we find here appear designed from start to finish to make it possible for people to have each other's affection if, and only if, each 'does his own',[36] i.e., performs to the best of his ability that complex of activities through which he is best fitted by nature and nurture to make his greatest possible contribution to his polis. In doing this he would fulfil the Platonic norm of *dikaiosynē*: he would discharge all of his obligations, and earn all of his rights. For our present purpose the latter is the important point. Whatever a man can rightly claim from others in the *Republic* is tied to the performance of his job. He can claim no benefit for himself except in so far as it would enable him to be a better producer.[37] This principle, upheld in the name of *dikaiosynē*, dovetails into a conception of *philia* according to which one is loved so far, and only so far, as he produces good. And here the question we raised a moment ago in the *Lysis* – 'produces good for whom?' – answers itself: Good for the whole community, which plays no favourites, distributing the social product to its producers with scrupulous impartiality, taking from each according to his ability and giving to each according to the needs of his job.

This moral philosophy Karl Popper has called 'collectivist or political utilitarianism'. 'Plato', he writes, 'recognizes only one ultimate standard [of justice], the interest of the state . . . *Morality is nothing but political hygiene* [my italics].'[38] But for Plato, as for Socrates before him, the supreme goal of all human endeavour is the improvement of the soul – and that means its *moral* improvement.[39] So the interest of the state would count for nothing unless it were strictly subordinate to this end.[40] The excellence of a state, its very legitimacy, would be judged by that standard:

> The sum and substance of our agreement comes to this: By what means can the members of our community come to be good men, having the goodness of soul that is proper to men? . . . This is the end to whose attainment all serious effort must be directed throughout life. Nothing which could hamper this should be given preference. In the end one should rather overturn the state, or else flee from it into exile, rather than consent to submit to the servile yoke of baser men – one should endure any fate rather than suffer the state to change to a polity which breeds baser human beings. (770C–E)[41]

To be true to what Plato says so explicitly here and assumes throughout the *Republic*, one would have to say not that morality is political hygiene but that politics is moral hygiene. Yet even so what Popper says is not entirely without foundation. One feels intuitively that something is amiss in Plato's ultramoralistic polity. But just what? The present analysis suggests an alternative diagnosis:

Consider what would happen in this utopia if someone through no fault of his own were to cease being a public asset. One of the philosophers, let us say, becomes permanently disabled and can no longer do his job or any other work that would come anywhere near the expected level of productive excellence. And to plug a possible hole in the hypothesis, let us preclude any higher spin-offs from the misfortune. It is not the case, for instance, that the man's character has been so purified during his illness that those who now come to visit him leave his bedside morally braced and elevated: that would be tantamount to shifting him to another job, the propagation of virtue. Our hypothesis is that neither in this nor in any other way can this man recoup his place as a producer. What may he then claim, now that he may no longer ground his claims on the needs of his job, but only on the value of his individual existence? As I read the *Republic*, the answer is: Nothing. In Book III Asclepius is pictured as follows:

> He would rid them of their disorders by drugs or by the knife and tell them to go on living as usual, so as not to impair their civic usefulness. But where the body was diseased through and through he would not try, by diet and by finely graduated evacuations and infusions, to prolong a miserable existence . . . Treatment, he thought, would be wasted on a man who could not live in his ordinary round of duties and was thus useless to himself and to the polis. (407DE; translation after Cornford)

What are we to say? That this 'political Asclepius' (497E) is not the divinity we know from other sources, the culture-hero of a vocation pledged to 'love of mankind' (*philanthrōpia*)?[42] This would be true. But it would miss the point that Plato could say exactly what he did and still credit his reconditioned Asclepius with *philanthrōpia*. If men are to be loved for their productiveness and for no other reason, why should there be breach of love in the refusal of medical treatment to the unproductive?

For another sidelight on what is morally disquieting about *philia* in the *Republic*, consider what would happen to the individual's freedom in that utopia. We know how highly this was prized in Plato's Athens. We know the current estimate of the positive side of freedom: guaranteed participation in the process by which political decisions were reached. 'There is no better way to define the proper sense of "citizen",' says Aristotle, 'than in terms of having a share in judgement and office.'[43] He holds that to deny a man such a share would be to treat him as though he were no better than an alien or a slave.[44] And we know how highly the negative side of freedom – the right to protected privacy – was esteemed. In Thucydides Pericles boasts that daily life in Athens is free from censorious constraint,[45] and Nicias, calling on his commanders to do their utmost for Athens in her hour of supreme peril,

reminded them that their fatherland was the freest in the world and that in it everyone had the right to live his daily life without orders from anyone.[46]

What would be left of all this in the *Republic*? Participatory democracy vanishes without a trace. So does free speech and, what Plato realizes is at least as important, free song, free dance, free art.[47] The rulers lose all right to personal privacy. Even their sex-life belongs to the state. For the greater part of their adult years intercourse is permitted them only for purposes of eugenic breeding, with partners assigned them by state officials. The end in view is the communizing – one might almost say the homogenizing – of their value-preferences, their likes and dislikes:

Can we say that anything would be a greater evil for a polis than what breaks it up and makes it many instead of one? Or any good greater than what binds it together and makes it one?
We can not.
And is it not the community of pleasure and of pain that binds it together – when so far as possible all the citizens are pleased or pained alike on the same occasions of gain or loss?
Quite so.
Whereas it is the privatization[48] of these feelings that breaks the bond – when some are intensely pained, while others are overjoyed at the very same things befalling the polis or its people?
Yes indeed.[49]

Plato's community is to approach the unity of affective experience in a single person: When a man hurts his finger, we don't say that his finger feels the pain, but that *he* 'feels the pain in his finger'; so too in 'the best ordered polis . . ., when any citizen is affected for good or ill, this kind of polis will feel the affection as its own – all will feel pleasure or pain together' (462D–E).

Now that persons who love each other should respond sympathetically to each others' mishaps and triumphs, that each should rejoice when his fellows have cause for joy and grieve when they have cause to grieve, is only what we would expect. So from the fact that A and B are *philoi* we may expect that A will be pleased at B's pleasure and pained at B's pain. But to say this is not to say that each will be himself pleased or pained at those (and only those) things which please or pain the other.[50] Let A admire and B dislike the mixolydian mode and Sappho's lyrics. Then some things in their world which thrill A will chill B. Would it follow that they cannot be friends or lovers? Why should it? Why should not personal affection imply tolerance, even tender regard, for such differences? So it would, if it did mean wishing another's good for his own sake. For then A would have good reason for wishing that B should have what B himself deems material to the fulfilment of his own unique personality – pleased at the thought of B's having it, though A himself would only be pained if it were forced on him. To work out a *modus vivendi* in which such differences are respected might well involve practical difficulties. It would call for reciprocal adjustments and concessions. But these would be felt as implementations of mutual love, not as denials of it. This possibility does not occur to Plato. He takes it for granted that diversity of valuational response – 'privatization' of feelings – would be a disruption of the love-bond,[51] a sign of mutual indifference or hostility. So the constraint on personal freedom at its deepest level – the freedom to feel whatever it be one wants to feel, whose suppression would justify that of so many other kinds of freedom – becomes not only compatible with what Plato understands by *philia*, but its indispensable ideal condition. He could not have reached this result if he had thought of love as wishing another person's good for just that person's sake, looking upon the loved one's individual being as something precious in and of itself.

IV

If – to recall the diction of the *Lysis* – we may not accord to any person we love the status of *prōton philon*, whom, or what, may we 'really' and 'truly' love? The sections of the *Republic* I have so far discussed give no more of an answer than does the passage about the *prōton philon* in the *Lysis*. Only when we come to the treatise on metaphysics and epistemology, which starts with the introduction of the Theory of Ideas in the latter part of Book V, do we get at long last what we have been looking for.[52] We get it when Plato starts talking of the philosophers as lovers of the Ideas.[53] He uses for this purpose not only *philein* (479E, with *aspazesthai*), but also *eran* which is so much stronger.[54] From just these data in the *Republic* we could have inferred that now the *prōton philon* is the Idea. But we have also the *Symposium* and the *Phaedrus*, either of which would confirm this inference to the hilt. I shall be content to work with the former, and there only with the metaphysical core of the dialogue – the part in which the priestess-prophetess, Diotima, instructs Socrates in 'the things of love'.[55] She begins with things Socrates says he knows already:

We love only what is beautiful.
In loving it we desire to possess it in perpetuity.
We desire to possess it because we think it good and expect that its possession would make us happy.[56]

Then she goes on to ask (206B1–3):

This being the aim of love,[57] in what way and by what activity is it to be pursued if the eagerness and intensity of the pursuit is to be (properly) called 'love'?

Socrates has no idea of what she is driving at.[58] She tells him: 'Birth in beauty'. She explains:

All human beings are pregnant (*kyousin*)[59] in body and in spirit, and when we reach maturity our nature longs to give birth. But this we can do only in the presence of beauty, never in that of ugliness.[60] There is something divine about this. In pregnancy and in birth the mortal becomes immortal. (206C)

Beauty stirs us so deeply, Plato is saying, because we have the power to create and only the beauty we love can release that power. He puts this, to begin with, into his interpretation of physical heterosexual love. Being himself an invert, with little appreciation of passionate love between the sexes for purposes other than procreation,[61] all he sees in feminine beauty is the lure to paternity. He accepts this as an authentic, if low-grade, form of creativity. Then, turning to other ranges of experience, he holds that what we love in each of them is always some variety of beauty which releases in us the corresponding power of 'birth in beauty'. Living in a culture which accepts the pederast[62] and does not constrain him, as ours did Proust, to falsify the imaginative transcript of his personal experience, transvesting Alfred into Albertine, Plato discovers a new form of pederastic love,[63] fully sensual in its resonance,[64] but denying itself consummation,[65] transmuting physical excitement into imaginative and intellectual energy. At the next level, higher in value and still more energizing, he puts the love of mind for mind, expecting it to prove so much more intense than skin-love that mere physical beauty will now strike the lover as a 'small', contempt-ible, thing.[66] Still higher in ordered succession come the beauty of poetry, of political constitutions, of science, and of philosophy. Ascending relentlessly, the lover will come to see at last 'a marvellous sort of Beauty' (210E) – the Platonic Idea of Beauty. 'And all our previous labours', says Diotima, 'were for this.'[67] All previously encountered objects – bodies, minds, institutions, works of the imag-ination or of science – were loved as a means of moving closer step by step to this 'marvellous sort of Beauty'.

Here we find ourselves in the thick of Plato's ontology, so let us stop to get our bearings. For every generic character which spatio-temporal objects may have in common, Plato posits an ideal entity in which particular things 'participate' so long as they have that character. We are thus offered a tripartite ontology:

(1) the transcendent, paradigmatic Form: say, the Form of Justice;
(2) the things in our experience which may have or lack the corresponding character – the persons, laws, practices, states, which may or may not be just;
(3) the character of those things – the justice they instantiate if they are just.[68]

That (1) is radically distinct (or, as Aristotle was to put it, 'exists separately')[69] from (3) I take to be the crux of this ontology. But what exactly does this 'separation' mean? Plato never made this fully clear. Had he done so, he would surely have seen how treacherous is one of the ways in which he tends to represent it in his middle dialogues, thinking of the Form as differing from its empirical instances not only categorially – as incorporeal, eternal, intelligibles would differ from corporeal, temporal, sensibles – but also as would an ideal exemplar from imperfect 'resemblances' of it.[70] This kind of language, if meant literally, would burden the Platonic Form with the logical difficulties of 'self-predication'[71] – an assumption which could not be generalized without contradiction, for then, e.g., the Form, Plurality, would have to be plural, and the Form, Motion, would have to be moving, contrary to the stipulation that each Form is unitary and immutable. Did Plato ever walk into this trap? The question has been hotly debated, and this essay is not the place to pursue the controversy. All I need say here is this: If Plato's ontology had been fashioned for narrowly logical, semantic, and epistemological purposes, he would have had no use whatever for exemplarism and we would have to read the language which suggests it as pure metaphor, freeing it from any self-predicative commitment. Suppose that just this had been Plato's intention. What would have been the consequence? A more coherent ontology, certainly – but a less fruitful one for other uses to which Plato put his Ideas, for his theory of love most of all. If Plato had seen in the Idea of Beauty just the character, not the paradigmatic instance of the character, then it would not have been for him the absolutely[72] and divinely[73] beautiful object of Diotima's discourse; it would not even have been beautiful – no more beautiful than ugly, as the character, Whiteness, being an abstract universal, a purely logical entity, is itself neither white nor of any other colour. How then could it have been love object par excellence in a theory which so strictly conditions love on beauty? What inspired that theory was a paradigm-form so splendidly and shamelessly self-exemplifying that its own beauty outshines that of everything else.

I cannot here formulate, let alone try to answer, the many questions that spring to mind when one ponders this theory that has done so much to mould the European imagination from Plotinus to Dante and from Petrarch to Baudelaire. A proper study of it would have to take account of at least three things about its creator: He was a homosexual,[74] a mystic, and a moralist. So to reach a balanced understanding of Platonic love – of the true original, not of that caricature confused with it by the illiterate and not infrequently by literati – one would need to pursue at the very least three complementary investigations:

First, a study of the effect which Plato's inversion would be likely to have on one who saw anal intercourse as 'contrary to nature',[75] a degradation not only of man's humanity, but even of his animality: even to brutes, Plato believes, 'nature' ordains heterosexual coupling.[76] This thought would poison sensual gratification for him with anticipatory torment and retrospective guilt. It would tend to distort his overall view of sexual fulfilment, while leaving him with raw sensitiveness to male beauty and heightening his capacity for substitute forms of erotic response.

Second, a study which would connect his theory of love with his religious mysticism, exploring the implications of the momentous fact that while Plato retains traditional deities and sets high above them in the *Timaeus* a creator-god of his own devising, none of these personal divinities stirs either awe or love in his heart, while the severely impersonal Ideas evoke both, but especially love, so much so that he speaks repeatedly of communion with them as an act of blissful and fertile conjugal union.[77]

Third, a study of the place of love in the pattern of inter-personal relations recommended in his moral philosophy.

Realizing what folly it would have been to spread myself in a single essay all over these three areas, I chose to concentrate on the third. That is why I started off with Aristotle, and then approached the *Symposium* via the *Lysis* and the *Republic*. My reason may be now apparent: What needs to be stressed most of all in this area is that Plato's theory is not, and is not meant to be, about personal love for persons – i.e., about the kind of love we can have only for persons and cannot have for things or abstractions. What it is really about is love for place-holders of the predicates 'useful' and 'beautiful' – of the former when it is only *philia*, of the latter, when it is *erōs*. In this theory persons evoke *erōs* if they have beautiful bodies, minds, or dispositions. But so do quite impersonal objects – social or political programmes, literary compositions, scientific theories, philosophical systems and, best of all, the Idea of Beauty itself. As objects of Platonic love all these are not only as good as persons, but distinctly better. Plato signifies their superiority by placing them in the higher reaches of that escalated figure that marks the lover's progress, relegating love of persons to its lower levels. Even those two personal attachments which seem to have meant more to him than did any others in his whole life – his love for Socrates in his youth and, later on, for Dion of Syracuse[78] – would be less than halfway up to the summit in that diagram. This is what we must keep in view, if we are to reach a fair assessment of Plato's conception of love, acknowledging its durable achievement no less than its residual failure.

V

Let me speak first of the achievement. Plato is the first Western man to realize how intense and passionate may be our attachment to objects as abstract as social reform, poetry, art, the sciences, and philosophy – an attachment that has more in common with erotic fixation than one would have suspected on a pre-Freudian view of man. So far as we know no earlier Greek had sensed this fact, though language had pointed the way to it by sanctioning as a matter of course the use of *eran*, no less than *philein*, for something as impersonal as love of country.[79] It is left to Plato to generalize this kind of *erōs* and to see that it may reach a mad[80] obsessive intensity which is commonly thought peculiar to sexual love. He discerns, as the link between such disparate involvements, the sense of beauty. He understands how decisive a role in the motivation of the most abstruse inquiry may be played by such things as the elegance of a deduction, the neatness of an argument, or the delight which floods the mind when a powerful generality brings sudden luminous order to a mass of jumbled data. He sees that the aesthetic quality of such purely intellectual objects is akin to the power of physical beauty to excite and to enchant even when it holds out no prospect of possession. And, instead of undertaking, as did Freud, to explain the attractiveness of beauty in all of its diverse manifestations as due to the excitation of lust, open or disguised, Plato invokes another drive, the hunger to create, and argues that this is what we all seek to appease in every activity propelled by beauty. That Plato's explanation is one-sided does not damn it. So is Freud's. Where comprehensive insight is denied us even partial glimpses of the truth are precious.

But, second, to return to Plato's view of that kind of love whose immediate object is a man or a woman, we can get out of it a subordinate thesis which has not only psychological but also moral validity. When he speaks of *erōs* for a person for the sake of the Idea, we can give a good sense to this at first sight puzzling notion, a sense in which it is true. It is a fact that much erotic attachment, perhaps most of it, is not directed to an individual in the proper sense of the word – to the integral and irreplaceable existent that bears that person's name – but to a complex of qualities, answering to the lover's sense of beauty, which he locates for a time truly or falsely in that person. I say 'truly or falsely' to call attention to a feature of Platonic love which has never been noticed, to my knowledge, in the rich literature on this subject. This feature can best be appreciated by contrast with romantic love – at any rate, with that brand of it whose textbook example is Rousseau.

'There is no real love without enthusiasm,' he writes in the *Émile*, 'and no enthusiasm without an object of perfection, real or chimerical, but always existing in the imagination.'[81] So if we do want 'real love', we must buy it with illusion. We must transfigure imaginatively the necessarily imperfect persons in whom we vest our love. We see in the *Confessions* that this is the recipe Rousseau followed himself in what he calls there 'the first and only love of my life, whose consequences were to make it unforgettable for the rest of my life and terrible in my recollection'.[82] What excited that high-temperature passion was scarcely the plain[83] and unremarkable young woman, Madame d'Houdetot. She served him only as a mannequin to wear his fantasies. A mood of frustration and self-pity had settled on him in his middle forties and had thrown him back, so he tells us, 'into the land of chimeras':[84]

Finding nothing in existence worthy of my delirium, I nourished it in an ideal world which my creative imagination soon peopled with beings after my own heart . . . Forgetting completely the human race, I made for myself societies of perfect creatures, as heavenly in their virtues as in their beauties.[85]

Presently Madame d'Houdetot moves into his private landscape. He had been 'intoxicated with a love without an object'. She provided one. 'Before long I had no eye for anyone but Madame d'Houdetot, but reclothed with all the perfections with which I had come to adorn the idol of my heart.'[86]

It would be a blunder to call this affair 'Platonic love', which it in fact was in the vulgar sense of the term – technically there was no infidelity[87] – and which it also approached as love for an ideal object. But no Platonist could have confused the idol of *his* heart with a Madame d'Houdetot. Even in the heat of passion the Platonic Idea does not lend itself to this kind of mistake. We see in the *Phaedrus* what keeps Plato's head clear even when his senses are enflamed.[88] It is the ontology of the paradigm-form. That harshly dualistic transcendentalism, which enraged Aristotle by its 'separation' of Forms from things and which nowadays drives analytical philosophers to despair when they try to make logical sense out of it, proves a sterling asset in this area. It sustains a kind of idealism less addicted to the pathetic fallacy than are most other kinds. It makes for a more truthful vision of that part of the world which we are all most tempted to idealize and so to falsify – the part we love. And it makes for a gain of another, no less important, kind: Freedom from the tyranny which even the unidealized love-object can exercise over a lover. Swann did not long idealize Odette.[89] But his love for her made a tortured, degraded, slave out of him while it lasted, and disabled his spirit for the rest of his life. If there is any place at all in Plato's diagram for a creature like Odette, it would be at just one level short of the bottom. At the next higher level Swann would have been once again free and whole.

But a sterling asset may be bought at a heavy cost. Plato's theory floods with the most brilliant light a narrow sector of its theme, and there points the way to authentic spiritual achievement. Beyond those limits the vision fails. Plato is scarcely aware of kindness, tenderness, compassion, concern for the freedom, respect for the integrity of the beloved, as essential ingredients of the highest type of interpersonal love. Not that Platonic eros is as 'egocentric' and 'acquisitive' as Nygren has claimed;[90] it is only too patently Ideocentric and creative. But while it gives no more quarter to self-indulgence than would Pauline *agape* or Kantian good will, neither does it repudiate the spiritualized egocentricism of Socratic *philia*.[91] That first description of the aim of eros in Diotima's speech – 'that one should possess beauty for ever' – is never amended in the sequel in any way which would make egoistic eros a contradiction or even an anomaly.[92] It is not said or

implied or so much as hinted at that 'birth in beauty' should be motivated by love of persons – that the ultimate purpose of the creative act
should be to enrich the lives of persons who are themselves worthy of
love for their own sake. The preceding analysis shows that Diotima's
failure to say or to suggest anything of the kind is no accidental oversight, but an integral feature of the structure of Plato's theory.

As a theory of the love of persons, this is its crux: What we are to
love in persons is the 'image'[93] of the Idea in them.[94] We are to love
the persons so far, and only in so far, as they are good and beautiful.
Now since all too few human beings are masterworks of excellence,
and not even the best of those we have the chance to love are wholly
free of streaks of the ugly, the mean, the commonplace, the ridiculous,
if our love for them is to be only for their virtue and beauty, the
individual, in the uniqueness and integrity of his or her individuality,
will never be the object of our love. This seems to me the cardinal flaw
in Plato's theory. It does not provide for love of whole persons, but
only for love of that abstract version of persons which consists of the
complex of their best qualities. This is the reason why personal affection
ranks so low in Plato's *scala amoris*. When loved as congeries of valuable
qualities, persons cannot compete with abstractions of universal significance, like schemes of social reform or scientific and philosophical
truths, still less with the Idea of Beauty in its sublime transcendence,
'pure, clear, unmixed, not full of human flesh and colour and other
mortal nonsense' (*Smp*. 211E1–3). The high climactic moment of
fulfilment – the peak achievement for which all lesser loves are to be
'used as steps'[95] – is the one farthest removed from affection for concrete
human beings.

Since persons in their concreteness are thinking, feeling, wishing,
hoping, fearing beings, to think of love for them as love for objecti-
fications of excellence is to fail to make the thought of them as *subjects*
central to what is felt for them in love. The very exaltation of the
beloved in the erotic idyl in the *Phaedrus* views him from an external
point of view. Depicting him as an adorable cult-object, Plato seems
barely conscious of the fact that this 'holy image'[96] is himself a valuing
subject, a centre of private experience and individual preference, whose
predilections and choice of ends are no reflex of the lover's[97] and might
well cross his at some points even while returning his love. Transposing
this from erotics to politics we see the reason for the tragedy of the
Republic; we see why its effort to foster civic love obliterates civil
liberty. The fashioner of this utopia has evidently failed to see that what
love for our fellows requires of us is, above all, imaginative sympathy

and concern for what they themselves think, feel, and want. He has, therefore, missed that dimension of love in which tolerance, trust, forgiveness, tenderness, respect have validity. Apart from these imperatives the notion of loving persons as 'ends in themselves'[98] would make no sense. No wonder that we hear of nothing remotely like it from Plato. Had such a thought occurred to him, his theory could have seen in it only conceptual error and moral confusion. On the terms of that theory, to make flesh-and-blood men and women terminal objects of our affection would be folly or worse, idolatry, diversion to images of what is due only to their divine original. We are a prey to this error, Plato would say, because of our carnal condition, burdened with incompleteness which fellow-creatures have power to complete;[99] were we free of mortal deficiency we would have no reason to love anyone or anything except the Idea: seen face to face, it would absorb all our love. Here we see the polar opposite of the ideal which has moulded the image of the deity in the Hebraic and Christian traditions: that of a Being whose perfection empowers it to love the imperfect; of a Father who cares for each of his children as they are, does not proportion affection to merit, gives it no more to the righteous than to the perverse and deformed. Not even Aristotle had any inkling of such a notion[100] – indeed, he less than Plato, whose God is impelled by love for Beauty to create and thereby to share his own goodness with his creatures,[101] while Aristotle's Prime Mover remains eternally complete in the stillness of his own perfection. Discerning the possibility of a kind of love which wishes for another's existence, preservation, and good for that other's sake, Aristotle thought only men could have it and only few men for few. To universalize that kind of love, to extend it to the slave, to impute it to the deity, would have struck him as quite absurd.

Though so much of what I have said here has been critical of Plato, this was only incidental to the effort to understand him. And since he is a philosopher whose separate ventures must be seen in the context of his synoptic vision, let me point out in closing how Plato's speculation structures love in the same way as it does knowledge in epistemology, the world-order in cosmology, the interrelations of particular and universal, time and eternity, the world of sense and the world of thought in ontology. In each of these areas the factors of the analytic pattern are the same: the transcendent Form at one extreme, the temporal individual at the other, and, in between, the individuals' immanent characters, projections of eternity on the flickering screen of becoming. And everywhere Plato gives the Form pre-eminence. In epistemology it is *the* object of knowledge; sensible particulars can only be objects of that low-grade cognitive achievement, opinion. In cosmology only the Forms represent completely lucid order; physical individuals, enmeshed in brute necessity, are only quasi-orderly, as they are only quasi-intelligible. In ontology there are grades of reality and only Forms have the highest grade. So too in the theory of love the respective roles of Form and temporal individual are sustained: the individual cannot be as lovable as the Idea; the Idea, and it alone, is to be loved for its own sake; the individual only so far as in him and by him ideal perfection is copied fugitively in the flux.

APPENDIX: Sex in Platonic Love

According to the *Concise Oxford Dictionary of Current Usage* (1954), Platonic love is 'purely spiritual love for one of the opposite sex'.[1] If we are to concede that this is what the term has come to mean today – we need not dispute the dictionary's authority – we should at least be careful to notice how far it has strayed away from what it meant for Plato. The first deviation – the notion that interpersonal eros is 'purely spiritual love' – passes unnoticed in the scholarly literature; so far from calling attention to it, some recent studies have actually endorsed it. Thus Gould (1963, 119) writes:

If they [the amorous couple in the *Phaedrus*] are truly lovers of wisdom, the only intercourse which will appeal to them is rational exploration together, to be companions in the adventures of the life of the mind.

And Irving Singer (1966, 80):

In the *Phaedrus* . . . the harmony of black and white finally yields to a purely spiritual bond from which all sexuality has been exorcised.

Such statements seem to have gone unchallenged, and it may not be amiss to point out that they are out of line with the clear implications of Plato's text.

Consider what happens in the passage these statements have in view: when the man first chances on the beautiful youth the 'erotic vision' provokes libidinous impulse in 'the whole' of his psyche: all of it – charioteer and white horse, no less than the black – is 'enflamed', is 'filled with the ticklings and pricklings of desire' (253E5–254A1).[2] The white horse (and *a fortiori* the driver) is 'held back by shame from leaping on the beloved' (254A2–3): the impulse is checked, not dissipated. Unchecked in the black horse, 'terrible and lawless deeds' would have ensued on the spot, were it not that the driver, falling back like a racer at the barrier, with a still more violent jerk breaks the bit from the shameless horse's teeth, bespattering its railing tongue and jaws with blood, throws it down on its legs and haunches, and punishes it. (254E)

This happens 'many times' (254E6) before the lecherous horse gives in.

Now would it be reasonable to think that Plato expects this liaison to start with such raw, all-but-overpowering, lust, and then become totally desexualized as it matures? If so, why does he tell us (255E) that the boy, when he comes to return the lover's passion, 'wants to see, touch, kiss, and share his couch', a desire which 'ere long, as one might guess, leads to the act', so that we now find the pair 'sleeping together'? Are we to suppose that such a thorough job of mortifying the flesh has intervened that kissing, embracing, and sleeping together now leaves the couple undisturbed by genital excitement? What comes next in Plato's story is not favourable to the hypothesis: the black horse in the boy's soul 'swells with desire' (256A2) when he embraces and kisses; he 'would not refuse to do his part in gratifying the lover's entreaties' (256A4–5) were it not that white horse and driver resist. So physical desire is still there in the boy, and *a fortiori* in the lover. It takes 'Olympic wrestling' (256B4–5) to keep it in check.

To put my thesis positively: that form of passionate experience invented by Plato, which should count as the original, and always primary, sense of 'Platonic love', is a peculiar mix of sensuality, sentiment, and intellect – a companionship bonded by erotic attraction no less than by intellectual give-and-take. Body-to-body endearment is one of its normal features, though always subject to the constraint that terminal gratification will be denied. And this interdict is itself only an ideal requirement; sternly mandatory for philosophers, it is applied more leniently to others. In lovers of the 'ambitious and less philosophic' way of life (256B–C) Plato expects lapses: 'When drunk or in some other careless hour, the insolent horses in their souls may catch them off their guard . . . and they may then choose and do what the vulgar take for bliss.' If this happens infrequently and against their best resolves, Plato's eschatology will not damn them – which means, among other things, that they still qualify as Platonic lovers:

> Those who have once got started on the heavenward journey no law would send to the dark pathways under the earth. But they shall walk together in a life of shining happiness and, when the time comes, they shall grow wings together because of their love. (256D)

Now let me take up the other point where the dictionary parts company with Plato on 'Platonic love': 'love for one of the opposite sex'. Here scholars have gone to the other extreme, suggesting that for heterosexual love Platonic eros has no place at all. Some of the finest studies have implied as much. J. A. Symonds, the Victorian invert, whose monograph cracked open Greek homosexuality for Englishmen of his generation, saw Platonic love as 'veiled sodomy' (1901, 54). Kenneth J. Dover, in his admirable monograph – as precise and sophisticated a piece of scholarship on its theme as has ever appeared in any language – says that 'Plato exploited exclusively homosexual emotion for his philosophical theory of eros' (1964, 39). I submit that this goes too far. Admittedly it fits everything in the *Phaedrus* and also *most* of what Plato put into the *pièce de résistance* of the *Symposium*, the speech of Diotima: boy-love forms the base of that escalated figure along which the lover rises to ever higher forms of love; he starts with the love of 'beautiful bodies', and if one reads attentively one will see that, sure enough, these bodies are male.[3] However, when Diotima undertakes to state the most general condition which the pursuit of Beauty has to meet to qualify as eros, her phrase, 'birth in beauty',[4] is all too patently a generalization of procreative – hence necessarily *heterosexual* – love. Let me dwell on this formula, for it is surely the most profound thing in the dialogue. Just before she had got Socrates to agree that eros is desire to possess the good, believing that it would bring its possessor happiness. One might have expected her to construe this along commonplace, hedonistic, lines – that what we want in love is pleasure and that beauty lures by promising pleasure. That is where she surprises us. For the picture of man as pleasure-chaser she substitutes an image of man as creator, producer, new-maker: ever 'pregnant',[5] carrying a burden from which he craves release, he thrills to Beauty because only in its presence can he find the longed-for deliverance.

This understanding of love has plainly a heterosexual paradigm. In the drive to reproductive coupling Plato recognizes the archetypal expression of eros, its most elemental and universal form. And he does not understate the emotional force of the drive:

> Don't you see how all living creatures, birds and brutes, in their desire of procreation are in agony when they take the infection of love, which begins with the desire of intercourse and then passes to the care of offspring, on whose behalf the weakest are ready to battle the strongest to the last and die for them, and will suffer the torments of hunger, or make any other sacrifice, to tend their young? (207B–C)

Gregory Vlastos

What is it then that prompted Symonds' and Dover's remarks and led that erudite philistine, John Jay Chapman, to stigmatize the *Symposium* as

> The *vade mecum* of those who accept and continue the practice it celebrates . . . a sort of lurid devotional book – the sulphurous breviary of the pederast? (1934, 133)

At most this: conjugal love, however intense, would still remain in Plato's scheme a spiritual dead end[6] – an impulse fully spent in reaching its immediate goal, generating no surplus energy to fuel flights into the empyrean. Suppose the man in the *Phaedrus*, long before meeting that boy, had loved a beautiful girl with whom he had reared in harmonious domesticity a brood of splendid children. There is not one word in Plato to suggest that this relation could have been at any point for the man, or for the girl, the start of a *vita nuova* – the take-off for the ascent diagrammed in the escalated figure. Platonic – as also, later, courtly, and still later, romantic – love is meant to be a life-transforming miracle, a secular analogue to religious conversion, a magical change of perspective that opens up new, enchanted, horizons. For Plato, for whom the spirit comes to life in words, the first decisive sign of the mutation would be a sudden loosening of the tongue, a new-found flair for intellectual talk. When do we hear of this? When the man who is 'pregnant in soul' encounters a 'noble and well-born' soul housed in a beautiful body, he then 'embraces the two in one, and in this man's company he straightway finds facility of speech about virtue and about what a good man ought to be and practise'.[7] This is what starts him off on the ascent whose terminus is the face-to-face encounter with the Idea of Beauty. There, at the peak, the homosexual imagery is dropped. Communion with the Idea is consummated in conjugal intercourse which 'will bring forth not images of beauty but realities' (212A). What started as a pederastic idyl ends up in transcendental marriage.

Notes

1. *Rhet.* 1380B35–1381A1.
2. *N.E.* 1166A2–5.
3. The second citation runs on: 'as mothers do for their children . . .' Parental affection is used to illustrate *philia* already in the first chapter of the Essay on *philia* (*N.E.* VIII.1). Cf. my reference to 1159A27–33 in the third paragraph of this essay.
4. As shown, e.g., by the fact that the translator is compelled to use 'love' when translating *philein* in the *Lysis* and that the commentators shift without apology to 'love' and 'beloved' when glossing *philein* and *philon*. I say that 'love' *covers* these Greek terms, bear-

ing in mind that its connotation is considerably wider, since it does also the work of *eran*, which overlaps with *philein*, but differs from the latter in three respects:

(i) *eran* is more intense, more passionate (cf. Plato, *Lg.* 837A: 'when either sort of *philon* becomes intense, we call it "*erōs*"');

(ii) *eran* is more heavily weighted on the side of desire than of affection (*desire, longing* are the primary connotations of *erōs*, *fondness* that of *philein*);

(iii) *eran* is more closely tied to the sexual drive (though *philein* may also refer to sexual love, for non-incestuous familial love one would have to turn to *philia* instead of *erōs*: cf. Plato, *Smp.* 179C: Alcestis had *philia* for her husband, and so did his parents, but 'because of her *erōs* for him, she so surpassed them in *philia*' that she was willing to die in his place, while they were not).

5. A useful term we owe to G. E. L. Owen.

6. 1155B29–31.

7. 'Ce simple croquis bouleversait Swann parce qui'il lui faisait tout d'un coup apercevoir qu'Odette avait une vie qui n'était pas tout entière à lui, ...' *A la recherche du temps perdu*, Vol. I of the Pléiade Edition (Paris, 1954), 240.

8. *N.E.* 8. 3–5, 1156A6 ff. These are 'accidental *philiai*', 1156A17–18. They are called *philia* 'by similitude' (1157A31–32) of the kind which is 'truly', 'primarily', and 'strictly' or 'chiefly' *philia* (loc. cit. A24 and 30–31), the only kind Aristotle considers 'complete' or 'perfect' *philia* (1156B34, 1158A11).

9. This is implied unambiguously in his discussion of what he calls 'complete *philia*' in 1156B7 ff., *malista philia* in 1157B1–1158A1.

10. *N.E.* 1159A27–28.

11. *N.E.* 1157B33.

12. Cf. n. 100, below.

13. *Eros and Agape* (English translation by P. S. Watson, Harper Torchbook edition, New York, 1969) – a distinguished, influential, and very one-sided book, whose treatment of the 'Greek' idea of love fails to reckon with the elementary fact that *philia* is a near-synonym of *agapē*, and that, regardless of what their philosophers said, Greeks, being human, were as capable of genuine, non-egoistic, affection as are we. Ignoring *philia* (save for a passing notice of the *Lysis* on p. 180, where Nygren translates the word by 'friendship' and uses the dialogue as further evidence 'of the egocentric nature of Eros' in Plato, 181, n. 3), he fails to take the slightest cognizance of Aristotle's conception of it.

14. [It is preceded by a whimsey in hyperbolic praise of 'wisdom': if we are wise we'll have the world at our feet ('all men, Greeks and barbarians, men and women, will allow us anything we want ... in those matters [in which we are wise] we shall be free ourselves and lords of others ...' [210B]). Socrates is talking with Lysis, a sweet, good-looking, good-natured teenager, whose critical powers, if any, are never in evidence in the dialogue. He chooses this eye-popping fantasy to bring somehow within the boy's ken the superlative attractions of Socratic *sophia*.]

15. Literally '*in* [or *of*] *the house*'; here 'family-relation, kinsman' in the extended sense of 'intimate', 'near and dear'.

16. Good examples in this citation of the unavoidability of the resort to 'love' when translating the verb *philein*.

17. His rendering for 210C5–8 reads: 'And shall we be friends to others, and will any others love us, in matters where we are useless *to them*? – Certainly not. – Then neither does your father love you, nor does anybody love anybody else, in so far as he is useless *to him*?' The italicized words answer to nothing in the Greek text. Similar mistranslation of the second sentence in the Pléiade translation by Robin (1950), '*En conséquence, ton père non plus,*

dans la mesure où tu ne lui es bon à rien, n'a donc pas d'amitié pour toi ...' (my emphasis). The passage had been correctly translated in the Budé translation by A. Croiset (1956).

18. It must have been an anticipation of this sequel that led Jowett to mistranslate the earlier passage.

19. The pronoun is not in the text. But the reflexive reference is definitely implied in the context: Thus Socrates observes at 217A that 'no one, while healthy, loves a doctor for the sake of health': so when persons 'love a doctor for the sake of health' it must be for the sake of the health *they* have lost and wish, with *their* doctor's aid, to regain. And cf. the next note.

20. 215BC. This is reinforced by the general formula in 218D7–9: When A loves B it is always for the sake of (*heneka tou*) something, x, and because of something (*dia ti*), y, where x ranges over goods and y over 'evils' remedied by the appropriate values of x. The 'evil' here stands for a remediable deficiency in A which B has power to remedy: '. . . that which desires, desires that of which it is in want . . . Hence that which is in want loves that of which it is in want . . .' (221D7–E2). This is Socrates' last word on this aspect of the topic (and, therefore, reassures us that the question in 215C3–4, 'But tell me, Lysis, in what way [*pēi*] have we gone off the track? Are we perchance wholly mistaken?' is not meant to invalidate everything in the preceding paragraph and, in particular, is not meant to impugn the statement that 'if one were in want of nothing one would feel no affection.')

This feature of the theory of *philia* in the *Lysis* is conserved and elaborated in what I take to be the Socratic component in the theory of eros expounded in the *Symposium*, i.e., in Socrates' dialogue with Agathon (199C–201C) and in the first part of his dialogue with Diotima (201D–206A): what we learn about love here is that it is caused by a deficiency in the lover and expresses the lover's longing for the good whose possession will relieve the deficiency. (For the shift in perspective at 206B, cf. Markus in n. 56 below, and paragraph 1 of Section IV of the present essay and n. 58.) This notion finds its complement in the thesis, emphasized in both dialogues (more briefly in the *Lysis* [216D–217A], at greater length in the *Smp.* [201B–204C], that the lover is in a condition intermediate between goodness and evil, or beauty and ugliness, hence *qua* lover neither good nor evil, neither beautiful nor ugly: if he were wholly the former, he would have no need to love.

21. [Is this consistent with Socrates' own love for his fellow-townsmen? It is. His interdependence with them would naturally generate affection for them in line with his own view of *philia* and warrant the *philanthrōpia* which, he says half-humorously in the *Euthyphro* (3D), makes him 'pour out to anyone anything I have to say'. However, in the *Apology*, where he explains with the deepest seriousness what it was that drove him to devote so large a part of his life to a mission to the unenlightened, the motive he cites is not love for those whose souls he sought to save – of such *philanthrōpia* there is not a word – but 'assistance to the god' (23B), 'tendance to the god' (23C), 'service to the god' (30A).]

22. R.-A. Gauthier and J. V. Jolif take no account of this passage when they see the *Lysis* as an expression of '*l'amour de bienveillance ou amour désintéressé*' (1958–9, 671; cf. 726). Since they do not argue for this extraordinary suggestion, one is reduced to surmise as to how it ever occurred to them that this is the message of the *Lysis*. What apparently suggested it to them is the example in 219E2–220B5 (cf. n. 23 below): they quote this passage in full (670–71) and cap the citation with a remark which shows that they are taking the father's love for the wine and his love for the son to stand respectively for '*amour de concupiscence*' and '*amour désintéressé*' without a word of explanation or argument to convince us that this is what Plato is illustrating in this passage. When he *says* he is illustrating is concern for an object which is valued not for its own sake, but for the sake of another (219E7–220A1). One wonders if they are confusing the difference between instrumental and intrinsic value (which is the immediate point of the example) with that between egoistic and non-egoistic

valuation, losing sight of the fact that the former difference would be as valid for the egoist as for anyone else: there is no reason in the world why an egoist should not attach intrinsic value to certain things, desiring them as ends (*his* ends), not as mere means.

23. Or 'phantoms'. In the terms of the accompanying example (219D5 ff.), the mistake would be to put such a value on wine as to refuse it to one's son when he is in mortal need of it, having drunk hemlock for which the wine is the only available antidote. In the analogy the father's love for the wine stands to love for his son as would love for a particular person to love for the *prōton philon*. It would be hard to think of a stronger way of making the point that in our love for persons we should *not* treat them as 'ends in themselves' (cf. the next note).

24. For an interpretation of this phrase see Vlastos 1962, 48–9, and notes. Aristotle's 'wishing another's good for his sake, not for yours', though still far from the Kantian conception of treating persons as 'ends in themselves', is the closest any philosopher comes to it in classical antiquity.

25. Just as 'it is not altogether true' that we set great stock by money, since we give it up readily when we find things we want to buy with it, so too 'it is only in a manner of speaking that we say we "love" what is loved for the sake of something else; it looks as though what is really loved is that very thing in which all of these so-called loves terminate' (209A2–B3). To say of another person that he or she is what we *really* and *truly* love would be to lapse, like the miser, into moral fetishism.

26. '. . . hence the good is loved?' (220B7) – a surprisingly casual and elliptical answer: it does not *say* that the good is the *prōton philon*, though this is doubtless what is meant. Socrates must think the proposition that the good is the *prōton philon* so truistic that it does not even call for a formal statement, let alone defence, in the present context. His attitude is perhaps understandable, given his standing conviction that the good is the only (real) object of desire (*Grg.* 467C5–468C7, which concludes, 'for we desire those things which are good, . . . while those which are neither good nor evil we do not desire, nor yet those which are evil'; cf. *Meno* 77C1–E4), and his present contention that 'desire is the reason (*aitia*) for love, and we love that which we desire and when we desire it' (221D2–4).

27. This is regarded as axiomatic in the Socratic dialogues, though never formally spelled out. It shows up, e.g., in the *Meno* (77C ff.), where the thesis that no one can desire evil things knowing that they are evil is proved by arguing that 'no one desires to be wretched and miserable' (78A4–5), or in the *Euthydemus* (278E2–282D: the protrepsis to philosophy), where it is argued that wisdom is the greatest of all goods because it alone enables us to use any other good in such a way as to make us happy, the presupposition of the argument being that anything will be good for any person if, and only if, it makes that person happy.

28. Though one would hardly guess this from much that has been written about Plato's social theory. Not a word about political *philia* in Plato in T. A. Sinclair, *Greek Political Theory* (London, 1951); in the Index under *philia* there are references to Protagoras and five other authors, but none to Plato. Sheldon Wolin, in his acute critique of Plato's political philosophy, *Politics and Vision* (Boston, 1960), duly reports (47) the doctrine of the *Politicus* that 'the end of the royal art was . . . a community bound together in "a true fellowship by mutual concord and by ties of friendship"' (311B9–C1); but nine pages later he says that 'it required the Christian notion of *agape* before there could be an idea of love as a force fusing together a community'. He evidently has no inkling of the fact that Plato expects *philia* to be just such a force. The same is true of the study of Plato's contribution to social theory, *Enter Plato* (New York, 1964), by the sociologist, Alvin W. Gouldner. He says that while Plato 'speaks well of friendship' (244), he 'removes love from the Pantheon of virtues . . . strip[s] it of moral relevance' (246). One wonders how so imaginative a student of Plato's social theory could say such things in view, e.g., of the fact that in the *Laws* the

three goals that are to guide all legislation are that the state should be intelligent, free, and 'phílē to itself' (693B–E, 701D; cf. also 628A–C, 697C, 698C, 699C, and especially 743C and 759B). Part of the trouble seems to be that he gets Plato *via* the Jowett translation, where *phílē* is turned into 'harmonious' or 'at unity with itself' and *philia* into 'friendship'. Yet even the Jowett translation might have given Gouldner reason to doubt that 'friendship' is what Plato means here. Thus in 698C one should be able to tell just from the context that Jowett's 'spirit of friendship' is a feeble understatement of what is being talked about: the embattled comradeship, the fraternal solidarity, that flared up among the Athenians at the time of the Persian invasion.

29. 451A2–8. And cf. 414E5–6, 'and they must think of the other citizens as their earth-born brothers'.

30. A. Bloom's happy rendering of *allotrios* (antonym of *oikeios*).

31. 463BC.

32. 424A; cf. 449C.

33. Cf. *Laws* 739C–740B, where thoroughgoing communism in both property and family is proclaimed as the ideal (it represents 'the best polis and laws, the most excellent constitution'), but private allotments and private families are accepted since the pure ideal would be 'beyond the capacity of people with the birth, rearing and training we assume' (740A).

34. 590C–D. Cornford, for once, misses the sense by a mile when he translates *homoioi* here by 'equal': the word could, of course, mean 'equal' in certain contexts; but equality between subject and ruler is the last thing Plato would tolerate, let alone commend; and that 'alike' is the sense here follows directly from its use in C8, to which 'governed by the same' in D6 alludes.

35. Which Plato accents strongly by using the word *doulos*, without meaning, of course, that the producers in the *Republic* are to be the chattel-slaves of the philosophers.

36. Cf. 'Justice and Happiness in the *Republic*' (hereafter abbreviated to '*JHR*') in my *Platonic Studies* (Princeton, new edition 1982), Sections II and III.

37. Thus the Guardians are denied individual property-rights because they would be 'more excellent craftsmen at their own job' (421C1–2) without, than with, such rights. Cf. *JHR*, III.2.

38. *The Open Society and Its Enemies*, Vol. I of the 4th edition (Princeton, 1963), 107 (and cf. 119). There have been many replies to this indictment. But it is not easy to rebut its thesis without endorsing antitheses which are still further from the truth. Thus R. B. Levinson (*In Defense of Plato* [Cambridge, Mass., 1953], 517) caps his critique (much of it pertinent) by calling on us to 'recognize Plato's altruistic concern for the welfare of the individual'; we are to see in 'every Platonic dialogue . . . a monument erected to his belief that individual men are important'.

39. *Lg.* 707D: '. . . unlike the majority of mankind, we do not regard mere safety and survival as matters of greatest value, but rather that men may become and be as virtuous as possible as long as they do survive'.

And 705E–706A: 'For I lay it down that only that law is rightly enacted which aims, like an archer, at this and this alone: how beauty [*to kalon*] should come about in consequence of it, passing over every other consideration, be it wealth or anything else devoid of beauty and virtue.'

40. *Lg.* 630C: '. . . every legislator worth his salt will legislate with no other end in view than to secure the greatest virtue [of the citizens]'.

41. And see the preamble to the laws in the opening paragraphs of *Lg.* V, where the rationale of the legislation is explained. (Here and in the preceding notes I have drawn on

the *Laws* where much that is implicit in the tightly constructed argument of the *Republic* is spelled out at length.)

42. Hippocrates, *Precepts*, 6: 'for if there is love of mankind, there is bound to be love of [one's] craft'.

43. *Pol*. 1275A22–3. By 'judgement' Aristotle must mean here effective judgement in political and legislative, no less than judicial, decisions (cf. *Thuc*. 2, 40, 2, *ētoi krinomen ge ē enthymoumetha*, where the latter 'must here be used of those who originate proposals', the former of those who judge [i.e., vote for or against] them [A. W. Gomme, ad loc.]; also *kritai*, 3, 37, 4, and *krinai* in 6, 39, 1). Aristotle goes on to explain (23–31) that under *archē* he includes that of the juror and of the ecclesiast, no less than that of the magistrate and of a member of the Council. Cf. 1275B 18–20 (much the same in 1278A 35–6, where 'sharing in honours' = 'sharing in *archē*' here).

44. *Pol*. 1275A7–8.

45. 'And we are free not only [1] in our public life but also [2] in the absence of suspicion (*hypopsian*) in the pursuit of our daily affairs. We feel no resentment at our neighbour if he does something for pleasure; we don't turn on sour looks which are painful even if they cause no damage' (2, 37, 2). The sense of *hypopsian* I take to be 'censorious watchfulness' (*LSJ s.v*. II). The 'sour looks' at those who choose a different style of life from ourselves (Croiset, '*regards chargés de blâme*') stand also for all those informal, extra-legal, pressures by which their life could be made miserable. For the recognition of [1] and [2] as distinct, though complementary, aspects of freedom, cf. Aristotle's account of liberty as the 'postulate' (*hypothesis*) of democracy: 'one [kind] of freedom is to rule and be ruled in turn . . . The other mark of democracy is to live as one wishes' (*Pol*. 1317B2–12).

46. *Thuc*. 7, 69, 2. Cf. Plato's account of the democratic ethos in *Rep*. 557B: there men are 'free and the polis is full of freedom and free speech, and one has the liberty to do what he likes. And where this liberty exists it is clear that each will make his own life according to his own private design – that which pleases him.' And cf. Aristotle in the preceding note.

47. The rulers 'must take the greatest care not to overlook the least infraction of the rule against innovation in gymnastic and in music counter to the established order . . . For a new form of music is to be feared as endangering the whole [of the social order]: for nowhere are the modes of music altered without affecting the most fundamental political usages . . . Here, in music, our guardians it seems must build their guard-house' (424B–C). Conceding that Homer is 'the first and most poetic of the tragic poets', we must banish him from our state: 'if you allow the honied Muse in song or verse, pleasure and pain will be king in your polis instead of law and consensus about the highest good' (607A).

48. No such word exists in English, as probably there was none in Greek when Plato wrote *idiōsis* here (no other occurrence is listed in *LSJ*). Shorey and Robin translate 'individualization', which is close enough. Cornford resorts to periphrasis: 'when such feelings are no longer universal'; so does Lee: 'When feelings differ between individuals.'

49. 462A9–C1. And cf. *Laws* 739C–D: the implementation of the maxim, 'friends have things in common' would require ideally 'driving by every means what is called "private" [*idion*] out of life, and contriving, if it were possible, that even things which nature made private should somehow become common – thus eyes and ears and hands would be expected to see and hear and act in common, and men would be as united as they could possibly be in what they praise and blame, rejoicing and grieving at the same things'.

50. The notion that friends are those who share each others' pleasures and pains is accepted by Aristotle, but only with the proviso which expresses what he himself considers definitive of *philia*: 'Your *philos* is he who shares your pleasures at what is good and grief at what is painful *for your sake, not for the sake of something else*' (*Rhet*. 1381A4–6).

The all-important phrase I have italicized is not present in *N.E.* 1166A6–8: 'And some [define the *philos*] as one who consorts with another and shares his preferences, or as one who shares the pains and pleasures of the one he loves.' But note that there is no indication here that this formula would be acceptable to Aristotle as a *definition* of *philia*. The evidence of the *Rhet.* shows that it would not: of the two formulae in 1166A2–10 only the first (A2–5, quoted in the text at n. 2, above) would be acceptable to Aristotle, since only this one states the condition which Aristotle uses to define *philos* in *Rhet.* 1380B35–1381A1 (quoted in n. 1, above), a context which leaves no doubt that Aristotle is speaking *in propria persona* (cf. 'let us define' here with 'some [define]' in *N.E.* 1166A6). That this remains the crucial condition of 'perfect' *philia* in the *N.E.* is clear e.g. at 1156B9–10: '*malista philoi* are those who wish good things for their friends for *their* sake'.

51. As breaking up the community, making it 'many' rather than 'one' (462AB); the same implication is in *Laws* 739C–D, where the citation in n. 49 goes on to speak of laws which maximize identity of pleasure and pain among the citizens as 'making the polis one so far as possible' (739D3–4).

52. 474C ff.

53. 501D: the philosophers are the 'lovers [*erastai*] of being and truth', i.e., of the Ideas; 490B: the philosopher's *erōs* for the Idea will lead him to a union with it which will give birth 'to intelligence and truth' (a passage which states in miniature the experience of the vision of the Idea of Beauty and union with it in *Smp.* 210E–212A).

54. Cf. above, n. 4 (i).

55. 201D5.

56. 204D–205A; 205E–206A11; 207A2. Nygren (op. cit., 180, n. 1) cites this passage to prove the 'egocentric' and 'acquisitive' nature of Platonic eros, taking no account of the fact that what Diotima has said so far is not meant to be the whole story: as yet she has not stated, has scarcely hinted at, that distinctive feature of Platonic eros which she proceeds forthwith to explain as 'birth in beauty' (to be discussed directly in the text above). For a corrective see R. A. Markus (1955, 219–30); Markus (225 ff.) calls attention to 'the radical change of perspective' when 'the new picture' of love 'as a begetting or procreating' is introduced. However, Markus goes a bit too far in the other direction when he remarks that while this new conception of love 'is at first grafted onto the original metaphor of desire-and-fulfilment, it very soon achieves independence' (loc. cit.). Diotima never cuts loose from the original description of eros as 'desire for one's perpetual possession of the good' (206A11–12); she brings in 'birth in beauty' to fill out, not to amend, that description (see next note), even asserting (206E8–207A2) that 'birth in beauty' *follows* (and 'necessarily'!) from that agreed-upon description. She claims that only through the immortalizing effect of 'birth in beauty' can one fulfil the desire to possess the good in perpetuity; how seriously she takes this implication shows up in her treatment of the Alcestis story: Alcestis' readiness to give her life for that of Admetus, which Phaedrus had explained as due to the intensity of her love for her husband (179C1), Diotima explains as due rather to her desire to win immortal fame for herself (208C–D). (A further point that should not escape notice is the force of the possessive pronoun in 206A11–12 and in the parallel phrase (to be cited in the next note) in 207A2. This is brought out well in Suzy Groden's translation (1970) of the two phrases: 'love is for the good to always belong to oneself', 'love is for the good to be eternally one's own'. It gets lost in the usual translations. Thus, to render the first phrase 'love is of the eternal possession of the good' [so Jowett, and similar renderings in Hamilton, Robin, Apelt & Capelle], fails to make it clear that what the lover desires is *his* possession of the good.)

57. Following Bury (against Burnet, Robin, and others) I accept Bast's emendation (favoured by Hermann and Schanz among others) of *touto* of the codices to *toutou*, since the

sense makes it clear that the reference of the pronoun in *diōkontōn auto* is not *erōs* itself, but its aim (love is the pursuing – not the object of the pursuit, which is the eternal possession of the good); and cf. 207A2, 'if love is for the good to be eternally one's own', where the object of 'is' is quite explicitly the aim of *erōs*, not *erōs* itself.

58. He replies, 'If I could [tell you the answer], Diotima, I should not be marvelling at your wisdom and coming to you to learn of this very matter.' This suggests that Plato is now introducing a doctrine which cannot be credited to the historical Socrates (cf. his use of a similar device in *Meno* 81A: Socrates learns of the doctrine of transmigration from 'priests and priestesses'). I see no justification for the view (F. M. Cornford, 'The Doctrine of Eros in Plato's *Symposium*', in *The Unwritten Philosophy* [Cambridge, 1950], 75) that 'the limit reached by the philosophy' of Socrates is indicated no earlier than in 209E4. If Plato had wanted to imply such a thing why should he have represented Socrates as stumped already at 206B?

59. For this striking image of male pregnancy [cf. 209B4 ff.: the *kyōn* is clearly male] there is no known precedent in Greek literature. The nearest thing to it is in Apollo's argument in the *Eumenides* (661 ff.) that the father is the true progenitor (*tokeus*), the mother serving only as 'nurse of the new-sown pregnancy [*trophos . . . kymatos neosporou*]' – a kind of human incubator.

60. Excising 'for birth is the intercourse of man and woman' as a gloss: cf. Bury ad loc. I find the defence of the text in S. Rosen, *Plato's Symposium* (New Haven, 1968), 247, n. 125, incomprehensible: 'it has the obvious function of serving as transition from homosexual to heterosexual generation' – how so, when there has been absolutely no reference to homosexual *generation* at all?

61. At least in the middle dialogues. There is a passage in the *Laws* (839AB) which suggests a better appreciation of conjugal love: one of his reasons there for prohibiting every other form of sexual gratification is that the restriction would make men fonder of their own wives. Cf. G. Grube, *Plato's Thought* (London, 1935), 118–19.

62. On this see Dover, 1964, 31–42, and the Appendix below.

63. I say 'new' because the doctrine of *sōphrōn erōs* (in which, it has been claimed, 'Euripides anticipates Plato' (Helen North, 1966, 73 ff. *et passim*),) is a doctrine of self-control, *not* of abstinence. The Uranian Aphrodite of Pausanias' speech in the *Symposium* is not meant to rule out intercourse, but to restrict it to a context in which intellectual and spiritual values prevail. Cf. Dover: 'But both good and bad [eros in Pausanias' speech] aim at the physical submission of the boy . . . [T]he difference . . . lies in the whole context of the ultimate physical act, not in the presence or absence of the act itself' (34).

64. See the Appendix below.

65. This is not said in the *Symposium* (cf. Grube, op. cit., 103–4) but it is suggested in the rebuff to Alcibiades' all-out attempt at seduction in 219B–D. It is unambiguously clear in *Phdr.* 250E and 255E–256E, as well as in *R.* 403BC. The latter is not contradicted in 468BC. The assumption that here Plato is 'allowing sexual licence, a completely free pick of sexual partners' to valorous warriors (Gouldner, 335) is based on a misreading of the text: *philein* does not mean 'intercourse' in this context (or in any other in Greek prose, to my knowledge) – for that Plato would have used *syngignesthai* (as in 329C2, 329C4, 360C1, 459D8, 560B5); *philein* and *haptesthai* are specifically allowed to chaste lovers in 403BC, where intercourse is clearly ruled out, as also in *Phdr.* 255E, where *haptesthai, philein*, and even *synkatakeisthai* are proper and will stop short of intercourse in the case of the 'victorious' lovers (256AB). (It should be noted that this interpretation of 468BC is entirely consistent with 'opportunity of more frequent intercourse with women' (460B) as an incentive to military prowess: this has to do not with *philein* but with eugenic breeding.)

66. 210C (a remarkable thing to say, considering the extreme susceptibility to physical beauty revealed in a passage like *Phdr.* 250C–E); and cf. *Symp.* 219C3–5.

67. 210E; cf. also 210A1 and 211C2.

68. Cf. Vlastos [1969], 76 ff.

69. Cf. *Metaph.* 1039A25 ff., and the references in Bonitz, *Index Aristotelicus*, 860A35–38.

70. For sensible instances 'resembling' their Form 'defectively' see *Phdo.* 74E1–4.

71. The assumption that the Form corresponding to a given character has that character.

72. *Symp.* 211A1–5.

73. *Symp.* 211E3.

74. The evidence tells strongly against classifying Plato as a bisexual (*pace* R. B. Levinson, op. cit., 119, n. 109): in every passage where Plato, voicing his own sentiment (through Socrates or through some other dramatic mouthpiece), alludes to sexual desire as an enthralling passion the context is homosexual: cf. Leonard Brandwood, *Word Index to Plato* (Leeds, 1976), *s.v. paidika* in all its inflections. And cf. the Appendix below.

75. *Phdr.* 251A1; *Lg.* 636B, 836B–C, 841D; and see next note.

76. *Lg.* 636B4–6 (England's text, defended by him ad loc.): 'And then again this ancient usage is thought to have corrupted the pleasure of sex which is natural not only for human beings but even for brutes'; *Lg.* 836B8–C6: 'If one were to follow nature in enacting the usage prior to Laius, stating that it was right to refrain from the same intercourse with men and boys as with women, calling to witness the nature of wild beasts and pointing out that male has no contact with male, since it is contrary to nature . . .' The same indictment of 'unnatural pleasure' in *Phdr.* 250E4–251A1: The sight of the beautiful boy incites the depraved lover 'to go after the fashion of a four-footed beast and sow generative seed (*paidosporein*); consorting with wantonness he has no fear or shame in running after unnatural pleasure'. This passage has been regularly given a heterosexual reading (most recently by Sir Kenneth Dover, *Greek Homosexuality* [Oxford, 1978], 163) because of its mention of *paidosporein* which R. Hackforth translates, 'beget offspring of the flesh'. But the word *can* carry its broader sense, as it must when used in conjunction with 'unnatural pleasure': cf. *Lg.* 841D: 'there should be no sowing of unhallowed and bastard seed with concubines, nor yet of barren [seed] with males contrary to nature', where 'contrary to nature' qualifies spilling of seed *only* in homosexual intercourse (to which alone 'unnatural' is applied: *Lg.* 636C, 836C). This gives good reason for giving a homosexual reading to *paidosporein* at *Phdr.* 250E5, as was done in antiquity: cf. Plutarch, *Amatores* 751D–E.

77. For the references see note 53 above *sub fin.*

78. On the latter see P. Shorey, *What Plato Said* (Chicago, 1933), 45. I see no good reason to doubt the authenticity of the epigram on Dion's death *ap.* Diogenes Laertius, 3, 30 (accepted by Shorey, loc. cit.; defended by C. M. Bowra, *A.J.P.* 59 [1936] 393–404) whose terminal line is 'Oh Dion, who has maddened my heart with *erōs*' (cf. 'maddened' here with the definition of love as 'madness' in the *Phdr.* 265A–266A *et passim*; cf. note 80 below).

79. Cf. Aristophanes, *Birds* 1316; *Thuc.* 2, 43, 1, with Gomme's comment *ad loc.*

80. Had I been able to work more intensively on the *Phdr.* in this essay I would have taken a crack at the extraordinary fact that here *erōs* is not only described, but *defined*, as *mania* by our ultra-rationalist, Plato, and is associated as *mania* in the closest terms with philosophy no less than with the mystic cults (which had been done also, though only in passing, in *Smp.* 218B). This convergence of *mania* and *nous* in love does not seem to intrigue commentators. Few of them notice the paradox at all or, if they do, they seem bent on explaining it away (thus J. Pieper [1964, 49 ff.] gives *mania* in the *Phdr.* a theological twist which hardly does justice to its psychological meaning; and even *qua* theology it is too one-sided: Pieper objects to 'madness' as the sense of *mania* because that 'suggests ties with the orgiastic Dionysian rites'). But even the above reference to the *Smp.* (not to refer to further

evidence, which exists in abundance) would show that those 'orgiastic Dionysian rites' could not have been entirely uncongenial to Plato.

81. *Œuvres Complètes*, vol. IV of the Pléiade Edition (Paris, 1969), 743. He goes on, a little later: 'Not all is illusion in love, I admit. But what is real consists of the sentiments with which it animates us for the true beauty it makes us love. This beauty is not in the object we love, it is the work of our errors. Well, what difference does that make? Would we be less willing to sacrifice all those base sentiments to this imaginary model?' For more statements, some of them quite remarkable, to the same effect elsewhere in Rousseau see M. Eigeldinger, *Jean Jacques Rousseau et la réalité de l'imaginaire* (Neuchâtel, 1962), Chapter 4, 'L'Amour et le pays des chimères'.

82. *Œuvres Complètes*, vol. I of the Pléiade Edition (Paris, 1959), 439. The references in the next five notes are to this volume.

83. 'Madᵉ la Comtesse de Houdetot . . . n'étoit point belle. Son visage étoit marqué de la petite vérole, son teint manquoit de finesse,' etc., 439. Compare Zulietta, 318–20.

84. 427. Erotic fantasy had been a habit of his since adolescence, 41.

85. loc. cit.

86. 440.

87. i.e., no genital intercourse. That there was physical contact of other sorts in abundance is stated openly enough in the *Confessions* (443–5; and see also the passages from the Correspondence in H. Guillemin's study, *Un Homme, Deux Ombres* [Geneva, 1943], Chapter IV, 'Fausse Route'). But there is plenty of this in Platonic love too: cf. note 65 above. Rousseau says that 'though at times carried away by my senses I sought to make her unfaithful, I never really desired this' (444); the lover depicted in *Phdr.* 254A ff. would not be human or truthful if he did not say the same *mutatis mutandis*.

88. Not that the lover in the *Phaedrus* is less combustible: the exaltation of the erotic object depicted here outruns anything in the *Confessions* or, to stick to Plato's own culture, anything in the whole of Greek prose and almost the whole of surviving Greek verse as well; it is matched only in Sappho (with whom Plato openly invites comparison, 235C3: cf. Fortenbaugh, 1966, 108–9): '[when he encounters the youth], first there comes upon him a shuddering and a measure of that awe which the [transcendental] vision had once inspired, then reverence as at the sight of a god: did he not fear being taken for a madman he would offer sacrifice to his boy-love as to a holy image and a god . . . ' (251A2–7; the translation mainly after Hackforth's).

Even so, the lover is in no danger of confusing the boy with the Idea or of decking him out with pseudo-attributes. In particular, there is no magnification of his moral or intellectual virtues, which are apparently not out of the ordinary, and the lover is not required to make believe that they are. His physical beauty is itself the 'divine' (*theoeides*, 251A2) thing in him, and this suffices.

89. Seeing her first as '*bonne, naïve, éprise d'idéal*', almost incapable of untruth (239), he soon discovers that she is cruel, sly, devious, deceitful, mercenary. Yet he remains as helplessly in love as before.

90. Cf. note 56 above.

91. Cf. Section II above and note that in the last analysis Socrates has just one reason for moral conduct: the perfection of his soul. In the *Crito*, his final reason for refraining from an unjust act (breaking gaol) is that to commit injustice would corrupt his soul (47C–48D). Cf. the argument against Polus and Callicles in the *Grg.*: against Polus he argues that one should abstain from wrong-doing because this would make one's own soul evil; also that when one has done wrong, one should welcome punishment which purges the evil in the soul, because the man with unpurged evil has suffered the greatest possible harm and is most wretched of men (477A–478E). Similarly he argues against Callicles that 'wrong-

doing is the greatest of evils to the wrong-doer' (509B) because it ruins his soul and, with one's soul ruined, one would be better off dead than alive (511E–512B). Plato never repudiates this motivation for moral conduct. He supports it to the hilt in the great argument that 'justice pays' in the *Republic*.

92. Cf. note 56 above.

93. This is most explicit in the *Phaedrus* (250E1 ff.), but also clear enough, by implication, in the *Symposium* also. This is all love for a person could be, given the status of persons in Plato's ontology.

94. Section IV above, the terminal paragraph.

95. 211C3 – an image for the idea that every other love is a means to the attainment of this one (an idea expressed no less than three times in two Stephanus pages, 210A–212B: cf. n. 67 above).

96. 251A6.

97. Which is what the boy's love turns out to be (255A ff.); he wants what his lover wants 'only more feebly' (255E2–3).

98. Cf. n. 24 above.

99. This is the point of Aristophanes' myth in the *Symposium*, as has often been noticed, and it is picked up and emphasized in another way in Diotima's speech (cf. n. 20 above).

100. Aristotle's conception of 'perfect *philia*' does not repudiate – does not even notice – what I have called above 'the cardinal flaw' in Platonic love. His intuition takes him as far as seeing that (a) *disinterested affection for the person* we love – the active desire to promote that person's good 'for that person's sake, not for ours' – must be built into love at its best, but not as far as sorting this out from (b) *appreciation of the excellences instantiated by that person*; (b), of course, need not be disinterested and *could* be egoistic. The limits of Aristotle's understanding of love show up in his failure to notice the ambiguity in 'loving a person for himself' (a phrase which may be used to express either (a) or (b): thus in *Rhet.* 1361B37 and 1381A5–6 'for himself' is used to express exactly the same thing which is conveyed by 'for his own sake' in 1380B36. But there are passages in which it is clearly used to express *only* (b): so, e.g., in *N.E.* 1157B3, 'but good men will be *philoi* for their own sake, i.e. in virtue of their goodness': here 'A and B are good men and A loves B for himself' implies 'A loves B because B is a good man and in so far as he is a good man.'

101. *Ti.* 29E–30B.

Notes to Appendix

1. Much the same, though in more guarded terms, in Webster's.

2. 253E5–254A1.

3. The 'beautiful bodies' in 210A are male: cf. 'giving birth to beautiful words' here with the 'fine words about virtue' induced by erotic passion at 209B, where boy-love is clearly in view; note 'a boy's beauty' in 210D2 and 'correct use of love for boys' in 211B5–6.

4. *Smp.* 206B ff.

5. Plato gets hold of this image in 206C (quoted above, first paragraph of Section IV), and keeps returning to it all through the sequel.

6. Cf. the concluding lines in Dover (1964, 40).

7. *Smp.* 209A–C; cf. 210C1–3.

Biographical Note

Gregory Vlastos has been Sage Professor of Philosophy at Cornell, Stuart Professor of Philosophy at Princeton and Mills Visiting Professor at the University of California at Berkeley. Currently (1983–4) he is Distinguished Visiting Professorial Fellow at Christ's College, Cambridge. He was John Locke Lecturer at Oxford in 1960, and Gifford Lecturer at St Andrews in 1981. He is a Fellow of the American Academy of Arts and Sciences, and Corresponding Fellow of the British Academy. His publications include *Platonic Studies* (1973 and 1982) and *Plato's Universe* (1979).

Further Reading

The following works are referred to in the essay only by the name of the author and the year of publication:

Bloom, Alan, *The Republic of Plato* (New York: Basic Books, 1968).

Cornford, F. M., *The Republic of Plato* (New York, 1955).

Croiset, Alfred, *Platon (Hippias Major, Charmides, Laches, Lysis)* (in the Guillaume Budé translation of Plato, 4th edn, Paris, 1956).

Dover, Kenneth J., 'Eros and Nomos', *Bulletin of the Institute of Classical Studies*, No. 11 (1964), 31–42.

Fortenbaugh, William W., 'Plato, *Phaedrus* 235C3', *Classical Philology* 61 (1966), 108–9.

R.-A. Gauthier and J. Y. Jolif, *Aristote, Éthique à Nicomaque* (Louvain, 1958–9).

Gomme, A. W., *Historical Commentary on Thucydides*, Book I (Oxford University Press, 1956).

Gould, Thomas, *Platonic Love* (London: Routledge & Kegan Paul, 1963).

Groden, Suzy, translation of Plato's *Symposium*, ed. John A. Brentlinger (Amherst, Mass., 1970).

Hackforth, R., *Plato's Phaedrus* (Cambridge University Press, 1952).

Markus, R. A., 'The Dialectic of Eros in Plato's *Symposium*', *Downside Review* 73 (1955), 219 ff.

Pieper, J., *Enthusiasm and Divine Madness*, trans. Richard and Clara Winston (New York: Harcourt, Brace, 1964).

Robin, Leon, *Platon, Œuvres Complètes*, Vol. I (Paris, 1950): the Pléiade translation of Plato.

Shorey, Paul, *Plato: The Republic*, 2 vols. (London, 1930–35).

Singer, Irving, *The Nature of Love, Plato to Luther* (New York: Random House, 1966).

Vlastos, G., 'Justice and Equality', in *Social Justice*, edited by Richard Brandt (Englewood Cliffs, N.J., 1962).

'Reasons and Causes in the *Phaedo*', *Philosophical Review* 78 (1969), 291 ff.

English translation of the whole of Plato's *œuvre* is available in Edith Hamilton and Huntington Cairns (eds.), *The Collected Dialogues of Plato* (including the Letters) (Princeton: Bollingen Books, 1961). Several of these are reprinted from the fourth (revised) edition of Benjámin Jowett's translation of Plato (Oxford University Press, 1953). Others are reprinted from translations by various authors, including R. Hackforth's of the *Phaedrus* and the *Philebus* (Cambridge University Press, 1952 and 1945); F. M. Cornford's of the *Theaetetus* and the *Sophist* (in his *Plato's Theory of Knowledge* [London: Routledge & Kegan Paul, 1933]) and of the *Parmenides* (in his *Plato and Parmenides* [London: Routledge & Kegan Paul, 1939]); Paul Shorey's of the *Republic* (Cambridge, Mass.: Harvard University Press [in the Loeb Classical Library], 1930 and 1935): A. E. Taylor's of the *Laws* (London: J. M. Dent, and New York: E. P. Dutton, Everyman's Library, 1934).

There are many alternative English translations of individual dialogues, some of which are superior to those included in the Hamilton and Cairns volume. Among the better ones are the following: R. E. Allen's of the *Euthyphro* (in his *Plato's 'Euthyphro' and the Earlier Theory of Forms* [London: Routledge & Kegan Paul, 1972]); G. M. A. Grube's of the *Euthyphro*, *Apology*, and *Crito* (in his *Trial and Death of Socrates* [Indianapolis: Hackett Publishing Company, 1975]); C. C. W. Taylor's of the *Protagoras* (Oxford: Clarendon Press, 1976); Rosamond K. Sprague's of the *Laches* and *Charmides* (Indianapolis and New York: Bobbs-Merrill, 1973 [in the Library of Liberal Arts]); R. Hackforth's of the *Phaedo* (Cambridge University Press, 1955); John McDowell's of the *Theaetetus* (Oxford: Clarendon Press, 1973); A. D. Lindsay's of the *Republic* (London: J. M. Dent; and New York: E. P. Dutton, 1935); F. M. Cornford's of the *Republic* (New York: Oxford University Press, 1945); R. G. Bury's of the *Laws* (Cambridge, Mass.: Harvard University Press [in the Loeb Classical Library]).

An excellent French translation of the Platonic corpus has been made for the Bibliothèque de la Pléiade by L. Robin and Joseph Moreau (all of the dialogues, except the *Parmenides* and *Timaeus*, are by Robin) (Paris, 1950).

M. F. Burnyeat

Aristotle: On Learning to Be Good

The main aim of Myles Burnyeat's inquiring and carefully speculative essay is to shed light on an absolutely essential and as it may seem obscure phase in the experience of an individual who subsequently comes to live the good life – the good life for man as conceived by Aristotle in the *Nicomachean Ethics*. That work has as much claim as any to being the most excellent in the long history of moral philosophy. Certainly it has been the most venerated, and it may be the part of Aristotle's philosophy which now gets most attention, which is to say a great deal. It consists, however, in scripts for his own lectures, scripts brought together by other hands. This is at least part of the reason for what is necessary, the considering of various scattered sections of the *Nicomachean Ethics* in order to come to and to examine Aristotle's view of the given prerequisite of the completed life of happiness and virtue.

To come to have a view of the prerequisite is to be enabled to understand better that of which it is a prerequisite, the completed life of virtue. It is also to come to have a view of those who have not satisfied the prerequisite, in particular the weak-willed, those who see the better course of action and yet follow the worse. The weak-willed or incontinent or akratic man, given certain assumptions about him, poses a troublesome philosophical problem. It is a secondary recommendation of Burnyeat's essay that he can be seen to be less troublesome than often supposed.

The *Nicomachean Ethics*, as he remarks, does not consist in sermons or argument directed to the wicked in the hope of getting them to mend their ways. Aristotle had little confidence in that kind of endeavour.

Aristotle, 384–322 B.C. Born in Stagira in northern Greece, the pupil of Plato and the founder of the Lyceum or Peripatos in Athens. His interests were wide, ranging over the main parts of philosophy and science, and among his attainments was the inauguration of the systematic study of logic. Remembering the death of Socrates he left Athens, 'in case the Athenians should sin a second time against philosophy'.

Nor are they directed to the morally immature, of whatever age. Rather, they are directed to those who already have acquired a certain morality. They do have a knowledge of what sorts of actions are virtuous. (pp. 55–7) What they do not have is a certain understanding of those actions, an understanding of what it is that makes actions just or magnanimous or courageous, or an understanding of how virtuous actions fit into the scheme of the good life for man. Thus, despite what they can be said to know, they have not in Aristotle's view actually acquired the virtues.

Having a knowledge of what sorts of actions are virtuous is the prerequisite of moving forward to the good life – which movement will be aided by Aristotle's lectures – but how does that knowledge come to be had? What happens in this essential phase? Aristotle's answer, in general, is well-known. A young man comes to have some approximation of the virtue of temperance by doing temperate things and thus falling into the habit of doing them. This is a matter of having a good upbringing. All of that, however, leaves the essential thing obscure. What explains why a good upbringing does not always produce the goods? Why is it that some individuals fall not into good habits but bad ones? Among the latter individuals, why is it that some see the better but do the worse? (pp. 58–9)

In terms of Aristotle's Greek, how is it that some individuals come to have a grip on 'the that' – how do they come to know, in some sense, that actions of one kind and another are virtuous? How do they come to this state, prior to having a grip on 'the because', prior to having an explanation of the very nature of the virtues and their part in the good life? (pp. 56–7) This is a matter not just of behaviour, but of knowledge, of seeing for oneself that certain things are true. (pp. 59–60)

The answer suggested, which is in part derived from a passage in the last chapter of the *Nicomachean Ethics* (p. 60), is that some individuals taste the *pleasures* of just action or temperate action or noble action. Pleasure or enjoyment in doing the right thing is what makes it comprehensible that some individuals, indeed many, come to have the prerequisite for further progress. There is the corollary that the state they come to be in can be misdescribed as merely a state of *knowing*, merely a state of having *learned*, what actions are in accordance with virtue. It is a mistake to intellectualize the state, to see it as only unimportantly a matter of feelings. What may happen in the course of a good upbringing is something which takes time, the acquiring of certain desires. These beginnings of morality are importantly unreasoned. (pp. 61–7)

This is the main but not the only thesis of the essay. A second thesis has to do with the weak-willed man. (pp. 67–74) In terms which Aristotle favoured, he may in a certain situation have two lines of thought. One is this: 'Insulting behaviour by others should be suitably answered; I have been insulted; I should act.' Another line of thought is this: 'Seeming insults need looking into before one acts; it seems that I have been insulted; I should take time to think.' Why does the weak-willed man act on the first syllogism rather than the second? The answer given is that it is a mistake to follow certain philosophers and to try to get the answer by looking into his head *now*, looking at him in his present situation of conflict. The answer is to be got from his past, and at bottom it is that he has not come to take pleasure in a certain kind of self-restraint. A third and less developed thesis of the essay has to do with the man of virtue, the individual who has come to a full knowledge of the good life, including the place of the virtues in it. Given his past – the essential phase we have been considering – he will to a considerable extent be a man of feeling and desire.

Burnyeat remarks that his paper is nothing but a prolegomenon to a reading of the *Nicomachean Ethics*. To be that thing – which at least it is – is to be a considerable thing.

Full details of works referred to in the article and footnotes, by title or author's name, are given in the note on further reading.

M. F. Burnyeat

Aristotle: On Learning to Be Good

The question 'Can virtue be taught?' is perhaps the oldest question in moral philosophy. Recall the opening of Plato's *Meno* (70a): 'Can you tell me, Socrates – can virtue be taught, or is it rather to be acquired by practice? Or is it neither to be practised nor to be learned, but something that comes to men by nature or in some other way?' This is a simple version of what was evidently a well-worn topic of discussion. Socrates' characteristic, but still simple reply is that until one knows what virtue is, one cannot know how it is (to be) acquired (*Meno* 71ab). I want to reverse the order, asking how, according to Aristotle, virtue is acquired, so as to bring to light certain features in his conception of what virtue is which are not ordinarily much attended to. Aristotle came to these questions after they had been transformed by the pioneering work in moral psychology which the mature Plato undertook in the *Republic* and later dialogues; by his time the simplicities of the debate in the *Meno* lay far behind. Nevertheless, about one thing Socrates was right: any tolerably explicit view of the process of moral development depends decisively on a conception of virtue. This dependence makes it possible to read a philosopher's account of moral development as evidence for what he thinks virtue is. In some ways, indeed, it is especially revealing evidence, since in problems of moral education the philosopher has to confront the complex reality of ordinary imperfect human beings.

My aim, then, is to reconstruct Aristotle's picture of the good man's development over time, concentrating on the earlier stages. Materials for the construction are abundant in the *Nicomachean Ethics*, but scattered; the construction will be gradual, its sense emerging progressively as the pieces come together from their separate contexts. I shall have

M. F. Burnyeat, 'Aristotle on Learning to Be Good', from *Essays on Aristotle's Ethics*, ed. Amélie Rorty (University of California Press, 1980). Reprinted with minor alterations with the permission of the author, editor and publisher.

to forgo extended exegesis of the various discussions from which Aristotle's remarks are extracted, but I trust that it is not necessary to apologize for the undefended interpretative decisions this will involve; such decisions are an inescapable responsibility of the synoptic enterprise.

Aristotle's good man, however, is not the only character I have in view. I am also interested in the conflicted akratic, the weak-willed (incontinent) man who knows the good but does not always achieve it in action. I want to place his problem too in the perspective of his development through time. And while I am not going to attempt anything like a full treatment of Aristotle's account of akrasia (incontinence, weakness of will), my hope is that the temporal perspective I shall sketch will remove one major source, at any rate, of the dissatisfaction which is often, and understandably, felt with Aristotle's account of the phenomenon.

In both cases, the good man and the akratic, we shall be concerned with the primitive materials from which character and a mature morality must grow. A wide range of desires and feelings are shaping patterns of motivation and response in a person well before he comes to a reasoned outlook on his life as a whole, and certainly before he integrates this reflective consciousness with his actual behaviour. It is this focus of interest that constitutes the chief philosophical benefit, as I conceive it, of what is a predominantly historical inquiry. Intellectualism, a one-sided preoccupation with reason and reasoning, is a perennial failing in moral philosophy. The very subject of moral philosophy is sometimes defined or delimited as the study of moral reasoning, thereby excluding the greater part of what is important in the initial – and, I think, continuing – moral development of a person. Aristotle knew intellectualism in the form of Socrates' doctrine that virtue is knowledge. He reacted by emphasizing the importance of beginnings and the gradual development of good habits of feeling. The twentieth century, which has its own intellectualisms to combat, also has several full-scale developmental psychologies to draw upon. But they have not been much drawn upon in the moral philosophy of our time, which has been little interested in questions of education and development.[1] In this respect Aristotle's example has gone sadly unstudied and ignored.

No doubt Aristotle's developmental picture is still much too simple, by comparison with what could be available to us. Let that be conceded at once – to anyone who can do better. What is exemplary in Aristotle is his grasp of the truth that morality comes in a sequence of stages with both cognitive and emotional dimensions. This basic insight is already sufficient, as we shall see, to bring new light on akrasia.

So let us begin at the beginning, which Aristotle says is 'the *that*'. This somewhat cryptic phrase occurs in an admitted digression (cf. 1095b 14) towards the end of I 4 of the *Nicomachean Ethics*. Aristotle has just begun the search for a satisfactory specification of happiness and the good for man when he pauses to reflect, with acknowledgements to Plato, on the methodological importance of being clear whether one is on the way to first principles or starting points or on the way from them (1095a 14–b 1). The answer to Plato's question is that at this stage Aristotle is travelling dialectically towards a first principle or starting point, namely, the specification of happiness, but in another sense his inquiry must have its own starting points to proceed from. As he explains (1095b 2–13),

> For while one must begin from what is familiar, this may be taken in two ways: some things are familiar to us, others familiar without qualification. Presumably, then, what *we* should begin from is things familiar to *us*. This is the reason why one should have been well brought up in good habits if one is going to listen adequately to lectures about things noble and just, and in general about political (social) affairs. For the beginning (starting point) is 'the *that*', and if this is sufficiently apparent to a person, he will not in addition have a need for 'the *because*'. Such a person has, or can easily get hold of, beginnings (starting-points), whereas he who has neither [*sc.* neither 'the *that*' nor 'the *because*'],[2] let him hearken to the words of Hesiod:
>
> > The best man of all is he who knows everything himself,
> > Good also the man who accepts another's sound advice;
> > But the man who neither knows himself nor takes to heart
> > What another says, he is no good at all.

The contrast here, between having 'the *that*' and having 'the *because*' as well, is a contrast between knowing or believing that something is so and understanding why it is so, and I would suppose that Aristotle quotes the Hesiodic verses in all seriousness. The man who knows for himself is someone with 'the *because*' – in Aristotle's terms he is a man of practical wisdom equipped with the understanding to work out for himself what to do in the varied circumstances of life – while the one who takes to heart sound advice learns 'the *that*' and becomes the sort of person who can profit from Aristotle's lectures. These lectures are no doubt designed to give him a reasoned understanding of 'the *because*' which explains and justifies 'the *that*' which he already has or can easily get hold of. What, then, is 'the *that*'?

The ancient commentators are agreed that Aristotle has in mind knowledge about actions in accordance with the virtues; these actions are the things familiar to us from which we must start, and what we know about them is that they are noble or just.[3] This fits an earlier statement (I 3 1095a 2–4, quoted below) that the lectures assume on the part of their audience a certain experience in the actions of life, because they are concerned with these actions and *start from them*. It also conforms to what I 4 says is the subject matter of the lectures for which knowledge of 'the *that*' is a prerequisite: things noble and just.

Now the noble and the just do not, in Aristotle's view, admit of neat formulation in rules or traditional precepts (cf. I 3 1094b 14–16, II 2 1104a 3–10, V 10 1137b 13–32, IX 2 1165a 12–14). It takes an educated perception, a capacity going beyond the application of general rules, to tell what is required for the practice of the virtues in specific circumstances (II 9 1109b 23, IV 5 1126b 2–4). That being so, if the student is to have 'the *that*' for which the doctrines in Aristotle's lectures provide the explanatory '*because*', if he is to be starting out on a path which will lead to his acquiring that educated perception, the emphasis had better be on his knowing of specific actions that they are noble or just in specific circumstances. I put it as a matter of emphasis only, of degree, because often, no doubt, moral advice will come to him in fairly general terms; a spot of dialectic may be needed to bring home to the young man the limitations and imprecision of what he has learned. But even where the advice is general, this need not mean he is taught that there are certain rules of justice, say, which are to be followed as a matter of principle, without regard for the spirit of justice and the ways in which circumstances alter cases. What Aristotle is pointing to is our ability to internalize from a scattered range of particular cases a general evaluative attitude which is not reducible to rules or precepts. It is with this process in view that he emphasizes in I 4 that the necessary beginnings or starting points, which I have argued to be correct ideas about what actions are noble and just, are not available to anyone who has not had the benefit of an upbringing in good habits.

We can put this together with some further remarks about 'the *that*' at the end of I 7 (1098a 33–b 4):

> We must not demand explanation [*sc.* any more than precision] in all matters alike, but it is sufficient in some cases to have 'the *that*' shown properly, just as in the case of starting-points. 'The *that*' is a first thing and a starting-point. Of starting-points some are seen by induction, some by perception, some by a certain habituation, and others in other ways again.

This time the wider context points to the outline definition of happiness or the good for man as the particular '*that*' which Aristotle has initially in mind. The search for a satisfactory specification of happiness and the good for man has just been completed, and Aristotle is reflecting on the extent to which he should claim precision and proof for his answer: it has the status of 'the *that*' merely, and, being general, no more precision than the subject-matter allows. Thus it would obviously be wrong to think of the notion of 'the *that*' as intrinsically tied to particular low-level facts. Nevertheless, in this passage the thesis that we have to start from 'the *that*' without an explanation, without 'the *because*', is reasserted for starting-points quite generally, and comp- lemented by a brief survey of various ways in which we acquire starting-points. We already know that in ethics good habits are a prerequisite for grasping 'the *that*'. It is now added that habituation is actually a way of grasping it, on a par with, though different from, induction, perception and other modes of acquisition which Aristotle does not specify (the ancient commentators fill out the list for him by mentioning intellectual intuition and experience).[4] Each kind of starting-point comes with a mode of acquisition appropriate to it; to give a couple of examples from the ancient commentators, we learn by induction that all men breathe, by perception that fire is hot. In ethics the appropriate mode for at least some starting-points is habituation, and in the light of I 4 it is not difficult to see which starting-points these must be.[5] The thesis is that we first learn (come to see) what is noble and just *not* by experience of or induction from a series of instances, nor by intuition (intellectual or perceptual), but by learning to do noble and just things, by being habituated to noble and just conduct.

In part, this is the well-known doctrine of II 1 and 4 that we become just or temperate by doing, and becoming habituated to doing, just and temperate things. But the passages we have examined from I 4 and 7 add to those chapters a cognitive slant. It turns out that Aristotle is not simply giving us a bland reminder that virtue takes practice. Rather, practice has cognitive powers, in that it is the way we learn what is noble or just. And on reflection we can see that this addition is quite in accord with II 1 and 4, even demanded by them. For according to II 4 the ultimate goal towards which the beginner's practice is aimed is that he should become the sort of person who does virtuous things in full knowledge of what he is doing, choosing to do it for its own sake, and acting out of a settled state of character (1105a 28–33). The beginner would hardly be on the way to this desirable state of affairs if he was not in the process forming (reasonably correct) ideas as to the nobility or justice of the actions he was engaged in; if you like, he must be on his way to acquiring a mature sense of values.

Let me skip here to VII 3 where at 1147a 21–2 Aristotle has an interesting remark about learners in general:

> Those who have learned a subject for the first time connect together[6] the propositions in an orderly way, but do not yet know them; for the propositions need to become second nature to them, and that takes time.

We shall come later to the significance of this learner as one of Aristotle's models for the state of mind of the akratic man. At present I want simply to connect the thought in VII 3 of ideas or beliefs becoming second nature to someone with the thought in II 4 of the learner in morals as someone who is tending towards a firmly established state of character which includes, and therefore must in part have developed out of, convictions about what is noble and just. The fully developed man of virtue and practical wisdom understands 'the *because*' of these convictions – in terms of I 4's contrast between things familiar without qualification and things familiar to us, he has knowledge or familiarity in the unqualified sense – but this state is preceded by the learner's knowledge (in the qualified sense) of 'the *that*', acquired by habituation so that it is second nature to him. Although only at the beginning of the road to full virtue, the learner has advanced to a stage where, having internalized 'the *that*', he has or can easily get hold of the type of starting-point which is seen by habituation.

Thus the picture forms as follows. You need a good upbringing not simply in order that you should have someone around to tell you what is noble and just – you do need that (recall the Hesiodic verses) and in X 9, and again in the *Politics* VIII 1, Aristotle discusses whether the job is best done by one's father or by community arrangements – but you need also to be guided in your conduct so that by doing the things you are told are noble and just you will discover that what you have been told is *true*. What you may begin by taking on trust you can come to know for yourself. This is not yet to know *why* it is true, but it is to have *learned that* it is true in the sense of having made the judgement your own, second nature to you – Hesiod's taking to heart. Nor is it yet to have acquired any of the virtues, for which practical wisdom is required (VI 13, X 8 1178a 16–19), that understanding of 'the *because*' which alone can accomplish the final correcting and perfecting of your perception of 'the *that*'. But it is to have made a beginning. You can say, perhaps, 'I have learned that it is just to share my belongings with others,' and mean it in a way that someone who has merely been told this cannot, even if he believes it – except in the weak sense in which 'I have learned such and such' means simply that such and such was the content of the instruction given by parent or teacher.

This is a hard lesson, and not only in the moralist's sense. How can I learn that something is noble or just by becoming habituated to doing it? Is it not one thing to learn *to* do what is just and quite another to learn *that* it is just? Clearly, we need to look further at what Aristotle has to say about learning to do what is noble and just. Let us begin again at the beginning presupposed by Aristotle's lectures. For more is said about good upbringing and its benefits in X 9, the very last chapter of the *Nicomachean Ethics*, which is specifically devoted to moral education.

In this chapter Aristotle gives an explanation (1179b 4–31) of why it is that only someone with a good upbringing can benefit from the kind of argument and discussion contained in his lectures.

Now if arguments were in themselves enough to make men good, they would justly, as Theognis says, have won very great rewards, and such rewards should have been provided; but as things are, while they seem to have power to encourage and stimulate the generous-minded among our youth, and to make a character which is well-bred,[7] and a true lover of what is noble, ready to be possessed by virtue, they are not able to encourage the *many* to nobility and goodness. For these do not by nature obey the sense of shame, but only fear, and do not abstain from bad acts because of their baseness but through fear of punishment; living by passion they pursue the pleasures appropriate to their character and the means to them, and avoid the opposite pains, and have not even a conception of what is noble and truly pleasant, since they have never tasted it. What argument would remould such people? It is hard, if not impossible, to remove by argument the traits that have long since been incorporated in the character; and perhaps we must be content if, when all the influences by which we are thought to become good are present, we get some tincture of virtue.

Now some think that we are made good by nature, others by habituation, others by teaching. Nature's part evidently does not depend on us, but as a result of some divine causes is present in those who are truly fortunate; while argument and teaching, we may suspect, are not powerful with all men, but the soul of the student must first have been cultivated, by means of habits, for noble joy and noble hatred, like earth which is to nourish the seed. For he who lives as passion directs will not hear argument that dissuades him, nor understand it if he does; and how can we persuade one in such a state to change his ways? And in general passion seems to yield not to argument but to force. The character, then, must somehow be there already with a kinship to virtue, loving what is noble and hating what is base.[8]

This important and neglected passage is not rhetoric but precise argument,[9] as I hope eventually to show. My immediate concern is the student Aristotle wants for his lectures. He is someone who already loves what is noble and takes pleasure in it. He has a conception of what is noble and truly pleasant which other, less well brought-up people lack because they have not tasted the pleasures of what is noble. This is what gives his character a kinship to virtue and a receptiveness to arguments directed to encouraging virtue.

The noble nature here described – Aristotle's prospective student – we met earlier as the person with a starting point. He is one who has learned what is noble ('the *that*') and, as we now see, thus come to love it. He loves it because it is what is truly or by nature pleasant. Compare I 8 1099a 13–15:

> Lovers of what is noble find pleasant the things that are by nature pleasant; and virtuous actions are such, so that these are pleasant for such men as well in their own nature.

This is from a context which makes clear that the word 'love' is not idly used; Aristotle has in mind a disposition of the feelings comparable in intensity, though not of course in every other respect, to the passion of a man who is crazy about horses. And the point he is making is that what you love in this sense is what you enjoy or take pleasure in. But equally he insists (X 9 1179b 24–6) that the capacity for 'noble joy and noble hatred' grows from habituation. I should now like to suggest that the prominence given to pleasure in these passages is the key to our problem about how practice can lead to knowledge.

There is such a thing as learning to enjoy something (painting, music, skiing, philosophy), and it is not sharply distinct from learning that the thing in question is enjoyable. Once again we need to eliminate the weak sense of 'learn', the sense in which to have learned that skiing is enjoyable is simply to have acquired the information, regardless of personal experience. In the strong sense I only learn that skiing is enjoyable by trying it myself and coming to enjoy it. The growth of enjoyment goes hand in hand with the internalization of knowledge.

There is also such a thing as learning to enjoy something properly, where this contrasts with merely taking pleasure in it. This is a hard subject, but I can indicate roughly what I mean by a few examples of not enjoying something properly: enjoying philosophy for the sense of power it can give, enjoying a trip abroad because of the splendid photographs you are taking on the way, enjoying a party because you are meeting important people, letting a symphony trigger a release of sentimental emotion. Aristotle's virtue of temperance is about the proper enjoyment of certain bodily pleasures having to do with taste and touch. These are things that any man or beast can take pleasure in, but not necessarily in the right way. Take the example of the gourmand who prayed that his throat might become longer than a crane's, so that he could prolong his enjoyment of the feel of the food going down (III 10 1118a 26–b 1): this illustrates the perversion of a man who takes more pleasure in brute contact with the food than in the flavours which are the proper object of taste. Aristotelian temperance is also concerned with sexual relations –

> *All* men enjoy in some way or other good food and wines and sexual inter-course, but not all men do so as they ought. (VII 14 1154a 17–18)

And this again is a thought we can understand, however difficult it might be to elaborate.

Now Aristotle holds that to learn to do what is virtuous, to make it a habit or second nature to one, is among other things to learn to enjoy doing it, to come to take pleasure – the appropriate pleasure – in doing it. It is in the light of whether a man enjoys or fails to enjoy virtuous actions that we tell whether he has formed the right disposition towards them. Thus II 3 1104b 3–13 (but the whole chapter is relevant):

> We must take as a sign of states of character the pleasure or pain that ensues on acts; for the man who abstains from bodily pleasures and delights in this very fact is temperate, while the man who is annoyed at it is self-indulgent, and he who stands his ground against things that are terrible and delights in this or at least is not pained is brave, while the man who is pained is a coward.[10] For moral excellence is concerned with pleasures and pains; it is on account of the pleasure that we do bad things, and on account of the pain that we abstain from noble ones. Hence we ought to have been brought up in a particular way from our very youth, as Plato says, so as both to delight in and to be pained by the things that we ought;[11] this is the right education. (cp. I 8 1099a 17–21, II 9 1109b 1–5, III 4 1113a 31–3, IV 1 1120a 26–7, X 1 1172a 20–23)

Such passages need to be received in the light of Aristotle's own analysis of pleasure in Books VII and X (cf. especially X 3 1173b 28–31): the delight of the temperate man who is pleased to be abstaining from overindulgence, or that of the brave man who is pleased to be standing up to a frightful situation, is not the same or the same in kind as the pleasure of indulgence or the relief of safety. The character of one's pleasure depends on what is enjoyed, and what the virtuous man enjoys is quite different from what the non-virtuous enjoy; which is not to say that the enjoyment is not as intense, only that it is as different as the things enjoyed. Specifically, what the virtuous man enjoys, as the passage quoted makes very clear, is the practice of the virtues undertaken for its own sake. And in cases such as the facing of danger, cited here, and others, the actions which the practice of the virtues requires *could* only be enjoyed if they are seen as noble and virtuous and the agent delights in his achievement of something fine and noble (cf. III 9 1117a 33–b 16). That is why his enjoyment or lack of it is the test of whether he really has the virtues.

Next, recall once more the statement in II 4 that virtue involves choosing virtuous actions for their own sake, for what they are. If we are asked what virtuous actions are, an important part of the answer must be that they are just, courageous, temperate, etc. and in all cases noble. (It is common to all virtuous actions that they are chosen because they are noble: III 7 1115b 12–13, IV 1 1120a 23–4, IV 2 1122b 6–7,[12] *EE* 1230a 27–9.) Accordingly, if learning to do and to take (proper) enjoyment in doing just actions is learning to do and to enjoy them for their own sake, for what they are, viz. just, and this is not to be distinguished from learning that they are enjoyable for themselves and their intrinsic value, viz. their justice and nobility, then perhaps we can give intelligible sense to the thesis that practice leads to knowledge, as follows. I may be told, and may believe, that such and such actions are just and noble, but I have not really learned for myself (taken to heart, made second nature to me) that they have this intrinsic value until I have learned to value (love) them for it, with the consequence that I take pleasure in doing them. To understand and appreciate the value that makes them enjoyable in themselves, I must learn for myself to enjoy them, and that does take time and practice; in short, habituation.

Back now to X 9. We have come to see that the young person there spoken of as a true lover of what is noble is not simply someone with a generalized desire to do whatever should turn out to be noble, but someone who has acquired a taste for, a capacity to enjoy for their own sake, things that are in fact noble and enjoyable for their own sake. He has learned, really learned, that they are noble and enjoyable, but as yet he does not understand why they are so. He does not have the good man's unqualified knowledge or practical wisdom, although he does have 'the *that*' which is the necessary starting point for acquiring practical wisdom and full virtue. He is thus educable. According to X 9 argument and discussion will encourage him towards virtue because he obeys a sense of shame (*aidōs*) as opposed to fear. What does this mean?

Aristotle discusses shame in IV 9:

> Shame should not be described as a virtue; for it is more like a feeling than a state of character. It is defined, at any rate, as a kind of fear of disgrace . . .
> The feeling is not becoming to every age, but only to youth. For we think

young people should be prone to the feeling of shame because they live by feeling and therefore commit many errors, but are restrained by shame; and we praise young people who are prone to this feeling, but an older person no one would praise for being prone to the sense of disgrace, since we think he should not do anything that need cause this sense. (1128b 10–12, 15–21)

Shame is the semi-virtue of the learner. The learner is envisaged as a young person who lives by the feelings of the moment and for that reason makes mistakes. He wants to do noble things but sometimes does things that are disgraceful, ignoble, and then he feels ashamed of himself and his conduct.[13] Now Aristotle holds that all young people (and many older ones) live by the feeling of the moment and keep chasing after what at a given time appears pleasant. A sample statement is the following from VIII 3 1156a 31–3:

The friendship of young people seems to aim at pleasure; for they live under the guidance of emotion, and pursue above all what is pleasant to themselves and what is immediately before them. (cp. I 3 1095a 4–8)

The point about those of the young who have been well brought-up is that they have acquired a taste for pleasures, namely the pleasures of noble and just actions, which others have no inkling of. The less fortunate majority also live by the feelings of the moment (X 9 1179b 13, 27–8), but since they find no enjoyment in noble and just actions, the only way to get them to behave properly is through fear of punishment (X 9 1179b 11–13). They will abstain from wrongdoing not because it is disgraceful, not because of what the actions are, unjust, but simply and solely as a means of avoiding the pains of punishment. Whereas the well brought-up person has an entirely different sort of reason for avoiding them. In so far as he realizes they are unjust or ignoble, they do not appear to him as pleasant or enjoyable; in so far as he does not realize this and so desires and perhaps does such things, he feels badly about it, ashamed of his failure. The actions pain him internally, not consequentially. He is therefore receptive to the kind of moral education which will set his judgement straight and develop the intellectual capacities (practical wisdom) which will enable him to avoid such errors.

The fundamental insight here is Plato's. For in discussing the development in the young of a set of motives concerned with what is noble and just, we are on the territory which Plato marked out for the middle part of his tripartite soul. The middle, so-called spirited part strives to do what is just and noble (*Rep.* 440cd), and develops in the young before reason (441a; cp. Ar. *Pol.* 1334b 22–5). It is also the seat of shame: implicitly so in the story of Leontius and his indignation with himself for desiring to look on the corpses, explicitly in the *Phaedrus* (253d, 254e). The connection with anger, which we shall also find in Aristotle, is that typically anger is this same concern with what is just and noble directed outwards towards other people (cp. *EN* V 8 1135b 28–9). Aristotle owes to Plato, as he himself acknowledges in II 3, the idea that these motivating evaluative responses are unreasoned – they develop before reason and are not at that stage grounded in a general view of the place of the virtues in the good life – and because they are unreasoned, other kinds of training must be devised to direct them on to the right kinds of object: chiefly, guided practice and habituation, as we have seen, but Aristotle also shares with Plato the characteristically Greek belief that musical appreciation will teach and accustom one to judge rightly and enjoy decent characters and noble actions through their representation in music (*Pol.* 1340a 14 ff.). In both cases the underlying idea is that the child's sense of pleasure, which to begin with and for a long while is his only motive, should be hooked up with just and noble things so that his unreasoned evaluative responses develop in connection with the right objects.

To say that these responses are unreasoned is to make a remark about their source. The contrast is with desires – the reasoned desires to which we shall come shortly – which derive from a reflective scheme of values organized under the heading of the good. But where desires and feelings are concerned, the nature of the response and its source are connected. It is not that the evaluative responses have no thought component (no intentionality): on the contrary, something is desired as noble or just, something inspires shame because it is thought of as disgraceful. The responses are grounded in an evaluation of their object, parallel to the way appetite is oriented to a conception of its object as something pleasant; in this sense both have their 'reasons'. The point is that such reasons need not invariably or immediately give way or lose efficacy to contrary considerations. There are, as it were, pockets of thought in us which can remain relatively unaffected by our overall view of things. This is a phenomenon which the century of psychoanalysis is well placed to understand, but the Greek philosophers already saw that it must be central to any plausible account of akrasia. It is that insight which backs their interweaving of the topics of akrasia and moral development.[14]

From all this it follows not only that for a long time moral development must be a less than fully rational process, but also, what is less often acknowledged, that a mature morality must in large part continue to be what it originally was, a matter of responses deriving from sources other than reflective reason. These being the fabric of moral character, in the fully developed man of virtue and practical wisdom they have become integrated with, indeed they are now infused and corrected by, his reasoned scheme of values. To return to temperance:

As the child should live according to the direction of his tutor, so the appetitive element should live according to reason. Hence the appetitive element in a temperate man should harmonize with reason; for the noble is the mark at which both aim, and the temperate man desires the things he ought, as he ought, and when he ought; and this is what reason directs. (III 12 1119b 13–18; cp. I 13 1102b 28, IX 4 1166a 13–14)

This is Aristotle's version of the psychic harmony which Plato sought to establish in the guardians of his ideal republic.

But Aristotle, as X 9 makes clear, draws an important conclusion from the requirement of unreasoned beginnings which is not, perhaps, so evident in Plato (though we shall come back to Plato in a while). In Aristotle's view it is no good arguing or discussing with someone who lacks the appropriate starting-points ('the *that*') and has no conception of just or noble actions as worthwhile in themselves, regardless of contingent rewards and punishments. To such a person you can recommend the virtues only in so far as they are required in a given social order for avoiding the pain of punishment. That is, for essentially external, contingent reasons. You cannot guarantee to be able to show they will contribute to personal goals the agent already has, be it power, money, pleasure or whatever; and even if in given contingent circumstances this connection with some antecedent personal goal could be made, you would not have given the person reason to pursue the virtues for their own sake, as a *part* of happiness, only as a means to it.

This casts some light on what Aristotle takes himself to be doing in the *Nicomachean Ethics* and why he asks for a good upbringing as a condition for intelligent study of the subject. If he is setting out 'the *because*' of virtuous actions, he is explaining what makes them noble, just, courageous and so on, and how they fit into a scheme of the good life, not why they should be pursued at all. He is addressing someone who already wants and enjoys virtuous action and needs to see this aspect of his life in a deeper perspective. He is not attempting the task so many moralists have undertaken of recommending virtue even to those who despise it – his lectures are not sermons, nor even protreptic argument, urging the wicked to mend their ways. X 9 shows he did not think that sort of thing is much use; some, perhaps most, people's basic desires are already so corrupted that no amount of argument will bring them to see that virtue is desirable in and for itself (cp. III 5 1114a 19–21). Rather, he is giving a course in practical thinking to enable someone who already wants to be virtuous to understand better what he should do and why.[15] Such understanding, as Aristotle conceives it, is more than merely cognitive. Since it is the articulation of a mature scheme of values under the heading of the good, it will itself provide new and more reflective motivation for virtuous conduct. That is why Aristotle can claim (I 3 1095a 5–6, II 2 1103b 26–9, II 4 1105b 2–5, X 9 1179a 35–b4) that the goal of the study of ethics is action, not merely knowledge: to become fully virtuous rather than simply to know what virtue requires.[16] Someone with a sense of shame will respond, because he wants to do better at the right sorts of things. Someone with nothing but a fear of punishment will not respond; the only thing to do with him is tell him what he will get into trouble for.

After these rather general remarks about the character of Aristotle's enterprise, we can begin to move towards the topic of akrasia. We need first to round out the picture of the motivational resources of the well brought-up young person. For the unreasoned evaluative responses with which his upbringing has endowed him are not the only impulses that move him to act. Being a human being he has the physiologically based appetites as well. The object of these is, of course, pleasure (III 2 1111b 17, III 11 1118b 8 ff., III 12 1119b 5–8, VII 3 1147a 32–4, VII 6 1149a 34–6, *EE* 1247b 20) but they can be modified and trained to become desires for the proper enjoyment of bodily pleasures; this, we saw, is what is involved in acquiring the virtue of temperance. There are also instinctive reactions like fear to be trained into the virtue of courage. In a human being these feelings cannot be eliminated; therefore, they have to be trained. It would also be wrong to omit, though there is not room to discuss, the important fact that Aristotle in Books VIII and IX takes seriously his dictum that the human being is by nature a social animal: friendship is itself something noble (VIII 1 1155a 29), and among the tasks of upbringing and education will be to give the right preliminary shape to the feelings and actions bound up with a wide range of relationships with other people.[17]

That said by way of introduction, we can consider a passage which takes us from moral education to akrasia (I 3 1095a 2–11):

Hence a young man is not a proper hearer of lectures on political science; for he is inexperienced in the actions that occur in life, but its discussions start from these and are about these; and, further, since he tends to follow his passions, his study will be vain and unprofitable, because the end aimed at is not knowledge but action. And it makes no difference whether he is young in years or youthful in character; the defect does not depend upon time, but on his living, and pursuing each successive object, as passion directs. For to such persons, as to the incontinent, knowledge brings no profit; but to those who form their desires and act in accordance with reason knowledge about such matters will be of great benefit.

Reason will appeal and be of use to the well brought-up student because he is ready to form his desires in the light of reasoning; that we have already discovered. Other people, the immature of whatever age, form desires in a different way, and this is what happens in akrasia; or rather, as we shall see, it is one half of what happens in akrasia. We have here two kinds of people, distinguished by two ways of forming desires. What are these two ways of forming desires and how are they different?

As Aristotle describes what he calls deliberation (cf. especially III 2–4), it is a process whereby practical thought articulates a general good that we wish for and focuses it on a particular action it is in our power to do, thereby producing in us a desire to do this thing. A desire is formed by the realization that the action will fulfil one of the ends endorsed by our reasoned view of the good life, and this more specific desire – more specific, that is, than the general wish from which it derived – is what Aristotle calls choice:

> The object of choice being one of the things in our own power which is desired after deliberation, choice will be deliberated desire of things in our own power; for when we have decided as a result of deliberation, we desire in accordance with our deliberation.[18] (III 3 1113a 9–12)

Or, to paraphrase his remarks in a later book (VI 2 1139a 21–33), choice is desire pursuing what reason asserts to be good.

So much for the forming of desires in the light of reasoning, which means: reasoning from the good. If a piece of practical reasoning does not relate to one's conception of the good, Aristotle does not count it deliberation, nor its outcome choice. But that does not mean he denies that reasoning and thinking are involved when desires are formed by the alternative process mentioned in I 3. On the contrary, he describes such thinking in some detail, as we shall see if we now turn to his discussion of akrasia in Book VII.

The akratic (weak-willed) man is one who acts against his knowledge (judgement) and choice of the good;[19] he has a reasoned desire to do one thing, but under the influence of a contrary desire he actually does another. Clearly, however, this contrary desire itself needs to be generated if we are to understand how it fixes upon some particular object and fits into an adequate explanation of the akratic's behaviour. Equally clearly, at least one main purpose Aristotle has in VII 3 is to exhibit akratic behaviour under a standard pattern of explanation which he schematizes in the practical syllogism. His model case turns on the point that bodily appetite can supply a major premise of its own having to do with the pleasant rather than the good ('Everything sweet is pleasant' or 'Sweets are nice'). That is to say, appetite sets an end which is not integrated into the man's life plan or considered scheme of ends, his overall view of the good. Unlike the self-indulgent man, whose (perverted) reason approves of every kind of sensual gratification as good in itself, the akratic is tempted to pursue an end which his reasoned view of life does not approve. But he acts, Aristotle emphasizes (VII 3 1147a 35–b 1), under the influence of a sort of reason and an opinion. His action is to be explained on the standard pattern by a combination of desire and thought, articulated in the syllogism 'Sweets are nice; this is a sweet; so I'll have this'. For the akratic this is only half the story – we have explained the action he actually performs but not the conflict behind it – but it is presumably the whole story of the immature people in I 3. They form desires and undertake actions not in accordance with reason because their ends are simply things that strike them as pleasant at a given moment; they have no steady conception of the good to reason from.[20]

But there are other sources of incontinence than the bodily appetites; most notably, the unreasoned evaluative responses we met before as an important characteristic of the well brought-up beginner. A parallel procedure to the one we have just followed will give us a picture of the sort of error that makes Aristotle's prospective student ashamed of himself. What in him is a mistake is one half of the conflict involved is non-appetitive akrasia.

The details appear in VII 6 1149a 25–b 2:

Spirit seems to listen to reason to some extent, but to mishear it, as do hasty servants who run out before they have heard the whole of what one says and then mistake the order, or as dogs bark if there is but a knock at the door, before looking to see if it is a friend; so spirit on account of the warmth and hastiness of its nature, no sooner hears – even though it has not heard an order – than it springs to take revenge. For reason or imagination informs us that we have been insulted or slighted, and spirit, reasoning as it were that anything like this must be fought against, boils up straightway; while appetite, if reason or perception merely says that an object is pleasant, springs to the enjoyment of it. Therefore spirit follows reason in a sense, but appetite does not.

The description, which owes much to Plato (*Rep.* 440cd again),[21] implies the usual pattern of practical thought and reasoning: 'Slights and injustices must be fought against; I have been wronged/slighted; so I should take revenge.' Aristotle does not specify in detail the better syllogism which must also be present if this is to be a case of full incontinence, but we can supply the order which spirit does not stop to hear, e.g. 'It is better to wait and investigate an apparent wrong before taking revenge; this is an apparent wrong; so wait and investigate.' As in Plato, the over-eager dog in us[22] is concerned with what is noble and just, with honour and self-esteem, without taking thought for the consequences or the wider view.

If, then, these evaluative responses are in us as a result of our upbringing, and the bodily appetites are in us as a part of our natural inheritance as human beings, the seeds of akrasia are going to be with us as we enter Aristotle's lecture room. He will encourage us to think about our life as a whole, to arrive at a reasoned view of the good for man, but to begin with, until our understanding of 'the *because*' has had a chance to become second-nature with us, this will be superimposed upon well-established, habitual patterns of motivation and response which it will take time and practice to integrate with the wider and more adult perspective that Aristotle will help us achieve.

This seems to me important. I think many readers feel that Aristotle's discussion of akrasia leaves unexplained the point most in need of explanation. What they want to know is why the better syllogism is overcome. Not finding an answer they look for one in what Aristotle says in VII 3 about the akratic's knowledge and the way this is not used, not had, or dragged about. And then they are dissatisfied because no adequate answer is to be found in the discussion of *that* issue, for the good reason, I believe, that none is intended. The treatment of knowledge pinpoints what is to be explained. It is not itself the explanation. Even in the relatively easy case where a man simply fails to bring to bear on the situation (fails to use) some knowledge that he has, the fact of his failure requires explanation: he was distracted, over-anxious, in haste, or whatever. For the more difficult cases Aristotle announces his explanation at 1147a 24–5:

Again, we may also view the cause as follows with reference to the facts of human nature.

Thus Ross's translation, but I think that the scope of 'also' is the whole sentence,[23] which means this: we may also give an explanation of the phenomenon we have been endeavouring, with some difficulty, to describe. The explanation that follows is in terms of the two syllogisms, which together account for the conflict, and one of which explains the action the akratic man performs. But the outcome of the conflict might have been different. In the continent man it is; his action is to be explained by the better syllogism. So what determines whether it is appetite or reason that is victorious?

I submit that the question is misguided, at least so far as it looks for an answer to the immediate circumstances of the conflicted decision. If there is an answer, it is to be found in the man's earlier history. We must account for his present conflict in terms of stages in the development of his character which he has not yet completely left behind. For on Aristotle's picture of moral development, as I have drawn it, an important fact about the better syllogism is that it represents a later and less established stage of development. Hence what needs explanation is not so much why some people succumb to temptation as why others do not. What calls for explanation is how some people acquire continence, or even better, full virtue, rather than why most of us are liable to be led astray by our bodily appetites or unreasoned evaluative responses. It is no accident that Aristotle gives as much space to the akratic as a type of person as to isolated akratic actions, and it is characteristic of him that he measures the liability to incontinence by comparison with the normal man. Thus VII 10 1152a 25–33:

> Now incontinence and continence are concerned with that which is in excess of the state characteristic of most men; for the continent man abides by his resolutions more and the incontinent man less than most men can.
>
> Of the forms of incontinence, that of excitable people is more curable than that of those who deliberate but do not abide by their decision,[24] and those who are incontinent through habituation are more curable than those in whom incontinence is innate; for it is easier to change a habit than to change one's nature; even habit is hard to change just because it is like nature, as Evenus says:

> > I say that habit's but long practice, friend,
> > And this becomes men's nature in the end.

I trust that this second set of verses will by now reverberate in their full significance.

Given this temporal perspective, then, the real problem is this. How do we grow up to become the fully adult rational animal that is the end towards which the nature of our species tends? How does reason take hold on us so as to form and shape for the best the patterns of motivation and response which represent the child in us (III 12 1119a 33 ff.), that product of birth and upbringing which will live on unless it is brought to maturity by the education of our reason? In a way, the whole of the *Nicomachean Ethics* is Aristotle's reply to this question, so that this paper is nothing but a prolegomenon to a reading of the work. But I would like, in conclusion, to make a few brief comments concerning one important aspect of the process.

Consider II 3 1104b 30–35:

There being three objects of pursuit[25] and three of avoidance, the noble, the advantageous, the pleasant, and their contraries, the base, the injurious, the painful, about all of these the good man tends to go right, and especially about pleasure; for this is common to the animals, and also it accompanies all objects of pursuit; for even the noble and the advantageous appear pleasant. Again, it has grown up with us all from infancy; which is why it is difficult to rub off this feeling, dyed as it is into our life.[26]

There are three irreducibly distinct categories of value for the fully virtuous man to get right – the three we have been discussing. Pursuit of pleasure is an inborn part of our animal nature; concern for the noble depends on a good upbringing; while the good, here specified as the advantageous,[27] is the object of mature reflection. We have seen that each of the three categories connects with a distinct set of desires and feelings, which acquire motivating effect at different stages of development. It has also become clear that Aristotle's insistence on keeping these distinctions is a key tactic in his vindication of akrasia against Socratic intellectualism.

Historically, the greatest challenge to the intelligibility of akrasia was the argument mounted by Socrates in Plato's *Protagoras* (351b ff.), which showed that weakness of will is unintelligible on the assumption, precisely, that there is only one 'object of pursuit' – one category of value, within which all goods are commensurable, as it were, in terms of a single common coinage. Pleasure was the coinage chosen for the argument, but the important consideration was that if, ultimately, only one factor counts – call it F – and we have measured two actions X and Y in terms of F and X comes out more F than Y, there is nothing left to give value to Y to outweigh or compensate for its lesser quantity of F. The supposed akratic cannot possibly find reason to do Y, the less valuable action, rather than the better action X, because Y offers him less of the only thing he is after: pleasure or whatever else the F may happen to be. If what Y offers is less of the only thing the man seeks, pleasure, its offering that pleasure cannot intelligibly function as a reason for doing Y instead of the admittedly more attractive X.[28] The moral is close to hand: Y must offer something different in kind from

X if the temptation and the man's succumbing to it are to be intelligible. Plato came to see this, and in the *Republic* it was in part to make akrasia and other forms of psychological conflict intelligible that he distinguished different objects of pursuit for the three parts of the soul. The passage quoted is Aristotle's version of that Platonic insight.[29]

However, the fact that there are three irreducibly distinct categories of value need not mean that one and the same thing cannot fall under two or more of them at once. To vindicate akrasia it is necessary only that this need not happen. The continent and the incontinent man do find the good and the pleasant or, in the anger case, the good and the noble in incompatible actions. Therein lies their conflict. The self-indulgent man, on the other hand, has no use for the noble and identifies present pleasure with his long-term good (cf. III 11 1119a 1–4, VII 3 1146b 22–3, VII 7 1150a 19–21, VII 8 1150b 29–30, VII 9 1152a 5–6). It would seem to follow that what we need to do to become fully virtuous instead of merely continent or worse is to bring those three categories of value into line with each other. We have already seen how a good upbringing makes the noble a part, perhaps the chief part, of the pleasant for us. Aristotle's lectures are designed to take the next step and make the noble a part, perhaps the chief part, of one's conception of the good (cp. *EE* 1249a 11). That is why in II 4 he makes it a condition of virtue that virtuous actions be chosen for their own sake. Choice, which is reached by deliberation from a conception of the good, includes a desire for them as good in themselves as well as noble and pleasant. But then he adds a further condition, and rightly, since choice by itself is compatible with incontinence and indeed continence. The further condition is that all this must proceed from a firm and unchangeable character. That is, it is second nature to the virtuous man to love and find his greatest enjoyment in the things he knows to be good (cf. VIII 3 1156b 22–3). In him the three categories of value are in harmony. They have *become* commensurable in terms of pleasure and pain, but not in the objectionable way which led to Socratic intellectualism, since the virtuous person's conception of what is truly pleasant is now shaped by his independent, reasoned conception of what is good; just as it was earlier shaped by his father's or his teacher's advice about what is noble. Indeed, one definition of the noble given in the *Rhetoric* (1366a 34) is to the effect that the noble is that which, being good, is pleasant because it is good (cp. *EE* 1249a 18–19). And with all three categories in harmony, then, and then only, nothing will tempt or lure him so much as the temperate or brave action itself. Nothing else will seem as pleasurable. That is how Aristotle can assert (VII 10 1152a 6–8) that the fully formed man of virtue and practical wisdom cannot be akratic. Quite simply, he no longer has reason to be.[30]

Notes

Reference by name alone, without page number, are to a commentator's note on or translator's rendering of the passage under discussion. (See Bibliography, p. 77.)

1. One exception is John Rawls, *A Theory of Justice*, Chapters VIII–IX, but the exception which most completely exemplifies what I am looking for is Richard Wollheim, 'The Good Self and the Bad Self: The Moral Psychology of British Idealism and the English School of Psychoanalysis Compared'; it is noteworthy that he too has to go to the history of philosophy – specifically, to F. H. Bradley – to find a serious philosophical involvement with developmental questions.

2. *Contra* Aspasius, Stewart, Burnet, Ross and Gauthier-Jolif, who take Aristotle to be speaking of a person of whom it is true neither that he has nor that he can get starting points.

3. So Aspasius, Eustratius, Heliodorus *ad loc.* and *ad* 1098a 33–b 4. Stewart agrees. Burnet's proposal that 'the *that*' is the much more general fact that the definition of happiness is such and such is right for I 7 (see below), but at the moment the definition of happiness is the first principle or starting point we are working towards. For some remarks on this and other misunderstandings of I 4, see W. F. R. Hardie, *Aristotle's Ethical Theory*, 34–6, although Hardie's own suggestion ('the *that*' is 'a particular moral rule or perhaps the definition of a particular moral virtue') also errs on the side of generality.

4. Some scholars (Peters, Grant, Stewart, Gauthier-Jolif) keep the modes of acquisition down to the three explicitly mentioned by reading *kai allai d' allōs* (1098b 4) as a summary rather than an open-ended extension of the list: 'some in one way, some in another', rather than 'others in other ways again'. The rendering I have preferred has the support of Ross as well as the ancient tradition.

5. Not, or at least not in the first instance, the definition of happiness, as Burnet thinks: although this is 'the *that*' which initiates the passage, it was secured by argument, not habituation, and Aristotle has turned parenthetically to a survey of wider scope (cp. T. H. Irwin, 'First Principles in Aristotle's Ethics', 269 n. 18). Of course, the starting points in question and the habituation they presuppose will lead further (cf. especially VII 8 1151a 15–19), but we are still at the beginning of Aristotle's lectures and of the progress they are designed to encourage.

6. Ross translates 'string together', and at the time of writing may not have intended the disparaging note the phrase now sounds. The fact is, the verb *suneirein* is not invariably, or even usually, disparaging in Aristotle's vocabulary. It is disparaging at *Met.* 1090b 30, *De Div.* 464b 4, but not at *Top.*158a 36–7, *Soph. El.* 175a 30, *Met.* 986a 7, 995a 10, 1093b 27, *De Gen. et Corr.* 316a 8, 336b 33, *De Gen. Anim.* 716a 4, 741b 9, *Probl.* 905a 19.

7. Ross translates 'gently born', which has aristocratic overtones irrelevant to the argument, even if Aristotle's sympathies happened to run in that direction. In fact, in the *Rhetoric* (1390b 22–5) Aristotle says that most of the products of noble birth are good for nothing, and he makes a sharp distinction between noble birth (*eugeneia*) and noble character (*gennaiotēs*). His view in the *Politics* is that it is likely that good birth will go with moral merit, but no more than that (*Pol.* 1283a 36 in its wider context from 1282b 14).

8. From here on I quote Ross's translation, corrected in a few places.

9. Strictly, the argument occurs twice, each paragraph being a distinct version, as Rassow saw ('Zu Aristoteles', 594–6). But all that shows is that Aristotle thought the material important enough to have had two goes at expressing it satisfactorily.

10. Strictly, as Grant observes, doing the right thing with reluctance and dislike is rather a sign of continence (self-control) than of vice proper (cf. III 2 1111b 14–15, *EE* 1223b 13–14, 1224b 16–18); the attributions of self-indulgence and cowardice should not be pressed.

11. The reference is to Plato, *Laws* 653a; cp. also *Rep.* 395d, featuring the idea that habit becomes second nature.

12. In the first and third of these passages Ross rather misleadingly translates 'for honour's sake'.

13. The connection between shame and the desire to do what is noble is very clear in the Greek. Shame is felt for having done *aischra* (things disgraceful, ignoble, base) and *aischra* is the standard opposite of *kala* (things noble, fine, honourable). Hence to do something from fear of disgrace is not incompatible with doing it for the nobility of the act itself. This is made clear at III 8 1116a 27–9, on 'citizenly' courage: the only thing that is 'second best' about this form of courage is that the citizen soldier takes his conception of what is noble from the laws and other people's expectations (1116a 17–21) rather than having his own internalized sense of the noble and the disgraceful (cp. III 7 1116a 11–12).

14. For a twentieth-century philosophical discussion which makes interesting use of Greek ideas to bring out the significance of the different sources of desire, see Gary Watson, 'Free Agency'. Watson goes so far as to claim (pp. 210–11) that there are desires carrying absolutely no positive favouring of their object, not even an idea that it is pleasurable. But the cases he cites (a mother's sudden urge to drown her bawling child in the bath, a man who regards his sexual inclinations as the work of the devil) cry out for treatment in terms of the thought of pleasure having to be kept unconscious.

15. An example to the point is the celebrated argument in I 7 which uses considerations about the distinctive activity (*ergon*) of man to show that happiness is activity in accordance with virtue: it is not an argument that would appeal to anyone who really doubted or denied that he should practise the virtues – so much is made clear in the closing pages of Book I of Plato's *Republic*, where Thrasymachus remains totally unmoved by an earlier version of the same argument – but it would say something to the reflective understanding of someone with the basic moral concerns which Aristotle presupposes in his audience. (Irwin, 260–62 seems to be more optimistic.)

16. Not that Aristotle ever suggests that attendance at lectures such as his is the only way to get practical wisdom, nor that attendance is sufficient by itself for developing the needed intellectual virtues. But he is serious about aiming to help his students in that direction, in a quite practical way. This is the solution to the traditional problem (most sharply formulated by Joachim, 13–16) about why Aristotle failed to recognize that the *Ethics* is not itself practical but a theoretical examination *of* the practical. The real failure here is in the impoverished conception of practical reason which finds it a puzzle to accept the practical orientation of Aristotle's enterprise (see further, Irwin, 257–9).

17. Here again Aristotle borrows from the middle part of Plato's tripartite soul: the *Republic* (375a ff.) likened the guardians to noble dogs, with special reference to their warm and spirited nature, and in the *Politics* (1327b 38–28a 1) Aristotle expressly alludes to the *Republic* when he suggests that the capacity of the soul in virtue of which we love our familiars is spirit (*thumos*).

18. It might be objected that Aristotle did not need to make choice a new and more specific desire. Given a wish for X and the realization that Y will secure X, explanation is not furthered by adding in another desire; it should be enough to say that the man wanted X and saw Y as a way of securing it (for intimations of this line of argument, see Thomas Nagel, *The Possibility of Altruism*, Chapters 5–6). But a new and specific desire is not explanatorily redundant in Aristotle's scheme if it helps to explain the pleasure taken in a virtuous act, a pleasure which ought to be more specific to the particular action than the pleasure of simply doing *something* to fulfil one's wish to be virtuous.

19. Against knowledge or judgement: VII 1 1145b 12, VII 3 1146b 24 ff.; against choice: VII 3 1146b 22–4, VII 4 1148a 9–10, VII 8 1151a 5–7, VII 10 1152a 17.

20. That this is the point, not a denial that they engage in practical thinking at all, is clear from X 9 1179b 13–14: 'living by passion they pursue the pleasures appropriate to their character and *the means to them.*' Cp. VI 9 1142b 18–20, *EE* 1226b 30.

21. This is one of the reasons why it seems preferable to translate *thumos* 'spirit' throughout, rather than 'anger' (Ross).

22. The dog image of 1149a 28–9 brings with it an allusive resonance to large tracts of Plato's *Republic*: cp. n. 17 above.

23. Compare W. J. Verdenius, '*kai* belonging to a whole clause'. A good parallel in Aristotle is *An. Post.* 71b 20–22, where *kai* emphasizes not the immediately following *tēn apodeiktikēn epistēmēn*, which merely resumes *to epistasthai* and the point that this must be of necessary truths, but rather the subsequent characterization of the premises from which these necessary truths are derived; that is the new point signalled by *kai* (here I am indebted to Jacques Brunschwig).

24. For these two forms of akrasia, see VII 7 1150b 19–22.

25. Ross's translation 'choice' badly misses the point, since not every pursuit (*hairesis*) is a choice (*prohairesis*) in the technical sense explained earlier. Note that this means that Aristotle does not endorse in every particular the commonplace (*endoxon*) which forms the famous first sentence of *EN*: he does not, strictly, think that every action aims at some good – for one thing, akratic action does not.

26. The dyeing metaphor is yet another allusion to Plato's treatment of these topics: cf. *Rep.* 429d–430b.

27. Perhaps because Aristotle is making argumentative use of a commonplace (*endoxon*): cf. *Top.* 105a 27, 118b 27. For the sense in which the advantageous = the good is the object of practical wisdom see VI 5 1140a 25–8, VI 7 1141b 4–8: the man of practical wisdom deliberates correctly about what is good and advantageous to himself with reference to the supreme goal of living the good life; but of course the same equation can be made when the deliberation concerns a more particular end (VI 9 1142b 27–33).

28. Here I can only sketch my account of the *Protagoras* argument, but various people have independently been propounding similar accounts for quite a time and the key idea is beginning to emerge in print: see, for example, David Wiggins, 'Weakness of Will, Commensurability, and the Objects of Deliberation and Desire'.

29. In a different context (*Pol.* 1283a 3–10) Aristotle expressly denies that all goods are commensurable (*sumblēton*); similarly *EE* 1243b 22, *EN* IX 1 1164b 2–6. Earlier in life Aristotle may have been tempted to think otherwise. *An. Pr.* 68a 25–b 7 is a sketch towards a calculus of preference relations as envisaged in *Top.* III 1–3, where 116b 31–6 aspires to cardinal measurement, not just a relative ordering. Yet it is difficult to judge how far Aristotle thought he could take the project, for *Top.* 118b 27–37 seems to be clear that there is no question of quantitative commensurability across the three categories of the noble, the pleasant and the advantageous. Hence when Aristotle at *De An.* 434a 8–9 says that deliberation requires the measurement of alternatives by a single standard, it is important that in the context he is concerned to mark the difference between rational agents and unreasoning animals, for which purpose the simplest achievement of deliberative calculation will suffice. *anagkē heni metrein* need not be generalized to all deliberation.

30. This paper was one result of the leisure I enjoyed from my tenure of a Radcliffe Fellowship. I am grateful to the Radcliffe Trust for the gift of the Fellowship and to University College, London, for allowing me to take it up. The paper has been improved by discussions at a number of universities (London, Cambridge, Reading, Sussex, Princeton, Berkeley, and the University of Massachusetts at Amherst) and by the comments of David Charles, James Dybikowski, Martha Nussbaum, Amélie Rorty, Richard Sorabji

and Susan Khin Zaw. I only regret that to deal adequately with all their criticisms would require the paper to be even longer than it is. But perhaps my greatest debt is to the members of my graduate seminar at Princeton in 1970, from whom I received my first understanding and appreciation of Aristotle's ethics.

Biographical Note

Myles Burnyeat is a fellow of Robinson College, Cambridge, before which he was a lecturer in philosophy at University College, London. He has held visiting appointments at Princeton, Harvard, Cornell and Pittsburgh. He was awarded a Radcliffe Fellowship in 1974, and has contributed to philosophical and to classical journals.

Bibliography

Aristotle, *Nicomachean Ethics*, trans. W. D. Ross; Aspasius, *In Ethica Nicomachea quae supersunt commentaria*, ed. G. Heylbut (Berlin, 1889); Burnet, John, *The Ethics of Aristole* (London, 1900); Eustratius, *Eustratii et Michaelis et Anonyma in Ethica Nicomachea commentaria*, ed. G. Heylbut (Berlin, 1892); Gauthier, René Antoine, and Jolif, Jean Yves, *L'Éthique à Nicomaque*, 2nd edition (Louvain and Paris, 1970); Grant, Sir Alexander, *The Ethics of Aristotle*, 4th edition (London, 1885); Hardie, W. F. R., *Aristotle's Ethical Theory* (Oxford University Press, 1968); Heliodorus, *In Ethica Nicomachea paraphrasis*, ed. G. Heylbut (Berlin, 1889); Irwin, T. H., 'First Principles in Aristotle's Ethics', *Midwest Studies in Philosophy* 3 (1978), 252–72; Joachim, H. H., *Aristotle – the Nicomachean Ethics* (Oxford University Press, 1951); Nagel, Thomas, *The Possibility of Altruism* (Oxford University Press, 1970); Peters, F. H., translation of *Ethica Nicomachea*, 10th edition (London, 1906); Rassow, H., 'Zu Aristoteles', *Rheinisches Museum* N.F. 43 (1888), 583–96; Rawls, John, *A Theory of Justice* (Oxford, 1972); Ross, Sir David, translation of *Ethica Nicomachea* in *The Works of Aristotle Translated into English*, Vol. IX (Oxford, 1925); Stewart, J. A., *Notes on the Nicomachean Ethics* (Oxford, 1892); Verdenius, W. J., '*kai* belonging to a whole clause', *Mnemosyne* 4th Ser. 29 (1976), 181; Watson, Gary, 'Free Agency', *Journal of Philosophy* 72 (1975), 205–20; Wiggins, David, 'Weakness of Will, Commensurability, and the Objects of Deliberation and Desire', *Proceedings of the Aristotelian Society*, N.S. 79 (1978–9), 251–77; Wollheim, Richard, 'The Good Self and the Bad Self: The Moral Psychology of British Idealism and the English School of Psychoanalysis Compared', *Proceedings of the British Academy* 61 (1975), 373–98.

Further Reading

The Nicomachean Ethics of Aristotle, trans. and with an introduction by W. D. Ross (World's Classics); W. F. R. Hardie, *Aristotle's Ethical Theory* (2nd edition); A. Rorty (ed.), *Essays on Aristotle's Ethics*; J. R. Ackrill, *Aristotle The Philosopher*

Anthony Kenny

Aquinas: Intentionality

The primary subject of Anthony Kenny's paper is fairly described as the nature of thought, and in the main what can be called its aboutness. His primary subject is therefore not Aquinas's doctrine about the nature of thought. However, it is Kenny's conviction, for which his paper provides evidence, that a philosophical inquiry into thought can be advanced towards its own proper end by attention to the *Summa Theologica*. The kind of attention he gives to it is in accordance with his conviction, and hence is meticulous and is guided by the expectation that there is truth to be found. Finding the truth depends in part on persisting with the scholastic conceptions which express it rather than abandoning them for post-medieval conceptions which are likely at least to distort it. The attention given to Aquinas, none the less, is not such that the expectation which informs it, the expectation of finding truth, cannot be defeated. In part it is defeated. Aquinas's doctrine is found in several ways to be naïve and unsatisfactory. In these respects the insights of Wittgenstein are to be preferred. The bringing together of these two thinkers, further, is not the enterprise of having two authorities rather than one. Aquinas and Wittgenstein give greatly different emphases to the problem of thought, and their accounts do indeed conflict. To judge how they can be brought together is to have a third account.

What is it that makes a thought *about* something? What makes a thought of mine *about* or *of* my father, or *about* or *of* redness? The same question arises in connection with sense perception and with such things as pictures and maps. What explains that the visual image I now have is of my balcony, or that Carrogis's portrait of Hume is of Hume? A natural answer is that aboutness has to do with resemblance, but the

St Thomas Aquinas, 1225–74. Of Italian origin, lectured at Paris, and served as adviser to the Papal Court. The great reconciler of Greek philosophy with Christianity, and the principal founder of Catholic philosophy. Said to have had the affection even of his adversaries.

answer faces great difficulties. Is the true portrait of one of two truly identical twins a portrait of the other?

The puzzling and difficult account given by Aquinas of aboutness or intentionality involves in part the Aristotelian conception of a form of a thing. A form can exist in several ways. It can exist individualized and in ordinary matter. It then has existence in nature. It can also exist in an immaterial and universal way in the mind, then having what can be called intentional existence. What makes one of my thoughts about or of a horse is partly the existence of the form of horse in my mind, which form is in fact also realized in nature. There, it is what makes a horse a horse. This is not to be taken as an explanation of aboutness in terms of resemblance. The explanation is at bottom a matter of one thing, a form, and not two things, two existences of it. In certain cases there may not even be two existences of a form, as in the case of my thinking of a satyr.

What sort of thing is a form itself? Kenny approaches this question from a direction suggested by another contemporary philosopher, Peter Geach. A start is made by way of assimilating a form to a concept of a certain kind, one for which such a wholly general predicate as '. . . is a horse' stands. A form of this generic kind, a form strictly speaking, is to be distinguished from an individualized form, the form of a particular individual. (p. 83) The distinction, I take it, is suggested by the distinction between, say, heaviness and the heaviness of a particular existing table.

The same account of aboutness or intentionality gets partial expression in terms of Aquinas's assertion that what may seem to be two things are in fact one – his assertion of the identity of what can be called the act of a perceptible object and the act of its perceiver (pp. 83–4), or the identity of the object of thought and the activity of the thinker (p. 86). This, in part, and by way of example, is to the effect that the sounding of the dinner gong, in my ears, is one and the same thing as the hearing of the dinner gong. That is, as Kenny expresses it, by way of another example, the action of such a sensible object as a piece of sugar upon my sense is one and the same event as the operation of my sense upon the object, my tasting the sweetness. The general claim of identity in act, however, has to do not only with sensation but with thought itself. '. . . the actualization of an object of thought is the same thing as the actualization of the capacity for thinking.' (pp. 84–5 and 86–7) The capacity for thinking is identified as our 'receptive intellect', the mind in its role as storehouse of thoughts and ideas. (p. 85)

In coming to his own understanding of the identity-claim, Kenny considers the understanding of another contemporary philosopher, Bernard Lonergan. (pp. 84–5). He takes it that the claim does involve forms, which is not disputed. However, he also takes it that Aquinas's view is that there is not just one form in question. What the view then comes to is that if a person has a thought of a thing, or perceives a thing, the form of his thought or perception must be *similar* to the form of the thing. (pp. 85–6) In Kenny's view this is mistaken. It is clear that Aquinas asserts there is but one form in question.

Aquinas's doctrine is not that there is one individualized form which occurs in some horse, and also occurs in my mind. In the world there are only individualized forms. In thought, as distinct from perception, there is only universal or substantial form. (pp. 87–8) The real object of an human knowledge, as distinct from perception, is form of this kind. Hence there is no intellectual knowledge of individual things. How then do we think of particular things, such as Socrates? The answer of Aquinas is that we depend somehow on sense impressions. We place a universal form 'within a context of sensory imagery'. (p. 88)

This is not to say that Aquinas is to be regarded as an idealist, in the particular sense of maintaining that we have no direct understanding or knowledge of reality, but only of our own immaterial, abstract and universal ideas. He is to be regarded as maintaining that we have no strictly intellectual access to the world. Kenny takes this to mean the truth that language by itself, the infinity of descriptions in it, does not allow us to pick out or individuate individuals. What is also necessary is sensory experience. (pp. 89–90) The latter is emphatically not a matter of perceiving true forms in reality. Forms are the creatures of the agent intellect, which is distinct from the receptive intellect.

The summary, in modern terms, of the whole of Aquinas's account of the intentionality of thought is therefore that the aboutness of one of my thoughts is a matter of the universal forms in which I think, and the sensory context in which my thought occurs. (pp. 90 and 92–3)

However, Aquinas's views on sensory context are weakened significantly by, above all, his confused theory of mental images. Furthermore, his attempt to explain the aboutness of thought partly by reference to mental images faces the difficulty that mental images by themselves do not enable us to individuate things any more than do descriptions in language. Some more direct connection with the world is necessary, a connection which for Wittgenstein is connected with behaviour. (p. 91)

At this point Kenny turns to the second question raised by the nature of thought. What makes a particular thought *my* thought? The question is particularly pressing for Aquinas. His only answer to it again has to do with mental images, and is unsatisfactory. (pp. 93–4) Kenny ends his paper, whose economy of expression and careful distinctions demand and repay close reading, with a final résumé and appraisal of Aquinas on aboutness, and a final characterization of the nature of the forms themselves. Aquinas, he remarks, avoids both the Platonic notion of the true forms somehow existing outside the mind, and the notion that we are somehow cut off from the real world, imprisoned in our own ideas.

Anthony Kenny

Aquinas: Intentionality

In section V of the *Philosophical Grammar* Wittgenstein sets himself a problem.

That's *him* (this picture represents *him*) – that contains the whole problem of representation.

What is the criterion, how is it to be verified, that this picture is the portrait of that object, i.e. that it is *meant* to represent it? It is not similarity that makes the picture a portrait (it might be a striking resemblance of one person, and yet be a portrait of someone else it resembles less).

When I remember my friend and see him 'in my mind's eye' what is the connection between the memory image and its subject? The likeness between them?

. . . Here we have the old problem . . . the problem of the harmony between world and thought.

In this paper I will say something about Wittgenstein's answer to his own question, his account of the harmony between world and thought. But mainly in the paper I will discuss an older solution to this old problem, to the question what makes a picture of X a picture *of X*, what makes an image of X an image *of X*, what makes a thought about X be *about X*?

One of the most elaborate, and also one of the most puzzling accounts of the harmony between the world and thought is Aquinas's doctrine of the immaterial intentional existence of forms in the mind. According to Aquinas, when I think of redness, what makes my thought be a thought of redness is the form of redness. When I think of a horse, similarly, it is the form of horse which makes the thought be a thought of a horse and not of a cow. What makes the thought of a horse the thought of a horse is the same thing as makes a real horse a horse: namely, the form of horse. The form exists, individualized and

Anthony Kenny's paper, 'Aquinas: Intentionality', is published here for the first time, with his permission.

enmattered, in the real horse; it exists, immaterial and universal, in my mind. In the one case it has *esse naturale*, existence in nature; in the mind it has a different kind of existence, *esse intentionale*.

What are we to make of this strange doctrine? The first question which arises is: what is a form? One of the most illuminating accounts of Aquinas's doctrine of forms is given by Geach in his paper 'Form and Existence' (*Proceedings of the Aristotelian Society*, 1961). This contains a useful comparison between Frege's theory of functions and Aquinas's theory of forms. Just as Frege regarded a predicate, such as '. . . is a horse' as standing for a particular kind of function, namely a concept, so Aquinas held that a general term such as 'horse' standing in predicate position referred to a form. The form which is referred to by the predicate which occurs in the sentence 'Socrates is wise' may be referred to also by the phrase 'the wisdom of Socrates'; but this latter expression must not be construed as 'wisdom, which belongs to Socrates', just as 'the square root of 4' does not mean 'the square root, which belongs to 4'. 'The wisdom of Socrates', in Geach's terminology, refers to an *individualized* form; the expression which indicates the generic form, the form strictly so called, is not 'wisdom' nor 'the wisdom of Socrates' but 'the wisdom of . . .' (cf. *Summa Theologica*, 1a, 3, 2 ad 4; 1a, 50, 2). 'Wisdom' *tout court* means nothing in heaven or earth; wisdom is always *wisdom of*; as Aquinas puts it, it is of something (*entis*) rather than itself something (*ens*). Against Plato's doctrine that the form signified by a general term is 'one over against many', Aquinas insisted that the question 'one or many' is itself only intelligible if we ask it in relation to a general term that signified a form or nature.

Geach admits that the account which he gives of individualized forms does not accord in all respects with Aquinas's language; but it is a most interesting analysis in its own right, whether or not it is to be found in its worked out form in Aquinas's writings. Geach treats Aquinas as Aquinas treated Aristotle – improving his insights, tactfully masking his confusions, charitably resolving his ambiguities. This may exasperate historians, but it is the philosophically rewarding way to read a classic text. But in some cases Geach benignly interprets Aquinas in a way which fathers on him interpretations which fall foul of what Aquinas says explicitly elsewhere. This is the case, as I shall try, later, to show, when Aquinas's doctrine of form is expounded by Geach in the context of intentional existence.

Another author who has contributed greatly to the exposition of Aquinas's theory of intentionality in recent years is the Canadian Jesuit Bernard Lonergan. In his book *Verbum*, Lonergan links the doctrine of intentionality with the Aristotelian theorem of the identity in act of knower and known. In Aristotle's *De Anima* we are told, as Lonergan summarizes, that

the one operation, sensation, is effected by the sensible object and received in the sensitive potency; as from the object it is action; as in the subject, it is passion; thus, sounding is the action of the object and hearing the passion of the subject, and so by the theorem of identity, sounding and hearing are not two realities but one and the same. (p. 147)

Because of differences between Greek and English vocabulary, Aristotle's point is easier to illustrate with an example such as taste. A piece of sugar, something which can be tasted, is a sensible object; my ability to taste is a sensitive potency; the operation of the sense of taste upon the sensible object is the same thing as the action of the sensible object upon my sense; that is to say, the sugar's tasting sweet to me is one and the same event as my tasting the sweetness of the sugar. The sugar is actually sweet, but until put into the mouth is only potentially tasting sweet: the scholastic jargon for this was to say that the sugar, outside the mouth, was sweet 'in first act' but not 'in second act'. It is the second actuality, sweetness in second act, which is at one and the same time the sugar's tasting sweet and the tasting of the sweetness of the sugar. (Something like black coffee, which can be made sweet if you put sugar into it, is not sweet either in first act or second act, but only in potentiality.)

Aquinas adopted this Aristotelian theorem, and frequently states it in its Latin version: *sensibile in actu est sensus in actu*. But he also emphasizes the corresponding doctrine about thought as well as the theorem about sensation. Not only is the actualization of a sensible object the same thing as the actualization of the sense-faculty; so too the actualization of an object of thought is the same thing as the actualization of the capacity for thinking. *Intelligibile in actu est intellectus in actu*.

The meaning of the slogan, however, according to Lonergan, has undergone a change. The meaning is not the original Aristotelian identity in second act, but rather assimilation at the level of ideas, or, as they are called by Aquinas, *species*. Knowing, according to Lonergan, is essentially a matter of assimilation: like is known by like.

Its grounds in Aristotelian theory are reached easily: as the thing is the thing it is in virtue of its form or species, so too a thought is the ontological reality it is in virtue of its own form or species; so further, unless the form of the thing and the form of the thought were similar, there would be no ground for affirming that the thought was a thought of the thing. (p. 148)

The similarity must be a similarity not at the level of matter, but of form: it must be an immaterial assimilation.

The senses are receptive of sensible forms without the matter natural to those forms, much as wax is receptive of the imprint of a seal without being receptive of the gold of which the seal is made. In human intellect immaterial assimilation reaches its fulness in immaterial reception: not only is the matter of the agent not transferred to the recipient, as the gold of the seal is not transferred to the wax; not only is the form of the agent not reproduced in matter natural to it, as in sensation; but the form of the agent object is received in a strictly immaterial potency, the possible intellect. (p. 149)

'Possible intellect' is a transliteration of the Latin '*intellectus possibilis*', which is Aquinas's term for the intellect in its role as storehouse of thoughts and ideas. 'Receptive intellect' might be a more illuminating English term for it. This intellect, Lonergan tells us, summarizing Aquinas,

is not the form of any organ; it has no other nature but ability to receive; it stands to all intelligible forms as prime matter stands to all sensible forms; and precisely because it is in act none of the things to be known, it offers no subjective resistance to objective knowing.

The substance of Lonergan's account of intentionality, then, is as follows. If A is to know X, then the form of A's knowing must be similar to the form of X which is known, but it must also be different. It must be similar in essence, if X is to be known; but it must be different in mode, if A is to be a knower and not merely the known.

Modal difference of form results from difference in recipients: the form of colour exists naturally in the wall, but intentionally in the eye, because wall and eye are different kinds of recipient; similarly angels have a natural existence on their own but an intentional existence in the intellects of other angels. (p. 151)

Intentional existence and immaterial existence are not the same thing. A pattern exists, naturally and materially, in a coloured object; it exists, intentionally and materially, in the eye or, according to Aquinas, in the lucid medium. Gabriel is a form which exists immaterially and naturally in its own right; it exists immaterially and intentionally in Raphael's thought of Gabriel. The characteristic of intellectual thought, whether of men or angels, is that it is the existence of form in a mode which is both intentional and immaterial.

I leave Aquinas's account of angelic understanding to those who are better acquainted than I with angels; I want to consider his thesis as a thesis about human thought. According to Lonergan's interpretation, the theory is essentially that the form of X when X is thought of is similar to the form existing in an object which is really X. But on Geach's interpretation the doctrine of intentionality should not be treated as a doctrine of the similarity of forms, but as a doctrine of the identity of forms. Geach puts the matter thus:

> What makes a sensation or thought of an X to be *of an X* is that it is an individual occurrence of that very form or nature which occurs in an X – it is thus that our mind 'reaches right up to the reality'; what makes it to be a *sensation* or *thought* of an X rather than an actual X or an actual X-ness is that X-ness here occurs in the special way called *esse intentionale*, and not in the 'ordinary' way called *esse naturale*.

So for Geach we have not just similarity but identity of forms. To be sure, my thought of a horse and the form of that horse grazing in the field are two *occurrences* of the form; but they are two occurrences of the *same* form, every bit as much as two occurrences of the form of horse in two horses grazing side by side.

Which is the correct interpretation of Aquinas, Lonergan's or Geach's? In my view, neither interpreter has the matter wholly right, and a third interpretation is possible which is both a more accurate account of Aquinas and a more plausible account of the nature of intentionality.

Lonergan is not successful in establishing that there is a shift of meaning between the two slogans *sensus in actu est sensibile in actu* and *intellectus in actu est intelligibile in actu*. Geach is right that the same theorem of identity is being enunciated both in the case of sensation and of understanding. Aquinas is committed to the identity of the objects of thought and the activity of the thinker just as he is to the identity of the activity of a sense-object and the activity of the sense-faculty. But there is no doubt that the doctrine about thought is more difficult to understand than the doctrine about sensation, and it is not surprising that Lonergan should attempt to adulterate it.

In stating the theorem with regard to the senses earlier I said that a piece of sugar was a sensible object. This is not strictly correct: it is the piece of sugar *qua* sweet ('*dulce*', 'the sweet') which is the sensible object; it is the sweetness of the sugar whose actuality is identical with the taster's tasting, not the sugar itself. In the case of a secondary quality such as sweetness, it is easy enough to accept the theorem of identity in second act. We can understand that the secondary quality in act is one and the same as the activity of the appropriate sense; the sweetness of X just is the ability of X to taste sweet. (It is related, of course, to various chemical properties and constituents of X; but that relation, unlike the relation to the activity of tasting sweet, is a contingent one.) But suppose that I think of the redness of X: can it be said that the redness of X just is the ability that X has to be thought of as red? Surely not, so how can the doctrine of identity in act apply to thought as well as to sensation?

To see how, we must recall that for Aquinas the real object of all human knowledge is form. The senses perceive the accidental forms of objects that are appropriate to each modality: with our eyes we see the colours and shapes of objects; with our noses we perceive their smells; colours, shapes, and smells are accidental forms or accidents, as opposed to substantial forms, the forms which locate things in their appropriate species. The accidental forms which are perceived by the senses are individual forms – it is the colour of *this rose* that I see and even the most powerful nose cannot take in the smell of the universal *sulphur*. Substantial form, on the other hand, is grasped not by the senses but by the intellect: the proper object of the human intellect is the nature or form of material things. Material things are composed of matter and form, and the individuality of a parcel of matter is not something that can be grasped by the intellect. The intellect can grasp what makes Socrates a man, but not what makes him Socrates; it can grasp his form but not his matter; or rather, more strictly, it grasps his nature by grasping the form plus the fact that the form must be embodied in some matter or other of the right kind. But because it is matter which is the principle of individuation, the form which is grasped by the intellect is universal, unlike the individual accidental forms which are the objects of sense-perception.

This feature is neglected in Geach's presentation of the theory that the form of the thought is the same as the form of the object of thought. Geach argues that we must make a real distinction between form and existence: in the case of each individualized form there is a distinction between the form and its *esse*. But Aquinas's doctrine of intentionality does not provide grounds for such a distinction, contrary to what Geach says. It is no part of Aquinas's doctrine that there is one same individualized form of horse which occurs in a particular horse, say Eclipse, with *esse naturale*, and occurs also in my mind with *esse intentionale*. What we have are two different individualizations of the same form, not two different existences of the same individualized form. The form, in the mind, is individuated by its thinker.

Anthony Kenny

Geach writes:

> When Plato thinks of redness, what exists in Plato is not a certain *relation* to redness or red things, but *is* redness, is an individual occurrence of the very same form of which another individual occurrence is the redness of this rose.

There is an equivocation in the sense of 'individual occurrence' here. The occurrence of redness in a particular rose is an individual occurrence because it is an occurrence of redness in a particular rose: it is the redness of *this rose*. The occurrence of redness when Plato thinks of redness is not individual by being the thought of the redness of any particular thing, but by being a thought thought by a particular thinker, namely Plato. It was a constant doctrine of Aquinas that thought, as such, is not directly of individual things at all, neither of individual forms like the redness of Socrates nor of individual substances like Socrates himself (e.g. *Summa Theologica*, 1a, 86, 1). When I think of Socrates there is no form of Socrateity having intentional existence in my mind; unlike Duns Scotus who believed in individual essence, *haecceitas*, Aquinas would have denied that there was any such form. According to Aquinas, when I think of Socrates there is in my mind only the universal form of humanity; I can use this form to think of Socrates only by placing it within a context of sensory imagery (*phantasmata*). The individual humanity of Socrates has *esse naturale* in Socrates but it does not have *esse intentionale* in my mind or in anyone's mind; the universal, humanity, has *esse intentionale* in my mind, but it does not have *esse naturale* in Socrates or in any human being. In neither case do we have one same individualized form with two different modes of *esse*. So the doctrine of intentionality is not, as Geach represents it, a doctrine of two modes of existence of the same individualized form. For in thought there are no individualized forms, only universals.

An accurate account of Aquinas's theory of intentionality has to give full weight to his thesis that there is no intellectual knowledge of individuals.

Aquinas wrote:

> Plato thought that the forms of natural things existed apart without matter and were therefore thinkable; because what makes something actually thinkable (*actu intelligibile*) is its being non-material. These he called ideas. Corporeal matter, he thought, takes the form it does by sharing in these, so that individuals by this sharing belong in their natural kinds and types; and it is by sharing in them that our understanding takes the forms that it does of knowledge of the different kinds and types. But Aristotle did not think that the forms of natural things existed independently of matter, and forms existing in matter are not actually thinkable. (*Summa Theologica*, 1a, 19, 3)

Forms existing in matter, Aquinas says, are only thinkable in the same way as colours are visible in the dark. Colours are perceptible by the sense of sight; but in the dark colours are only perceptible potentially, they are not actually perceptible. The sense of vision is only actuated – a man only sees the colours – when light is present to render them actually perceptible. Similarly, Aquinas says, the things in the physical world are only potentially thinkable or intelligible. An animal with the same senses as ours perceives and deals with the same material objects as we do; but he cannot have intellectual thoughts about them – he cannot, for instance, have a scientific understanding of their nature. To explain our ability to do so we have to postulate a species-specific capacity for abstract thought; what Aquinas calls the agent intellect, the *intellectus agens* which he contrasts with the receptive intellect or *intellectus possibilis*. We, because we can abstract ideas from the material conditions of the natural world, are able not just to perceive but to think about and understand the world.

Does this mean that Aquinas is an idealist? Does he mean that we never really know or understand the world itself, but only our own immaterial, abstract, universal ideas? Aquinas was not a representative idealist: he explicitly rejected the thesis that the intellect can know nothing but its own ideas. But Aquinas's thesis does mean that he is anti-realist in one of the many senses of that term. And though he did not think that we can know nothing but our own ideas, he rejected equally the idea that our knowledge of material objects could be something which was purely intellectual. In this, I believe, his instinct was sound, if we identify 'intellectual' with 'linguistic'.

When I think of a particular human being, there will be, if I know her well, very many descriptions I can give in language to identify the person I mean. But unless I bring in reference to particular times and places there may be no description I can give which would not in theory be satisfiable by a human being other than the one I mean; I cannot individuate simply by describing her appearance, her qualities. Only perhaps by pointing, or taking you to see her, can I make clear which person I mean; and pointing and vision go beyond pure intellectual, linguistic, thought.

Similarly, Aquinas thought, if I bring in spatio-temporal individuating references I have left the realm of intellectual thought: from the point of view of a pure spirit there would be no such framework.

Our intellect cannot have direct and primary knowledge of individual material objects. The reason is that the principle of individuation of material objects is individual matter; and our intellect understands by abstracting ideas from such matter. But what is abstracted from individual matter is universal. So our intellect is not directly capable of knowing anything which is not universal. (*Summa Theologica*, 1a, 86, 1)

It is by linking universal intellectual ideas with sensory experience that we know individuals and are capable of forming singular propositions such as 'Socrates is a man'.

If Plato was wrong, as Aquinas thought he was, then there is not, outside the mind, any such thing as human nature as such; there is only the human nature of individual human beings like Jack and Jill. But because the humanity of individuals is form embedded in matter, it is not something which can, as such, be the object of intellectual thought. In Aquinas's terminology, an individual's humanity is 'intelligible' (because a form) but not 'actually intelligible' (because existing in matter). It is the agent intellect which, on the basis of our experience of individual human beings, creates the intellectual object, humanity as such. This, then, is the sense in which Aquinas, though not an idealist, is anti-realist. The ideas are not intermediate entities which represent the world: they are modifications of our intellect consisting in the acquired ability to think certain thoughts. But the universals which the ideas are ideas of are themselves things which have no existence outside the mind, as universals. Their only existence is their ability to occur in thoughts. Thus the actuality of the universal thoughts is one and the same thing as the actuality of the capacity for intellectual thought. *Intelligibile in actu est intellectus in actu.*

Putting Aquinas's doctrine in modern terms, we might say that our thoughts have the sense they have because of the universal forms in which we think; they have the reference they have to individuals because of the sensory context in which they occur. In *Philosophical Investigations*, II, xi, Wittgenstein wrote:

'at that word we both thought of him'. Let us assume that each of us said the same words to himself – and how can it mean MORE than that? – but wouldn't even those words be only a *germ*? They must surely belong to a language and to a context, in order really to be the expression of the thought *of* that man.
If God had looked into our minds he would not have been able to see there whom we were speaking of.

If by 'mind' we mean 'intellect' Aquinas would have agreed. To see my reference to an individual, God would have to look outside the intellect to the *phantasmata*.

It is not altogether clear what Aquinas means by *phantasmata*: I have been translating his references to them by vague and benign phrases such as 'reference to a context of sense and imagination'. I believe that in Aquinas's dicta about phantasms there is combined a correct and important insight about the relation between the intellect on the one hand and the imagination and senses on the other, with a confused theory about the nature of the imagination and the character of mental imagery.

Aquinas often states that phantasms are necessary not only for the acquisition of concepts but also for their exercise. In this life at least, it is impossible for us to think any thought except by attending to phantasms. We can see this, he says, if we reflect that injury to the brain can impede thought, and if we remember that we all conjure up images when we are doing our best to understand something. However dubious these arguments may be, it does seem to be true that there must be some exercise of sense or imagination, some application to a sensory context, if we are to be able to pin down someone's habitual knowledge or beliefs to an exercise on a particular occasion. He need not recite to himself his belief in his imagination, or see its content in his mind's eye perhaps; but at least something in his sensory experience or conscious behaviour must occur for it to be possible to latch the thought onto a date and time.

Attention to phantasms is, according to Aquinas, necessary for any thought, even of the most abstract and universal kind. But a special type of relationship to phantasms (*reflexio supra phantasmata*) is needed if the thought is to be a thought concerning individuals rather than universals. In a manner which remains mysterious, Aquinas seems to have thought that only the appropriate accompanying mental imagery would differentiate a thought about Socrates from a thought about Plato or about any other human being. Even if this is so, it seems that the same questions about individuation could arise about the mental imagery as arise about the thought, unless we relate the imagery in some way to a transaction in the world outside the imagination. This brings us back to the question of Wittgenstein's with which we began: what makes an image of X an image of X? Wittgenstein's own answer to his problem goes as follows:

How can I know that someone means (a) picture as a portrait of N?
Well, perhaps he says so or writes it underneath.
What is the connection between the portrait of N and N himself?
Perhaps that the name written underneath is the name used to address him.
The image of him is an unpainted portrait.
In the case of the image too I have to write his name under the picture to make it the image of him.

Aquinas's theory of the imagination is in some sense naïve and unsatisfactory: he calls the imagination an inner sense and his picture of how it operates is modelled far too closely on the operation of the senses. He seems to have thought that an inner sense differed from an outer sense principally in having an organ and an object inside the body (in the brain) rather than outside. Wittgenstein and others have shown how misleading this picture of the imagination is. If we are to accept Aquinas's view that it is *phantasmata* which give reference to individuals, we have to fill out his account with the kind of considerations which Wittgenstein adduces.

While Aquinas's account of the imagination seems unacceptable, he has a clear grasp of the relationship between the intellect and the imagination when thought takes place in mental images or in subvocal speech. In such cases it is not the imagery that gives content to the intellectual thought, or meaning to the words which express the thought. It is the intellect that gives meaning to the imagery – whether imagined words or pictures or mental images – by using it in a certain way. In the book of our thoughts it is the intellect that provides the text; the mental images are illustrations. (Cf. *Philosophical Investigations* 663.)

We can sum up Aquinas's doctrine of intentionality thus. Both sense-perception and the acquisition of intellectual information are matters of the reception of forms in a more or less immaterial manner by a human being. In both perception and in thought a form exists intentionally. When I see the redness of the setting sun, redness exists intentionally in my vision; when I think of the roundness of the earth, roundness exists in my intellect. In each case the form exists without the matter to which it is joined in reality: the sun itself does not enter into my eye, nor does the earth, with all its mass, move into my intellect.

A sensory form exists in one manner in the thing which is outside the soul, and in another manner in the sense itself, which receives the form of sensible objects without their matter – the colour of gold, for instance, without the gold. (1a, 84, 1c)

But intentional existence is not, as such, completely immaterial existence. The form in the eye lacks the matter of gold, but not the matter of the eye; it is an individualized form, not a universal. And according to Aquinas the redness exists intentionally not only in the eye but in the lucid medium through which I see it.

But matters are different with the forms of thought. In the intellect there is no matter for the forms to inform. The receptive intellect indeed has no other nature than its ability to be informed by forms existing intentionally; if it had, it would be incapable of understanding whatever shared its nature, as coloured spectacles prevent one from discriminating white light from light of their own colour (*Summa Theologica*, 1a, 75, 2; 87, 1). The occurrence of concepts and thoughts in the intellect is not a case of the modification of any matter: there is no moulding of mysterious mental material. If the intellect were composed of matter and form, the forms of things would be received into it in all their concrete individuality, so that it would know only the singular, as the senses do, which receive forms of things in a physical organ (*Summa Theologica*, 1a, 75, 5).

Aquinas's doctrine of the intentional existence of forms remains one of the most interesting contributions ever made to the philosophical problem of the nature of thought. Suppose that I think of a phoenix. There seem to be two things which make this thought the thought it is: first, that it is a thought of a phoenix, and not of a cow or of a goat; secondly that it is my thought and not your thought or Julius Caesar's. These seem to be the two essential properties of any thought: to have a content, and to have a possessor. Of course thoughts may have other properties too – e.g. they may be profound or childish, exciting or depressing, and so on – but the two things essential to any thoughts seem to be that they should be somebody's thoughts and that they should be thoughts of something. Any theory of the nature of thought must give an account of both these features.

Theories of thought propounded at different times emphasize different members of this pair of features. From the time of Descartes until comparatively recently the problem 'What makes my thoughts *my* thoughts' has comparatively rarely struck philosophers as problematic at all; but many have sought to give a solution to the problem of the relation of a thought to what it is a thought of. Does a thought become a thought of *X* by being *like X*? Or is the relationship between thought and its object some other relationship? How can it be a relationship at all, since we can have thoughts of what does not exist, like my thought of a phoenix, and there is nothing in such a case for my thought to be related to? Moreover, even if we could agree on the relationship – say resemblance – and concentrate on the cases where there are things to be related to – say horses – there is still the problem: what *has* the relationship?

A statue of a horse is a piece of stone or bronze, resembling, with greater or less success, a real horse; but in the mind there is nothing corresponding to the stone or the bronze to bear the resemblance. Aquinas's answer, that what makes the thought of a horse the thought of a horse is not any resemblance, but an occurrence of the same thing which makes a horse a horse, makes easier the question concerning the content of the thought; but it makes more striking the question: what makes A's thought of a horse *A's* thought? There is nothing in the content of a thought that makes it one person's thought rather than another's. Innumerable people besides myself believe that two and two makes four; when I believe this what makes the belief *my* belief?

The question was a very lively one in Aquinas's time and the subject of much controversy between Latin and Arab interpreters of Aristotle. Aquinas insisted, against the Averroists, that such a thought is my thought, and not the thought of any world-soul or supra-individual agent intellect. But to the question what makes them *my* thoughts his only answer is the connection between the intellectual content of the thought and the mental images in which it is embodied. It is because these mental images are the products of my body that the intellectual thought is my thought. This answer seems unsatisfactory for many reasons. Wittgenstein, who reawoke philosophers to the importance of the question of individuating the possessor of a thought, was surely better inspired when he urged us to look at the expression of a thought to supply the criteria for individuating its possessor. Aquinas has nothing of value to offer in the search for such criteria: his significance for the modern reader here is that he alerts one to the existence of the problem.

But if we make allowances for this lacuna in Aquinas's theory, can we say that in other respects the thesis of intentionality can be regarded as a sound philosophical account of the nature of thought?

The theorem that the activity of a sensible property is identical with the activity of a sense-faculty seems to be strictly true only of secondary qualities like taste and colour; it is only of these that we can say that their only actualization, the only exercise of their powers, is the actualization of sense-faculties. A primary quality, like heaviness, can be actualized not only by causing a feeling of heaviness in a lifter, but in other ways such as by falling and exerting pressure on inanimate objects.

But the intellectual equivalent of the theorem of identity in second act still seems defensible as a formulation of a particular kind of anti-realism. The actuality of the object of thought is the actuality of the power of thinking. That is to say, on the one hand, the intellect just is the capacity for, the locus of, intellectual thought; it has no structure or matter; it is just the capacity for thought. (Or, if we say it has a structure, all that this can mean is that it is a capacity which can be stratified, hierarchically, into other abilities and powers.) On the other hand, the object of intellectual thought, redness as such, is something which has no existence outside thought. Or so we must say unless we are prepared to embrace the Platonism which Aquinas rejected.

Of course material objects are not to be identified with universals. They are objects which are thinkable in potency: their thinkability, their intelligibility, is their capacity to be brought under the universal concepts of the intellect's creation.

It is a commonplace to distinguish between two concepts of concept, or *Begriff*. There is an objective one associated with Frege (a *Begriff* as something 'out there', mind-independent, the reference of a predicate) and a subjective one associated with Wittgenstein (a concept as for example the learnt mastery of a word in a language).

If Aquinas is right, the two kinds of *Begriff* are facets of the same item. The redness of *this* has existence outside thought; it has its own history and causal interactions; but redness as such has no existence outside thought. Redness as such is not something I think *of*, as I think of Napoleon; it is something, rather, which I think, when I think of redness without thinking of the redness of any particular object. The thinkability of the redness of *this* is its ability to be abstracted by the human abstractive power, the species-specific ability to master language, the *intellectus agens*.

I have attempted to combine Aquinas's theory of intentional exist-ence with the *prima facie* very different account of intentionality sketched by Wittgenstein. The resulting theory, if I am right, has the merit that it enables one to avoid the realist idealism of Platonism without falling into the conceptualist idealism of many anti-realists, past and present.

Biographical Note

Anthony Kenny has been Master of Balliol College, Oxford, since 1978, before which time he was a Fellow of the college, and a lecturer at Exeter and Trinity Colleges. He was educated partly at the Gregorian University in Rome, ordained as a priest in 1955, and returned to the lay state in 1963. He has given the Gifford Lectures, as well as other estab-lished lectures, and been a visiting professor at Chicago, Washington, Michigan, Stanford and Rockefeller. His books include *Action, Emotion and Will* (1963), *Descartes* (1968), *The Five Ways* (1969), *Wittgenstein* (1973), *The Anatomy of the Soul* (1974), *Will, Freedom and Power* (1975), *The Aristotelian Ethics* (1978), *Freewill and Responsibility* (1978), *Aristotle's Theory of the Will* (1979), *The God of the Philosophers* (1979) and *Aquinas* (1980). He is a Fellow of the British Academy.

Anthony Kenny

Further Reading

Summa Theologica, trans. the Fathers of the English Dominican Province (2nd revised edition, London, 1920; reissued New York: Benziger, 1947); *Basic Writings of St Thomas Aquinas*, ed. A Pegis (New York: Random House, 1945); *St Thomas Aquinas: Philosophical Texts*, selected and translated T. Gilby (London: Oxford University Press, 1951).

G. E. M. Anscombe and P. T. Geach, *Three Philosophers* (Oxford University Press, 1961); F. C. Copleston, *Aquinas* (Harmondsworth: Penguin Books, 1955); B. Lonergan, *Verbum: Word and Idea in Aquinas* (London: Notre Dame, 1967).

Thomas Nagel

Hobbes: His Concept of Obligation

Hobbes's *Leviathan*, sometimes too emphatically described as a response by a prudent and indeed fearful man of the seventeenth century to the terribleness of civil war, has very certainly transcended any such beginning. Its central conclusion is indeed that we must give over our individual rights to the absolute government of a civil society for fear of the alternative, a state of nature – a state which in Hobbes's worn but still splendid line would be one where the life of man is 'solitary, poor, nasty, brutish and short'. Such a contract, however, with an absolute government, is not the only social contract to which Hobbes's arguments are relevant. The fact that the *Leviathan* is of relevance to more liberal political views, however, is but one reason for its acceptance as one of the greatest of works of political philosophy. It offers, to mention but one further thing, an account of what motivates us to action, a deterministic account in terms of selfishness which lies in the history of many subsequent doctrines. It is an account that does not stand separate from but is somehow integral to his politics.

Howard Warrender's book, *The Political Philosophy of Hobbes*, is recognized as providing an understanding or interpretation of Hobbes of exemplary clarity and strength. It gives what can be regarded as a defence of Hobbes against a charge of immorality – a charge, by the way, laid against him during his lifetime by the University of Oxford. Warrender's account, and a quite contrary account, are the subject-matter of Thomas Nagel's paper reprinted here. It is a paper of force and persuasiveness. This philosophical dispute is one where each of the parties is well-armed.

The dispute concerns what Hobbes called laws of nature. Such a law

Thomas Hobbes, 1588–1679. Born at Malmesbury and educated at Magdalen College, Oxford, he lived in England but made long visits to the Continent. Of scientific interests and inspired by geometry, his greatest attainments are perhaps in his political philosophy. Redoubtable controversialist, but more successful against bishops than mathematicians.

Thomas Nagel

is characterized by him as 'a precept, or general rule, found out by
reason, by which a man is forbidden to do what is destructive of his
life, or taketh away the means of preserving the same . . .'. In the
Leviathan he specifies nineteen natural laws. The first is that men are
'to seek peace and follow it' and the second is to the effect that they are
to enter into a social contract with a government of the kind that
Hobbes favours. Others are to the effect that punishments must be
directed to the prevention of future harm, that judges are to be of a
certain impartiality, and so on. Warrender's book, as Nagel begins by
saying, has in the main to do with the system of obligations including
and based upon his natural laws. (p. 100)

The dispute has to do with the nature or character of these precepts
or general rules, or, what comes to the same, with why we ought to
abide by them. It is Nagel's view that the natural laws have nothing
to do, certainly nothing significant, with moral obligation. They are
essentially precepts or general rules which appeal to the selfishness of
men, their rational self-interest. The instruction, 'seek peace and follow
it', given Hobbes's philosophy, must be understood as an instruction
which appeals to our self-interest rather than as an instruction as to
what is right, what morally we ought to do. So too with the natural
law that we ought to give over our rights to a government. Hobbes's
way of speaking, and much of his terminology, is fundamentally
misleading.

Nagel's argument for this conclusion begins with the general definition itself of natural laws given by Hobbes and mentioned above.
Whatever he may imply elsewhere, the definition certainly contains no
explicit suggestion that natural laws are *moral* obligations. (p. 101) The
definition is consonant with Hobbes's general theory of what motivates
us to action in every case. What moves a man to action is always 'some
good to himself', above all his own self-preservation. It is true that
Hobbes speaks of both a man's right and a man's duty of self-
preservation. These facts raise difficulties for the view of Hobbes as an
amoralist, in his philosophical theory, but they are surmountable
difficulties. (pp. 102–4).

The alternative account offered by Warrender is that Hobbes took
laws of nature to be moral obligations, and that the reason for abiding
by them is that they are commands of God. Self-interest enters into the
situation only in a secondary way. Since we *are* self-interested, and the
natural laws do serve our self-interest, we are indeed able to act on
them. '. . . the reason why I *can* do my duty is that I am able . . . to
see it as a means to my preservation; but the reason why I *ought* to do

my duty is that God commands it.' Self-interest is taken to be no more than a necessary condition of action of the right kind, as the fact that a man is not tied up is ordinarily taken as a necessary condition or 'validating condition' of, say, praise or blame with respect to the question of his giving aid to someone else who is wounded. Hobbes's view is to be seen as resting on the belief, as it can be expressed, that *ought* implies *can*, perhaps that one can only hold a man responsible for not having done something if he could in fact have done it.

This is disputed by Nagel, by way of the contrast between a man whose pathological fear of water prevents him from saving a drowning person, and, on the other hand, all men as conceived by Hobbes. It is our nature that we can *never* do otherwise than seek our own personal good, and this must ruin any attempt to ascribe to Hobbes the view that we have moral obligations. The belief that *ought* implies *can* works in favour of rather than against the view that Hobbes's doctrine is of an amoral rather than a moral kind. (pp. 104–7).

There follows a consideration of various other passages in the *Leviathan* which may seem to cut against that conclusion. One raises the question of a distinction, insisted on by Nagel, between something's being a law and its being morally obligatory. (pp. 106–7) Another pertains to another distinction, between counsel and command. (pp. 108–9) The paper ends with two principal questions, the first of which is that of the place of God in Hobbes's system if it is indeed true that his natural laws must be taken as appeals to self-interest. The answer given includes Hobbes's determinism, in which God serves as a first cause. This determinism, of course, is partly expressed by way of his theory of motivation.

The other principal question is that of whether a system of principles, precepts or instructions could in fact be a moral system in virtue of being the commands of a person, divine or otherwise. It is possible not merely that this is not sufficient to make it a moral system, but that it is sufficient to make it not a moral system. If so, the attempt to see Hobbes's natural laws as moral laws, by taking them as God's commands, necessarily fails. (pp. 111–12)

These are but some of the strands of thought in Nagel's compelling view of Hobbes. As in the case of other pieces of philosophy in this book, it strives to give a true view of its essential subject-matter, the thought of a great philosopher, and in so doing contributes to contemporary reflection on the questions which concerned him.

Thomas Nagel

Hobbes: His Concept of Obligation

Howard Warrender's book, *The Political Philosophy of Hobbes*,[1] is a piece of careful scholarship, intelligent exegesis, and clear presentation, and also a major contribution to our understanding of Hobbes's ideas. The interpretation of Hobbes has always been full of disagreement and confusion, and Mr Warrender's thorough examination of Hobbes's system of obligation brings real clarity to the field, clearing up many traditional difficulties and establishing a coherent framework for any further discussion of Hobbes's political theories. Warrender provides new insight into the nature and relation of the various types of obligation described by Hobbes. He shows that, according to Hobbes, we have a basic obligation to obey the laws of nature, that all our other obligations can be deduced from it, and that no new sort of obligation arises in society which did not exist in nature. After this examination of the system has been accomplished, however, there remains another problem which must be solved to complete the analysis of Hobbes's ideas. It is this problem which I should like to discuss, and it is stated by Warrender himself:

> To proceed beyond this point, however, to ask in turn, why the individual ought to obey natural law, is to make a new departure and the treatment of this problem is an addendum to, rather than a continuation of, the main argument which has been outlined in the first two Parts of this work. What has been examined above is the substructure of the obligation to obey natural law, in the sense of the pattern of consequences that derive from it; whereas the investigation of the ground of this obligation is concerned solely with its superstructure. Although the acceptance of different solutions to the question of the ultimate ground of obligation in Hobbes's theory, gives a different significance to his pattern of rights and duties, it does not in itself change that pattern, nor prejudice the account of it in the form in which it has been presented.[2]

Thomas Nagel, 'Hobbes's Concept of Obligation', *The Philosophical Review*, Vol. LXVIII, No. 1, Whole number 385, 1959. Reprinted without alteration with the permission of author and editor.

Warrender asserts that although he will venture to make some comments on this question, he feels unsure about them, much less sure than he does about his views concerning Hobbes's *system* of obligation. But he says rightly that the system can be successfully investigated without an analysis of the central concept and its grounds. So although I shall disagree with some things he says concerning the concept of obligation in Hobbes, I do not consider this a fundamental criticism of the book, since it is an issue quite separate from those to which Warrender directs himself primarily and with which he has dealt so admirably. The reason I shall frequently put my comments on the concept of obligation in Hobbes in the form of criticisms of views suggested by Warrender is that he has formulated the problems very clearly and has produced the most exhaustive and compelling arguments I have seen in support of a view in opposition to mine.

I shall attempt to show that genuine moral obligation plays no part in *Leviathan* at all, but that what Hobbes calls moral obligation is based exclusively on considerations of rational self-interest. Many people have rejected the view that Hobbes appeals solely to self-interest and have tried to reconcile the apparent presence of such a theme with a moral interpretation of Hobbes's concept of obligation. I shall try to show how such attempts fail and to produce an interpretation under which I feel his views become consistent.

One cannot miss the arguments in *Leviathan* based on self-interest. An egoistic theory of motivation permeates the entire book. I shall not attempt to trace it in detail, since the arguments are in no way hidden. They come out with particular clarity in the exposition of the laws of nature, which delineate our basic obligations and from which all others are derived. Hobbes defines a law of nature as 'a precept, or general rule, found out by reason, by which a man is forbidden to do that which is destructive of his life, or taketh away the means of preserving the same; and to omit that by which he thinketh it may be best preserved'.[3] He then goes on to derive nineteen such laws, and the justification of every single one of them is based on the argument that disobedience to the law will lead men into the state of war, which is for every man a dreadful prospect.

The egoistic theory of motivation is clearly expressed in Hobbes's explanation why certain rights are inalienable. 'Of the voluntary acts of every man, the object is some good to himself. And therefore there be some rights which no man can be understood by any words or other signs to have abandoned or transferred. As first a man cannot lay down the right of resisting them that assault him by force, to take away his life; because he cannot be understood to aim thereby at any good to himself.'⁴ The stipulations about what sorts of covenants one can and cannot be conceived to have made, when a covenant becomes void, when one is obliged to perform and when not, can, I think, be looked on as the construction of a practice of covenants in which it is possible to take part without ever acting contrary to one's own interests, and one which it is consequently possible for men to adopt. I think that it is a mistake to feel that because the right of self-defence sets a limit to obligation, it implies the understanding that there exist some truly moral obligations which must be so limited. It can be thought of merely as a logical consequence of Hobbes's self-interested concept of obligation. In Hobbes's language, it is one's moral obligation to follow the dictates of reason towards self-preservation and longer life. Certain acts, self-destruction for example, can never serve as means to self-preservation. Therefore killing oneself or not protecting oneself against harm can never be morally obligatory.

Warrender feels that there are in Hobbes two separate systems, a theory of motivation and a theory of obligation, the former having self-preservation as the supreme principle, based on the fact that all men will regard death as their greatest evil, and the latter based on the obligation to obey natural law regarded as the will of God. He explains the egoistic appearance of the theory of obligation on the grounds that it must be consistent with the theory of motivation, but he claims that self-preservation is a 'validating condition' of obligation and not a ground of obligation. He defines such a condition as one which must be satisfied if a ground of obligation is to be operative.⁵ Common examples of validating conditions are such things as sanity and maturity, which, although they certainly do not constitute grounds of obligation, must be present in an individual before he can be obliged.

Warrender expresses his purpose in the statement that 'If the fundamental principle which the individual is obliged to follow is one which enjoins peace rather than self-preservation as such, his duties are given a more social and less self-regarding appearance.'⁶ He thinks it can be shown that Hobbes does not feel that we are obliged primarily to insure our own preservation.

In support of this he argues first that according to Hobbes we have a right to self-preservation; but right and duty are in the same matter inconsistent, because right is the liberty to do or forbear, the absence of obligation. Therefore we cannot have a duty to self-preservation.⁷ But I maintain that Hobbes's position is not nearly so clear as this; that it appears in fact to be self-contradictory. For on the first page of

Chapter 14 of *Leviathan* Hobbes makes the following sequence of assertions: first, that the right of nature is the liberty that each man has to preserve his own life; second, that a law of nature is a precept by which a man is forbidden to do what is destructive of his life, or to omit that by which he thinks it may be preserved; third, that since right is the liberty to do or forbear, whereas law binds you to do one particular thing, law and right differ as much as obligation and liberty, which are in one and the same matter inconsistent.[8] I confess that I do not know what is intended, but I do not think that it is possible on this basis to show that Hobbes felt we do not have an obligation to preserve ourselves.

Warrender argues also, 'If self-preservation were meant to be taken as the principal duty of each individual, one would expect Hobbes to have regarded the precept that we should defend ourselves as a law and not as a right, and that we *ought* to use the advantages of war where peace is unobtainable. As his words stand, however, the fundamental law of nature is not "preserve thyself", but "seek peace", and the further laws of nature are derived from the latter precept.'[9] Warrender wishes to interpret the laws of nature not as maxims for individual preservation but as principles for the constant preservation of men in multitudes, based on concern for the conservation of society or of men in general. This makes him discount the ample evidence to the contrary. He realizes, for instance, that after listing the laws of nature Hobbes says that there are other things tending to the destruction of individuals which are also forbidden by the law of nature. He says they are not here relevant, since the discussion is about civil society. This indicates that the basic precept of the laws of nature is self-preservation and not preservation of society, but Warrender claims that these self-destructive actions can be considered harmful to the community, through destruction of the rational faculties, and so forth. I do not deny that they can be so considered, but I do not think it plausible that Hobbes considers them contrary to natural law for that reason alone.

Warrender admits also that at times Hobbes describes the laws of nature as precepts by which a man is *forbidden* to do that which is destructive to his life. But he says that this is not an accurate statement of Hobbes's position, and that he is more accurate when he calls them the articles of peace. This can certainly not be decided on the basis of the relative frequencies of the two descriptions. He sees that the laws which Hobbes lists as the fundamental obligations of man all bear directly on society and the general welfare. And it is a strict system of laws, not just a collection of random advice. I do not wish to deny this,

but it seems to me that Hobbes derives them carefully from considerations of individual self-interest. It is the fact that the laws of nature are
on the surface typically moral precepts, which inclines Warrender to
deny that they are prudential maxims which each man should obey for
his own sake.

He gives the following explanation of the role of self-interest in
Hobbes:

> The laws of nature, that command the individual to seek peace, keep cove-
> nants, etc., are from one point of view rational maxims for self-preservation;
> and one answer to the question of why the citizen should obey the civil law, is
> that obedience constitutes the best means to his preservation . . . This answer,
> given in terms of self-preservation, however, is concerned with motive and not
> with obligation . . . this consideration does not ensure their obligatory character;
> it is only in their aspect of being commands of God that they are laws and hence
> oblige. Thus the reason why I *can* do my duty is that I am able . . . to see it as
> a means to my preservation; but the reason why I *ought* to do my duty is that
> God commands it.[10]

Warrender interprets Hobbes as saying that there is a class of actions
to which men can be prudentially motivated, a subclass of these which
tend to self-preservation, and a subclass of these which tend to peace
and not merely to the individual's self-preservation. These last can be
considered the commands of God and consequently obligatory, because
we are previously obliged to obey Him and not because they are
conducive to self-interest. I shall discuss first what Warrender says
about self-interest in Hobbes, setting aside temporarily his contention
that the ground of obligation lies in the command of God.

Warrender inserts into Hobbes's moral doctrine certain validating
conditions of obligation which he says are made necessary by Hobbes's
egoistic theory of will, feeling, like Taylor, that Hobbes's obligation
can retain a moral sense if a separation is made between the two theories
of obligation and of will. He says that what a man cannot, according
to Hobbes, be obliged to do derives from an analysis of what is implied
in being obliged. Any law, to oblige, must satisfy the validating
conditions for obligation, which 'may be summarized by the statement
that the individual cannot be obliged where this is logically impossible'.[11] Among these are the conditions that the law must be knowable,
that the author must be known, and that if a man is in serious danger
of death, he is excused if he acts against the law to save himself. I would
certainly agree with everything that Warrender says up to this point,
but I disagree with his claim regarding the source of these validating
conditions. He says that the last condition derives from the logical fact

that, to be obliged, a person must be capable of having an adequate motive to obey the law (which he claims is involved in the notion that ought implies can), plus the empirical fact that since men perform only those actions which they believe to be in their own best interest, only in very rare circumstances can anyone have an adequate motive to contribute to his own destruction or not to resist others in their attempts on his life. All obligatory actions must be at least *capable* of being regarded by the individual concerned as in his best personal interest; therefore self-destruction and the like are never obligatory. This is Warrender's way out of saying that self-interest is the ground of Hobbes's obligation.

But is this condition really, as Warrender says, a logical extension of the belief that ought implies can? It may perhaps be admitted that if someone were incapable of having an adequate motive to do a certain thing, then he could be said to be *unable* to do it. It might even be that we should for this reason absolve him from obligation to do it. If someone with a pathological fear of water stands by while another person drowns, we may be less hard on him than we should be on a normal individual, though I do not think that the sense in which it may be said that he cannot act otherwise is the same as that involved in 'Ought implies can.' When we say, 'He couldn't have done it; therefore he wasn't obliged,' we usually mean to point out that even had he wished to do it, he would not have succeeded. He is excused from failure to act because his failure was no indication of his wishes.

But the person who is so afraid of water that nothing can motivate him to enter it may be, in other respects, quite normal morally, and subject to all the usual sorts of obligations. Consider, on the other hand, the case of the Hobbesian man. He can do something voluntarily only if he thinks it is in his own best personal interest. There are certain self-destructive actions which are incapable of being regarded as in his best personal interest, so they are impossible for him as voluntary acts. Warrender feels that if this is true of someone, then he cannot be obliged to perform those acts.

I feel that there is a difference between this case and that of the hydrophobe. This difference is obscured if we consider only those actions to which the Hobbesian man can *never* be sufficiently motivated. It seems then very similar to a phobia for some particular set of actions. But these few actions which he can never perform voluntarily constitute only a small part of the Hobbesian man's malady. He can never perform *any* action unless he believes it to be in his own best interest. Unlike the hydrophobe, who has a small kink in the cloth of his moral behaviour, the rest of which is quite normal, the Hobbesian man is incapacitated not only in relation to a few specific actions.

We may ascertain that the hydrophobe understands moral obligation by observing his behaviour in ordinary circumstances. If he is prepared to sacrifice his own interests somewhat in order to keep promises, help people in distress, and so forth (so long as the performance of duty does not involve his entrance into water), then we know that he has a moral sense. But we have no such behaviour on which to base a similar judgement of the man who never acts contrary to his interests. His case is not that of an otherwise normal individual who is incapable of a few isolated actions. The fact that the egoist is totally incapable of a few specifiable actions is only one aspect of his incapacity for a whole way of behaving. He is susceptible only to selfish motivation, and is therefore incapable of any action which could be clearly labelled moral. He might, in fact, be best described as a man without a moral sense.

Warrender's and Taylor's admission of Hobbes's feeling that no man can ever act voluntarily without having as an object his own personal good is the ruin of any attempt to put a truly moral construction on Hobbes's concept of obligation. It in a way excludes the meaningfulness of any talk about moral obligation. It deprives it of any room to work. Moral obligation is something that plays a part in deliberations, and it has an influence in situations in which a person might not perform an action if he considered only his own benefit, whereas the consideration of a moral obligation, to help others, for example, leads him to do it anyway. Nothing could be called a moral obligation which in principle never conflicted with self-interest. But according to the theory of motivation which Warrender attributes, I think correctly, to Hobbes, the only thing by which men are ever motivated is the consideration of self-interest. So a genuine feeling of moral obligation can never play a part in their deliberations. And if Hobbes acknowledges as a factor in human motivation anything which he *calls* moral obligation, then it must be some consideration of self-interest.

It is Warrender's view that our obligation to the laws of nature derives from a duty to obey the commands of God. This functions both as an explanation of the final ground of obligation and as a refutation of the position that obligation in Hobbes is based on self-interest.[12] The statement of Hobbes on which he bases his interpretation is the following remark about the laws of nature, which follows his development of them:

These dictates of reason, men use to call by the name of laws, but improperly: for they are but conclusions, or theorems concerning what conduceth to the conservation and defence of themselves; whereas law properly is the word of him that by right hath command over others. But yet if we consider the same theorems as delivered in the word of God, that by right commandeth all things, then are they are properly called laws.[13]

It is based on Hobbes's definition of law: a law is a command addressed to one previously obliged to obey the commander. So if we are to call the laws of nature laws, they must be the commands of someone to whom we are previously obliged, and who can this be but God?

Warrender interprets this (and I want to make it clear that this is just an interpretation) as meaning that only as the commands of God are the laws of nature *obligatory*.[14] He says that for the atheist the laws of nature in the state of nature, and consequently in society as well, are just prudential maxims, guides to his preservation, but that he cannot consider them as laws becasue they are not the commands of someone to whom he acknowledges a duty to obedience, and consequently they cannot be said to *oblige* the atheist. Warrender accuses those commentators who identify Hobbes's whole theory of morals and politics virtually with this atheistical viewpoint of passing over the assertion that the natural laws are laws as they proceed from God. But he is mistaken. Nowhere does Hobbes say that only the commands of an authority can be *obligatory*. All he says is that only the commands of an authority can be *laws*. This is all that is maintained in any of the passages cited by Warrender to support his view, nor have I been able to find anything more in Hobbes's writings. There is a difference between denying that they derive their status as *laws* because they proceed from God and denying that they derive their *obligatory* status because they proceed from God. I wish to deny the latter and to maintain that Warrender has no grounds in Hobbes for affirming it. I think it quite consistent with Hobbes's system to say that the laws of nature can be considered the commands and laws of God, but I do not think that saying they have this sort of obligation is in contradiction to the notion that Hobbes's primary ground of obligation is prudential. I believe that he considers even our obligation to obey God a prudentially grounded one. I shall not say more on this point until later on. But at any rate, this is not to claim that Hobbes was an atheist or that he thought that no obligations could derive from God's commands.

Hobbes is in the passage in question drawing some sort of distinction between the laws of nature as maxims of prudential behaviour and as the commands of God, but it may be nothing more than the unimportant distinction, based on the definition of law, that only as the commands of someone in authority *can they be properly called laws*.

(These are Hobbes's own words.) We are obliged to obey them in several ways: basically on prudential grounds, but also as the commands of God and of the sovereign, though these also reduce, I believe, to a prudential basis. My interpretation is that after developing the laws of nature he makes, as an afterthought, a comment on usage; he says that his calling these precepts 'laws' is not strictly correct, since only the commands of an authority are properly called laws.

Warrender feels that the distinction being drawn is that as prudential maxims they are not obligatory while as laws they are. The only thing which I can imagine might be construed as favourable to the view that Hobbes has this in mind is the distinction drawn between counsel and command, in Chapter 25 of *Leviathan*, where Hobbes says that a man can be obliged to obey a command which is uttered only for the commander's benefit, 'But he cannot be obliged to do as he is counselled, because the hurt of not following it is his own.'[15] There is nothing else in the entire book similar to this passage, nothing to indicate a belief on Hobbes's part that obligation could not be derived from self-interest. But this one passage seems to imply that the ground of obligation cannot be self-interest but must be the authority of a commander. It seems to imply, in fact, that one cannot be obliged to obey any precept for which the hurt of not obeying is one's own. This would entail that one could not be obliged to obey the laws of nature, so that this interpretation of the passage involves a result so drastic that it is not to be accepted lightly. I think that if we consider the passage more closely, however, it will be seen why this restriction need not apply to the laws of nature.

'A man may be obliged to do what he is commanded, as when he hath covenanted to obey,' writes Hobbes, and he says that if one covenants to obey counsel, 'then is the counsel turned into the nature of a command.'[16] Hobbes is describing a difference between two types of imperative utterance. (The chapter concerns counsel and the position of counsellors.) He says that if we obey a man's counsel it is because we want to, and if we are obliged to obey him, then we do not do so because we happen to consider each of his commands to be in our own interest, but because we are obliged to obey *him*, so it is no longer counsel but command. He is analysing the concepts of counsel and command in terms of the very different sorts of reasons for which we obey the two sorts of imperatives. In one case we obey because the individual precepts seem to us directed to our own benefit; in the other case we obey because we are obliged in general to obey the precepts of that particular individual. But this does not exclude the possibility that our general obligation to obey him whom we have covenanted to obey is based finally on self-interest. All that is meant, I think, is that it is logically excluded that we should be obliged to do whatever someone tells us and that it should at the same time be called counsel. This can apply as well to the commands of God as to those of the civil sovereign. But it is quite irrelevant to the obligatory status of anything other than imperatives uttered by a person of some sort. Hobbes does not claim, as Warrender seems to think, that the only possible source of an obligation to do something is that it is the command of someone in authority. He is just making a mild grammatical observation of somewhat restricted scope.

It is possible to think of the laws of nature as something other than either command or counsel. Warrender feels that to call them prudential maxims is to classify them as counsel, and so to make them necessarily non-obligatory in Hobbes's system. But when Hobbes speaks of counsel, he means the counsel of some particular person. Hobbes would not, I think, deny that a set of maxims like the laws of nature, although not being commanded by anyone to anyone, could still be obligatory. In fact, I believe that he considers our basic obligations to be not to authority but to a set of principles, the laws of nature, and that our obligations to authority derive from these.

If, however, I deny that God is the ground of obligation, what can I say about the position which God occupies in Hobbes's theory in relation to the laws of nature and the obligations of men? I believe that He plays several roles.

One is that of the omnipotent ruler of the kingdom of God by nature, of whom Hobbes speaks in Chapter 31. His subjects in this kingdom are those who believe that He exists and governs, with rewards and punishments for obedience and disobedience. He promulgates His laws by the dictates of natural reason, by revelation, and through prophets. Hobbes claims that His right to reign and our obligation to obey Him have nothing to do with His having created us and our consequent gratefulness to Him but springs solely from His irresistible power. He says that it is just as if one man in the state of nature had had the power to subdue all the rest by himself. Since every man in the state of nature has a right to all things, this man could just have taken over. The only thing that prevents this from happening in fact is that no man is that strong, so that the establishment of a sovereign requires that all others lay aside their right to all things. 'Whereas if there had been any man of power irresistible, there had been no reason why he should not by that power have ruled, and defended both himself and them according to his own discretion. To those therefore whose power is irresistible, the dominion of all men adhereth naturally by their excellence of power; and consequently it is from that power that the kingdom over men, and the right of afflicting men at his pleasure, belongeth naturally to God Almighty; not as creator, and gracious; but as omnipotent.'[17] What could be clearer? We must obey, or else. One might even consider God Himself as being in the state of nature. But He is in no danger in the war of all against all, so He need not follow those laws of nature drafted as principles by which weaker individuals might preserve and lengthen their lives. We possess a duty to worship God, says Hobbes, 'By those rules of honour that reason dictateth to be done by the weak to the more potent men, in hope of benefit, for fear of danger, or in thankfulness for good already received from them.'[18]

Warrender admits that this interpretation fits in well with the theory of human motivation but claims that it does not properly acknowledge the truly moral tone of Hobbes. Whether there is, as Warrender and A. E. Taylor maintain, a truly moral tone in Hobbes is a view which I consider quite open to question. But whatever truth it may contain, it cannot change the strictly prudential sense which the concept of obligation has in his system.

Another role which God plays is that of the cause of all things. All men's desires, passions, and appetites are caused in the last analysis by God's will, so that their actions actually proceed by necessity. In this sense, 'When we ascribe to God a will, it is not to be understood as that of a man, for rational appetite; but as the power by which he effecteth every thing.'[19] By controlling our individual desires he controls our collective actions. In Chapter 17 Hobbes describes how this works with social animals like bees. They can act together for the common good just by following their own private inclinations. But man, who is a proud and critical being, must devise principles of civil government in order to live in this way. Nevertheless, even these dictates of reason, and the basic desires from which they are derived, are present in human beings by the will of God. Since according to Hobbes we can act only in what we take to be our interests, and all our actions are determined by the will of God, we can be said to have an obligation to obey only in the far-fetched sense in which stones might be said to have an obligation to roll downhill. And this is not in any sense a moral obligation. Or if we forget about the deterministic side of the theory, we might say that men have an obligation to seek their own benefit in certain ways devised by God (by following the laws of nature and setting up civil society), which are rationally the best ways, and consequently the ones by which, acting selfishly, men will be acting in the public interest. But this again is not a moral obligation. The reason an individual chooses to obey the laws of nature will still be totally selfish.

The one role, at any rate, which I wish to deny that God plays in Hobbes's theory of obligation is that of the ground of moral obligation, which Warrender and Taylor have claimed resides in His word. The obligation to obey God does not seem to me to occupy the central position in Hobbes which Warrender attributes to it. Warrender argues that all moral obligation is based on the natural law, and that the laws can be obligatory only in their status as the commands of God, to Whom we are previously obliged. He says that the question becomes finally whether the ultimate, unquestionable appeal regarding what our obligations are is to be made to the authority of a person or to that of a rule. Even leaving aside the contention that it is not a system of moral obligation at all, it seems to me clearly based far more on laws than on commands. The laws of nature are obligatory by themselves. They may also be the commands of God, and may derive some obligation from that. But Hobbes does not derive them by saying, 'We are obliged to do whatever God commands; he has commanded these laws; therefore these are our basic obligations.' He says that the laws of nature are immutable and eternal because war will always destroy life and peace will always preserve it, not because God will never change His instructions.[20] It is a mistake to say that God is the ultimate appeal for Hobbes, for, if that were so, then all things which He ordered would be of equal obligatoriness, and whenever He changed his orders, our obligations would change. The essentials of Hobbes's system are a set of principles concerned mainly with the preservation of human society, and if those principles were changed, it would not be the same system.

I feel also, although with some uncertainty, that a system of obligation which has at its apex the authority of a person, and not a principle, cannot properly be called a moral system. I wish to mention this point (although I shall not discuss it thoroughly) because Warrender believes that in establishing this sort of ground for Hobbes's concept of obligation, he is showing it to be *moral* obligation. When it is a legal system that is under examination, then the question of whether the apex is a law or a person is certainly present. We settle it by observing what people in the system finally appeal to. But if it is a moral system, and the final authority turns out to be a person, I am inclined to say that it is not really moral at all. This is not because I feel that this sort of appeal must be based on self-interest or fear. When a father says that a child should do something 'just because I said so!'

he need not be referring to any physical sanctions attached to his commands, but to simple, basic, personal authority. Many people, as Warrender has pointed out, feel this to be the only ground of obligation, and they act upon it in ways very similar to those in which I act on what I take to be the grounds of obligation. The strength of feeling is no less in the one case than in the other, and guilt and blame and praise play similarly active roles in both sorts of discourse. I wish to deny that the other sort is properly called moral, partially because rational consideration and human feeling play no part in it in deciding what is right and what is wrong, and also because of the possibility that such a belief should result in the person's accepting as moral laws a set of precepts completely different from those which I accept as moral, since it is possible that the being whom he feels obliged to obey may command anything whatever, and it will then be moral law. It is part of the concept of morality that certain precepts must be included in a system of rules if we are to call it a moral system. There must be precepts concerning kind and fair treatment of others, precepts against inflicting unnecessary suffering, and so on. Nothing can be called a ground of morality which admits the possibility that these precepts might not be among our obligations.

I think I have shown that, in the system of obligations which is developed in *Leviathan*, what Hobbes calls moral obligation is based entirely upon self-interest. Not once in *Leviathan* does he appeal to concern for others as a motive, but always to self-interest. Yet he is clearly interested in the welfare of humanity; the book is directed at the problems of society. One might even wish to say that these are moral feelings on his part, and that they are in a sense expressed in the work. But I think that one must consider this moral aspect of Hobbes's sentiments as something quite separate from the system which he propounds. His theory of motivation, according to which men act for none but selfish reasons, precluded his writing a hortatory work which appealed to altruistic motives. So the *Leviathan* tells men how they may act in their own best interests, such that if all of them act in the same way, they will all benefit together. If Hobbes had proved that certain institutions and practices promoted the general welfare, and had then said that every man was obliged to work for their establishment regardless of whether they happened to be in his own particular interest, then the concept of obligation involved could be called moral. But nothing of this sort is said. Given Hobbes's theory of motivation, one cannot expect to find reference to genuine moral obligation in a book in which he is trying to convince people to do certain things; and this, I believe, is why Warrender's attempt is bound to fail. The temptation to try comes from the idea that Hobbes must have felt morally about the matter to write a book like this, which is quite possibly a reasonable conclusion. But questions about Hobbes's feelings must not be confused with questions about the sense of his text.

Warrender feels that Hobbes needs to be saved from the stigma of having based his arguments for political obligation upon self-interest. I myself do not feel that there is anything strange about basing a system of political *theory* on considerations of self-interest and justifying various governmental institutions and practices by Hobbes's methods. I agree that to call it, as Hobbes does, a system of moral obligation is a mistake. As an attempt to analyse moral concepts *Leviathan* fails. But if one wishes to construct a system of social and political behaviour which it is hoped all men may find it feasible to adopt, it seems natural to appeal to the sort of far-seeing, rational self-interest on which Hobbes bases his system. And it is very important to differentiate between this sort of appeal to self-interest and another sort. When Hobbes says that a law of nature is 'a precept, or general rule, found out by reason, by which a man is forbidden to do that which is destructive of his life, or taketh away the means of preserving the same; and to omit that by which he thinketh it may be best preserved',[21] one might feel entitled to say that the laws of nature are equivalent to the one command, 'Preserve yourself'. And this strikes one naturally as a very odd general precept on which to found a social system. As we would ordinarily understand the simple precept 'Preserve yourself', if everyone followed it the result would be essentially Hobbes's war of all against all, with all men striving only for their immediate benefit, to the general detriment of mankind. One might obey it by getting a gun and shooting anyone who obstructed one's interests. But realizing this, and realizing most importantly of all that the strongest human motivation he has to work with is self-interest, Hobbes tries to discover what men can do with this motivation which will better their state by extracting them from the war of all against all. His laws of nature are precepts which take into account that men in the state of nature striving just for their individual good, unlike the bees, do not produce an optimum state of affairs in terms of human security and survival. The laws of nature do not enjoin men to renounce the basic motivation to seek their own immediate benefit. They urge the establishment of conditions such that the results of men's acting from this same motivation will differ from the universal condition of war. And they contain

113

qualifications to insure that in no case can adherence to them be opposed to the self-interest of the particular individual. That is, it is not the case merely that if all men follow these rules, the result will be to the general good, but also that a single man following them, even if no one else does, will not jeopardize his own welfare. Therefore it is to every man's advantage to follow the rules; they are in fact the best and most rational way in which a man can act in his own interest. So it is in a sense true to say that they amount to the precept 'Preserve yourself', but this is also very misleading. Taken as the essence of a set of rules 'dictating peace, for a means of the conservation of men in multitudes', it is quite different from the same injunction addressed to just one individual. There are at least two sorts of appeal to self-interest in the justification of the adoption of a set of rules for behaviour. And one is far more refined than the other and has an important application in the construction of political systems.

Notes

1. Oxford, 1957.
2. p. 278.
3. *The English Works of Thomas Hobbes*, ed. by Sir William Molesworth (London, 1839–45), III, 116–17. All references to Hobbes are to this edition.
4. ibid., p. 120.
5. Warrender, p. 14.
6. ibid., p. 218.
7. ibid., pp. 214–15.
8. Hobbes, III, 116.
9. Warrender, p. 216.
10. Warrender, pp. 212 f. This division is also made by A. E. Taylor, 'The Ethical Doctrine of Hobbes', in *Philosophy*, XIII (1938), 408.
11. Warrender, p. 94.
12. It is to be found in Taylor, and some of the relevant arguments are made by Michael Oakeshott, *Hobbes's Leviathan*, edited with an introduction (Oxford, 1946).
13. Hobbes, III, 147. This view is expressed in several places throughout Hobbes's writings. See also *Leviathan*, III, 251; *De cive*, II, 49–50; *De corpore politico*, IV, 109.
14. pp. 97–8.
15. Hobbes, III, 241.
16. ibid., p. 241.
17. ibid., p. 346.
18. ibid., p. 350.
19. ibid., p. 352.
20. ibid., p. 145.
21. ibid., pp. 116–17.

Biographical Note

Thomas Nagel has been professor of philosophy at New York University since 1980. Before that he taught at Princeton University and the University of California at Berkeley. His books are *The Possibility of Altruism* (1970) and *Mortal Questions* (1979).

Further Reading

Hobbes, *Leviathan*, many editions; Hobbes, *De homine* and *De cive*, translated as *Man and Citizen* (New York: Doubleday, 1972).

    Howard Warrender, *The Political Philosophy of Hobbes* (Oxford: Clarendon, 1957); Keith Brown, ed., *Hobbes Studies* (Oxford: Blackwell, 1965); J. W. N. Watkins, *Hobbes's System of Ideas* (London: Hutchinson, 1965); David Gauthier, *The Logic of Leviathan* (Oxford: Clarendon, 1969).

Bernard Williams

Descartes: Cogito and Sum

Beyond question the greatest of French philosophers, Descartes founded his work principally on his Method of Doubt, at bottom the resolve to produce a philosophy by first discarding any belief about which he could generate a doubt. The rational way to truth, the way of the Pure Enquirer, was to begin by attempting to suspend judgement about everything except the absolutely indubitable. Pursuing this scepticism, which itself raises large philosophical issues, he required of himself that he give up belief in all material things and very nearly everything else, including the existence of God.

There was something that had to be taken as indubitable or certain. He expressed it in 'Cogito ergo sum' or 'I am thinking, therefore I exist', perhaps the most famous sentence in philosophy. On this foundation he proceeded to build a structure of argument. Its conclusions included what had been put aside in the initial scepticism, including an acceptance of the material world and God. The foundation, 'I am thinking, therefore I exist', is the subject-matter of the chapter which follows. It comes from Bernard Williams's *Descartes: The Project of Pure Enquiry*, the most individual, tireless and acute book on Descartes in many decades. Its author never succumbs to the philosophical temptation to give up pursuit of the valuable but elusive, or of further essential distinctions.

The chapter does not contain all of Williams's examination of or his final conclusion about the *cogito* – that is, the argument expressed by 'I am thinking, therefore I exist'. It contains quite enough to establish a great deal, including the fact that the *cogito*, for all its force, is far indeed from being a truth that is plain and simple.

René Descartes, 1596–1650. Born at La Haye in France, educated at a Jesuit college, lived mainly in Holland, lastly in Sweden. Regarded as the first of the Rationalist philosophers, also a mathematician. Died in Stockholm, to which Queen Christina had asked him to grace her court.

What does the certainty that somehow attaches to the *cogito* come to? One kind of understanding or kind of certainty is *incorrigibility*. If I have a belief that I am thinking, or a belief that I exist, or indeed if I wonder about or doubt those things, then it must be that it is true that I am thinking or that I exist. (p. 121) If I do the further thing of asserting that I am thinking, or that I exist, then my assertions are certain in a related way. They are *self-verifying*, which is to say that if I make the assertions, it must be that they are true. (pp. 121–2). Williams considers and questions a view of the *cogito* and in particular of the self-verifying nature of 'I exist' by itself, which depends on the philosophical notion of a performative utterance. Such a linguistic act – saying the sentence 'I promise' in the right circumstances is an example – has the peculiarity that it is the performance or act which the sentence seems to describe.

A great shortcoming of at least one version of the performative view of the *cogito*, which view makes 'I exist' somehow like 'I promise', is that it seems to imply that my act of thinking the proposition that I exist makes that proposition true. (pp. 122–3) That cannot be right. A related line of thought in fact takes us away from the notion of a performative utterance. (p. 123) A further shortcoming of such understandings of the *cogito* is that they conflict with what seems to be the case, that Descartes's argument involves two propositions, not only 'I exist' but also 'I am thinking'. The proposition 'I exist' does not seem to be presented as somehow self-recommending. There is at least the semblance that it stands to 'I am thinking' as conclusion to premise. Indeed, putting aside the performative view, since 'I exist' itself involves both incorrigibility and self-verification, we seem not to have a kind of certainty which gives any role in the argument to 'I am thinking'. Certainly we do not have an inference from 'I am thinking', taken as an explicitly made self-reflexive statement used in an argument, to the conclusion 'I exist'.

There is a third way or sense in which a thing can be certain. It can be *self-evident*. A proposition's having this property is for there to be someone such that if the proposition is true, the person believes it. (p. 124) *This* certainty is had by 'I am thinking', which is where we want to start, but at least at first sight not by 'I exist'. As it turns out, being self-evident is something that is true of many propositions about conscious states or activities generally, including for example one's having the sensation of touching something. (pp. 124–5) The certainty which is a proposition's being self-evident is bound up with the states or activities being such things as necessarily are present to consciousness.

After considering some connections between the given kinds of certainty (pp. 127–30) and in particular connections having to do with the ideas of subconscious or unconscious mental states, which ideas conflict sharply with one of Descartes's views (p. 130), and after considering Descartes's need for self-evident propositions in his subsequent argument (pp. 131–2), we come to the fundamental and baffling question noticed earlier, whether the *cogito* is to be taken as expressing an inference, as the word 'therefore' certainly suggests. The answer given is that it involves a bare statement of necessity or an 'eternal truth'. (pp. 134–6) It transpires that the content of this truth, in terms of the English language, is that the pronoun 'I' – as against 'you' or 'he' – is such that a genuine use of it attaches or latches onto something. Here, although there are considerable complications, we have a fourth kind of certainty, and, in a sense, an inference.

The last section of the chapter (pp. 137–42) has to do with an objection raised to the premise of the inference by an eighteenth-century philosopher and various successors. It is that the most that Descartes can claim is not 'I am thinking' but rather the lesser thing 'There is thinking going on'. Rather than the 'personal' claim, only the 'impersonal' claim is allowed to him by his commitment to the Method of Doubt.

The lesser claim is not easy to understand – is there a clear thought in the words 'There is thinking going on'? If we say yes, we must also allow that the meaning or content of this lesser claim seems to require a supplementation that in fact turns it into the larger personal claim. Moreover, we are driven further. In order to make sense of personal reports of thought, we need to do something different. We need in a way to assert the existence of a thinking subject, as distinct from the occurrence of a thought whose content includes an 'I'. (p. 141)

Descartes, however, is not taken by Williams as victorious. He has by his scepticism limited himself, so to speak, to accepting a realm which has in it only thought-events. If one stays in this realm, it seems one cannot assume the existence of thinking subjects. But then – as we have just seen in considering the eighteenth-century criticism – there seems to be no possibility of making sense of, or indeed making, reports of thought – one cannot make sense of the very stuff of the given realm. The *cogito*'s prospects of success look pretty uncertain.

The arguments by which Williams proceeds to this conclusion –

The abbreviated references to Descartes's works in the text are explained in the note on further reading which follows it. In some cases references are made to the volume and section number of named works.

arguments taken up again later in his book – are exceptional pieces of philosophy. They are difficult for the good reason that they go beyond what is philosophically conventional, and not by the easy way of relaxing the standards of the subject. They advance the persistent subject of a Cartesian foundation for our beliefs.

Bernard Williams

Descartes: Cogito and Sum

The Method of Doubt, radically and generally applied, leaves Descartes, it seems, with nothing. God, the world, his own body, the past, all seem to have succumbed to it; all might be illusions. Is there anything at all that he can know to be true, that can survive the process of doubt? At this point Descartes makes the reflection which brings the Doubt for the first time to a halt, and which sets him off in the opposite direction, on the path of positive knowledge.

> I have convinced myself that there is nothing at all in the world, no heaven, no earth, no minds, no bodies; have I not then convinced myself that I do not exist? On the contrary: there is no doubt that I existed, if I convinced myself of anything. – But there is some deceiver, in the highest degree powerful and ingenious, who uses all his efforts to deceive me all the time. – Then there is no doubt that I exist, if he is deceiving me; let him deceive me as much as he likes, he can never bring it about that I am nothing, so long as I think that I am something. So after every thought and the most careful consideration, I must hold firm to this conclusion: that the proposition *I am, I exist*, must be true, whenever I utter it or conceive it in my mind.

This is a translation of what Descartes wrote, in the original Latin version, near the beginning of the *Second Meditation* (VII 25, HR1 150). But the French translation of the *Meditations* – which, the work of the Duc de Luynes, appeared in 1647 and had been seen and approved by Descartes[1] – presents a more complex version of the second sentence:

> Certainly not: I certainly existed, if I convinced myself, or simply if I thought anything. (IX–1 19)

This emphasis brings out more strongly a connection that is already implicit, between Descartes's assurance that he exists, and his thinking.

Bernard Williams, '*Cogito* and *Sum*', Chapter 3 of *Descartes: The Project of Pure Enquiry* (Harmondsworth: Penguin Books, 1978). Reprinted with the permission of author and publisher. Slight alterations to text.

This connection is basic; but in the *Meditations* the claim that he is thinking is not itself offered as something of which he is certain – only the proposition 'I am, I exist' is explicitly said to be that.[2] In the famous words of the *Discourse*, however, his thinking is offered both as part of what is certain, and also as the ground, so it seems, of the assurance that he exists (Part iv: VI 32, HR1 101):

. . . I noticed that, while I was trying to think that everything was false, it was necessary that I, who was thinking this, should be something. And observing that this truth: *I am thinking, therefore I exist* was so firm and secure that all the most extravagant suppositions of the sceptics were not capable of overthrowing it, I judged that I should not scruple to accept it as the first principle of the philosophy I was seeking.

Cogito ergo sum, 'I am thinking, therefore I exist' – the *cogito*, as it is often known – is not only the most famous but the most discussed of Descartes's sentences, and there has been much controversy about the ground of the certainty that it seems to possess; whether it is, as it seems to be, an inference; and what content can be found in the proposition 'sum', from which Descartes is to extract quite ambitious metaphysical conclusions. Here we shall be principally concerned with the certainty of 'cogito' and of 'sum', and with the connection between them.

Since Descartes is prepared to regard 'cogito' and 'sum' as equally and independently certain, it is reasonable, in trying to explain or ground their certainty, to look in the first place for some characteristic that they both possess. Both possess the property of being *incorrigible*: if anyone believes that he is thinking, or again, that he exists, then necessarily he has a true belief. Moreover, they both have another property which is closely related to their incorrigibility, and contributes to it: each of them is *self-verifying*, in the sense that if anyone asserts the proposition, then that assertion must be true.[3] The basis of this is particularly clear in the case of 'cogito', where it can be seen as the limiting case of a phenomenon displayed by other propositions. 'I am writing' will be true if I write it, but not if I say it; conversely with 'I am saying something'. 'I am making a public utterance' (in a rather strained sense of that sentence, perhaps) will be true whether I say it or write it, but not if I merely think it. 'I am thinking' is at the very end of that road: it will make a true assertion whatever mode it is asserted in, publicly or merely to myself. It can be true, of course, even if it is not *asserted* at all but merely if it is entertained or considered or doubted: for all of these are modes of thought, so the fact that I doubt or consider anything, and in particular, doubt or consider the proposition that I am thinking, will make it true that I am thinking. However, this by itself will not yet give me any true beliefs, since merely to consider or doubt something is not yet to believe anything. The Pure Enquirer will have a true or certain belief only when he advances to asserting something, for example that he is thinking, and here the self-verifying property of 'cogito' as asserted gives him inevitably a true belief. Since 'I am thinking', and also 'I exist', in this sort of way necessarily make true assertions, 'I am not thinking' and 'I do not exist' necessarily make false ones. They do not, however, make assertions that are *necessarily false*, in the sense of being logical falsehoods or self-contradictions. A logical falsehood is false in all possible states of affairs, its contradictory true in all possible states of affairs; but Descartes does not believe, either now or later in his reflections, that his thought or his existence are in any such way necessary features of the universe. He might not have existed; but in any state of the world in which he did not exist, of course he could not then think, believe, assert etc. that fact. The denials of 'I am thinking' and 'I exist' are not logical false-hoods, but pragmatically self-defeating or self-falsifying – we might compare someone's saying 'I am absent' in a roll-call. Descartes himself is not only committed to their not being logical falsehoods, but he is clear that they are not: '*I am, I exist*, must be true, *whenever I utter it or conceive it in my mind.*'

Several writers have emphasized this aspect of the incorrigibility possessed by 'cogito' and 'sum'.[4] It is with regard to this aspect that Hintikka has used the notion of a 'performatory' or 'performative' interpretation of the *cogito*. This term, however, can be seriously misleading. The main use of 'performative' in recent philosophy has been to cover certain uses of language by which the very act of uttering a sentence, in a correct context, constitutes the act to which the sentence refers: 'I hereby warn you . . .', 'I bid . . .', 'I promise . . .', are well-known examples. If the term 'performatory' is applied to the *cogito*, this might suggest, by a kind of analogy to these examples, that it is the very act of thinking the proposition that makes the proposition true. This might suggest, further, that the peculiar certainty that the thinker possesses about the proposition is the product of the fact that he has made it true – on the lines, perhaps, of Vico's favourite thought, *verum et factum convertuntur*, it is only what one oneself produces that one can know through and through.[5] But none of this can be on the right lines. For while a sense might be defended in which I make it true that I am thinking, by thinking, there is no sense in which I make it true, by doing anything, that I exist; nor could Descartes have thought so, who emphatically insists that he could not be self-created. Now Hintikka does not himself seem to mean that the 'performatory' interpretation of the *cogito* involves the idea of *making these propositions true*; though he does rather misleadingly say that the relation of 'cogito' to 'sum' is 'rather comparable with that of a *process* to its *product*',[6] and also speaks of the 'act of thinking through which the sentence *I exist* may be said to verify itself'.[7] What he rather seems to mean is that it is the *indubitability* of 'I exist' which 'results'[8] from the act of thinking. But it is not clear how this is to be taken. If it just meant that Descartes could not recognize 'I exist' to be indubitable unless he thought it, this would not make any special point: he could not recognize any proposition to be indubitable without thinking it. Hintikka makes it clear that he means more than this. The idea is perhaps rather that the very act of thinking it *provides the grounds*, in some way, for recognizing 'I exist' as indubitable. This seems nearer to what is needed, but it also begins to narrow the gap between a 'performative' interpretation and some alternatives to it.

A distinctive mark of a 'performative' interpretation, as Hintikka discusses it, seems to be this, that it does not regard the *cogito*, in its fundamental form, as expressing a relation between *two* propositions. There is the one proposition, 'sum', of which Descartes becomes certain, but the other proposition, 'cogito', is not essential, as a reflexive thought of Descartes's, at all. What is essential is just that Descartes should be thinking, and it will be that thinking, and not a reflexive proposition recording it, which will somehow bring the indubitability of 'sum' before him. The *Meditations* formula, in which 'cogito' is not itself presented, will then be primary and more accurately express the nature of the *cogito*. But if we are to say that the thinking is not just the occasion of recognizing 'sum' to be indubitable, but that it provides, in any sense at all, grounds for that recognition, it is hard to see how a full reconstruction of Descartes's thought can avoid expressing those grounds explicitly: that is to say, it will actually display the reflexive proposition 'cogito', and the *cogito* will involve two propositions. It does not follow from that that the relation between the two has to be one of inference; but it does remove one of the more compelling reasons one might have for denying that it was an inference, namely that the supposed premiss never appeared as a proposition at all.

We shall come back later to the question of whether the *cogito* can be an inference, and whether Descartes thought it was. Before that, however, we should look at a quite different aspect of the *cogito*, which involves a different way in which certainty comes into the matter. The 'self-verifying' property applied to both 'cogito' and 'sum'; and the fact that it applied to 'sum' in its own right contributed to the point we have just considered, that the role of 'cogito' as a proposition which is itself reflexively thought may seem not essential. We now turn to a different property related to certainty, and this, by contrast, undoubtedly requires the presence of a proposition other than 'sum' – out of the two, 'cogito' and 'sum', it is 'cogito' that it applies to. This property I will label 'being evident': that a proposition is *evident* (with respect to *A*) means that if it is true, then *A* believes it. It is, so to speak, the converse of incorrigibility, as I have defined that. A proposition can be both incorrigible and evident, as Descartes takes 'I am thinking' to be: in that case, *A* will believe it if and only if it is true. 'I exist', however, while it is incorrigible, cannot be assumed to be evident (in this special sense) at this stage, without anticipating the answers to many questions that will come later. It will turn out, eventually, to be in Descartes's view an evident proposition, because his existence will turn out to be that of an essentially (and constantly) thinking thing, so that his existence will be as evident as Descartes always takes his thinking to be. But he cannot assume yet that his existence is such that if he exists, he must believe that he does – it might be possible, as common-sense would suggest, for him to exist without believing anything.

As an *evident* proposition, 'cogito' is not just one peculiar item, but rather the representative of a large class of different propositions. It is an important point that in Descartes's usage the Latin verb *cogitare* and the French verb *penser* and the related nouns *cogitatio* and *pensée*, have a wider significance than the English *think* and *thought*. In English, such terms are specially connected with ratiocinative or cognitive processes. For Descartes, however, a *cogitatio* or *pensée* is any sort of conscious state or activity whatsoever; it can as well be a sensation (at least, in its purely psychological aspect) or an act of will, as judgement or belief or intellectual questioning. As he puts it in the more formal exposition of the *Principles* (i 32):

All forms of consciousness (*modi cogitandi*) that we experience can be brought down to two general kinds: one is cognition (*perceptio*), or the operation of the intellect; the other is volition, the operation of the will. Sensation, imagination and pure intellection are just various forms of cognition; desire, aversion, assertion, denial, doubt, are various forms of volition.

These various forms of *cogitatio* are not something that Descartes introduces only at a later stage of his philosophy. Already in the *Second Meditation* he is prepared to say, soon after the proof of his existence in the *cogito*, that he can be certain that a whole variety of purely mental operations must actually belong to him as he experiences them. He describes himself, on the strength of the *cogito* alone, as a 'thinking thing' (*res cogitans*) (VII 27, HR1 152); to this description we shall have to return later, but what matters for the present is the way in which Descartes is prepared to interpret this, which sheds some light on the meaning of the *cogito* itself. He goes on (VII 28, HR1 153):

What then am I? A thinking thing. What is that? One that doubts, under-stands, asserts, denies, is willing, is unwilling, which also imagines and feels.

This is quite a number of things, if they all belong to me. But why should they not? Am I not the being who is now doubting almost everything; who nevertheless understands something, and asserts this one thing to be true, who denies the others, who wants to know more, and does not want to be deceived, who imagines many things, sometimes against my will, and who is aware of many things as though they came by the senses? What is there in all this which is not just as true as that I exist – even if all the while I am asleep, even if the being who created me deludes me to the full extent of his power?[9] Can any of this be distinguished from my thought (*cogitatio*)? Can any of it be separated from myself? It is so self-evident that it is I who doubts, understands, and desires, that there seems no way in which it can be more clearly explained.

Further, it is also I who imagines; for even if (as I supposed) none of the things that I imagine is true, yet this power of imagination really exists and forms part of my thought. Finally, it is I who have sensations, that is to say, who is aware of objects as though by the senses, since indeed I see light, I hear noise, I feel heat. – But all these objects are unreal, since I am dreaming. – Let it be so; certainly it seems to me that I see, I hear, and I feel heat. That cannot be false; that is what in me is properly called sensation; and in this precise sense, sensation is nothing but thought.

In this passage, Descartes takes two important steps. First, he claims that there is a whole range of specific *cogitationes* of which he is certain. They are specific both as types of *cogitatio* – doubting, willing, imag-ining – and, further, in their content: he is doubting, willing or imag-ining some particular thing. In the previous discussion, we considered 'cogito' only in its unspecific form, 'I am thinking'; but Descartes is also prepared to include among his certainties such specific propositions as 'I am denying that I have a body' or 'it seems to me as though I can feel heat'. This is the first step. The second, instanced by this last example, is that among these *cogitationes* he is prepared to include some that he identifies as the purely mental element in experiences which earlier he treated as presupposing the existence of his body and the physical world, and hence to be ruled out by the Doubt (VII 27, HR1 151). Now he is prepared to 'shear off' a purely mental experience, and call that 'sensation' (cf. *Princ.* i 66). He can be certain of the existence of this, he claims, merely as a mental phenomenon, even though he remains in doubt whether such experiences are related to physical bodies through physical organs of sense.

All these kinds of *cogitatio* are accepted just as such, and their acceptance rests on no more than what was available at the moment of the *cogito*. Though Descartes refers to them only after he has proved his own existence, they are in a sense bound up with the 'I am thinking' part of the *cogito*: these *cogitationes* are part of what Descartes considers as self-evident when he says that the existence of his thought is self-evident. This makes a difference to the interpretation of the *cogito*. The unspecific proposition 'I am thinking' is, like 'I exist', self-verifying, and its incorrigibility can be traced to that; but 'I am uncertain whether God exists' or 'it seems to me as though I can see a red patch' are not self-verifying, and if they are incorrigible (as Descartes believes) then it is for a quite different sort of reason. One thing that helps to bring out the difference between this kind of proposition, and the self-verifying ones, is that these can be used to tell a lie. 'It all looks fuzzy', 'I feel cheerful', 'I believe what you say', can all in various ways be used to deceive, but 'I exist', and the others, for obvious reasons, cannot. The difference does not of course suggest that the evident kind of proposition is less certain than the self-verifying, but it illustrates how the basis of its certainty is something different.

Descartes takes those operations of the mind to be immediately obvious to the thinker, and the thinker to have immediate access to them. In our terminology, he regards some propositions about such states as both incorrigible and evident, and the states as being necessarily present to consciousness. It may seem artificial to treat matters such as this in the terminology of 'propositions': it may seem more natural merely to speak of the states that he is in, and of the fact that he is certain that he is in those states, and this is indeed how Descartes puts it in the *Second Meditation*. But the formulation explicitly in terms of propositions brings out something which is important and which is indeed implicit in Descartes's own treatment, that his certainty depends not just on what states he is in, but on how they are described. Take some state described as his having an experience *as of* seeing a table, or its seeming to him that he sees a table: then under that description, Descartes claims, he is certain of it. But that very same experience *could* be caused by the physical presence of a table, and if it is described in such a way as to imply that it is so caused – for instance, if it is described as the experience *of seeing a table* – then he is not certain of it. Similarly, if he claims that it seems to him now that he had dinner last night, then his claim will be certain, but if he describes that experience as *recalling having dinner last night*, then his claim, strictly taken, will not be, by the standards of the Doubt, certain. So, by Descartes's own provisions, there is no way of avoiding the point that the same experience or state can be characterized in different ways, and that how it is characterized is relevant to the possibility of certainty; it is this that forces on us the language of propositions. The most radical way in which this comes up we have already taken for granted: that these propositions are *in the first person*. If there were someone else to comment on Descartes's state of mind, they would refer to the same state in the third person as Descartes refers to in the first person, but their statements would not possess his certainty.[10]

What Descartes has acknowledged in this passage of the *Second Meditation* is that some (first-person, present tense) propositions about the mental life are certain. We have already partly interpreted that acknowledgement as involving the claims that these propositions about the mental life are both incorrigible and evident, and that the mental states are present to consciousness.

It will be worthwhile pausing here, before taking up further questions about 'cogito', 'sum', and the connection between them, to examine briefly some relations between these properties of *being incorrigible* and *being evident*, and to chart some larger claims about the mental that Descartes does, or will eventually, make. Descartes's introduction of this class of propositions at this stage is, so to speak, the thin end of the wedge so far as his views about the mental life are concerned, and it is as well to be warned of the wedge's full size.

It is important, first, that the fact that these propositions are incorrigible does not entail, just in itself, that they are evident. It could be the case, in principle, that whenever I believed that I wanted a certain thing (for instance), I did want that thing, but nevertheless not the case that whenever I wanted something, I believed I did – the thought, on some occasions, might not occur to me at all. This possibility tends to escape notice because of the first-personal formulations that we are dealing with, which tend inevitably to imply that the matter has come up for me. But if we just consider what has to be the case for me to want something, then we can reflect that *that* could be the case without a belief in any way having occurred to me to the effect that it was the case. This will be so even if we agree (ill-advisedly, in fact) that propositions of the form 'I want X' are incorrigible.

It will also be so, whether or not we think that what has to be the

Bernard Williams

case if I want something involves some conscious experience such as a feeling. Whether that is so or not is a separate question. In fact it is false that every want involves such an experience, but even if it did, it might still be possible for one to have that feeling without making any judgement, or forming any belief, to the effect that one had a certain want. An interesting case in this connection is pain. It would be generally agreed that pain is a conscious experience: one who is in pain feels something. Now it may, further, be true that a language user who is in pain will believe that he is in pain, unless perhaps he is in such a reduced state that he has lost effective hold on his language use. If one possesses and can use the concept *pain*, its application to oneself will be elicited by one's being in pain, and in this, pains importantly contrast with wants. But non-language-users can be in pain (though Descartes denied it); they have no concept of pain they can apply to themselves, and to them we cannot in all seriousness ascribe, in addition to their pain, a belief that they are in pain.[11]

Further, the fact that some conspicuous group of propositions about the mental life are incorrigible or evident of course does not mean that all such propositions are so, or that incorrigibility and evidence are necessary conditions of the mental. There are many propositions, quite obviously about the mental life, for which it is quite implausible to claim it: that one is in love, for instance, or that one is not jealous, or that one can bring to mind the colour violet. The list of supposed certainties which Descartes gives in the *Meditation* already shows signs of going too wide.

In particular, there are subconscious or unconscious mental states or processes. We must get one difficulty out of the way first: in the sense of 'evident' that I am using, a proposition could even be *evident* and yet, in principle, refer to a state that was unconscious. It will of course follow from its being evident, by definition, that if one is in the state, one will believe that one is; but to guarantee that the state is not unconscious, one has to add a further requirement that that belief is not itself unconscious. Similarly, one cannot just say that unconscious or subconscious states are mental states that one is in without knowing that one is in them. How best to use these notions, where and how to employ the concepts of unconscious knowledge or belief, are not matters calling for verbal legislation – they are questions of what will be the most fruitful theory of such states. For Descartes's purposes, however, we can agree to leave this particular problem on one side, and take 'belief' in the definitions of incorrigibility and the rest as relating to conscious belief.

Even allowing for that, there is nothing to stop there being a mental state or process, propositions about which were *incorrigible*, but which could sometimes nevertheless be subconscious. A possible example of this combination is *noticing*. On the one hand, it is quite plausible to claim that if one believes one has noticed something, then one has done so (though one may be wrong in one's description of what one has noticed); but one can notice things subconsciously, i.e. notice them without consciously believing that one has, and without the noticing being an event in conscious experience.

If we take 'unconscious' processes, as opposed to 'subconscious' ones, to relate to processes *in the unconscious*, as postulated by some psychoanalytical theory, which will connect the notion of the unconscious with the notion of repression, then propositions about these processes cannot be incorrigible. It will not of course follow that they have been ruled out as mental processes. However, if there is some mental item, some propositions about which have already been accepted as incorrigible – let us say, for the sake of argument, wishes – then there is likely to be a real difficulty in saying also that some unconscious state is a wish in the same sense. If there is a difficulty about that, this will leave two options. One might perhaps have reason for saying that statements about unconscious states did not mean the same as corresponding statements about conscious states; one might have more reason, though, for saying that 'wish' (for example) did mean basically the same in conscious and in unconscious connections, but that people were wrong who, like Descartes, thought that propositions about wishes were incorrigible. Here again, what there will be reason for saying will be a matter of successful theory (for instance, on the question whether there is any class of wishes which could be marked off as conscious or as unconscious just in virtue of their content). That we do not as a matter of fact know what we have reason for saying here is evidenced by those philosophers who, having made a generalization about the incorrigibility of some class of mental propositions, so often add desperately '(except in Freudian connections)'.

The fact, then, that some propositions about the mental life are in the highest degree certain does not tell us all that much about the mental in general. But in fact Descartes will go on to hold that these characteristics apply quite generally: that it is a mark of propositions about the mental life that they are incorrigible and evident, and that mental states are fully available to consciousness. (Signs of this are perhaps already to be seen in the generous list of psychological properties introduced in the *Second Meditation*.) There are indeed some mental states that we can accept as coming near to Descartes's model, as paradigms of privacy from others and of immediate access for the thinker. Above all, where *privacy* is the principal focus of the question, one paradigm is provided by certain episodic verbal thoughts and images – the kind of thing to which the old saying 'a penny for your thoughts' particularly applies. Pains and other bodily sensations, which have particularly been discussed by philosophers in these connections, present a slightly different contrast between the situations of subject and of observer. In the case of episodic thought, the contrast centres on the point that overt expression of thought or fantasy seems in the standard case to be an entirely voluntary matter; when such an episode occurs in my thought, it seems entirely up to me whether I give it any distinctive overt expression at all (of course this does not mean that whenever I express my thought – for instance, in expressing my opinion, or just in thinking out loud – there has to have been such an inner episode which I have chosen to express). In the case of pains, this is not the centre of the contrast: pains, or at least severe pains, tend to express themselves. In their case, the contrast that especially attracts the idea of privacy is another one, the difference between being in pain and believing that someone else is – a type of difference which is far less dramatic in the case of thoughts, and indeed may vanish.

Although there are these paradigms of privacy – of more than one type, as I have suggested – it is vitally important that there is no useful or even viable concept of the mental or the psychological which takes these as the determining paradigm, and relegates everything else to some non-psychological category, to not being part of the mental life. Descartes's dichotomy of everything into the mental and the physical, and his equation of the mental with the conscious, form jointly one of the most damaging, as well as one of the most characteristic, features of his developed system.

For the present, however, we are following Descartes as the Pure Enquirer in the search for certainty, and he does not need at this stage these extravagant conclusions about the mental. He just seeks some certainties, and in some first-personal, present tense, propositions about the mental life, as well as in the unspecific 'I am thinking', he finds some. But here an important question begins to surface. The terms we have been using, *incorrigible*, *evident*, etc., are of course our terms, not Descartes's. Descartes speaks of things that are certain, or indubitable, or – in a phrase he repeatedly uses – things that he 'very clearly and distinctly perceives' to be true. Such things, he supposes, will meet his need, and will stop the Doubt. But can a proposition's merely being incorrigible be enough to stop the Doubt? Or even the Pure Enquirer's seeing that it is incorrigible? Must he not, rather, be *certain* that it is incorrigible? – and whatever that certainty might consist in, it would not consist in another level of the incorrigible, since the claim that a given proposition is incorrigible or, again, evident is not itself incorrigible or evident.

These problems are not just difficulties for us and for our terminology. They are very important difficulties for Descartes's theory of knowledge, and for the construction of the Pure Enquirer's project.* Being incorrigible, or being evident, or being both, are not in fact enough for the indubitability that Descartes wants. However, we can discuss most of the issues, and in particular, some differences between different bases of certainty, adequately in these terms.

Descartes has, then, under the *cogito* two propositions ('cogito' and 'sum' themselves) which are self-verifying and incorrigible, and others ('cogito' and the specific psychological propositions) which are incorrigible and evident. Does he, for his future progress, need both sorts? The former sort (its interest to recent philosophers notwithstanding) is not essential to him; but the latter is, for two reasons. As we saw, he could, relying on its being self-verifying, acquire 'sum' as a certainty without the reflective proposition 'cogito' occurring to him at all; but without the reflective proposition he could not acquire *sum res cogitans*, which is essential in the coming step in his argument, and which he takes as including the more specific mental functions. Second, when at a later stage he proceeds from his own existence to the existence of something other than himself, he must essentially start from the contents of his own mind: there is nowhere else for him to start from. In particular, he has to rely on knowing *that he has the idea of God*, and this proposition he regards as a certainty of the psychological, immediate access, sort.

It might be wondered whether he has to regard it in that light, or whether he might not, in fact, treat 'I have an idea of God' as self-verifying. Descartes's formal account of what *having an idea* is, is this:

Idea is a word by which I understand the form of any thought, that form by the immediate awareness of which I am conscious of the said thought: in such a way that, when understanding what I say, I can express nothing in words, without that very fact making it certain that I possess the idea of that which these words signify. (*II Rep.*: def. II: VII 160, HR2 52)

---

* Editor's note: The difficulties are discussed further in Chapter 7 of Williams's book.

Someone might argue: if one says 'I have an idea of God' and understands the meaning of those words, then (by this definition) what he says must be true. But if he does not understand the meaning of his words, then he is not asserting that proposition at all. So the proposition 'I have an idea of God' (or, indeed, the idea of anything else), if asserted, must be true, i.e. is self-verifying. Descartes in fact comes close to this conclusion in his answer to an anonymous objector (letter to Mersenne, July 1641: III 392, K 105). But there must be something wrong with this argument: it cannot be that one who says, for instance, 'I have no idea what a geodesic is' has said something pragmatically self-defeating – what he says could, quite clearly, be true. The answer to the argument is that statements to the effect that one has or lacks a certain idea are, in so far as they relate to words and their meanings, to be taken on the lines of statements in which words are mentioned rather than used. 'I have no idea what a geodesic is' will be, on this line, roughly equivalent to something like 'I do not know what "geodesic" means', and the assertion of that in no way presupposes its falsehood. Similarly, 'I know what "God" means', the (very rough) equivalent of 'I have an idea of God', is not self-verifying. It is an interesting and difficult question, what kind of self-knowledge is involved in the knowledge of propositions of this sort,[12] but it *is* a kind of self-knowledge, and Descartes needs that kind of knowledge to be able to proceed, eventually, beyond himself.

We can now turn to the question of whether the *cogito* expresses an inference; and, first, whether Descartes supposed that it did. Its form is trivially that of an inference, in the sense that it contains the word 'therefore'; and Descartes is happy to refer to it in inferential terms, for instance in the *Discourse on the Method*:

(seeing that) . . . from the very fact that I was thinking of doubting the truth of other things, *it followed* very clearly and very certainly that I existed . . . (Part iv: VI 32, HR1 101)

and again, in replying to a correspondent who, like many others, had pointed out that the argument of the *cogito* was anticipated by St Augustine:[13]

. . . it is a thing which in itself is so simple and natural, *to infer* that one exists from the fact that one is doubting, that it could come from the pen of anyone . . . (Letter to Colvius, 14 November 1640: III 248, K 84)

Yet the situation is more complex than these off-hand remarks might suggest. Elsewhere, Descartes is very emphatic that in some sense, at least, the *cogito* is not an inference:

When someone says, *I am thinking*, therefore *I am*, or *I exist*, he does not conclude his existence from his thought as if by the force of some syllogism, but as a thing which is self-evident: he sees it by a simple inspection of the mind. This is clear from the fact that, if he deduced it by the syllogism, he would already have to know this major premiss: everything that thinks is, or exists. But on the contrary, he learns this proposition from what he perceives in himself, that it is impossible that he should think, if he does not exist. For it is the nature of our mind to form general propositions from the knowledge of particular ones. (*II Rep.*: VII 140, HR2 38)

Two things at least emerge clearly from this statement. One is that Descartes does not regard the *cogito* as a *syllogistic* inference, that is to say, an inference of the form 'All *A*'s are *B*'s; I am an *A*, therefore I am a *B*'; though of course, since not all inferences are syllogistic, the possibility remains open that the *cogito* is some other sort of inference. The second thing that emerges is that Descartes, in saying this, is not merely making a psychological point – he is not merely saying that the experience of grasping the *cogito* is that of an instantaneous insight, rather than that of a mental passage from one proposition to another. It is true that elsewhere Descartes is concerned with psychological aspects of logical inference; in the early work, the *Regulae*, he has a distinction between 'deduction' and 'intuition' which is certainly psychological, since the question 'can I judge of the validity of a complex piece of reasoning by intuition or by deduction?' comes down to the question 'can I conceive the whole chain of this reasoning in one act of the mind?'; and he makes the point that familiarity with a piece of reasoning may eventually enable one to see the whole thing intuitively, whereas at first one could grasp it only by deduction, that is to say, step by step.

However, it is clear that it is not merely this psychological distinction between intuition and deduction that Descartes is relying on in the passage just quoted about the *cogito*. The point that he is making is not just that he does not as a matter of fact conduct a syllogistic inference, but that he is in no position to, since such inference would involve relying on a premiss which he is in no position to know. What is rather less clear is what he supposes this impossibility to consist in. He says that the difficulty would be that he would have to presuppose a general proposition, but that he could only get to know this general proposition from the particular one which he perceives to be true in his own case. But this is a misleading way to represent the situation, since it makes it sound as though one arrived at the general proposition 'everything that thinks, exists' by some sort of induction based on observing that each particular thing that thinks also exists, which is absurd. Descartes regards the connection between thinking and existing as a necessary connection. He makes this clear even in the passage just quoted; for he says that what he observes in his own case is that it is *impossible* that he should think without existing, and this already imports the notion of necessity. But if it imports the notion of necessity, does it not import the notion of generality? For clearly it is not Descartes's view that this impossibility of thinking without existing could be peculiar to his own case – rather, in reflecting on his own case, he sees that in general it is impossible to think without existing. But if he supposes that he can grasp this general statement of impossibility at this stage, what becomes of his answer that the *cogito* cannot be a syllogistic inference because it would have to rely on a general proposition which he does not yet know to be true?

In my view, the answer to this depends on distinguishing between the syllogistic major premiss 'everything that thinks, exists', and the statement of impossibility 'it is impossible to think without existing' (or, what comes to the same thing, the statement 'in order to think, it is necessary to exist'). The first Descartes denies to be presupposed by the *cogito*; the latter he is prepared to admit as presupposed. And there is a reason behind this distinction. As he puts it in the *Principles*:

> When I said that this proposition: *I am thinking, therefore I exist* is the first and the most certain that presents itself to one who conducts his thoughts in order, I did not for all that deny that it was necessary first to know what thought was, and certainty, and existence, and that in order to think it is necessary to exist, and other similar things; but, because these are notions so simple that in themselves they do not give us knowledge of any existent thing, I did not think that they had to be taken into account here. (*Princ.* i 10; see also a letter to Clerselier, June 1646, on what is meant by 'a first principle': IV 444–5, K 196–7)

Thus the point is that 'in order to think, it is necessary to exist' does not make any reference to anything existing in the world: it is a bare statement of necessity which can, on Descartes's view, be intuitively grasped. This property it shares with certain other statements, all of which Descartes is prepared to admit the mind can grasp, as abstract necessities, before it comes to know of anything actually existent in the world:

> . . . when one says that it is impossible that one and the same thing should both be and not be at the same time; that what has been done cannot be undone; that one who thinks cannot fail to be or to exist while he thinks; and many similar things: these are merely (eternal) truths, and not things that are outside our mind . . . (*Princ.* i 49)

The bare statement of necessity is thus all right as a presupposition of the *cogito*, since it makes no existential claim. Correspondingly, what is wrong with the syllogistic premiss 'everything that thinks exists' seems to be that it does make an existential claim; and while Descartes does not explicitly say this, it can perhaps be elicited from the denials and admissions already quoted. Moreover, this would be entirely in line with the traditional logic of the syllogism, since that logic does ordinarily presuppose that general propositions of the form 'All *A*'s are *B*'s' should refer to *A*'s that actually exist. On this doctrine, to assert anything of all thinking things would be to presuppose that there actually were some thinking things in existence, which Descartes is clearly in no position to presuppose; moreover, it would be paradoxical, since it is unclear what the premiss, so taken, would be saying, in asserting existence of things presupposed to exist. It is probably these points that he wishes to emphasize in preferring generally the statement of necessity, or 'eternal truth', to the syllogistic premiss form; together with the point, which is important to him, that the mind basically grasps eternal truths as they are presented in particular examples, rather than in an abstract formulation – which is not to deny that it grasps them *as general truths*.

It is this second point that Descartes seems to have stressed in the conversation he had with a young man called Burman who on 16 April 1648 came to question him on his philosophy. In that one place, however, Descartes admits that 'everything that thinks, exists' is presupposed by the *cogito* (V 147, C p. 4). Perhaps Burman (whose notes we rely on) made a mistake, or, very probably, Descartes did not always use these verbal forms strictly to mark the distinction. It is hard to reconcile the texts on any view, but the main point seems to me still to be that there is a real, and relevant, distinction between the 'eternal truth' and a standard syllogistic premiss.[14]

What is the content of the 'eternal truth'? It looks as though it is an application of a very general principle, that in order to do or be anything, or to have any predicate, it is necessary to exist – a principle which modern logic usually expresses in the form '$Fa \rightarrow (Ex)(x = a)$'.[15] In this form, the principle has nothing specially to do with thinking, nor with the first person. But the *cogito* has got something specially to do with thinking; and it also has something specially to do with the first person – the fact, pointed out by Kenny,[16] that Descartes also expresses *cogito*-like reflections in the third person, or, in the *Recherche de la Vérité* (X 515, HR1 316), in the second person, relates only to other persons' first-personal reflections, and does not subtract from the point that all the force of the reflection lies in its first-personal form. We can see how special features of thinking, and of the first person, co-operate in the *cogito* with the general principle.

The mere assertion or presentation of propositions of the forms 'he is *F*' or 'you are *F*' does not guarantee truths corresponding to 'he exists' and 'you exist': 'he' and 'you' might miss their mark altogether – there might be no one I was speaking about, or to. But assertion or thought involving 'I' seems not to be subject to this hazard: where there is assertion, or indeed any other genuine presentation, of a proposition involving 'I', there is some assertor or thinker for the 'I' to latch on to. Sometimes we are presented with sentences including 'I' where we cannot take seriously the application of 'I' – as with an ingeniously instructed parrot, or with the machine which says 'I speak your weight'. But in these cases, equally, we cannot take seriously the presented sentences as assertions or expressions of thought. So a peculiarity of the first person is involved in the *cogito*. As it can be expressed with reference to the English language: with regard to 'I', unlike other pronouns, the mere fact that it is used in genuine thought is enough to guarantee that it does not miss its mark.

But if that is so – why, in particular, 'I am thinking'? *Respiro ergo sum*, 'I am breathing, therefore I exist', would surely be just as good – a difficulty put to Descartes, in different forms, more than once. A quick answer to this would be that in the case of 'I am breathing' Descartes would not know the proposition to be true, since breathing and similar activities presuppose the existence of his body, a belief suspended in the Doubt; whereas 'I am thinking' can be known to be true, in virtue of the sort of considerations we have already examined, such as its incorrigibility. But does the assertion *need* to be true? The principle we now have, with regard to the first person, is that if a proposition containing 'I' is genuinely asserted or thought, then 'I' cannot miss its mark. This does not require the proposition to be true, only to be genuinely thought: false thoughts require thinkers as much as true ones. So would it not do for Descartes to start by asserting or entertaining any proposition about himself, for instance the possibly false proposition 'I am breathing', and conclude from that that he exists?

In one sense, the answer is 'yes', but it is a sense that precisely illustrates the peculiarity of the *cogito*. For he would draw his conclusion in such a case not from the content of the proposition regarded in the abstract, but rather from the fact that he was asserting, or entertaining, it; that is to say, from the fact that he was thinking it. So this line brings us back again to 'cogito' as the basic premiss: to entertain the proposition that one is breathing is just another *cogitatio*. The process that leads from *the thinking of* 'I am breathing' to 'I exist' will, if it is made fully explicit, actually display the reflexive proposition 'I am thinking . . .'. It will display it in the context 'I am thinking that I am breathing' (or '. . . about the possibility that I am breathing' etc.); and so will emerge, as we saw above (p. 126), as an incorrigible proposition of the psychological kind. This is very much what Descartes himself says in a letter of March 1638 (II 37; cf. also *V Rep.*: VII 352, HR2 207):

When one says 'I am breathing, therefore I exist', if he wants to conclude his existence from the consideration that breathing cannot go on without the breather existing, his conclusion is of no value, since he would have to have proved already that it was true that he was breathing, and this is impossible, if he has not already proved that he exists. But if he wants to conclude his existence from the belief or opinion that he has that he is breathing, in the sense that, even if this opinion were not true, all the same one sees that it is impossible that one should have it, unless one existed, then his conclusion is very sound, since this opinion that we are breathing presents itself to our mind before that of our existence, and we cannot doubt that we have the opinion while we have it. And to say in *this* sense 'I am breathing, therefore I exist,' is just the same as 'I am thinking, therefore I exist'. And if one is careful, one will find that all the other propositions from which we can in this way conclude our existence come back to this one . . .

But this line of argument also shows how, in a more basic sense, 'I am breathing' is really no replacement for 'I am thinking'. Since it is not the content of 'I am breathing', but the fact that I am thinking of it, that leads to the truth of 'I exist' – a connection which, reflexively spelled out, emerges as 'I am thinking "I am breathing", therefore I exist' – we can see that the fact that 'I am breathing' is itself a first-personal proposition is not what is doing the work. In any sense in which 'I am breathing, therefore I exist' expresses the probative force of the *cogito*, so does 'it is raining, therefore I exist'. The first, unlike the second, constitutes a valid argument, but it is not the premiss of *that* argument which is doing the work. The work is done by a premiss which is produced by reflection on the point that I think 'I am breathing'; but, equally, it could be produced by reflection on the point that I think 'it is raining'.

The first-personal form, 'I am thinking', is essential; but what right to it has Descartes got? It has repeatedly been suggested, for example by the eighteenth-century philosopher and aphorist Georg Lichtenberg, that the most that Descartes could claim was 'cogitatur', 'there is some thinking going on' – like, in Lichtenberg's own comparison, 'there is lightning'. This idea, taken up by Ernst Mach, has recurred in a number of philosophies in this century, particularly of empiricist outlook. This is an important line of objection, and it may seem an attractive one, but more closely considered it turns out to share with Descartes his deepest error.

The objection is that in saying 'I am thinking' Descartes is saying too much. It assumes, that is to say, that there are two possible states of affairs, one more substantial than the other, which can be represented respectively as 'I am thinking' and 'thinking is going on', and that Descartes had no right to assert the more substantial rather than the less substantial. That is how those two states of affairs would be represented from the Enquirer's point of view; but the complaint against Descartes is that in asserting the more substantial rather than the less, the Enquirer is claiming more than he should about *what is objectively the case*, and this implies that the difference between the two states of affairs can also be represented from a third-personal point of view, as that between 'thinking is going on' and '*A* thinks', where '*A*' is a name, which could be used from a third-personal perspective, of whatever it is in the more substantial state of affairs that is doing the thinking. The point about what I am calling 'the third-personal perspective' is not of course that if the more substantial state of affairs obtained, there would actually have to be another person, still less another person who knew about it and could apply the name '*A*'. It is merely that, invited to grasp in the abstract the supposed difference between these two states of affairs, we grasp it in terms of there being, in the more substantial state of affairs, a thinker who could in principle be labelled '*A*', while in the less substantial state of affairs there is no such thinker.

It is not at all clear that we really can grasp this supposed difference in the abstract, but let us at least pretend that we make enough of it to continue. Suppose, then, that the following are true:

(T1) It is thought: *P*   (T2) It is thought: *Q*

Will it follow that the following is true?

(T3) It is thought: *P* and *Q*

However slight our grasp on the impersonal formulation, we must surely grant that T3 cannot follow: a distinct thought-content is involved in T3, and there is nothing in the occurrence of the two thought-events T1 and T2 to determine that *that* thought ever occurred at all. The thoughts T1 and T2 could be, as we might hopefully put it, 'separate'. But if thoughts can be, or can fail to be, 'separate' in this way, then a difficulty emerges for the impersonal formulation. It can best be illustrated if we extend the range of possible thought-events a little, to include that class of psychological phenomena which Descartes is at present accepting as described by the first-person forms 'I am doubting', 'I am willing' etc. While the present line of objection to Descartes will of course reject the 'I' from each of these, it has no reason to reject the idea that there are corresponding differences in the states of affairs which these forms (misleadingly) represent – differences which will have to emerge in properly impersonal representations of those states of affairs. So we shall need a class of 'non-I' or impersonal formulations, which we might put as: 'it is willed: *P*', it is doubted: *Q*?', etc.

We may now consider the following combination:

(T4) It is thought: it is not doubted whether *Q*
(T5) It is doubted: *Q*?

Is the thought reported at T4 true or false? Unless more is put in, nothing prevents its being straightforwardly made false, by the state of affairs T5. But granted what has just been said about T1, T2 and T3, it cannot be the case that the thought in T4 should have to be false just because of T5: we must want it to be possible that T5 be as 'separate' from T4 as T2 can be from T1. T5 can falsify T4, we will want to say, only if the doubt-event T5 is not 'separate' from the thought-event T4, or, one might say, if they both occur in the same thought-world (whatever that might turn out to mean).

The obvious reaction to this problem is to relativize the content of T4 so that it refers only to its own thought-world; to make it say, in effect

(T6) It is thought: it is not doubted here whether *Q*.

But the 'here' of T6 is of course totally figurative – nothing in the construction has given us places for these disembodied thoughts to occur at, let alone to serve as a basis for linking them up. So what might do better than 'here'? Further reflection suggests very strongly that, if the job can be done at all, there could be no better candidate for doing it than the Cartesian 'I'. The content of the impersonally occurrent thought needs, it seems, to be relativized somehow; and there is no better way of relativizing it than the use of the first person. So the objector – assuming all the time that we can follow him at all – seems to have been wrong in saying that the *content* of the Cartesian thought should be impersonal rather than first-personal. However, this does not eliminate the possibility (if, again, we can understand it at all) that what is *objectively happening* is impersonal rather than substantial. That is to say, we have a reason now for preferring

(T7) It is thought: I am thinking

to

(T8) It is thought: thinking is going on;

but no reason so far for rejecting T7 in favour of

(T9) *A* thinks: I am thinking.

If the position we have now reached were the final one, the situation would be very odd. The objector would be wrong, it seems, about the required *content* of the Cartesian thought, but right about the state of affairs (or at least, the minimal state of affairs) involved in its being thought. It would follow from this that the first-personal content, even though it was correct and indeed requisite, might well represent a state of affairs which could not be described from the third-personal point of view as '*A* is thinking'. It would follow that Descartes could not make an inference from 'I am thinking' to 'I exist', if that, in its turn, were taken to represent (as Descartes takes it to represent) a state of affairs which could be third-personally represented as '*A* exists' ('there is such a thing as *A*'). It might then be unclear whether there was any sense at all in which 'I exist' could be got from 'I am thinking', but at any rate it would not express any substantial truth expressible in a third-personal form. The objection to Descartes seems to have failed at one level but succeeded at another; the result is that the relation between the two levels is very obscure, and we have lost our bearings on the connections between the thought-content 'I am thinking' and the state of affairs: *A is thinking.*

It is an uncomfortable position; but we do not have to, indeed cannot, remain in it. If we press further the same line of argument that got us this far, we shall find that the position has to be given up; but this does not mean the victory, after all, of Descartes over his objector, but rather the failure of them both. The device we have used to deal with the problems of 'separateness', that of relativizing the content of the impersonally occurring thoughts, only *appears* to be of help: by itself, in fact, it can achieve nothing at all. This can be seen if we compare the case of literal place. If someone seeks by relativization to save the following two statements from contradicting one another:

it is raining   it is not raining

he will achieve nothing by merely adding 'here';

it is raining here   it is not raining here

raise as big a problem as the first pair, unless we advance a stage further and make clear whether 'here' does or does not indicate the same place in the two cases. Thus

It is stated (thought) in place A: it is raining here
It is stated (thought) in place B: it is not raining here

yield statements which have a chance of both being true at once. Similarly with the figurative mental 'here', if we return to that for a moment: the relativized thought of T6,

it is not doubted here whether Q

does not in fact help by itself, because we have no way of specifying where, so to speak, 'here' is. So the relativization, if it is to do anything at all, cannot be confined to the content of thought-events; it must be attached, and in a third-personal, objective form, to the statements of their occurrence, so that T6 becomes rather

(T10) It is thought at place A: it is not doubted here whether Q.

But just as the 'here' in the content was totally figurative, and the best possible candidate for its replacement seemed to be the Cartesian 'I'; so some less figurative replacement is needed for 'at place A' in the statement of the thought's occurrence – and it is natural to conclude that nothing less than a personal name, or some such, will do as a replacement, so that T10 will give way to

(T11) A thinks: I am not doubting whether Q.

At this point we shall have returned completely to substantial formulations, and the programme of introducing impersonal formulations in their place will have finally collapsed.

The last step, however, may perhaps be too big. There might possibly be some replacement for the figurative 'places' which served the purposes of effective relativization, but did not go so far as introducing a subject who thinks. If there is an effective replacement less ambitious than 'A thinks', we shall still be left with some version of the problem about the relation between the 'I think' in the content of the thought, and what is objectively involved in the state of affairs

Bernard Williams

which constitutes its being thought. The question whether there could
be a replacement which fell short of '*A* thinks' is not one that I shall
pursue further. The point is that *some* concrete relativization is needed,
and even if it could fall short of requiring a subject who has the
thoughts, it has to exist in the form of something outside pure thought
itself.

The thought-event formulation we have been examining requires the
notion of objectively existing thought-events, and in supposing that it
can start out merely from the idea of thoughts as experienced, and from
that achieve the third-personal perspective which is necessary if this
notion is to apply, it shares a basic error with Descartes. There is
nothing in the pure Cartesian reflection to give us that perspective. The
Cartesian reflection merely presents, or rather invites us into, the
perspective of consciousness. Descartes thinks that he can proceed from
that to the existence of what is, from the third-personal perspective,
a substantial fact, the existence of a thinker. The objection I have been
discussing tries to find a fact which is less substantial; but that, too, will
have to be capable of being regarded from the third-personal perspective if it is to be an objective fact, and the mere perspective of consciousness no more gives us a way of getting to that kind of objective fact,
than it gives us a way of getting to Descartes's more substantial fact.
This is not a verificationist point; the question is not about how anyone
could come to know that various separate thought-events were occurring – it is a question about the coherence of the conception, of what
it is one is invited to conceive.

If we have no help from anything except the pure point of view of
consciousness, the only coherent way of conceiving a thought
happening is to conceive of thinking it. So, sticking solely to the point
of view of consciousness, we are forced back to a position in which
there is, in effect, only one such point of view: events either happen
for it, or they do not happen, and there is no way of conceiving of such
events happening, but happening (so to speak) elsewhere. But this is
what the objector, as much as Descartes, must need.

Notes

1. Descartes's first biographer, Adrien Baillet (*Vie de Descartes*, ii 171–3), says that the
French version is actually preferable, because Descartes took the opportunity of the translation to introduce corrections and additions; see IV 194.
2. *Regulae* iii (X 368, HR1 7) offers as two *separate* propositions which can certainly be
known to be true by the intuitive light of reason, *that one exists*, and *that one thinks*.

3. For a detailed discussion of epistemological concepts introduced in this chapter, see Appendix 1 of *Descartes*, from which this extract is taken.

4. For various accounts of this kind, see e.g. A. J. Ayer, 'Cogito ergo sum', *Analysis* vol. 14 (1953–4), 17–33, and *The Problem of Knowledge* (London, 1958), pp. 45–54; John Passmore, *Philosophical Reasoning* (London, 1964), pp. 60–64; my own 'La Certitude du *cogito*', *Cahiers de Royaumont* IV (Paris, 1962), translated as 'The Certainty of the *cogito*' in W. Doney, ed., *Descartes, A Collection of Critical Essays* (New York, 1967); J. L. Mackie, 'Self-Refutation – a Formal Analysis', *Philosophical Quarterly* vol. 14 (1964), 193–203; G. Nakhnikian, 'On the Logic of cogito Propositions', *Nous* III (1969), 197–210. The term 'existentially inconsistent' has been introduced by J. Hintikka for the negations of these propositions, in his well-known article, '*Cogito, ergo sum*: Inference or Performance?', *Philosophical Review* LXXI (1962), 3–32, reprinted in Doney, op. cit., pp. 108–40, and see also *PR* LXXII (1963), 487–96; but his very unsatisfactory formulation of that notion has been well criticized by F. Feldman, 'On the Performatory Interpretation of the *cogito*', *PR* LXXXII (1973), 345–63.

5. For the importance of this thought in Vico's (profoundly anti-Cartesian) philosophy, see Isaiah Berlin, *Vico and Herder* (London, 1976), especially pp. 15 ff.

6. Doney, p. 122; Hintikka's emphasis.

7. Doney, p. 122.

8. ibid.

9. That is to say, the malicious demon: as Descartes explained to Burman (V 151, C p. 9), at this stage of his progress he is not yet clear that his creator is really God.

10. For more detailed discussion of 'proposition' here, see Appendix 1 of *Descartes*.

11. Some philosophers deny that anyone can be said to believe or, again, know that he is in pain; on the ground that '*A* believes that he is in pain' or '*A* knows that he is in pain' and their first-personal versions, 'have no standard use in the language'. With regard to knowledge, the claim is anyway false: the thought, concerning a suspected malingerer, that he knows whether he is in pain, is entirely in place. But in any case it is a hopelessly weak kind of ground.

12. Cf. *Must We Mean What We Say?* by Stanley Cavell, in his book of that title: New York, 1969.

13. For historical material on this point, see É. Gilson, *Commentaire*, pp. 295 ff. See also the admirable passage from Pascal quoted by Gilson (p. 299), which ends: '. . . this saying is as different in [Descartes's] writings, compared with the same saying in others to whom it occurred in passing, as a man full of life and strength is different from a corpse.'

14. John Cottingham, in his valuable edition of the *Conversation with Burman*, puts all the weight on the point about grasping general truths in particular cases, and denies any important distinction between the 'eternal truth' and the syllogistic premiss. This seems to me not to give enough weight to *Princ.* i 10, quoted above, in particular to Descartes's admission that 'it is necessary *first* to know . . . that in order to think it is necessary to exist.'

15. Hintikka (Doney, pp. 113–14) denies that Descartes can invoke this principle without circularity. But the example which Hintikka invokes to illustrate the possible consistency of '*Fa*, but *a* does not exist' – 'Hamlet thought, but Hamlet did not exist' – is well answered by Kenny (p. 61); while Feldman (op. cit., pp. 355 ff.) has argued that any reconstruction of the *cogito* on Hintikka's own lines which is not trivial will itself rely on the principle.

16. A. Kenny, *Descartes: A Study of His Philosophy* (New York, 1968), p. 47.

Biographical Note

Bernard Williams is Provost of King's College, Cambridge. He was Knightbridge Professor of Philosophy at Cambridge from 1967 to 1979; before that Professor of Philosophy at Bedford College, London, Lecturer at University College, London, and Fellow of All Souls and of New College, Oxford. His books are *Morality* (1971), *Problems of the Self* (1973), *Utilitarianism: For and Against* (with J. J. C. Smart, 1973), *Descartes: The Project of Pure Enquiry*, from which the excerpt in the present book is taken, *Moral Luck* (1981), and, as editor, with A. C. Montefiore, *British Analytical Philosophy* (1966), and, with Amartya Sen, *Utilitarianism and Beyond* (1982).

Further Reading

The Philosophical Works of Descartes, ed. E. S. Haldane and G. R. T. Ross (Cambridge University Press, 1911). Most comprehensive English translation. Abbreviated above to 'HR' with volume and page number following, e.g. 'HR1 150'. Descartes, *Œuvres*, ed. Charles Adam and Paul Tannery (Paris). Standard French edition. Abbreviated above merely by mention of volume and page, e.g. 'VII 261'. *Descartes: Philosophical Letters* (Oxford University Press, 1970), translated by Anthony Kenny. Abbreviated above to 'K' with page number. John Cottingham (ed.), *Descartes' Conversation with Burman* (Oxford University Press, 1970). Abbreviated to 'C' with page number, e.g. 'C p. 26'.

Descartes: Philosophical Writings, trans. Norman Kemp-Smith (London: Macmillan, 1953); *Descartes: A Collection of Critical Essays*, ed. W. Doney (New York: Doubleday, 1967); H. G. Frankfurt, *Demons, Dreamers and Madmen: The Defence of Reason in Descartes' 'Meditations'* (New York: Bobbs-Merrill, 1970); A. Kenny, *Descartes: A Study of His Philosophy* (New York: Random House, 1968).

Timothy L. S. Sprigge

Spinoza: His Identity Theory

It is possible, as the history of philosophy so readily attests, to conceive all of what exists as consisting in an infinite number of things, or in two things or at any rate two kinds of things, or in one thing. Leibniz did the first, Descartes the second and Spinoza the third. Such a summary of conceptions of the contents of reality, incomplete as it is, says exceedingly little, mainly because the word 'thing' can be put to a number of uses, involving different principles of counting. Indeed, given different uses of the word, reality can perfectly well be taken as consisting in an infinite number of things, *and* the same reality in two or two kinds of things, *and* also in one thing. Spinoza's one thing, in his famous and frustrating description of it, is *God or Nature*. It somehow has or consists in *attributes*, an infinite number of them, of which we know only two. These two, which are *of* the one thing, somehow have to do with mentality and physicality. They are spoken of as Thought and Extension, and the first is also spoken of yet more grandly as Divine Intellect. There are also *modes*, also of the one thing, these including things in the mundane sense, say mushrooms and chairs, and also the bodies and minds of persons.

It is Timothy Sprigge's purpose in the paper that follows to defend an understanding of Spinoza's monism, and to go some way to defending the understanding as giving truth about reality. He does not join most contemporary philosophers, at least most of those who write in English, in being disinclined to speculative metaphysics, let alone speculative metaphysics of the largest kind. He finds in Spinoza, further, not only truth about reality, but something that philosophers of this century, anyway those who write in English, have largely abandoned to more vibrant spirits, which is to say a philosophy of life. He

---

Benedict de Spinoza, 1632–77. Born of Jewish parents in Holland, where he lived, working as a lens-grinder. Rationalist in philosophy and life. After winning a lawsuit about it, he abandoned his inheritance, accepting only a 'good bed and good linen'.

takes Spinoza neat. It can be said of such a way with the great philosophers, conceivably, that some of those who eschew it fall into something near enough to contradiction. That is the near-enough contradiction of taking the work of the great philosopher to be different in kind from, say, outmoded science, and therefore to be venerated, and yet averting one's eyes from his principal doctrines.

One and it seems the fundamental question raised by Spinoza's *Ethics*, which propounds his monism and is certainly not given over to ethics, is the relationship of the attributes of mentality and physicality to one another, and also their relationship to God or Nature, also called Substance. There is the further question of how certain modes – say my mind and my body – are related, and how they are related to God or Nature.

An answer to be put aside is what is called the subjective interpretation of Spinoza. Here, the physicality and mentality of God or Nature are taken as of the order of appearances-to-us rather than reality. They are most importantly facts about us, subjective facts, rather than facts about reality. The true essence or nature of reality is neither physical nor mental, and not in any way to be perceived or understood. (p. 150) This is incoherent. Mentality is reduced to appearance – but an appearance is an appearance *to* mentality, *to* a mind.

There is a second answer to the question of how Spinoza saw the two attributes as related. There is physicality, and it is a matter not of appearance but of objective reality, and there is mentality, of which the same is to be said, and the two somehow *correspond* to one another. Each is related to the other as a map to what it maps. (p. 150) Further, in line with Spinoza's plain denial of interaction between the mental and the physical (p. 156), there is no causal connection between them, and they are not identical one with the other. (p. 152) Sprigge finds this answer unpersuasive. There is no satisfactory explanation of the correspondence or mapping. (pp. 151–2) There are other difficulties, one of which is that Spinoza's own words tell decisively against understanding him in the given way. (p. 153)

Sprigge takes it that we need a synthesis of the subjective and the objective answers. There is indeed but one thing in question, which seems denied by the objective answer, and physicality and mentality are objective facts. To think of what exists as physical is to grasp it as it is. Equally, to think of it as mental is to grasp it as it is. This, of course, needs further explaining. There is one way in which it is *not* to be understood. The view is not, so to speak, that there are three things in question: a bare particular or substratum or substance, and two properties of it, the physical and the mental. There are several reasons against this. Sprigge's different view involves the difficult notion of the essences of things, including the essence of God or Nature. Essences, I take it, may be described as possibilities, to the extent that that is helpful, but when they are actualized they are none the less somehow identical with the actualizing things. (pp. 154–5)

Enlargement of this account of the relation between the attributes, and between them and God or Nature, and of the relation between such modes as my body and my mind, is advanced by way of consideration of Spinoza's idea of the mental. In Section II of the paper, and following sections, there is consideration of what can fairly be called an attempt to water down Spinoza. It is one which reduces the attribute of Thought to propositions, which is to say abstract objects not existing in any ordinary way. They are not in space or time, but can be said to be contents of mental events. Spinoza's reality, on this view, involves the physical, which is spatio-temporal, and propositions about it. As Sprigge maintains, to my mind rightly, this is not Spinoza. Mentality, for Spinoza, is indeed to be described as consciousness or mentality, a series of mental events. There is no alternative, then, given the oneness of Thought and Extension, to a traditional view of Spinoza. He is to be regarded as a panpsychist, one who holds that all *individual* things are conscious or sentient. Fortunately, this is not to hold that mushrooms, say, are conscious. It is to go in that direction.

Section IV of the paper carries further the given account of Spinoza. The identity in which the attributes of Thought and Extension are involved, and in which particular mental and physical modes are involved, has to do with thought on the mental side which is *of* simultaneous changes on the physical side. One of my thoughts, further, is also a thought on the part of God or Nature. Two large problems which Sprigge takes to be raised by this account, which has within it an Identity Theory of our minds and brains, are considered in Sections IV and V. In Section VI, there is a further speculation, promised earlier, as to the claim of identity in connection with modes, attributes, and God or Nature. This is related to Leibniz's view of reality as consisting in an infinite number of extensionless monads.

The summary given in Section VII is that those modes which are our minds are presentations of states of those modes which are our bodies, and in particular our brains; the presentations are identical with states or processes of our brains; they are the states or processes 'as felt from the inside'; the presentations belong to a cosmic presentation of the entire physical world; this cosmic presentation – the God of God

147

or Nature – is identical with the entire physical world; it is the physical world 'as felt from the inside'. It is one recommendation of this view, to return to the matter of philosophies of life, that it gives a place to the religious aspirations of mankind.

The view is one alien to ordinary ways of thinking about the world. It is alien to mine. What is more in need of saying is that none of seeming naturalness, or ordinariness, or fashion, or dominance in a philosophical tradition, or the conviction of most of a century's philosophers, is a guarantee either of truth in a world-view, or, perhaps, of its possible use and fertility.

Timothy L. S. Sprigge

Spinoza: His Identity Theory

I

Of all great philosophers, Spinoza is (as is often said) the most variously
interpreted. This is exemplified by the tendency for both absolute
idealists and materialists of various different sorts to claim him for their
own, or to claim at least that their philosophies provide the proper
home for the further development of his profoundest insights. Is this
a sign of vagueness and incoherence in his thought, or of a richness
which does better justice to the universe than any more one-sided
philosophy?

Larger questions as to the coherence of his thought must be left on
one side here, but on the question as to whether an idealist or a
materialist Spinoza is nearer to the truth, there is an easy answer. If an
idealist is one who thinks that all is Thought, then Spinoza is an idealist,
while if a materialist is one who thinks that all is Matter, then Spinoza
is equally a materialist. It is in respect of its viability as, in effect, a
synthesis of idealism and materialism that I shall be examining
Spinoza's theory of the attributes of Thought and Extension here, and
I shall claim that it is still very much a 'living option'.

There is, of course, a controversy which has lasted a good century,
as to how Spinoza viewed the relations between these two attributes
(and also the other unknown attributes) and their joint inclusion in (or
perhaps derivation from) the essence of God or Nature. There are two
contrasting extremes of interpretation, and a variety of intermediate
positions. The two extremes are described as the subjective and the
objective interpretations.[1]

The subjective interpretation ascribes to Spinoza a thesis which may
be put briefly thus. Everything there is, apart from Nature itself
(together with its absolutely all-pervasive characteristics), is a finite
mode of, that is, a fragment or perhaps rather partial manifestation or

Timothy L. S Sprigge, 'Spinoza's Identity Theory', *Inquiry*, 20, 1977. Reprinted with the
permission of the author and editor. Addition made to footnote 2.

state of this one true individual. Nature as a whole, and each such fragment or partial state thereof, has an essence or nature the true being of which we cannot grasp, but which we can think of with a certain aptness as either a mental whole or fragment, or a physical (extended) whole or fragment. What I call my body, for example, is a certain fragment or state of Nature which I can aptly think of as spread out in space and moving about according to certain physical laws; what I call my mind is a certain fragment or state of Nature, which I can aptly think of as a mind having ideas which follow according to certain laws of thought; and, in fact, it is the same fragment of reality in both cases cognized in different ways, both with some aptness but both failing to get at the reality in its ultimately true character. Both are ways in which a single reality presents itself or appears to us, the difference between them being wholly a matter of how the thing appears and not of how it is.

In contrast to this, we have the 'objective' interpretation. According to this, my body is a physical fragment of a vast, or rather infinite, physical whole, and my mind is a fragment of a vast, or rather infinite, mental whole. The physical whole does not merely appear as physical; rather it is physical, having all the properties the term normally implies. Likewise is the mental whole, really mental, not just apparently mental; it is an infinite system of thoughts constituting a cosmic mind. As for God or Nature, or, to be more precise, as for *Natura Naturata*,[2] that is a still more all-comprehensive unity, being made up of the whole physical world, the total cosmic mind, and other unknown realities or attributes each 'infinite in its own kind'; all these attributes being thought of as quite distinct, but as corresponding structurally so as to map each other, so that there is a part of the mental whole mapping every part of the physical whole, such as my body. This interpretation is 'objective' (in the modern sense) because the existence of, and difference between, the mental and the physical is not taken as a matter of how things appear but of how they are. They appear so because they are so.

Neither interpretation is very promising either as a view of the world or as an account of Spinoza's meaning. Certainly the subjective version of Spinoza is not at all satisfactory. To begin with, it is internally incoherent. It makes sense to say, with Leibniz, that the extended world is the appearance (to certain monads) of the system of monads as a whole, since the reality of the monads is not itself reduced to an appearance. It does not make sense to say, as the subjective interpretation would have Spinoza say, that both extendedness and mentality are ways in which a substance whose true essence includes neither property, appears to mind, since this both implies and denies that there is something whose true essence is mind. This applies equally whether the attributes are supposed to be ways in which the infinite substance appears to itself *qua* infinite percipient, or only ways in which it appears to certain of its finite modes. Either supposition implies that something is really a mind to which things appear.

Of course, philosophers can hold views in which others find incoherence, but the subjective interpretation conflicts sharply with Spinoza's express claim that the human mind can form adequate ideas of its own modifications and those of its body (V P4 and C)[3] and of all that he says about the 'common notions' (II P 38–40). Undoubtedly, Spinoza believes that knowledge of the world *qua* physical and knowledge of the world *qua* mental both give true insight into the nature of things.

It is worth while, none the less, to bear in mind Wolfson's contention that those commentators were wrong who rejected the subjective interpretation on the grounds that it was anachronistic because it looks at Spinoza through Kantian spectacles and uses a distinction between phenomenon and noumenon which is quite alien to seventeenth-century thought. Wolfson showed, as against this, that the subjective interpretation fits in well with the positions of certain medieval Jewish theologians whose theories about the attributes of God would have been familiar to Spinoza.[4] Besides, if Leibniz could, in effect, contrast phenomenon and noumenon, why could not Spinoza have done so too?

Still, the subjective interpretation is unsatisfactory for the reasons given, and it is time to turn to the objective interpretation. This is put forward by Wolf in the following words.

> Spinoza's view seems sufficiently clear. Substance (or Nature or God) is the unified totality of Attributes . . . The only difference between the Attributes and Substance is that our intellect can by an act of abstraction think of one of the Attributes apart from the rest, whereas in reality all the Attributes are essentially together . . . According to Spinoza, the intellect (unlike the imagination) gives real knowledge or knowledge of the real. It is therefore entirely unwarranted to read into Spinoza the distinction between what a known Attribute is *realiter* and what it is *in intellectu* [as those do for whom] the Attributes were not regarded by Spinoza as real, objective characters of Substance, but only as our (subjective) ways of conceiving it.[5]

The thesis which the objective interpretation ascribes to Spinoza does not have quite the almost self-contradictory character as that ascribed to him by the subjective interpretation, but it can hardly be called a very persuasive position. If the attributes are really utterly distinct realms of being which share a common structure without there being any bond whether of causality or identity between them, what explanation can there be of the fact of their parallelism, and what possible reason can there be for us to believe in it? The only answer which seems to have been suggested is that they all follow from, and in some sense express, the same single essence of Substance, which imposes the same abstract form on the structures realized in these different media. But this is to say that the essence of Substance is some other thing, quite distinct from the attributes, which map each other in virtue of the fact that all map their common source. That seems to deprive the objective interpretation of its main *raison d'être* as against the subjective interpretation, namely that it rescues the essence of Substance from being some unknowable reality distinct from the attributes. Thus the objective interpretation either makes Substance, in respect of its own essence, a mere aggregate of realms which map each other for no apparent reason, or a transcendent unknown source from which these realms emanate. The latter alternative seems the more logical, but it clashes with Spinoza's propensity to speak of each attribute as somehow actually being the essence of Substance.

Even if we take it as just a fundamental fact of reality that the attributes do map each other, without this being explicable by any bond of identity or causality, there is a still more fundamental difficulty. Things which belong together in a whole must be related to each other in some manner, and it is obvious that for Spinoza the different attributes do belong together in a single whole, as Wolf admits in talking of Substance as their unified totality. Yet it is hard to see how they can be related to one another, while each remaining infinite in its own kind, since relatedness seems to imply some ability on the part of the terms related to 'bound' (*terminare*) each other, or at least to be both bounded by some common thing which lies between them, yet any such meeting at a boundary seems to be precisely what is denied of distinct attributes when they are described as each infinite in its own kind (I Def. 2). This difficulty is not obviated by saying that all the attributes issue from an essence of Substance which is distinct from them, since then each attribute must be bounded by this essence, a difficulty which I doubt whether description of this essence as a causal act[6] or an infinite potency[7] can remove. Here is a difficulty which does not arise on the subjective interpretation, since for it there is no need of a relation between different attributes which brings them into a single whole, since they are, in truth, simply one reality differently described or conceived.

It may be suggested that we are forgetting that it is the essential nature of Thought to be about something. Although Thought is not in any sort of causal relation to Extension it is – or rather some of it is – Thought *of* Extension; it consists, in part, of ideas to the effect that certain things are so in the extended world. Thus Thought is assertive, and in so far as it is true, as all Thought is when taken in its completeness in God, what it asserts is so; hence the physical world will be as the Divine Thought or Infinite Intellect asserts it to be, and there will be a correspondence turning neither on identity nor causal influence.

This will certainly not explain whatever parallelism there may be between the various non-mental attributes, and it would reduce any unity they had together in Substance to the fact that the singleness of the attribute of Thought might allow them to be held together in the knowledge of the Divine Intellect. It is doubtful, however, if the Divine Intellect could remain one if there was no unity among its ideata. Moreover, even if we forget about the attributes other than Thought and Extension, the objective interpretation of Spinozism leaves the relation between idea and ideata altogether obscure. Why should the one reflect the other if there is no bond between them?

The question of its internal coherence aside, the objective interpretation does not square easily with what Spinoza says.

> Thus, also, a mode of extension and the idea of that mode are one and the same thing expressed in two different ways – a truth which some of the Hebrews appear to have seen as through a cloud, since they say that God, the intellect of God, and the things which are the objects of that intellect are one and the same thing. (II P 7 S)

The objective interpretation quite loses sight of the identity asserted here, which implies far more than a parallelism of the numerically distinct.

Since both these interpretations fail, we must either decide that Spinoza had no coherent position at all, or look for another. Our best hope would seem to lie in some sort of synthesis of the two, since, after all, each can muster a good deal of evidence in its favour.

It is easier to construct such a synthesis than one might expect. Surely the subjective interpretation is right in holding that, for Spinoza, the very same reality we think of as being the extended world as a whole, or some part thereof, is also mental reality as a whole, or some part thereof. But surely the objective interpretation is right in holding that, for Spinoza, when we think adequately about either Extension or Thought we grasp reality as it is, and not merely as it appears.

153

Combining these positive aspects of each interpretation, I suggest that, for Spinoza, the conception of any or all concrete existence as extended represents one correct way of grasping it, showing us how it really is, and the conception of it as mental represents another correct way of grasping it, showing us how it really is. Likewise with the other attributes, for any minds able to think in terms of them. The distinction between the attributes is a conceptual one (whether the concepts be entertained by finite or infinite mind) but it is a distinction between different valid concepts, not a distinction between concepts which misrepresent reality.

As an interpretation of Spinoza's actual position this appears to square well with what he says, particularly in the crucial scholium just quoted, while doing justice to much that can be brought in support of each of the other two interpretations of which it is a synthesis. As a theory of the world it has, of course, its own difficulties. If the properties connoted by extendedness and mentality are utterly distinct, can one reality meaningfully be said to possess both?

There is one way in which we might expect to be able to give an affirmative answer which is unsatisfactory both as interpretation and as a theory of reality. One might think of mentality and extensity as attachments belonging to a certain single thing which is something in its own right aside from both of them. This is a common way in which properties of objects are thought of; a thing is thought of as having its colour and as having its shape, but as being itself something distinct from either of them, a bare particular as it is sometimes called. This can hardly be our clue to the way in which Substance can have two attributes, for it would make attributes belong together with modes as things which are in another thing in the sense of I, A1. That, on the contrary, each attribute is a thing which is in itself is made quite clear by I P10 which affirms that 'each attribute of a substance must be conceived through itself', and that, as is clear from the phrasing of I Def. 3, comes to the same as saying that it is 'in itself'. It follows that the sense in which Extension and Thought are both attributes of one and the same substance cannot be explained by saying that they are distinct properties which it possesses in any sense where a thing is thought of as having an inner being which somehow stands apart from its properties. In some sense, Substance as Natura Naturans must be both extensity and cognitivity, and as Natura Naturata must be both the whole extended universe and the systematic whole of all Thought.

But is it Substance, or the essence of Substance, with which each attribute is somehow identical? One may say (I think) that, for Spinoza, an individual is the same thing as its essence, in the case of modes as well as of Substance, but that there is a difference in what is being presupposed in the case when we speak of the thing's essence and in the case when we speak of the thing itself. When we speak of a thing's essence, we imply either that it does not exist, or that its existence is in doubt, or that its existence is something we are to affirm, as opposed to presupposing it in saying something else about this same item, as is the case when we speak of the thing itself rather than of its essence. The essential point is that an existing thing is a certain essence actualized or existing, not something other than the essence, since what exists is the essence. If that essence were not actualized, did not exist, it would be merely an essence and not also a thing.[8] Existence is a privilege or a tribulation which comes to essences, not to things of some other sort which have essences. To distinguish a thing from its essence is merely to insist that its status as an essence leaves the matter of its existence open. In the case of God, of course, there is no real sense in which his existence can be left open, in which his status as an essence stands apart from his status as an existence. None the less, we may speak of his essence, in as much as we may wish to demonstrate that his existence is a necessary truth without begging the question in a merely verbal way by speaking of him as an existence from the start.

The sense, then, in which the conceptions of Substance as Extension and as Thought are distinct, but equally correct and all-embracing, conceptions of Substance as it really is, is one which demands a deeper identity between the attributes than that of merely being properties of a thing distinguishable from both. That Spinoza believed that there was some such deeper identity seems reasonably clear. But is there any way in which such a belief might be true? In Section VI of this essay I shall argue that there is.

II

Any interpretation of Spinoza's theory of the relation between the attributes will be related to the view taken of his conception of each known attribute considered separately. The most usual way of taking Spinoza's conceptions of Thought and Extension treats them as in basic essentials Cartesian. Extension covers all that sort of reality which has shape, or is a whole within which shapes can be carved out, while Thought covers all sorts of consciousness, where consciousness consists in a series of mental acts, and is that same reality which William James was later to christen the stream of consciousness (in spite of various contrasts in the way in which the thinkers of such different periods describe it).

If this is correct, Spinoza's denial of the possibility of interaction between Thought and Extension (as in III P 2) is in much the same spirit as the following passage from a writer of the late nineteenth century.

> Let us try to imagine an idea, say of food, producing a movement, say of carrying food to the mouth . . . What is the method of its action? Does it assist the decomposition of the molecules of the grey matter, or does it retard the process, or does it alter the direction in which shocks are distributed? Let us imagine the molecules of the grey matter combined in such a way that they will fall into simpler combinations on the impact of an incident force. Now suppose the incident force, in the shape of a shock from some other centre, to impinge upon these molecules. By hypothesis it will decompose them, and they will fall into the simpler combination. How is the idea of food to prevent this decomposition? Manifestly it can do so only by increasing the force which binds the molecules together. Good! Try to imagine the idea of a beefsteak binding two molecules together. It is impossible. Equally impossible is it to imagine a similar idea loosening the attractive force between two molecules.[9]

This way of relating Spinoza to Descartes and later discussions regarding mind–body dualism, parallelism, occasionalism, and so forth has not gone unchallenged. Albert Balz, for example, argued with considerable vigour that ideas or modes of Thought are not, for Spinoza, psychological events at all but logical entities or pure concepts, and that the so-called parallelism of the attributes is simply the principle that the 'system of concepts corresponds with the orderly system of nature' and has nothing to do with psycho-physical parallelism as commonly understood. For Spinoza, Balz seems to maintain, thinking and feeling, regarded as temporal occurrences, belong to the attribute of Extension.[10]

E. M. Curley has given an account of the attribute of Thought somewhat akin to Balz's.[11] He holds that ideas or modes of Thought are, for Spinoza, the same as what later philosophers call true propositions, items with a logical rather than a psychological status. On this interpretation, all that Spinoza means when he says that all things are animate (II P 12 S) is that there are true propositions about them. Consciousness arises only when there are further propositions (ideas of ideas) about these primary propositions which affirm that their truth is known. I'm not sure I follow this, but the implication seems evident that the actual knowing does not itself belong to the attribute of Thought and that consciousness does so only if (very oddly) it is identified not with knowing but with the logical entity which is the truth that it occurs. It's not very clear where the knowing itself belongs in this case (or where the fact of its occurrence belongs, as Curley would say, who identifies modes of Extension with facts rather than with things) except in the attribute of Extension, which is precisely Balz's view.

Wolfson's interpretation is along the same lines to some extent, though it is more of an Aristotelian one, according to which the soul is the form of the body.[12] This doesn't carry quite the same suggestion that even those modes of Thought which constitute the states of a human soul are logical abstractions rather than concrete psychical phenomena, since an Aristotelian form is thought of, however confusedly, as the sort of thing which, in the special case of higher organisms, may rise to being a form of consciousness. None the less, Wolfson makes it clear that, as he understands it, a mode of the attribute of Thought need not be a phase of consciousness, and that the only sense in which all things are supposed to be animate is that they all have forms, be it only 'the form which endows matter with corporeality or tridimensionality'.

It will be as well to centre attention on what we may perhaps call the formalist interpretation of the attribute of Thought in its strongest form, as certainly advocated by Balz, according to which modes of Thought are never identifiable with phases of concrete psychical reality. On such a view, Natura Naturata, *qua* Thought, is the system of true propositions about, or of concepts applicable to, the world, such as need never be affirmed by anyone or have evoked any feelings, while Natura Naturans, *qua* Thought, will, presumably, be the essence of logical coherence as the determinant of the truth about the world as the one complete set of logically coherent propositions or concepts. One interest of this interpretation is in its pointing up similarities between Spinoza and Hegel.

A special appeal of this interpretation for some seems to be that it appears to rescue Spinoza from what they consider the slur of being a panpsychist. The scholium of II P 13, in which it is said that all individuals 'are animate, although in different degrees', since everything so far said about that idea of a man's body in God which is his soul will be true of the idea in God of every other thing, has proved an embarrassment to many commentators, who do not like to suppose that someone so hard-headed as Spinoza believes something they think so soft-minded as that everything is sentient. All this comes to, according to the formalist interpretation, is that there is a truth about everything or that everything has a form or character.

In the case of Balz and Curley, moreover, it is not only the ascription of sentience to individual physical things of the kind we usually call inanimate which is satisfactorily avoided by their interpretation; we also remove from Spinoza's teaching the doctrine that there is a cosmic consciousness of which our own experience is a fragment.

When Spinoza says such things as that 'we are parts of a thinking thing, whose thoughts – some in their entirety, others in part only – constitute our mind' or that 'the human Mind is part of a certain infinite intellect',[13] absolute idealists naturally take this as a formulation of precisely their own view that a human mind is a mere fragment of an infinite consciousness which grasps all things in their totality, so that my consciousness is a component in the absolute consciousness some-what as one of my sensations is a component in *it*. For the formalist interpretation, however, it means merely that the truth about a human organism is a little piece of the truth about the world as a whole, a piece which contains not only some few complete syllogisms but also many conclusions whose premises belong to different groupings of truths or concepts.

I am convinced that the main drift of these anti-Cartesian interpretations of the attribute of Thought are wrong. They confuse the contrast between Thought and Extension with one between Essence and Existence. Proposition 8 of Part II, and the proof of immortality later based on it, make it plain that the attribute of Extension is, so to speak, the womb of all possible shapes and movements, and thus contains the essences of all possible physical things, just as the attribute of Thought is the womb of all possible sorts of thinking, and thus contains the essences of all possible 'ideas'. The relation between essence and existence holds within each attribute. It is true that, on Curley's account, the modes of Thought are true propositions rather than essences, but it is true, none the less, that to see the distinction between the attributes as one between facts on the one hand, and true propositions on the other, is to render it much more like a contrast between existence and essence than between two different sorts of essences together with their actualizations.

The truth is, surely, that individual modes of Thought are existences or occurrences quite as concrete as individual modes of Extension, and that the infinite idea of God as it exists at any moment is the unified totality of the ideas or states of consciousness occurring at any one moment just as the face of the universe is the unified totality of the physical as at a moment. If so, I do not see how one can deny that

Spinoza is in the good company of such as Leibniz and Whitehead in being a kind of panpsychist.

III

If one is wondering how Spinoza's panpsychism might be developed in more detail, a question arises about the unity of the individual consciousness. God has a certain idea of my body, a certain sense of how far the formula regarding the proportion of motion and rest which constitutes my physical essence, is safe or at risk in its continuing applicability to the corpuscles which are, either directly or at some remove (by being parts of parts of parts . . .) my physical parts. Now that idea, though it has a certain complexity, also has a special unity, of a sort much discussed since Spinoza's time, such as makes it into an individual consciousness. There seems no compelling reason why the kind of apparent cut-off-ness of an individual human consciousness from the rest of cosmic sentience, should pertain likewise to the ideas of every other physical individual. It might be, for example, that though God has an idea of a mushroom, so that his awareness of its fate is a definite item within his total sentience, it is not an item which has any such sense of its own apartness as does the idea of a human body. That might give a sense in which the mushroom is not sentient, or in which it is animate to a different degree from us. Whatever may be true of a mushroom, there are relatively arbitrary ways of conceptually carving up the physical continuum which would hardly yield objects the most convinced panpsychist would think of as sentient as wholes.

Spinoza has often been thought neglectful of problems concerned with the unity of the individual consciousness, but anyone interested in Spinozism as a system possibly still viable in its more basic features must consider how it might best deal with them. The matter really needs discussion in the light of modern science, but Spinoza's own approach to the matter is not, as it happens, so very unclear.[14] A portion of the physical world is an individual to the extent that it has a character which it behaves so as to preserve against outside influences. Presumably it is only of physical individuals in this sense that there are ideas which possess even an approximation of mental unity. These ideas will necessarily also answer to a more intrinsic criterion of mental unity, in as much as they will have a character, their cognitive purport, which they will tend to preserve against other ideas in the general welter of cosmic Thought.

IV

This last phrase is suggestive, deliberately, of just that sort of romantic pantheistic conception of our minds as elements in an infinite ocean of universal feeling from which the formalistic interpretation would seek to rescue Spinoza. Such a Spinoza, it is doubtless thought, is fit for a Goethe, a Wordsworth, or even a Whitehead, but not for a contemporary philosopher, and it does indeed seem a little remote from the seventeenth-century Dutch Jew who poured scorn on the music of the spheres. One should bear in mind, however, that the logic of a philosopher's position is not always the same as that of his personal mood. Spinoza does not sound much like Wordsworth, but the logical implications of his theorems are, in many respects, such as to harmonize with a romantic insistence on the universe as instinct with life and feeling throughout.

Still, though the formalist interpretation of the attribute of Thought is wrong, it does draw attention to an important feature of Spinoza's position which explains the essentially unromantic cast of his pantheism. I am referring to the highly intellectualistic view which he, like Descartes and Leibniz, takes of consciousness. Modes of Thought are, indeed, items in the stream of consciousness, but then the stream of consciousness consists, for Spinoza, essentially of judgements, of intellectual affirmations – or at least of disjointed fragments of such – rather than of 'pure experience'. It is consciousness as described by Brentano rather than James.

For Curley the attribute of Thought, together with its modes, is the system of true propositions, and an individual's mind is the truth about it. This appears to me wrong only as long as one is expected to think of these propositions as unaffirmed and unentertained. Think of these truths as ideas actually entertained within a cosmic mind, the Divine Intellect, and you have exactly Spinoza's position. One may equally call them concepts, but concepts actually entertained in acts of living Thought, and thereby, on Spinoza's view, necessarily affirmed as having application in reality. One's own mind is that portion of the Divine Consciousness which consists in its ideas about the fate of my organism.

The question arises whether a mode of Thought can have any other individuating feature besides the idea it affirms, the objective essence it incorporates. The third axiom of Part Two of the *Ethics* might seem to suggest that love, desire, and so forth incorporate both an idea of something and a feeling towards it, such as makes an object loved rather than hated, or whatever. However, when we turn, in Part Three, to the definitions of joy, sorrow, and desire, and of all other emotions, such as love, in terms of them, it seems, after all, as though all distinctions between modes of Thought are matters of their objective essence, since joy is the idea of the physical fact that the body passes to a greater perfection, sorrow that it passes to a lesser, and desire, on its mental side, is not a particular feature of certain modes of Thought but their general tendency to persist in whatever their character is.

We may picture the total state of God or Nature on the Thought side, as it exists at any one moment, somewhat like this. It consists in the affirmation of an infinite set of propositions of two broad sorts. First, there are all the propositions which specify the general characteristics of Extension, and of all the other attributes. So far as Extension goes, these are the basic principles of mathematical physics together with all that they entail or render in principle possible. Affirmation of these propositions is unchanging. The other propositions affirmed at any moment are specifications of the precise state of things as it then momentarily is; in particular, a specification of the exact state and mutual relations of all the fundamental particles of the universe, as well as of the over-all character of the larger systems they thereby form. From all these propositions taken together, the Divine Intellect deduces another set of propositions of the same general sort, in which the specifications of the state of things subject to change is altered. (This is very much Curley's account, subjected to the very considerable revision indicated. It is important, however, not to press the kind of analogy with deduction from laws of nature and state descriptions as conceived by our contemporary philosophers of science to quite the extent that Curley does, since for Spinoza the propositions or ideas about changing things will of themselves logically imply, by being a kind of determination of, the propositions about the unchanging features of Extension. The essence of a finite mode includes its producibility within a system governed by certain laws, and thus implies them.) The process of God's passage by deduction from the one set of propositions to the other parallels an actual change of the world thereby described from the one total state to the other. The speed with which God's mind works is the speed of the universe (though it will always contain the ideas of all things produced and to be produced, but not now existing).

The consciousness of any individual body is God's affirmation of certain propositions about it which specify what is going on in it, especially in so far as this is a matter of the way in which it is being affected by other bodies in ways which assist or hinder it in its individual drive for survival, which increase or decrease its 'perfection'. It has rightly been suggested that Spinoza's position becomes more promising if we take the body of which my consciousness is the idea to be the brain.

It must be admitted that, as an account of the nature of one's consciousness, this does not square too obviously with the impressions provided of it by introspection. I am not thinking of any general objections there may be to the notion of one's individual sentience being a component in cosmic sentience, but to the notion of its being a component of this particular sort. Does it not imply that my consciousness should have as complex an internal articulation as does my body or brain? Does it not imply that introspection should reveal the fundamental laws of matter (a consequence which Spinoza would seem actually to draw)[15] as well as the brain's own detailed make-up? Admittedly, what is God's awareness of my body/brain is my awareness rather of what is acting on it, but even so, it would seem that, on Spinoza's view, the character of the former should be something one could read off from the character of one's consciousness.

Certainly some of his formulations do seem to imply these patently absurd ideas, but there are also indications of a more obscure, but less unlikely, thesis, for which what is in question under the title of my body is not the aggregate of its physical parts, but rather a certain formula, considered not as an abstraction but as something actualized in virtue of the relations between its (the brain's or body's) constituents which is about, or rather is, a certain ratio of motion to rest.[16] My mind, then, would not be God's affirmation of a proposition detailing the precise states and relations of my physical parts, but an affirmation simply specifying this formula and its present prospects of there being particles, or complexes of complexes of complexes of . . . such, which conform to it, or on which it can impose itself. Of course, God will affirm its actualization only in the light of his affirmations about the more detailed activity of the physical parts to which it applies, but it is the formula itself, or rather the ratio which it specifies, which, not as some kind of merely abstract entity, but as a feature really present in the physical world, is the body whose existence and prospects are reported in those divine affirmations which are my consciousness.

V

But there are still grave difficulties. The colourfulness, literal and metaphorical, of our sense experience and the plangency of our emotions are hardly what one associates with thoughts about a world specifiable entirely in terms of shape, motion, rest, etc., whether the thoughts concern details or only a certain general upshot. They might represent feelings in the Divine Intellect, about the world of Extension, but we have seen that, for Spinoza, feelings are merely further thoughts about Extension.

I can see just two ways in which Spinoza's theory could be brought into line with the actual quality of our experience. Either he is bound to take a much more exotic view of the nature of body than the largely Cartesian position with which one has good reason to associate him, or he must think of the relations between ideas and that which they characterize as less transparent than we have so far thought of them as being.

The first of these views might be arrived at by giving an assent perhaps more complete than Spinoza did himself to his statement that 'the human body exists as we perceive it' (II P13 C). Since we do not, in fact, perceive it as a pattern of elementary particles, or of complexes ultimately composed of these, even if at some remove, nor indeed as some kind of ratio of motion and rest having merely mathematical characteristics, but rather as something incorporating such qualities as colour and pain, this statement suggests that these do somehow qualify the body as it really is.

But just what qualities do we perceive the body as having? Is it the body-image which is just one part of my total perceptual field whose character we need to consider, or is it rather the whole of my perceptual field, indeed the total contents of my consciousness, which constitutes '*Corpus humanum, prout ipsum sentimus*'? Clearly the latter, since it is the whole of my mind which is the presentation to God of my body. The visual presentation of the tree, which I see, is not for God, and in truth, a presentation of the tree as it really is, but of my body as modified by the tree. Similarly, the visual presentation of my hand is in truth a presentation to God not of it but of the physical process corresponding to my seeing it. The only sense in which Spinoza could think that the body exists as we perceive it is one in which our mental activity gives us a view of the physical processes underlying it as they actually are. Certainly the idea they give of these physical processes will normally be most inadequate, but this must mean for Spinoza that it is so incomplete in what it tells us as to be misleading considered in isolation, not that there is anything wrong in its purely positive content. For Spinoza an inadequate idea of a bodily process must be included as a positive component in any adequate idea thereof, and be correct when cognized in context.[17]

C. D. Broad presented an account of Spinoza's theory of mind and body which would cohere well with what I have called, somewhat slangishly, an 'exotic' view of the body, though he does not himself associate it with any such view.[18] He represents Spinoza as holding that every act of consciousness is an act of direct acquaintance with a sensum, and that this sensum is, in fact, a modification of one's body, and he interprets Spinoza's claim that Thought and Extension are finally identical, as the view that the distinction between sensum and acquaintance is ultimately a false abstraction, each being but one side of the whole concrete event. Such a theory, when combined with Spinoza's view that there is nothing positive in error, implies that the specific sensory qualia experienced in perception are somehow literally present in the physical processes underlying consciousness. It also suggests that pleasure and pain, as felt, are the literal 'in itself' of some aspect of what goes on as the body's vitality is promoted or hindered.

It is of interest to note that much better sense can be made, on this interpretation, of what Spinoza says about the 'common notions' than might at first appear. It is not unplausible to say that our total perceptual field, including its extension by imagination, conforms to Euclid, and that the primary constituents of consciousness are all located in such a field. (This is, after all, a main plank of Kant's philosophy.) If one believes this and also believes that 'Euclid is true', one might well explain one's knowledge of Euclid's axioms, by saying that they are known as characterizing every space which can be immediately presented, and that thus one can give no flesh to any alternatives. Unless on some such lines as these, namely that consciousness provides an exemplar of basic geometrical laws, it is not easy to understand the relevance of Spinoza's claim that what is equally in the part and in the whole is conceived adequately. Even if we are today persuaded that real physical space is not Euclidean, I would still say that if it had been, Spinoza would have provided a better explanation of our supposed knowledge of such a fact than did Kant. For both of them, the fact that we can have no consciousness which does not exhibit the truth of Euclid, and that we can discover this by free mental activity without the need to check with the external world, seems to be the key fact. It is no more question-begging to say that it is the universe which imposes its character on our free mental activity than our forms of intuition which impose themselves on the universe. If it is objected to Spinoza that we have no guarantee that the part is in this respect an adequate key to the whole, it may equally be objected to Kant that we have no guarantee that our forms of intuition may not change and falsify our expectations.

It is surprising how much of what Spinoza says fits in well with Broad's interpretation taken together with an 'exotic' view of the body, surprising because it might seem to conflict with Spinoza's broadly Cartesian outlook in physics, though I am not sure there is any real clash with any explicit affirmation. (To insist, as in I, Appendix, that the aesthetic qualities we enjoy in things perceived are not really located in them is not necessarily to deny that they are physically located in us.) In any case, if we interpret, or develop, Spinozism along these lines, we bring it close to certain theories advanced by Bertrand Russell and Herbert Feigl, according to which our experience is an immediate awareness of states of the brain from the inside, states which answer to the universal laws and forms of physical reality but actualize them in their own particular concrete way, having like everything their own special individual quality.

The second way in which Spinozism may be taken as understanding the actual quality of our lived experience in its colourfulness and plangency is more conventional. Colour, smell, charm and so forth may be thought of as essences whose whole status it is to be exemplified *objectively* as presentations to modes of the attribute of Thought and which have no formal status in physical reality. Essentially it is the Lockean view of secondary qualities.

We can only make sense of this, however, if we take a rather different view of the relation between idea and ideatum than we have so far understood Spinoza to be taking. I have assumed so far, and not without justification, that an idea differs from its ideatum not in any qualitative way but in the one essentially formal feature that a certain essence which in the ideatum is there formally as its character figures in the idea objectively as its object or content. In short, the difference between X the ideatum and the idea of X is always just the same difference as that between Y the ideatum and the idea of Y. No individuality is allowed to ideas as renderings of their ideata, no question of different systems of ideas using different modes of projection or codes of representation. Not that there was any thought of denying that Paul's idea of Peter might be different from John's, still less from Peter's, but then in each case the primary ideatum of the idea is really different, a state of Paul's body as acted on by Peter, or of John's or of Peter's own, and it is this relation between the ideas which form our mind, and their primary ideata, the modifications of our body or brain, which concerns us.

If Spinozism is not to be associated with the exotic view of the body of which we have spoken, these assumptions about the relation between ideas and their primary ideata must be revised. We must say instead that a physical fact which completely lacks a certain form or quality may be the primary ideatum of an idea which incorporates it. On this view, a quality of pleasure, for example, is a way in which an increase in the vitality of an extended thing is registered in God's mind without the pleasure in any way duplicating something present in physical reality, and a quality of red may be God's way of registering a fact about events in the eye or brain which in no way incorporate it in themselves. The assumption would be, of course, that the formal essences of extended things would also be present objectively in the Divine Intellect. God, in short, would have ideas of two sorts, those which presented the sheer literal truth about the physical, and ideas which registered in a fresh medium, original to the attribute of Thought, the general upshot of various processes of extraordinary complexity. A human consciousness would be a series of ideas of the latter sort in which God registered its body's fate with feelings of an inherently suitable but also essentially novel sort.

Such an idea is rather attractive, and it avoids exoticizing the body, but it certainly does not fit the general tenor of Spinoza's treatment of idea and ideatum.

Of these two ways of seeking to reconcile Spinozism with the actual facts of immediate experience, I believe the former leaves more of his system standing. Whether Spinoza can be said to have held either position or not, the logic of his system forces a choice between them, a choice not to be eluded by a reference to the inadequacy of the ideas about our bodies in which our minds consist, since inadequacy for Spinoza implies only the need for a supplementation, such as they do in fact receive within the total context of the Divine Intellect.

VI

I will conclude with my promised suggestion as to a way in which it might in fact be true that Thought and Extension are identical, that ideas of extended things are one with their primary ideata.

My mind, for Spinozism, is God's idea of my body, or at least of certain modifications thereof, an idea which is included in that system of ideas which constitutes the Divine Intellect. Combine this with the view that the objects of God's intellect are one with his ideas of them (the view ascribed with apparent approval to 'some of the Hebrews') and one comes up with the proposition that my mind is one with certain modifications of my body as they really are rather than as they appear to someone else whose body is affected by them. My idea of Peter is not Peter, but, considered as God's idea of a modification of my body which is what, when considered rightly in the light of the whole, it is, it *is* somehow identical with its ideatum. My proposal is that we interpret this identity in a quite simple way and say that God's ideas of those modifications of my body are just the same thing as the modifications themselves, counting as physical in view of their structural properties (and at the level of the first kind of knowledge in view of the way in which they are presented to an external finite observer) and as mental in view of the feeling aspect which gives them their concrete individuality.

This interpretation follows naturally from that 'exotic' view of the body to which we have already felt drawn. For that view all the features which introspection reveals as factors in my consciousness are presentations to God of states of my body as they really are, though they are set for him in a much fuller context than for me whose mind they form. My final proposal is simply that these presentations to God of certain states of the body are not in the last analysis distinct from the states they present to him, being the same reality as God's experience of them. This is not to deny that it will be in virtue of different aspects of the character of this single reality that it is describable on the one hand as consisting of certain corporeal modifications and on the other as an experience of them.

Understood in this way, Spinoza's position becomes closer to that of Leibniz than it is usually thought of as being. Leibniz, it has been suggested,[19] held in succession two somewhat different views: first, that bodies are really aggregates of monads, possessing physical properties, secondly, that really there are no bodies, but that aggregates of monads appear as such to certain of the monads themselves. The former view has some kinship to the position under discussion.

But there are important differences. For Leibniz, even on his earlier view, the same thing is never both mental and physical; ideas are only found in minds, which are single monads, while extended things are composed always of aggregates of monads, which are not individually physical. For Spinozism, on our interpretation, every physical individual is also a mental individual, and vice versa. Both elementary corpuscles and the wholes they form are identical with those ideas of them which constitute their minds or mental aspect.

Besides Spinozistic monism and Leibnizian monadism lose none of their mutual contrariety. For Spinoza an individual mind, being a certain mode of Substance, *qua* Thought, is an abstraction from a single psychical whole just as, physically considered, it is an abstraction from a single physical whole, and is therefore most unlike one of Leibniz's monads. Both points of view have their problems as well as their rationale. We may find it hard to believe, with Spinoza and Bradley, that our minds can belong together in a single psychical whole. Yet surely these philosophers are right in claiming that there can be no dynamic transactions between things which do not belong together in a whole, since the very idea of things as standing in relation demands a shift of attention from the conception of them as separate things to the conception of the totality they participate in forming. It was, indeed, largely because he shared this opinion that Leibniz conceived his monads as without mutual influence. Whatever its difficulties, the monistic position seems more satisfactory as alone allowing the real interactions between things which we cannot seriously question.

How far the view of the ultimate relation between the physical and the mental here too briefly adumbrated approaches to Spinoza's own often obscure view of the matter remains doubtful. What I do claim is that it provides a way in which his chief doctrines about mind and body may actually be true, and integrates strikingly with the main features of his philosophy.

It fits in well, for one thing, with what he says about the idea of an idea. Here he appears to insist strongly on the absolute identity of the idea which is the ideatum and the idea which is of it, seeming to hold that it is one reality which is self-aware (II P 21 S, etc.). This self-awareness is a matter of degree, and to the extent that it increases – partly by relating itself more articulately to the other ideas in my mind – it belongs to that system of adequate ideas in virtue of which a man is active (V P 3). Since he insists that the relation between the idea of an idea, and the idea which it is of, is the same as the relation between an idea of extension and the extension which it is of (II P 21), the thesis is strongly suggested that a phase of physical existence as it is in itself and the immediate awareness of that phase of physical existence are identical in the most absolute sense, being one thing which has both an aspect of physicality and an aspect of awareness of that physicality, aspects which it is suitable from a conceptual point of view to treat separately, but which are each false abstractions set up as complete realities in their own right.

I also believe that our interpretation will assist us in grasping how the form of a physical explanation is supposed to be related to the form of a psychological explanation. The idea that, in the study of man, we should keep these two sorts of explanation rigidly apart, often thought of as Spinozistic, is not borne out by his actual practice in Parts Three and Four of his *Ethics*. It would seem rather that for Spinoza the proper study of man involves a unitary treatment of mind and body in which we recognize that we are studying one process with two aspects and use the more obvious aspect of any particular process to illuminate the other, without confusing ourselves with an attempt to find the locus of interaction between them. What is certainly mistaken is the tendency one sometimes encounters to regard Spinoza as virtually an epiphenomenalist for whom the mind is just some sort of passive register of physical fact.[20] The key to this whole issue seems to lie in the relation between propositions 12 and 28 of Part Three, but I cannot pursue the matter.

But there is a serious difficulty, already touched on, which should be considered again in the light of the interpretation advanced in this section. If the idea which has a body as its primary ideatum really is that body as it is considered from the inside and with respect to its aspect as a form of sentience, then it would seem that my consciousness, being an idea which has my body or brain as its primary ideatum, should contain parts corresponding to each of its physical parts. Yet this seems clearly not to be so.

We suggested above that the physical whole of which my mind is the idea may not be so much the mere aggregate of its physical parts as a formula which their relationship to one another actualizes, such as can be considered a physical reality in its own right. Yet it remains strange that one cannot find out the character of this formula simply by introspection, and that Spinoza was evidently not troubled by this.

We may have made the matter appear more troublesome than it is by talking as though the human mind was the idea of the human body itself rather than of certain of its modifications. The former is indeed what is suggested by II P13, and at other places, but the implication of II P19 seems to be that though God has an idea of my body as a whole it is only the ideas of certain of its modifications which form my ordinary daily consciousness. (The remainder, or some of it, might be identified with my unconscious, though for Spinoza it may have a more mysterious character as the inheritance into which I shall enter at death.)

Yet this hardly solves the problem. The affections of the body or brain which my consciousness must be regarded as registering have a complexity which it certainly does not seem to reproduce, a matter as obvious to Spinoza as to us today.

The following suggests itself. God has complete cognitive awareness as to how the particular formula definitive of me is prospering in the physical world, and he follows its successes and failures, in its struggle to remain actualized, with appropriate emotions. My conscious mind consists not in his knowledge but in his feelings about what he knows.

The suggestion may appeal if we are still concerned to rescue Spinoza from an exotic view of the body, and it is not unplausible to look upon the consciousness of an organism as Nature's way of feeling about it, but it is not very Spinozistic to ascribe ideas to God which, however much they may combine with adequate ideas of what is really going on, can be no part of them, presenting qualities completely absent in their ideata. In any case, such a suggestion would mean a complete abandonment of the literal interpretation of the identity claim concerning my consciousness and my body, or certain of its affections, which we are developing.

There is (I believe) an alternative which preserves this identity, one which points up the links between Spinozism and absolute idealism. There are grave difficulties to the whole notion of relations between genuinely distinct individuals, as was clear to Spinoza, Leibniz, and Bradley, and which Russell and others – though I cannot argue the point here – have failed to dissipate. The idealist solution has been to say that things can be related to one another only through being objects of a unified thought. As a comment about ideas there is no reason why Spinoza should not have accepted this, and have agreed that ideas of individual things can only combine so as to be ideas of larger wholes, composed of their ideata in relation, if there is a further idea about these ideas and about the way their ideata are mutually related. But that seems to imply that there must be a physical equivalent of this further idea which unites the physical parts into a physical whole. We can only think of this as some kind of physically actualized form of unity of the kind discussed above. On the present view, the unifying idea and the physical form, will be the very same thing, and one's consciousness will be what it is like for itself.

It would, indeed, be thoroughly confused to suppose that the basic togetherness of distinct finite individuals in one world of Thought or Being, could consist in the existence of another concrete individual, since clearly it will then need to be related to them. I am assuming, however, that for a monist all ideas, and all those ideata which are those ideas in another aspect, are mere abstractions from the unity of the one total reality, and that this forms their original togetherness. It may still be true that intermediate unities can only be cut out of the one whole of ultimate parts by some hierarchical arrangement of the kind suggested. If so, it would seem that the consciousness of an organism as a whole could be an idea at a higher level than the idea of its parts, a concept applied to those parts by the Divine Intellect without being merely the aggregate of its concepts of each. There will indeed be such an aggregate concept but it will be the subject, so to speak, of a proposition of which the concept which is my consciousness will be the predicate, and the affirmation of this whole proposition will be one with the physical fact which it affirms. Granted in any case that Spinoza's identity theory requires a view of physical nature which gives it a nature not purely mathematical or geometrical, it does not seem impossible to think of one's consciousness as an idea which plays this sort of role in God's thought.[21]

VII

How promising is an identity theory of a Spinozistic sort? The essential propositions are three: first, that our mind consists wholly in presentations of states of our body, more particularly our brain; secondly, that these presentations actually are those states of the body as felt from the inside; thirdly, that they belong to a cosmic whole of presentation which forms a presentation of the physical world which also is this totality as felt from the inside.

That a hypothesis along the lines of the first two propositions is a promising one, suggested by a host of empirical and conceptual considerations, is revealed in the contemporary vogue of the 'identity' theory. But there are features of Spinoza's view which make it superior to this. First, it incorporates the still essentially valid Cartesian recognition that one cannot possibly specify mind as a special sort of complication in the physical world as Armstrong, or for that matter Hobbes, would do. In this respect Spinoza stands closer to Herbert Feigl and the later Bertrand Russell, though with more concern for the intentionality of consciousness, than to Smart, Armstrong, or Putnam. Secondly, it recognizes that one cannot regard man as a natural object, as one should, without some complementary adjustments in one's view of so-called inanimate nature; the physical and the mental must be brought together everywhere or not at all. Thirdly, by associating the first two propositions with the third, it gives a rational place to the religious aspirations of mankind by interpreting the universe as a concrete spiritual as well as material unity. Spinoza's theology has much in common with the absolute idealisms of Hegel, Bradley, and others; and, in our own century, with the views of Whitehead and Teilhard de Chardin, granted in all cases the fundamental shift to an evolutionary rather than a 'steady state' universe. Absolute idealism has fallen into discredit not, I believe, because of any weakness in its essential principle that terms in relation must be comprehended in a whole at least as concrete as themselves, but because its postulation of the Absolute as being the concrete unity in which all things are comprehended went with an essentially anti-scientific point of view and was part of a last ditch defence of a man-centred universe. Spinoza remains a rather solitary witness, in Western thought, to the possibility of a sterner sort of Absolutism, in which the inanimate world, so called, is not a mere backcloth to human culture; it is an absolutism, incidentally, fitted to inspire sentiments of concern to the ecological movement,[22] though it must be admitted that Spinoza's own seventeenth-century attitude to the non-human environment was exploitative rather than cherishing. Still, if a rational theology with any serious ontological content has any future, it will need to be an interpretation of the natural cosmos which exhibits it as having properties such as make it a proper focus for religious feeling, in short, to be a kind of Spinozism.

A word should be said finally as to the infinitely many unknown attributes of Substance of which Spinoza speaks. There is no reason why an interpretation of Spinoza should explain the actual 'how' of their existence, but if it did not make some sense of their possibility its claims to be a development of Spinozism would be considerably reduced. On this topic too I find Curley's commentary extremely helpful when modified in the light of a much more 'absolutistic' reading of Spinoza. If Nature somehow mentally grasps itself as a whole, in a mental grasp in which our consciousnesses somehow figure as elements, one may well grant that this grasp may incorporate system-atizations other than that of any physical science we can conceive, systematizations which are ways in which the same phenomena really are organized, and which may, for all we know, actually be used by other finite minds.

Notes

1. Subjective interpretations were advanced by J. E. Erdmann (*Grundriss der Geschichte der Philosophie*, Band II, Berlin: W. Hertz, 1896) and H. A Wolfson (*The Philosophy of Spinoza*, New York: Schocken, 1934, Vol. 1, Ch. IV). Proponents of an objective interpretation include A. Wolf ('Spinoza's Conception of the Attributes of Substance', *P.A.S.*, Vol. XXVII, reprinted in S. P. Kashap [ed.], *Studies in Spinoza*, University of California Press, Berkeley/Los Angeles/London, 1972); Francis S. Haserot ('Spinoza's Definition of Attribute', *The Philosophical Review*, Vol. LXII [1953], reprinted in Kashap, op. cit.); and Martial Gueroult (*Spinoza: I Dieu*, Paris, 1968). See also Alan Donagan's excellent 'Essence and the Distinction of Attributes' (in Marjorie Grene [ed.], *Spinoza: A Collection of Critical Essays*, Garden City, N.Y.: Anchor Books, 1973).

2. The attribute of Extension is not, strictly, the whole physical world as it exists at any one time, rather is it extensity itself. Similarly the attribute of Thought is cognitivity itself rather than the cosmic mind or infinite intellect of God. The physical world and the mental world as concrete and shifting wholes are rather infinite modes, perhaps the ones Spinoza calls the 'face of the whole universe' and 'the idea of God' – though there is controversy on these points. Since I am not much concerned with the relation between *Natura Naturata* and *Natura Naturans* ('nature natured' and 'nature naturing', the former, to put it roughly, being nature as a system of things in certain states as a result of the principles of activity built into them, the latter being nature as the principles of activity built into things with that system as a result) I shall allow myself a little looseness, as I think Spinoza does himself, and speak sometimes of the attributes of Extension and Thought when I mean the whole actualization of them, ever shifting in detail though the same in general character and richness of being.

3. All abbreviated references in the present paper are to the *Ethics*. 'V P4 and C' stands for: *Ethics*, Pt V, Proposition 4 and Corollary. 'Def.' stands for 'Definition', 'S' for 'Scholium', 'A' for 'Axiom'.

4. Wolfson, op. cit., p. 147, and ff.

5. Wolf, op. cit., on pp. 17–18 of Kashap, op. cit.

6. Gueroult, op. cit. p. 238.

7. A. E. Hallett, *Creation, Emanation and Salvation: A Spinozistic Study*, The Hague: Nijhoff, 1962, Ch. 1.

8. But perhaps its idea would be an existing idea rather than the mere essence of one. (Cf. II P8 with C. and S.)

9. Chas. Mercier, *The Nervous System and the Mind*, London/New York: Macmillan, 1888, p. 9. Quoted by William James in *Principles of Psychology*, Vol. 1 (1890), p. 135.

10. Albert G. A. Balz, *Idea and Essence in the Philosophy of Hobbes and Spinoza*, AMS Press, Inc., 1967, p. 1 (first published N.Y. 1918).

11. E. M. Curley, *Spinoza's Metaphysics*, Cambridge, Mass.: Harvard University Press, 1969, Ch. 4.

12. Wolfson, op. cit., Chs. VII and XIII.

13. TdIE (Vloten and Land, MCMXIV, Tomus Primus, p. 23) and Ep. 22.

14. Cf. Def. before Lemma IV after II P13 and III P6 and 7.

15. Cf. II P39.

16. Def. and Lemmas IV and V, following II P13.

17. Cf. IV P1 S.

18. C. D. Broad, *Five Types of Ethical Theory*, London: Routledge & Kegan Paul, 1930, Ch. II, 'Spinoza' at pp. 16–23. Broad does not consider the possibility of an 'exotic' view

of body and hence thinks Spinoza's theory that error is solely negative is incompatible with his theory of mind and body.

19. Cf. Montgomery Furth, 'Monadology' at pp. 121–3 of its reprint (from *The Philosophical Review*, 1967), in H. G. Frankfurt (ed.), *Leibniz: A Collection of Critical Essays*, Garden City, N.Y.: Anchor Books, 1972.

20. David Bidney, *The Psychology and Ethics of Spinoza* (1962), p. 59.

21. It could even be argued that a kind of summing-up of a mass of physical details could occupy the same space as the details. Cf. John B. Cobb, *A Christian Natural Theology*, Philadelphia: Westminster Press, 1965, pp. 82 and ff.

22. Since writing this I have heard E. M. Curley reading a paper on this topic arguing a rather contrary case.

Biographical Note

T. L. S. Sprigge has been Professor of Logic and Metaphysics at the University of Edinburgh since 1979. Before that he taught philosophy at the University of Sussex. He edited the *Correspondence of Jeremy Bentham*, Vols. 1 and 2 (1968), and is author of *Facts, Words and Beliefs* (1970), *Santayana: An Examination of his Philosophy* (1974) and *The Vindication of Absolute Idealism* (1983), which last he regards as presenting a sort of Spinozism.

Further Reading

Spinoza, *Ethics*, ed. James Gutmann (New York: Hafner, 1949); Stuart Hampshire, *Spinoza* (Harmondsworth: Penguin Books, 1951); E. M. Curley, *Spinoza's Metaphysics* (Cambridge, Mass.: Harvard University Press, 1969); Errol Harris, *Salvation from Despair* (Atlantic Highlands, N.J.: Humanities Press 1974); Marjorie Grene (ed.), *Spinoza: A Collection of Critical Essays* (Garden City, N.Y.: Anchor Books, 1979). Books and articles of great interest on Spinoza are innumerable.

J. L. Mackie

Locke: Primary and Secondary Qualities

The judgement once given by a philosopher who was apt to take his terms from cricket, that Locke does not come in the first eleven of the great philosophers, does get a good deal of support. As J. L. Mackie allows in the introduction to the book from which the following selection comes, Locke is frequently accused of muddle and inconsistency. As he allows near the beginning of the selection, it is widely believed among philosophers that, whatever Locke said about primary and secondary qualities, it is wrong. That is, whatever distinction he really did attempt to make between the shape, size, number and motion or rest of, say, the chairs in a room, and, on the other hand, their qualities which somehow involve our perceptual experience or sensations of them in a different way, such as their colour, feel, temperature and so on, that distinction is mistaken.

It is Mackie's contention that the facts are otherwise. In his characteristically cogent, economical, clear and wholly independent discussion – the first chapter of his *Problems from Locke* – he concludes that Locke had good reasons for drawing the distinction he did, and that something close to it is correct. Given this, by the way, a conflict between scientists and many philosophers, those philosophers who have taken against Locke on the subject of primary and secondary qualities, is to be resolved in favour of the scientists. The distinction between the two kinds of qualities has been a persistent assumption of science, and in particular physics. The chapter gives a part, a large part, of Mackie's defence of Locke. The remainder of it has to do with what is certainly integral to the distinction, and is itself subject to a good deal of philosophical suspicion, a representative theory of perception a certain theory of our perceptual experience.

John Locke, 1632–1704. Born in Somerset and an undergraduate at Christ Church, Oxford, where he was after a Senior Student. The first of the British Empiricists. Known not only for his work in epistemology, but for his political philosophy. Of a Puritan family. 'His death was like his life, truly pious, yet natural, easy and unaffected.'

The distinction has to do with our experience of physical things, by sight, touch and so on, and the properties of those things. We do take the colour and the smoothness of a cup, as well as its shape and size, to be qualities of the cup. The distinction intended by Locke in Mackie's view of him, put most simply, is that our experience of the shape and size of the cup resembles actual properties of the cup, but that our experience of its colour and smoothness does not stand in such a resembling relation to any actual properties of the cup. However, this is not at all properly reported as the view that colour and smoothness and other secondary properties are 'wholly in the mind', or 'have no existence outside the mind'. There are actually properties of the cup that are essential to its colour and smoothness. The essential point is that they do not stand to our experience in the resembling way that other properties stand to our experience of the shape and size of the cup. There is the upshot, however, that what can be called our ordinary beliefs about physical objects include a general and systematic mistake. We do indeed take it that secondary qualities are *of* or *in* things in more or less the way that primary qualities are of or in things. They are not.

The distinction is set out more precisely by way of the notion of a power of a thing. To say a thing has a power to do such and such, in Mackie's view, is to say that the thing would do such and such if certain conditions obtained. It would do such and such in certain circumstances. That is to say that the thing has certain properties that are a partial cause of such and such. These properties are the basis or ground of the power. To say that hot water has a power to dissolve the wax on candlesticks is to say that the conjoining of hot water and certain other things is a complete or sufficient cause for dissolved wax. Properties of the water are a partial cause, and the basis of the power.

Secondary qualities of things are certain powers of things. They are powers to produce our experience, as well as certain other changes in the world. Neither the powers nor their bases can be said to resemble our experience – colour-as-seen, softness-as-felt, and so on. As for primary qualities of material things, say shape or size, they are not powers but are intrinsic features of the things. They do resemble our experience – shape and size and so on as we perceive them.

In the first section of the chapter, this distinction is expounded, and then the question considered of how it stands to what Locke actually says in the *Essay Concerning Human Understanding*. Mackie notes Locke's inconsistencies in his use of the terms 'quality' and 'idea' – in a wide use of the latter term, it is taken to stand both for contents of our experience, what might now be called concepts, and also actual prop-

erties of things. His loose usage is not at all fatal to his doctrine. It is
one thing that enables Berkeley to think, mistakenly, that he has refuted
the doctrine. It is summed up in the diagram on p. 187.

The second section sets out and examines arguments for the
primary–secondary distinction. The first and strongest of these, as
might be expected, derives from science, not only that of Locke's day
but also our contemporary science. Locke himself in effect offered this
argument, and four others. The four, in so far as they do not depend
on the first, are open to objections of several kinds. A line in the last of
them, although not mistaken, led Berkeley to another failing attempt
at refutation. Locke does not suppose, despite the line (p. 192), that
primary qualities are unlike secondary ones in that primary qualities do
not give rise to sensory illusions.

Others of Berkeley's objections to the distinction – all of which were
attempted in support of his own grand conclusion that *all* physical
properties are 'in the mind' – are the subject of the third section. Several
of these objections beg the very question at issue: whether things in fact
are as they are perceived, whether all of the properties we attribute to
them are in fact had by them in the same way. However, one objection
does give rise to a serious problem, having to do with the supposed
primary quality of solidity. It is that feature of a thing which has the
power to keep other things out of a given space. But *this* feature of the
physical world is not something of which we can be said to have a
resembling idea. Hence there is one property of things which in fact
cannot be regarded as either primary or secondary. This necessary
concession, however, like the weakness of some of Locke's arguments,
does not destroy his distinction.

The fourth and fifth sections of the chapter have to do with two other
doctrines about the properties of things, and the bearing of these
doctrines on Locke's distinction. The first has to do with the fact that
some qualities are open to only one kind of perception or sensation,
and other qualities are open to more than one. It raises Molyneux's
problem: Could a blind man, who had distinguished shapes by touch,
distinguish them by sight alone if he regained it? These matters do not
endanger Locke's distinction, although they require that it be qualified
in a second way. Finally, Mackie considers a doctrine owed to Jonathan
Bennett, in which primary and secondary qualities are distinguished in
a way different from Locke's. It is a view of great interest, not easily
grasped by way of a brief exposition. It is not taken to be one to which
Locke's must give place.

To return to the introduction to *Problems from Locke*, Mackie mentions that he had indeed originally intended to give less attention to Locke's solutions. He was led, however, by the strength of Locke's discussions, to give them greater attention. Mackie's account of Locke on primary and secondary qualities illustrates those strengths, as it also illustrates his own.

J. L. Mackie

Locke: Primary and Secondary Qualities

1. Locke's distinction and the representative theory of perception

The suggestion that primary qualities are to be distinguished from secondary qualities is one that seems to bring science and philosophy into head-on collision. Primary qualities like shape, size, number, and motion have been treated very differently by physicists, at least since the seventeenth century, from secondary qualities like colours, sounds, and tastes. But philosophers have on the whole accepted arguments that would show either that no such distinction can be drawn at all or at least that none can be drawn in the way in which we are initially tempted to draw it. For that way of drawing it presupposes a representative theory of perception, a contrast between percepts or sense-data or ideas as immediate objects of perception and material things which are the more remote or indirect objects of perception, and there are well-known philosophical objections to any such theory.

There is no doubt that Locke asserted, though he did not invent, some distinction between primary and secondary qualities. Whether he adopted a representative theory of perception is a question on which commentators disagree. The two topics cannot be completely separated . . . However, I shall keep these topics as much apart as possible, carrying the discussion of the primary/secondary distinction as far as I can carry it on its own . . .*

---

* In the chapter of *Problems from Locke* which follows the one reprinted here, Mackie firmly defends a representative theory of perception. It is one of which he says – to refer to A. D. Woozley's reported opinion below – that certainly it 'cannot be refuted by . . . objections . . . plain to the first-year student'. (Editor's note)

J. L. Mackie, 'Primary and Secondary Qualities', Chapter 1 of *Problems from Locke* (Oxford: Clarendon Press, 1976). With the permission of Joan Mackie and the publisher.

It is widely believed among philosophers that, whatever Locke said about primary and secondary qualities, it is wrong. It is still more widely believed that, if he held a representative theory, he was wrong there too. He has, indeed, defenders. But they commonly argue either that he did not hold a representative theory or else, conceding that he did hold one, that it is a relatively unimportant part of what he said. For example, Jonathan Bennett, while he speaks of a 'veil-of-perception doctrine', says that the word 'doctrine' is misleading if it suggests something which Locke was 'consciously concerned to expound and defend', and that 'Locke's treatment of the appearance/reality distinction is not prominent in the *Essay*'; he says also that 'something true and interesting is misexpressed' by Locke's thesis about primary and secondary qualities, and goes on to defend a distinction which, though it largely coincides with Locke's, is at least initially quite different in principle.[1]

Similarly, Gilbert Ryle, while utterly condemning the representative theory, admits that one of Locke's uses of the term 'ideas' belongs with that theory: the term is used to denote 'certain supposed entities which exist or occur "in the mind"', certain 'supposed mental proxies for independent realities'; but to have expounded and popularized this theory is no part of Locke's greatness as a philosopher. A. D. Woozley goes further, denying that Locke held what is usually called the representative theory, pointing out that Locke himself criticized that theory as stated by Malebranche, and remarking 'It would be hard to understand why anybody should want to rate Locke an important philosopher if his whole theory rests on errors so elementary that a first-year student has no difficulty in spotting them.'[2]

In opposition to such views, I shall try to show that Locke's own primary/secondary distinction is fairly clear and interesting in its own right, that Locke had good reasons for drawing it, and that something close to it is correct – something closer, for instance, than Bennett's initial distinction...

Locke does, however, present his primary/secondary distinction in a somewhat misleading way, and his use of terms is, as he admits, inconstant. It may therefore be better first to state the substance of his view in somewhat different terms, and only afterwards to show how his words and phrases fit into this picture. Let us, then, suppose that Locke intended to say something like this:

There are material things extended in three-dimensional space and lasting through time. In this room, for example, there are several chairs: each of them has a specific shape and size and position, and is at any time in some definite state of rest or motion. The group of chairs in this room at any time has a certain number. Also, each chair is made up of a great many tiny particles which move about rapidly even when the chair as a whole is at rest. Material things also appear to have many other properties; they differ from one another, we say, in colour, hardness, temperature, and so on. But the real differences which these descriptions reflect consist wholly in the arrangement and motion of the tiny particles of which these material things are composed. Such things are also solid or impenetrable in that each keeps any other out of the place where it is. There are admittedly apparent exceptions: for example, water soaks into or through a sponge or a block of sandstone. But this shows merely that in such large-scale things there may be spaces between the particles: the particles of one thing or quantity of stuff may find their way between the particles of another. But each ultimate particle is completely solid and completely excludes any other particle from the same place. Thus the properties which material things, large or small, have in themselves are shape, size, position, number, motion-or-rest, and solidity. More exactly, each particle has solidity, each large-scale thing has some approximation to solidity, each thing large or small has some determinate shape, some determinate size, is at some place and is in some determinate state of rest or motion, while each group of things has some determinate number.

Material things interact with one another in regular causal ways: hence we can say that each thing has various powers. To say that a certain thing has a certain power is just to say that it would affect or be affected by another thing of a certain sort in some specific manner. A power is not the cause of such an effect; rather to have the power is to be such as to cause the effect. The cause – or, more accurately, a partial cause, since the effect will also depend upon *other* things – will be some set of properties, of the sorts already mentioned, of the thing that has the power: it will generally be, or at least include, some set of such properties of the minute parts of that thing, of the collection of particles of which it is composed. These properties which constitute the cause can be called the ground or basis of the corresponding power.

Material things also interact with our sense-organs and, through them, with our minds in ways that give rise to those states in us which we call the having of sensations and perceptions. That is, material things have powers to produce sensations and perceptions in us, and these powers, like any others, have grounds or bases in the intrinsic properties of the things. Also, our sensations and perceptions have what we can call their experiential content: we have sensations of pain, heat,

J. L. Mackie

and cold, and perceptions of coloured shapes, of rough or smooth and variously shaped surfaces, of impacts, pressures, and resistances, of sounds, tastes, smells, and so on. This experiential content is at most times very complex; commonly we do not attend to it or talk about it as such, but rather attend to and talk about the material things, with their properties and what they do, which we take it to reveal to us; but we can attend to the experiential content itself, and it is then most naturally referred to by such phrases as 'how it looks to me' or '. . . feels to me' or '. . . sounds to me', and so on. This experiential content is partly as of properties of the sorts already noted as belonging to material things – solidity and determinations of shape, size, motion-or-rest, and number. I have a visual perception as of a circular shape in what I take to be a saucer and of which I also have tactual perceptions as of something solid, thin, and concave. But this content is also partly as of other features – colours, sounds, heat, cold, smells, pain, and the like. Shape, size, position, number, motion-or-rest, and solidity, just as they occur as elements in this experiential content, can also belong to material things. The saucer can be circular just as I see it as circular, it can be thin just as I feel it as thin, what I see as a group of three chairs may indeed be three chairs. Of course we can make mistakes, distortions and illusions can occur. I may see as elliptical the saucer which in itself is circular, and it may feel thicker than it is. But we sometimes perceive shapes and so on pretty correctly: material things often have very nearly the shapes etc. that we see or feel them as having. And even when we make mistakes, they have other *shapes*, for example, other determinate properties that belong to the same determinable (that is, shape in general) as those which occur as elements in our experiential content. We also commonly ascribe to material things colours as we see colours, as they occur as elements in our experiential content, and again heat, cold, roughness, and so on as we feel them; we ascribe tastes as we taste them to bits of food and to liquids, smells as we smell them to spatial regions; and I think of the ticking sound as I hear it as coming to me from the clock. But this is all a mistake, a systematic error. All that is out there in reality is the shape, size, position, number, motion-or-rest, and solidity, which occur as properties both of large-scale things and of their minute parts (though perhaps there is also some substance or substratum to which these properties belong). . .It is these properties, especially those of the minute parts of things, that cause the corresponding sensations and perceptions whose qualitative content we wrongly ascribe to external things. On the other hand pain as we feel it, though it may be caused by an external object, say by a needle sticking into my finger, is not ascribed to that external object; rather it is commonly ascribed to the part of one's body in which, as we say, the pain is felt.

But how does this view connect with what Locke says? How is it to be translated into his terminology? First, what about 'ideas'? His official definition of 'idea' is very wide: 'whatsoever is the *object* of the understanding when a man thinks'.[3] This could include real, external, independent things considered as objects of thought, and also, as Locke says, what has been meant by such terms as 'phantasm', 'notion', and 'species', or what might now be called concepts – someone's idea of blue, say, or of murder – and again it could include what I have called experiential content. Locke certainly uses it to refer to the elements that form the content of a sensory perception while we are having it, but also to remembered images, imaginary constructions, and concepts, apparently without realizing the difficulty of making a single sort of item do all these jobs. But he does take some care to make his meaning clear. When he is about to introduce the distinction between primary and secondary qualities, he first distinguishes between ideas – the word must here be used in a broad sense – 'as they are ideas or perceptions in our minds' and 'as they are modifications of matter in the bodies that cause such perceptions in us', and proposes to call only the former *ideas*.[4] That is, he is introducing a narrow sense of 'ideas' in which these are to be 'perceptions in our minds' and not 'modifications of matter'. One would expect him here to call the latter *qualities*, but in fact this is not what he proposes to do; rather he says that he will give the name *qualities* to the various powers of objects to produce ideas in us. But immediately afterwards his usage is partly inconsistent with this proposal, for what he identifies as *primary qualities* are 'solidity, extension, figure, motion or rest, and number', and these are not powers: rather they are intrinsic properties of things which may be the grounds or bases of powers, and they are 'modifications of matter in the bodies . . .'. *Secondary qualities*, however, of which he gives as examples 'colours, sounds, tastes, etc.', he does identify with powers: they are 'nothing in the objects themselves, but powers to produce various sensations in us by their primary qualities, i.e. by the bulk, figure, texture, and motion of their insensible parts'.[5]

In this often-quoted remark 'nothing . . ., but' means (despite the comma) 'nothing except'; but many students and some commentators have read it as if 'but' were the conjunction, and so have taken the first part of the remark as saying that secondary qualities are not in the objects at all. This leads easily to the view that secondary qualities are 'in the mind', that is, that they are a species of what Locke has called ideas in the narrow sense. Other passages, too, lend some colour to this view; but it is clearly a misinterpretation of the doctrine which Locke is trying to expound. It might, indeed, be regarded as a merely verbal distortion of Locke's main way of speaking: obviously we could, quite harmlessly, use the phrase 'secondary qualities' to refer to what Locke would rather have called our ideas of secondary qualities, and find some other term to refer to the powers of things to produce these ideas. But historically it has not been harmless. For example, this distortion was used by Berkeley in constructing a specious argument for his own position (*Hylas: . . . secondary qualities*, have certainly no existence without the mind . . . *Philonous*: But what if the same arguments which are brought against secondary qualities, will hold proof against these also? *Hylas*: Why then I shall be obliged to think, they too exist only in the mind.[6]) By 1929, according to Reginald Jackson, this distortion had become the current usage of the term 'secondary qualities'.[7]

But this is not the way in which Locke generally uses the phrase. His official terminology is that while there are ideas both of primary and of secondary qualities, and all such ideas are in our minds, the primary qualities are the intrinsic properties of material things, large or small – that is, shape, size, number, motion-or-rest, and solidity – and the secondary qualities are powers of material things, whose basis is the primary qualities of the minute parts of those things. Locke includes under the heading 'secondary qualities' both powers to produce ideas of colours and so on in us and powers to produce changes in other bodies, for example the power of the sun or of a fire to melt wax.[8]

Locke says that shape, size, etc. 'may be called real, original, or primary qualities, because they are in the things themselves, whether they are perceived or no'. This would seem to suggest, by contrast, that the secondary qualities are neither real nor original, and are not in the things themselves, or perhaps anywhere, unless they are perceived. But to give Locke a consistent view we must read this as meaning merely that the secondary qualities are powers to produce (especially) perceptions, not that they are themselves those perceptions or ideas.

Locke's list of primary qualities varies a little, and often includes 'texture'. But I take it that the texture of, say, the surface of a body is just the way in which the smaller parts at or near that surface are arranged: this, like 'situation', would be covered by the inclusion of position in the original list, with the understanding that this includes both absolute and relative position.

Locke also says that 'the ideas of primary qualities . . . are resemblances of them, and their patterns do really exist in the bodies themselves; but the ideas produced in us by these secondary qualities have no resemblance of them at all'.[9] He means, surely, that material things literally have shapes as we see shapes, feel shapes, and think of shapes, that things move in just the sort of way in which we see, feel, and think of things moving, and so on. But he cannot mean that we never make mistakes, never suffer from illusions, with regard to primary qualities. Essentially what he must be claiming is that material things have, for example, shapes which are determinations of the same determinable or category, shape in general, as are the shapes seen, felt, or thought of. Thus I may be wrong in thinking that this table-top is square, and my seeing of it as a non-rectangular parallelogram is indeed distorted (but of course in a standard, familiar way which does not tend to make me judge wrongly, and does not even prevent me from – in another sense – seeing it as square at the same time); but a physical table-top *could* have a shape of either of these sorts, and this one does have some shape that belongs to the same family as these. The contrast that Locke is drawing is with, for example, colours. It is not that we sometimes make mistakes about colours – for example, wrongly match two different shades of blue under artificial light – but that even under ideal conditions, when we are as right as it is possible to be about colours, colours as we see them are totally different not only from the powers to produce such sensations, with which Locke equates the secondary qualities, but also from the ground or basis of these powers in the things that we call coloured. This ground, Locke thinks, will be only some arrangement and motion of the minute parts of the surfaces of these things: no colour as we see colour, no determinate within that category at all, is literally in or on the things, even when they are illuminated, nor is any determinate of that category in the light that comes from the things to our eyes. Similarly, and even more obviously, there is nothing of the same category as a sound as we hear it either in a vibrating gong or around it: sound as we hear it is nothing like a wave motion in the air. It is, of course, a trivial logical point that our ideas of secondary qualities, colours as we see them, sounds as we hear them, and the like, cannot be or resemble powers. But it is not trivial that they do not resemble the grounds of the powers: this is a non-obvious but, Locke thinks, real difference between the secondary qualities and the primary ones.

Someone might argue that primary qualities too should be identified with powers. A square object has the power to produce the idea of squareness in me in favourable conditions of observation. Admittedly there are such powers. But we also need a term to refer to the intrinsic features of things which form the grounds or bases of their various powers, and it is this job that is done by the phrase 'primary quality'. A large part of the basis of a thing's power to produce the idea of squareness will, moreover, be its literally being square, its having a shape-quality which is just like the shape-quality which we find in the experiential content to which the thing gives rise. The ideas of primary qualities resemble the grounds of the powers to produce those ideas.

The inclusion of solidity in the list of primary qualities does, indeed, make it difficult to sustain this distinction between intrinsic qualities and powers, for solidity, as Locke himself explains it, seems to be just the power to keep other things out. Yet after almost conceding that solidity is just impenetrability, which is obviously a power, Locke withdraws and suggests that '*solidity*... carries something more of positive in it than *impenetrability*; which is negative, and is perhaps more a consequence of *solidity* than *solidity* itself'.[10] That is, he wants solidity to be the ground of the power, not the power itself.

That this is the distinction which Locke is trying to draw between primary and secondary qualities will, I believe, be evident from a careful and unprejudiced reading of Chapter 8 in Book II of the *Essay* itself. This account agrees also with that given by Reginald Jackson in a classic article which, I think, has never been superseded. And essentially the same view was put forward by Robert Boyle, from whom Locke took the very terms 'primary qualities' and 'secondary qualities'.[11] It is true that Boyle, like Locke himself, shows some tendency to oscillate in his application of the term 'secondary quality': though he usually applies it to the relevant power, he sometimes applies it to the ground of that power, and sometimes to the resulting idea. But the substance of the view does not depend on the decision where a certain label is to be attached, nor need it be undermined by careless inconstancy in labelling. What matters is the claims made about what sorts of entities are or are not there, and what relations hold or do not hold between them.

There is, indeed, a possible objection to part of my interpretation. I have ascribed to Locke the view that there is a systematic error in our ordinary thinking, in that we ascribe colours as we see them, tastes as we taste them, and so on to material things, in effect that we mistake secondary qualities for primary ones. But a primary/secondary distinction could be introduced not as an error theory but as an analysis of what we ordinarily think and say; it could be argued that there are differences already implicit in the ways we handle qualities of the two sorts. Knowing well that a piece of cloth looks a different colour in different lights and even at different angles, and even apart from this may look a different colour to different people, we may already treat 'This is crimson' as the ascription of a power rather than as the claim that there is in the cloth an intrinsic feature that resembles one of our colour ideas. But Locke at least offers his distinction as a correction, not as an analysis, of our ordinary concepts. Whereas the power of the sun to melt wax is recognized as just a power, the secondary qualities 'are looked upon as real qualities in the things thus affecting us', we are 'forward to imagine that those ideas are resemblances of something really existing in the objects themselves'.[12] And on the whole I think he is right. Though we cannot treat secondary qualities in exactly the same way as primary ones, yet our dominant ordinary view gives them much the same status, and if Locke's way of drawing the distinction, at least, is to be defended, it must be in opposition to everyday assumptions.

Diagram (i) may help to make plain both the substance of Locke's distinction and the official terminology which he employs, not quite consistently, in presenting it.

If this is the distinction Locke was trying to draw, it is clear in what way it presupposes a representative theory of perception. It is formu-

Intrinsic features of material things = 'P.Q.'	Powers of material things	Items 'in minds'
Shape, size, number, position, solidity, motion-or-rest (i) on large scale = ground of power (i)	(i) Power to produce ideas of P.Q.	Shapes etc. as we see and feel them = 'Ideas of P.Q.'
(ii) of minute parts = ground of powers (ii) (iii) and (usually) (iv)	(ii) Power to produce ideas of S.Q. (iii) Power to produce pain, sickness, etc.	Colours as we see them, sounds as we hear them, etc. = 'Ideas of S.Q.'
	(iv) Power to produce changes in other things	Pain, Sickness, etc.
	Powers (ii), (iii), & (iv) = 'S.Q.'	

Diagram (i)

lated in terms of a contrast between ideas in minds – here especially elements in the content of a present sensory perception – and intrinsic features of external material things. It is being assumed that the latter are causally responsible for the former, and hence that we can speak of powers, wnose grounds are such intrinsic features, to produce those ideas, among other things. The principle of this primary/secondary distinction is that the ideas of primary qualities resemble the grounds of the powers to produce them while the ideas of secondary qualities do not. While our ideas of qualities of both kinds correspond to and systematically represent real differences in external things, it is with the primary qualities alone that our ideas fairly faithfully depict what is there in the things.

But did Locke have any good reasons for drawing this distinction? Can its coherence be defended against well-known philosophical objections? Should we now accept it, or anything like it, as correct?

2. Arguments for the distinction

It is clear that Locke adopted the distinction as part of the 'corpuscularian philosophy' of Boyle and other scientists of the time whose work Locke knew and admired.[13] It had long been known that sound is a vibration in the air, and Hooke, Huygens, and Newton were trying out wave and corpuscular theories of light. In the development of any such theory it is simply superfluous to postulate that there are, in material objects, in the air, or in the light, qualities which are at all like sounds as we hear sounds or colours as we see colours. And though science has changed the details of its accounts since the seventeenth century, the broad outlines of its message on this issue have remained the same: the literal ascription of colours as we see colours, and the like, to material things, to light, and so on, forms no part of the explanation of what goes on in the physical world in the processes which lead on to our having the sensations and perceptions that we have, but, by contrast, the features actually used in the construction of such explanations still include spatial position and arrangement and motions (of various sorts) of items most of which are countable at least in principle. Despite the change from a Newtonian to an Einsteinian space–time framework, physics still recognizes, on a large scale, countable things with at least relative positions and extensions and motions, and despite the Quantum Theory, it still recognizes, on a small scale, particles with something like these spatio-temporal determinations. Solidity, it is true, no longer plays anything like the part it played in Boyle's theory, but is replaced by electromagnetic fields or attractive and repulsive forces; but fairly close relatives of all the other Boyle–Locke primary qualities still figure among the data of physical explanation, whereas no resemblances of our ideas of secondary qualities figure among these data.

But stressing the scientific support for the distinction may invite a facile but mistaken shelving of it as being merely of physical, not philosophical, importance. 'The doctrine of primary and secondary qualities is', says O'Connor '. . . nothing but some scientific truths dangerously elevated into a philosophical doctrine.'[14] It is often suggested that the so-called primary qualities are merely those in which physicists are specially interested, perhaps because they lend themselves more than others to measurement and to use in mathematically formulated theories, but that those of us who have other interests need not defer to such base mechanical preferences. But to say this is to miss the point. The physical considerations do not concern merely features which are scientifically interesting and important; they show that there is no good reason for postulating features of a certain other sort, namely thoroughly objective features which resemble our ideas of secondary qualities. Does this mean that the physicists are telling us that grass is not really green and that blood is not really red, and that we have to take such dogmatism lying down? That would be a misleading way of putting the question. Of course grass and blood differ in some respect which is related to the different colour sensations that we get in looking at them in ordinary conditions in a good light. We could use colour-words in such a way that this, along with some family of similar resemblances and differences, was all that we meant in saying that grass is green, that blood is red, and so on. Over-reliance on the Wittgensteinian thesis that we need 'outward criteria' might lead to the conclusion that this is how we already do and must use colour-words, that only thus can their use form part of a public language. The physicist has nothing to say that would undermine this use. But I have no doubt that most people who use colour-words are commonly inclined to believe something more than is enshrined in this publicly establishable use, something that may be indicated by saying that colours as we see them belong intrinsically to the (illuminated) surfaces of material objects. The physicist (seventeenth- or twentieth-century) can point out that he has no need of this hypothesis. But admittedly physics does not itself tell us that no such properties are there. This denial is a further, philosophical, step; but it is one which is at least prima facie reasonable in the light of the successes of physical theory.

We might further explain and defend the Lockean view about secondary qualities by considering what it would be like for it to be false and for us to have evidence of its falsity – for example, what would be required to justify our taking colours to be primary qualities. For this two steps would be needed. First, we should want a scientific case for postulating the existence of qualities with the spatial structure of colours, either in addition to or instead of the hypothesized micro-structures to which physicists would at present refer in explaining colour phenomena. Secondly, we should need some reason for believing that the postulated surface-covering quality of redness was, qualitatively, as we see it – that is, that different people, and even members of different species, if not colour-blind, all see red alike (it is not the case that you see red as I see green, for example), and that their red-seeing was veridical not only in that they would agree with one another in judgements about what things were red, and not only in that there was some objective feature to which those judgements corre-sponded, but also in that this feature was just as they all perceived it. But in fact not even the first of these two requirements is satisfied, so the question whether the second is satisfied does not even arise.

Physics, then, gives us no reason for taking colours as primary qual-ities, and much the same can be said about sound-qualities, tastes, smells, heat, and cold. And the philosophical principle of economy of postulation then supplies a reason for not introducing supposedly objective qualities of kinds for which physics has no need. Perhaps the strongest argument for Locke's distinction, therefore, is based partly, though not wholly, on physics.

Locke himself, however, was not a physicist, and he says repeatedly that it would be contrary to the design of his essay to 'inquire philo-sophically into the peculiar constitution of bodies'.[15] Yet he does not merely take over the primary/secondary distinction from Boyle, he argues for it, and his arguments are rather a mixed bag, good, bad, and indifferent.

First, in introducing the distinction, Locke picks out, as what he will call primary, such qualities

as are utterly inseparable from the body, in what estate soever it be; such as, in all the alterations . . . it suffers . . . it constantly keeps; and such as sense constantly finds in every particle of matter which has bulk enough to be perceived, and the mind finds inseparable from every particle of matter, though less than to make itself singly be perceived by our senses.[16]

Locke is here making two points: that when a body is changed or divided it, or its parts, if they are big enough to be seen, can still be seen to have shape, size, and the other primary qualities, and that even if the parts are too small to be seen, we still have to think of them as having shape, size, and so on. But the contrast he is drawing seems to depend on an unfair comparison between determinable qualities on the primary side and determinate ones on the secondary side. The determinate shape, size, and so on of a material thing are as alterable as its determinate colour; and while, no matter how you knock a thing about, cut it up, and so on, either it or its parts will still have some shape, some size, and so on, it seems equally true that so long as the parts are big enough to be seen it or they will still have some colour. We can regard heat-or-cold, or temperature, as a determinable analogous to motion-or-rest: a thing's determinate temperature is separable from it, but so is its determinate state of rest or motion, and just as it will always have *some* motion-or-rest, so it will also have *some* temperature. But if we carry division to the point where the separate particles are no longer perceivable by the senses, it seems circular to appeal to the fact that the mind will still give each particle some shape and size, but not, perhaps, any colour or any temperature. If the mind discriminates thus, it will be because it has already adopted the distinction: this cannot be the evidence upon which the distinction itself is based. Despite the prominent place given to it, this is therefore almost worthless as an argument; at best it might provide part of what is meant in calling a quality primary. But even in this respect it is misleading; as we have seen, what is central in the notion of a primary quality is that it is an intrinsic feature of material things, but is also a resemblance of some idea – that is, at least of the same category as some features that figure within the contents of our experience – and that it is something that the best physical theory will find it necessary to use as a starting-point of explanation. But clearly a feature could satisfy all these requirements even if it disappeared when things were divided beyond a certain point.

Secondly, and much more usefully, Locke does refer in outline to the physical considerations which provide the best support for the distinction – the causal processes involved in perception, the likelihood that 'some singly imperceptible bodies' come from seen objects to the eyes, and so convey some motion to the brain. We can conceive, Locke says, that God should annex the ideas of colours to motions to which they have no similitude; but the theology is dispensable: all he needs here is the principle that the sensation-effect need not resemble its cause, as we know it does not when pain is produced by the motion of a piece of steel dividing our flesh. Similarly, we need light to see colours; things have no colour in the dark. But no one, Locke thinks, will suppose that the light produces colours as qualities of what we call coloured objects. It is a much more plausible hypothesis that different surface textures merely reflect different rays of light.[17]

A third argument of the same sort is weaker though more picturesque. If you pound an almond, the taste and colour change, but 'what real alteration can the beating of the pestle make in any body, but an alteration of the texture of it?'[18] Someone might well reply that if there were intrinsic colour-as-we-see-it and taste-as-we-taste-it qualities, the beating could alter them, and that in any case it might easily release differently coloured and differently tasting liquids previously shut up in the cells of the nut. The most that Locke should have said is that the result of this experiment is consistent with his view.

A fourth argument draws an analogy between ideas of secondary qualities and pain and nausea. Everyone will admit that there is nothing like pain or nausea in the materials that produce them in us, so why should we suppose that there must be something like colours as we see them, sounds as we hear them, and so on in the objects that produce these ideas in us? This shows, indeed, that there may well be a pattern of relationships such as Locke describes for secondary qualities, where in virtue of some basis in an object it has the power to produce in us a sensation whose content is quite unlike that basis; but it gives no reason for supposing that colours, sounds, and so on conform to this pattern whereas shapes, sizes, motions, and so on do not. This argument shows that there may be secondary qualities, but not that the line between primary and secondary qualities is to be drawn just where Locke draws it. There is no obvious respect in which colours etc. are more akin to pain and nausea than shapes are.

Fifthly, Locke shows how his theory enables us to explain such illusions as our feeling the same water as hot with one hand but as cold with the other: if our feelings of warmth and cold arise from changes in the motion of minute parts of our 'nerves and animal spirits', it is easy to see how the lukewarm water could produce these different feelings by speeding up the relevant motions in the one hand and slowing down those in the other.[19] In itself this is a good argument, though of course just part of the 'corpuscularian philosophy'. But Locke throws in, for contrast, the remark that 'figure' – that is, shape – 'never produce[s] the idea of a square by one hand [and] of a globe by another'. Though literally correct, this is unfortunate because it has led careless readers from Berkeley onwards to think that Locke is founding the primary/secondary distinction on the claim that secondary qualities are subject to sensory illusion while primary qualities are not. It is then easy for Berkeley to reply that illusions also occur with respect to primary qualities like shape, size, and motion, and hence that there can be no distinction between the two groups of qualities; and then, adding the further misinterpretation (noted above) that secondary qualities exist only in the mind, to conclude that Locke himself would be required, for consistency, to admit that the primary qualities also exist only in the mind. But of course Locke's argument does not rest on any such claim that illusions affect only the secondary qualities; he himself records illusions that affect primary qualities like size and number;[20] it is rather that the corpuscular theory is confirmed as a scientific hypothesis by its success in explaining various illusions in detail. The explanations which it gives of illusions about secondary qualities make use of the assignment, to the powers to produce the corresponding ideas, of bases which do not resemble those ideas; but the same is not true of the explanations which it would give of illusions about primary qualities. The latter explanations still involve the assignment to material objects of qualities of just the same category as those that occur within our experiential content.

The arguments that Locke explicitly offers, then, add up to something of a case for the primary/secondary distinction, but not to a very strong one. Its best support comes from the success of a certain programme of physical explanation, success which indeed has come mainly after Locke's time. But even in Locke's time it had had some successes, though he does not consider it any part of his task to report them, and it had a fair degree of initial plausibility. Science, including popular science, has, I think, constantly adhered to something like the Boyle–Locke distinction; but philosophers have, in the main, been hostile to it, believing that there are powerful, perhaps even overwhelming, arguments on the other side, in particular those first put forward by Berkeley.[21] What are these objections, and are they really so forceful?

3. Arguments against the distinction

Berkeley develops at great length the argument that illusions occur equally in our perception of primary qualities. But this, as we have seen, is simply beside the point, since the distinction does not rest at all upon the mere fact that illusions occur with the secondary qualities. A second argument runs thus: '. . . if you will trust your senses, is it not plain all sensible qualities co-exist, or to them appear as being in the same place? Do they ever represent a motion, or figure, as being divested of all other visible and tangible qualities?' The answer is, of course, that they do not, but that it is an *ignoratio elenchi* to appeal to 'the senses' and how they 'represent' things, that is, to what we find in the content of sensory or perceptual experience, against a theory whose whole point is that things are in many respects not as they are sensorily perceived. A third argument takes the issue further: 'it is impossible even for the mind to disunite the ideas of extension and motion from all other sensible qualities' – that is, we cannot even conceive an extended moving thing without giving it some colour or some other secondary quality. In so far as this is just an appeal to what we can or cannot imagine, it is hardly relevant. If, as the second argument has stressed, we always experience extended things as having either colours-as-we-see-them or tactile surface qualities as we feel them, it is not surprising if our imaginings are similarly restricted. But behind this there is a more serious conceptual problem. Nearly all the primary qualities which Locke lists are, in a broad sense, geometrical ones. Shape, size, texture, motion-or-rest, and number are all only aspects of the spatio-temporal patterning or distribution or arrangement of some stuff (or stuffs). Each of these, and even all of them together, are essentially incomplete: there must be something that occupies some spatio-temporal regions and not others. It would be useless to draw the boundary of a certain shape if there were no difference between what was on one side of the boundary and what was on the other. But have we not forgotten about solidity? This is not a purely geometrical feature; could it not be the item of which each specific extension is the extension? Locke says 'This is the idea [that is, quality] that belongs to body, whereby we conceive it to fill space.'[22] As Hume forcibly pointed out, if solidity is just impenetrability, the power to exclude other things of the same sort, it cannot do this job. If two things are to keep each other out of the regions they occupy, each must be not only something other than just a specific region, but also something other than the ability to keep others out of that region.[23] But, as we have seen, Locke's view is that solidity is not just impenetrability, not just a power but the ground of this power. However, this creates a difficulty for Locke's claim that solidity is a primary quality in the sense that the quality itself resembles the idea we have of it. If solidity is the space-filling feature which makes the difference between body and empty space and enables each body to keep other bodies out, then we do not have a simple, adequate idea of it, but only the indirect and relative notion of it as the supposed or inferred ground of a power which is itself learned from its manifestations.

In the Boyle–Locke theory primary qualities are meant to play two roles: they are meant to be objective features which resemble the ideas to which they give rise in us, and to be the features that a viable physical theory will use as starting-points of explanation. What our argument shows is that a complete list of items that play the former role is not a complete list of the items that are needed to play the latter. But it does not show that the qualities Locke has listed as primary ones, other than solidity, cannot play both roles. Nor does it show (as Hume thought) that any of the present secondary qualities has to be taken over and transferred to the 'primary' list for the second purpose. Rather, the additional basic physical feature will be something that should not be, and perhaps is not, on either the primary or the secondary list because it does not appear in our ordinary experiential content at all. And of course there may be more than one such feature. Locke's solidity should not have been on either list: it is an inferred physical property. Modern physics will not indeed use this; but electric charge is one feature which has come into physical theory to play a corresponding part, and mass (rest mass) is perhaps another. Neither of these is an immediate object of any of our senses, so neither can be called a primary quality in the sense of an intrinsic feature of material things which is also a 'resemblance' of some ordinary pre-scientific idea.

Developed in this way, then, this Berkeley–Hume objection does indeed point to a revision needed in Locke's account of primary qualities, especially the distinction of their two roles and the recognition of some items which play the second role but not the first. But this objection does not show any need to break down the distinction between primary and secondary qualities. But, it may be said, this is the wrong way to develop the objection. Whether or not physical theory needs further space-occupying properties, which may well be initially quite unknown to us, we need, for a coherent account of what we perceive and can imagine, some *known* space-filling property or properties to make the difference between body and empty space *for us*. And since this cannot be one of Locke's primary qualities (solidity having been removed from the list) and cannot be unknown or unperceived, it must be one (or more) of the secondary qualities. But this need not be conceded. Visually, indeed, it is as coloured that we are able to pick out space-occupying material things. Tactually, it is as having certain felt surface qualities. But what if I feel over the surface of a rigid body, say the top, edge, and the underside of a table-top, not directly with my fingers but with some instrument, such as a pencil? Can I not thus detect a shape without being aware of any quality that fills that shape other than the power, impenetrability? Although this was not an adequate candidate for the space-occupying role from the point of view of physical theory, it is adequate in relation to this other, experiential, way of developing the difficulty. Impenetrability could conceivably be all that made the difference *for us* between body and empty space. But even if this were not so, how would it matter? We should merely be brought back by another route to Berkeley's thesis that neither our senses nor our imaginations ever represent to us collections of primary qualities alone without secondary qualities, and this would be irrelevant as an argument against Locke's view, the whole point of which is that things are not as they are sensorily perceived, that we need to revise and correct the picture of the world which we initially acquire by the use of our senses.

Berkeley's other arguments against the distinction amount to little more than ingenious satire and rhetoric – for example, the way in which Philonous traps Hylas into saying (in attempting to defend Locke's view) that real sounds are never heard, but may – since they are wave motions – possibly be seen or felt. The Lockean view is at variance with initial common-sense opinions, and it is not easy to express it naturally and coherently in the ordinary language whose primary function is to make statements within the framework of those common-sense opinions. The term 'sound' is thus initially employed both to denote a feature that forms part of the content of our experience – or at least that is of the same category as features that do so – and to denote a supposed independently existing entity. But Locke's account of secondary qualities is precisely that with them nothing plays both these roles; someone who adopts that account must then either say that there are no sounds or else use the word to denote one or other of the items that (in his opinion) do exist but violate its linguistic connection with the other. It will be awkward for him to express his view; but this is no good argument against that view, but rather a glaring example of an invalid way of appealing to ordinary language to settle a philosophical issue.

None of these arguments of Berkeley's, then, tells at all forcibly against Locke's distinction. But in examining them we have shown up an assumption which Locke makes but which is implausible from the start. His primary qualities have to do two jobs: they have to be the constituents of the physical world (and hence the starting-points of explanations in the best possible physical theory), but they also have to be features of which some of our ideas are 'resemblances', that is, they have to be of categories which are fairly correctly depicted in the way in which we sensorily perceive the physical world. But there is little reason to suppose that every real constituent, even basic constituent, of physical things will be recorded in our perceptions, and we have found an argument which shows that physical theory must postulate at least one constituent feature (to be the extension-occupier) of which no pre-scientific idea that we have is a resemblance. It is interesting to note that Locke at least once explicitly left room for such a development, remarking that our ideas of secondary qualities depend 'upon the primary qualities of their minute and insensible parts or, if not upon them, upon something yet more remote from our comprehension'.[24]

But there is still a major difficulty for the distinction as Locke drew it. It is formulated within the framework of a representative theory of perception which distinguishes sharply between ideas in our minds and any externally real things, while postulating that our ideas are causally produced by those external things acting upon our sense-organs and through them on our brains, and yet assumes that we can speak intelligibly about resemblances between some of our ideas and those external realities. It is in terms of this theory that primary qualities are distinguished in status from secondary ones, that though we have ideas of both sorts, the corresponding realities in the one case resemble the ideas, but not in the other, that the primary qualities really are *qualities*, and are themselves the ground or basis of the powers to produce the corresponding ideas, whereas the secondary qualities are mere powers, whose ground or basis is the primary qualities of minute parts. But the representative theory has been severely criticized and is widely believed to be completely untenable; if so, this must be fatal for any distinction between primary and secondary qualities that is developed within its framework.

This is the most serious difficulty for Locke's distinction; but I shall postpone discussion of it . . .* I shall consider two distinctions which are related to Locke's distinction between primary and secondary qualities, but which do not require any sort of representative theory and which could therefore survive criticisms which might be fatal to the distinction as Locke drew it.

---

* As noted earlier, Mackie discusses the difficulty in the following chapter of his book, and concludes it can be overcome. (Editor's note)

4. Aristotle's distinction and Molyneux's problem – common and special sensibles

First, there is a distinction which goes back at least to Aristotle between objects of perception which are perceived by more than one sense – perhaps by all, but at least both by sight and by touch – and those which are perceived by one sense only.[25] This distinction coincides fairly closely with Locke's: Aristotle mentions as 'common sensibles' motion, rest, shape, size, number, and unity, while colour, sound, and flavour are examples of the 'special sensibles'. There is no doubt that there is a distinction which can be drawn in these terms quite innocently, without commitment to any further theory about the objective status of these various items. On the other hand, this difference might be taken as a piece of evidence supporting Locke's distinction, as a datum of experience for which Locke's account provides an explanation. If material things themselves literally have shape, size, and so on, it is not surprising that we can become aware of their shapes, sizes, and so on, more or less accurately, by way of more than one sensory channel; and if, for example, shapes as we see them and shapes as we feel them both resemble shapes as material things actually have them, intrinsically, they will naturally resemble one another. But if our idea of some secondary quality is merely a causal product of the interaction of something external with some sense-organ and some part of the central nervous system and does not resemble anything external, then it is on the whole to be expected that it will be peculiar to that particular sense.

This suggestion, however, faces some exceptions and problems. Some qualities seem to be common to the senses of taste and smell – there can be a sour smell as well as a sour taste. Are these, then, to count as common sensibles? If so, our argument from Aristotle's distinction to Locke's would suggest that sourness is to be a primary quality, whereas it is obviously a secondary one for Locke. But this is easily explained away. The mechanisms of the senses of taste and smell are so similar and so closely related that the same ground in the material object – presumably in minute particles floating in the air as well as in the food – can give rise to similar ideas by way of the two mechanisms.

A more serious question is whether the primary qualities really are common sensibles to sight and touch, for example whether visual and tactual ideas of shape really resemble one another. Locke himself discusses Molyneux's problem, whether a man born blind, who has learned to distinguish by touch a cube and a sphere of the same metal and of about the same size, and who then acquires the sense of sight, would be able to tell which was which of a cube and a sphere by sight alone, before he had touched them.[26] Locke agrees with Molyneux that the man would not be able to do this. Berkeley also agreed, and developed this answer by maintaining that the visual ideas of the two shapes are quite different from the tactual ideas of them, and that it is only experience that enables us to correlate visual with tactual ideas, and so to expect a certain tactual impression where we have had the correlated (but intrinsically quite different) visual one. On Berkeley's view there is, at least primitively, no one common sensible *shape* (or size, and so on: though Berkeley is evasive about number, attempting to brush it aside as 'entirely the creature of the mind'):[27] the name of any particular shape, say 'square', stands for a pair of correlated ideas, one visual and one tactual, and what Aristotle takes as the perceiving of some one object through two senses is really the separate perceiving, by each of the two senses, of an idea special to that sense, accompanied by an inference to or expectation of the correlated idea which is peculiar to the other sense.[28]

Did Locke, then, in giving the same answer to Molyneux's problem as Berkeley gave later, commit himself to the denial that shape, for example, is a common sensible? I think not, for if we pay attention to the context in which he refers to the problem we can see that his reason for the negative answer to Molyneux's question is quite different from Berkeley's. Locke uses it to illustrate the thesis that 'the ideas we receive by sensation are often in grown people altered by the judgment, without our taking notice of it'; in other words, perception is modified by unconscious automatic interpretation, and we owe this to experience. For example, where all that we see (in one sense) is 'a plane variously coloured' we get the impression of a convex surface; 'the judgment . . . frames to itself the perception of a convex figure . . .' We can infer that Locke's reason for saying that Molyneux's man would not be able, before touching the objects he was now seeing for the first time, to say which was the sphere and which the cube is that this man would not have acquired automatic interpretations of various patterns of shading as indicators of three-dimensional shapes such as spherical convexity or the corner of a cube projecting towards the viewer. As Locke says, quoting Molyneux himself, 'he has not yet attained the experience that what affects his touch so or so must affect his sight so or so; or that a protuberant angle in the cube, that pressed his hand unequally, shall appear to his eye as it does in the cube'. But this would leave open the possibility that two-dimensional shape should be a common sensible for sight and touch.

In fact, Molyneux's question is confusing, because it raises more than one issue. The issues would be discriminated if we were to ask two separate questions: first, whether Molyneux's man would be able to say which was which of two flat plates, one square and one circular, placed with their flat surfaces at right angles to his line of sight, and secondly, whether he would be able to say which was which of a flat circular plate (still so placed) and a sphere. Berkeley would, of course, answer 'No' to both questions. But it would be more plausible to say 'Yes' to the first question and 'No' to the second. This affirmative answer to the first question would rest on the assumption that (two-dimensional) squareness and circularity can each be detected both by sight and by touch, or again that a circle as seen and a circle as felt share the genuinely common feature of being the same all round, whereas a square, whether seen or felt, has the contrasting feature that its four corners are different from its four sides. But the negative answer to the second question would rest on the view that there is no feature genuinely common to convexity as felt and to the shading by which an artist represents convexity – something like the latter being all that Molyneux's man could see when he looked at the sphere for the first time.

In fact there is some (admittedly inconclusive) experimental evidence in favour of an affirmative answer to our first question.[29] R. L. Gregory reports the case of a man who was not indeed totally blind, but with no useful vision, not from birth but from the age of ten months, and whose sight was restored by corneal grafts. It appears that he could recognize ordinary objects by sight, could tell the time by a seen clock-face, having previously learned to tell the time by touching the hands of a large watch with no glass, and could recognize capital letters which he had learned by touch. Provided that we can discount his experiences up to the age of ten months and such vision as he had between that age and the operation, this man's performance disproves Berkeley's thesis that the objects of sight have, initially, nothing in common with the objects of touch – of course 'touch' must here be taken to include kinaesthesis. But it says nothing against Locke's thesis that only an experienced correlation enables us to interpret shading as relief. Gregory's report does not include any direct answer to our second question, but it does say that the man had no impression of depth from the Necker cube and similar line-drawings. This indirectly supports a negative answer to our second question, since it shows that the man did not respond to a remotely analogous visual indication of depth. There is, then, some evidence in favour of Locke's negative answer to the precise question with which he was concerned. If a man like

Molyneux's could, contrary to what Locke thought, also distinguish a sphere from a flat circular plate, it could only be by some innate or instinctive faculty of interpreting shading as relief. This is not impossible, but it would be much more surprising than the reported achievements which show only an ability visually to recognize two-dimensional shapes and patterns previously learned by touch.

I conclude that Locke could, consistently with his negative answer to Molyneux's question in the context in which he discussed it, hold that we get the same idea of shape from both sight and touch, provided that this is confined to two-dimensional shape. This view is intrinsically plausible, and such empirical evidence as there is supports it against Berkeley's thesis. If there are thus common sensibles for sight and touch, we can take Aristotle's distinction innocently in its own right. But we can also take it, more interestingly, as evidence that supports Locke's more speculative distinction between primary and secondary qualities.

This discussion does, however, force us to qualify Locke's claim that our ideas of shapes resemble the intrinsic qualities of objects which causally produce those ideas. This will hold for both visually and tactually acquired ideas of two-dimensional shape, and perhaps for some tactually acquired ideas of three-dimensional shape. It may hold also for visually acquired ideas of three-dimensional shape, but only in so far as these ideas are the product of unconscious interpretation based on experience, 'a settled habit . . . performed so constantly and so quick, that we take that for the perception of our sensation which is an idea formed by our judgment'. Something similar would apply, I believe, to most tactual perception of three-dimensional shape. We have had to learn both to see and to feel things as making up a three-dimensional Euclidean world. Only by an unconsciously sophisticated performance do we form those ideas of three-dimensional shapes which resemble the intrinsic shape-qualities of the things that give rise to them.

5. Bennett's distinction

Another way of distinguishing primary from secondary qualities has been introduced and defended by Jonathan Bennett.[30] Primary qualities such as size have far more complex connections with our experiences, with the ways in which things interact, than do secondary qualities. Consequently someone can be colour-blind without its being brought home to him by any ordinary conjunction of other experiences that there is anything wrong, whereas to suppose that someone could be size-blind without its showing up almost at once we should have to suppose a fantastically complicated systematic distortion of his perceptions as compared with those of other people. It is therefore a contingent matter that we agree as well as we do about what tastes bitter or what looks green. Bennett mentions phenol-thio-urea as a substance that tastes intensely bitter to three people out of four but which is tasteless to the rest; consequently selective breeding or mass surgery could bring it about that everyone found it bitter or again that no one did. Describable and easily understandable procedures could bring it about that this stuff was, or was not, bitter in just as unambiguous a way as lemons are now sour or sugar sweet. Bennett admits that secondary qualities have some causal connections with other aspects of our experience: red apples are more squashable than green ones, different colours reflect light of different wavelengths, and so on; but these are relatively few and unimportant, and are no obstacle to our basing colour descriptions simply on how things look, and flavour descriptions simply on how they taste.

There is no doubt a difference between qualities in such a degree of causal connectedness, but a primary/secondary distinction based simply on this would be very different from Locke's. Bennett's distinction is one of degree only, not of kind or status. It would lead to the conclusion that the primary qualities are of special importance for a description of the natural world, and particularly for a science or technology that is interested in causation, in bringing things about; but it would not lead to the conclusion that material things as they are in themselves can be completely described in terms of primary qualities – including those of their minute parts – alone.

At least in his original article Bennett thinks that this difference is to the advantage of his distinction as against Locke's: 'Locke is *wrong*', he says, 'in that part of each claim which Berkeley *accepts*', that is, in suggesting that 'secondary qualities . . . sit looser to the world than is usually thought', for example that 'things do not really have temperatures'.[31] But this last is a misleading way of putting Locke's thesis: of course things really differ in ways which our feelings of them as hot or cold roughly indicate, and which our measurements with thermometers discriminate better, but Locke may still be right if what he means is that heat as we feel heat and coldness as we feel coldness are not present in the things themselves in the same way as their shape (or, we might now add, their mass).

In his article, Bennett emphasizes only this difference of degree of interconnectedness. Later, in his book, he distinguishes what he calls Locke's *analytic thesis* from his *causal thesis*.[32] The analytic thesis is that a statement attributing a secondary quality to a thing is equivalent to a counterfactual conditional, of the form: 'If *x* stood in relation *R* to a normal human, the human would have a sensory idea of such and such a kind.' That is, the analytic thesis equates secondary quality statements with attributions of powers to things. The causal thesis is that 'in a perfected and completed science, all our secondary-quality perceptions would be causally explained in terms of the primary qualities of the things we perceive'.

Whatever else the analytic thesis is, it is not analytically true. This is obviously not what ordinary secondary-quality statements as naïvely used *mean*. It is, however, what Locke is proposing that they should mean. But what supports this recommendation? Why should we give this sort of meaning to secondary-quality statements but not give a similar powers meaning to primary-quality statements? Bennett strangely seems to suggest that it is his distinction between degrees of interconnectedness that would justify this discrimination. But I see no reason why it should, if there is no difference in status between the two sets of qualities. At most, what it would justify is the use of a more complicated sort of powers meaning for primary-quality statements: a primary quality would be a many-track or multiply-manifested disposition whereas a secondary quality would be a single-track or singly-manifested one.[33] But to justify the more extreme difference of giving a powers meaning to secondary-quality statements but not to primary-quality ones at all we need rather something like the causal thesis. For if the causal thesis were true, then the literal attribution of colours as we see them (and so on) to things would serve no explanatory purpose; it would therefore be unjustified; and only by limiting secondary-quality statements to a powers meaning could we keep them strictly true, whereas primary-quality statements could still be strictly true with a non-dispositional meaning. So although the analytic and the causal thesis can be distinguished, they go together very naturally in Locke's thought: it is the latter that supports the former, and supports it far better than Bennett's distinction of degree would. These two theses together, then, with the naturally associated view about what is and what is not really there, constitute the most important and interesting, but admittedly speculative and controversial, distinction between primary and secondary qualities. Bennett's distinction, like

J. L. Mackie

Aristotle's, points to a real and not very controversial difference: but it gains in significance when it is seen as a preliminary step towards the Boyle–Locke distinction – or some modernized variant of this.

The phenol argument, indeed, would support Locke's distinction rather than Bennett's. If one (genetically or surgically producible) physiological condition makes people classify phenol-thio-urea along with gall, aloes, quinine, and other paradigmatically bitter-tasting things, whereas another physiological condition makes people classify it away from these and along with water, pure alcohol, fish fingers, the flesh of battery chickens, and other paradigmatically tasteless things, then it is less plausible to suppose that flavours as we taste them are ever actually in the things. A similar powerful argument about colours is given by J. J. C. Smart.[34] Even for people with normal vision, there is no simple correlation between seen colour and wavelength of light: the colour-sensation produced by pure light of a certain single wavelength can also be produced by various appropriate mixtures of light of quite different wavelengths, and it is therefore most improbable that there is any single quality, an objective 'resemblance' of, say, my sensation of a particular shade of green, in all the things, or all the light-rays, that give me this sensation; and if it is unlikely that such an objective *quale* is in all of them, it is also unlikely – because quite gratuitous to postulate – that it is in any of them.

There is, then, in the end a strong case for a distinction between primary and secondary qualities which is essentially that of Boyle and Locke, backed up by further arguments from physics of the same general sort as those which they used, but revised by the relegation of solidity to the status of a power and by the recognition of objectively real and physically important properties which are not resemblances of any of our ordinary ideas . . .

Notes

1. 'Substance, Reality, and Primary Qualities', *American Philosophical Quarterly*, ii (1965), reprinted in *Locke and Berkeley*, ed. C. B. Martin and D. M. Armstrong, especially pp. 91, 104–5.

2. G. Ryle, 'John Locke on the Human Understanding', in *Tercentenary Addresses on John Locke*, ed. J. L. Stocks, reprinted in *Locke and Berkeley*; A. D. Woozley, editor's introduction to Fontana edition of Locke's *Essay*, pp. 26–7.

3. I. i. 8. (Editor's note: This note, and the following ones of this form, giving Book, Chapter and Section, refer to Locke's *Essay Concerning Human Understanding*, 5th edition, as reprinted in the Everyman Library, ed. John Yolton.)

4. II. viii. 7.

5. II. viii. 10.

6. First Dialogue in *Three Dialogues between Hylas and Philonous*.

7. 'Locke's Distinction between Primary and Secondary Qualities', in *Mind*, xxxviii (1929), reprinted in *Locke and Berkeley*.

8. II. viii. 26.

9. II. viii. 15.

10. II. iv. 1.

11. For Jackson's article, see note 7 above; for Boyle's view, see 'The Origin of Forms and Qualities according to the Corpuscular Philosophy', *Works*, vol. iii.

12. II. viii. 24–5.

13. See e.g. the Epistle to the Reader at the beginning of the *Essay*.

14. 'Locke', by D. J. O'Connor, in *A Critical History of Western Philosophy*, ed. D. J. O'Connor, p. 210.

15. e.g. II. xxi. 73.

16. II. viii. 9.

17. II. viii. 12–13 and 19, also IV. xvi. 12.

18. II. viii. 20.

19. II. viii. 21.

20. e.g. he notes how distance affects apparent size, and how differently we should see things if we had microscopic eyes (II. xxi. 63; II. xxiii. 12), and he mentions 'that seeming odd experiment of seeing only the two outward ones of three bits of paper stuck up against a wall . . .' ('An Examination of P. Malebranche's Opinion of Seeing All Things in God', *Works*, vol. 9, p. 216).

21. Especially in the First Dialogue.

22. II. iv. 2.

23. *Treatise*, Bk I, Pt IV, Sect. 4 (hereafter I. iv. 4).

24. IV. iii. 11.

25. Aristotle, *De Anima*, 418^a. 9–24; 425. 14–21.

26. II. ix. 8.

27. *A New Theory of Vision*, §§ 47–9, 96–105, 110–11, 132–6, etc.

28. op. cit., § 109.

29. R. L. Gregory, *Concepts and Mechanisms of Perception*, pp. 65–129 (reprint of monograph by R. L. Gregory and Jean Wallace, *Recovery from Early Blindness: a Case Study* (1963)).

30. 'Substance, Reality, and Primary Qualities'. Bennett also discusses the issue in *Locke, Berkeley, Hume: Central Themes*, pp. 88–111.

31. *Locke and Berkeley*, p. 109.

32. *Locke, Berkeley, Hume: Central Themes*, pp. 94–5, 102–6.

33. For this distinction, see G. Ryle, *The Concept of Mind*, pp. 44–5, also my *Truth, Probability, and Paradox*, pp. 122, 145–8.

34. *Philosophy and Scientific Realism*, pp. 66–75.

Biographical Note

John Mackie, who died in 1981, was a Fellow in Philosophy at University College, Oxford, and before then Professor of Philosophy at the University of Otago, the University of Sydney and the University of York. His books include *Truth, Probability and Paradox* (1973), which has to do with fundamental questions in logical theory, *The Cement of the Universe:*

J. L. Mackie

A Study of Causation (1974) and *Ethics: Inventing Right and Wrong* (1977). He also published
many articles in various branches of philosophy, including the philosophy of science and
the philosophy of religion.

Further Reading

J. L. Mackie, *Problems from Locke* (Oxford University Press, 1976), especially Chapter 2;
Locke, *An Essay Concerning Human Understanding*, fifth edition, as in the Everyman Library
edition, ed. John Yolton; Reginald Jackson, 'Locke's Distinction Between Primary and
Secondary Qualities', *Mind*, xxxviii, 1929, reprinted in *Locke and Berkeley, A Collection of
Critical Essays*, edited by C. B. Martin and D. M. Armstrong (London: Notre Dame, 1968);
J. L. Mackie, *Truth, Probability and Paradox* (Oxford University Press, 1973); Berkeley,
Three Dialogues Between Hylas and Philonous, in his *Philosophical Works* (London: Dent, 1975),
ed. M. R. Ayers; J. F. Bennett, *Locke, Berkeley, Hume: Central Themes* (Oxford University
Press, 1971)

Ian Hacking

Leibniz and Descartes: Proof and Eternal Truths

It is sometimes said of Leibniz that his philosophy was formed as the modern world dawned, and that it brings together the past and the future of his century. There is more of the past in his metaphysics, a monadology according to which the reality behind the world's appearance consists in monads, these being sentient, active and indestructible entities without extension or shape, unconnected with one another but proceeding according to a pre-established harmony ordained by God. There is more of the future in his logic and mathematics, and his philosophical reflection on them. He is indeed said to have founded formal logic. More particularly, in the view of Ian Hacking, whose Dawes Hicks Lecture on Philosophy to the British Academy appears below, Leibniz had a grip on an idea that can be regarded as the very keel of rigorous inquiry of a certain kind since his time, the idea of a proof. It cannot be said that he originated it. There remains the fact, in Hacking's view, and as he begins by saying, that Leibniz knew what a proof is, and his predecessor Descartes, also a mathematician, did not. Also, if Leibniz was too much attached to proof, Descartes in effect rejected it.

Hacking's lecture is directed in part to establishing this distinction in knowledge and attitude of the two philosophers. It is also directed to the answering of a certain question. How did it come about that the conception of a proof emerged when it did? This had to do, he takes it, at least as much with history as with any man's invention. It had to do, in fact, with a certain malaise in seventeenth-century thought about scientific knowledge and its method. In seeking to establish the distinction and to answer the question, Hacking's concern is the history of philosophy and its explanation. It is to understand the philosophical

Gottfried Wilhelm Leibniz, 1646–1716. Born in Leipzig, worked in service of Archbishop of Mainz and then as librarian. The third of the Rationalists. Also a mathematician, he invented the differential calculus independently of Newton. Met Spinoza, died neglected.

207

past, and hence a concern different from those of many of the other contributors to this book. However, he is also moved by, and gives some expression to, a conjecture, which is that the preconditions of the emergence of a conception, such as that of a proof, fix what can be done with them, the subsequent possibilities in inquiry and argument. (pp. 211–13) This has relevance to our contemporary philosophy of mathematics. (pp. 222–3)

Leibniz took it, as we now do, that a proof in logic is a matter of *form*, not a matter of the subject-matter or content of particular propositions. Any proposition *p*, and any other proposition *q*, are such that if it is true that if *p* then *q*, and if it is the case that *p*, then *q* is true. Further, the proof of *q* begins with a proposition prior to if *p* then *q*, and *p*, which proposition is some version of the Law of Identity: *A* is *A*, or everything is what it is, or if something is true it is true. (p. 212) This conception of a proof, essentially our own today, was also correctly seen by Leibniz to involve the further ideas of a finite number of steps, and of a mechanical method of checking correctness, which gives a kind of guarantee of correctness. The idea of a proof was fundamental to a project to which he gave attention throughout his life, that of establishing a kind of universal, formal and indeed numerical language – the Universal Characteristic – in which all knowledge could be ordered and seen in its logical relations. (pp. 213–14, 221) The project of the Universal Characteristic, evidently, lies in the history of our contemporary logical systems.

There is a further view of proof to which Leibniz came. It is that a proof has, so to speak, a yet more fundamental role than that of establishing the truth of a proposition. A proof is essential to the full *understanding* of a proposition. (p. 214) One gets in a proof an analysis of the concepts out of which the proposition is constructed. A proof, it might be said, determines what a proposition *is*, as well as establishes its truth. A yet stronger view is also visible in Leibniz, that the truth of a proposition does not consist in correspondence to facts or objects, but in fact consists in its relation to other propositions, in effect in its having a proof based in the Law of Identity. The correspondence view, in mathematics, involves abstract or ideal objects and is the Platonism of which Hacking speaks. (p. 222) The Leibnizian view is closely related to modern doctrines on mathematics (Intuitionism, Constructivism and Formalism) which also make a close connection between the very ideas of proof and truth.

Descartes has a conception of the connection between truth and proof which is fundamentally different from that of Leibniz. Descartes, in

Hacking's estimate, took proof to be simply irrelevant to truth. Truth depends on a kind of intuition, on clearly and distinctly perceiving what is the case. It is a matter of the natural light of reason. A proof may help one to see the truth, but is inessential either to an understanding of the proposition proved or to its truth. A proof is close to what a later mathematician called 'gas', a rhetorical flourish aimed at stimulating all that matters, perception of a truth. (pp. 214–15) It is natural for Descartes, then, to have a certain attitude to the question of God's relation to the Eternal Truths. The latter are taken as the truths of arithmetic, algebra and geometry, and usually certain scientific laws. Eternal truths, for Descartes, are subject to God's will, and not independent of it. He could, if he had chosen, have made a five-sided square. Descartes's view of truth and God has consequences for the long-running controversy over whether Descartes's reasoning in a fundamental part of his philosophy is circular, of whether the premise used to establish an essential conclusion does itself already depend on that conclusion. (pp. 215–16)

After a consideration of Descartes's further views in connection with proof, Hacking offers his explanation of the emergence, in Leibniz, of the modern conception of a proof. It is an explanation having to do with seventeenth-century science, which is also pertinent to Descartes's contrary attitude to proof. The medieval conception of science, derived from Aristotle, was that of beginning with settled First Principles, above all Eternal Truths, and demonstrating that certain things follow. This view of science, although involving an ontology which took First Principles somehow to exist in reality, made it akin to the enterprise of giving a proof, in the modern sense. In the seventeenth century, however, science began to belie this picture of itself. (pp. 218–19) In place of First Principles and the like, there was speculation and hypothesis. Descartes himself exemplifies the change. The picture of science as a demonstrator of truth was belied by the practice of science and its new aim, in a way less grand, of making warranted predictions. Leibniz, like Descartes, responded to the unsettling 'evaporation of truth', the malaise troubling seventeenth-century reflection on human inquiry and knowledge. Leibniz saw that there could be a persistence with demonstration in a limited part of that inquiry and knowledge: the formal or non-empirical part. His response is conservative, the saving of what is of value by limiting its pretensions. In making this response he elaborated the idea of formal proof as we know it. (pp. 221–2) Descartes, by contrast, radically abandoned the ideal of demonstration, disconnecting truth from proof and the like.

(pp. 220–21) It was fundamentally reflection on the course of science, then, or a lesser awareness of it, that issued by way of Leibniz in our conception of proof. This is an explanation more fundamental than another mentioned earlier by Hacking, the algebraizing of geometry. (p. 213)

Hacking's speculation, which in the end issues in strong reflections on the sterility of contemporary philosophy of mathematics, is both audacious and persuasive. Its details, which do require an independent knowledge of the philosophy of mathematics and the like, do not obscure its main lines. It does indeed bring into a more precise focus the place of Leibniz as precursor, and rather more than precursor, of the future.

Ian Hacking

Leibniz and Descartes: Proof and Eternal Truths

Leibniz knew what a proof is. Descartes did not. Due attention to this fact helps resolve some elusive problems of interpretation. That is not my chief aim today. I am more interested in prehistory than history. Leibniz's concept of proof is almost the same as ours. It did not exist until about his time. How did it become possible? Descartes, according to Leibniz, furnished most of the technology required for the formation of this concept, yet deliberately shied away from anything like our concept of proof. I contend that Descartes, in his implicit rejection of our idea of proof, and Leibniz, in his excessive attachment to it, are both trying to meet a fundamental malaise in seventeenth-century epistemology. I speak of a malaise rather than a problem or difficulty, for it was not formulated and was perhaps not formulable. But although these unformulated preconditions for the concept of proof are forgotten and even arcane, many facts of the resulting theories of proof are familiar enough. Leibniz was sure that mathematical truth is constituted by proof while Descartes thought that truth conditions have nothing to do with demonstration. We recognize these competing doctrines in much modern philosophy of mathematics. The way in which the two historical figures enacted many of our more recent concerns has not gone unnoticed: Yvon Belaval deliberately begins his important book on Leibniz and Descartes with a long chapter called 'Intuitionisme et formalisme'.[1] There are plenty more parallels there for the drawing. I find this no coincidence, for I am afflicted by a conjecture, both unsubstantiated and unoriginal, that the 'space' of a philosophical problem is largely fixed by the conditions that made it possible. A problem is individuated only by using certain concepts, and the preconditions for the emergence of those concepts are almost

Ian Hacking, 'Leibniz and Descartes: Proof and Eternal Truths', Dawes Hicks Lecture on Philosophy to the British Academy, 1973. *Proceedings of the British Academy*, Volume LIX (1973). With the permission of the author and the British Academy.

embarrassingly determining of what can be done with them. Solutions, countersolutions, and dissolutions are worked out in a space whose properties are not recognized but whose dimensions are as secure as they are unknown. I realize that there is no good evidence for the existence of conceptual 'space' nor of 'preconditions' for central concepts. Nothing in what follows depends on succumbing to the conjecture that there are such things. The Dawes Hicks lecture is dedicated to history and I shall do history, but I do want to warn that my motive for doing so is the philosophy of mathematics and its prehistory.

In saying that Leibniz knew what a proof is, I mean that he anticipated in some detail the conception of proof that has become dominant in our century. He is commonly said to have founded symbolic logic. He occupies the first forty entries in Alonzo Church's definitive *Bibliography of Symbolic Logic*. I do not have that logical activity in mind. Most seventeenth-century wrestling with quantifiers, relations, combinatorics, and the syllogism seems clumsy or even unintelligible to the most sympathetic modern reader. In contrast Leibniz's ideas about proof sound just right.

A proof, thought Leibniz, is valid in virtue of its form, not its content. It is a sequence of sentences beginning with identities and proceeding by a finite number of steps of logic and rules of definitional substitution to the theorem proved.[2] He experimented with various rules of logic and sometimes changed his mind on which 'first truths' are admissible. He was not able to foresee the structure of the first order predicate logic. He unwittingly made one of our more beautiful theorems – the completeness of predicate logic – into a definition through his equivalence between provability and truth in all possible worlds. My claim for Leibniz is only that he knew what a proof was. He was not even good at writing down proofs that are formally correct, for by nature he was hasty, in contrast to Descartes who despised formalism and who is nearly always formally correct.

The Leibnizian understanding of proof did not much exist before his time. Yet so well did Leibniz understand proof that he could offer metamathematical demonstrations of consistency using the fact that a contradiction cannot be derived in any number of steps from premises of a given form.[3] He understood that a proof of a necessary proposition must be finite, and made an important part of his philosophy hinge on the difference between finite and infinite proofs. We owe to him the importance of the definition of necessity as reduction to contradiction, and the corresponding definition of possibility as freedom from contradiction, understood as the inability to prove a contradiction in finitely many steps. Proof is not only finite but computable, and the checking of proofs is called a kind of arithmetic. Leibniz even saw the importance of representing ideas and propositions by a recursive numbering scheme.[4] His invention of topology is motivated by a theory of the notation needed for valid proof.[5] He is not alone in any of these observations but he did have the gift of synthesizing and stating some of their interconnections. In asking how these ideas became possible it is immaterial whether they are the ideas of a single man. It suffices that they are novel and become widespread in the era of Leibniz, but it is convenient to have an Olympian figure who so perfectly epitomizes this new understanding.

Leibniz himself has a plausible explanation of why the concept of proof emerged at this time. Insight into the nature of proof is not to be expected when geometry is the standard of rigour. Geometrical demonstrations can appear to rely on their content. Their validity may seem to depend on facts about the very shapes under study, and whose actual construction is the aim of the traditional Euclidean theorems. A Cartesian break-through changed this. Descartes algebrized geometry. Algebra is specifically a matter of getting rid of some content. Hence in virtue of Descartes's discovery, geometrical proof can be conceived as purely formal. Leibniz thought that Descartes had stopped short, and did not see his way through to a completely general abstract Universal Characteristic in which proofs could be conducted,

and which renders truth stable, visible and irresistible, so to speak, as on a mechanical basis . . . Algebra, which we rightly hold in such esteem, is only a part of this general device. Yet algebra accomplished this much – that we cannot err even if we wish and that truth can be grasped as if pictured on paper with the aid of a machine. I have come to understand that everything of this kind which algebra proves is due only to a higher science, which I now usually call a *combinatorial characteristic*.[6]

'Nothing more effective,' Leibniz ventures to say, 'can well be conceived for the perfection of the human mind.' Insight becomes irrelevant to recognizing the validity of a proof, and truth has become 'mechanical'. Two trains of thought parallel this conception of proof. One has long been known: Leibniz's belief that there exists a proof, possibly infinite, for every truth. Sometimes readers have inferred that the Universal Characteristic was intended to settle every question whereas in fact Leibniz continues the letter quoted above saying that after the Characteristic is complete, 'men will return to the investigation of nature alone, which will never be completed'. The second train of thought concerns probability. Leibniz did often say that when the Characteristic is available disputes would be resolved by calculation. Sometimes these calculations would be *a priori* demonstrations but more usually they would work out the probability of various opinions relative to the available data. In surprisingly many details Leibniz's programme resembles the work of Rudolf Carnap on inductive logic.[7] I shall argue at the end of this lecture that the Leibnizian conceptions of proof and probability have intimately related origins. For the present I shall restrict discussion to proof.

Although the conception of proof and probability is partly familiar, there is a point at which most admirers of Leibniz stop:

> Every true proposition that is not identical or true in itself can be proved *a priori* with the help of axioms or propositions that are true in themselves and with the help of definitions or ideas.[8]

'Every' here includes all contingent truths. Moreover, Leibniz thought one does not fully understand a truth until one knows the *a priori* proofs. Since the 'analysis of concepts' required for proof of contingent propositions is 'not within our power', we cannot fully understand contingent truths. In these passages Leibniz is not giving vent to some sceptic's claim that only what is proven is reliable. Leibniz is no sceptic. He is not even an epistemologist. You need a proof to understand something because a proof actually constitutes the analysis of concepts which in turn determines the truth, 'or I know not what truth is'.[9] Moreover a proof gives the reason why something is true, and indeed is the cause of the truth. Truth, reason, cause, understanding, analysis, and proof are inextricably connected. It is part of my task to trace the origin of these connections. The connections are not automatic then or now. To illustrate this we need only take the contrasting doctrines of Descartes.

Leibniz thought that truth is constituted by proof. Descartes thought proof irrelevant to truth. This comes out nicely at the metaphorical level. Leibniz's God, in knowing a truth, knows the infinite analysis and thereby knows the proof. That is what true knowledge is. Leibniz's God recognizes proofs. Descartes's God is no prover. A proof might help a person see some truth, but only because people have poor intellectual vision. It used to be held that angels did not need to reason. Although commendably reticent about angels, Descartes has just such an attitude to reasoning. He is at one with the mathematician G. H. Hardy,

> Proofs are what Littlewood and I call gas, theoretical flourishes designed to affect psychology . . . devices to stimulate the imagination of pupils.[10]

Naturally Descartes says little about demonstration. Much of what he says is consistent with the doctrines advanced in the *Regulae*. Intuition and deduction are distinguished. Elementary truths of arithmetic can be intuited by almost anyone. Consequences may also be intuited. Deduction requires the intuition of initial propositions and consequential steps. The modern reader tends to equate intuition and deduction with axiom and theorem proved, but this is to see matters in a Leibnizian mould. The Cartesian distinction is chiefly psychological. One man might require deduction where another would intuit. In either case the end product is perception of truth. Some Cartesian scholars have recently debated whether the *cogito ergo sum* is inference or intuition or something else again.[11] Descartes does give varying accounts of this famous *ergo* but it is completely immaterial to him whether one man needs to infer where another intuits directly. The point of the *cogito*, as the *Discourse* informs us, is to display a truth one cannot doubt. Then one may inquire what, in this truth, liberates us from doubt. The intuition/inference/performative controversy is misguided because Descartes is indifferent to what sort of 'gas' induces clear and distinct perception. However you get there, when you see with clarity and distinctness you note that there is no other standard of truth than the natural light of reason. Leibniz, although granting some sense to 'what is called the natural light of reason',[12] inevitably observed that Descartes 'did not know the genuine source of truths nor the general analysis of concepts'.[13]

The Cartesian independence of truth from proof is illustrated by Descartes's unorthodox view on the eternal truths. These comprise the truths of arithmetic, algebra, and geometry, and usually extend to the laws of astronomy, mechanics, and optics. Contemporary authorities like Suarez taught that eternal truths are independent of the will of God. All the eternal verities are hypothetical. If there are any triangles, their interior angles must sum to two right angles. Since God is free to create or not to create triangles, this hypothetical necessity is no constraint on his power.[14] Descartes, although cautious in expressing opinions at odds with received doctrine, disagreed. The eternal truths depend upon the will of God, and God could have made squares with more or fewer than four sides. As we might express it, the eternal truths are necessary, but they are only contingently necessary.

Even if God has willed that some truths should be necessary, this does not

215

mean that he willed them necessarily, for it is one thing to will that they be necessary, and quite another to will them necessarily.[15]

I very much like the way that Émile Bréhier[16] uses this theory about eternal truth in order to explain away the Cartesian 'circle' alleged, in the first instance, by Arnauld. The circle goes like this: from the clarity and distinctness of the third meditation it follows that God exists, but clarity and distinctness can be counted on only if there is a good God. Many commentators interrupt this simple-minded circle by saying that God's veracity is not needed when we are actually perceiving truth with clarity and distinctness. God comes in only when we turn our minds to another thought. This leaves open the question of the role that God plays when we are thus distracted. There are several competing interpretations. André Gombay uses this comparison.[17] In moments of passionate love a man (such as the husband in Strindberg's play, *The Father*) cannot doubt his wife is faithful. But at more humdrum moments he doubts her love. What is his doubt? (*a*) His memory is playing tricks; the feeling of passionate certainty never occurred. (*b*) He remembers correctly his passionate conviction, but subsequently feels that he was misled by his passion. No matter how convinced he was then, he was wrongly convinced. (*c*) She was true to him at that passionate moment, but is no longer so. In the case of Cartesian doubt, recent commentators correctly rule out doubts of kind (*a*): God is no guarantor of memory. Gombay, probably rightly, favours (*b*). But doubt of kind (*c*) is instructive. Bréhier proposes that God is needed to ensure that an 'eternal truth', once perceived clearly and distinctly, *stays* true.

No set of texts tells conclusively for or against the Bréhier reading. This in itself shows how far Descartes separates proof from truth. What would happen to the proof of p if p, previously proven, went false? We can imagine that in the evolution of the cosmos Euclid's fifth postulate was true, relative to some assigned metric, and subsequently ceased to be true. At least this remains, we think: if a complete set of Euclidean axioms is true, the Pythagorean theorem is true too. That necessary connection between axiom and theorem cannot itself be contingent. Descartes disagreed. God is at liberty to create a Euclidean non-Pythagorean universe. We owe to Leibniz the clear statement that if not-p entails a contradiction then p is necessary and indeed necessarily necessary. Descartes grants that it is unintelligible how p can entail contradiction and still be true. But this unintelligibility shows the weakness of our minds. Leibniz caustically dismisses this view of modality.[18] It betrays, he thought, a lack of comprehension of the very concepts of necessity, contradiction, and proof.

Not only did Descartes acknowledge no dependence of necessary truth on proof; he also challenged accepted modes of presenting proof. He favoured 'analysis' rather than 'synthesis'. His doctrine is sufficiently hard to understand that Gerd Buchdahl distinguishes radically different Cartesian meanings for 'analysis',[19] but even if Descartes ought to have distinguished meanings of the word, he intended to be unequivocal. Synthesis is deduction, whose paradigm is Euclid. Deduction may bully a reader into agreement, but it does not teach how the theorem was discovered. Only analysis can do that. Descartes subscribed to the standard myth that the Greeks had a secret art of discovery.[20] The new algebraic geometry rediscovered it. He called it analytic geometry, as we still do. Its method is to:

suppose the solution already effected, and give names to all the lines that seem needful for the construction . . . then, making no distinction between known and unknown lines, we must unravel the difficulty in any way that shows most naturally the relations between these lines, until we find it possible to express a quantity in two ways.[21]

Then we solve the equation. Analysis is a mode of discovery of unknowns, and the arguments of the *Geometry* show how solutions can be obtained. Descartes thought that the physicist postulating causes on the basis of observed effects may be doing analysis, and he maintained that the *Meditations* furnish another example of analysis.

The Cartesian notion of analysis underwent strange transformations. The fact that Euclidean synthesis was deemed to depend on content as well as form is well illustrated by Descartes's own observations that in geometry the primary notions of synthetic proofs 'harmonize with our senses'. The point of all those 'minute subdivisions of propositions' is not even to ensure that the proof is sound. It is to render citation easy 'and thus make people recollect earlier stages of the argument even against their will'.[22] Synthetic proofs work partly because we have sensible representations of what we are proving and are thus unfit for metaphysics which uses abstract concepts. Yet by a strange inversion, it is Cartesian analysis that enables Leibniz to argue that proof is entirely a matter of form, and to apply this thought to deductive proof in general, including synthesis. Moreover, what he calls the analysis of concepts proceeds by what Descartes would have called synthetic demonstration!

Descartes wanted good ways to find out the truth and was indifferent to the logical status of his methods. This is well illustrated by yet another kind of 'analysis'. Traditionally science was supposed to proceed by demonstration of effects from causes stated in first principles. In practice the more successful scientists were increasingly guessing at causes on the basis of effects according to what we can now call 'the hypothetico-deductive method'. When challenged Descartes said that this too is a kind of 'demonstration', at least according to 'common usage', as opposed to the 'special meaning that philosophers give' to the word 'demonstration'. In reality, says Descartes, there are two kinds of demonstration, one from causes to effects, in which we prove the effect from the cause, and the other from effect to cause, in which we explain the effect by postulating a cause.[23]

There was a pressing practical problem for the second kind of so-called demonstration. As his correspondent put it, 'nothing is easier than to fit a cause to an effect'. To which Descartes replied that 'there are many effects to which it is easy to fit separate causes, but it is not always so easy to fit a single cause to many effects'. This thought was worked up by Leibniz into the theory of 'architectonic' reasoning.[24] We seek those hypotheses that would be attractive to the Architect of the World, who has a mania for maximizing the variety of phenomena governed by laws of nature, while minimizing the complexity of those selfsame laws.

On such questions of method there does not seem, in perspective, very much at issue between the two philosophers. But they have radically different theories of what they are finding out. Leibniz supposes that truths are constituted by proof, and so proof is essentially linked to truth, while Descartes imagines that truths exist independently of any proof. However, we shall not find the origin of this difference in what might be called the philosophy of mathematics, but in what we should now call the philosophy of science. The very success of scientific activity in the early seventeenth century had created a crisis in man's understanding of what he knows. In the medieval formulations, adapted from Aristotle, knowledge or science was arrived at by demonstration from first principles. It demonstrated effects from causes, and its propositions were universal in form and were necessarily true. In giving the causes, it gave the reasons for belief, and also the reasons why the proposition proved is true. As well as arithmetic and geometry, science included astronomy, mechanics, and optics. This did not mean that one was supposed to do all one's mechanics *a priori*, for it might need ample experience to grasp the first principles of the universe. Francis Bacon furnishes a good example of a thinker trying to preserve this old ontology, insisting that instead of being dogmatic, the scientist must survey large quantities of experiences before he ventures to guess at the axioms, common notions, and first principles. What one is aiming at, however, is a body of universal and necessary axioms which will, when recognized and understood, have the character of self-evidence.

Bacon's methodology is a despairing attempt to save the old theory of truth on its own ground. Increasingly men of science are not doing what they are supposed to be doing. Among what I shall call the high sciences, astronomy, mechanics, and optics, there is a dogmatic school maintaining the Aristotelian physics. It is shattered by new theories which do not merely contradict the old physics but do not even have the same kind of propositions that the old physics sought after. Moreover, among the low sciences, medicine and alchemy, whose practitioners are what Bacon scornfully called the empirics, there has developed a set of practices and concepts that are unintelligible on the old model of knowledge.

Descartes's curious assertions about 'false hypotheses' illustrate how far he has come from traditional views. He says at length in his *Principles*, and throughout his life to various correspondents, that the chief hypotheses of his physics are strictly false, and may be regarded as a kind of fable.[25] It is common to construe this as a safety net spread out after the Galilean scandal. Is it? Hypotheses serve as the basis for deducing true effects, but are not themselves to be asserted as true. Many ancient writers, including Archimedes, base their demonstrations on hypotheses that are strictly false, or so Descartes says. Perhaps he is merely seeking bedfellows in support of political caution. I see no reason to think so. Leibniz says that if they worked Descartes's 'false hypotheses' would be like cryptograms for solving the regularity of phenomena,[26] and he also says that Descartes is just wrong in changing the direction of physics to a search for false hypotheses. In short the Cartesian view was taken literally by the next generation of readers.

If Descartes means what he says everything has been turned upside down. Science was to make the world and its truths intelligible. From universal first principles concerning essence and cause and the true being of things one was to deduce the effects and their reasons, making intelligible the variety of general phenomena present to us. The first principles were to get at the very core of truth. But now the core evaporates, turns into a mere sham, a cryptogram of falsehoods. New merits have to be found for science, chief among them, in the seventeenth century, being the virtue of predictive power. In the traditional theory of truth, predictive power did not matter much because science was demonstrating necessities. When it abandons its ability to give reasons and causes by way of first principles, all it can do is provide us with predictions.

The evaporation of truth is what I have called the malaise or even the crisis in the early seventeenth century. We have been accustomed, especially in Britain, to notice the epistemological worries of the period. In fact men wrote treatises not of epistemology but of methodology. The methodology was an attempt to tell how to do what was in fact being done, and how to do it better. The Cartesian titles such as *Rules for direction of the mind*, or *Discourse on Method*, are characteristic of the time. Underneath these works runs not the problem of British empiricism-scepticism, 'How can I ever know?' It is rather, 'What is knowledge, what is truth, are there such things?'

Reconsider the situation of Descartes. We have usually read him as an ego, trapped in the world of ideas, trying to find out what corresponds to his ideas, and pondering questions of the form, 'How can I ever know?' Underneath his work lies a much deeper worry. Is there any truth at all, even in the domain of ideas? The eternal truths, he tells us, are 'perceptions . . . that have no existence outside of our thought'.[27] But in our thought they are, in a sense, isolated perceptions. They may be systematized by synthesis but this has nothing to do with their truth. The body of eternal truths which encompassed mathematics, neo-Aristotelian physics and perhaps all reality was a closely knit self-authenticating system of truth, linked by demonstration. For Descartes there are only perceptions which are ontologically unrelated to anything and moreover are not even candidates for having some truth outside my mind. One is led, I think, to a new kind of worry. I cannot doubt an eternal truth when I am contemplating it clearly and distinctly. But when I cease to contemplate, it is a question whether there is truth *or* falsehood in what I remember having perceived. Bréhier suggested that demonstrated propositions may go false. It seems to me that Cartesian propositions, rendered lone and isolated, are in an even worse state. Perhaps neither they nor their negations have any truth at all. They exist in the mind only as perceptions. Do they have any status at all when not perceived? When demonstration cannot unify and give 'substance' to these truths, the constancy of a veracious God who wills this truth suddenly assumes immense importance. We have long been familiar with the role of God as the willing agent that causes Berkeley's perceptions. We know Leibniz required the mind of

God as the arena in which the essences of possible worlds compete for existence, saying indeed that

neither the essences nor the so-called eternal truths about them are fictitious but exist in a certain region of ideas, if I may so call it, namely in God himself.[28]

I am suggesting that Descartes's veracious God is needed not just to guarantee our beliefs, but also to ensure that there is some truth to believe. I do not claim this as a worked out Cartesian thought but rather as an underlying response to the breakdown in the traditional conception of knowledge.

Descartes was almost ingenuously radical. Faced by the fact that the new science was not Aristotelian knowledge or *scientia*, he abolished the traditional concepts even where they did work, namely in arithmetic and geometry. Leibniz, in contrast, was ingeniously conservative. The merit of the old system was that it gave us some understanding of the nature and interconnection of truths. The demerit was the inadequacy of the implied methodology of doing physics by deduction. So Leibniz grafted a new methodology on to the old theory of demonstration. Demonstration was formerly the key to both ontology and method. Leibniz restricts it to the former. It is turned into the theory of formal proof. In the old tradition only universal propositions are subject to demonstration. In the new practice, only what we now call pure mathematics fits this model. But Leibniz, making proof a matter of ontology, not methodology, asserts that all true propositions have an *a priori* proof, although in general human beings cannot make those proofs. This is to resolve the open question as to the nature of truth. Hence his careful distinction between finite and infinite proofs, the importance of form over content, and all the rest of Leibniz's rendering truth 'mechanical'. The universal characteristic, you will recall, 'renders truth stable, visible, and irresistible, as on a mechanical basis'. The new science that was not *scientia* had made truth totally unstable. The concept of formal proof was intended to restore the balance.

The ingenuity of Leibniz's eclecticism shows itself in another direction. The Universal Characteristic, as I have said, was to be the vehicle of finite deductions and of probability calculations of inductive logic. Whereas demonstration is the tool of what was traditionally called knowledge, probability, in medieval times, pertained to a quite different realm, opinion. The low sciences of alchemy and medicine are the artisans of opinion and the forgers of probability – or so I argue at

Ian Hacking

length in my book, *The Emergence of Probability*. Those thoroughly alien hermetical figures of the Renaissance did more: they actually engendered a concept of inconclusive evidence derived from facts, as opposed to testimony. The high sciences related to experience in a hypothetico-deductive or one might say 'Popperian' way. That is, they concerned themselves with the deductive connections between experienced effects and conjectured causes. The low sciences were too inchoate for that, and created what, in recent times, has been called probability and induction. Leibniz puts the antique theory of demonstration into the realm of ontology. Finite demonstrations become the topic of mathematics, now rendered formal. Architectonic reasoning is his version of the hypothetico-deductive method. Inductive logic is the rationalization of what Bacon dismissed as mere empiricism. The vehicle for all these parts of methodology is the Universal Characteristic. It is a vehicle that cheerfully carries finite proofs and calculations of probability, and yet is a coarse and inadequate mirror of the very nature of truth, the infinite proof.

Carnap and Popper have recently re-enacted the tension between Leibniz's inductive logic and his architectonic reasoning. My topic today is proof, not probability. I claim that the concept of formal proof was created in the time of Leibniz to overcome quite specific breakdowns in traditional ontology. The Cartesian concept of anti-proof has the same origin. These concepts were devised, almost unwittingly, to fill a vacuum. We still employ those concepts but live in a vacuum that those concepts cannot fill. Consider the sterility of modern philosophy of mathematics – not the collection of mathematical disciplines now called the foundations of mathematics, but our conflicting theories of mathematical truth, mathematical knowledge, and mathematical objects. The most striking single feature of work on this subject in this century is that it is very largely banal. This is despite the ample fertilization from the great programmes and discoveries in the foundations of mathematics. The standard textbook presentations of 'Platonism', constructivism, logicism, finitism, and the like re-enact conceptual moves which were determined by an ancient and alien problem situation, the disintegration of the concept of *scientia* and the invention of the concept of evidence culminating in the new philosophy of the seventeenth century. We have forgotten those events, but they are responsible for the concepts in which we perform our pantomime philosophy.

Take, for example, the most seemingly novel, and also the most passionately disparate of contributions, Wittgenstein's *Remarks on the*

Foundations of Mathematics. He invites us to destroy our very speech, and abandon talk of mathematical truth and knowledge of mathematics and its objects. We are asked to try out language in which mathematics is not 'true', our discoveries are not 'knowledge' and the 'objects' are not objects. Despite this fantastic and perplexing attempt to get rid of all these inherited notions, Wittgenstein ends up with a dilemma that is essentially Leibniz–Cartesian. On the one hand he suggests, in quite the most radical way, that mathematical 'truth' is constituted by proof, and on the other he is obsessed by just the intuitions that so impressed Descartes. Hardly anyone thinks he has achieved a synthesis of these notions. There is a reason for this. He rejects that antique triptych, truth, knowledge, and objects, but works in the space created by that earlier period, and is driven to employ the concepts created then for the solution of quite other problems, and which are fettered by their need to solve those other problems. The 'flybottle' was shaped by prehistory, and only archaeology can display its shape.

Notes

1. *Leibniz critique de Descartes*, Paris, 1960.

2. This frequently occurring theme is expressed, for example, in the letter to Conring of 19 March 1678, *P*. I, 194. See also *P*. VII, 194 and *O*. 518. On the importance of form rather than content, see the letters to Tshirnhaus, e.g. May 1678, *M*. IV, 451. (*P*. = *Die Philosophischen Schriften von G. W. Leibniz*, ed. G. Gerhardt. *O*. = *Opuscules et fragments inédits de Leibniz*, ed. L. Couturat. *M*. = *Mathematische Schriften*, ed. G. Gerhardt.)

3. For example in notes written in November 1676, intended for discussion with Spinoza. *P*. VII, 261.

4. *Lingua Generalis*, February 1678, *O*. 277. Cf. L. Couturat, *La Logique de Leibniz*, Paris, 1901, ch. III.

5. To Huygens, 8 September 1679, *M*. II, 17; cf. *P*. V, 178.

6. To Oldenburg, 28 December 1675, *M*. I, 84.

7. For references see my 'The Leibniz–Carnap program for inductive logic', *Jl. Phil.* lxviii, 1971, 597.

8. *P*. VII, 300.

9. To Arnauld, 14 July(?) 1686, *P*. II, 56.

10. 'Mathematical Proof', *Mind*, xxviii, 1928, 18.

11. For example, H. G. Frankfurt, 'Descartes' discussion of his existence in the second meditation', *Phil. Rev.* 1966, 333. A. Kenny, *Descartes*, New York, ch. 3. Jaako Hintikka, '*Cogito ergo sum*, inference or performance?', *Phil. Rev.* lxxi, 1962, 3–32. I agree with André Gombay, from whom I have much profited in conversation about Descartes. '*Cogito ergo sum*, inference or argument?' in *Cartesian Studies*, ed. R. J. Butler, Oxford, 1972.

12. To Sophia Charlotte, 1702, *P*. VI, 501.

13. To Philip, December 1679, *P*. IV, 282.

14. F. Suarez, *Disputationes Metaphysicae*, 1597. Cf. T. J. Cronin, *Objective Being in Descartes and in Suarez*, Analecta Gregoriana 154, Rome, 1966.

223

15. To Mesland, 2 May 1644. Other texts on eternal truths are as follows. To Mersenne, 6 May and 27 May 1630 and 27 May 1638. Reply to *Objections* V and VI. *Principles* xlviii–xlix.

16. 'La création des vérités éternelles', *Rev. Phil.* cxxiii, 1937, 15.

17. 'Counter privacy and the evil genius', read to the Moral Sciences Club, 30 May 1973.

18. *Monadology*, § 46.

19. *Metaphysics and the Philosophy of Science*, Oxford, 1969, ch. 3.

20. At the end of the reply to the second set of *Objections*.

21. From the beginning of the *Geometry*.

22. op. cit., n. 2.

23. To Morin, 13 July 1638.

24. *Tentamentum Anagogicum*, 1696, *P.* VII, 270.

25. *Principles*, xliii–xlvii, and, e.g., To Mesland, May 1645.

26. To Conring, 19 March 1678, *P.* I, 194.

27. *Principles*, I. xlviii.

28. 'On the radical origination of things', 23 November 1697, *P.* VII, 305.

Biographical Note

Ian Hacking was born in 1936 in Vancouver, Canada. He studied mathematics and physics at the University of British Columbia, and philosophy at Cambridge University. He has taught at British Columbia, Makerere University, Uganda, Cambridge and Stanford University, where he was Henry Waldgrave Stuart Professor of Philosophy. He is now at the Institute for the History and Philosophy of Science and Technology, University of Toronto. His books include *Logic of Statistical Inference* (1965), *The Emergence of Probability* (1975), *Why Does Language Matter to Philosophy?* (1975), and *Representing and Intervening* (1983).

Further Reading

Other interpretations of Descartes on eternal truths: E. Bréhier, 'The Creation of Eternal Truths in Descartes' System', in *Descartes*, ed. W. Doney (New York: Doubleday, 1967); H. Frankfurt, 'Descartes on the Creation of Eternal Truths', *The Philosophical Review* 86 (1977); J. Etchemendy, 'The Cartesian Circle', *Studia Cartesiana* 2 (1982).

The best overview of Leibniz's work is found in L. Loemker, *Leibniz's Philosophical Papers and Letters* (Dordrecht, 1970).

The following three anthologies contain important articles and bibliography: H. Frankfurt, ed., *Leibniz* (New York: Anchor Books, 1972); R. S. Woolhouse, *Leibniz, Metaphysics and Philosophy of Science* (Oxford University Press, 1981); M. Hooker, ed., *Leibniz* (Baltimore, Md: Johns Hopkins University Press, 1982).

Other articles by Ian Hacking on Leibniz: 'Substance' in H. Frankfurt (ed.), op. cit.; 'A Leibnizian Theory of Truth', in M. Hooker (ed.), op. cit.; 'Infinite Analysis', *Studia Leibnitiana* 6 (1974); 'A Leibnizian Space', *Dialogue* 14 (1975); 'The Identity of Indiscernibles', *Journal of Philosophy* 72 (1975).

M. R. Ayers

Berkeley: His Immaterialism and Kant's Transcendental Idealism

Berkeley's place in the history of philosophy is due, above all, to the measure of success he had in an unlikely enterprise, that of arguing against the existence of matter, as ordinarily understood. *Esse est percipi*, to be is to be perceived. Material objects exist only through being perceived. What we have experience of, beyond ourselves, is no more than 'ideas', these being subjective, fleeting things akin to what philosophical descendants of Berkeley, hardly any so audacious as he, have often called sense-data. However, this view does not reduce all of our conscious experience to a level. On the contrary, the view of the sensible world as importantly mind-dependent is taken to enable us to assert a certain distinction between appearance and reality. We can defeat a scepticism which denies this distinction, and reduces all to illusion. The real, as distinct from the illusory, consists in those of our ideas, which if they are owed to us, are also owed to God's causing them in us in conformity with laws of nature. Berkeley's arguments for his immaterialism, as he himself called it, are of several kinds, but have generally been taken to have relatively little to do with the question of the nature of space. That is the question, at bottom, of whether space is to be regarded as wholly independent of the things in it. Can it be conceived in an absolute way, without any reference whatever to things in it, or is its conception somehow dependent on them?

Kant's place in the history of philosophy is owed in part to a ramified doctrine which appears to be in a way similar to Berkeley's. Our experience of things is, so to speak, largely our doing. Again, as with Berkeley, things are to an important extent mind-dependent. Space and time are 'in us', imposed by us. So too are what we ordinarily take to

George Berkeley, 1685–1753. Born in Kilkenny of an English family, educated partly at Trinity College, Dublin, became Fellow of Trinity and Bishop of Cloyne. Second of the British Empiricists. Spent several years in Newport, Rhode Island, hopeful of funds from the British government to establish a missionary college.

M. R. Ayers

be other fundamental properties and relations of things. Kant does allow the existence of something outside our self-organized experience, noumena as against phenomena, but denies we can have any knowledge of it. However, it follows from his doctrine, transcendental idealism, that our conscious experience is not all on a level. We can distinguish, in it, between appearance and reality. Reality, unlike illusion, is a matter of location in space and time, and being subject to natural law. There is no need to succumb to a scepticism which allows that all might be illusion.

The parallelism between Berkeley and Kant, as even so adventurously brisk a summary indicates, is not complete, but it does evidently exist. It leads to the idea that Berkeley influenced Kant significantly. However, Kant himself took pains to deny or at any rate to minimize the parallelism, and he does so in terms which have led some to suppose that he was only dimly aware of the content of Berkeley's philosophy. In particular, he accused Berkeley of degrading all that exists for us, without differentiation, to 'merely imaginary entities'. The 'British Empiricist' is assigned the belief that 'all knowledge through the senses and through experience is nothing but illusion, and only in the ideas of pure understanding and reason is truth'. Furthermore, Kant appears to take Berkeley as having relied exclusively, in his argument for his immaterialism, on a denial that any sense can be made of space as absolute.

Michael Ayers, in the paper reprinted here, is concerned to offer a limited defence of Kant. This he does by extending and elaborating an argument, begun by others, that there is good reason for Kant's declaration of difference between his own philosophy and that of his predecessor. Further, it is at least possible to understand reasons or possible reasons for Kant's assigning to Berkeley the argument beginning from a rejection of absolute space. However, if Ayers is concerned to deal with the worth of Kant's view of Berkeley, it is perhaps true to say that that concern is a means to a further end: the better understanding of each of Berkeley and Kant. It is his conviction that the greatest value to us of the work of the great philosophers depends on a kind of historical approach. They are to be considered in their contexts, and in their own terms. It is not too much to say, perhaps, that the greatest value to us of the great philosophers is to be secured by following the history of philosophy in a close and comparative way. It is then to be expected that profit from Berkeley, or from Kant, is to be got not by an independent consideration of either, but by considering both together, and along, not only with such others as Descartes, but with philosophers now regarded as minor figures. This method, which takes philosophical thinking about past masters closer to scholarship than certain other methods, has distinctive virtues, and vigorous defenders of them. It is fair to say, I think, that it is a method which presents a greater challenge to those readers who are less familiar with the great philosophers. They are not brought out of their time. It is more necessary in the case of the following excerpt, as against most of the others in this book, to have some direct acquaintance with the philosophers themselves, and to some extent with subsequent reflection on them.

In Section 2 of his paper, Ayers supports the contention that Kant is not guilty of oversight or blunder in not concerning himself with Berkeley's distinction between appearance and reality. Rather, Kant takes it that the premises of Berkeley's argument, although Berkeley mistakenly thinks otherwise, do commit him inevitably to the conclusion that all is illusion. The argument assigned to Berkeley is roughly that a conception of space as absolute is a necessary condition of there being material objects, which *are* conceived as spatial in this way, but that such a conception of space is absurd, for various reasons, and hence there are no material objects – all our experience is illusory. There is some reason for assigning this argument to Berkeley, who did indeed disdain absolute space, involving as it does the idea that there can be an idea of all of space as wholly empty. Also, despite his appearance–reality distinction, Berkeley in all his works does characterize all of what we experience as no more than 'inert, fleeting, dependent' ideas. Still, there remains a secondary puzzle about Kant's characterization both of Berkeley and of other thinkers. (pp. 233–4) It is closely considered in the remainder of Section 2.

A principal contention of the following section is that Kant's strenuous distinction between himself and Berkeley is also owed to the fact that he unlike Berkeley does allow the existence of something other than God outside of our experience. There is 'transcendental otherness', noumena, however preserved from our knowledge. Kant's appearances are appearances *of* something. (This part of his doctrine is in some analogy with Locke's idea that while colours, say, are in our minds and not in objects, our colour vision is none the less of something.) Kant links this intrinsic intentionality of sensory awareness to its being, for us, awareness of things in space. There is no counterpart to these features of transcendental idealism in Berkeley's immaterialism, and this does make a significant distinction between the two theories.

Section 4 provides further understanding of Kant's insistence that a denial of absolute space is fundamental or important to Berkeley's doctrine. This has to do with what is taken as entering into the view of space as absolute, which is that it is *infinitely* divisible, and that the motion of a thing is not relative to other objects, but is absolute. Ayers proposes that Kant is not wrong to locate Berkeley firmly among those philosophers, Zeno, Malebranche, Bayle and others, for whom the famous paradoxes of infinite divisibility were important sceptical tools. He seeks to show that a central Berkeleyan argument, which is commonly supposed to rely entirely upon an analogy between primary and secondary qualities, in fact presupposed in Berkeley's mind the infinite divisibility of space. So a further important difference between Berkeley and Kant consists in their quite different responses to the paradoxes of infinite divisibility.

Section 5, having to do with time rather than space, is concerned both with Kant's famous 'Refutation of Idealism' (and its possible origins in Locke and Leibniz) and with Berkeley's extremely subjectivist view of time. By showing that the latter gives some justification to Kant's charge that Berkeley 'degrades bodies to mere illusion', Ayers concludes a distinctive inquiry not only into the relation between two philosophers, but into the nature, strength and uniqueness of the work of each.

M. R. Ayers

Berkeley: His Immaterialism and Kant's Transcendental Idealism

1. Introduction

Ever since its first publication critics of Kant's *Critique of Pure Reason* have been struck by certain strong formal resemblances between transcendental idealism and Berkeley's immaterialism. Both philosophers hold that the sensible world is mind-dependent, and that from this very mind-dependence we can draw a refutation of scepticism of the senses.

According to Berkeley, the scepticism which makes philosophy ridiculous 'vanishes if we annex a meaning to our words, and do not amuse ourselves with the terms *absolute*, *external*, *exist* and such like . . . . I can as well doubt of my own being, as of the being of those things which I actually perceive by sense'.[1] Ideas of sense constitute 'real things': i.e. ideas caused in us by God in conformity with the principles or rules which we call the laws of nature. It is their evident external causal origin, their givenness, together with their regular association with other ideas in the order of nature, which constitute the criteria by which 'real' or 'external' things are to be distinguished from 'chimeras and illusions on the fancy'.[2]

According to Kant's Fourth Paralogism, which appeared only in the First Edition of the *Critique*, since space as the form of outer sense is 'in us', what is given in space by the senses is in us too, but it nevertheless constitutes physical reality. It can be distinguished from mere illusion because a condition of determinate location in space and time is conformity with law, so that we can employ as our criterion of reality the rule, 'Whatever is connected with a perception according to empirical laws is actual.'[3]

Both Berkeley and Kant distinguish two senses of 'external'. For Berkeley, the word may mean 'absolutely independent of mind', in

M. R. Ayers, 'Berkeley's Immaterialism and Kant's Transcendental Idealism', from *Idealism Past and Present*, Royal Institute of Philosophy Lectures, Series 13, 1981, edited by Godfrey Vesey. Reprinted by permission of author and editor.

which sense there are no external physical objects; or it may simply mean 'externally caused' or causally independent of us, like ideas of sense.[4] He attributes the error in the ordinary man's view of physical reality to the assumption that what is external in the second sense is external in the first.[5] Similarly for Kant, 'external' may denote, first, 'that which as thing in itself exists apart from us', in which transcendental sense 'external' objects are entirely unknown; or it may denote 'things which are to be found in space', in which empirical sense 'external' objects are indubitably experienced. The 'transcendental realist' opens the door to scepticism by assuming that what is external in the second sense is also external in the first: i.e. that objects in space are thereby independent of mind.[6] Scepticism of the senses Kant calls 'empirical idealism', to which the antidote is a combination of 'transcendental idealism' (i.e. recognition of mind-dependence) with 'empirical realism' (i.e. employment of determinate existence in space under law as the criterion of reality). Despite differences in their arguments, these and other parallels make it natural to suppose that Berkeley had a not insignificant influence on Kant's thought.

Kant's own later efforts to distinguish his theory from Berkeley's, however, have convinced many readers that there was not in fact any such influence. Paradoxically, that is not because of his success in clarifying the difference between them, but because of his supposed abysmal failure. The Second Edition of the *Critique* and the *Prolegomena to Any Future Metaphysics* contain such seemingly inept characterizations of immaterialism that generations of commentators have held that their author could not have read Berkeley's main works, a conclusion which has been supported by the claim that neither the *Principles* nor the *Three Dialogues Between Hylas and Philonous* was available in German translation until after the First Edition of the *Critique*.

This traditional view of the relationship between the two philosophers has been challenged by contributors to a discussion initiated some years ago by Colin Turbayne.[7] Turbayne points out that (as well as *Siris*) *De Motu* and Eschenbach's translation of the *Three Dialogues* were readily available while Kant formulated his own theory. He further argues that Kant's criticism can all be read as intelligible attempts to bring out genuine differences from Berkeley, provided that we take them to be founded, not so much on explicit doctrines, as on what Kant sees as the inevitable consequences of explicit doctrines. For Kant, Berkeley *in effect* believes these things. But in Turbayne's view Kant's main argument against scepticism of the senses, the argument which explains the term 'transcendental idealism', is not importantly different from Berkeley's. He believes that from all Kant's criticisms only minor or else irrelevant differences emerge, the significance of which Kant disingenuously exaggerates in a disreputable perversion of Berkeley's doctrines. Other commentators, however (in particular Gale Justin and Henry Allison[8]), have since argued persuasively that Kant does locate a fundamental line of distinction between himself and Berkeley. At the same time it seems in general to be agreed that Kant's criticisms do distort their object. In this paper I want to support and extend Allison's general position, but I also want to look again at the question of distortion. Since in the first part of my paper points which others have made and the additional points and modifications which I should like to make myself are sometimes rather entwined, I shall not spend time surveying previous arguments in detail. In the second part of the paper I shall be more on my own.

2. Absolute Space and Reality

Let us start with two notorious passages in the Second Edition of the *Critique*. First, in the Transcendental Aesthetic,[9] Kant claims that, if we ascribe objective reality to the forms of outer and inner sense, then the world of experience is 'transformed into mere illusion'.

For if we regard space and time as properties which, if they are to be possible at all, are to be found in things in themselves, and if we reflect on the absurdities in which we are then involved, in that two infinite things, which are not substances, nor anything actually inhering in substances, must yet have existence, nay, must be the necessary condition of the existence of all things, and moreover must continue to exist, even although all existing things be removed – we cannot blame the good Berkeley for degrading bodies to mere illusion.

Secondly, in the preamble to the Refutation of Idealism,[10] Kant distinguishes two forms of 'material' (i.e. empirical) idealism. The material idealist

declares the existence of objects in space outside us either to be merely doubtful and indemonstrable or to be false and impossible. The former is the *problematic* idealism of Descartes, which holds that there is only one empirical assertion that is indubitably certain, namely, that 'I am'. The latter is the *dogmatic* idealism of Berkeley. He maintains that space, with all the things of which it is the inseparable condition, is something which is in itself impossible; and he therefore regards the things in space as merely imaginary entities. Dogmatic idealism is unavoidable, if space be interpreted as a property that must belong to things in themselves. For in that case space, and everything to which it serves as condition, is a non-entity.

All this may seem clear enough evidence of distortion on Kant's part, whether deliberate or unwitting. Both passages suggest that Berkeley treats all objects of the senses as illusions, ignoring his distinction between illusion and reality. Together they imply that one of Berkeley's arguments is of the form: 'Absolute space is a condition of the existence of bodies. Absolute space is an absurdity. Therefore bodies do not exist.' It is true that Berkeley does attack absolute space, in the form in which it is maintained by Newton, in the *Principles*, in *De Motu*, in *Siris* and, briefly and directly, in the *First Dialogue*. But no modern reader of all these works would naturally suppose that this attack constitutes the chief ground of his rejection of independently existing bodies.

How then might Kant's account of Berkeley be justified or excused or even understood in other terms than ignorance or dishonesty? The chief lines of the argument which emerges from recent discussion are as follows. First, Kant may have known of Berkeley's reality/illusion distinction but refused to be put off by it. It is for him a mere sop provided by someone who does not grasp that the only explanation which can do justice to the empirical reality of bodies is in terms of their determinate existence in space and time. Thus Kant regarded critics who assimilated him to Berkeley as having utterly failed to grasp the logic of his own account of the concept of empirical reality. Secondly, it is said that Kant's one-sided reading of Berkeley, supposing that he approached him through *De Motu* and *Siris*, would have made the attack on space seem more important to the critique of matter than it is.

In support of this second point it might be mentioned that in one passage in *Siris* Berkeley hints at just the kind of argument which Kant ascribes to him: 'From the notion of absolute space springs that of absolute motion; and in these are ultimately founded the notions of external existence, independence, necessity and fate.'[11] Berkeley has just cited Plotinus with approval as 'affirming that the soul is not in the world, but the world in the soul'. He thus seems to be suggesting that the belief in mind-independent bodies arises because people think of space rather than mind as the receptacle or container of bodies. In his earlier works, however, he ascribes belief in the mind-independence of ideas of sense to their involuntariness. The rival to the soul as that in which sensible objects exist is there not space but material substance, which is postulated by those who see that sensible qualities need a support but who do not grasp that what 'supports and contains' the entire sensible world is perceiving spirit.[12] So although the diagnosis of our mistake which is proposed in *Siris* is in one way typical of Berkeley, in another way it does not seem to fit in with his earlier arguments at all well. To attribute the *general* belief in mind-independence to the *philosophical* doctrine of absolute space is, moreover, a bit odd. One might speculate that in *Siris* Berkeley was less interested in explaining that ordinary belief than in expressing his increasing conviction that Newtonian metaphysics represented the chief philosophical impediment to the acceptance of immaterialism.

It seems very possible that, after the criticism of the first edition of the *Critique*, Kant searched through translations of Berkeley for evidence of his misapprehension of the connection between the concepts of space and of empirical reality, hitting upon this passage from *Siris* as peculiarly revealing. One reason for thinking so lies in the apparent origin of another notorious characterization of Berkeley, that well-known 'British Empiricist', as driven by the principle that 'all knowledge through the senses and through experience is nothing but illusion, and only in the ideas of pure understanding and reason is truth'.[13] For this passage seems to be nothing but a mildly tendentious paraphrase of *Siris*, 264 (cf. 253 and 303 f.). Berkeley's editor, T. E. Jessop, seems quite right to argue that all such denigration of the senses in *Siris* is entirely compatible with the arguments of the earlier works.[14] In all the works, after all, the objects of the senses are characterized as 'inert, fleeting, dependent beings'. In *Siris* he makes the point that the senses are incapable of carrying us beyond such low-grade objects to the principles of science, which call for a rational 'discursive faculty', or to the independent, permanent, substantial realities, spirit in general and God, which are grasped by pure intellect.[15] It is just this Platonic conception of pure intellect penetrating beyond the sensible to the immaterial and ultimately real which Kant rightly opposes to his own principles. But the present point is that Kant takes his characterizations of Berkeley from Berkeley's mature reflections upon his own theory. It is difficult to see how they could prove ignorance of that theory.

That having been said, both Kant's diagnostic characterization of dogmatic idealism in the Second Edition of the *Critique* and its possible original in *Siris* have a rather puzzling feature. For they seem to imply that transcendental realists, as such, believe in absolute space, in some strong sense of 'absolute', as an independent entity. Yet, as both Kant and Berkeley would very well know, some transcendental realists, such as Aristotle and Descartes himself, approached space in a reductionist spirit, explaining it as no more than an attribute of bodies in some way abstractly considered. For Descartes, 'the same extension which constitutes the nature of body likewise constitutes the nature of space'.[16] Body and the space it occupies are logically distinguishable as species from genus, but are not ontologically distinct. Consequently the notion of a vacuum is a contradiction. Movement, i.e. change of place, is defined relatively to surrounding bodies. The rival doctrine of absolute space as an entity achieved respectability as a consequence of powerful anti-Cartesian arguments. Hobbes did not go all the way in this respect. He poured scorn on the 'childish' *a priori* arguments against a vacuum, and argued that there is no difficulty in a conception of space empty of all bodies. Such a conception is an abstraction from our experiential conception of body: it is 'the phantasm of a thing existing without the mind simply',[17] equivalent to the idea of the *possibility* of external body. But it is distinct from the idea of body, and is required in order that body 'may be understood by reason, as well as perceived by sense'.[18] It enters into the definition of motion, for example, which is not merely relative. Yet Hobbes carefully emphasizes that space is not a thing, but is simply nothing. There is an empty space between two bodies precisely when there is nothing between two bodies which do not meet. Others, however, like Gassendi and Henry More, went much further in their rejection of the reductionist view. What can be computed cannot be nothing. Gassendi produces the principle that space and time are neither substance nor accident: consequently 'all being is substance or accident or place in which all substances and all accidents exist, or time, in which all substances and all accidents endure'.[19] He simply swallows the traditional objection that to treat space as real is to allow something other than God which is uncreated and infinite. The Cambridge Platonist, Henry More, avoids that problem by identifying space with the immensity of God, quoting what was to become Berkeley's favourite text, 'in whom we live, move and have our being'. He calls space a logical rather than physical entity, a necessary condition of existence of every particular thing whatsoever, body or spirit. Its necessity is an aspect of the necessity of God to the existence of finite beings.[20] Newton was writing in this tradition when he distinguished between sensible or relative space on the one hand, and real or absolute space on the other,[21] a distinction present in a slightly different form in Locke's *Essay Concerning Human Understanding*[22] and explicitly attacked by Berkeley.[23] Newton also supplied some famous physical arguments for accepting absolute motion (i.e. that absolute space has effects) as well as the suggestion in the *Optics* that space is, as it were, the sensorium of God.[24]

The difficulty, then, is this. Descartes certainly held that space and time, if they exist at all, are properties of things in themselves. But he did not accept the 'absurdities' in which, according to Kant, such a belief is involved. For these absurdities are simply explicit elements of *anti*-Cartesian doctrines. The only coherent interpretation of Kant's argument seems to be this: 'Transcendental realism implies the doctrine of absolute space as an independent entity, even if this is not understood by all transcendental realists. It makes dogmatic idealism unavoidable for them logically, even if not psychologically.' The relation between Descartes and Berkeley would accordingly appear like this: 'Berkeley recognizes certain features of our conception of space which make it inappropriate to things in themselves, but Descartes fails to recognize these particular features. Consequently Descartes sees nothing objectionable in our conception of space – he simply does not analyse it accurately. *Qua* problematic idealist, however, he raises the question whether anything external corresponds to our conception. But Berkeley rejects our very conception of space, and with it our conception of empirical reality: i.e. he reduces all sensory representation to illusion.'

3. The Criteria of Reality in Berkeley and Kant

If this interpretation is right, then it must presumably have seemed irrelevant to Kant that Berkeley cobbled up his own accounts of space on the one hand and of reality on the other, arguing that they do justice to what matters in our ordinary conceptions. But the question remains why Kant should have taken such a dismissive line, rather than more sympathetically treating Berkeley as a transcendental idealist who has been driven into a wrong analysis of our ordinary, mind-dependent conception of space by a failure to see that mind-dependence explains and makes innocuous the otherwise 'absurd' attributes of absolute space. It can only be this question, if anything, which keeps alive accusations of dishonesty and lack of generosity on Kant's part.

Perhaps what makes the difference for Kant is that, unlike Descartes, Berkeley explicitly attacks the right, logically inescapable conception of space *at all points*, as the conception of an impossible object. For, as others have remarked, the properties mentioned in his direct criticisms of Berkeley are not the only properties of space which for Kant are inescapable but which Berkeley refuses to swallow. There are also its being the common object of the senses, its being infinitely divisible, and its being *a priori*, a property manifested in the possibility of the *a priori* science of geometry. All these properties are, of course, recognized, and swallowed, by Descartes. For Berkeley, on the other hand,

experience can have no criteria of truth because its phenomena (according to him) have nothing *a priori* at their foundation, whence it follows that experience is nothing but sheer illusion; whereas with us, space and time (in conjunction with the pure concepts of the understanding) prescribe their law to all possible experience *a priori* and, at the same time, afford the certain criterion for distinguishing truth from illusion therein.[25]

Kant's claim that he is sharply distinguished from Berkeley by his ability to derive the criteria of reality *a priori* (first from the conditions of objective existence in space and time and ultimately from the necessary unity of apperception) has been well discussed by others, and I do not have much to add. I should, however, like to give further emphasis to the point that Kant's explanation of the paradoxical properties of space, like his explanation of reality, essentially involves transcendental otherness. Space is the way things in themselves impinge on us. Empirical externality is the mode of representation of transcendental externality. To take just one example, the paradox of the purely relational difference between isomorphic incongruent figures is explained as follows: 'There is no intrinsic difference between such figures, only a relational one. The understanding assures us that there cannot be things which differ only relationally, but this "can well be the case with mere appearances".'[26] Kant does not mean that there can be entities comparable to Berkeley's ideas which differ only relationally: he means that an absolute difference may *appear* as a merely relative difference. That is the proof that spatiality, which allows such merely relational differences, is a form of appearance. Kant's appearances are therefore, as he continually says, necessarily appearances *of* something, whereas Berkeley's ideas have no such intrinsic intentionality.

This point may seem at odds with the most 'Berkeleyan' passages, such as the Fourth Paralogism, in which Kant seems to make a sharp separation between transcendental object and empirical object, as if we could concern ourselves with the existence of the latter without any reference at all to the former. But Kant is struggling with a notably difficult area in the topic of intentionality, as we may remind ourselves if we make the comparison ('altogether insufficient' as he says it is) with secondary qualities such as colours. If what typically causes the sensation of blue is (say) a certain micro-texture of the surface of objects, is it or is it not the case that we can perceive that surface micro-texture? In a way we can, since we see it as blue. Yet in a way we cannot see it at all, and it does not appear to the closest inspection. In a way blue is the appearance on the one hand, distinct from surface micro-texture, the reality, on the other. Yet in a way the blueness of an object just *is* a certain surface structure as it appears to sight. Locke had this trouble with secondary qualities, and Kant accordingly has it with bodies. Just as Locke is led to suggest that 'blue' has two meanings, for appearance and for reality, so Kant is led to talk as if he were giving 'body' two meanings in the same breath:

> I do indeed admit that there are bodies outside us, i.e. things which, although wholly unknown to us as to what they may be in themselves, we know through the representations which their influence on our sensibility provides for us, and to which we give the name of bodies. This word therefore means the appearance of that for us unknown but none the less real object.[27]

Thus despite the famous dictum about sensations without concepts,[28] Kant's sensory ideas or representations essentially contain something which points beyond themselves: they are not wholly 'blind' effects. Their spatiality is what makes them intrinsically *capable* of truth and falsity. The concepts of the understanding come into play at the stage of distinguishing *between* truth and falsity. Testing for illusion is testing empirically, which of course means causally, that a part of space is for a time filled in such and such a way.

This admirable, profound connection of the intentionality of our sensations with their being sensations of things in space was not without antecedents. Hobbes, as we have seen, held that to form the idea of pure space just is to focus on the perceived externality or otherness of things. Very possibly it was Hobbes's view which stimulated Berkeley's concern to deny that distance from the perceiver, or 'outness', is immediately perceived. The perception of distance is explained by Berkeley as a hypothetical judgement about future sensations based on a regular association between ideas of the same or different senses in the past.[29] There is no other sort of 'outness' than that. Spatial externality thus does have a certain, rather accidental connection with his criteria of reality, but only because of the role of constant conjunction between ideas in his account of both. The sole theoretical basis for the connection is the notion of a divine language through which God forewarns us of the future course of experience.

It may help us to understand why space and reality should be so disconnected in Berkeley's system if we remember the influence on him in particular of Locke's theory of perception. Locke holds that we have immediate sensory knowledge of the *existence* of external objects, but strictly limited sensory knowledge of their *nature*. In what he calls 'actual sensation' we are immediately aware that 'exterior causes' are acting on us through the senses, but in this 'sensitive knowledge' we conceive of such causes or powers purely through their effects.[30] Locke does of course believe that the external powers to cause sensory ideas belong to bodies in space. He holds that ideas of space 'resemble' their causes, and distinguishes primary from secondary qualities in this respect. Yet he treats such beliefs as subsequent hypotheses or reasonable physical speculations not included in immediate perceptual knowledge itself. His general theory of representation is purely causal: simple ideas represent in thought their regular causes.[31] Such a theory treats sensations as blank data rather than as intrinsically intentional states. More accurately, it treats sensations as if the sole respect in which they are intrinsically intentional is causal. External objects are presented in sensation solely as the possessors of powers to cause sensory effects. Hence Berkeley can claim that those powers might as well belong to a spirit, indeed that that is the only intelligible hypothesis.[32] But Locke's theory of perception is inadequate. For all sensation is, as such, sensation of things in space, whether of things distant from the body, in contact with the body or, as in the case of pain and other bodily sensations, within the body itself. Unless 'external objects' were presented in sensation not only as causes of sensations but as objects in space, no particular object could possibly be identified as the single possessor of a number of experienced qualities, or the cause of a number of sensations. The philosophical issue is obviously too large for the present context, but the necessary connection between the spatiality and the intentionality of sensation is one of the things which Kant offers to explain by the doctrine that space is the form of outer sense, but which goes unrecognized by Berkeley.

4. Infinite Divisibility in Berkeley and Kant

Kant, then, represents Berkeley as primarily a critic of objective space who thereby deprives himself of the material for a conception of objective reality. Obsessed with space in his destructive arguments, Kant's Berkeley unduly neglects it in his botched-up account of 'real things'. Is the first part of such a characterization as inept as it might, *prima facie*, seem? I shall argue that it in fact places Berkeley, not at all inappositely, within a tradition to which arguments about space were indeed of central importance, the tradition which, as Kant says, stretches from the Eleatic School.[33] Other members of that tradition, contemporary with Berkeley, were Pierre Bayle and Arthur Collier, both of whom attack our notion of objective space as vigorously as Zeno can seem to do himself. Bayle, who certainly influenced Berkeley, remarks with respect to pure space that 'an unmovable, indivisible and penetrable extension' is 'a nature of which we have no idea, and is besides repugnant to the clearest ideas of our mind'.[34] Collier's *Clavis Universalis* was, in its German translation, bound in with Berkeley's *Three Dialogues*,[35] and significantly favours antinomies. One is to the effect that 'an external world, whose existence is absolute' would have to be 'both finite and infinite' in extent.[36] Both Collier and Bayle devote considerably more space to an argument even more characteristic of the tradition to which they belong. Objective extension would have to be infinitely divisible, which is absurd, and objective motion is by all our lights impossible.[37]

The topic of infinite divisibility was central to the topic of the objective determination or measurement of space and time. On the evidence of the *Principles* and *Three Dialogues*, however, one might think that it was a topic, like that of pure space, with no more than a minor role in Berkeley's argument. That appearance is misleading. Both in early and late works a concern with infinite divisibility constitutes a major preoccupation at the heart of his objections to Newtonianism.[38] But it also permeates one of his most famous arguments of all.

In the *First Dialogue* Berkeley finds contradictions arising from the conjunction of three propositions. First, the presupposition accepted by Hylas at this stage of the argument (while he represents the naïve realist) that the real size of an object is the size it is perceived to be. Secondly, the ordinary assumption that when two observers of different sizes, such as a mite and a man, perceive the same object, then they both perceive its size. (The same goes for the two eyes of one observer, 'looking with one eye bare, the other through a microscope'.) And thirdly, the principle that an object's real size is at any one time single and determinate. Philonous concludes that all determinations of extension are sense-relative, and that independent material objects could not possess determinate size and shape. A similar point is made about motion, and a further argument demolishes the suggestion that an absolute extension and an absolute motion are abstractible in thought from their sense-relative determinations, great and small, swift and slow. Hylas is thus left to defend belief in a material substance to which not even extension and motion can be attributed.[39]

The structure of the *First Dialogue* can make it seem that Berkeley simply extends to primary qualities the mechanists' arguments about secondary qualities. 'Was it not admitted as a good argument', Philonous asks in direct, if unfair allusion to Locke, 'that neither heat nor cold was in the water, because it seemed warm to one hand and cold to another?'[40] Yet Philonous can only make this appeal because poor Hylas currently represents Berkeley's common man, who assumes, prior to argument, that whatever particular colour or size is immediately perceived is independently real. The corresponding argument in the *Principles* is less misleading in more than one respect. First, an extension of the mechanists' arguments against secondary qualities is there taken to prove only the sceptical conclusion that 'we do not know by sense which is the true extension or colour of the object'. Secondly, the analogy with secondary qualities is drawn only *after* an independent argument that determinates of extension and motion are sense-relative. This latter claim rather surprisingly receives as its sole credential the statement that it is 'allowed' by modern philosophers.[41] Now we might reasonably wonder how 'modern philosophers' could possibly both allow that size and speed are relative to perception and at the same time distinguish sense-independent primary qualities such as size and motion from sense-relative secondary ones. In fact what Berkeley is doing is placing two different arguments to be found in mechanist philosophers face to face in confrontation. The first has to do with the limitations of the senses and infinite divisibility. Even by itself, in Berkeley's view, it leads to absurd consequences.

The authors of the Port Royal *Logic*, while on the fashionable topic of the limitations of our faculties, invite us to boggle at the implications of matter's being infinitely divisible. A grain of wheat contains a whole universe, which may itself contain proportionately smaller grains of wheat, and so *ad infinitum*. We cannot even in thought identify 'any part, no matter how small, that does not have as many proportional parts as does the whole world'. Immediately before this sally against atomism we have been told that the senses cannot inform us of the 'true and natural' or 'absolute' size of a body, as the existence of lenses is evidence:

Our very eyes are spectacles, and how do we know whether they diminish or magnify the objects we see or whether the artificial lenses believed to diminish or magnify objects may not on the contrary give their true size? Nor do we know whether others perceive an object to be the same size as we do. Two people agree that a given body measures only five feet, but each may have a different idea of a foot.[42]

These two lines of thought came to be combined by Malebranche in a single sceptical argument. Because of the infinite divisibility of matter, 'nothing but infinities are to be found everywhere'. Yet our ideas of objects are 'proportionate to the idea we have of the size of our body, although there are in these objects an infinite number of parts that they do not disclose to us'. We cannot, that is to say, indefinitely divide the immediate object of vision: 'As far as vision is concerned, a mite is only a mathematical point. It cannot be divided without being annihilated.' Microscopes, together with the thought that 'our own eyes are in effect only natural spectacles' and that there could be microscopically small perceivers, should convince us that 'we must not rely on the testimony of our eyes to make judgements about size'. Indeed, 'nothing is either large or small in itself'.[43]

Like Malebranche, Bayle combines the topics of size and infinite divisibility, including a long and elaborate exposition of geometrical paradoxes of infinity taken by themselves to prove the impossibility of extension. He returns to the 'spectacles' passage from the Port Royal *Logic*, making the very tendentious comment that it concedes outright that determinate size is relative to the senses in just the way in which, according to 'modern philosophers', colours, heat, cold and so forth are sense-relative.[44]

All these discussions make it easy to understand Berkeley's claim, as tendentious as Bayle's, that 'modern philosophers' allow that determinate size is relative, although the *Logic* and even Malebranche are in fact arguing something rather different. But very like Malebranche, if to different effect, Berkeley ties the relativity of sensible size together with the infinite divisibility of extension by imagining an infinitely variable sense by means of which the realist's infinity of worlds within worlds, parts within parts of matter, might be observed. From the doctrine of infinite divisibility,

it follows, that there is an infinite number of parts in each particle of matter, which are not perceived by sense. The reason therefore, that any particular body seems to be of a finite magnitude, or exhibits only a finite number of parts to sense, is . . . because the sense is not acute enough to discern them. In proportion therefore as the sense is rendered more acute, it perceives a greater number of parts in the object, that is, the object appears greater, and its figure varies, those parts in its extremities which were before unperceivable, appearing now to bound it in very different lines and angles from those perceived by an obtuser sense. And at length, . . . when the sense becomes infinitely acute, the body shall seem infinite. During all which there is no alteration in the body, but only in the sense. Each body therefore considered in itself, is infinitely extended, and consequently void of all shape or figure.[45]

This argument is explicitly an elucidation of the earlier discussion of sense-relativity and primary and secondary qualities in §11. Consequently it irresistibly suggests that infinite divisibility is also in Berkeley's mind in the *First Dialogue*. Unlike Bayle, of course, Berkeley does not conclude baldly that extension does not exist. The absurdities and contradictions are supposed to attach only to *external* and *independent* extension, to the belief that each physical thing has a single determinate extent variously perceptible by various observers under a variety of conditions. Once it is recognized that what really has extension is each separate idea which goes to constitute the 'thing', the problems vanish. For the contrast between contradictory, independent extension and untroublesome, sense-dependent extension, the contrast which runs through all Berkeley's arguments against the former, involves in his mind a positive doctrine about the latter. That is the doctrine of *minima sensibilia*, which we may reasonably suppose was inspired both by Malebranche and by Locke's suggestion that 'sensible points' are the ultimately 'simple' ideas of extension.[46] Berkeley concluded that the extension of an idea, or sensible extent, is not infinitely divisible, since it is composed of a finite number of *minima*. *Minima* are parts without parts – otherwise they would not be *minima*. Consequently the *minima* of mites and men are equal, and microscopes do not enable us to see more of them. Mites and men simply see different extensions, while the microscope 'presents us with a new scene of visible objects'.[47]

For Kant, on the other hand, as for orthodox Cartesians, infinite divisibility is mathematically proved and hence undeniable: 'the proofs are based upon insight into the constitution of space, in so far as space is . . . the formal condition of the possibility of all matter'.[48] Yet at the same time, it is necessary to conceive of the composition of substances as a composition of indivisible simples. The evident clash of these supposedly evident principles constitutes the Second Antinomy, the explanation of which, according to Kant, lies in the fact that external substances are necessarily experienced in a successive synthesis of spatial appearances. If matter is infinitely divisible then the conception of the *complete* appearance of a thing is impossible, since it is impossible to complete the task of conceiving the possible appearances of its separable parts: on the other hand, to deny infinite divisibility is to claim what is manifestly untrue, that that task could be so completed that every discernible part had actually been discerned in experience. Kant's solution seems to be that the interminable synthesis of possible appearances which is a necessary feature of experience of things in space does not correspond to a feature of things in themselves. To experience an infinitely divisible object in space is not to experience an object with an infinite number of parts – but it is not to experience an object with a finite number of parts either. The answer to the question whether an object in space has a finite or an infinite number of spatial parts is necessarily indeterminate, like a similar question about the size of the universe. The question is therefore meaningless.[49]

The difference between the two solutions is characteristic of both philosophers. Kant embraces the paradoxical property of objective extension which Berkeley, retreating to the supposedly unproblematic subjective impression, rejects outright. Yet Kant's discussion is obviously a kind of commentary on the sceptical tradition within which Berkeley wrote. One might conclude that Kant was better educated than most of us to understand the *First Dialogue*.

5. The Determination of Space and Time and the Refutation of Idealism

All these issues relate to a general problem about the measurement and objective determination of space and time, and so can bring us round to the topics of the Refutation of Idealism. One discussion which seems likely to have influenced Kant considerably here was Leibniz's commentary on Locke's *Essay*.

Locke, in his account of ideas of determinate size, employs a model very like that of the Port Royal *Logic*, although without the sceptical consequences. Thus 'Men for the use and by the custom of measuring, settle in their Minds the Ideas of certain stated lengths, such as an Inch, Foot, Yard', etc. Using these as elements, we can construct an idea of any distance whatsoever, even of a quasi-infinite or indefinite distance.[50] Leibniz protests, rather profoundly, that there cannot be a distinct idea corresponding to each precise 'stated length'. 'For no one can say or grasp in his mind what an inch or a foot is. The signification of these terms can be retained only by means of real standards of measure which are assumed to be unchanging, through which they can always be re-established.'[51]

Leibniz's further discussion might suggest that this assumption of immutability depends on the assumption of immutable laws. For example, he considers the suggestion that a universal relationship, such as the length of a pendulum whose swing would take exactly one second at a specified latitude, should be used as a dependable unit of length. And it is clear that any doubt whether a particular physical standard, such as the standard metre, has changed length would have to be resolved (and would in principle always be resolvable) by means of scientific theory. So to have the notion of a foot is roughly speaking (ignoring complications having to do with the 'division of linguistic labour'[52] and so forth) to know how to determine a certain unit of physical measurement. And the possibility of physical measurement presupposes that the world is law-governed; and that might imply, and would certainly in Leibniz's time have been taken to imply, that it is composed of a law-governed substance or substances. Since the existence of determinate extension seems to presuppose the possibility of physical measurement, and it seems that extension is necessarily determinate, it also seems that we have here a proof that an extended world is necessarily law-governed, consisting of law-governed substance.

This argument is not advanced by Kant, still less by Leibniz. But a roughly parallel argument relating to time does appear in the *Critique*, in the Analogies. The seeds of something like this argument already exist in the *Essay* because Locke sees it as a special problem about the measurement of time that 'we cannot keep by us any standing unvarying measure of Duration', as we can of extension. A convenient measure of time must be 'what has divided the whole length of its Duration into apparently equal Portions, by constantly repeated Periods'. He first argues, however, that the succession of ideas itself gives us the idea of determinate duration, and supplies us with our first sense of 'constantly repeated periods'. For unless that were so, it would never have occurred to us, for example, that one diurnal or annual revolution of the sun was equal to the next. 'The constant and regular Succession of Ideas in a waking Man is, as it were, the Measure and Standard of all other Successions.' The primitive unit of time, the period from one idea to the next, Locke calls an 'instant'. Yet he does recognize that subjective judgements of time can be checked against objective phenomena, and he also sees that, whatever regular motion we choose as our measure, the judgement that it does measure the 'one constant, equal, uniform Course' of 'Duration itself' relies upon the judgement that 'the Cause of that Motion which is unknown to us, shall always operate equally'. In other words, he recognizes that measurement of time ultimately presupposes immutable substances and laws of nature.[53]

Leibniz, as we should expect, protests against the notion of the primitive subjective clock: 'Changes in our perceptions prompt us to think of time, and we measure it by means of uniform changes.' He seems to mean that our primitive sense of time is not a determinate measure of time. We need for that something much closer, and more evidently closer, to the operation of basic laws. He also makes the point that yardsticks are only relatively unchanging, so that they do not after all represent a fundamental distinction between time and space.

These arguments supply some of the ingredients of the Analogies and the Refutation of Idealism. (Another ingredient, which I shall ignore, is the traditional Aristotelian derivation of the measurement of time from a primitive division of time into *before* and *after* by the point *now*.) In the First Analogy Kant argues that the objective determination of time requires something permanent: succession must be conceived as the permanent undergoing change in accordance with law. The Refutation adds roughly the following argument: If I am to think of myself as more than a bare logical subject, I must have experience of myself as a thing with determinate duration in time. In that case, as well as the succession of my ideas or states of consciousness, something permanent must be the object of my senses. Inner sense, however, perceives only states of consciousness – no permanent self is perceived. I can only locate my states in determinate time by relating them to those permanent material objects, changing or moving relatively to one another as the sun moves in relation to the earth, which are perceived by outer sense. Only in this way can I think of the self or subject of my states as having determinate duration, with successive states objectively ordered in time. Hence to accept one's own existence in time as indubitably given but to doubt that of external motions and clocks is incoherent, for to do the latter is to doubt the very perceptions which make experience of a permanent self possible. The concept of an enduring substance cannot be empirically employed in relation to the self unless it is first employed in relation to physical objects.

We can easily see why this argument is directed against Descartes, for whom the concept of absolute duration is quite unproblematic. The duration of a substance, whether matter or spirit, is for him not distinct from its being. The concept of duration is, moreover, prior to the concept of measurable time, which is a creation of the mind.[54] But consideration of Leibniz on Locke may also help to illuminate Kant's intentions. For Locke holds that something merely subjective, the succession of ideas, can give us a measurement of duration. A sceptic of the senses who thinks of the self as a substance in time must adopt Descartes's and Locke's presuppositions. Kant in effect turns an endorsement of Leibniz's objection to Locke into an anti-sceptical argument: i.e. we must turn to matter and the laws of physics for the possibility of that measurement of duration without which the concepts of duration and of time, of substance and of change in a substance, are empty and inapplicable. The argument presupposes that there is no identifiable empirical nature of the soul as there is of matter. Nothing in psychology corresponds to Newtonian physics. In this reasonable view there are once again echoes of such earlier writers as Gassendi, Malebranche and Locke.[55]

Kant presents the Refutation of Idealism as a proof of the existence of external objects in response to the 'problematic idealism' of Descartes. Berkeley is first set on one side with the claim that his position has already been refuted in the Transcendental Aesthetic. But there are two reasons why the Refutation might in any case be supposed an inappropriate argument against Berkeley. For any argument will work only against those who accept what it presupposes as undisputed, and the Refutation makes two such presuppositions which Berkeley rejects. First, it assumes the *concept* of a material permanent undergoing change, a concept which is not impugned by Descartes's scepticism but which Berkeley finds unintelligible and self-contradictory. Secondly, it assumes that the sceptic, like Descartes, sees the self as a substance with objectively determined duration, its states being objectively determined in time. Yet, although for Berkeley the self is a substance, on his official view he does not allow it objective duration or see its states as objectively determined in time – any more than he sees sensible bodies as objectively determined in space.

It may not always seem that Berkeley does reject objective or absolute time. For example, in an argument against absolute motion or velocity he claims that it is 'possible ideas should succeed one another twice as fast in your mind as they do in mine'.[56] Yet this argument is dialectical and *ad hominem*. It appeals, for example, to the Lockean principle that time is measured by the succession of ideas, understood to mean merely that we measure or estimate time that way. Berkeley himself actually holds to this principle in a much stronger, ontological sense: each spirit has its own time, determined or constituted by the succession of its own ideas. There is a temporal *minimum*, the instant from one idea to the next, which is without duration: 'the duration of any finite spirit must be estimated by the number of ideas or actions succeeding each other in that same spirit or mind'.[57] It would follow that the speed of the succession of ideas cannot vary from one person to another, and the only relevant intersubjective comparison possible would be between the length of time (i.e. number of ideas) between two given ideas in one person with the time between two other ideas in another person. Consequently no question of intersubjective simultaneity would be meaningful. Berkeley cannot allow, for example, that when two observers perceive, as we say, the same physical event or object, they have the ideas in question at the same time (or, for that matter, at different times). If a Berkeleyan does allow that such questions could arise, then, as the briefest reflection reveals, he will be plunged into contradictions. Berkeley's intersubjective 'reality' is so disintegrated that even time does not bind together the ideas which are supposed to constitute a real thing.

Whether Kant knew of Berkeley's extreme and wildly implausible retreat into subjectivity in the case of the determinations of time (as I have suggested he very probably did recognize the parallel move in the case of determinations of extension) is perhaps doubtful enough. Nevertheless it is one of the features of Berkeley's system which would seem fully to justify, not only Berkeley's exclusion from the scope of the Refutation of Idealism, but the charge that, with whatever sophistication, he 'degrades bodies to mere illusion'.

Notes

1. *Principles of Human Knowledge*, I, 87–91.

2. *Principles*, I, 30–34.

3. *Critique of Pure Reason*, trans. N. Kemp Smith (New York: St Martin's Press, 1965), A376.

4. *Principles*, I, 90.

5. *Principles*, I, 56.

6. *Critique*, A373.

7. C. M. Turbayne, 'Kant's Refutation of Dogmatic Idealism', *Philosophical Quarterly* (1955); republished as 'Kant's Relation to Berkeley' in *Kant Studies Today*, L. W. Beck (ed.) (La Salle: Open Court, 1969).

8. G. D. Justin, 'On Kant's Analysis of Berkeley', *Kant Studien* (1974); H. E. Allison, 'Kant's Critique of Berkeley', *Journal of the History of Philosophy* (1973). Margaret Wilson, in 'Kant and the Dogmatic Idealism of Berkeley', *Journal of the History of Philosophy* (1971), had argued that Kant's criticisms do correspond to important differences from Berkeley but also indicate that Kant did not know Berkeley's theory well.

9. *Critique*, B70 f.

10. *Critique*, B274 f.

11. *Siris*, 271.

12. Cf. *Principles*, I, 7, 73 f., etc.

13. *Prolegomena to Any Future Metaphysics*, trans. P. G. Lucas (Manchester: Manchester University Press, 1962), 374. Numerical reference follows the pagination of the Berlin Academy edition of the Collected Works.

14. *The Works of George Berkeley, Bishop of Cloyne*, A. Luce and T. Jessop (eds.) (London: Nelson, 1953), V, 14 ff.

15. For explicit mention of 'pure intellect' in earlier works cf. *Three Dialogues between Hylas and Philonous*, I (*Works*, II, 153) and *De Motu*, 53. But the well-known theory of

'notions' is also endorsement of a quasi-Cartesian pure intellect (without innate ideas). Cf. *Principles*, I, 27 f., 89, 140 and 142; *Three Dialogues*, III, 232 f.

16. *Principles of Philosophy*, II, trans. E. Haldane and G. Ross (New York: Dover, 1955),10 f.

17. *Elements of Philosophy*, II, vii, 2.

18. *Elements*, II, viii, 1.

19. *Syntagma*, Second Part, I, ii, 1, as translated by C. Brush, *Selected Works of Pierre Gassendi* (New York: Johnson Reprint Corp., 1972).

20. Cf. *Divine Dialogues*, I.

21. *Principia Mathematica*, Def. VIII Schol.

22. op. cit., II, xiii, 10.

23. *Principles* I, 110–16, etc.

24. *Optics*, qu. 28.

25. *Prolegomena*, 374 f., quoted by Allison, 60.

26. *Prolegomena*, 286.

27. *Prolegomena*, 289.

28. *Critique*, A51 (B75). In Kemp Smith's translation, 'intuitions without concepts are blind'.

29. *Essay towards a New Theory of Vision*, 45 *et passim*.

30. Cf. *Essay*, IV, xi, 2, etc. I do not mean to imply that it is not also helpful towards understanding Berkeley to consider Descartes's rather different account of perceptual beliefs, and in fact *Principles of Philosophy*, II, 1, seems to set the scene rather neatly for the Berkeleyan theory. But Berkeley does allude specifically to the features of Locke's account described here.

31. Cf. *Essay*, II, xxx, 2; II, xxxi, 2; etc.

32. Cf. *Three Dialogues*, III, 239; *Theory of Vision Vindicated*, 11 ff.; *Philosophical Commentaries*, 80, 112.

33. *Prolegomena*, 374.

34. Cf. *Historical and Critical Dictionary*, article 'Leucippus'.

35. See Turbayne, 226.

36. *Clavis Universalis*, II, iii.

37. Bayle, *Dictionary*, article 'Zeno'; Collier, *Clavis*, II, iv.

38. On the one hand, in the early notebooks known as *Philosophical Commentaries*; on the other, in *The Analyst* and *A Defence of Free-Thinking in Mathematics*.

39. *Three Dialogues*, I, 188 ff.

40. *Three Dialogues*, I, 189. Cf. Locke, *Essay*, II, viii, 21.

41. *Principles*, I, 11.

42. Arnauld and Nicole, *Logic, or the Art of Thinking*, IV, i, as translated by J. Dickoff and P. James (Indianapolis, 1964).

43. *Search After Truth*, I, vi, as translated by T. Lennon and P. Olscamp (Columbus: Ohio State University Press, 1980).

44. *Dictionary*, article 'Zeno'.

45. *Principles*, I, 47.

46. *Essay*, II, xv, 9.

47. *New Theory of Vision*, 85; cf. *Three Dialogues*, III, 245.

48. *Critique*, A439 (B467).

49. *Critique*, A487 f. (B515 f.) and A505 (B533).

50. *Essay*, II, xiii, 4.

51. *New Essays on Human Understanding*, II, xiii, 4, trans. P. Remnant and J. Bennett (Cambridge: Cambridge University Press, 1981).

52. Cf. H. Putnam, 'Meaning and Reference' in *Mind, Language and Reality* (Cambridge: Cambridge University Press, 1975).

53. *Essay*, II, xiv.

54. *Principles of Philosophy*, I, 55 ff.

55. Cf. Gassendi, *Objections to Descartes' Meditations*, II, 6, 9; Malebranche, *Search after Truth*, III, ii, 7; Locke, *Essay*, IV, iii, 16 f.; IV, iii, 29; IV, vi, 14.

56. *Three Dialogues*, I, 190.

57. *Principles*, I, 98.

Biographical Note

M. R. Ayers has been Tutorial Fellow in Philosophy at Wadham College, Oxford, since 1965. He has held visiting posts at the University of California, Berkeley (1964 and 1979), and at the University of Oregon, Eugene (1970–71). He has published on a variety of topics, including freewill, identity, philosophy of mind, John Locke and the historiography of philosophy. He has come increasingly to believe in the value of approaching philosophical issues through the history of philosophy. A recent book (with J. Rée and A. Westoby) is *Philosophy and Its Past* (1978). He gave the British Academy Dawes Hicks lecture for 1981 on *Locke's Logical Atomism*, and is writing a book on Locke.

Further Reading

Satisfactory texts of Berkeley's philosophical works are: (1) *The Works of George Berkeley, Bishop of Cloyne*, ed. A. A. Luce and T. E. Jessop (London: Nelson, 1948-57); (2) *George Berkeley: Philosophical Works Including the Works on Vision*, ed. M. R. Ayers (London: Dent, and Totowa, N.J.: Rowman and Littlefield, 1975) (based on (1) above); (3) *Berkeley: Works on Vision*, ed. C. M. Turbayne (Indianapolis: Bobbs-Merrill, 1963); (4) *Berkeley: Principles, Dialogues and Correspondence*, ed. C. M. Turbayne (Indianapolis: Bobbs-Merrill, 1965).

Ayers discusses other, in some ways more central aspects of Berkeley's philosophy in 'Substance, Reality and the Great, Dead Philosophers' (*American Philosophical Quarterly*, 1970) and in the introduction to (2) above. A good critical survey of many issues in the interpretation of Berkeley is presented in *Berkeley: The Philosophy of Immaterialism* by I. C. Tipton (London: Methuen, 1974). The main bibliography of writings on Berkeley is T. E. Jessop's *A Bibliography of George Berkeley* (2nd edn revised and enlarged, The Hague: 1973), which is kept up to date in the *Berkeley Newsletter* of Trinity College, Dublin.

Barry Stroud

Hume: Action, Reason and Passion

Hume is often regarded as the greatest of sceptics, or at any rate without peer since the Greeks. He put into question the foundation of our general beliefs about the world, thereby beginning the still-continuing history of the problem of induction: on what good basis do we extrapolate from limited evidence to general truths? To Barry Stroud, the author of the prize-winning book of which a chapter is reprinted here, his aim is better regarded as positive. Like Marx or Freud, he advances a new theory of man, an account of human nature. His hope was to do for human existence what he took the new science of the seventeenth century and particularly Isaac Newton to have done for the physical world. He would make man the subject of scientific study, not *a priori* theorizing.

Fundamental to such an enterprise must be an explanation of human action. What sort of explanation is there of what we do? The responses to this question include two large ones which Hume considers. One in its traditional expression is that we have freewill. Our actions derive from our free choices and decisions. The other response, often related to the first, is that our actions are sometimes or often subject to reason or rationality, and perhaps always can be. They sometimes do not derive from our passions or feelings and perhaps need not ever do so. Hume's view of the doctrine of freewill is closely considered in the first part of the chapter below, and his view of the elevation of reason over the passions in the second.

The answer of freewill denies that we ourselves are subject to causation in the way of the physical world. Determinism is false. We are

David Hume, 1711–76. Born in Scotland and lived mainly in Edinburgh. The greatest of the British Empiricists. Also a historian and man of letters. Recovered from the fact that his *Treatise* 'fell deadborn from the press' but failed, on account of his opinions, ever to get a professorship. Perhaps the greatest of British philosophers, of whatever outlook or tradition.

not caused to do as we do, but rather, when we are about to act, there are two possibilities open to us. My action is not the end-effect of a causal sequence each of whose parts was the only thing that could have happened then, given what went before. Hume thinks otherwise (pp. 254–7) and believes he must do so if he is to persist in his hope of founding a science of human nature (p. 257). If it really were true that our decisions and actions were not part of a causal order, and hence were unpredictable not only in practice but also in theory, there could be little possibility of a science of man. Still, it is a hard fact that we *do* regard ourselves as having more than one possibility open to us when we are about to act. Hume must explain away this seemingly fundamental belief.

Hume's view of the elevation of reason over the passions is partly summed up in famous passages from his *Treatise of Human Nature*. (1) '... reason alone can never be a motive to any action of the will . . .' (2) Reason 'can never oppose passion in the direction of the will . . . Reason is, and ought only to be the slave of the passions, and can never pretend to any other office than to serve and obey them . . . 'Tis not contrary to reason for me to prefer the destruction of the whole world to the scratching of my finger. 'Tis not contrary to reason for me to chuse my total ruin to prevent the least uneasiness of an *Indian* or person wholly unknown to me.' My actions cannot spring from reason on any occasion. Reason merely serves to enable me to acquire, perhaps by planning, that to which my passions move me. Further, it is not even that my passions conflict with and always overcome by reason. There can be no conflict between reason and passion. They are not sorts of things that can ever conflict.

Hume attempts in three ways to deal with what he takes to be the false belief that we are free in a way inconsistent with causation. His first explanation in one version (pp. 257–9) is roughly that our ordinary idea of freedom is in fact of something perfectly consistent with causation, but that somehow we confuse our ordinary idea with another. We confuse a freedom we in fact usually have with a freedom we always lack. We usually have what the medievals called liberty of spontaneity: we can usually do as we choose, uncoerced by others and unconstrained by such things as prison walls. We do not have what was called liberty of indifference, which somehow involves two or more possibilities really being open to us when we act. Perhaps this supposed freedom has never been clearly explained, but philosophers have sometimes spoken of the 'creative choices' of the Self. The second explanation Hume offers of what he takes to be our false belief is that we do not feel, about our own actions, that they are the effects of unbroken causal sequences. We do not feel this about ourselves, whatever view we take of others. (pp. 259–61) The third explanation, at bottom, is that we take people to be responsible for their actions, responsible in such a way as requires the liberty of indifference. (p. 261)

With respect to the supposed confusion of our ordinary idea of freedom with something else, Hume takes it that he needs to do no more than point it out. As for the mentioned feeling of freedom, it does not guarantee that we actually have the given freedom. A faulty argument is involved. As for the third consideration, Hume argues audaciously that indeed we are responsible for our actions: they are *ours*. But to be such, far from being somehow uncaused, they must be caused by our characters, wants, desires and so on. Responsibility is not only consistent with determinism, but demands it.

It is Stroud's strong contention (p. 258) that (1) Hume does not explain how or where our supposed confusion comes about, which raises doubt of there being a confusion, and (2) he does not explain what leads us to the mentioned faulty argument. Is it a fact which throws doubt on Hume's contention that we mistake our ordinary idea of a freedom we really have? We are invited to see (3) that in several ways Hume's seemingly powerful argument about responsibility requires further and deeper reflection. It may be, then, taking into account these three matters, that causation and our idea of freedom are not compatible, and hence that there is a challenge to a science of man. Stroud is inclined to the view that freedom and causation are indeed not compatible.

The second section of the chapter, after sketching the traditional place given to reason rather than passion in explaining action, and Hume's denial, allows what seems plausible, that a preference or propensity, or an aversion, is always required for an action. (p. 269) I would be mistaken to take this as conceding Hume's claim that reason alone can never be a motive or spring to action. For what is a preference? It seems not to be, or not to need to be, a felt passion or feeling. Might it not be the result of reason alone rather than a passion? Hume denies this, since he denies that reason alone, whatever the intermediaries, can ever be a motive to action at all, alone or with anything else. He also denies that reason and passion can ever conflict. That they can is also part of the traditional conception, according to which not only may reason without the obstruction of passion issue in action, but it also may conflict with passion, and issue in action by overcoming it.

His arguments for his several denials rest on his conceptions of reason and passion. (pp. 270–73) In effect he identifies reason with what can also be called its contents or objects: propositions. A proposition is not a particular thought, where the latter is understood as a mental event which occurred at a particular time and presumably place. A proposition is the content of a thought, *that such-and-such is the case*, which is true or false and may be the content of many particular thoughts. A proposition itself is not in space or time. Such entities, sometimes called abstract objects, can no more be causes than can, say, the number 12, and so they cannot be a motive to action. As for conflict, it consists in two propositions or like things being in disagreement. But a passion is conceived by Hume to be other than propositional. It is not a claim as to how things are. Hence there can be no conflict between reason and passion.

Stroud questions Hume's conception of reason, which in concentrating on propositions entirely leaves out the idea of a mental process. (p. 274) Indeed, there are grounds for thinking that Hume must accept reason in the sense of a mental process. (pp. 274–7) Reason in this sense *can* be causal, *can* have effects. If so, there is also the possibility of some kind of conflict between reason so conceived and passion.

In the end, then, in Stroud's view, Hume does not establish that a preference cannot spring from reason. (p. 276) Nor does he deal with the uncomfortable fact that we are not always aware of a passion before we act. (pp. 277–8) He cannot succeed by mistakenly running together the idea of having a preference with that of being subject to a passion or feeling. (pp. 278–81) A preference may in fact be regarded as a disposition or tendency, as distinct from an experienced feeling. Hume's theory of ideas, discussed fully elsewhere in Stroud's book, is such that mental or psychological phenomena are limited to items in or before the mind. This leads him to what appears to be the mistaken identification of having a preference and being subject to a passion. It seems also to lie behind his identifying reason with propositions.

There remains the seeming truth that every action has a preference in its background. Hume's work points to this truth. But, in Stroud's persuasive view, involving distinctions which deserve close attention, the truth does not establish that action never derives by way of a preference from reason, or that reason cannot overcome passion since conflict is out of the question. Hume's large arguments make possible, and call for, more inquiry.

Barry Stroud

Hume: Action, Reason and Passion

> Yes, Nature's road must ever be prefer'd;
> Reason is here no guide, but still a guard:
> 'Tis hers to rectify, not overthrow,
> And treat this passion more as friend than foe:

Hume is a scientist of man who believes that every event has a cause. Most of us are perhaps inclined to agree, at least with respect to the happenings of brute physical nature. In any case, we do not believe that inanimate bodies have anything we would regard as freedom or liberty – that they can change the direction or speed of their motion, for example, independently of the causal forces operating on them. Hume claims that the same thing holds for those parts of nature that involve 'actions of the mind'. This includes not just 'mental events' alone, but human actions generally.

He thinks that what naturally and inevitably leads us to believe in causality in the inanimate world also leads to the same belief with respect to human actions. We come to think of certain physical events as necessarily or causally connected when we have observed a constant conjunction between events of those two types in the past. But if that is so, then it is obvious that human affairs are just as much cases of 'necessary operations' as is the behaviour of bodies. There is just as much uniformity in human affairs as in inanimate nature. The 'regular operation of natural principles' is equally obvious in both realms. (p. 401).[1]

This is not to say that every human being is the same as every other, or that everyone acts the same way in a given situation. It means only that every human action is an instance of some uniformity, just as is

Barry Stroud, 'Action, Reason and Passion', Chapter 7 of *Hume* (London: Routledge & Kegan Paul, 1977). Reprinted, with small alterations, by permission of the author and publisher.

every event involving only inanimate objects. The principle that like causes produce like effects is equally true for both sorts of events. And the existence of uniformities is not incompatible with immense variety both in inanimate nature and in human behaviour. The world would be either a dreary or a chaotic place if it were. A certain sequence of events makes one tree bear apples and another tree bear plums, but we do not conclude that they are not caused to bear the particular fruits that they do. We attribute their different products to different internal structure. Similarly there are differences in the sentiments, actions and passions of different human beings. For example, those of the members of one sex are 'distinguished by their force and maturity, the other by their delicacy and softness' (p. 401).[2]

But there also seems to be considerable evidence against the uniformity Hume claims to find in human behaviour. He himself puts the objection this way:

For what is more capricious than human actions? What more inconstant than the desires of man? And what creature departs more widely, not only from right reason, but from his own character and disposition? An hour, a moment is sufficient to make him change from one extreme to the other, and overturn what cost the greatest pain and labour to establish. Necessity is regular and certain. Human conduct is irregular and uncertain. The one, therefore, proceeds not from the other. (p. 403)

Hume thinks this objection shows something about human behaviour, but not that it lacks causes. It shows that there is a great deal we do not know about human beings and how they operate. Although, given our knowledge of a person's character, motives, aims, and so on, his actions are often as predictable as inanimate physical events, it must be admitted that this is not always so. According to Hume that is because of the great complexity of the contributing factors in most human actions, and our insufficient knowledge of them. But there are also many occasions on which we lack the appropriate knowledge about inanimate physical objects as well. Our inability to predict the outcome of a turn of the roulette wheel, for example, does not lead us to believe that its operations are not really caused after all. There we are quite willing to attribute our failure to lack of knowledge rather than to the absence of causality, and Hume thinks the same is true of human action.

But he is not content simply to point out that there is in fact uniformity in human behaviour. He thinks that what we all say and do in dealing with other human beings shows that all of us actually believe in the uniformity as well, despite what we feel inclined to say about man's freedom. We continually form beliefs about the future behaviour of people on the basis of what we know about them – their 'motives, tempers, and circumstances' (p. 401). If we did not do this, how could we have any human contact at all? How could we rely on other people, or try to act ourselves in accord with what we expect them to do?

All politics, commerce, in fact, even simple communication depends on our making inferences from what we know of a person to what we think he is about to do. A prince who imposes a tax on his subjects expects their compliance; a man who gives his order for dinner expects the waiter to bring it; and so on (p. 405). These expectations are acquired through inferences from what is known or believed about people, and Hume says they are all causal inferences. I think the waiter will bring my dinner because he wants to keep his job, and because he believes that bringing my dinner is required for him to keep his job. And these inferences, like all causal inferences, are made on the basis of past observations of constant conjunctions between people having particular 'motives, tempers, and circumstances' and their acting in certain ways.

Naturally, such expectations are not infallible. Many of our conclusions about what people will do are based on assumptions for which we do not always have very strong grounds, and even if we do, we sometimes turn out to be wrong. But that is no surprise, nor does it reveal anything special about human behaviour. We often make mistakes in our expectations about inanimate objects as well.

That we really believe in causality in both the human and the inanimate domains is further confirmed by the fact that we often put reasoning about human actions together with reasoning about physical events to reach a conclusion about the necessity or impossibility of certain occurrences.

A prisoner, who has neither money nor interest, discovers the impossibility of his escape, as well from the obstinacy of the gaoler, as from the walls and bars with which he is surrounded; and in all attempts for his freedom chuses rather to work upon the stone and iron of the one, than upon the inflexible nature of the other. The same prisoner, when conducted to the scaffold, foresees his death as certainly from the constancy and fidelity of his guards as from the operation of the ax or wheel. His mind runs along a certain train of ideas: The refusal of the soldiers to consent to his escape, the action of the executioner; the separation of the head and body; bleeding, convulsive motions, and death. Here is a connected chain of natural causes and voluntary actions; but the mind feels no difference betwixt them in passing from one link to another. (p. 406)

All that is required for such inferences to be convincing is that we have observed the appropriate constant conjunctions in the past. Whether they are conjunctions involving only 'mental' phenomena, or only inanimate phenomena, or one of each, is irrelevant to our acquiring the beliefs we do.

So Hume thinks that if we observe human behaviour we will inevitably believe that human actions are caused, and that they arise 'of necessity' out of their antecedents. Only if that is so, he thinks, can human actions be explained. In the absence of causality there would simply be no answer to the question why a particular action occurred. That would leave the science of man with nothing to say – the action in question would be literally inexplicable or unintelligible. Hume wants to explain everything that happens – and especially human thoughts, feelings and actions – as part of a natural causal order. It is a condition of our fully understanding what goes on, and therefore a condition of the success of Hume's science of man.

But the idea that actions arise of necessity out of their antecedents has also been thought to conflict with another important and familiar aspect of human life – man's freedom, or liberty. Hume is not unaware of this tension in our thought about ourselves and others, and he tries to explain its source. He does so by trying to account for people's dissatisfaction with 'the doctrine of necessity' and for the attractiveness of 'the doctrine of liberty', in so far as liberty is thought to conflict with necessity.

What he says on this subject is important and famous. Hume's writings provide one of the main sources of today's widely shared belief that an action's being caused or necessitated by its antecedents is perfectly compatible with its being a free action.[3] He finds three distinct factors that lead people mistakenly to suppose that the two are incompatible.

The first, not surprisingly, is confusion or misunderstanding. In the *Treatise* Hume describes it as a confusion between two different kinds of liberty, but in the *Enquiry* he thinks it is simply a misunderstanding of what liberty is. We often think of someone as acting unfreely when he is forced 'against his will', for example by violence or the threat of violence, to do something by somebody else. Of such a person we can perfectly justifiably say 'he had to do it', 'he couldn't have done anything else' or 'he had no alternative', and these are taken as denials of his liberty with respect to that action. But in the normal course of everyday events, when for example I cross the street and buy some ice cream with no one threatening, imploring, requesting or even suggesting anything, it is very difficult to think that I had no alternative, that I had to do it or that I could not have done otherwise. It seems to be a perfect case of absence of force or constraint or whatever was responsible for the lack of liberty in the first kind of case. The implication Hume draws is that, in the absence of what makes liberty absent in the first kind of case, liberty is present.

What is present in the example of my crossing the street for ice cream is 'the liberty of *spontaneity*' – 'that which is oppos'd to violence' (p. 407) – which Hume in the *Treatise* regards as liberty in 'the most common sense of the word' and the only kind of liberty 'which it concerns us to preserve' (pp. 407–8). We are concerned to minimize the power of others over us, and to structure our communities to reduce opportunities for people to impose their wills upon us in conflict with our own. Hume thinks that, somehow, because of the great importance the liberty of spontaneity has for us, we tend to confuse it with something quite different, viz. 'the liberty of *indifference*'. This latter sort of liberty *is* incompatible with necessity and causes, and so our failure to distinguish the two kinds of liberty leads us mistakenly to deny that human actions are caused. Of course, if Hume is right about our confusions then we are wrong to draw the conclusion that free human actions are uncaused, but he offers no explanation at all of exactly how our intense concern with 'the liberty of spontaneity' leads us to confuse it with the absence of causality. Recent writers have concentrated more on that aspect of the Humean diagnosis,[4] but there is a puzzling blank at that point in Hume's actual account.

In the *Enquiry*, there is no mention of a confusion between two kinds of liberty at all. The 'liberty of spontaneity' is said to be the only kind there is.

> For what is meant by liberty, when applied to voluntary actions? We cannot surely mean that actions have so little connexion with motives, inclinations, and circumstances, that one does not follow with a certain degree of uniformity from the other, and that one affords no inference by which we can conclude the existence of the other. For these are plain and acknowledged matters of fact. By liberty, then, we can only mean *a power of acting or not acting, according to the determinations of the will*; that is, if we choose to remain at rest, we may; if we choose to move, we also may. Now this hypothetical liberty is universally allowed to belong to every one who is not a prisoner and in chains. Here, then, is no subject of dispute. (*E*, p. 95)[5]

This again does not begin to explain why people are inclined to deny causal determination of human actions in the name of liberty. It simply advances a view about what 'liberty' means, thus attributing the perennial dispute about liberty and necessity to some still unspecified confusion or misunderstanding.

The view about what 'liberty' means, or about the nature of that liberty that we are concerned to preserve, is expressed very briefly in this passage, and it can hardly be described as a subtle or profound analysis of the concept. A man from whom money is demanded with a gun at his head certainly has 'a power of acting or not acting, according to the determinations of the will'. If he chooses not to give the money, he may, and if he chooses to give it, he may. The penalties will be much greater on the one alternative than on the other, but which alternative is realized now depends on his will. So this example would seem to count as a case of liberty, given Hume's explanation of it, although it is clearly a case in which the kind of liberty Hume says it concerns us most to preserve is absent. The quest for liberty is more than an effort to stay out of prison or out of chains.

Hume is not concerned to offer a complete account of the precise nature and limits of what he calls the liberty of spontaneity. He says that it is one – or perhaps the only – sense of the word 'liberty', but he does not even begin to explain what that sense is, or how our failure to understand it properly leads us mistakenly to think it is incompatible with causality. Consequently he can hardly be said at this point to have shown, or to have established, that liberty and necessity are compatible.

He offers two other explanations of people's opposition to the idea that human actions are caused. We often have what Hume calls '*a false sensation or experience*' of the absence of necessity or determination in action (p. 408), and hence we conclude that there is no such thing. For Hume necessity is not an objective property of the relation between events we regard as causally connected; nor is it a characteristic possessed by any 'agent', whether animate or inanimate. The *observer* of human actions believes that particular actions are caused by their antecedents when he has observed constant conjunctions between antecedents of those kinds and actions of those kinds. He then feels 'a determination of the mind' to pass from the idea of one of those things to the idea of 'its usual attendant'. But in *performing* an action, Hume says, we often do not feel any such determination; in fact, we are often 'sensible' of a certain 'looseness or indifference' (p. 408), and so we tend to regard our action as completely free or uncaused;

as liberty, when opposed to necessity, is nothing but the want of that determination, and a certain looseness or indifference which we feel, in passing, or not passing, from the idea of one object to that of any succeeding one. (*E*, p. 94n)[6]

Why do we experience this 'looseness or indifference' in the case of our own actions? It cannot be because we lack experience of, and hence know nothing of, the conjunction between wants and beliefs of certain kinds and actions of certain kinds, since we do not feel the same 'looseness' when we observe the same kinds of actions performed by others. It cannot be a mere lack of exposure to instances of relevant generalizations that is responsible for the lack of the feeling of causality in our own case. Nor can it be our involvement in, and concentration on, the action at hand, since it is not a condition in general of having a feeling of causal determination, or of getting causal beliefs, that one explicitly rehearse and consider the past experience from which the feeling or belief naturally arises. Animals get expectations on the basis of experience just as people do – automatically, without deliberate excogitation. How then is it possible for us to be so immune to the pressures of past and present experience in the case of our own actions, especially if Hume is right about our causal beliefs arising from a 'feeling of determination'? Somehow, when we are acting, that feeling deserts us.

Hume does not give a satisfactory explanation of this phenomenon. He is mainly interested in showing that, whatever its source, it does not imply that human actions are not caused by the 'motives, temper, and situation' of the agent. He points out, quite rightly, that if we are confronted with two alternatives A and B, and we do A, we nevertheless have no difficulty in forming an idea of our having done B instead. And that is enough to persuade us that we could have done B instead of A, and hence that we were not causally determined to do A. But why are we so easily persuaded? According to Hume it is because we are confident that, if anyone challenges us to show that we really could have chosen B, we think we will have met the challenge if we set up the situation again and choose B *this* time. There seems no other way conclusively to prove the existence of a power that was not exercised. Since we could not do both A and B at the same time, it might seem that the only proof left to us is to do B at some later time, thus showing that we can do it, and then conclude that we could have done it earlier, and hence that our doing A was not causally determined.

Hume has little difficulty in showing that this 'experiment' is useless to demonstrate an absence of causality in the first action. The first time I was merely presented with two alternatives, and the wishes, desires and motives I had at the time led me to take A. But the second time the situation is quite different. For instance, the question of my liberty has arisen; I want to demonstrate my freedom, and I think the way to do so is to choose B this time. Obviously, the fact that doing B naturally issues from this second set of wants and beliefs does not imply that my doing A was not the effect of the set of wants and beliefs I had the first time. The fact that I do B the second time does not imply that the wants and beliefs I had the first time were not sufficient to cause me to do A. Hume suggests that it is only because we somehow mistakenly believe that that implication holds that our experiences in acting lead us to deny 'the doctrine of necessity'. He admits that 'we may imagine we feel a liberty within ourselves' (p. 408), but taken alone that proves nothing about whether or not we actually have that liberty. The experiences must be accompanied by some inference in order to establish our liberty, but at this point Hume does not explain how or why we could ever be led to make the particular faulty inference he attributes to us.

I think it is only when he reaches the third possible source of the attractiveness of 'the doctrine of liberty' that Hume begins to approach a more realistic account of what actually makes us regard liberty and necessity as incompatible, but even there what he says is brief and not fully satisfying diagnostically.

There seems little doubt that many people are opposed to 'the doctrine of necessity' because they think its truth would undermine religion and morality, and show them to be nothing but illusions. That would not in itself imply that 'the doctrine of necessity' is false, but it does explain why many people are not disposed to accept it.

The explanation can be made more specific. Opposition to 'the doctrine of necessity' involves more than just a taste for old things, or a fondness for the traditional ways. It is widely believed that, as Hume puts it, 'necessity utterly destroys all merit and demerit either towards mankind or superior powers' (p. 411). If the actions of a man or a god arise of necessity out of their antecedents, it is felt that that agent was not free not to perform the actions in question, and hence cannot legitimately be praised or blamed for them. Praise or blame – or responsibility of any sort – for an action is rightly ascribed only if the agent could have done otherwise. But if human actions are events which arise of necessity out of their antecedents then, if their antecedents have occurred, the actions in question *must* occur, they could not fail to occur, there is no alternative to their occurring. So 'the doctrine of necessity' is rather naturally taken to imply the absence of alternatives to what happens, and 'the doctrine of liberty' requires alternatives. Whatever might be wrong with this way of thinking, it is plausible to suggest that something like it is behind the feeling that liberty and necessity are incompatible, and therefore that the truth of 'the doctrine of necessity' would undermine morality and ascriptions of responsibility. What exactly does Hume say about this source of the apparent conflict?

I have already mentioned his suggestion that there is a confusion or conflation of two different senses of 'liberty' somewhere in our thinking about the conflict, but he does not point to any particular place at which the alleged confusion occurs, or explain why and how we are led to make it. And he does not give a very careful explanation of what 'liberty' or 'could have done otherwise' actually mean; nor does he show that they are consistently applicable to actions that arise of necessity out of their antecedents. Those are the sorts of tasks the successful completion of which would seem to have the greatest chance of resolving once and for all 'the question of liberty and necessity – the most contentious question of metaphysics, the most contentious science' (*E*, p. 95). And they would seem to be all that is needed for clearing away this felt obstacle to the success of the science of man. But Hume virtually ignores them, and he does so partly because he thinks we must all in fact accept 'the doctrine of necessity' in order to ascribe responsibility at all. It is not merely that liberty and the ascription of responsibility are compatible with necessity – they actually require it; they would make no sense without it. So for Hume to concentrate on establishing only their compatibility would be for him to concentrate on establishing much less than what he regards as the whole truth.

His argument for the stronger conclusion goes as follows. We only praise or blame someone for something *he* does. The action must be *his* action, not somebody else's, and it must not be something that merely happens to him but otherwise has no connection with him at all. If a man's 'actions' were not caused, they would not be the effects of anything at all, and so they would not be the effects of his character, wants, desires, motives, etc. But if an 'action' does not proceed from a man's character, wants, desires, motives, etc., then there is no connection between the 'action' and the man who is said to have done it. If an event which we regard as an action of a particular man is in fact not connected with him in any way, then the fact that it occurred 'can neither redound to his honour, if good, nor infamy, if evil' (p. 411). The event might involve the man in the sense that it is something occurring in or on or near a certain human body, but that is not enough to justify our attributing the event to the man as in some sense 'his', and therefore holding him responsible for its occurrence. Of course, we might regard it as unfortunate or bad that the event occurred, but that is not to hold a particular man responsible for it. So thinking of actions as being done by someone, or as being his, hers or theirs, requires a belief that the actions are effects of other things that are going on in, or are true of, particular human beings. Therefore, only if 'the doctrine of necessity' is true can a person rightly possess merit or demerit for his actions, since *his* actions are those that are caused by his character, wants, desires, motives, and so on. Everyone who ascribes responsibility must believe in 'the doctrine of necessity'.

This argument raises a number of issues. It seems undeniable that in order for an action to be the action of a particular agent, it must in some way issue from the motives, wants, beliefs, character or other dispositions or attributes of that particular agent. Only then does it make sense to attribute that action to that agent, and thus to hold him responsible for it. But that is a very vague admission. It leaves open the fundamental question of precisely *how* an action 'issues from' certain characteristics of the agent. Hume's view that the ascription of responsibility requires 'the doctrine of necessity' is based on the plausible idea that the wants, beliefs, character, etc., of an agent are the *causes* of his actions. But one could be wrong in taking the relation between them to be straightforwardly causal without being wrong about the weaker and vaguer, and apparently undeniable claim that the ascription of actions and responsibility to an agent requires that those actions in some way or other 'issue from' the wants, beliefs, character, etc., of that agent.[7]

Hume thinks he has good reason to believe that a person's actions are events that are caused by, or arise of necessity out of, their antecedents, such as the person's wants, beliefs and other propensities. As a scientist of man, he notices constant conjunctions between a certain sort of person's wanting and believing such-and-such and his doing certain things, and he then comes to believe that phenomena of those two sorts are causally connected. And that is why he concludes that 'the doctrine of necessity', or of the causal origin and explanation of human actions, is what is required for the attribution of those actions to particular agents.[8] Hume's causal theory of action is a natural outcome of his conception of science, and in particular of the science of man.[9]

The whole question of the nature of human action – its genesis and explanation – is very complicated, and remains in a highly unsettled state. I return in the next section to a discussion of some aspects of Hume's causal theory, in particular the nature of wants or desires and their role in the 'production' of actions. For the moment I want to concentrate on another point relevant to his treatment of the dispute about liberty and necessity.

Suppose Hume were absolutely right. Suppose that the only way we could make sense of the attribution of actions to agents was by taking those actions to be caused by the wants, beliefs or other characteristics of those agents. Then if we also were still inclined to believe that 'the doctrine of necessity' is incompatible with liberty and hence responsibility, some of the things we believe would have to be false. Both sides simply could not be true. But that is typically the beginning, rather than the end, of a philosophical problem. Hume would have provided us with a dilemma – perhaps even an antinomy – which demands solution. Our minds would be 'uneasy' in such a situation and would 'naturally seek relief from the uneasiness'. And Hume does not really offer us any relief.

We need a demonstration, and not merely an unsupported assertion, that liberty and necessity are perfectly compatible. The ascription of responsibility requires that the agent could have done something other than what he did at the time, and we need an account of what that requirement comes to, and how it could be fulfilled even though the action that occurred arose of necessity out of its antecedents. Granted, those who suspect an incompatibility here do not have an unproblematic account in clearer terms of what 'could have done otherwise' means, but one does have enough of a sense of what the requirement involves to notice deficiencies in candidates actually offered by compatibilists.

If it is causally necessary that if an A occurs then a B occurs, then if an A occurs, a B must occur. The occurrence of something other than a B is not possible if an A has occurred, given that it is causally necessary that if an A occurs then a B occurs. That is to say, given the way the world is – the causal connections which hold in it and the state of affairs that obtains when that A occurs – there is no alternative to a B's occurring. Of course, it is, in itself, *possible* for a B not to occur – that involves no contradiction or absurdity. The world might simply explode or come to an end right after the A occurs. That is simply Hume's point that no two events are such that the occurrence of one of them can be deduced from the occurrence of the other. But a B occurs' does follow logically from the conjunction of 'an A occurs' and 'it is causally necessary that if an A occurs then a B occurs'. So if the causally impossible, but still possible, situation in which an A occurs and a B does not occur were realized, it would follow that it is not the case that it is causally necessary that if an A occurs then a B occurs.

That is to say that it is a contingent fact, which could have been otherwise, that the causal connections which hold in our world do hold. But *if* a causal connection does hold between As and Bs and an A occurs, then a B cannot fail to occur. No alternative to a B is possible in such a world after an A has occurred. If no B occurred it would follow that the world is not as the causal statement says it is.

But surely to say that, at the time of the A's occurrence, an agent in that situation could have brought about some alternative to a B, is to say at least that an alternative to a B was possible in that situation in that world.[10] And that is what 'the doctrine of necessity' denies. Some compatibilists, armed with an analysis of 'X could have done otherwise', would reject the implication from 'X could have done otherwise' to 'an alternative to what X did was causally possible at the time of X's action' on the grounds that liberty consists only in the absence of constraint, or coercion or the like, and has no implications about physical or causal possibility.

The dispute is not one I wish to enter into further. I say only that this particular denial of the implication by compatibilists seems, as it stands, clearly mistaken. It is difficult to see how someone could have done otherwise at the time of action if no alternative to what he did was causally possible at that time. But, more important for present purposes, Hume does not actually argue for any such claim, nor is he in a position to do so without a more realistic account of 'the liberty of spontaneity', or of the meaning of 'X could have done otherwise'. Consequently he is not in a position to point to the place at which a fallacy occurs in the reasoning I have roughly sketched in favour of incompatibility between liberty and necessity. I do not say that there is no mistake in the reasoning – only that Hume does not identify it and give us the relief from conflict which we all seek.

Hume sometimes betrays more of a sense of the conflict than he officially allows one can have. He realizes that he has not silenced all possible objections.

It may be said, for instance, that, if voluntary actions be subjected to the same laws of necessity with the operations of matter, there is a continued chain of necessary causes, pre-ordained and pre-determined, reaching from the original cause of all to every single volition of every human creature. No contingency anywhere in the universe; no indifference; no liberty. While we act, we are, at the same time, acted upon. The ultimate Author of all our volitions is the Creator of the world, who first bestowed motion on this immense machine, and placed all beings in that particular position, whence every subsequent event, by an inevitable necessity, must result. (*E*, pp. 99–100)

This is an example of some theological difficulties apparently implied by 'the doctrine of necessity' – it is one of the reasons the doctrine has been thought to be dangerous to religion. Hume tries half-heartedly to deal with one of the theological problems, but he confesses a failure to resolve them all, and the tone of his remarks suggests that he regards that as so much the worse for religion and theology (*E*, p. 103). But for some reason he does not even consider a non-religious form of the same kind of determinism. If the theological version can seem plausibly to lead to the conclusion that God is the only responsible agent, as Hume admits, then a fully secularized version could equally plausibly lead to the conclusion that there are no responsible agents at all.

Leaving 'the original cause' out of the picture, it is easy to see 'the doctrine of necessity', when applied to everything that happens, as implying a description of a world in which 'there is a continued chain of necessary causes' extending from time immemorial to 'every single volition of every human creature' and thus leaving no alternatives, 'no indifference, no liberty' anywhere in the universe. Surely that is the worry of many who see 'the doctrine of necessity' as a threat to man's liberty – their opposition comes from more than an embarrassment at having to admit that God is the place where the buck stops.

And there seems to be at least some good reason for worry. Many sorts of actions for which agents were held responsible in the past are no longer so regarded. Greater knowledge of certain kinds about what makes people act as they do leads us to ascribe to them only diminished responsibility for those actions, or perhaps no responsibility at all. Our greater sensitivity to psychological factors in everyday life and the increased use of psychiatric testimony in the courts are sufficient proof of the point. And knowledge of the causes of human behaviour is growing. It is quite likely that the connection between the growth of our knowledge and the corresponding shrinking of the domain of responsibility is due at least in part to our belief that certain kinds of causal knowledge about human actions tend to show that the actions could not have been avoided, and to our belief that a person is not responsible for something he could not have avoided doing. And that seems to be genuine moral progress. It is wrong to blame or punish people for what they could not have avoided doing.

Once again, we might be extremely confused in thinking that some causal explanations of action show that the agent could not have done otherwise and so ought not to be blamed, but the fact is that we do think so, and our ascriptions of responsibility to some extent reflect that fact. I have already said that Hume does not identify and expose the

source of any such confusion. Nor does he address himself in any detail
to the question of exactly how certain kinds of causal explanations can
and do lead us to withhold ascriptions of responsibility. That is one
place to look for a resolution of the dispute about liberty and necessity.
It requires a much closer scrutiny of our actual practices of praising,
blaming and excusing than Hume gives us, and some explanation of
how and why the domain of moral responsibility is thought to contract
as we learn more about the causes of human behaviour. If we withhold
blame from a psychopath, for example, not merely because his behaviour was determined, but rather because it was determined in some
particular way, then what is the distinction we are using between events
determined in an exonerating way and those determined in such a way
that the agent remains responsible?

These are familiar, which is not to say easy, questions. I do not
suggest that it is impossible for a determinist to answer them. But
certainly Hume does not answer them; nor does he make much of a
beginning. That is probably because they do not embody his real
concerns. The general strategy of his 'reconciling project' is not new.
It is found in all essential respects in Hobbes.[11] Hume thinks his only
original contribution to the dispute is his novel conception of necessity –
it 'puts the whole controversy in a new light' (Hume, *Abstract*). His
main aim throughout is to establish that uniformities, and therefore
necessities, are present to the same degree in human affairs as in the
operations of inanimate matter, since for him that is a necessary
condition of there being a science of man. The possibility of such a
science is what he is interested in, so 'the doctrine of liberty' is dealt
with only to the extent that it might seem to count against that
condition's being fulfilled. A demonstration that liberty and responsibility actually require 'the doctrine of necessity' erases any threat from
that quarter. *A fortiori*, it secures the weaker point that they do not
conflict, but it does so without explaining how that compatibility is
possible, and therefore without fully resolving what has been felt to be
the perennial dispute. But if we know that liberty and necessity must
be compatible, then the 'attempt to introduce the experimental method
of reasoning into moral subjects' can proceed.

Although every human action is an event that has a cause, and the
science of man seeks the causes of human behaviour, it is not part of
Hume's aim in any of his philosophical writings actually to explain
any particular actions that have occurred. He wants only to lay the
foundations for such specific investigations by showing that they are

possible and that they will all have a certain general structure. Something can be said in advance about the *kinds* of causes human actions have, and the *sorts* of ways they bring about their effects, and Hume tries to sketch some general principles. What he says appeals primarily to psychological phenomena, understood in terms of the theory of ideas, but there is nothing in his general programme to exclude physiology from the total theory of man.

Just as in other parts of his philosophy, so here too there is a negative and a positive aspect to the overall plan. And here too the theory of ideas plays a large role in the negative phase. In outlining a general theory of action and morals, Hume discusses from another angle the role of reason in human life. His verdict is no more optimistic here than elsewhere. He starts by asking how human actions are actually brought about.

We do things of various sorts in all kinds of different circumstances, so it might seem very difficult to say anything illuminating in general about human action. Is there anything interesting in common between a man's tying his shoelace this morning and his choosing a certain profession or mode of life after years of experiment and deliberation? Hume thinks there is, and that it has profound implications for those who believe that man is a rational animal in the traditional sense.

When we reflect on the great variety of human actions it seems obvious that at least some of them, and often the most important ones, are the result of a great deal of thought. Thousands of hours of information-gathering, hypothetical reasoning, and deliberation went into the invasion of France on D-Day, for example, and finally the event occurred. Isn't something like that also often the case for individual human beings who deliberate and then decide what to do? They seem to be trying to determine or discover what they should do, or what is the best thing for them to do, and it seems as if they often succeed, and then, as a result of that discovery, act. In short, it seems that men often try to be as rational or reasonable in their actions as they can. They think about what they are about to do, and try to make their actions as much the result of rational, informed thought as possible.

The importance of rational or reasonable action is enshrined in the traditional moral precept that we ought to keep our emotions and passions under the control of our reason; men are thought to be virtuous in so far as they conform themselves to the dictates of reason. No man can always achieve this ideal, any more than a man can always believe only what he has the best reasons for believing – interest and passion will sometimes intervene – but in so far as a man is most human he will follow the guide of his reason. Rational men act in accord with their knowledge and informed beliefs.

Hume thinks this conception of reason and its relation to action is completely mistaken, just as he thinks the traditional Cartesian conception of how we come to believe things on the basis of reason could not possibly be right. He tries to demonstrate that by showing:

first, that reason alone can never be a motive to any action of the will; and *secondly*, that it can never oppose passion in the direction of the will. (p. 413)

This is an attempt to prove that what has been thought to be an important factor in the genesis of action is never *alone* sufficient to do what it has been thought to do. If the proof is successful we will have to change our view of the role of reason in action, and also come to see more clearly those causal factors that are actually most important in the production of action.

Reasoning is a process of arriving at beliefs or conclusions from various premisses or bits of evidence, and according to Hume there are only two general kinds of reasoning – demonstrative and probable. Mathematics, or demonstrative reasoning generally, is certainly useful in almost all areas of human life, but he thinks that in itself it has no influence on action, since it is always employed to achieve 'some design'd end or purpose' (p. 414). It can be used to direct our judgements concerning cause and effect, but that is all. And asking how we arrive at those judgements of cause and effect leads us to the second kind of reasoning – the 'experimental' or probable. But it too can only direct our impulses or actions; it does not produce them. If we already have an 'end' or 'purpose', then of course we can use reasoning of either kind to help us discover the best or most appropriate means of achieving it.

'Tis obvious, that when we have the prospect of pain or pleasure from any object, we feel a consequent emotion of aversion or propensity, and are carry'd to avoid or embrace what will give us this uneasiness or satisfaction. 'Tis also obvious, that this emotion rests not here, but making us cast our view on every side, comprehends whatever objects are connected with its original one by the relation of cause and effect. Here then reasoning takes place to discover this relation; and according as our reasoning varies, our actions receive a subsequent variation. But 'tis evident in this case, that the impulse arises not from reason, but is only directed by it. (p. 414)

As a way of showing that reasoning alone can never produce action, this is hardly a conclusive argument. It says only that when we already have a 'propensity' towards a certain end, the only role reason can play in action is to guide us in choosing the appropriate means to that end. In the cases Hume describes it is clear enough, as he says, that 'the impulse arises not from reason, but is only directed by it', because they are described as cases in which we start out with an antecedent 'propensity' and then look around for a way (or the best way) to satisfy it. If we have a 'propensity' or 'aversion' already, then perhaps there is nothing left for reason to do but 'direct' it, but it must be shown that all cases of human action are like this – that reason alone can *never* produce action.

Hume claims that there must be what he calls 'propensities' or 'aversions' present in every case of action, and so the 'prospect' of a certain end, or the 'mere' belief that it will be forthcoming, can never alone produce action. And that seems plausible when we consider that:

> It can never in the least concern us to know, that such objects are causes, and such others effects, if both the causes and effects be indifferent to us. Where the objects themselves do not affect us, their connexion can never give them any influence . . . (p. 414)

Here Hume is saying that in order to perform any action, or to be moved to perform it, we must be 'affected' in some way or other by what we think the action will lead to; we must not be indifferent to the effects of the action. We must in some way want or prefer that one state of affairs obtain rather than another if we are to be moved to bring about that state of affairs. And that seems extremely plausible.

We often come to believe something by reasoning, and that discovery alone does not lead us to act, for just the reason Hume gives. I might find out by observation and reasoning that there is a large juicy water-melon in the next room. I also know by reasoning what I must do in order to get some – I must get up and walk into the next room, try to get someone to bring me some, or some such thing. But clearly all that knowledge, both categorical and hypothetical, is not alone sufficient to lead me to do anything as long as I do not *want* any water-melon. If I do not want any to eat, or to give to someone else, or to use as a paperweight or for anything else, then all the knowledge I admittedly have will not lead me to try to get it. Without a want or desire, or at least a preference for water-melon over its absence, I will do nothing, however much knowledge I have acquired by reasoning. This is part of what Hume has in mind when he says that no discovery of causes or effects would concern us or affect us in any way if we were indifferent to those causes or effects.

But he wants to establish a stronger conclusion. He is trying to show that reason alone is impotent in the sphere of action – that it alone can never lead to action. And he can show that only if he can show that our being concerned by, or being affected by or our not being indifferent to, a certain course of action, is itself something that cannot be the result of some process of reason or reasoning. This can be put in another way.

'Propensities' or 'aversions' are for Hume the causes of all actions. If we could arrive by reason alone at various 'propensities' or 'aversions', then, we could be led by reason alone to act, since propensities and aversions are what cause actions, and if reason alone could bring about those states that are the causes of actions, then reason alone could be the cause of action after all. So in order to establish his thesis of the impotence of reason in action Hume must show that no propensities or aversions could be arrived at by reason alone. It would seem that whether or not that could be established would depend on what sort of things propensities or aversions are. Hume calls them 'emotions' or 'passions', and thus contrasts them directly with anything that could be arrived at by reason. But that is precisely what is in question. If to call something a passion or emotion is to assign it to a different 'faculty' and thus to imply that it could not be arrived at by reason, then it must be independently settled whether or not propensities (i.e. the causes of action) *are* passions or emotions in that sense. Hume thinks they must be.

His main argument, if successful, would establish that conclusion about propensities only indirectly. That is no shortcoming in this case, since it would do so by establishing the stronger thesis about reason and action that Hume is most interested in. He claims to be able to prove that reason alone could never lead to action, and that an action could never be 'opposed to' or 'contrary to' reason. And from that it would follow that, whatever the causes of actions are, whatever 'faculty' propensities and aversions are to be assigned to, they cannot be the sorts of things that are arrived at by reason. If they were, then action could proceed from reason alone; but Hume tries to argue independently that it cannot. If that argument is successful, the propensities or aversions that produce action must be 'emotions' or 'passions', and not the sorts of things that can be arrived at by reason.

Not only do 'conclusions of reason' and the 'propensities and aversions' that are the causes of action belong to different faculties. Hume thinks it is a mistake to think of them as even possibly in conflict with each other. In order for reason to conflict with passion in the direction of the will, reason would have to be 'pushing' the agent or creating an impulse in a direction opposite to that in which passion is 'pushing' the agent. And if reason is perfectly inert, and cannot produce any impulses at all, then obviously it cannot be opposed to passion in the production of action.

Thus it appears, that the principle, which opposes our passion, cannot be the same with reason, and is only call'd so in an improper sense. We speak not strictly and philosophically when we talk of the combat of passion and of reason. Reason is, and ought only to be the slave of the passions, and can never pretend to any other office than to serve and obey them. (p. 415)

This famous passage is the heart of Hume's theory of action, and therefore of his theory of morals as well.

His main argument for it is very complicated, and he gives it twice, in two different forms.

A passion is an original existence, or, if you will, modification of existence, and contains not any representative quality, which renders it a copy of any other existence or modification. When I am angry, I am actually possest with the passion, and in that emotion have no more a reference to any other object, than when I am thirsty, or sick, or more than five foot high. 'Tis impossible, therefore, that this passion can be oppos'd by, or be contradictory to truth and reason; since this contradiction consists in the disagreement of ideas, consider'd as copies, with those objects, which they represent. (p. 415)

When he comes to refer back to this argument in the first section of Book III, 'Of Morals', Hume repeats it as follows:[12]

Reason is the discovery of truth or falshood. Truth or falshood consists in an agreement or disagreement either to the *real* relations of ideas, or to *real* existence and matter of fact. Whatever, therefore, is not susceptible of this agreement or disagreement, is incapable of being true or false, and can never be an object of our reason. Now 'tis evident our passions, volitions, and actions, are not susceptible of any such agreement or disagreement; being original facts and realities, compleat in themselves, and implying no reference to other passions, volitions, and actions. 'Tis impossible, therefore, they can be pronounced either true or false, and be either contrary or conformable to reason. (p. 458)

In order to try to understand what Hume is getting at, let us say that the sorts of things that are true or false are 'propositions'. They are 'representative' entities in that they represent things to be a certain way, and they are true if and only if things are as the proposition represents them to be. Only propositions, so understood, are the proper 'objects of reason'. Hume appears to be saying that the only way something could be opposed to, or in conflict with, reason is by being opposed to, or in conflict with, one of the 'objects of reason'. But something can be in conflict or contradiction with a particular proposition only if it differs in truth-value from that proposition, and so whatever can be in conflict or contradiction with a proposition must be something that itself has a truth-value. And the only things that have truth-values, the only things that are either true or false, are 'representative' entities such as propositions.

But a passion or emotion is what Hume calls an 'original existence, compleat in itself'; it is not a proposition at all. When I have a certain passion, then I am in a particular state; I undergo a certain 'modification of existence'. And Hume concludes that passions do not 'represent' things to be a certain way; they just exist, or are felt. My being angry is a state or condition I am in, just as is my being more than five feet high. Therefore passions and emotions are said to be incapable of truth or falsity, and hence incapable of being in conflict with, or in opposition to, any of the 'objects of reason'. Those 'objects' are propositions that are either true or false, so there could be no such thing as a conflict or combat between reason and passion.

Of course we do speak of actions, and even passions, as being 'unreasonable', or contrary to reason, but Hume thinks that is just a loose way of speaking and is quite compatible with his view. He thinks an action is said to be 'unreasonable' only when it is 'accompany'd with' some judgement or proposition which is itself 'unreasonable' or 'contrary to reason'. If we do or feel something only because we believe that *p*, and it is in fact false that *p*, then our action or passion might be said to be unreasonable. It is unreasonable for a man to be searching the swamps of Florida for the fountain of youth, because there is no such thing; it is unreasonable for a man to try to get his car to move only by beckoning it with his finger. In the first case the man has a false belief about what exists, and in the second he has a false belief about the appropriate means for achieving one of his ends. But in both cases, Hume says it is because of the falsity of the proposition believed that his action or passion is called 'unreasonable'. Strictly speaking, no actions or passions themselves can be unreasonable or 'contrary to reason'.

> 'Tis not contrary to reason to prefer the destruction of the whole world to the scratching of my finger. 'Tis not contrary to reason for me to chuse my total ruin, to prevent the least uneasiness of an *Indian* or person wholly unknown to me. 'Tis as little contrary to reason to prefer even my own acknowledg'd lesser good to my greater, and have a more ardent affection for the former than the latter . . . In short, a passion must be accompany'd with some false judgment,

in order to its being unreasonable; and even then 'tis not the passion, properly speaking, which is unreasonable, but the judgment. (p. 416)

The argument obviously turns on the contention that the only 'objects of reason' are propositions, or things that are 'representative' and can be true or false. Since only 'original existences' or 'modifications of existence' can cause something to happen, Hume thinks that the objects of reason, and therefore reason itself, can have no such influence. Now there is no doubt that the objects of reason, so understood, can never cause anything. Propositions are at best abstract entities with no location in space or time, and so they cannot themselves cause anything that happens in space and time. They are not 'original existences' or 'modifications of existence'. That part of Hume's argument is perfectly correct. What is questionable is his further assumption that reason is somehow to be understood simply as the totality of the 'objects of reason', i.e. as a set of propositions. That seems to leave out altogether the notion of reason as a faculty of the mind, or reasoning as a mental process.

Hume does say that reason is the *discovery* of truth or falsehood, and that implies that the activities of reason or reasoning involve more than just the 'objects of reason'. They involve our taking a certain 'attitude' towards some 'objects of reason', or our 'operating' with or on them in certain ways, or our 'getting into a certain position' with respect to them. To discover that something is so is to come to believe it. *What* a person believes is either true or false, but his discovering or believing it is not. That is just as much a state of the person, or a 'modification of existence', just as 'non-representative' and incapable of having a truth-value, as is his being angry or his being more than five feet tall. So although the 'objects of reason' – the things that are true or false – cannot cause action, and therefore cannot be opposed to passion in the production of action, it does not follow that reason or reasoning alone cannot cause action. For all Hume has shown so far, it is possible for the discovery by reasoning of the truth of a certain proposition to lead one to act, even though that proposition itself cannot cause anything.

There are good reasons for Hume to agree with this assessment of his argument. For one thing, it seems that one belief – one 'believing' – can be in conflict with another in the same way that one passion or propensity can be in conflict with another. A mother can believe that her son is a good boy while also believing that he has just committed his seventh robbery and assault, and that good boys don't do such things. There can be conflict, or tension, even felt tension, between believings. This is not to say only that all the propositions believed cannot be true together. That is so, but the conflict I am referring to cannot be understood purely in terms of the truth-values of the propositions believed. It is a conflict or tension between two different 'original existences' or 'modifications of existence', and it is just as familiar in the case of beliefs, or believings, or inclinations to believe, as it is in the case of passions or emotions. If, as it seems, believing something can have such effects even though the propositions involved do not, and if, as Hume allows, we can discover or come to believe things by reason or reasoning, then the argument considered so far does not show that it is impossible for reason or reasoning alone to cause action.

Hume's own positive theory to the effect that 'belief is more properly an act of the sensitive, than of the cogitative part of our natures' (p. 183), supports this verdict. He describes the state of believing that *p* as that of having a certain *feeling* or *sentiment* towards the idea of *p*, or of 'holding' the idea of *p* in the mind with a certain sentiment or feeling. Sentiments and feelings can certainly conflict, and can cause action, so if Hume is to show that beliefs arrived at by reason or reasoning cannot cause action, he needs some independent argument for the impotence of those particular sentiments or feelings that are beliefs arrived at by reason. The admitted fact that the 'objects of reason' or the 'objects' of belief are not 'original existences, compleat in themselves', will not suffice.

Furthermore, if Hume's argument showed that no passions or actions, but only propositions, can be contrary to reason, or unreasonable, it would also show that no *beliefs* can be contrary to reason or unreasonable either. Someone's believing something is not itself a proposition that is either true or false, any more than his being more than five feet tall has a truth-value. To believe something, or to be more than five feet tall, is simply to be in a certain 'state'. If the 'reasonableness' or 'unreasonableness' of a belief is solely a matter of the truth-value of what is believed, as Hume suggests, then *how* someone comes to discover or believe something – what procedures he follows, how careful and thorough he is, and so on – is irrelevant to the question of the reasonableness of his belief. But is an unreasonable belief simply one that is false? Surely a person can quite reasonably believe something that is, unknown to him and to everyone else, false, or quite unreasonably (e.g. superstitiously) believe something that is actually true. Hume never thoroughly discusses this distinction.

He holds the sceptical view that we have no reason to believe any of the things we believe; that we are mistaken in thinking that we have

275

any good reasons for believing what we do. And so it might be thought that Hume can gladly accept the conclusion just arrived at to the effect that no *beliefs*, as well as actions or passions, can be contrary or conformable to reason. But that is not so. To accept that conclusion would deprive him of a way of making the very point he insists on about the role of passion or feeling in the production of action. He establishes his sceptical conclusion by showing that, contrary to appearances, the best possible reasons anyone could ever get for any of his beliefs about the unobserved are never good enough to give him any reason to believe what he does rather than its negation; the grounds for each are equal. But the consequence just deduced from Hume's latest argument is much stronger than that. It says that beliefs are simply not the sorts of things that could possibly be reasonable or unreasonable. It is not just that the best possible reasons there could be are, alas, not good enough, but that believings, not being propositions, are no more capable of being reasonable or contrary to reason than are my passions, my actions or my height.

But the whole point of Hume's discussion of the production of action is to contrast feelings or passions with discoveries by reason, and to argue that the former are always the dominant factor and that the latter alone can never cause action. And the kinds of discoveries by reason he has in mind include at least ordinary beliefs about the behaviour of things in the world around us arrived at by straightforward causal reasoning. He wants to show that even my well-based belief that there is a large, juicy water-melon in the next room, say, can never alone lead me to do anything. Observing various things and making causal inferences from them on the basis of past experience is all part of what Hume means to include under the rubric 'reason or reasoning' when he contrasts it with passion or feeling.[13] The assumption is that to acquire a belief by reasoning is not in itself to be 'influenced' or 'affected' one way or the other. In short, it is not to have a 'propensity' or 'aversion' to any action. And without a 'propensity' or an 'aversion' no action occurs.

Hume still has not established that to acquire a belief by reasoning is not in itself to have a 'propensity' or 'aversion'. That conclusion does not follow from the fact that the 'object' of belief, the proposition that is either true or false, has no causal influence. Nor can he easily concede that believings are simply not the sort of things that could be reasonable or unreasonable, since that would put believings and feelings into the same class, and deprive him of the desired contrast between feelings and beliefs arrived at by reason. How then does he know that our coming to believe something as a result of reasoning never by itself causes us to act and that a feeling or passion is always present?

Hume finds that sometimes 'we feel an . . . emotion of aversion or propensity' (p. 414) and this might suggest that we are *directly aware* of the second and dominant factor in the causality of all action. Perhaps we notice by direct inspection, as it were, that we have the propensity, and notice that it is different from the 'mere' belief or 'prospect'. This would be the best possible evidence we could have for the presence of the two different factors, and there is no doubt that we often have such feelings. We sometimes *feel* impelled to act; we even speak of feeling 'uncontrollable' passions, and on those occasions, perhaps, we can directly find a passion which we take to be the cause of our action. But Hume's thesis is that passions or emotions – states that are not arrived at by reasoning – are *always* present in the production of action, and it is difficult to believe that I am overcome with emotion when I simply decide to cross the road or when I decide to write down something I have just found out. I am certainly not aware of any emotion or passion impelling me to act in such cases – they seem the very model of cool, dispassionate action.

Hume agrees that direct inspection or introspection does not always yield a passion as the cause of action. He thinks that although it often seems to us as if there is no passion or emotion involved, nevertheless in such cases we are wrong. There is a passion there, although it is entirely natural that we should miss it.

'Tis natural for one, that does not examine objects with a strict philosophic eye, to imagine, that those actions of the mind are entirely the same, which produce not a different sensation, and are not immediately distinguishable to the feeling and perception. Reason, for instance, exerts itself without producing any sensible emotion; and except in the more sublime disquisitions of philosophy, or in the frivolous subtilities of the schools, scarce ever conveys any pleasure or uneasiness. Hence it proceeds, that every action of the mind, which operates with the same calmness and tranquility, is confounded with reason by all those, who judge of things from the first view and appearance. Now 'tis certain, there are certain calm desires and tendencies, which, tho' they be real passions, produce little emotion in the mind, and are more known by their effects than by the immediate feeling or sensation. These desires are of two kinds; either certain instincts originally implanted in our natures, such as benevolence and resentment, the love of life, and kindness to children; or the general appetite to good, and aversion to evil, consider'd merely as such. When any of these passions are calm, and cause no disorder in the soul, they are very readily taken for the determinations of reason, and are suppos'd to proceed from the same faculty, with that, which judges of truth and falshood. Their nature and principles have been suppos'd the same, because their sensations are not evidently different. (p. 417)

We do not simply *feel* 'calm passions'; their existence and efficacy is not discovered by direct inspection.

But Hume says "'tis certain' that there are such passions and desires; they feel to us just like 'determinations of reason', but he claims to know they are not. This does not cohere very well with his fundamental principle that we cannot be wrong about the contents of our own minds at a given moment.

For since all actions and sensations of the mind are known to us by consciousness, they must necessarily appear in every particular what they are, and be what they appear. Every thing that enters the mind, being in *reality* a perception, 'tis impossible any thing shou'd to *feeling* appear different. This were to suppose, that even where we are most intimately conscious, we might be mistaken. (p. 190)[14]

Apparently we are often mistaken about whether or not a certain calm passion is before the mind. On the basis of the feeling or sensation alone we often think that only a 'determination of reason' is leading us to act, but in fact, unknown to us, it is a calm passion. Hume is willing to forget one of the foundations of the theory of ideas in order to support his account of the role of reason in action, although, as we shall see, his theory of action takes its shape primarily from the theory of ideas.

He says that the calm passions are 'more known by their effects than by the immediate feeling or sensation', but what are the effects by which such passions are known to exist? The only candidates would seem to be the actions or inclinations which the calm passions actually cause. But if the calm passions are known to exist from the fact that certain actions or inclinations occur, and the fact that those passions are the causes of those actions or inclinations, then there must be some independent way to discover that calm passions are the causes of those actions and inclinations. If we knew that passions were always involved in the production of every action we could infer from the occurrence of an action that a passion existed, even if it was not 'violent' enough to be felt. That is in effect what Hume does. But he still has given no such independent justification. The question of whether a separate passion is in fact involved in the causality of every action is precisely what is at issue.

There is considerable truth in the passage about calm passions just quoted, but it is not obvious that the idea that having a 'propensity' is a matter of having a certain feeling or passion is part of that truth. Even

Hume's own examples of the calm 'passions' do not clearly support that idea. He says there are certain 'calm desires and *tendencies*' which are of two distinct kinds: either 'certain *instincts* originally planted in our natures' or 'the general *appetite* to good, and *aversion* to evil, consider'd merely as such'. It is quite plausible to suggest that involved in the causality of every action there must be certain *tendencies*, *instincts* or *appetites*. Without tendencies or urges to do something of one sort rather than another how could we ever be led to do anything at all? But Hume thinks appetites or desires are themselves passions or feelings.

For example, he speaks of kindness to children as a passion or emotion – one of those 'instincts originally implanted in our natures'. But to have that 'instinct', it would seem, it would be enough for one to be moved to act and disposed to feel certain things on certain occasions; for example, to treat children kindly, to try to prevent harm from coming to them, to feel distress when they might be harmed or in danger, and so on. Being the sort of person who tends to act and feel in those ways is what it is to be a person who is kind to children. But being that sort of person does not require any particular feeling, sensation or passion which is itself the feeling or passion of kindness to children. People who lacked the appropriate tendencies or dispositions would not be thought of as kind to children, but they would not be disqualified because there was a particular feeling or passion they lacked. But Hume says that such tendencies or propensities are passions or feelings.

He clearly thinks that to have a tendency to do a certain thing rather than some alternative is to *prefer* to do that thing, or not to be indifferent as between the alternatives. We could never be led to act unless we were not indifferent to what we think the act will lead to; that is what 'being moved' to act is. And from the true premiss that we would not act unless we preferred one thing over another, or were not indifferent, Hume appears to conclude that we are always moved to act by a passion. Or perhaps it is more accurate to say that he does not carefully distinguish his conclusion from that premiss. For him they seem to be just the same. This is confirmed by the famous passage considered earlier.

> 'Tis not contrary to reason to *prefer* the destruction of the whole world to the scratching of my finger. 'Tis not contrary to reason for me to *chuse* my total ruin, to prevent the least uneasiness of an *Indian* or person wholly unknown to me. 'Tis as little contrary to reason to *prefer* even my own acknowledg'd lesser good to my greater . . . (p. 416, my italics on verbs)

Barry Stroud

and he concludes:

> In short, a *passion* must be accompany'd with some false judgment in order to its being unreasonable. (p. 416, my italics)

This is supposed to be an illustration of how it is impossible, strictly speaking, for a passion to be contrary to reason. But Hume's examples are *preferrings* and *choosings*, and so they confirm his main thesis only if preferring one thing to another, or choosing one thing over another, is a matter of having a certain *passion*. But that is just what was to have been established.

The theory of ideas is probably at work here. Hume thinks that if you want something or have a propensity towards something then there must be something that is your want or your propensity, and that that thing must be a perception in the mind.

> It has been observ'd, that nothing is ever present to the mind but its perceptions; and that all the actions of seeing, hearing, judging, loving, hating, and thinking, fall under this denomination. The mind can never exert itself in any action, which we may not comprehend under the term of *perception* . . . (p. 456)

Wanting something is a case of what Hume calls 'the mind's exerting itself in action'; it is a certain kind of mental or psychological phenomenon, and he believes that there must be a perception before the mind if any psychological phenomenon is occurring. The perceptions involved in the case of wanting, preferring, and so on, are all impressions. In particular, they are those impressions of reflection which are emotions, feelings or passions.

I have argued that Hume does not prove, or even make very plausible, the contention that a feeling or passion must always be present for action to occur. Much of its attraction for him derives from the general framework of his unquestioned theory of the mind. But it is difficult to deny the intuitive idea from which he begins to the effect that no belief about the consequences of a certain course of action will lead me to do it unless I also want or prefer those consequences to obtain. If I am totally indifferent as between their presence or absence I will never be moved to bring them about or to prevent them from coming about, whatever I believe. So it seems that something in addition to the 'mere' belief must be present if any action is to occur. But none of this implies that the 'something in addition' is a particular mental item or event, even one that we perhaps do not notice when we 'judge of things from the first view and appearance'. And this is an important point about wants or propensities.

If one event B comes about as a result of another event A, then two things must be true: (i) A occurs, (ii) A causes B. If the first condition is not fulfilled then B does not happen as a result of A; and if the second condition is not fulfilled then B does not happen as a result of A, even though A happens. So we can distinguish two parts or aspects of the production of B, and hence say that the 'mere' occurrence of A is not alone enough to bring about B. At least one other condition must be fulfilled. But obviously none of this implies that if A occurs and B occurs then because A *could have* occurred without B, or *could have* occurred without causing B, there must have been some other event in addition to A which 'helped' cause B. In a world in which A causes B, the occurrence of A alone is enough. If that were not so, then on Humean principles it would follow that *no* event or state of affairs, however complex, would ever be enough in itself to cause any other event or state of affairs, so nothing would ever come about as a result of anything else. For any two events allegedly related as cause and effect Hume argues that it is always possible for the first to exist without the second. But if that implied that in order for the second to be brought about something else must be added to the first, then even the then-augmented 'cause', since it too *could* exist without the second event occurring, would still not be enough to bring the second about, and so on, and so on. This naïve appeal to possibility obviously proves nothing about causal insufficiency.

This shows that there is a way of understanding Hume's quite reasonable claim that no belief alone would lead me to act *unless* I also had a certain desire or preference, without taking it to imply the existence of two distinct items or events, in the mind or elsewhere. It can be quite true that there are two parts or aspects of the production of an action – belief and desire or propensity – without desires or propensities themselves being particular mental items. A 'mere' belief alone would never lead a person to act unless that person were such that, when he gets a belief of that kind, it leads, or tends to lead, to action. And being in some such dispositional state might be all that having a certain desire or propensity consists in. It need not be an additional mental item that itself produces the action.

I am suggesting that the intuitive idea from which Hume derives his theory of action is quite compatible with a non-Humean theory of desires or propensities. It might well be that to have a desire for or propensity towards E is simply to be in a state such that when you come to believe that a certain action will lead to E you are moved to perform that action. I am not interested in the details of such an account at the moment – obviously it is hopelessly crude and oversimplified as it stands[15] – but if some such theory is on the right track, then wanting, preferring or having a propensity need not be understood as a matter of a certain perception's being before the mind. Having a propensity will be nothing more than there being a disposition for certain things to occur in the mind when certain others occur there. We have seen earlier that Hume's pattern of psychological explanation must endow the mind with some dispositions or propensities which cannot themselves be understood in terms of the presence of actual perceptions, so not every psychological statement is such that its truth requires the existence of actual perceptions in the mind. The present suggestion about wants or propensities would be one further instance. If a person is not in a state such that, when he gets a certain belief he will be led to act in a certain way, then the 'mere' belief alone will not lead him to act in that way. He lacks the appropriate propensity or desire. And even if desires or propensities are understood as certain kinds of causal states, or dispositions – and not particular items felt or inferred to be in the mind – there is still a perfectly good sense in which without the desire or propensity the belief would never lead to action. If A occurs, but does not cause B, then B does not come about as a result of A's occurrence.

When Hume says that desires or propensities are passions or emotions he does not mean only that they are feelings. He is even more concerned to show that they are not arrived at by reasoning, and hence that reason alone can never produce action. And even on the non-Humean theory I have suggested, according to which desires are not feelings, he could still be right about the role of reason in action. There is not much independent argument on this point. I said that Hume does not distinguish the true premiss that we would not act unless we wanted or preferred one course of action over another from the questionable conclusion that we are always moved to act by a passion or feeling. And since for him passions or feelings are not the sorts of things that can be arrived at by reason, he thinks he has established that reason alone can never produce action. But there is at least one attempt to show more directly that reason must be supplemented by something not derived from reason if action is to occur. It is the claim that 'the ultimate ends of human actions can never, in any case, be accounted for by *reason*' (*E*, p. 293).

Ask a man *why he uses exercise*; he will answer, *because he desires to keep his health*. If you then enquire, *why he desires health*, he will readily reply, *because sickness is painful*. If you push your enquiries farther, and desire a reason *why he hates pain*, it is impossible he can ever give any. This is an ultimate end, and is never referred to any other object.

Perhaps to your second question, *why he desires health*, he may also reply, that *it is necessary for the exercise of his calling*. If you ask, *why he is anxious on that head*, he will answer, *because he desires to get money*. If you demand *Why? It is the instrument of pleasure*, says he. And beyond this it is an absurdity to ask for a reason. It is impossible there can be a progress *in infinitum*; and that one thing can always be a reason why another is desired. Something must be desirable on its own account, and because of its immediate accord or agreement with human sentiment and affection. (*E*, p. 293)

This is perhaps the best expression of Hume's conception of reason.[16] It does not deny that I can come by reasoning to have a certain want or propensity that I lacked before I engaged in the reasoning. Wanting good health, but not knowing how to get it, I can discover by experimental reasoning that exercise is the best way to get it, and thereby come to want exercise. Reasoning as I did is what led me to want exercise. But if I had not wanted health at the outset, the discovery that if one exercises then one stays healthy would not have resulted in my wanting exercise. A prior want, propensity or lack of indifference is always required in order for reasoning to provide me with wants. And if reasoning provides me with wants or propensities only if I have some prior want or propensity, then reasoning cannot provide me with all the wants or propensities I have. Something must be wanted on its own account, and not just as a means to, or as a way of, getting something else one wants.

Hume's examples here trace the chain of wants back to a desire for pleasure, or for the absence of pain, but there is no need for a view like his to incorporate only a monolithic doctrine of motivation. A Humean theory of the role of reason in action could be correct even if there were many different basic, underived wants. All that is required is that, for each action, there be at least one want or propensity in its causal ancestry that is not arrived at by reasoning. And that follows from the extremely plausible proposition that for every action there is a want or propensity in its production, together with the plausible principle that reasoning produces a want or propensity only if the agent also has some prior want or propensity. Those who see men as sometimes moved to act on the basis of reason alone must deny this latter principle, and also explain how considerations of reason alone can actually move someone to act.[17] They have tended to concentrate their hopes in the domain of morality.

Notes

1. All page numbers appearing alone in parentheses in the text refer to *A Treatise of Human Nature*, ed. L. A. Selby-Bigge (Oxford University Press, 1958).

2. It is not clear how basic Hume thinks these differences are, or what he thinks accounts for them. He compares them here with the differences among 'different trees, which regularly produce fruit, whose relish is different from each other' (p. 401). But he insists on the social origin of important differences among people when he writes: 'The skin, pores, muscles, and nerves of a day-labourer are different from those of a man of quality: So are his sentiments, actions, and manners. The different stations of life influence the whole fabric, external and internal; and these different stations arise necessarily, because uniformly, from the necessary and uniform principles of human nature. Men cannot live without society, and cannot be associated without government. Government makes a distinction of property, and establishes the different ranks of men. This produces industry, traffic, manufactures, law-suits, war, leagues, alliances, voyages, travels, cities, fleets, ports, and all those other actions and objects, which cause such a diversity, and at the same time maintain such an uniformity in human life' (p. 402).

3. For an early and influential expression of the idea that Hume did all that ever ought to have been needed in this subject, see Moritz Schlick, *Problems of Ethics*, tr. David Rynin (New York: Dover Publications, 1962), p. 143. For a more recent expression of the same idea see Donald Davidson, 'Freedom to Act', in Ted Honderich (ed.), *Essays on Freedom of Action* (London: Routledge &Kegan Paul, 1973), p. 139.

4. It has been widely believed, for example, that we tend to confuse laws of nature, which are discovered by science, with prescriptions or requirements, which we might feel we are somehow compelled to follow. This diagnosis has been offered by, for example, Schlick, op. cit., pp. 146–8; University of California Associates, 'The Freedom of the Will', in H. Feigl and W. Sellars (eds.), *Readings in Philosophical Analysis* (New York: Appleton Century Crofts, 1949), pp. 602–4; and A. J. Ayer, 'Freedom and Necessity', *Philosophical Essays* (London: Macmillan, 1959), p. 283.

5. All page numbers preceded by an 'E' in parentheses in the text refer to *Enquiries Concerning the Human Understanding and Concerning the Principles of Morals*, ed. L. A. Selby-Bigge (Oxford University Press, 1962).

6. This argument is reproduced almost *verbatim*, with only small alterations and improvements, from the *Treatise* (pp. 408–9).

7. It could be, for example, that actions 'belong' to a particular agent only if the wants, beliefs, etc., of that person contribute in a certain way to explanations of those actions, but the explanations in question are not causal or do not fit Hume's model of causal explanation. The controversy about the production and explanation of human actions is one of the most complicated issues in recent philosophy.

8. For an elaboration of the idea that Hume's causal theory of action is what leads him astray, and that his errors on that question undermine his support for the strong thesis that the ascription of responsibility requires 'the doctrine of necessity', see Philippa Foot, 'Freewill as Involving Determinism', *Philosophical Review*, vol. lxvi, 1957.

9. Hume's causal theory of action might also be seen as a result of the severe constraints imposed by his conception of the self. That conception leaves no room for a self or agent as the initiator of a causal sequence, and the idea of agency, or initiating, is of central importance in our ascriptions of responsibility. I owe this observation to Hans Sluga.

10. For a more detailed elaboration of the argument I sketch here see David Wiggins, 'Towards a Reasonable Libertarianism', Ted Honderich (ed.), op. cit., especially pp. 43–4.

11. Thomas Hobbes, *The English Works of Thomas Hobbes*, ed. Sir William Molesworth (London: John Bohn, 1839), vols. 4, 5.

12. Similar considerations are advanced in Francis Hutcheson, *Illustrations on the Moral Sense*, ed. Bernard Peach (Cambridge, Mass.: Harvard University Press, 1971), pp. 120–21.

13. This is perhaps further evidence for Kemp Smith's conjecture that Hume's views on action and morals were composed first, before generalizing the point to all cognitive activity in Book I of the *Treatise*. The 'reasoning' that Hume here contrasts with 'feeling' or 'passion' includes ordinary causal reasoning, the conclusions of which he here regards as 'calm and indolent judgments of the understanding' (p. 457), whereas in Book I he holds the more radical view that even those conclusions do not belong to 'reason' or to 'the understanding', but to 'the imagination'. However, the two different contrasts remain present in the *Enquiries* as well. The first *Enquiry* parallels Book I of the *Treatise* in contrasting 'reason' or 'the understanding' with 'sentiment or feeling', while the second *Enquiry* continues to contrast only the 'cool assent of the understanding', which 'begets no desire or aversion' (*E*, p. 172) with 'an active feeling or sentiment' (*E*, p. 290), which 'takes possession of the heart' (*E*, p. 172).

14. I have altered the passage as it appears in the text in accord with Hume's directions on p. 636.

15. There are great difficulties in any very simple dispositional theory of wants or desires, but there is no need for such a theory to be objectionably reductionistic or behaviouristic. It is quite likely, for example, that the notion of desire cannot be understood separately from that of belief, and vice versa. See, for example, Donald Davidson, 'Mental Events' and 'Psychology as Philosophy', in his *Actions and Events* (Oxford: Clarendon Press, 1980).

16. Very similar considerations, along with explicit reference to Aristotle, can be found in Hutcheson, op. cit., p. 123.

17. For the most interesting recent account of this type see Thomas Nagel, *The Possibility of Altruism* (Oxford University Press, 1970). Nagel grants that for every action there is a want, but he denies that at least one of the wants involved must always be underived or basic. The presence of what he calls 'motivated wants' is not enough, he claims, to establish Hume's conclusion. That is not to say that Nagel himself succeeds in explaining how rational considerations alone actually move people to act.

Biographical Note

Barry Stroud is Professor of Philosophy at the University of California, Berkeley, where he has taught since 1961. In addition to *Hume* (1977), from which the present selection is taken, he is the author of numerous philosophical essays on a variety of subjects, primarily within the theory of knowledge and the history of philosophy.

Further Reading

A. J. Ayer, 'Freedom and Necessity' in *Philosophical Essays* (London: Macmillan, 1959); M. Schlick, *Problems of Ethics* (New York: Dover, 1962), Chapter VII; D. Davidson, 'Freedom to Act' in T. Honderich (ed.), *Essays on Freedom of Action* (London: Routledge & Kegan Paul, 1973); P. Foot, 'Freewill as Involving Determinism', *Philosophical Review*, 1957; D. Wiggins, 'Towards a Reasonable Libertarianism' in T. Honderich, op. cit.; A. J. Ayer, 'Man as a Subject for Science' in *Metaphysics and Common Sense* (London: Macmillan, 1969); D. Davidson, 'Actions, Reasons and Causes' in *Essays on Actions and Events* (Oxford University Press, 1980); P. Ardal, *Passion and Value in Hume's Treatise* (Edinburgh University Press, 1966); J. L. Mackie, *Hume's Moral Theory* (London: Routledge & Kegan Paul, 1980), Chapter III.

P. F. Strawson

Kant: The *Critique of Pure Reason*

Kant's *Critique of Pure Reason*, despite its system perhaps as ungoverned and therefore intractable a book as philosophy has to offer, is divided by P. F. Strawson into three parts, different one from another. The first has to do with a set of ideas which is the necessary structure of any intelligible thought about the world and our part in it. These ideas set limits to what can be conceived, to the making of sense. A second part is the rejection of any claims to knowledge which go beyond our experience, what empirically we know. To escape experience is to escape significance, to go beyond sense. A third part makes a division between appearance and reality, and shuts us out from reality, leaves us within appearances. All of what we experience, even ourselves, consists not in noumena but in no more than phenomena.

In the preface to *The Bounds of Sense*, a book which is an exemplar of philosophical judgement, and whose introductory chapter is reprinted below, Strawson remarks that reading as well as re-reading the *Critique of Pure Reason* produces in one a commingled sense of great insights and great mystification. He finds the principal insights in the first of the three parts he distinguishes, which is not to say that it is free of mystification and misconception. In the other parts, or at any rate the third, it is at least true that the proportion of insight to both mystification and other error is reversed. The third part, indeed, is at war with the guiding idea of the second, and not victorious.

The first section of the chapter is a preliminary sketch along these lines, which sketch is filled in in what follows, the whole chapter thus providing a general review of the *Critique*. It is a sketch for a fuller picture given in the succeeding chapters of *The Bounds of Sense*. Both

---

Immanuel Kant, 1724–1804. Born and lived in Konigsberg, now Kaliningrad. University professor. Sometimes taken as having brought together British Empiricism and Continental Rationalism. Enviably quiet unmarried life, and sympathy for the American and French Revolutions.

the chapter and the book set a standard in philosophy, a standard for a fundamental kind of reflection on the great philosophical works of the past, of which the *Critique* indubitably is one. It is a kind of reflection informed, I think, by the idea that philosophy is not entirely unlike science, that there is also progress in philosophy, and hence that it is within the capability of its present to judge and indeed to discard parts of its past. This is to make true use of the achievement of the past, and to further the progress of philosophy. In considering the great works of philosophy there cannot be any imperative to the effect that they are to be considered in some non-judgemental way from within the world-views or the preoccupations of their makers. There can be an excess of sympathetic understanding.

The first of the three lines of thought in the *Critique*, separated out from the others and not in Kant's way run together with other things, most notably a doctrine about faculties of the mind, has at bottom to do with a number of variously related claims as to the necessary features of any intelligible picture of the world and our experience in it. The first claim is that it is impossible to conceive of experience in other than a temporal way, as somehow static or out of time. The second and the most fundamental claim is that each temporal sequence of experiences must have a common character or unity, such a one as allows a person or subject to distinguish between them and the owner of them, and in fact to see or to claim them as his. At least a part of the character or unity in question is that experiences do not consist in individual items of which it might be said that each in itself has sufficient properties to be a moment or part of consciousness. Rather, an experience consists in something's being classified, in its being put under a general concept. An experience *is* an instance of a type. (pp. 294–5, 300) A third claim is that experience must be conceived as *of* something else, which has an independent or objective existence. The remaining three claims are to the effect that the fundamental objects of experience must be taken as in space; that all objects as well as any experiences of them are at places within one space and occur at points in one time-order; and that the objects are relatively permanent and in causal relations with one another. The six claims, in various ways connected, together constitute a minimum, fundamental and general characterization of the world, and, above all, our role in it, a metaphysics of experience. It is elaborated by Kant in a number of ways. (pp. 302–6)

In virtue in particular of the third claim of the metaphysics of experience, there is the conclusion that the philosophical tradition of classical empiricism, exemplified by Hume, is fundamentally mistaken. Experience cannot be characterized in terms of a private stuff somehow complete in itself, transient ideas or sense-data. Experience, in the first instance, is that which is *of* objects, of that which has a reality independent of the facts of our access to it. (pp. 293–4)

The second line of thought, prised out of its encumbering context in the *Critique*, is different in not conflicting but in being consonant with classical empiricism. It conflicts with the philosophical tradition of transcendent metaphysics, Plato to Hegel and beyond. This line of thought has as its guide what is named by Strawson the principle of significance. This is that supposed ideas, including those of God and the soul, which lack a certain connection with the empirical world, are in fact without meaning of their intended kind, and, it might be said, not ideas at all in a certain standard use of that term. It is necessary that we know, about propositions making standard use of any putative idea, what states of affairs *given in experience* would make the propositions true. (pp. 291–2) It follows that speculation about certain transcendent realities, transcendent metaphysics, is in fact delusive. It is delusive, at any rate, if it is taken to amount to knowledge. Taken differently, it is regarded by Kant as essential both to the *Critique* and to more of his philosophy. (pp. 296–7, 306, 308 f.) In connection with religion, morality and the freedom of the will, Kant made essential use of propositions about supersensible reality. As for the delusive kind of speculation, its futility can be shown by the fact that it issues in contradiction. For example, no matter which of two opposed views we take concerning a beginning of the world, we end in contradiction. There is the difference between Kant and the classical empiricists that he does not merely deploy his principle of significance against transcendent metaphysics but rather advances a great deal of particularized argument. (Section 3)

The third line of thought involves Kant in going dramatically against his own principle of significance. The result, given what has just been said of the impossibility of knowledge of such things as God and the soul, comes as something of a shock to the system. Our ordinary experience of things, and our experience of others and ourselves, is experience of appearances, phenomena. Nature as we know it somehow made by mind. Strawson notes that this is not the cautious view that we cannot know any supersensible reality that may exist, but the view that there is just such a reality and that it is wholly beyond our knowledge. By contrast, such empiricists as Locke and Russell do allow us inferential knowledge of what they take to be beyond, or partly beyond, our experience. The Kantian doctrine does certainly issue in unintelligibility, notably in connection with space and time, which themselves are demoted to being but appearances. The doctrine is again bound up with Kant's idea of the faculties of the mind. It is in fact much closer to Berkeley's idealism, which reduces all reality to mentality, than Kant allows. (p. 295; Section 4)

The chapter concludes partly with a preliminary consideration of something of which Kant makes much, and which has been the concern of many of those who have written of the *Critique*. This is the existence of two sorts of *a priori* judgements, judgements known by us to be true independently of our experience. *A priori* judgements of the analytic kind, somehow typified by 'All bachelors are unmarried' and the like, are uncontroversial, or at any rate not controversial in the way of the others – of these others it cannot be said, for what it is worth, that their predicates are contained in their subjects. It is Strawson's view that Kant nowhere provides a clear distinction between two kinds of *a priori* judgements, and that the matter is not essential to the part of his work which remains of greatest importance, the first line of thought having to do with the necessary character of any intelligible reflection on the world and ourselves, and hence, as we might as well say, with the necessary character of the world and ourselves.

Strawson's emancipating way with the *Critique of Pure Reason* is not one which suits the inclinations of all philosophers. It begins from scholarship but is not an endeavour in it, and thus is a way wholly different from that of traditional historians of philosophy. They are, in my own view, often enough prone to find a lack of understanding in us when in fact there is a lack of clear matter to be understood. Beyond doubt, Strawson's way constitutes an advance of significance in our relationship with the philosophical past.

P. F. Strawson

Kant: *The Critique of Pure Reason*

1. Two Faces of the Critique

It is possible to imagine kinds of world very different from the world as we know it. It is possible to describe types of experience very different from the experience we actually have. But not any purported and grammatically permissible description of a possible kind of experience would be a truly intelligible description. There are limits to what we can conceive of, or make intelligible to ourselves, as a possible general structure of experience. The investigation of these limits, the investigation of the set of ideas which forms the limiting framework of all our thought about the world and experience of the world, is, evidently, an important and interesting philosophical undertaking. No philosopher has made a more strenuous attempt on it than Kant.

A central difficulty in understanding his attempt lies in the fact that he himself thought of it in terms of a certain misleading analogy. It is a commonplace of casual, and of scientific, observation, that the character of our experience, the way things appear to us, is partly determined by our human constitution, by the nature of our sense organs and nervous system. The workings of the human perceptual mechanism, the ways in which our experience is causally dependent on those workings, are matters for empirical, or scientific, not philosophical, investigation. Kant was well aware of this; he knew very well that such an empirical inquiry was of a quite different kind from the investigation he proposed into the fundamental structure of ideas in terms of which alone we can make intelligible to ourselves the idea of experience of the world. Yet, in spite of this awareness, he conceived the latter investigation on a kind of strained analogy with the former.

P. F. Strawson, 'General Review', Part 1, *The Bounds of Sense: An Essay on Kant's Critique of Pure Reason* (London: Methuen, 1966). Reprinted without alteration by permission of author and publisher.

Wherever he found limiting or necessary general features of experience, he declared their source to lie in our own cognitive constitution; and this doctrine he considered indispensable as an explanation of the possibility of knowledge of the necessary structure of experience. Yet there is no doubt that this doctrine is incoherent in itself and masks, rather than explains, the real character of his inquiry; so that a central problem in understanding the *Critique* is precisely that of disentangling all that hangs on this doctrine from the analytical argument which is in fact independent of it.

The separation of these two strands in the *Critique*, however, is only part of a wider task of division between what remains fruitful and interesting and what no longer appears acceptable, or even promising, in its doctrines. Accordingly, I shall begin this introductory survey by setting out, in rough opposition, the elements of this division. I shall follow this with a slightly fuller but still introductory account of some of the central themes of the work.

Like many of his predecessors and successors, Kant laid stress on the fact that the results hitherto achieved in philosophy contrasted unfavourably with those achieved in mathematics and natural science. If philosophy too was to be set 'on the sure path of a science', one requisite was that it should limit its pretensions; and a major instrument of this necessary limitation was a principle repeatedly enunciated and applied by Kant throughout the *Critique*. This is the principle that there can be no legitimate, or even meaningful, employment of ideas or concepts which does not relate them to empirical or experiential conditions of their application. If we wish to use a concept in a certain way, but are unable to specify the kind of experience-situation to which the concept, used in that way, would apply, then we are not really envisaging any legitimate use of that concept at all.[1] In so using it, we shall not merely be saying what we do not know; we shall not really know what we are saying.

This principle, which I shall refer to as Kant's principle of significance, is one with which empiricist philosophers have no difficulty in sympathizing. They sympathize just as readily with the consequence which Kant drew from it: viz. the complete repudiation of transcendent metaphysics. Whole regions of philosophy – regions of maximum pretension and minimum agreement – owed their existence, he maintained, to disregard of the principle of significance. Freed from the obligation to specify the empirical conditions of application of the concepts they used, philosophers might seem to be giving information about the nature of Reality as it is in itself, instead of as it appears in the limited and sense-bound experience of creatures such as ourselves; but their seeming knowledge was delusion, and the first task of a critical and scientific philosophy was to ensure that it was recognized as such. The first task of philosophy is to set its own limits.

Kant was not content merely to draw this general negative conclusion about the impossibility of transcendent metaphysics. He thought that the propensity to think in terms of ideas for which no empirical conditions of application could be specified was not merely a philosophers' aberration, but a natural and inevitable propensity of human reason. It was even, in some ways, a beneficial propensity. Certain ideas which had in themselves no empirical application or significance nevertheless inevitably arose in the course of scientific inquiry, and might even serve a useful function in stimulating the indefinite extension of empirical knowledge.[2] The illusion of *metaphysical* knowledge arose only when it was thought that there must be realities answering to these ideas and that it was possible to obtain knowledge of these realities by pure thought, unmixed with experience. It was in this kind of thinking that the principle of significance was violated. A substantial proportion of the *Critique* is devoted to showing how, in particular celebrated instances, we are tempted to violate the principle and to demonstrating the empty, and sometimes conflicting, character of the metaphysical knowledge-claims which result from our doing so.

Transcendent metaphysics, then, is declared in general, and demonstrated in detail, to be impossible as a form of knowledge, or, as Kant would say, as a science. But this does not mean that no form of scientific metaphysics is possible at all. On the contrary, there is a large positive task for a genuinely scientific metaphysics, a task which, according to Kant, can be discharged once for all, and which is at least partially carried out by him in the most original, interesting, and difficult part of the *Critique*. This is the task I have already referred to: the investigation of that limiting framework of ideas and principles the use and application of which are essential to empirical knowledge, and which are implicit in any coherent conception of experience which we can form. It is of course possible to feel and express scepticism, not only about the details of Kant's execution of this programme, but about the programme itself; it may be thought unlikely that such an inquiry could yield any but the slenderest results. But if these doubts are unjustified, and a fruitful inquiry of this kind is possible, then it will fully deserve the title of metaphysics. It will be, as metaphysics was always said to be, the most general and fundamental of studies; and its method will be non-empirical, or *a priori*, not because, like transcendent metaphysics, it claims to be concerned with a realm of objects inaccessible to experience, but because it is concerned with the conceptual structure which is presupposed in all empirical inquiries. This kind of investigation Kant sometimes calls 'transcendental', as distinct from 'transcendent', though he is by no means consistent in his use of this expression.

In his espousal of the principle of significance and in his consequential repudiation of transcendent metaphysics, Kant is close to the tradition of classical empiricism, the tradition of Berkeley and Hume, which has probably, at least in England, received its clearest modern expression in the writings of A. J. Ayer. But in the elaboration of his positive metaphysics of experience, Kant departs sharply from that tradition. The central problem of classical empiricism was set by the assumption that experience really offers us nothing but separate and fleeting sense-impressions, images and feelings; and the problem was to show how, on this exiguous basis, we could supply a rational justification of our ordinary picture of the world as containing continuously and independently existing and interacting material things and persons. Hume, it is true, rejected the problem in this form, holding that such a justification was impossible, but also unnecessary, since the gaps found, and left, by reason were filled by the helpful fictions of the imagination. Between the views of Hume, the most sophisticated of the classical empiricists, and those of Kant, there is a subtle and interesting parallelism. But there is also a great gap. For Kant rejected the basic empiricist dogma which Hume never questioned. He did not reject it in the spirit of naïve, or refined, common sense which has sometimes, in England, seemed to be the twentieth-century alternative to classical empiricism. His rejection took the form, rather, of a proof that the minimal empiricist conception of experience was incoherent in isolation, that it made sense only within a larger framework which necessarily included the use and application in experience of concepts of an objective world. Thus the execution of Kant's programme for a positive metaphysics is held to entail the rejection of what he calls 'problematic' idealism, even if such idealism is only the methodological starting-point, rather than the terminus, of philosophical reflection. Any philosopher who invites, or challenges, us to justify our belief in the objective world by working outwards, as it were, from the private data of individual consciousness thereby demonstrates his failure to have grasped the conditions of the possibility of experience in general. Philosophers as unlike in other respects as Descartes and Hume are held to be alike guilty of this failure.

These themes of the *Critique* which I have so far referred to have an evident harmony. Together they form, one might be tempted to claim, the framework of a truly empiricist philosophy, freed, on the one hand, from the delusions of transcendent metaphysics, on the other, from the classical empiricist obsession with the private contents of consciousness. Together they present the blander, the more acceptable face of the *Critique*. But it would be a very one-sided account of the work which referred to these themes alone. Their exposition and development is throughout interwoven with more questionable doctrines, one of the sources of which I have already indicated. It is true that Kant thought of himself as investigating the general structure of ideas and principles which is presupposed in all our empirical knowledge; but he thought of this investigation as possible only because he conceived of it also, and primarily, as an investigation into the structure and workings of the cognitive capacities of beings such as ourselves. The idiom of the work is throughout a psychological idiom. Whatever necessities Kant found in our conception of experience he ascribed to the nature of our faculties.

He prepares the ground for this ascription by the manner in which he presents a certain fundamental duality, inescapable in any philosophical thinking about experience or empirical knowledge. This is the duality of general concepts, on the one hand, and particular instances of general concepts, encountered in experience, on the other. If any item is even to enter our conscious experience we must be able to classify it in some way, to recognize it as possessing some general characteristics. To say that we must have general concepts in order for empirical knowledge to be possible is just to say that we must have such recognitional abilities as these. No less evidently, if these abilities are ever to be exercised, we must have material on which to exercise them; particular instances of general concepts must be encountered in experience. The importance of this fundamental duality is fully recognized by Kant. His word for awareness in experience of particular instances of general concepts is 'intuition'; and the point epitomized in his famous dictum, that 'thoughts without content are empty, intuitions without concepts are blind',[3] is one which he repeatedly emphasizes.

There are many idioms in which this inescapable duality can be expressed. Kant's idiom is psychological, the idiom of departments or faculties of the mind. He distinguishes between the *receptive* faculty of *sensibility*, through which we have intuitions, and the *active* faculty of *understanding*, which is the source of concepts; and thereby prepares the way for ascribing to these faculties, as their source, those limiting features which he finds in the notion of experience in general. Thus it seems that there is no conceivable way in which concepts could be instantiated in our experience except by our being aware of instances of them in space and time – or, at least, in time. Space and time themselves are accordingly declared to be 'in us', to be simply the forms of our sensibility, nothing but our ways of being aware of particular things capable of being brought under concepts. Again, it is argued that unless the concepts we employed in application to our experience implicitly involved the application of certain very general notions (the categories), it would be impossible that there should be any such thing as self-conscious awareness of the succession of experience in time. The applicability of these notions is, then, a further necessary condition of the possibility of anything which deserves the name of experience or empirical knowledge. But this necessity once more is presented as a consequence of our cognitive constitution; only it is assigned, this time, to our faculty of understanding, which is described as acting on our sensibility to bring about the satisfaction of its own requirements.

These allocations contain already the seeds of that disastrous model which, as we shall see, Kant had such powerful motives for prizing. The natural world as we know it, the whole content of our experience, is thoroughly conditioned by the features just referred to: our experience is essentially experience of a spatio-temporal world of law-governed objects conceived of as distinct from our temporally successive experiences of them. But all these limiting features alike simply represent ways in which things must appear in the experience of beings constituted as we are, with such a sensibility and such an understanding as ours. Of things as they are in themselves as opposed to these appearances of them, we have, and can have, no knowledge whatever; for knowledge is possible only of what can be experienced, and nothing can be experienced except as subjected to the forms imposed by our sensibility and our understanding.

This 'transcendental idealism', according to which the whole world of Nature is merely appearance, is sharply distinguished by Kant from other forms of idealism. The typical 'empirical' idealist, as Kant calls him, takes as certainly real the temporally successive states of consciousness and questions or denies the real existence, or our knowledge of the existence, of bodies in space. The transcendental idealist, on the other hand, is, Kant says, an empirical realist, according no superiority of status, as regards reality or certainty of existence, to states of consciousness over physical objects. When we see how Kant supports this claim, however, we must view it with scepticism. It is true that he grants us as immediate a knowledge of the physical objects of 'outer sense', whose form is space, as he does of the psychological states, the objects of 'inner sense', whose form is time. It is true, too, that he says that our inner-directed experience no more yields us knowledge of ourselves as we are in ourselves than our outer-directed experience yields us knowledge of other things as they are in themselves. But *these* parities do not really amount to according equal reality to bodies in space ('outer objects') and states of consciousness ('inner determinations'). The doctrine that the material and the mental constituents of the natural world are alike only appearances turns out, in the end, to bear with unequal weight on bodies and states of consciousness. Kant, as transcendental idealist, is closer to Berkeley than he acknowledges.

The doctrines of transcendental idealism, and the associated picture of the receiving and ordering apparatus of the mind producing Nature as we know it out of the unknowable reality of things as they are in themselves, are undoubtedly the chief obstacles to a sympathetic understanding of the *Critique*. We may be tempted by weakened interpretations of these doctrines, representing them as expository devices perhaps not wholly understood by their user. Thus the doctrine that we can have knowledge only of things as objects of possible experience, and not of things as they are in themselves, has a certain ambiguity; and we may be tempted, at times, by its subtler or ironical sense, which Kant himself seems, at times, almost to endorse. Again, we may be tempted to interpret the whole model of mind-made Nature as simply a device for presenting an analytical or conceptual inquiry in a form readily grasped by the picture-loving imagination. All such interpretations would, however, involve reading into much of the *Critique* a tone of at least half-conscious irony quite foreign to its character; and there are other, more decisive reasons for thinking that they would altogether fail to answer to Kant's intentions.

One of them is made clear enough in the Preface. As Kant there says, he is concerned not only to curb the pretensions of dogmatic metaphysics to give us supersensible knowledge; he is concerned also to curb the pretensions of sensibility to be co-extensive with the real. The proof of our necessary ignorance of the supersensible safeguards the interests of morality and religion by securing the supersensible realm from our scepticism as well as from our knowledge. There are other indications of a different kind, more important still in the present context, as being more immediately related to the main concerns of this *Critique*. Thus the principle of significance itself, as applied to the categories, is derived by Kant as a *consequence* of the nature of the part played by the faculty of understanding in ordering experience; and the very possibility of knowledge of necessary features of experience is seen by him as dependent upon his transcendental subjectivism, the theory of the mind making Nature. This indeed is the essence of the 'Copernican Revolution' which he proudly announced as the key to a reformed and scientific metaphysics. It is only because objects of experience must conform to the constitution of our minds that we can have the sort of *a priori* knowledge of the nature of experience which is demonstrated, in outline, in the *Critique* itself. Finally, Kant's claim to find in the solution of the first Antinomy decisive confirmation of the thesis of the ideality of space and time would be quite extraordinarily misleading if he meant by it no more than that the solution vindicated the application of the principle of significance to the question whether the world is or is not bounded in space and time.

Those interconnected doctrines which centre on the thesis of transcendental idealism are not the only obstacles to sympathetic understanding. Others are attributable in part to the state of scientific knowledge at the time at which Kant wrote. He believed without question in the finality of Euclidean geometry, Newtonian physics, and Aristotelian logic; and on these beliefs he founded others, still more questionable. Thus he believed that Euclidean geometry provided a unique body, not only of truths, but of necessary truths, about the structure of physical space; and in this belief found what seemed to him a further powerful argument for the thesis that space was transcendentally 'in us'. Kant's theory of geometry, though not defensible as a whole, contains valuable insights; and, being relatively independent of the main structure of the *Critique*, does not succeed in obscuring anything we may wish to preserve of that structure. It is otherwise with his conviction that what he took to be the presuppositions of Newtonian physics embodied conditions of the possibility of empirical knowledge in general; for the anxiety to arrive, by way of conclusion, at supposed *a priori* principles of natural science really does have the effect of obscuring what there is of substance in the arguments of a central, and crucial, section of the book, viz. the Analogies of Experience. As for the effect of Kant's uncritical acceptance, and unconstrained manipulation, of the forms and classifications of traditional logic, this is of a rather different kind. It may be held in part responsible for his boundless faith in a certain structural framework, elaborate and symmetrical, which he adapts freely from formal logic as he understands it and determinedly imposes on the whole range of his material. Over and over again the same pattern of divisions, distinctions, and connections is reproduced in different departments of the work. The artificial and elaborate symmetry of this imposed structure has a character which, if anything in philosophy deserves the title of baroque, deserves that title. But this is a feature which, though it may cause us unnecessary trouble and give us irrelevant pleasure, we can in the end discount without anxiety.

2. The Metaphysics of Experience

The heart of the *Critique of Pure Reason*, and its most difficult passages, are contained in the Division entitled Transcendental Analytic; for it is there, with some dependence on the earlier section concerned with space and time and called Transcendental Aesthetic, that Kant attempts to show what the limiting features must be of any notion of experience which we can make intelligible to ourselves. I shall try to indicate in outline the nature of this attempt and to estimate the degree of success it achieves.

Among the general theses which Kant assumes or argues for it is possible to distinguish the following:

1. that experience essentially exhibits temporal succession (the temporality thesis);

2. that there must be such unity among the members of some temporally extended series of experiences as is required for the possibility of self-consciousness, or self-ascription of experiences, on the part of a subject of such experiences (the thesis of the necessary unity of consciousness);

3. that experience must include awareness of objects which are distinguishable from experiences of them in the sense that judgements about these objects are judgements about what is the case irrespective of the actual occurrence of particular subjective experiences of them (the thesis of objectivity);

4. that the objects referred to in (3) are essentially spatial (the spatiality thesis);

5. that there must be one unified (spatio-temporal) framework of empirical reality embracing all experience and its objects (the thesis of spatio-temporal unity);

6. that certain principles of permanence and causality must be satisfied in the physical or objective world of things in space (the theses of the Analogies).

Of these theses the first is treated by Kant throughout as an unquestionable datum to which we cannot comprehend the possibility of any alternative; and as such we may be content to regard it. The second is seen by Kant as inseparably linked with the requirement of the conceptualizability of experience, with the requirement that *particular* contents of experience should be recognized as having some *general* character; and, so linked, may reasonably be seen as a standard-setting definition of what is to count as 'experience'. I doubt if any philosopher, even the most economical of empiricists, has ever in practice worked, or tried to work, with a more limited conception. This thesis, or standard-setting definition, serves as the premise of the Transcendental Deduction of the Categories, that section of the *Critique* which cost Kant, and costs his readers, the greatest labour, being one of the most abstruse passages of argument, as also one of the most impressive and exciting, in the whole of philosophy. The only other of the listed theses which is assumed rather than argued for by Kant is that which I have numbered (4), the spatiality thesis. In fact, this is scarcely distinguished by Kant as a separate thesis at all, though it should be. From the truth that objects of our experience conceived of as existing independently of experience of them are in fact spatial objects, it does not seem to follow immediately that the spatial is the only mode in which we could conceive of such objects. That the spatial is the only conceivable mode of existence of such objects might nevertheless perhaps be allowed if we stripped the concept of spatiality of its usual sensory associations and gave it a mainly formal meaning; and even if we allow the concept to carry its normal visual and tactile associations, it can still be maintained that the spatial mode is at least that *on analogy with which* any alternative mode of existence of independent objects of our experience would have to be conceived by us.

All the remaining listed theses are explicitly or implicitly argued for in the Analytic. The order of Kant's exposition may be misleading on this point. For in the Aesthetic, which precedes the Analytic, it is already affirmed that there is but one Space and Time, and it is at any rate natural to assume that the space there declared to be essentially one is the space of objects conceived of as existing independently of our experiences of awareness of them, since the thesis of spatial unity has no other plausible application. We might by this be misled into supposing that the Analytic starts with the assumption that experience is necessarily of independently existing objects forming a unified spatio-temporal system and seeks on this basis to establish further necessary conditions of the possibility of experience. This would be a false impression. The thesis of objectivity – which might be abbreviated to the statement that experience must include awareness of objects which form the topic of objective judgements – is certainly implicitly argued for in the Analytic, and so is the thesis that these objects must possess the kind of unity of relation provided for by the doctrine that they belong to a unitary spatio-temporal system.

The essential premise of the Analytic is, as I have already remarked, the thesis of the necessary unity of consciousness. This 'necessary unity' is called by many other names in the *Critique*. Kant's favourite expression for it is 'the transcendental unity of apperception'; and this unity of apperception or consciousness is sometimes also called a unity of 'self-consciousness'. Sometimes Kant's employment of this last phrase might give the impression that what he has in mind is some special kind of consciousness of self, different from such ordinary or empirical self-awareness as is expressed in the commonplace self-ascription of perceptions, feelings, etc. But this is not really so. He is concerned, as I have remarked, with the general conditions of the employment of concepts, of the recognition of the particular contents of experience as having some general character; and he regards these conditions as being at the same time the fundamental conditions of the possibility of ordinary or empirical self-consciousness. The fulfilment of these conditions sets a minimum standard for what is to count as experience; and the standard-setting requirement, Kant argues, can be satisfied by nothing less than this: that the temporally extended series of experiences which are to form the contents of a possible experience should be so connected among themselves as to yield a picture of a unified objective world, of which these experiences – or some of them – *are* experiences. The argument to this effect is developed in the Transcendental Deduction of the Categories and in certain sections of the Analytic of Principles; and again the order and detail of exposition are not such as to facilitate understanding. In the Deduction we find a repeated insistence that a certain connectedness and unity among our experiences is necessary to constitute them experiences of an objective and law-governed world; that the concepts of the objective which we apply in experience embody the rules of such unity; and that this rule-governed connection of experiences under concepts of the objective is precisely what is required for the necessary unity of consciousness, i.e. for the possibility of self-consciousness.

The force of these contentions is by no means immediately obvious. It becomes somewhat clearer when we turn to certain sections of the Principles, which are supposed to contain a more detailed working out of the implications of the Deduction; notably, to the argument called the Refutation of Idealism and the arguments of the Analogies. Experiences occur in temporal relation; but for *self*-consciousness to be possible ('consciousness of my own existence as determined in time'), it must at least be possible to distinguish between the order and arrangement of our *experiences* on the one hand and the order and arrangement which *objects* of those experiences independently enjoy. For this, in turn, to be possible, objects of experience must be conceived of as existing within an *abiding* framework within which they can enjoy their own relations of co-existence and succession and within which we can encounter them at different times, these encounters yielding the merely subjective order of our experiences of them. The abiding framework, of course, is spatial, is physical space; and Kant's immediate concern in the Refutation of Idealism is to point out that these necessary distinctions of temporal relation must be drawn *within* experience and hence we must be immediately, or non-inferentially, aware of objects in space. 'The consciousness of my existence is at the same time an immediate consciousness of the existence of other things outside me.'[4]

The fundamental thoughts which underlie the whole complex argument of these sections might be roughly expressed as follows. First, no one could be conscious of a temporally extended series of experiences as *his* unless he could be aware of them as yielding knowledge of a unified objective world, through which the series of experiences in question forms just one subjective or experiential route. Second, this conception, necessary to the possibility of self-consciousness, must be implicit in the character of the concepts actually employed, and directly applied, in experience. Not any set of concepts would by themselves suffice to yield, i.e. to demand, this conception. (For example, the jejune empiricist array of simple sensory quality concepts would not.) At least the concepts applied must include concepts of persistent and re-identifiable objects in space; and any objects which could fall under such concepts as these must exhibit some degree of 'regularity in their operations',[5] i.e. the changes to which they are subject must themselves, at least in general, be subject to causal law.

Kant supposed himself to have established stricter necessities than these. He certainly argued that the necessary distinctions between subjective and objective time-relations implied the necessary applicability within experience of concepts of permanence and causality. But he was not satisfied with the merely relative permanence of re-identifiable bodies in space, though this is in fact the most that the argument establishes; nor with any such weakened corollary about causation as I have suggested. From the argument for permanence in the first Analogy he derives a quantitative conservation principle which does not follow from it and is quite irrelevant to the satisfaction of those conditions which the argument shows must be satisfied; and in the famous argument of the second Analogy he claims to show that the experience of objective change, of succession as occurring in the objective world and not merely in the series of our subjective experiences, is possible only if every event is taken to be causally determined; but the crucial step in this reasoning can seem legitimate only if the critical faculty is numbed by the grossness of the *non sequitur*. In his determination to establish the principles which he regarded as the necessary foundations of physical science, Kant attempts, throughout the Analogies, to force from the argument more than it will yield.

Nevertheless the Transcendental Deduction, the Analogies, and the Refutation together establish important general conclusions. The standard-setting definition of experience (thesis (2)) is surely acceptable. There is, no doubt, reason to think that there are forms of sentience which fall short of this standard. But the fulfilment of the fundamental conditions of the possibility of self-consciousness, of self-ascription of experiences, seems to be necessary to any concept of experience which can be of interest to us, indeed to the very existence of any *concept* of experience at all. Kant's genius nowhere shows itself more clearly than in his identification of the most fundamental of these conditions in its most general form: viz. the possibility of distinguishing between a temporal order of subjective perceptions and an order and arrangement which objects of those perceptions independently possess – a unified and enduring framework of relations between constituents of an objective world. Almost equally important is his recognition that this distinction must be implicit in the concepts under which the contents of experience are brought, since there is no question of perceiving, as it were, the pure framework itself. These are very great and novel gains in epistemology, so great and so novel that, nearly two hundred years after they were made, they have still not been fully absorbed into the philosophical consciousness.

There is, of course, plenty of scope for further discussion of these themes. It may perhaps be held that Kant has not stated the *full* conditions for the possibility of empirical self-consciousness. To this it may be replied that he has stated the most fundamental conditions. Again, it may perhaps be questioned whether the thesis of objectivity really carries with it the thesis of unity in the unqualified form in which Kant asserts it. Even if the unity of consciousness demands the original context of one unified spatial (or quasi-spatial) world, does it not then possess a potentially wider scope? Could it not conceivably serve as a link between, say, spatially independent objective worlds? On fantasies which profess to exploit this potentiality, we may safely make the Kantian comment that readiness to allow our concept of the objective to range over spatially independent worlds would be altogether dependent on the possibility, if it is one, of representing them as systematically integrated in other ways; for Kant was surely right in insisting on the general connection between objectivity and systematic unity.

The above account of the central argument of the Analytic omits much that is to be found in the course of its development; and on these omissions I must now comment. The Transcendental Deduction of the Categories lies between a section which Kant subsequently refers to as the Metaphysical Deduction and a celebrated passage called the Schematism. To understand this arrangement, it is above all necessary to remember the importance which Kant attaches to the idiom of faculties, and in particular the seriousness with which he takes the duality of understanding and sensibility. Their co-operation is essential to experience, understanding as the source of concepts, sensibility as supplying the forms of intuition. Experience, empirical knowledge, is possible only when intuitions are brought under concepts, when empirical judgements are made. But the general functions of understanding can be investigated in abstraction from the modes of sensibility. In fact, there is already in existence a science which investigates those functions, viz. the science of formal logic. Since this science supplies us with a complete account of those forms into one or another of which all our judgements must fall, whatever their content, we may hope to find in these forms a clue to whatever necessities are imposed by understanding alone on the character of our experience. This investigation is not undertaken in formal logic itself, which simply offers us analytic truths about the logical relations between these forms, rules of formally valid inference; it abstracts altogether from any question about the conditions under which these forms can be *applied* to yield individually true or valid judgements about objects. By raising precisely this question in its most general form, Kant claimed to derive, from what he regarded as twelve fundamental propositional forms, twelve 'pure concepts of the understanding' or categories, each of which must have application in experience if true judgements of the corresponding forms were to be made. This is the 'Metaphysical Deduction' of the categories.

Now in the Transcendental Deduction, as we have seen, there is a general argument to the effect that the concepts under which we bring the contents of our experience must be such as to confer upon that experience a certain rule-governed connectedness or unity. Kant concludes that the general principles of that unity are precisely such as are secured by the necessary applicability in experience of the already derived categories. But the 'pure' categories, as derived in the Metaphysical Deduction, are derived, in complete abstraction from the modes of sensibility, simply from the requirements of understanding, the faculty of concepts. Therefore, to appreciate the actual significance of the categories in application to experience, which requires the co-operation of understanding *and* sensibility, we must interpret the pure categories in terms of the general form of sensible intuition. This is the role of the Schematism, which makes the transition from pure categories to categories-in-use by interpreting the former in terms of time. It is sufficient, in the Schematism, to give the interpretation in terms of time alone, without explicit mention of space; for it is the temporal character of experience that is invoked in the premises of the argument of both the Deduction and the Principles; that the application of the categories requires a framework which we cannot but conceive of as spatial (or on analogy with space) is something that emerges in the course of the argument.

It requires only moderate acquaintance with formal logic to be both critical of the list of forms which is to be the basis of Kant's derivation in the Metaphysical Deduction and sceptical of the whole conception of the derivation itself. It requires none at all to be astonished by most of the transitions from form to category that he actually makes. The list of twelve categories, in four sets of three, remains with us, however, to impose its own artificialities of arrangement at various stages in the book. The elucidation of what the necessary application of the categories is held to involve is contained in the chapter which follows the Schematism and which sets out the 'principles of pure understanding'. On the parts of that chapter which really do form, together with the Transcendental Deduction, one complex argument about the necessary unity and objectivity of experience (notably the Analogies and the Refutation of Idealism) I have already commented. Of the remaining principles, the Postulates of Empirical Thought contain instructions and warnings about the employment of the concepts of possibility and necessity in senses other than the narrowly logical, but add little that is new. The 'mathematical' principles (Axioms of Intuition and Anticipations of Perception) are held to state what are, from the point of view of the understanding, the necessary conditions of the application of mathematics to objects of experience; but their connection with the general themes of the Analytic is tenuous and is made, as far as it is made at all, through the concept of 'synthesis'.

Of that concept, though it figures largely in the Transcendental Deduction, especially in the first edition version, I have so far said nothing. I have treated the Deduction as an *argument*, which proceeds by analysis of the concept of experience in general to the conclusion that a certain objectivity and a certain unity are necessary conditions of the possibility of experience. And such an argument it is. But it is also an essay in the imaginary subject of transcendental psychology. Since Kant regards the necessary unity and connectedness of experience as being, like all transcendental necessities, the product of the mind's operations, he feels himself obliged to give some account of those operations. Such an account is obtained by thinking of the necessary unity of experience as produced by our faculties (specifically by memory and imagination controlled by understanding) out of impressions or data of sense themselves unconnected and separate; and this process of producing unity is called by Kant 'synthesis'. The theory of synthesis, like any essay in transcendental psychology, is exposed to the *ad hominem* objection that we can claim no empirical knowledge of its truth; for this would be to claim empirical knowledge of the occurrence of that which is held to be the antecedent condition of empirical knowledge. Belief in the occurrence of the process of synthesis as an antecedent condition of experience and belief in the antecedent occurrence of disconnected impressions as materials for the process to work on are beliefs which support each other and are necessary to each other. But, by hypothesis, experience can support neither belief; and since neither is necessary to the strictly analytical argument, the entire theory is best regarded as one of the aberrations into which Kant's explanatory model inevitably led him.

The discarding of the story of synthesis might seem to leave us with questions to answer: viz. when we speak of the necessary unity of experiences, what are the items so unified, and in what does their necessary unity consist? To these questions the answers are common-place enough and, indeed, implicit in what has already been said. First, the unified items are just the experiences reported in our ordinary reports of what we see, feel, hear, etc. No faithful reports of these experiences are in general possible which do not make use of the concepts of the objects which our experiences are experiences of. Second, the unity of these experiences under the rules embodied in the concepts of objects is just what is exemplified in the general coherence and *consistency* of our ordinary descriptions of what we see, hear, feel, etc. The employability of such concepts as these, hence the objectivity of experience in general, is necessarily bound up with the fulfilment of this requirement of consistency or unity. In telling the story of a dream, the requirement of consistency may indeed be waived; but the employment of concepts of objective reality in telling of a dream is a secondary employment, just because those concepts are then liberated from that condition of their use which makes them concepts of an objective reality.

3. Transcendent Metaphysics

After construction, demolition; after the Transcendental Analytic, the Transcendental Dialectic. This lengthy and imposing section of the *Critique* is substantially easier to understand than the Analytic and I shall devote proportionately less space to it.

The primary aim of the Dialectic is the exposure of metaphysical illusion; the primary instrument of exposure is the principle of significance. Kant advances, as I earlier remarked, a secondary thesis to the effect that certain ideas for which no empirical conditions of application can be specified and which are therefore a source of illusion if taken as relating to objects of possible knowledge may nevertheless have a useful, and even a necessary, function in the extension of empirical knowledge, when employed in a different way, which he entitles 'regulative'. Such ideas are those of God, and of the soul conceived of as a simple immaterial substance. Though it would be illusion to think we can have knowledge, or even form any definite conception, of objects corresponding to either idea, yet advances in psychology and in science in general, Kant holds, are assisted by, even dependent on, thinking of inner states *as if* they were states of an immaterial substance and thinking of the natural world in general *as if* it were the creation of a divine intelligence. So to think is to make a regulative employment of these ideas. Kant's contention that such a use of the ideas is natural, even necessary, to human reason, when it is busy with scientific matters, is evidently quite unplausible. But it becomes clearer why he should have held this view when we consider the general structure of the Dialectic.

For illusion, too, has a systematic structure. Nowhere indeed, does Kant's passion for system enjoy a more uninhibited indulgence than in the construction of the framework, again based upon formal logic, within which he treats the topics of the Dialectic. The logical frame-work itself is little more than a philosophical curiosity.[6] But some observation of genuine analogies and connections goes into its construction. Kant notes that it is typical of systematic rational inquiry to raise questions such that the answer to one such question may itself form the topic of another question of the same general kind. Thus it is typical of the scientific enterprise to seek for ever greater generality of explanation, to try to bring ever wider ranges of phenomena within the scope of a unifying theory; and this search for ever greater compre-hensiveness of explanation has parallels in other natural tendencies of both primitive and sophisticated inquiry, such as the tendency to press our investigations farther and farther into remoter regions of space and of past time, and to inquire ever more minutely into the composition of matter in general. We might name this parallelism by saying that all these types of inquiry have a *serial* character, that the items they disclose form a *series*, each item having a typical relation to its predecessor. Kant held that an inevitable concomitant of certain types of serial inquiry was the idea of the *totality* of the series of items disclosed in the course of the inquiry; and this conception seems to force upon us the necessity of a certain alternative. Either the series has an ultimate, limiting term – the absolute beginning of the world in time and its limits in space, the ultimate ground or condition of everything in Nature, the ultimate constituents of matter, etc. – or it has no limiting term, it is an infinite or unlimited series. Where this disjunction does seem forced upon us, Kant thought he could prove that embracing either limb of it led to contradiction; whence he called this division of the Dialectic the Antinomy of Pure Reason. His solution of these 'conflicts of pure reason with itself' turns on invoking the principle of significance. In operating with the concept of the series as a whole, we fail to consider whether any possible intuition, or experience, might answer to this concept. But there is, Kant maintains, no way in which experience could decide in favour of either limb of the disjunction. The question of which of the apparently necessary alternatives holds is empirically unsettleable; and hence the concept of absolute totality which seems to force the disjunction upon us has no empirical use. 'In its empirical meaning the word "whole" is always only comparative.'[7]

Kant treats his solution as a confirmation of the thesis of transcen-dental idealism. If space and time, and the world in space and time, existed as things in themselves, the disjunctions in each case would hold as necessary truths. Since the assumption that they do hold leads to contradiction, we have as good a proof as could be desired that space and time and the natural world do not exist as things in themselves, but only as appearances, are only in us, etc. This proof appears to rest on the premise that if things in space and time *were* things in themselves, then the principle of significance would not apply to them; they would be things of such a kind that concepts could be properly used of them without consideration of empirical criteria for their use. The conclusion that things in space and time are not such things as these *might* be construed as an ironically framed repudiation of the whole conception of 'things as they are in themselves' and an oblique affirmation of the autonomy of the principle of significance. If this were the correct construction, one could only think that the thesis of transcendental idealism is generally expressed with a misleading excess of irony. But irony, except of a cheerfully obvious kind, is not characteristic of Kant. What really emerges here is that aspect of transcendental idealism which finally denies to the natural world any existence independent of our 'representations' or perceptions, an aspect to which I have already referred in remarking that Kant is closer to Berkeley than he acknowledges.

Many other issues need to be raised in any detailed discussion of the Antinomies. The validity of the arguments Kant uses to derive the contradictions is highly questionable; and it is not so plain as it appeared to him that no empirical resolution of any of these 'conflicts of reason' is possible. Thus developments in physical science, unforeseeable at that time, appear to give empirical significance to the notion of physical space, and the world in space, as finite, though unbounded. These issues I now leave aside, to revert to the question of the general structure of the Dialectic.

Its unifying thesis, as I have already remarked, is that human reason is inevitably led, in the search for systematic knowledge, to entertain certain ideas of an *absolute* character, for which no empirical condition of application can be specified but which may have a useful regulative role in the advancement of knowledge. This thesis is a complex one, with four parts which must be clearly distinguished: (1) that the ideas in question all have the character which Kant expresses by the words *'absolute'* or *'unconditioned'* (e.g. an absolute totality, an absolutely first beginning, an ultimate, unconditioned ground, an absolutely simple constituent of matter, etc.); (2) that we are *inevitably* led, by the nature of systematic inquiry, to entertain such ideas; (3) that all such ideas are essentially *transcendent* of any possible experience; (4) that, in each sphere in which they arise, some such idea has *regulative utility*. Even in the case of the cosmological types of inquiry considered in the

Antinomies, this complex doctrine, as I indicated in the preceding paragraph, does not seem to be true in all its parts. But if we set on one side post-Kantian developments in science, some at least of these types of inquiry do seem to offer brilliant examples of the necessary inter-connectedness of these four features; and the Kantian suggestion that the appropriate regulative idea for science in these cases is that of the totality conceived as an unlimited series, setting a never completable task for inquiry, seems entirely reasonable.

The success of the general thesis in the case of cosmological inquiries must have encouraged Kant to form an exaggerated notion of its plausibility in what he regarded as the two other spheres of inevitable dialectical illusion: namely, theology and psychology. The history of philosophy certainly suggests that the belief that we can have knowledge of the soul as an absolutely unitary, enduring immaterial thing or substance is a natural, though not an inevitable, *philosophical* illusion. But it is false that this idea is one we are naturally led to entertain by the systematic empirical study of psychology, and equally false that it has any regulative utility in this connection. Again, the topic of God certainly gives plenty of scope for the notions of the absolute and the ultimate. God is absolutely necessary existence, absolute perfection, the ultimate ground of everything, etc. But it is only in so far as the idea of God rests upon notions treated of in the Antinomies, viz. those of absolute beginnings and original causes, that it is at all plausible to contend that we are inevitably led by reason to entertain such an idea; and even then, as Kant recognizes, this basis is inadequate to sustain the idea of God. There is, on the other hand, no plausibility at all in Kant's suggestion that the entire enterprise of science is necessarily conducted under the aegis of the idea of an intelligent creator, and that we are thus inevitably led to this idea by Reason's characteristic search for general explanations. Ideas of God, or of gods, have many sources, some of them not markedly connected with Reason; and the relating of any such idea to scientific explanation is something that presents an awkward problem to the theologian rather than a necessary inspiration to the scientist.

Kant's exposure, in the Paralogisms, of the metaphysical illusion of knowledge of the soul is of peculiar brilliance in itself, and also of particular interest because of its connection with the general argument of the Analytic. The target of attack is the doctrine that each of us can know of the existence, in his own case, of one persisting, purely immaterial, non-composite, thinking thing, the thing referred to by each of us as 'I'. The line of attack is that prescribed by the principle of significance. If we are to make any legitimate employment of the crucial concepts of unity or numerical identity through time, we must apply them, in the light of empirical criteria, to objects encountered in experience. But if we abstract entirely from the body and consider simply our experiences or states of consciousness as such (the contents of inner sense), it is evident not only that we do not, but that we could not, encounter within this field anything which we could identify as the permanent subject of states of consciousness. How, then, does the illusion arise? A slogan-like summary of Kant's answer would be: the unity of experience is confused with the experience of unity. It has already been argued that, for self-consciousness to be possible at all, there must be such unity among the members of a series of experiences as to constitute them experiences of a single objective world. Now while the fulfilment of this condition constitutes the basic ground of the possibility of self-consciousness, further conditions (it may be held) are required for the actual ascription of experiences to oneself. There must exist empirically applicable criteria of identity through time of a subject of experience. Such criteria do exist: as Kant himself seems to recognize, they involve the fact that 'the thinking being (as man) is itself . . . an object of outer sense',[8] i.e. a body in space. But we are tempted to overlook the relevance of such criteria by the fact that we do not actually have to employ them when we use the word 'I' in ascribing current or remembered experiences to ourselves. (When I am in pain, for example, I do not have to look and see that it is *I* who am in pain.) Thus we are tempted to think that we have knowledge of a continuing, identical subject, as such, knowledge which is independent of any empirical criteria of identity. We try, as it were, to abstract the force of 'I' from the background of empirical criteria which give it its power of referring to a continuing subject and yet still view it as possessing that power. But if we do perform this abstraction, there is nothing for the word to express except consciousness in general, or the general conditions of the possibility of experience. Thus we confound the unity of experience with the experience of unity; and thus there arises the illusion of knowledge of the soul as a persisting immaterial thing. But it is only an illusion; and if we succumb to it, we are powerless to defend such a view of the soul against rival and less flattering theories, since no empirical means of decision between them is available. Kant adds that it is essential to his own critical philosophy to demonstrate the emptiness of any such claim to knowledge; for if it were allowable, then our knowledge must have transcended the realm of experience and entered that of things as they are in themselves.

4. The Metaphysics of Transcendental Idealism

Something more must now be said of the doctrines of transcendental idealism. I have mentioned the anodyne interpretations by which we may be tempted and to which some of Kant's own observations give colour; and have said that, with whatever degree of reluctance, we must conclude that they do not answer, or do not steadily answer, to Kant's intentions. The doctrine is not merely that we can have no knowledge of a supersensible reality. The doctrine is that reality is supersensible and that we can have no knowledge of it. There are points in plenty at which the doctrine takes swift plunges into unintelligibility. Consider, for instance, the view that since space and time are nothing but forms of our sensibility, our awareness of all things in space and time, including ourselves, is awareness of things only as they appear and not as they are in themselves. We are aware, then, of ourselves in a temporal guise and hence only as we appear to ourselves and not as we are in ourselves. But what sort of a truth about ourselves is it, that we appear to ourselves in a temporal guise? Do we really so appear to ourselves or only appear to ourselves so to appear to ourselves? It seems that we must either choose the first alternative at once or uselessly delay a uselessly elaborated variant of it. Then is it a temporal fact, a fact about what happens in time, that we really so appear to ourselves? To say this would be to go back on our choice; for all that occurs in time belongs on the side of appearances. So it is not a fact about what happens in time that we really appear to ourselves in a temporal guise. I really do *appear* to myself temporally; but I do not really *temporally* appear to myself. But now what does 'really do appear' mean? The question is unanswerable; the bounds of intelligibility have been traversed, on any standard. Kant can scarcely claim that the fact is unalarming, on the ground that it agrees with the standard set by his own principle of significance, which is itself derived from the set of doctrines to which the present doctrine belongs. It is not a defence of an unintelligible doctrine that its unintelligibility is certified by a principle derived from it.[9]

This is but one instance of many incoherences into which these doctrines swiftly lead. But this kind of *ad hominem* criticism is not enough for understanding. We must see what notions are misapplied, what truths perverted, in these doctrines; and how they are misapplied or perverted. Here we must revert to the analogy, or model, mentioned at the beginning of this introduction. We know that to any being who is a member of the natural spatio-temporal world of science and everyday observation the spatio-temporal objects of that world can sensibly *appear* only by *affecting* in some way the constitution of that being. The way in which objects *do* appear, what characteristics they appear as having, depends in part upon the constitution of the being to which they appear. Were that constitution different, the same things would appear differently. These facts have seemed to many philosophers, e.g. Locke and Lord Russell, to be good reasons for denying that we are sensibly or perceptually aware of things as they really are, or are in themselves. For example, objects appear to be coloured, but, it is held, are not really coloured; what is really the case is that objects have certain physical properties, and we have a certain physical constitution, such that the effect of the former on the latter is to make objects appear to us coloured. This line of reasoning, though not compelling, is perfectly intelligible. We still know what is meant by 'objects as they really are'. They are objects thought of as endowed with only such properties as are ascribed to them in physical theories, especially the theories which supply explanations of the causal mechanism of perception. They are objects thought of as really possessing those (primary) properties which make them capable of appearing differently to beings differently equipped with sensory and nervous apparatus, but not as possessing those further (secondary) properties their apparent possession of which is explained by the effect of the primary properties on that apparatus.

This conception, though perhaps not attractive, is not unintelligible. The scientifically minded philosopher who embraces it departs, indeed, from some ordinary applications of the contrast between appearance and reality; for there are (as Berkeley complained) *no* circumstances in which things as he says they really are can *appear* as they really are. But he does not cut us off from empirical knowledge of things as they really are. The connection with sensible experience is still there; only it is less direct.

Kant's conception of the contrast between things as they are in themselves and things as they appear seems to have the same starting-point as the scientifically minded philosopher's conception of the contrast. They hold in common that, because we are aware of objects only in being affected by them and only as they appear as a result of our being so affected, we are not aware of objects as they are in themselves. But the next step is quite different. The scientifically minded philosopher does not deny us empirical knowledge of those things, as they are in themselves, which affect us to produce sensible appearances. He only denies that the properties which, under normal conditions, those things sensibly appear to us to have are included (or are *all* included) among the properties which they have, and which we know them to have, as they are in themselves. But Kant denies the possibility of any empirical knowledge at all of those things, as they are in themselves, which affect us to produce sensible experience. It is evidently consistent with, indeed required by, this denial to deny also that the physical objects of science *are* those things, as they are in themselves, which affect us to produce sensible experience. By assigning the whole spatio-temporal frame-work of the natural world to the receptive constitution of the subject of experience, by declaring the whole natural world to be mere appearance, Kant is able, in form, to reconcile these denials with the common starting-point, which he shares with the scientifically minded philosopher, for the application of the contrast between things as they are in themselves and things as they appear. But the price of the formal reconciliation is high. For the resultant transposition of the terminology of objects 'affecting' the constitution of subjects takes that terminology altogether out of the range of its intelligible employment, viz. the spatio-temporal range. The doctrine that we are aware of things only as they appear and not as they are in themselves because their appearances to us are the result of our constitution being affected by the objects, is a doctrine that we can understand just so long as the 'affecting' is thought of as something that occurs in space and time; but when it is added that we are to understand by space and time themselves nothing but a capacity or liability of ours to be affected in a certain way by objects not themselves in space and time, then we can no longer understand the doctrine, for we no longer know what 'affecting' means, or what we are to understand by 'ourselves'.

Kant indeed offers further information, but not further enlighten-ment, on the subject of 'affecting'. Any mode of awareness which is dependent on the existence of the object of awareness is one in which 'the subject's faculty of representation is affected by the object'. So awareness of things as they are in themselves ('non-sensible or intel-lectual intuition') would be a *creative* awareness which produced its own object; a kind of awareness which, 'so far as we can judge, can belong only to the primordial being'.[10] Kant points out that we are unable to comprehend the possibility of such a kind of awareness. He does not point out that whatever obscurity surrounds these notions surrounds also the entire doctrine that things in space and time are appearances.

The doctrines of phenomena and noumena, of transcendental idealism, of the ultimate subjectivity of the natural world, can, then, be understood in this sense: that we can trace the steps by which the original model, the governing analogy, is perverted or transposed into a form in which it violates any acceptable requirement of intelligibility, including Kant's own principle of significance. Further, we can understand the role of the resulting model or picture as a help to Kant in his wielding of more acceptable ideas: as appearing both to certify the principle of significance and to explain the possibility of his programme for a 'scientific' metaphysics of experience. We can even, and should, find room in philosophy for a concept which performs at least some of the negative functions of the Kantian concept of the noumenal. In rejecting the senseless dogma that our conceptual scheme corresponds at no point with Reality, we must not embrace the restrictive dogma that Reality is completely comprehended by that scheme as it actually is. We admit readily that there are facts we do not know. We must admit also that there may be *kinds* of fact of which we have, at present, no more conception than our human predecessors had of some kinds of fact admitted in our conceptual schemes but not in theirs. We learn not only how to answer old questions, but how to ask new ones. The idea of the aspects of Reality which would be described in the answers to the questions we do not yet know how to ask is one which, like the idea of the realm of the noumenal, though not in the same drastic style, limits the claim of actual human knowledge and experience to be 'co-extensive with the real'.

This seems to be the necessary, and not very advanced, limit of sympathy with the metaphysics of transcendental idealism. Though it is difficult to disentangle its doctrines from the analytical argument of Kant's positive metaphysics of experience, yet, when the disentangling operation has been carried out, it is remarkable how little those doctrines appear to have distorted that argument.

5. Conclusion

Many questions about the *Critique* and its problems are left so far untouched on in this brief account. I conclude by considering two, which are not unconnected with each other.

In the course of the *Critique* Kant frequently makes use of a certain distinction to which I have made no reference, the distinction between analytic and synthetic *a priori* propositions. Both types of proposition are said to have this in common, that they can be known by us to be, not only true, but such that no experience could possibly disconfirm or provide a counter-instance to them. In this respect, both types of proposition are contrasted with true empirical propositions, which are such that we can know them to be true only because, and in so far as, they are confirmed in experience. Kant holds that whereas the *a priori* character of analytic propositions presents no profound philosophical problem, it is far otherwise with *a priori* synthetic propositions. Indeed he says in the Introduction that the whole problem which the *Critique of Pure Reason* is devoted to solving can be epitomized in the question: How are *a priori* synthetic judgements possible?

It might be felt that more account should be taken of a distinction to which Kant attaches such importance. But it is doubtful whether this would in fact be advantageous. Kant nowhere gives an even moderately satisfactory theoretical account of the dichotomy between analytic and synthetic *a priori* propositions; nor can any be gleaned from his casually scattered examples. Among propositions generally counted as *a priori* there are, of course, many distinguishable subclasses; and in the history of controversy concerning such propositions, many philosophers have followed Kant at least to the extent of wishing to restrict the title 'analytic' to the members of one or more of these subclasses. But it is very doubtful indeed whether any clearly presentable general restriction of this kind would release into a contrasted class of synthetic *a priori* propositions just those types of proposition which Kant's epitomizing question was meant to be about. We can enumerate, as belonging to this intended class, truths of geometry and arithmetic and supposed *a priori* presuppositions of empirical science. But we can really form no general conception of the intended class except in terms of Kant's answer to his epitomizing question. What Kant means in general by synthetic *a priori* propositions is really just that class of propositions our knowledge of the necessity of which could, he supposed, be explained only by mobilizing the entire Copernican resources of the *Critique*, by appealing to the model of 'objects conforming to our modes of representation', i.e. to our sensibility's constitution and the understanding's rules. Since, as I have already argued, nothing whatever really is, or could be, explained by this model – for it is incoherent – it must be concluded that Kant really has no clear and general conception of the synthetic *a priori* at all.

Still, it might be said, there is a problem here, even if it is not happily stated in the form of Kant's epitomizing question. I have represented as the major positive achievement of the *Critique* the carrying out, or partial carrying out, of a certain programme. The programme was that of determining the fundamental general structure of any conception of experience such as we can make intelligible to ourselves. Whether or not we choose to entitle the propositions descriptive of that structure 'synthetic *a priori*', it is clear at least that they have a distinctive character or status; and Kant's Copernican theory was an attempt to explain that status. Is it not, after all, easy to read the very formulation of the programme – 'the determination of the fundamental general structure of any conception of experience such as *we* can make intelligible to ourselves' – in such a way as to suggest the Kantian-seeming thought that any necessary limits we find in such a conception are limits imposed by *our* capacities? And if we nevertheless discard, as incoherent in itself and failing in its purpose, the Kantian explanation of the feasibility of the programme, what other are we prepared to offer? To this I can only reply that I see no reason why any high doctrine at all should be necessary here. The set of ideas, or schemes of thought, employed by human beings reflect, of course, their nature, their needs and their situation. They are not static schemes, but allow of that indefinite refinement, correction, and extension which accompany the advance of science and the development of social forms. At the stage of conceptual self-consciousness which is philosophical reflection, people may, among other things, conceive of variations in the character of their own situation and needs and discuss intelligibly the ways in which their schemes of thought might be adapted to such variations. But it is no matter for wonder if conceivable variations are intelligible only as variations within a certain fundamental general framework of ideas, if further developments are conceivable only as developments of, or from, a certain general basis. There is nothing here to demand, or permit, an explanation such as Kant's. In order to set limits to coherent thinking, it is not necessary, as Kant, in spite of his disclaimer, attempted to do, to think both sides of those limits. It is enough to think up to them. No philosopher in any book has come nearer to achieving this strenuous aim than Kant himself in the *Critique of Pure Reason*.

Notes

1. 'All concepts, and with them all principles, even such as are possible *a priori*, relate to empirical intuitions, that is, to the data for a possible experience. Apart from this relation they have no objective validity' (B 195). Of the most general of concepts, the categories, Kant says that they 'allow only of empirical employment and have no meaning whatsoever when not applied to objects of possible experience, that is, to the world of sense' (B 724). These sentences are typical of dozens in the *Critique*. (The references here and later to the *Critique* are to the Kemp Smith translation, listed in the bibliography.)

2. This was not, in Kant's view, the only function of ideas which lacked empirical significance. He thought that the moral life depended on such ideas; but he sharply distinguished between moral thinking and the sort of thinking which aimed at knowledge. The

principle of significance, though to be interpreted strictly as far as theoretical speculations and claims to knowledge were concerned, had to be understood with certain reservations.

3. A 51/B 75.

4. B 276.

5. The phrase is adapted from Hume. See *Treatise of Human Nature*, Book I, Part IV, Chapter 2.

6. Its basis is a 'demonstration' that there are three, and only three, types of inevitable dialectical illusion, each correlated with one of three forms of deductive reasoning, and all springing from a unitary 'demand of reason', conceived as the faculty of mediate inference, for completeness in the premises of a given conclusion. Further elaborations are held to be determined by the fourfold division of the categories.

7. A 483/B 511.

8. B 415.

9. The incoherence of this doctrine is more fully displayed in Part IV, Section 4 of *The Bounds of Sense*.

10. B 72.

Biographical Note

Sir Peter Strawson has been Waynflete Professor of Metaphysical Philosophy at Oxford since 1968, before which he was a Fellow of University College, Oxford. His books include *Introduction to Logical Theory* (1952), *Individuals* (1959), *The Bounds of Sense* (1966), *Logico-Linguistic Papers* (1971), *Subject and Predicate in Logic and Grammar* (1974) and *Freedom and Resentment and Other Essays* (1974). He is a Fellow of the British Academy.

Further Reading

Kant in English translation: *Critique of Pure Reason*, N. Kemp Smith (London: Macmillan 1929); *Critique of Practical Reason*, L. W. Beck (Chicago University Press, 1949); *Critique of Judgment*, J. C. Meredith (Oxford University Press, 1953); *Groundwork of the Metaphysic of Morals*, trans. as *The Moral Law*, H. J. Paton (London: Hutchinson, 1966); *Selected Pre-Critical Writings*, G. B. Kerferd and D. E. Walford (Manchester University Press, 1968); *Prolegomena*, P. G. Lucas (Manchester University Press, 1953); *Metaphysical Foundations of Natural Science*, Ellington (Indianapolis and New York: Bobbs-Merrill, 1965).

Some books on Kant: J. Bennett, *Kant's Analytic* (Cambridge University Press, 1966); J. Bennett, *Kant's Dialectic* (Cambridge University Press, 1974); C. D. Broad, *Kant: An Introduction* (Cambridge University Press, 1978); P. F. Strawson, *The Bounds of Sense* (London: Methuen, 1966); R. C. S. Walker, *Kant* (London: Routledge & Kegan Paul, 1978).

Collections of essays: T. Penelhum and J. J. MacIntosh, *The First Critique* (Belmont, California: Wadsworth, 1969); R. C. S. Walker, *Kant on Pure Reason* (Oxford University Press, 1982).

Alasdair MacIntyre

Hegel: On Faces and Skulls

A principal aim of Alasdair MacIntyre's resolute, individual and unfettered paper is to support the view that no physical science can give a causal or otherwise lawlike explanation of our rational reflections, our self-consciousness, our characters and character-traits, others of our dispositions including certain of our feelings, and above all our actions. The view, perhaps, is not that *no* mental facts can be given such an explanation – our ordinary sensations can perhaps be so explained. Rather, what might be called the most important mental facts, those that have to do with a self-consciousness or reflectiveness of a rational of judgemental kind, cannot be explained as effects of sufficient causes which are, say, physical states or processes of the brain. MacIntyre is therefore opposed to what are perhaps the most challenging forms of determinism, those that do assert that all mental facts are in causal or other lawlike connection with physical rather than other mental facts about persons.

Hegel's immediate concern, in the relevant part of *The Phenomenology of Spirit*, was with what we now recognize to be two bad sciences, physiognomy and phrenology. The first set out to establish that a man's character, conceived as a set of determinate traits, can be systematically read off from his facial features, such as the set of his eyes. Phrenology involved the view that mental facts are somehow correlated in a lawlike way with specific parts or locales of the brain, and that these in turn stand in connection with areas of the cranial bone or skull, the notorious bumps and hollows. One can proceed, then, from the study of a man's skull to conclusions about mental facts, notably his character. It is MacIntyre's contention that Hegel's rejection of physiognomy and

---

Georg Wilhelm Friedrich Hegel, 1770–1831. Born in Stuttgart, professor mainly at Berlin. Known partly as philosopher of history, which he regarded as the development of Spirit. Influenced, among many others, Kierkegaard and Marx. Regarded by many as a defender of the State, by some few as a liberal constitutionalist.

phrenology is not as irrelevant now as those discredited sciences. (pp. 325–8) Rather, his fundamental arguments against them are relevant to their successors. They are relevant to contemporary neuro-physiological determinisms. Such doctrines share the view that there are physical states, processes or events of persons which are sufficient causes of human action, character and the like. If MacIntyre does not conclude that Hegel's understanding of action, character and so on is correct, and that determinisms which make them themselves into effects or lawlike correlates are false (pp. 332–3), the tendency of his paper is unmistakably towards that conclusion.

A principal theme of the paper, true to Hegel, is that we cannot conceive of action, character and so on in such a way that we get items that can count as effects or as lawlike correlates of physical facts. Hegel did not oppose physiognomy and phrenology by anything like the arguments of its contemporary critics: arguments which assert a dualism of mind and matter, and deny that mental facts can have physical causes. Rather, it was Hegel's conviction that actions, character and the like do not have a nature such that they can enter into causal or lawlike generalizations which link them with physical facts about the person. This is so for the reason that actions and character are not fixed and determinate. For generalizations of the given kind to be possible, we do require things which have a fixed and determinate nature.

One relevant fact in this connection is that actions as we conceive them are not mere physical movements or sequences of movements. They are no more such than facial expressions, say an expression of gloom. Actions and expressions are not physical movements which we independently perceive, and then use as premises or bases for a conclusion about something else, a man's intentions or character or other 'inner' facts. 'There is nothing more to his character than the sum total of what he does.' (pp. 322–3) A second relevant fact is that we only make sense of the idea of character-traits within a given context, and indeed within a given culture. That is as true of the idea of an action. There is no relevant determinate thing common to excusable killing in self-defence and gratuitous or pointless killing. (pp. 324–5) Thirdly, our characters and much else are subject to our own self-consciousness. It is a fact that through his own reflection on himself a man has the possibility of exchanging what he is for what he is not. (p. 325)

A second theme in MacIntyre's paper has to do with a view related to what has been under criticism, but involving scientific or lawlike generalizations of a different kind about action. It may be thought that a man's character-traits or dispositions have physical bases but also that it is possible to establish explanatory generalizations having to do with his dispositions rather than their bases, together with something else: the situation in which he acts. If it is not possible to proceed to an explanation of his action from such dispositions as his desire to avoid humiliation, it is possible to proceed from the premise of his dispositions and his personal situation, perhaps his relation to another person. However, in this talk of situations we again lack the sort of thing that could enter into generalizations of the kind pursued. Again there is a want of fixity and determinateness. (pp. 327–9)

This is in part a matter of the fact that a particular situation is not a matter of properties then obtaining, but also a matter of the past: our very conception of the situation involves the past. (p. 329) What somehow contributes to the agent's act is a view of the present in the light of the past. Furthermore, there is an absolute particularity about a situation. There is what can be called its ultimacy of concreteness.

This is approached by way of the established philosophical proposition that it is not a *property* of a thing, alongside its colour or weight, that *it exists*. To say that a thing exists is to say of a description, a specification of a set of properties, that there is something that falls under that description or specification. MacIntyre adds something to the established philosophical proposition. It is that one cannot suppose either that in saying that a situation *occurs* one is assigning a property to it. It follows that one cannot, in saying that a man responded to some occurrence, characterize *that* situation generally. (pp. 329–30)

Furthermore, in connection with action-generalizations, there is the fact noticed already that through self-consciousness I am aware of what I am and, more important, what I am not, and hence there is the possibility of altering my behaviour. (pp. 331–2) To accept this and the previous considerations against the supposed action-generalizations is not to deny all possible causal explanations in the neighbourhood of action. For one thing, movements can be caused, but they are not actions. (pp. 330–31)

The last section of the paper offers a further Hegelian objection to both sorts of generalization about action, character and the like. It is that action is to be conceived not merely as goal-directed, but as directed to goals which get their formulation in the course of the action. This rules out a predictive explanation of action. There are also considerations having to do with rational judgements of the present and hence the alteration of the future, and with a historical understanding of actions. This latter relates in part to what was said above of the past entering into the definition of present situations.

There can be little doubt that Hegel catches hold of and gives expression to a view of our lives which will not soon disappear. MacIntyre presses forward strongly with that view. If it is one from which it is possible to dissent, as I do, it is also possible to see the necessity and the profit of giving it close attention. It is not at all a condition of recognizing good or indeed great philosophy that it secures one's agreement.

Alasdair MacIntyre

Hegel: On Faces and Skulls

The Phenomenology of Spirit was written hastily. It is notorious that one outcome of this is that arguments are compressed, that the relation of one argument to another is often unclear, and that paragraphs of almost impenetrable obscurity recur. The commentator is therefore liable to feel a certain liberty in reconstructing Hegel's intentions; and the exercise of this liberty may always be a source of misrepresentation, perhaps especially when Hegel's arguments are relevant to present-day controversies. None the less, the risk is sometimes worth taking, for although it is true that to be ignorant of the history of philosophy is to be doomed to repeat it, the joke is that we are doomed to repeat it in some measure anyway, if only because the sources of so many philosophical problems lie so close to permanent characteristics of human nature and human language. It is in this light that I want to consider Hegel's arguments about two bad sciences – physiognomy and phrenology – and their claims to lay bare and to explain human character and behaviour, and the relevance of those arguments to certain contemporary issues.

1

Physiognomy was an ancient science that in the eighteenth century enjoyed a mild revival, especially in the writings of Johann Kaspar Lavater (1741–1801). The central claim of physiognomy was that character was systematically revealed in the features of the face. Character consists of a set of determinate traits; and the face, of a set of determinate features. In some cases the cause of the face's being as it is is the character's being as it is; but in other cases certain experiences, such as the experiences incurred in certain occupations, may leave their

Alasdair MacIntyre, 'Hegel on Faces and Skulls', *Hegel: A Collection of Critical Essays* (Garden City, N.Y.: Doubleday, 1972), edited by Alasdair MacIntyre. Reprinted without alteration by permission of author and publisher.

marks both on the character and on the face. In this latter type of case the features of the face are not effects of the traits of character, but remain revelatory of character.

In his discussion of physiognomy, Hegel begins by noting that its adherents assert that their science makes a different type of claim from that made, for example, by the adherents of astrology. Astrologers assert that types of planetary movements and types of human actions are correlated in certain regular ways; the connection is purely contingent and external. But the face is an *expression* of human character; what a man is, appears in his face. Hegel next notes the difference between this claim as it is made by the physiognomist and this claim as it is made in everyday life. Part of our ordinary human relationships is to read off from each other's faces thoughts, moods, and reactions. But we do not treat the facial expression simply as a sign of something else, the outer as a sign of something inner, any more than we treat the movement of the hand in a human action as a sign of something else, the inner meaning of what is done, the intention. We treat the expression of the face and the movement of the hand as themselves actions, or parts or aspects of actions. In this connection Hegel makes four points.

It is not what the face is, its bone structure or the way the eyes are set, that is the expression of character or action; it is what the face does that is such an expression. We are therefore not concerned with mere physical shapes, but with movements that are already interpreted. This leads on to Hegel's second point. A man's character is not something independent of his actions and accessible independently of his actions. There is nothing more to his character than the sum-total of what he does. Hegel here sides with Ryle in *The Concept of Mind* in his enmity to the notion of dispositions as causes of the actions that manifest them. The conjoint force of these two points is as follows:

When we see someone with a sad expression on his face, we do not infer to an inner sadness he feels on the basis of an observed correlation between such a physical arrangement of the facial features and inner states of sadness. We read or interpret the expression as one of sadness in the light of the conventions in our culture for interpreting facial expressions. Notice that we have to learn how to do this in alien cultures, and that no amount of correlating one observable characteristic with another in the search for regularities would assist us in the task of such learning. There is thus a difference between seeing a set of physical features and seeing that set as a face and as a face with a particular expression, just as there is a difference between seeing a string of physical shapes and seeing that string as an English sentence and as a sentence with a particular meaning. To learn how to read a face or a sentence is not to follow rules justified by observation that embody a correlation between two sets of items, one of which is the physical features or shapes.

What Hegel's argument has done so far is to show that the physiognomist's treatment of the face as expressive of character, and the physiognomist's treatment of the face as (at least sometimes) the effect of character, cannot be combined without damaging inconsistency. Hegel's two next points are still more damaging to the claim of physiognomy to go beyond the prescientific understanding of facial expression to a scientific knowledge of the causal relations allegedly underlying that expression. He points out sharply how the rules that we use in everyday life in interpreting facial expression are highly fallible. We can express Hegel's point in this way: if someone is apparently glaring at me and I accuse him of being angry with me, he has only to retort that he was thinking of something quite different and I shall have no way to rebut him by appeal to some set of rules for interpreting facial expression. Hegel quotes Lichtenberg: 'If anyone said, "Certainly you behave like an honest man, but I can see from your face that you are compelling yourself to do so and are a villain underneath," there is no doubt that every brave fellow so greeted will reply with a box on the ear.'

Finally – although Hegel makes this point earlier in the discussion – our dispositions of character, as expressed in our actions, speech, and facial expressions, are not simply given as physical features are given. My bone structure can be altered by surgery or violence, but at any given moment it is simply what it is. But my character is not determinate in the same way as my bone structure, and this in two respects: First, a disposition to behave in a particular way always has to be actualized in some particular context, and the nature and meaning of the action that manifests the disposition is in many cases unspecifiable apart from that context. If I strike a man dead when he attacks me murderously, my action does not have the same nature and meaning as when I strike a man dead in a fit of bad-tempered gratuitous aggression. Dispositions that are actualized independently of context are like tendencies to sneeze or to produce compulsive movements; their manifestations will be happenings that in virtue of their independence of context cannot be viewed as intelligible behaviour, except perhaps as nervous habits. But about my action produced in a context, we can ask if it is appropriate or inappropriate in the light of the norms defining intelligible behaviour in such a context; indeed this is a question that any agent can ask about his own actions. In asking this, he has to characterize his actions in such a way that he becomes self-conscious about what he is doing.

An agent, for example (my example, not Hegel's), may find himself performing a set of multifarious individual actions. Becoming conscious of the character of these, he becomes aware that his over-all conduct is jealous, let us say, or cowardly. But now he is able to place, indeed cannot but place, his conduct *qua* jealous or *qua* cowardly in relation to what Hegel calls 'the given circumstances, situations, habits, customs, religion, and so forth', i.e., in relation to the relevant norms and responses of his culture. But to do this is to provide himself with reasons, perhaps decisive reasons, for altering his conduct in the light of those norms and responses and of his own goals. It is of the nature of the character traits of a rational agent that they are never simply fixed and determinate, but that for the agent to discover what they are in relation to his unity as a self-conscious agent – that is, what they are in his personal and social context – is to open up to the agent the possibility of exchanging what he is for what he is not.

Moreover, the agent who does not change his traits may change their manifestations. Indeed, for him to become conscious that he manifests certain traits and so appears in a certain light, is to invite him to do just this. The relation of external appearance, including the facial appearance, to character is such that the discovery that any external appearance is taken to be a sign of a certain type of character is a discovery that the agent may then exploit to conceal his character. Hence, another saying of Lichtenberg, in *Über Physiognomik*, which Hegel also quotes: 'Suppose the physiognomist ever did have a man in his grasp; it would merely require a courageous resolution on the man's part to make himself again incomprehensible for centuries.'

2

But who now is likely to be impressed by the claims of physiognomy? Reading Lavater's *Physiognomische Fragmente zur Beförderung der Menschenkenntniss und Menschenliebe*, with all its romantic whimsy – Lavater on the basis of a youthful acquaintance associated piercing eyes with power of memory, for instance – one might well ask, ought anyone ever to have been impressed by such claims? Part of the answer is that we ought in any case to be interested in bad sciences if only in order to illuminate the contrast with good ones. The study of astrology, physiognomy, or phrenology is justified in so far as it helps us to understand the character of chemistry and physiology. But part of the answer concerns the way in which certain issues may be raised in precisely the same way by bad sciences such as phrenology and physiognomy as by good ones such as genetics or neurophysiology.

In the case of phrenology some of the central theses actually survive in the history of physiology into the present day. It was, for instance, a central thesis of phrenology that different features of the brain were localized in different areas of the brain. This thesis is still controversial, of course, but the empirical neurophysiological and neuroanatomical evidence seems to be against it, especially if localization is understood in anything like the terms in which the phrenologists understood it. There is secondly the thesis, distinctively phrenological, that the different areas of the brain correspond to different areas of the cranial bone, and that the shapes of these areas, the famous bumps of the phrenologists, reveal the different degrees of development of each area of the brain. It is scarcely necessary to remark that this empirical contention is false. There is finally the thesis that the local activity of the brain is the sufficient cause and explanation of behaviour, and that therefore the shape of the cranium allows us to predict behaviour.

Buried in these dubious contentions is one that is less obviously dubious, that is indeed familiar and widely accepted. I mean of course the thesis that there are biochemical or neural states of affairs, processes, and events, the occurrence and the nature of which are the sufficient causes of human actions. This thesis wore phrenological clothing in 1807; today its clothing is as fashionable as it was then, only the fashions are not what they were. Moreover, when Hegel attempted to rebut the claims of physiognomy and phrenology, he did so in such a way that if his rebuttal is successful it would hold against the thesis that I have just stated, whatever its scientific clothing.

At this point, someone may object to my metaphor. The thesis, so it may be protested, does not merely wear scientific clothing, it is itself part of science; and, being a scientific thesis, it is an empirical question, and purely an empirical question, whether it is true or false. My reply to his point, and what I take to be Hegel's reply to this point, occupies a large part of the rest of the paper. But it is worth noting initially that the thesis *has* survived the most remarkable changes in our empirically founded beliefs about the anatomy, physiology, and chemistry of the human body, and that if it is a thesis in natural science, it is certainly not a thesis at the same level as the contention that the shape of the brain is partly the same as that of the cranium or that the nucleic acids play a specific part in reproduction.

In the debate about phrenology in the early nineteenth century, the attempt to challenge the thesis was undertaken by a number of writers very different from Hegel, and his project deserves to be sharply distinguished from theirs. The standard statement of the phrenological position was taken from the writings and lectures of Franz Joseph Gall (1758–1828) and his pupil J. C. Spurzheim, who developed Gall's doctrine, later claiming both that he had in fact originated some of the basic ideas and also that his doctrine was very different from that of Gall. Gall and Spurzheim drew maps of the cranium locating not only character traits but abilities in different parts of the brain, and their manifestations in what they took to be the corresponding parts of the skull. Examples of traits are secretiveness, combativeness, and acquisitiveness; examples of abilities are the power of speech and the power of imagination. Gall was charged by his critics with determinism, materialism, and consequently atheism. Both Gall and Spurzheim denied these charges, Spurzheim seeking to show that they held of Gall's version of phrenology but not of his. The critics in question, notably Francis Jeffrey, the editor, and Brougham, the lawyer, fastened all their attention on the alleged causes, seeking to show that the mental cannot have a physical, or more specifically a physiological, cause. To show this, they rely on a simple dualism of matter and mind, and the vapid naïveté of Gall's and Spurzheim's science is matched only by the vapid naïveté of Jeffrey's and Brougham's philosophy.

The spirit of their attack on phrenology is as alien to the spirit of Hegel's attack as any could be. Hegel's opposition to Cartesian dualism is of so thoroughgoing a kind that he would have to reject all the premises of Jeffrey's and Brougham's attacks. Nor is Hegel interested in showing that there cannot be physiological causes of the type cited by the phrenologists. His whole attention is focused not on the existence or non-existence of the alleged causes, but on the character of their alleged effects.

Hegel deploys a number of arguments that are closely allied to his arguments against physiognomy in the interests of his conclusion that 'it must be regarded as a thoroughgoing denial of reason to treat a skull bone as the actuality of conscious life . . .' What Hegel means by this is indicated by his further contention that 'It is no use to say we merely draw an inference from the outer as to the inner, which is something different . . .' Hegel wants to say that if we regard the traits of a rational agent as belonging to the type of item that can stand in a genuinely causal relation to anatomical or physiological or chemical states, then we are misconceiving the traits of a rational agent. Why does Hegel think this? We can usefully begin from a point that Hegel did not make in his discussion of physiognomy.

Traits are neither determinate nor fixed. What does it mean to say that they are not determinate? 'Just as, e.g., many people complain of feeling a painful tension in the head when thinking intensely, or even when thinking at all, so it might be that stealing, committing murder, writing poetry, and so on, could each be accompanied with its own proper feeling, which would over and above be bound to have its peculiar localization.' Hegel's discussion in terms of the localization of feeling has of course a specific reference to contemporary phrenology; but what he goes on to say about local feelings can easily be translated into a thesis about particular dispositions. 'Feeling in general is something indeterminate, and that feeling in the head as the centre might well be the general feeling that accompanies all suffering; so that mixed up with the thief's, murderer's, poet's tickling or pain in the head there would be other feelings, too, and they would permit of being distinguished from one another, or from those we may call mere bodily feelings, as little as an illness can be determined from the symptom of headache if we restrict its meaning merely to the bodily element.'

What would the corresponding theses about dispositions be? Let us consider points from two of Hegel's examples – those of the murderer and of the poet. A given murderer, for instance, commits his crime because he fears his own humiliation by losing his beloved. If we are to look at the traits and other qualities manifested in his action, they do not include a disposition to commit murder, but such things perhaps as a general intolerance of suffering, a disposition to avoid specific kinds of humiliation, his love for the girl, and so on. The same dispositions might explain to precisely the same extent the same person's outbidding others in giving to a deserving cause in order to impress the same girl. But just this fact puts in question the use of the word 'explain'. Hegel makes this point in relation to phrenology: 'And again his murderous propensity can be referred to any bump or hollow, and this in turn to any mental quality; for the murderer is not the abstraction of a murderer . . .'

Suppose that to this the reply is made that the same given set of dispositions may well produce quite different actions, but that this is because the agent is responding to quite different situations (although in some sense, in my example, the situations are certainly the same).

So that we explain the particular action by reference to a conjunction of the set of dispositions and some feature of the situation. We then explain the acts in an entirely familiar and unproblematic way by appealing to a generalization of the form 'Whenever such and such a set of dispositions and such and such a type of situation are ignored, such and such an action will occur.' To cite human traits in such an explanation would be precisely parallel to citing the dispositional properties of physical objects in explaining physical events.

But this is to suppose that what the agent is responding to is some conjunction of properties and not the specific historical situation. An empiricist would generally not be prepared to draw this contrast; for him, there is nothing to any specific historical situation but a set of properties, the conjunction of which may as a matter of contingent fact be unrepeated, but which is in fact repeatable. Why, then, does Hegel insist on the contrast and deny this characteristic empiricist contention?

A particular historical situation cannot on Hegel's view be dissolved into a set of properties. One reason for this is that such a situation has to be characterized in terms of relations to earlier specific events and situations. There is an internal reference to the events and situations that constitute its history. So the English revolt against Charles I not only has as key properties specific reactions to particular acts of Charles I, but responses to events and situations in the past as recent as acts of Elizabeth and as far off as Magna Charta and the Norman Conquest. Now, to respond to a particular situation, event, or state of affairs is not to respond to any situation, event, or state of affairs with the same or similar properties in some respect; it is to respond to *that* situation conceived by both the agents who respond to it and those whose actions constitute it as particular.

Suppose that to this position some empiricist were to respond as follows: that the agents treat the situation as particular and that the situation is partially constituted and defined by reference to the particular events and situations, does not show that everything relevant to explanation cannot be expressed in terms of repeatable properties. But this reply fails to notice one key point. Hegel would be the last to assert the ultimacy of unanalysed and unanalysable particulars (such as Russell's logical atoms). But he does assert what we may call the ultimacy of concreteness. What the ultimacy of concreteness amounts to is this: just as there are good conceptual reasons for holding that existence is not a property, so there are good conceptual reasons for holding that occurrence at some specific time and place is not a property.

By a property I mean that kind of attribute which a subject of the appropriate type (appropriate for that type of attribute) may or may not possess, which a given subject may possess at one time but not at another, and which may (although it need not) be possessed by more than one subject. On such an account of properties, existence fails to count as a property, because the appropriate type of subject cannot either possess it or fail to possess it and because the appropriate type of subject cannot possess it at one time but not at another. On the same account of properties, occurrence at some specific time and place (e.g., at 3 p.m. in the year 1776 at the point where the Greenwich meridian crosses the south bank of the Thames) fails to count as a property, because any subject of the appropriate type (events, situations, states of affairs) cannot possess any particular example of this attribute at one time but not at another and because any particular example of this type of attribute cannot be possessed by more than one subject.

It is properties about which we construct genuine empirical generalizations of such forms as $(x) (\phi x \supset \psi x)$ and $(x) (\phi x \supset \psi y)$, in which the values of variables of the type of ϕ and ψ are property-ascribing predicates. But it is on Hegel's view universals particularized in their concrete occurrence to which we respond in our actions – both those concrete particulars which we actually encounter and those which are the counterpart in the actual world to the intentional objects of our beliefs, attitudes, and emotions. A poet does not take pride in his having written some poem that has properties of such and such a kind, but in his having written *this* poem. A murderer did not strike out at anyone who happened to have such and such properties but at *this* person. Just because this concreteness is not constituted by a mere collection of properties, it evades causal generalizations and so makes causal explanation, whether phrenological or neurophysiological, inapplicable.

Note what Hegel is *not* saying. Hegel is not asserting that the movements of the murderer's hand or the poet's hand do not have causal explanations. Nor is he asserting that it is impossible that there should be agents with responses only to the abstract universal and not to the concrete. It is just that in so far as someone did respond to presentations of properties with the degree of uniformity that would warrant the construction of causal generalizations, he would not be at all like characteristic human agents as we actually know them and they actually exist. It is a contingent empirical fact about human beings that they are as they are and not otherwise, but in Hegel's philosophy there is no objection to taking notice of such contingent empirical facts. None the less, Hegel is not denying that it is logically possible for some human actions to have causes, and he is not denying that some human actions do or may have physiological causes. Let me draw a parallel with another type of case.

Some Africans who believe in witchcraft point out that to explain the onset of a disease by referring to bacterial or virus infection leaves unexplained such facts as that Jones should have been afflicted by such an infection immediately after quarrelling with Smith. 'What is the cause of that conjunction?' they inquire, pointing out that Western science gives no answer. Now, if indeed it were true that every event had a cause, that event which is Jones-going-down-with-measles-on-the-day-after-he-quarrelled-with-Smith would presumably have a cause. But no champion of natural science feels affronted by the assertion that this is not an event with a cause or an explanation, although the event that is Jones-going-down-with-measles certainly has a cause and an explanation. So also, when Hegel allows that a certain kind of causal explanation will not give us the understanding that we require of self-conscious rational activity, his argument does not require him to deny that many properties of the agents engaged in such activities will have such explanations.

I now return to Hegel's point that traits are not determinate or fixed. I have argued that the indeterminacy of traits is an indeterminacy vis-à-vis any action or given set of actions. From the fact that an agent has a given trait, we cannot *deduce* what he will do in any given situation, and the trait cannot itself be specified in terms of some determinate set of actions that it will produce. What does it mean to say that traits are not fixed? Let me reiterate the crucial fact about self-consciousness, already brought out in Hegel's discussion of physiognomy; that is, its self-negating quality: being aware of what I am is conceptually inseparable from confronting what I am not but could become. Hence, for a self-conscious agent to have a trait is for that agent to be confronted by an indefinitely large set of possibilities of developing, modifying, or abolishing that trait. Action springs not from fixed and determinate dispositions, but from the confrontation in consciousness of what I am by what I am not.

It is a failure to notice this that on Hegel's view most of all underlies those would-be sciences that aspire to give to observation the same role in the study of human beings that it has in inquiries into nature. For what we can observe in nature is, so to speak, all that there is to discover; but what we can observe in human beings is the expression of rational activity, which cannot be understood as merely the sum of the movements that we observe. (For a Hegelian, Hume's failure to discover the character of personal identity is the result of his fidelity to the methods and criteria of observation.) From Hegel's position, a radical thesis about experimental psychology would follow.

For a large class of psychological experiments, a necessary condition for experimental success is that the stimulus that is administered or the situation with which the agent is confronted shall have its effect independently of the agent's reflection on the situation. The situation or the stimulus must be the same for all experimental subjects; so one subject's envisaging the situation in a particular way must not constitute that situation a different one from that which it is for a subject who envisages that situation in some quite different way. Now, there is a real question as to whether this requirement can ever in fact be satisfied except in experiments in which the stimulus is purely physical (for example, a variation in intensity of light) and the response purely physiological (for example, a constriction of the pupil). But this question I shall put on one side. What Hegel would assert is that even if such experiments are possible, they are so different from the key situations in which rational agents operate, that any inferences from the behaviour of such experimental subjects to behaviour outside the experimental situation will be liable to lead us into error.

3

Whatever else the arguments in this paper may or may not establish, they do seem to show that between the Hegelian mode of understanding human action and the mode that has dominated modern thinking about the relevance of such sciences as neurophysiology and genetics, there is a basic incompatibility. Hence, the refutation of Hegelianism in the relevant respects would be a prerequisite for that mode of thought and not merely that frivolous, positivistic refutation to which Hegel has so often been subjected and that he himself adequately characterized. Whether a more adequate refutation is possible, I shall not discuss here. What I do want to do, in conclusion, is to try to characterize Hegel's alternative mode of understanding inquiry into human action.

Three features of Hegel's account stand out: The first is the way in which each stage in the progress of rational agents is seen as moving towards goals that are only articulated in the course of the movement itself. Human action is characteristically neither blind and goalless nor the mere implementation of means to an already decided end. Acting that is the bringing about of such an end by a calculated means certainly has a place, but a subordinate place, in human activity. That it is only in the course of the movement that the goals of the movement are articulated is the reason why we can understand human affairs only after the event. The owl of Minerva, as Hegel was later to put it, flies only at dusk. The understanding of human beings is not predictive in the way that natural science is.

The second feature of Hegel's account is the role of rational criticism of the present in the emergence of the future. Hegel did not believe that the future followed from the present simply as its rational sequel; this he denies as strongly as Voltaire does. But it is in the working out of the failure of the present to satisfy the canons of reason that the future is made. It is this which involves Hegel in seeing history as composed of sequences in which the actions that constitute later stages of the sequence involve reference to, and thus presuppose the occurrence of, actions that constituted earlier stages of the same sequences. The sequences that constitute history are themselves discrete and can stand in the same logical relation to each other as can the stages of a single sequence. But the doctrine that all the sequences of history constitute a single movement towards the goal of a consciousness of the whole that is absolute spirit and that by its consciousness of the whole of history constitutes that whole into a single rational totality, is a thesis certainly held by Hegel to be the key to his whole doctrine; yet, Hegel's other doctrines as to human history do not seem in any way to entail his doctrine about the Absolute, and to be unwilling to admit the truth of that doctrine ought not to be a source of prejudice against Hegel's other doctrines.

The third feature of Hegel's account relates closely to his criticism of physiognomy and phrenology. Historical narratives are for Hegel not a source of data to be cast into theoretical form by such would-be sciences. Instead, Hegel sees our understanding of contingent regularities as being always contributory to the construction of a certain kind of historical narrative. History, informed by philosophical understanding, provides a more ultimate kind of knowledge of human beings than inquiries whose theoretical structure is modelled on that of the natural sciences. It is outside the scope of this paper to develop or to assess Hegel's view on this matter, but a concluding remark may be in place.

It concerns the question: if history is not a matter of general laws and of theories, in what sense does it give us understanding at all? The Hegelian reply is that the self-knowledge of a self-conscious rational agent has always to be cast in a historical form. The past is present in the self in so many and so important ways that, lacking historical knowledge, our self-knowledge will be fatally limited. Moreover, this type of self-knowledge could never be yielded by theoretical sciences that aspire to explain behaviour in terms of physiological structures and processes. It is in fact just because our history constitutes us as what we are to so great an extent, that any explanation that omits reference to that history, as did and do the explanations of phrenology and neurophysiology, may explain the aptitudes and conditions of the human body, but not those of the human spirit.

Biographical Note

Alasdair MacIntyre teaches philosophy at Vanderbilt University. He is the author of *A Short History of Ethics*, *Against the Self-Images of the Age* and *After Virtue*. He has given the Carlyle Lectures at Oxford and was recently Henry Luce Professor at Wellesley College.

Further Reading

Hegel's Phenomenology of Spirit, trans. A. V. Miller (Oxford University Press, 1952), with a useful analysis of the text by J. N. Findlay.

　Jean Hyppolite, *Genesis and Structure of Hegel's Phenomenology of Spirit*, trans. S. Cherniak and J. Heckman (Evanston, Ill.: Northwestern University Press, 1976), the best commentary. W. V. Quine, *Word and Object* (New York: Wiley, and London: Chapman & Hall, 1960), Chapter 6, gives an argument which is relevant to Hegel: that such conceptions of action etc. as Hegel's are irremediably unscientific and must be replaced.

Richard Wollheim

Mill: The Ends of Life and the Preliminaries of Morality

Reading John Stuart Mill's great founding essay *Utilitarianism*, let alone reading it in conjunction with others of his writings such as the essay *On Liberty*, is to become uncertain or indeed perplexed about his moral philosophy. He professes to be a utilitarian and to be committed to the Principle of Utility. It is easy enough to produce the sentence that the Principle of Utility is the principle which enjoins us always to choose, from the range of possibilities, the particular action or policy which will produce the greatest balance of happiness over unhappiness, counting everyone affected by the action, or the greatest balance of pleasure over displeasure, or of utility over disutility, or of satisfaction over dissatisfaction. But, if only for the reasons that happiness, pleasure, utility and satisfaction may be taken to be different things, and that Mill gives his support to 'higher' as against 'lower' forms of these things, we have in that sentence nothing clear, no single principle.

Moreover, a reading of Mill is bound to disturb the idea that he was indeed given over in his thinking and his advocacy to any single moral principle. His morality does not seem to be in that sense monistic. He appears to value other ends than the maximization of happiness, pleasure, utility or satisfaction. He is fervent in his defence of individualism and of liberty, committed to truth and to reason, to fairness and variety, and often when he represents these as subordinate to the Principle of Utility, as being merely means to the end of the greatest happiness or whatever, he is unpersuasive in his arguments, and his declarations seem overborne by his own convictions as expressed on other pages. They are the convictions, as it must seem, of a pluralist in morality.

Richard Wollheim, in the following paper taken from a volume of

John Stuart Mill, 1806–73. Born in London, and worked there as civil servant. Now known for ethics, politics and logic. Briefly a Member of Parliament. A principal but reluctant Utilitarian. Esteemed women.

papers in honour of Sir Isaiah Berlin, makes a signal attempt to make sense of Mill's moral philosophy, and to do so in a way which captures the complexity, the perceptive feeling, the tensions and indeed the very proper uncertainty of that philosophy – an uncertainty whose concealment or subtraction would indeed have diminished it. Wollheim's enterprise is speculative. There seems little chance of establishing the nature of Mill's morality by a constrained attention to his official declarations of intent and the like, or by mechanically dividing his life into doctrinal phases. If Wollheim's inquiry is speculative, however, it is guided by a determination to keep in view, and to give the best possible rendering of, the fundamental character and the commitments of Mill's philosophy. They are indicated, if no more than indicated, by Mill's line that it is utility 'in the largest sense' to which he gives adherence, utility 'grounded in the permanent interests of man as a progressive being'.

A part of the burden of the second section of the inquiry is that Mill's mental crisis of 1826 can be seen as exemplifying a disenchantment with utilitarianism conceived in a traditional way. Here, it is indeed taken to be a morality of a single principle, and one which has the unique recommendation among moralities of satisfying not only some sum total of desires of persons affected when an agent acts in accordance with it, but also the agent's own desires. Traditional utilitarianism ceased to satisfy Mill, essentially for the reason that in its generality and abstractness it does not come into contact with the human experience which must be the true subject-matter and somehow the determinant of morality. Mill therefore revised utilitarianism, and in effect produced what can be called two other utilitarianisms. That is not to say, however, that one was succeeded in time by the other. Both, according to Wollheim's idea, persisted in his thinking.

The first of these enriches traditional utilitarianism by giving a place to such secondary principles, values or ends as the education of the mind and family affection. However, these are subordinate to what is primary in this hierarchical utilitarianism, the principle of the maximization of pleasure. When there is conflict between what is recommended to us by the primary principle of hedonism, and what is recommended by, say, family affection, it is family affection which must give way. To act on family affection is usually but not always a means to the end – which is taken to be a sufficiently clear and serviceable end – specified by the primary principle.

The second utilitarianism to be discerned in Mill's thought – complex utilitarianism – is also pluralistic. It might be said that unlike the first it is truly pluralistic. As sketched in the fourth section below, complex utilitarianism involves *a* principle of utility, which is not the principle of the maximization of pleasure, and also secondary principles, and the latter are not subordinate to the former. It is not the case that conflicts arise such that the cultivation of sexual love, say, or the maintenance of personal dignity, are sacrificed to the primary principle. The secondary principles – a group of which may provide a kind of summary of one individual's conception of his own utility or well-being – are in complex relation with the primary principle. A large part of this relationship is that they in fact give content to the primary principle. It is elucidated by reference to them. This utilitarianism, further, since it depends essentially on the fact of conceptions by individuals of their own happiness, requires some theory of human nature, a theory best acquired through a satisfactory developmental psychology.

If complex utilitarianism is unlike the other in giving an ineliminable role to developed thoughts, feelings and attitudes – undeniable values of diverse kinds – it might be thought to pertain only to those individuals who have come to a certain maturity. That is, they have come to have adequate or fulfilling conceptions of their own well-being. In Section V, this problem is dealt with by taking complex utilitarianism to be but one of three parts of a certain ethical outlook. This ethic also has within it a part which pertains to that period or area of the lives of individuals which is not directed by their own full conceptions of happiness. Here, there is a place for the monistic utilitarianism which Mill is taken to have come to see could not be the whole of his morality. There is also a place here for the hierarchical utilitarianism which gives sway to the principle of the maximization of pleasure. Finally, this ethical outlook contains a part which has a certain priority. It bears on both the others, enjoining us to arrive at and to maintain our individual conceptions of our happiness. The three parts of the ethic are therefore associated with happiness, pleasure and, in a wide sense, education.

Wollheim completes his enlarged understanding of Mill by considering several of his injunctions taken to illustrate the third part of the given ethic. In so doing he completes a proposal which requires attention not only as a view of the most compelling of the utilitarians but also as a contribution to ongoing moral philosophy.

Richard Wollheim

Mill: The Ends of Life and the Preliminaries of Morality

I

In the introductory chapter of *On Liberty* John Stuart Mill claimed that for him utility was the ultimate appeal on all ethical questions, and that he renounced any advantage that might accrue to his argument from considerations of abstract right.[1] In 'John Stuart Mill and the Ends of Life' Isaiah Berlin challenges Mill's claim.[2] He puts it forward as his view that, though Mill avowed a commitment to utility, the commitment is not real. In support of the avowed commitment Mill was compelled to stretch the notions of happiness and pleasure to the point of vacuity. Meanwhile his real commitment was to various distinct values such as individual liberty, variety, and justice. These values may at a number of places make demands that coincide with those of utility – in so far, that is, as these themselves are coherent – but they cannot be given a consistently utilitarian interpretation.

In many writings Berlin has urged upon us a single message of great power and moment. It is that human values are necessarily many, not one, and that of the many values there is not one to which the others are properly subordinate. Values come in systems, and systems of value possess the kind of complex structure that allows the different constituent values to interact. What morality rejects is monism, and the pluralism within which it can find accommodation is a pluralism of a loose kind or pluralism without hierarchy.

It is worth pointing out that this message, which has profound and subversive implications for both practical and theoretical thinking yet to be absorbed, relates exclusively to the internal nature of an individual's morality. It says nothing about the relations between the

Richard Wollheim, 'John Stuart Mill and Isaiah Berlin: The Ends of Life and the Preliminaries of Morality', from *The Idea of Freedom: Essays in Honour of Isaiah Berlin* (Oxford University Press, 1979), edited by Alan Ryan. Reprinted without alteration by permission of author, editor, and publisher.

moralities of different individuals, and specifically it does not say that there must or even can be a multiplicity of such moralities. Berlin himself, who has always held to a version of voluntaristic meta-ethics, probably believes in this kind of pluralism too. But the pluralism here under discussion is perfectly compatible with the belief in a single system of values, to which the different systems of value held by different individuals ought to conform and upon which they may be expected to converge. The message that I have attributed to Berlin is consistent, as far as I can see, with ethical objectivism and even ethical realism.

Now, once Berlin's message is clearly before us, it is plausible to think that his reading, or re-reading, of Mill derives from it. The derivation would take roughly the following course: Berlin finds Mill a sympathetic thinker with many of whose views on moral and social topics he finds himself in deep agreement; he finds it impossible to believe that these views could be arrived at on the basis of the monistic morality that utilitarianism must insist on; therefore, whatever he may profess, Mill is not really committed to utilitarianism; rather he is committed to a pluralistic morality, moreover to a loosely pluralistic morality, and it is from this that his best thinking depends.

In this essay I want to tread a narrow path. I accept wholeheartedly Berlin's strictures upon moral monism and indeed upon anything other than a loose form of pluralism in morality. I share his high opinion of Mill, who for me also is a sympathetic thinker on moral and social topics. However, I reject Berlin's reading of Mill and I accept Mill's claim about himself. In other words, I believe that Mill did remain a utilitarian and I think that he certainly continued to think of utility as he said he did: that is, as the ultimate appeal on all ethical questions. But the crucial qualification here is, to my mind, provided by Mill himself when he goes on to say that he intends utility 'in the largest sense' or utility 'grounded in the permanent interests of man as a progressive being'.[3] For it is central to my way of thinking about Mill that this significantly extends the notion of utility, that it is vital to the understanding of Mill's revision of utilitarianism, and that it does not, as Berlin thinks, stretch the notion of utility to the point of vacuity. For me it is just this qualification, properly understood, which explains simultaneously how Mill remained a utilitarian and how he emerged as an interesting and sympathetic thinker. And, by qualifying the notion of utility as he does, Mill, to my mind, produces not only a more plausible morality, but a morality that can be more plausibly regarded as utilitarian, than that constructed upon the cruder notion or notions of utility held alike by his immediate predecessors and many of his numerous successors.

A residual question remains: Berlin insists upon the diversity of human values. Mill ascribes complexity to the single value to which he subscribes. Given that Mill in talking of complexity succeeds in doing justice to everything that Berlin has in mind by diversity, given that Mill shows that utility, properly understood, can lay claim to the appropriate complexity, is he still right to think of utility as the complex value appropriate to occupy the central place in morality? I shall not attempt an answer to this residual question.

II

In 1826 John Stuart Mill underwent a severe mental crisis, to which so much of his earlier life contributed, and from which so much of his later life was to draw benefit. Mill himself wrote of the crisis as an event in his intellectual development. It was clearly more than this, but it was also this, and it is solely as an event in his development as a moral philosopher that I wish to consider it.

One day Mill found himself putting to himself the following question:

Suppose that all your objects in life were realised; that all the changes in institutions and opinions which you are looking forward to, could be completely effected at this very instant: would this be a great joy and happiness to you?[4]

He did not have to wait long for an answer. The question was posed, and

an irrepressible self-consciousness directly answered 'No!' At this my heart sank within me: the whole foundation on which my life was constructed fell down. All my happiness was to have been found in the continual pursuit of this end. The end had ceased to charm, and how could there ever again be any interest in the means? I seemed to have nothing left to live for.

One striking detail about the incident, or about Mill's telling of it, is the way in which Mill frames the original question. For he does not ask, as one might expect, Do I still find the utilitarian ideal a good ideal? Am I in accord with it as a moral or political objective? Instead he asks whether the realization of utilitarian objectives will give him pleasure, whether the satisfaction of the utilitarian ideal will in turn satisfy him, and at first this might strike the reader as a peculiarly personal or poignant touch, showing how deeply this crisis of belief affected his whole being and how it had shaken the more drily abstract way of looking at things which had been natural to him. The briefest reflection will show that this is a misinterpretation of Mill. In framing the question as he did, just what Mill shows is how firmly he still stood within the utilitarian framework. For, according to utilitarianism, it is a constraint upon morality that, for any given moral judgement, general or particular, there should be a precise match between the content of the judgement, or what it obliges an agent to do, and its motivational force, or its capacity to incite the agent – the agent, that is, who has fully understood it – to act in conformity with it. Further, utilitarianism prided itself on being a morality – indeed the only morality – which could meet this constraint. By assigning content to the moral judgement in the way in which it did – that is, as what would result in the greatest net balance of pleasure over pain for its recipients – it claimed to provide the agent with a uniquely good motive for putting it into practice – that is, the prospect of the greatest net balance of pleasure over pain for him too. Accordingly Mill was accepting one cardinal tenet of utilitarianism and using it to challenge another when he began to suspect that the fulfilment of the utilitarian ideal would not bring him happiness. As this suspicion hardened into certainty, his mental crisis peaked.

Mill's recovery from depression coincided with the attempt he made over the subsequent years to bring the content and the motivational force of utilitarianism back into line. Or – as it might more realistically be put, for Mill never really took altogether seriously the idea that there could be a morality which, once properly grasped, would prove irresistible – with the attempt he made to recapture motivational appeal for utilitarianism. Reflection must have shown that there were in principle two ways of doing this. Starting from the simple Benthamism with which he had become so thoroughly disillusioned, either he could rethink the content of utilitarian morality, so as to enhance its appeal, or he could put forward a revised account of human motivation with the aim of showing that utilitarian morality, content unchanged, had after all the capacity to move to action.

There was an evident difficulty for Mill in pursuing the second course. It would have required him to deny the most crucial experience of his life. In rewriting human motivation he would have had to rewrite his own motivation, and he would have had to say that, at the very moment when he was utterly convinced that the ideals in which he had been brought up no longer moved him, he did in fact have a motive, however best described, for acting on them, the deliverances of self-

341

consciousness notwithstanding. In other words, Mill would have extricated himself from his mental crisis only at the expense of unlearning the lesson it seemingly had taught him, and it is no surprise that, in his attempt to recapture motivational appeal for utilitarianism, he chose the first course.

Mill's revision of the content of utilitarian morality can most conveniently be considered if it is looked upon as falling into two stages. The two stages are not chronological stages, and there are good reasons for thinking that Mill's thought is ill-suited to chronological study – which, it is no accident, his detractors greatly favour.[5] Mill was a very perceptive thinker, and he often ran ahead of himself in grasping the conclusions to which his current thinking would lead him. At the same time he was very preoccupied with the impression that his words might make on a reader, and sometimes, in order to dispel the suspicion that he had abandoned the leading ideas of his earlier years, he would use phraseology which no longer consorted well with his actual thinking. To consider then, as I propose to do, the shift that Mill effects in utilitarian morality as falling into two stages – one of which is the shift from a morality that employs a monistic conception of utility to one that employs a conception of utility that is pluralistic but with hierarchy, and the other is the shift from a morality that employs a conception of utility that is pluralistic but with hierarchy to one that employs a conception of utility that is pluralistic and without hierarchy – is not to advance a historical thesis. Evidences of the later stage are already to be found in the essay on Bentham (1838), while the earlier stage still leaves its mark on *Utilitarianism* (1861).

In explicating the revision that Mill effects upon the content of utilitarian morality, I shall do so with an eye to the two questions that may be raised about it. The first is: Does this shift in content succeed in restoring appeal to utilitarianism? The second is: Is this shift really a shift within utilitarianism, or isn't it, rather, a shift out of utilitarianism?

Finally, with Mill's revision of utilitarianism fully before us I shall draw attention to a corollary that Mill appended to utilitarianism. Its effect is to show that utilitarian morality may be set within a larger framework of ordinances. This larger framework I shall call an ethic, and that Mill proposed a three-tiered ethic is, I shall suggest, one of the most interesting, as well as one of the more neglected, aspects of his work as a moral philosopher.

III

In our consideration of Mill's revision of utilitarianism, there is one problem, which might be expected to have priority for someone out to revise utilitarianism, which we do not have to trouble ourselves with. For reasons whose adequacy need not detain us, Mill took the problem as solved. The problem is that of the transition from a purely egotistic morality, which is the form in which, according to a well established tradition, utilitarianism initially proposes itself, to a non-egotistic morality: that is, to a morality which enjoins the maximization of pleasure but is indifferent to whom it is to whom the pleasure accrues, and, specifically, is blind to the distinction between agent's pleasure and the pleasure of others.[6] For the purposes of this essay this transition is assumed.

The first stage in the shift that Mill effects in the content of utilitarian morality consists in the move from a monistic conception of utility to a conception of utility that is pluralistic but with hierarchy. Alongside the primary principle of hedonism, or the maximization of pleasure, secondary principles make their appearance. Examples of such secondary principles would be the education of the mind, the cultivation of sexual love and family affection, patriotism, the maintenance of personal dignity, or the attachment to beauty, and, of course, it must be appreciated that these secondary principles, like the primary principle, may be non-egotistic. Secondary principles fix the agent's ends – their ends are his ends – but there is no reason why his ends should be self-interested or exclusively for him. However, what is characteristic of this stage of Mill's thinking, and what defines it, is that secondary principles are strictly subordinate to the primary principle, and it is because of this subordination that the pluralism brought about by the introduction of secondary principles is hierarchical.

In order to see how hierarchy manifests itself, let us take as the central case – for it is the clearest case – that in which a moral agent invokes utilitarian morality in order to decide how he ought to act.[7] Once we have grasped how hierarchy manifests itself here, we can use this understanding in order to grasp the effects of hierarchy in what may be regarded as derivative cases: that is, where a moral agent decides whether he has acted as he ought to have, or where a moral critic decides how others ought to act or whether they have acted as they ought to have.

Now in the central case, the moral agent in reaching a decision may consult the primary principle; alternatively he may consult one or other or more of his secondary principles. Let us suppose that he consults secondary principles. He does so, and he arrives at a decision. Then it is open to him to consult the primary principle and arrive at a decision on the basis of it. It is not required of him to do so, but, other things being equal – that is, the costs not being prohibitive – it is a rational course of action. It is so just because, should the two decisions diverge, then what he ought to do is given by the decision arrived at on the basis of the primary principle. The original decision must be abandoned. Of course, if the secondary principles have been at all carefully thought out, such divergences will be a rare thing. Nevertheless, should they occur, the primary principle operates in the agent's reasoning as though it were the only principle in the field, and this is one way in which secondary principles show themselves to be subordinate to the primary principle, or in which hierarchy manifests itself.

This way is the straightforward way, and to see the oblique way let us now suppose that the agent, in reaching a decision how he ought to act, consults the primary principle. In such a case what he will do is that he will survey the various actions that are practicable for him, he will assign to each the consequences that it is most likely to have for himself and for others, and he will calculate for each of these consequences the net balance of pleasure and pain that it is likely to produce, and then arrival at a decision will be a matter of selecting that action whose consequences maximize pleasure or produce the greatest net balance of pleasure over pain. Non-egotism is preserved by indifference to whom it is to whom the pleasure accrues. Now, in computing the pleasure and pain for each action, the agent will have to consider how his action interacts with the actions of others, and therefore he will need to know the courses of action on which those others who are affected by the action are embarked. However, these courses of action will themselves have been decided upon in one or other of two ways: either on the basis of the primary principle or on the basis of some one or more of the secondary principles of the person embarked on it. Let us now suppose that all the courses of action on which those others affected by the agent's action are embarked have been decided upon on the basis of secondary principles, and that this is known to the agent. All persons affected by his action are acting on secondary principles. In that case in computing the pleasure and pain that his action is likely to produce the agent will surely find it natural to equate, for each person, pleasure with the achievement of the end or ends fixed by the secondary principle or principles on which that person is acting. This determines the way in which, at any rate in the first instance, the agent will consider the interaction of his action with the actions of others. But, once again, this calculation having been made, though it is not required, it is, other things being equal, rational for the agent to make a complementary calculation. This time, in computing the pleasure and pain that his action is likely to produce, the agent, one allowance apart, ignores the fact that those others whom his action affects have decided upon the courses of action on which they are embarked on the basis of secondary principles. He assumes all persons affected by his action are acting on the primary principle, and in consequence, for each person, he equates pleasure, not with the achievement of the end or ends fixed by the secondary principle or principles on which that person is in point of fact acting, but just with whatever the primary principle enjoins for him – the one allowance that the agent makes being that he still has to count as pain for each person any disappointment he might experience from frustration of the secondary principle or principles on which he is actually, if misguidedly, acting. On this new assumption the agent will arrive at a fresh decision how he ought to act, and should the two decisions diverge, it is the second decision that he should prefer. He should, in other words, act as though the primary principle operates, this time not in the agent's reasoning, but in the reasoning of others, as the only principle in the field. Here we have the other way in which secondary principles show themselves to be subordinate to the primary principle, or in which hierarchy manifests itself.

The subordination of the secondary principles to the primary principle at this stage in Mill's thinking has, as a consequence, that the ends fixed by the various secondary principles stand to the end fixed by the primary principle in a special relationship: they stand as means to end. The agent's ends are, and are to be assessed as, means to pleasure. This means–end relationship totally coheres with the motivation that prompts this first shift in the content of utilitarian morality. This motivation is essentially practical, and is best expressed by Mill when he talks of utility as 'too complex and indefinite an end'[8] for a moral agent always to have had to take stock of in calculating what he ought to do or what would be best for himself and others. Such a calculation remains a calculation about utility, but it might be more practical to arrive at an answer by working it out in terms both simpler and more definite than utility. These terms are just what secondary principles provide through fixing subsidiary aims.

If Mill's first revision of utilitarian morality makes it easier for the agent to operate, it also does more than this, and it is this additional thing it does that enhances the appeal of utilitarian morality. For the revision brings it about that an agent, in deciding what he ought to do, has no longer to regard as irrelevant a whole body of thoughts, and also the attitudes and feelings connected with these thoughts, had by him or had by others, and which must be reckoned by any sensitive person as amongst the most interesting that either he or they are likely to entertain. I refer, of course, to those thoughts which define either his ends or the ends of others, for these thoughts must now enter into his calculations in so far as he thinks of pleasure accruing to himself or to them through the satisfaction of secondary principles upon which they act. So far, but no further. This body of thoughts acquires relevance for his calculations, but the relevance is merely provisional. Once it seems to the agent that pleasure is less likely to accrue this way, once the ends of the secondary principles no longer convince him as the best means to the end of the primary principle, then these thoughts cease to have a claim upon his attention. He may, indeed he must, put them out of his mind.

The purely provisional way in which these thoughts enter into the agent's calculations, and, correspondingly, the way in which they can be appropriately displaced by the direct thought of pleasure or utility, attest, of course, to the hierarchy that at this stage constrains the new-found pluralism of utilitarian morality. But they attest to something else as well. They attest to the degree to which the concept of pleasure, or happiness, or utility – and so far I have not found it necessary to distinguish between them – is itself found quite unproblematic. More specifically, the concept is not felt to require any of the interesting thoughts I have just referred to, or the ends fixed by secondary principles, for its elucidation. All this, however, is to change as utilitarian morality undergoes its second revision, to which we may now turn.

IV

The second stage in the shift that Mill effects in the content of utilitarian morality consists in the move from a conception of utility that is pluralistic but with hierarchy to one that is pluralistic and without hierarchy. Not merely do secondary principles appear alongside the primary principle but now they are not subordinate to it. The ends fixed by the secondary principles no longer stand to the end fixed by the primary principle in the means–end relationship. Or at least they no longer stand to it exclusively in this relationship. They also serve to elucidate it.

That the ends fixed by the secondary principle now serve to elucidate the end fixed by the primary principle has the implication that by now the latter end, or utility, has ceased to be unproblematic. And this is so. It is characteristic of utilitarianism under its second revision that utility is found problematic, but it is important to grasp how. The point is not that – or is not merely that – Mill, the moral philosopher, finds utility problematic. Rather, in his moral philosophy Mill reconstructs the fact that the moral agent finds, indeed must find, utility problematic. It then goes on to represent how the moral agent tries to resolve the problem for himself. He is represented as trying to make utility unproblematic by subscribing to secondary principles.

Why the moral agent finds utility problematic is to do with the highly abstract nature of the concept. Grasping this highly abstract concept, the agent finds that it doesn't contribute, in the way that utilitarianism leads him to believe that it should, to a decision how he ought to act. Even with all requisite information at his disposal, he will still have an inadequate grasp of what he should do to maximize utility. The abstract concept utility needs to be filled out, and this filling out can be thought of in two parts. In the first instance, the moral agent is required to have what might be thought of as a conception of his own utility. Only then can he consider how his utility is to be advanced. This conception is, however, not something that can be given to him or that he can learn. It is something that has to be formed, and it is formed through the process of trial and error. He tries out various secondary principles and finishes by subscribing to those whose ends give him or teach him what he wants. But, in the second instance, the moral agent requires that others have – that is, others form – a conception of their own utility, for only then can he consider how he is to advance their utility. And, once again, this conception is one that they have to form, they form it through trial and error, and it is codified in their secondary principles.

But it is one thing to believe that utilitarian morality cannot be successfully pursued unless each forms a conception of his own utility and that such a conception is formed through subscribing to secondary principles, and another thing, and evidently unjustified, to equate the subscription to just any set of secondary principles with the formation of a conception of one's own utility. Surely there must be some constraint upon the secondary principles subscribed to. More specifically, there must be some constraint upon the ends that these principles fix. To put the point another way: It may very well be that the pursuit of morality requires the subscription to secondary principles; but what has to be true of the secondary principles for the morality that they permit to be truly thought of as a utilitarian morality?

Actually it is an exaggeration to say, as I have said, that at this stage of Mill's revision of utilitarian morality utility is found problematic, if this is taken to mean that utility is found altogether problematic. There remains an unproblematic aspect of utility, and to mark the distinction that is at stake here it would be useful to employ the traditional distinction between pleasure and happiness. Unproblematically utility connotes pleasure, where pleasure is thought of as a kind of sensation or adjunct of sensation, and so long as utility is given this highly restricted interpretation, the moral agent may arrive at utilitarian decisions about how he ought to act without either his forming for himself or others' forming for themselves conceptions of their own utility. Such decisions are decisions about the maximization of the privileged sensation or adjunct of sensation. It is only when the moral agent appreciates that utilitarian decisions cannot be circumscribed in this way that utility becomes problematic for him. Any issue from this problematic situation is possible only if two conditions are met. In the first place, utility must be recognized to connote more than just pleasure. It also connotes, and it must be perceived to connote, happiness. Secondly, for the concept of utility in its broader connotation to gain application, it is required that the agent and others form conceptions of their own utility. This they do, as we have seen, through subscribing to secondary principles. If, however, we now ask what these secondary principles must be like, or what is the constraint laid upon the ends fixed by secondary principles if the conception to which these principles contribute is to be regarded as a conception of the person's utility or if the morality that they help to constitute is to be regarded as a utilitarian morality, the answer is easier to find. The constraint appears to be this: the ends fixed by the various secondary principles must be systematically related to pleasure.

But to say that the ends of the secondary principles must be systematically related to pleasure if utilitarianism is to be safeguarded does not say enough. There are various ways in which the ends of secondary principles may be systematically related to pleasure. For instance, some moral philosophers would argue that the systematic relationship is to be of a conceptual kind. The ends must derive from the concept of pleasure. I wish to suggest that the systematic relationship must be of a genetic kind. And I also wish to suggest that this is how Mill thought of the matter. In other words, utilitarianism as revised by him requires that it is possible to arrange pleasure and the ends fixed by the secondary principles of a moral agent on one and the same dendrogram, where the ends lie on the branches, pleasure is at the base of the tree, and the diagram as a whole represents the emergence of the moral agent according to the best available theory of human nature.[9]

From this last point an important consequence follows. To be able to say what it is for a morality that consists in a primary principle enjoining the maximization of utility and various secondary principles not subordinate to the primary principle to be overall a utilitarian morality presupposes that one has in one's possession a developmental psychology of a certain richness. It is only through such a psychology that one can tell whether the secondary principles appropriately relate to the primary principle. It is unnecessary to observe that Mill did not have such a psychology. He conceded the point – notably in the essay *The Subjection of Women* – and in at least one place he gave it as his opinion that the lack constituted the biggest single gap in contemporary knowledge.[10] However, there is a passage where he clearly recognizes just what has to be the internal structure of a morality that is pluralistic and without hierarchy and also utilitarian, and how this structure presupposes a theory of human nature. I refer to the passage in *Utilitarianism*, widely ridiculed, in which Mill talks of higher and lower pleasures.[11] To see how this passage bears upon the present issue, the reader needs to orientate himself appropriately. For generally this passage is read for what Mill has to say about the difference between higher and lower pleasures, or how it is that one pleasure can vary qualitatively from another. But the passage can also be read for what Mill has to say about what higher and lower pleasures have in common, or why it is that both are kinds of pleasure. Roughly, Mill's view is that higher and lower pleasures are both kinds of pleasure because they are functionally equivalent at different levels of a person's psychological development – which, of course, is also, to the same degree of roughness, just the reason why one kind of pleasure is qualitatively superior to the other. Thereby Mill throws everything on to the question of psychological development and how its levels are to be identified and what lies on each level. Given his lack of a psychological theory, Mill is naturally unable to answer these questions, but what is crucial for the proper interpretation of Mill is that he saw just what it is that was necessary if such answers were to be produced or where they were to come from.

I shall call utilitarianism under its second revision, or where its content is given by the primary principle of hedonism and various secondary principles not subordinate to but elucidatory of it, 'complex utilitarianism', and I turn to the question how, or how far, complex utilitarianism restores appeal to utilitarianism.

The crucial way in which complex utilitarianism restores appeal to utilitarianism is that it compels – it doesn't just permit, it compels – the moral agent, in deciding what he ought to do (or in coming to any related decision), to take account of what I have already called thoughts that are amongst the most interesting that human beings entertain: that is, thoughts definitive of the ends fixed by secondary principles, whether the agent's own or of others. And in taking account of these thoughts the agent is also required to take account of the feelings and attitudes that group themselves around those thoughts. And the account that he is required to take of these mental constellations is something that is by now ineliminable. It is not merely provisional, and it is not to be set aside in deference to some consideration which overrides secondary principles and their aims. Utilitarianism at last pays attention to man in his full complexity as a developed human being, and it would have to be a very gloomy or very desiccated self-consciousness that returned the answer 'No' to the question whether the pursuit of man's happiness, when man is thus envisaged, was an end that held out promise of great joy.

V

However, it might now seem that utilitarianism under its second revision, or complex utilitarianism, gains, or regains, appeal, but only at the cost of scope. Let me explain.

A moral agent, we are now told, has to take ineliminable account of both his and others' secondary principles. But this is impossible unless both he and others have secondary principles, and furthermore – for otherwise the account he takes of them would be eliminable – hold them not subordinately to the primary principle. He and they must have formed conceptions of their own happiness, and they must more-over have knowledge of each other's conceptions. But this is not a universally satisfied condition: it represents an achievement, first of all, in the life of the species, and then, secondly, in the life of the individual. Complex utilitarianism gains its appeal from the way in which it pays respect to the full faculties of man: but, by the same token, it appears to lose its hold when man has not entered into possession of his full faculties. In its attempt to do justice to the developmental nature of man, complex utilitarianism takes on or acquires a developmental nature. Or so it might seem. Is this so, and is this how Mill saw it?

Mill, we know, like his father and like Bentham, professed to think that any non–utilitarian morality was ultimately untenable. But did he think that utilitarian morality held in those circumstances – whether of general history or of personal biography – in which it did not hold appeal?

Explicitly Mill never raised the question. But implicitly – or so I believe – he must have, just because he supplied the question with an answer, and an answer which, as I have already said, constitutes one of the most interesting and also most neglected aspects of his work as a moral philosopher. For what Mill did was to set complex utilitarianism within a larger structure, appropriately thought of as a three-tiered ethic, and to each tier of which he then assigned distinct conditions under which it held or in which it obliged the agent to act in conformity with it.

On one tier of this ethic, the uppermost tier, there is utilitarianism proper, by now glossed as complex utilitarianism. Complex utilitarianism enjoins the maximization of utility, as utility is elucidated in the moral agent's conception of happiness and in the conceptions of happiness entertained by the various recipients of his action. Complex utilitarianism holds when, or in so far as, people have indeed formed their own conceptions of happiness, know of the conceptions of others, and pursue utility accordingly. It holds just when men have entered into possession of their full faculties. On the tier below this, or the middle tier, there is simple utilitarianism, where this includes both utilitarianism employing a monistic conception of utility and utilitarianism employing a conception of utility that is pluralistic but with hierarchy. Simple utilitarianism holds when, or in so far as, men have not formed conceptions of their own happiness, and pleasure rather than happiness is what they pursue for themselves and others. It is the ethic of men whose faculties are still undeveloped. Then, on the third tier, the lowermost, there is what I shall call 'preliminary utilitarianism', and I claim that it is one of the most innovative aspects of Mill's ethical thought that he identified and found a place for preliminary utilitarianism. What preliminary utilitarianism enjoins is whatever is necessary for people either to form, or, having formed, to maintain, conceptions of their own happiness – or, for that matter (though I shall not pursue this aspect), envisagements of other people's conceptions of their own happiness. The conditions under which preliminary utilitarianism holds are disjunctive: that part which is concerned with the formation of people's conceptions of their own happiness holds when such conceptions are not fully formed, and that part which is concerned with the maintenance of such conceptions holds just when they are formed. Preliminary utilitarianism invariably holds. And, finally, when the injunctions of preliminary utilitarianism conflict with the injunctions of either simple or complex utilitarianism – whichever is relevant – then, unless the cost in utility is too severe, the injunctions of preliminary utilitarianism take priority. Education up to the point where happiness can be attained is more important than the attainment either of pleasure or of happiness.

I shall end by drawing attention to the three separate places where Mill argues for policies or practices on the basis of preliminary utilitarianism.

Two occur in the essay *On Liberty*.

The first passage is in chapter 4, where Mill, having divided the actions of the agent into the 'self-regarding' (his phrase) and the 'other-regarding' (not his phrase), exempts the former altogether from the sphere of State intervention. For this exemption might not be the verdict reached by appeal either to simple or to complex utilitarianism, and for two distinct reasons. In the first place, though it is a matter of dispute just how Mill effected the division, it seems as though self-regarding actions are not to be equated with those which in no way impinge upon others. They must be those actions which affect others, if they do, only in some discountable fashion.[12] Accordingly there is always the possibility that a self-regarding action is in its net effect more adverse than some other action practicable for the agent. Why should not such an action, on grounds of utilitarianism, either simple or complex, be the object of State intervention? Secondly, self-regarding actions, however defined, have an effect upon the agent. Why should not utilitarianism decide that those with a benign effect upon him ought to be enforced by the State and those with a malign effect upon him be prohibited? Mill's counter-argument seems to be that self-regarding actions are crucial to those 'experiments of living' without which individual conceptions of happiness would either not be formed or, having been formed, wither away.[13] Here we witness a case of preliminary utilitarianism overruling either simple or complex utilitarianism.

The second passage is to be found in chapter 2, where Mill discusses liberty of opinion, which once again is treated as total. Mill's argument in favour of total liberty of opinion appeals to two considerations: truth and rationality. In both cases the content of the appeal is subtle, but the question arises: Why should a utilitarian, even a complex utilitarian, set such supreme value on truth and rationality? These may, of course, and almost certainly will be, amongst the ends fixed by secondary principles of the various citizens. But does this fully explain the strength of Mill's commitment? It seems that preliminary utilitarianism must make its contribution to the argument, in that, if it does not overrule utilitarianism proper, at least it supplements it.

The third passage is in *Considerations on Representative Government*. Mill says that representative government is the ideally best form of government in that it is 'the one which in the circumstances in which it is practicable and eligible is attended with the greatest amount of beneficial consequences, immediate and prospective'. Here, it might seem, speaks utilitarianism proper. But not so. For as Mill develops the argument, he brings forward two criteria by which the merit of political institutions is to be judged. One concerns the way in which they 'organize the moral, intellectual, and active worth already existing, so as to operate with the greatest effect in public affairs'.[14] If that sounds like the voice of utilitarianism, what are we to make of the second criterion? For this concerns the way in which political institutions 'promote the general mental advancement of the community'. If this can in part be put to utilitarianism proper – and this I do not deny – in part it attests to the influence of preliminary utilitarianism.

It is not surprising that critics are to be found who will see in these passages evidence of Mill's backslidings from utilitarianism. Given their failure to perceive the complex character of Mill's commitment to utilitarianism – more complex, it now turns out, than a mere commitment to complex utilitarianism – their criticisms are altogether understandable. However concern for the proper interpretation of Mill requires us to reject them. Properly interpreted, Mill can be shown to concur not only with Berlin's concern for a loose pluralism in morality but also with his other, no less urgent, no less generous, and certainly related, concern for the all-important value of liberty. But that is another though not all that different a story.

Notes

1. *Collected Works of John Stuart Mill*, ed. J. M. Robson (Toronto/London, 1963–) (hereafter *J.S.M.*), vol. 18, p. 224.
2. Isaiah Berlin, *John Stuart Mill and the Ends of Life* (London, 1959), reprinted in his *Four Essays on Liberty* (London, 1969).
3. *J.S.M.*, loc. cit. (note 1 above).
4. John Stuart Mill, *Autobiography* (London, 1873), pp. 133–4.
5. e.g. Introduction to *Essays on Politics and Culture*, ed. G. Himmelfarb (New York, 1962); G. Himmelfarb, *On Liberty and Liberalism* (New York, 1974): cf. John Rees, 'The Thesis of the Two Mills', *Political Studies* 25 (1977), 369–82.
6. In two early essays – the 'Remarks on Bentham's Philosophy' (1833), which appeared anonymously, and 'Sedgwick's Discourse' (1835) – Mill sets himself against the identification of utility with selfish or self-regarding interest. In the earlier essay he uses this point

as a criticism of Bentham, in the later essay he uses it in defence of Bentham against his critics. Both essays are to be found in *J.S.M.*, vol. 10.

7. For ease of exposition I write throughout as though utilitarianism were to be construed as act-utilitarianism. I tend to believe that this is correct, but all my examples can fairly readily be converted so as to concord with rule-utilitarianism.

8. *J.S.M.*, vol. 10, p. 110.

9. At two different places in his edition of his father's *magnum opus* Mill seeks to forestall those who criticize the view that evolved ends derive from the pursuit of pleasure on the grounds that the two kinds of end are unresembling, by pointing out to such critics that, when the genetic derivation is lengthy, 'the resulting feeling always seems not only very unlike any one of the elements composing it, but very unlike the sum of those elements'. James Mill, *Analysis of the Phenomena of the Human Mind*, ed. John Stuart Mill (London, 1869), vol. 2, p. 321; cf. p. 252.

10. 'Of all difficulties which impede the progress of thought, and the formation of well-grounded opinions on life and social arrangements, the greatest is now the unspeakable ignorance and inattention of mankind in respect to the influences which form human character.' John Stuart Mill, *The Subjection of Women* (London, 1869), pp. 39–40. The missing science Mill had talked about under the name 'ethology' in book 6, chapter 5 of his *System of Logic*.

11. *J.S.M.*, vol. 10, pp. 210–13.

12. J. C. Rees, 'A Re-reading of Mill on Liberty', *Political Studies* 8 (1960), pp. 113–29; Alan Ryan, 'Mr McCloskey on Mill's Liberalism', *Philosophical Quarterly* 14 (1964), 253–60; C. L. Ten, 'Mill on Self-Regarding Actions', *Philosophy* 43 (1968), 29–37; Richard Wollheim, 'John Stuart Mill and the Limits of State Action', *Social Research* (1973), 1–30.

13. *J.S.M.*, vol. 18, p. 261.

14. *J.S.M.*, vol. 15, p. 392. Some interesting observations on the interlock between Mill's concern with the formation of character and his political views are to be found in R. J. Halliday, 'Some Recent Interpretations of John Stuart Mill', *Philosophy* 43 (1968), 1–17, reprinted in *Mill: A Collection of Critical Essays*, ed. J. B. Schneewind (New York, 1968).

Biographical Note

Richard Wollheim is Professor of Philosophy at Columbia University. He was Grote Professor of the Philosophy of Mind and Logic at University College, London, before which he was Lecturer and then Reader in the college. His books include *F. H. Bradley* (1959), *Art and Its Objects* (1968), *A Family Romance* (1969), which is a novel, *Freud* (1971) and *On Art and the Mind* (1973). He is a Fellow of the British Academy.

Further Reading

John Stuart Mill, *Three Essays*, ed. with introduction by Richard Wollheim (Oxford University Press, 1975); John Stuart Mill, *Autobiography* (London: 1873).

F. H. Bradley, *Ethical Studies* (Oxford: 1876, 1927); J. F. Stephen, *Liberty, Equality, Fraternity* (London: Cambridge University Press, 1967); J. C. Rees, 'A Re-reading of Mill on Liberty', *Political Studies* 8, 1960; J. B. Schneewind (ed.), *Mill: A Collection of Critical Essays* (New York, London: Notre Dame, 1970); Richard Wollheim, 'John Stuart Mill and the

Limits of State Action', *Social Research* 40, 1973; H. L. A. Hart, *Law, Liberty and Morality* (Stanford University Press and Oxford University Press, 1963); Gertrude Himmelfarb, *On Liberty and Liberalism: The Case of John Stuart Mill* (New York: Knopf, 1974); Isaiah Berlin, *Four Essays on Liberty* (London: Oxford University Press, 1969); John Gray, *Mill on Liberty: A Defence* (London: Routledge, 1983).

Allen W. Wood

Marx: The Critique of Justice

Karl Marx condemned capitalism, the system in which some men own only what he called their labour power, and others own such means of production as factories. He condemned capitalism, as he said, partly because the members of the first class, the working class, are exploited and are subjected to a servitude which is such that they are rightly called slaves. They are also impoverished materially, mentally and morally. They are alienated, which means in but one part that they are deprived of all satisfaction in their labour. Their existence, in short, is wretched. Those who own means of production, the capitalist class, are by contrast exploiters, slave-masters, and live in wealth, comfort and idleness. They have great possibilities of personal fulfilment.

Is capitalism then unjust? Does it offend against principles of justice or fairness or equality? Marx's answer was that it is *not* unjust. He attacked those other critics of capitalism whose essential claim is that capitalism is unjust or unfair or offends against a principle of equality. He spoke of it as just. (pp. 369–70) He castigated demands for 'a just wage' or 'a fair day's wage for a fair day's work', and dismissed appeals to the rights of man.

Allen Wood, in the following essay, gives what is perhaps the best available account of why Marx, despite his condemnation of capitalism, did not take it to be unjust, and spoke of it as just. Wood also seeks to argue, I think, that Marx was right. That is, Marx had a conception of justice which is the correct or defensible or rational one, and it does not at all follow from this conception that capitalism, while it exploits, enslaves and so on, is unjust. Moreover, it cannot be said that the dispute between Marx and other critics of capitalism, or between him

---

Karl Heinrich Marx, 1818–83. Born in Germany, lived in a number of European cities, finally London. Economist and sociologist, and philosopher. Also a revolutionary, true to his view that what the world needs is not philosophizing about, but changing.

and anyone who takes exploitation, misery and the like to be unjust, is only a verbal dispute. It is not the case that words are being used differently, and that fundamentally there is agreement about the nature of a thing. There is dispute of a factual kind about the nature of a thing. (p. 375)

The first of the four sections of the essay contrasts two conceptions of human life and society. The first conceives of our lives and societies in terms of law, government, political system, rights, various related institutions and morality. This is the juridical or legal, or political, conception of society. This traditional conception is such that society is properly described as 'the body politic' and indeed is nearly identified with the state.

Out of Marx's view of man's nature as *productive* there arises his view of society as a mode of production. (p. 364) This complex whole somehow has as basic to it means or forces of production and certain relations connected with them. (p. 363) These are relations between men and means of production, and relations between men and men having to do with means of production, most notably the relation of capitalist and worker in the capitalist society. If law, government, political system, rights, various institutions and morality also enter into and 'regulate' a society conceived as a mode of production, they are none the less a 'superstructure', somehow less fundamental than means and relations of production – than man's life as a producer of things. (pp. 362–4) Wood, while he requires this proposition of fundamentality for his further argument, is keen not to overstate it. (pp. 364–6)

The burden of the second and perhaps the crucial section of the essay, a burden anticipated in the first (p. 362), is that the condemnation of anything as unjust, the use of a principle of justice, fairness or equality, is fundamentally a matter of the laws of morality which are aspects of a particular society, such a particular mode of production as capitalism. To talk of justice can be to do no more than talk of laws and rules that are 'expressions' or 'aspects' or 'dependent moments' of a mode of production while it persists. To see justice in this way – Marx's way – is in a way not to diminish it. It is accepted as playing a significant supporting role of a regulating kind in the given mode of production. Laws support the mode of production and serve its development or history. (pp. 368–70) Their justice consists in their having that function.

There is therefore no rational or defensible principle of justice independent of a mode of production, and perhaps good for all places and times. Any offering of such a thing is the offering of what is meaningless. To attempt to turn real justice, an expression or aspect of this or that mode of production or epoch, into an independent principle, perhaps the work of a philosopher, is to engage in mystification and misbegotten glorification. To suppose that capitalism can be judged this way, because of its awfulness, is to do this sort of thing. It is to try to judge it by way of what is empty and useless.

Justice clearly seen, then, is a subordinate if significant feature of a society. Justice is misconceived and glorified when its somehow subordinate role is not seen or is denied. Its subordinate role is the essential premise from which there follows the conclusion that capitalism cannot be condemned as unjust. To condemn it as unjust, as the thought might briskly be expressed, must be to say absurdly that it is condemned by its own laws and the like, which clearly it is not, or to say as absurdly that it is condemned by some fantasy-principle unconnected with social reality. No such thing is worth attention. All that is of importance, in so far as justice is concerned, is the reality of laws and the like which are parts of the superstructure of a society.

The third section of the essay has to do in part with Marx's view as an economist of the nature of capitalism. It is a view opposed to that of classical economists, who did criticize capitalism as unfair or unjust. On Marx's view, which resists summary, the increase in value which results when something is worked on – by a labourer who sells his labour to a capitalist – does with perfect reason go to the capitalist. To be led into glorified or mystical condemnation of this as unjust is to do something which derives in part from somehow mistaken economic conceptions. Also, it derives from failing to see that there is blunder in applying to capitalism Locke's idea that a man has a right to the ownership of something if he has mixed his labour with it. (pp. 372–8) There is no point whatever, given these and the previous considerations, in attempting to argue for what will come, the breakdown of capitalism and the revolution, by way of ideas of justice. The breakdown and revolution will not be owed to such ideas, but rather will result inevitably from the nature of capitalism itself. (pp. 381–8)

The fourth section gives Marx's own condemnation of the capitalist epoch, mentioned above. It is an epoch of exploitation, servitude, alienation and misery. Does this condemnation derive from a principle of justice which Marx has disdained, but which somehow operates in his thinking? It does not, and no such principle, or any moral principle whatever, can be used in a summation of his condemnation.

Wood's essay, to repeat, is perhaps more instructive and persuasive than any other on Marx on justice. It has that excellence despite what some will suppose, as certainly I do myself, that Marx's view is mistaken. The essay, further, is an admirable introduction to Marx's philosophy as a whole, one which succeeds in bringing its nature before us.

Allen W. Wood

Marx: The Critique of Justice

When we read Karl Marx's descriptions of the capitalist mode of production in *Capital* and other writings, all our instincts tell us that these are descriptions of an unjust social system. Marx describes a society in which one small class of persons lives in comfort and idleness while another class, in ever-increasing numbers, lives in want and wretchedness, labouring to produce the wealth enjoyed by the first. Marx speaks constantly of capitalist 'exploitation' of the worker, and refers to the creation of surplus value as the appropriation of his 'unpaid labour' by capital. Not only does capitalist society, as Marx describes it, strike us as unjust, but his own descriptions of it themselves seem to connote injustice.

When we look in the writings of Marx and Engels for a detailed account of the injustices of capitalism, however, we discover at once that not only is there no attempt at all in their writings to provide an argument that capitalism is unjust, but there is not even the explicit claim that capitalism is unjust or inequitable, or that it violates anyone's rights. We find, in fact, explicit denunciations and sustained criticisms of social thinkers (such as Pierre Proudhon and Ferdinand Lassalle) who did condemn capitalism for its injustices or advocated some form of socialism as a means of securing justice, equality, or the rights of man. We even find, perhaps to our surprise, some fairly explicit statements to the effect that capitalism, with all its manifold defects, cannot be faulted as far as justice is concerned. Whatever else capitalism may be for Marx, it does not seem that it is unjust.

The fact that Marx does not regard capitalism as unjust has been noted before.[1] But Marx's reasons for holding this view, and the concept of justice on which it rests, have been less frequently understood. It is of course true that Marx and Engels do not say much about

Allen W. Wood, 'The Marxian Critique of Justice', *Philosophy and Public Affairs*, Vol. 1, No. 3, 1972. Reprinted without alteration by permission of author and editor.

the manner in which social or economic justice may be actualized, and that they do not concern themselves greatly with the ways in which just social institutions may be distinguished from unjust ones. And if, as I wish to argue, the attainment of justice does not, in itself, play a significant role in either Marxian theory or Marxist practice, these omissions are neither serious nor surprising. Nevertheless, Marx and Engels did take seriously the concept of justice and did have a place for it in their conception of society and social practice. Both were in fact highly critical of what they took to be the misuse of this concept in social thought, its 'mystification' and ideological 'glorification'. This Marxian critique of justice may be viewed as an attempt to clarify the role of the concept of justice in social life and to prevent its ideological abuse. Much can be learned, I think, by tracing this critique to its roots in the Marxian conceptions of society and social practice, and viewing it in relation to Marx's own reasons for denying that capitalism is unjust while at the same time calling for its revolutionary overthrow.

I

The concept of justice has traditionally played an important role in theories of the rational assessment of social institutions. It is commonly felt that justice is the highest merit any social institution can possess, while injustice is the gravest charge which could ever be lodged against it. It seems to be no exaggeration to say that to both the philosopher and the common man justice has often appeared, as Engels once put it, 'the fundamental principle of all society, . . . the standard by which to measure all human things, . . . the final judge to be appealed to in all conflicts'.[2] Why is such importance attached to the concept of justice? 'Justice' (*Gerechtigkeit*), according to Marx and Engels, is fundamentally a juridical or legal (*rechtlich*) concept, a concept related to the law (*Recht*) and to the rights (*Rechte*) men have under it. The concepts of right and justice are for them the highest rational standards by which laws, social institutions, and human actions may be judged from a juridical point of view.[3] This point of view has long been regarded as being of particular importance for the understanding and assessment of social facts. It is not too much to say that the traditional Western conception of society is itself a fundamentally juridical conception. The social whole, according to this tradition, *is* the 'state' or 'body politic', the framework within which human actions are regulated by legal and political processes. The study of society in this tradition has been, above all, the study of these processes; the ideal society, since Plato's time, has been conceived of as the ideal *state*; and social practice, in its highest form, has been thought to be the skilful fashioning of a state through the giving of just laws, or the regulation of the actions of citizens by a wise government. The social life of man, according to this tradition, is his life in relation to the political state; man as a social being is man in relation to those powers which promulgate laws, guarantee rights, and issue juridical commands. Granted this conception of society, it is quite understandable that right and justice should be taken as the fundamental social principles, the highest measure of all social things.

The source not only of Marx's critique of justice, but also of the fundamental originality of his social thought, is his rejection of this political or juridical conception of society. Marx tells us in his preface to *A Contribution to the Critique of Political Economy* that the origins of his social thought lay in the discontent he felt with this conception as a student of law and the philosophy of law, and particularly of Hegel's *Philosophy of Right*. His critical reflections, he tells us – and we can see it for ourselves in the articles and manuscripts produced by Marx in the course of the year 1843 – 'led to the result that juridical relations [*Rechtsverhältnisse*], like forms of the state, are to be grasped neither through themselves nor through the so-called universal development of the human spirit, but rather are rooted in the material relations of life, whose totality Hegel . . . comprehended under the term "civil society"'.[4] The social whole, the fully concrete unity of social life was, in Hegel's view, to be found in the political state; the sphere of men's material activities and interests, civil society, was treated by Hegel as a system of social processes taking place *within* the political whole and dependent on it. Marx reversed this relationship. Human society, he maintained, is a developing system of collective productive activity, aimed at the satisfaction of historically conditioned human needs; its institutions, including juridical and political ones, are all aspects of this productive activity. As early as 1844 Marx tells us that 'Religion, the family, the state, the law [*Recht*], morality, science, art, etc., are only particular modes of production and fall under its general law.' And in the *German Ideology* Marx and Engels reject 'the old conception of history which neglects real relationships and restricts itself to high-sounding dramas of princes and states'.[5]

The key to Marx's transformation of Hegel's concept of society is found in the Marxian conception of human practice. Human society, according to the Marxian view, is a fact of nature. But it is nevertheless characterized throughout by the essential quality of man as a natural phenomenon, by productive activity or labour, which distinguishes man from the rest of the natural world. 'Men begin to distinguish themselves from animals when they begin to *produce* their means of life, a step conditioned by their bodily organization.'[6] 'The animal,' says Engels, 'merely *uses* external nature and brings about changes in it merely by his presence in it; man makes it serviceable to his ends through such changes, he *masters* it. This is the final and essential distinction between men and other animals, and it is labour which effects this distinction.'[7] The essential feature of labour for Marx and Engels is its purposiveness, the fact that it is the expression of *will*. Labour, says Engels, is that by which men 'impress the stamp of their will upon the earth'.[8] Man alone, Marx points out, 'makes his life-activity itself an object of his will and consciousness'.[9] And again, in *Capital*, he says: 'What distinguishes the worst architect from the best of bees is that he raises his structure in his head before he builds it in wax. At the end of the labour process a result comes about which at the beginning was already in the representation of the labourer, which was already present ideally.'[10] But human productive activity, according to Marx, always takes place in particular historical circumstances. At a given point in human history, men are possessed of determinate methods and capacities for subjecting nature to their will – methods and capacities which they have inherited from previous generations through a specific process of historical development. These productive forces (*Produktivkräfte*), as Marx calls them, correspond to, and are expressed in, determinate relationships between men, within which alone these forces, in their historically given form, can be applied to nature. These relationships Marx calls production relations (*Produktionsverhältnisse*). Because men are not free to choose the degree of their mastery over nature at a given stage in history, they are also not free to choose the form these production relations will take. Hence production relations are, in Marx's words, 'necessary and independent of their will'.[11]

Human productive activity, however, not only transforms nature; it also transforms man himself.[12] In altering nature and in developing his productive forces, man acts on himself as well. Human history, for Marx, consists above all in the development and transformation of human nature. The activity of labour itself is for Marx essentially man's self-production.[13] This is because the employment of productive forces is not just a means to human ends, but is rather 'a determinate kind of activity of individuals, a determinate way of expressing their life, a determinate *mode of life*. As individuals express their life, so they are. What they are is bound up with their production, and *what* they produce with *how* they produce.'[14] Men produce by adopting determinate modes of collective activity, modes which in turn act upon them and change them. As they satisfy their needs by productive activity, therefore, they are at the same time producing new forms of activity and new needs. 'The production of new needs,' say Marx and Engels, 'is the first historical act.'[15]

Human productive activity, therefore, is a complex historical process composed of many interdependent factors acting upon and reacting with one another. Men's needs, their productive forces, their production relations are all decisive moments in it, but none of them is independent of the others. At a given stage in history these interdependent factors form a whole, a complex system of human activity with a kind of relative stability. Such a historically conditioned system of productive activity has its own characteristic forms of social and cultural life, and within it men have a characteristic human nature, distinguishing this system from the preceding system of activity out of which it arose historically and from the succeeding system into which it will eventually pass over. Such a historically conditioned social whole is called by Marx a 'mode of production' (*Produktionsweise*).

The Marxian conception of society is sometimes described as 'economic determinism'. By this it is often meant that Marx's theory takes one aspect of social life (the 'economic' aspect) to be the crucial one on which all others depend. Marx, according to this account, either reduces all of social life to economics, or he regards the rest of social life as an epiphenomenon of economics, or else as a series of effects proceeding entirely from 'economic' causes. This interpretation of Marx, it seems to me, is fundamentally mistaken. There is no space here to deal with this issue in the depth it deserves, but I would like at least briefly to suggest why it seems to me wrong to understand Marx's 'determinism' in this simplistic way. In the first place, Marx did not regard himself primarily as a political economist; he thought of himself rather as a *critic* of political economy, attempting to preserve what was valuable in classical political economy within a more comprehensive theory of society and history. He criticizes political economists for the one-sidedness of their approach to social phenomena, for their failure to see the interconnection between the different factors in social life. When Marx refers to production relations as 'economic' relations, he does not mean to isolate one 'aspect' of social relations as the crucial one, but simply to emphasize that all such relations are *forms* of human productive activity, and should be viewed in their connection with production.

Marx does say that 'the mode of production conditions social, political, and spiritual life-processes'. He also says that 'it is not men's consciousness which determines their being, but on the contrary their social being which determines their consciousness'.[16] But he does not mean to reduce social, political, and spiritual processes to processes of production, as some philosophers have tried to reduce mental phenomena to physical ones. Nor does Marx mean to say that 'production', regarded as one factor among others in the social process, is in general the *cause* of the remaining social institutions. Marx's point here can best be understood if we keep in mind that his conception of society is a transformation of Hegel's conception, and can best be brought out by looking at Hegel's own anticipation of it early in the *Philosophy of Right*. Hegel is speaking about the function of legislation in the state, and says: 'Legislation must not be considered abstractly and in isolation, but rather must be seen as a dependent moment in one totality, in its connection with all the other determinations which make up the character of a nation and an epoch.'[17] Legislation, according to Hegel, is one of the 'determinations' (*Bestimmungen*) which make up a nation and an epoch, one of the dependent moments in a totality. To be properly understood, therefore, it must not be treated as something independent of this totality, or something intelligible on its own, but rather must be viewed as a partial process within the total process. The totality of national life in a given epoch could, in this sense, be said by Hegel to determine and to condition the laws of the nation. It would, however, be either incorrect or unintelligible to say that for Hegel legislation could be *reduced* to the totality of national life. Hegel is not reducing legislation to anything; he is rather attempting to appreciate its richness by noting its connection with other factors in national life. Nor is it at all plausible to attribute to Hegel the view that legislation is a mere 'epiphenomenon' of national life. Legislation, in Hegel's view, might very well be said to be caused by specific factors within the totality of national life, but this is a result of the fact that legislation is itself a determination or dependent moment within this organic totality.

The organic whole of social life in a given historical epoch is of course not for Marx a nation or political state, but a mode of production. This whole is called a mode of *production* because human life is essentially productive activity. And Marx explicitly distinguishes 'production' in this comprehensive sense from 'production in its one-sided form' as one of the elements or 'determinations' of the total process.[18] Not only human needs, modes of commerce and exchange, and property relations, but also men's political life, religion, morality, and philosophical thought are moments, phases, determinations of human productive activity. Like the more narrowly 'economic' categories of exchange and consumption, they are 'elements in a totality, distinctions within a unity . . . There is an interaction between the various moments. This is the case with every organic whole.'[19] Legal and political structures are therefore called 'superstructures' by Marx; they are structures which are dependent on and hence 'built upon' the mode of production within which they operate as regulative institutions.[20] These institutions owe their existence and their form to the mode of production within which they operate, to the specific manner in which they regulate existing production relations and serve the needs of given individuals. Law and politics may indeed affect and condition these other moments of the social process, but they are also affected and conditioned by them. They 'mirror' or 'reflect' the productive social life they regulate.[21] The task of comprehending them is not that of reducing political or juridical facts to economic facts, but that of discovering empirically the 'connection [*Zusammenhang*] of the social and political structure with production'.[22]

I have been claiming that Marx's conception of society is founded on a reversal of the Hegelian relationship between social production (civil society) and the political state. I have argued that just as for Hegel civil society was a partial process within the totality of national political life, so for Marx the state was a partial process reflecting the life of civil society. This claim needs to be clarified and qualified, however. For it was not an 'eternal truth' for Marx (nor, *mutatis mutandis*, for Hegel) that the political life and productive activity of man stand in this relationship to one another. Marx did not believe, in fact, that the identification of the social whole with the political state was necessarily false under all historical circumstances. In the *Grundrisse* he distinguishes three general types of society, the tribal, the oriental, and the ancient, which because they were rooted in the common ownership of means of production by the political whole or its representative involved no separation of the political state from civil society. In such societies the productive and political life of man was an immediate unity, and the productive activity of the individual was indistinguishable from his participation and membership in the political *Gemeinwesen*, the tribe, state, or polis. Thus from a Marxian viewpoint ancient political science, such as we find in Plato's *Republic* or Aristotle's *Politics*, cannot be faulted for conceiving of the social whole as identical with the laws, customs, and institutions of the polis. In ancient society, the social life of man was his political life, and it was quite correct to say, as Aristotle did, that the 'way of life' of a people was its *politeia*.

The differentiation of the political state from civil society was made historically possible, Marx believed, by the introduction of commodity exchange into the productive life of society, and the resulting opposition between the form of common property corresponding to the tribal *Gemeinwesen* and the form of private property corresponding to the exchange of commodities. This opposition, present already in the oriental and ancient productive modes, made possible in Marx's view the alienation of the state from civil society which characterized feudal production, and which reaches its extreme form in the fragmented life of capitalist civil society. Here the state, which began in immediate unity with the process of social production, has become a distinct institution operating within this process, which nevertheless still claims to represent society in its totality. The existence of the political state as a determination and alienated reflection of man's productive life is therefore not an eternal truth about the nature of society, but a historical truth about those European societies which have passed through feudal to capitalist production.

The importance of human productive activity in the Marxian conception of society, however, transcends this historical process, or rather represents a principle of social life which emerges with increasing clarity from it. Only when the sphere of human productive activity as such emancipates itself from the limiting regulatory forms of political life can the universal character of man's social being as cooperative labour become apparent to him. Hence it was Marx's view that social production, the true basis of all society, could not be appreciated as such by the ancient world, and only emerged with clarity in the economic life of the capitalist mode of production. This is why Marx repudiated the tendency of other thinkers, such as Rousseau and Hegel, to idealize the political life of the ancient world and to long for its restoration or to conceive of the modern state as a principle of social unity to be imposed on the fragmented world of capitalism. Instead, Marx saw implicit in the modern emancipation of civil society from the state the possibility of establishing men's cooperative labour itself as the basis of a new form of *Gemeinwesen*. It is this notion of the replacement of the political state by a new form of community based on labour which lies at the root of Marx's belief that in communist society the state will be abolished and transcended (*aufgehoben*).

Allen W. Wood

II

The concept of justice, as we have seen, is in the Marxian account the highest expression of the rationality of social facts from the *juridical* point of view. This point of view, however, is always the point of view of one of the dependent moments of a given mode of production, the sphere of political authority or *Staatsrecht*. Marx, as we have seen, rejected the Hegelian notion that the organic unity of society is to be in any sense identified with the regulatory functions of the political state. Just as little is the state a power acting on the mode of production from outside, determining its form and controlling its historical destiny. The political state is rather a power acting *within* the prevailing mode of production, it is one of the instruments of production fashioned by the historical past and employed in the present by given individuals to satisfy their historically conditioned needs. The state is an expression, a determination, of the prevailing mode of production. Its point of view, the juridical one, and the conceptions of right and justice which express this point of view, are rationally comprehensible only when seen in their proper connection with other determinations of social life and grasped in terms of their role within the prevailing productive mode.

For all his detailed study of social reality and his profound concern with the rational assessment of it, we find no real attempts in Marx's writings to provide a clear and positive conception of right or justice. This relative neglect of juridical concepts and principles does not derive from a personal aversion to 'moral preaching' or from an 'amoral' attitude towards social reality, as some have suggested. It is due rather to Marx's assessment of the role of juridical conceptions in social life. Because Marx regarded juridical institutions as playing only a supporting role in social life, he attached considerably less importance to juridical conceptions as measures of social rationality than most previous social thinkers were inclined to do. The juridical point of view, for Marx, is essentially one-sided, and to adopt it as the fundamental standpoint from which to judge all social reality is to adopt a distorted conception of that reality. But it is not true that Marx tells us nothing about justice as a rational social norm. In *Capital* he says: 'The justice of transactions which go on between agents of production rests on the fact that these transactions arise as natural consequences from the relations of production. The juristic forms in which these economic transactions appear as voluntary actions of the participants, as expressions of their common will and as contracts that may be

368

enforced by the state against a single party, cannot, being mere forms, determine this content. They merely express it. This content is just whenever it corresponds to the mode of production, is adequate to it. It is unjust whenever it contradicts that mode. Slavery, on the basis of the capitalist mode of production, is unjust; so is fraud in the quality of commodities.'[23]

This passage by no means amounts to a clear statement of a Marxian 'theory of justice', but it is nevertheless quite illuminating. For although Marx speaks in the passage only of the justice of 'transactions', the account he gives is general enough to apply to actions, social institutions, even to legal and political structures. And what he says about the justice of transactions does suggest several important theses regarding the concept of justice and its proper function in social theory and practice.

First, as we should expect, Marx views the concept of justice in terms of its function within a given mode of production. The employment of this concept by human thought and its application to social practice are always dependent moments of the process of production. The rational validity of any such employment is, for Marx, always measured in terms of the prevailing mode of production. The political state and the concept of law and right associated with the public regulation of society are for Marx both determinations of the prevailing mode of production and alienated projections of it. They mirror or reflect production, but in a distorted and mystified way. The state gives itself out as the true representative of society, and *Rechtsbegriffe* pretend to constitute the foundation for the rationality of social practice, based either on the autonomous rationality of the state or on unconditioned rational principles of 'right' or 'justice' beyond which no rational appeal can be made. But in Marx's view the real *raison d'être* of juridical institutions and concepts can be understood only from the more comprehensive vantage point of the historical mode of production they both participate in and portray. Justice, therefore, as a *Rechtsbegriff*, always requires explication from beyond 'juristic forms'. A determination of the justice of transactions or institutions demands, rather, an appreciation of their function in production. When Marx says that a just transaction is one that corresponds to the prevailing mode of production, he means, I think, that it is one which plays a concrete role in this mode, one which functions as an actual moment in the productive process. Just transactions 'fit' the prevailing mode, they serve a purpose relative to it, they concretely carry forward and bring to actuality the process of collective productive activity of human individuals in a concrete historical situation. The judgement whether a social institution is just or unjust depends, then, on the concrete comprehension of the mode of production as a whole, and on an appreciation of the connection between this whole and the institution in question. This is perhaps why Engels says that 'social justice or injustice is decided by the science which deals with the material facts of production and exchange, the science of political economy'.[24]

Secondly, then, justice is not a standard by which human reason in the abstract measures human actions, institutions, or other social facts. It is rather a standard by which each mode of production measures *itself*. It is a standard present to human thought only in the context of a specific mode of production. Hence there are no general rules or precepts of 'natural justice' applicable to any and all forms of society. The ownership of one man by another, for example, or the charging of interest on borrowed money are not in themselves just or unjust. Under the ancient mode of production, the holding of slaves was, as Aristotle argued, both right and expedient. Usury, on the other hand, was essentially foreign for the most part to this mode of production; and where it involved simply making a profit on the momentary distress of another, it was certainly unjust. Under capitalist production, however, direct slavery is unjust; while the charging of interest on borrowed capital is perfectly just.

Thirdly, it is clear that Marx followed Hegel in rejecting a formal conception of justice. For Marx, the justice or injustice of an action or institution does not consist in its exemplification of a juridical form or its conformity to a universal principle. Justice is not determined by the universal compatibility of human acts and interests, but by the concrete requirements of a historically conditioned mode of production. There *are* rational assessments of the justice of specific acts and institutions, based on their concrete function within a specific mode of production. But these assessments are not founded on abstract or formal principles of justice, good for all times and places, or on implicit or hypothetical contracts or agreements used to determine the justice of institutions or actions formally and abstractly. Abstracted from a concrete historical context, all formal philosophical principles of justice are empty and useless; when applied to such a context, they are misleading and distorting, since they encourage us to treat the concrete context of an act or institution as accidental, inessential, a mere occasion for the pure rational form to manifest itself. But the justice of the act or institution is its concrete fittingness to *this* situation, in *this* productive mode. The justice of transactions, Marx says, is not a matter of form, but a matter of content. The justice of an institution depends on the particular institution and the particular mode of production of which it is a part. All juridical forms and principles of justice are therefore meaningless unless applied to a specific mode of production, and they retain their rational validity only as long as the content they possess and the particular actions to which they apply arise naturally out of and correspond concretely to this productive mode.[25]

Finally, the justice of acts or institutions does not depend for Marx on their results or consequences. We might think, for instance, that just acts and institutions would tend to make people happier than unjust ones. But this is by no means necessary. For if a mode of production rests on the exploitation of one class by another, then it seems likely that just institutions under that mode will tend in general to satisfy the needs of the oppressors at the expense of the oppressed. But if this is Marx's view, we might at least be tempted to think that he would agree with Thrasymachus that justice is what is in the interest of the stronger, i.e., of the ruling class. And we may be inclined to think also that he would agree with Hume that those acts and institutions are just which contribute to the preservation, stability, and smooth functioning of society, i.e., of the prevailing mode of production. For, we might argue, if a transaction is to arise naturally out of the existing production relations, to correspond to the prevailing mode of production and play a concrete role in it, then it must serve, or tend to serve, the interests of the ruling class under that mode, and it must contribute, or tend to contribute, to the security and stability of the existing order of things. Now in the short run this may very well be so, and just transactions may even be carried on in many cases with the conscious intention of furthering the interests of a certain class or maintaining the stability of the existing order. But if, as Marx believes, there is an inherent tendency in each mode of production itself towards mounting instability, increasing social antagonism and conflict, and ultimately towards its own eventual overthrow and abolition, then in the long run those very transactions which are most just, which are most intimately a part of a specific mode of production, must also contribute in an essential way to its instability and eventual destruction. For Marx, a transaction is just on account of its function within the whole, and not on account of its consequences for the whole.

There is no reason, it seems to me, to regard the Marxian concept of justice as a relativistic one. It is true that whether a given transaction or institution is just or unjust will depend for Marx on its relationship to the mode of production of which it is a part, and that some institutions which are just in the context of one mode of production would be unjust in the context of another. But one does not have to be a relativist to believe that the justice of an action depends to a great extent on the circumstances in which the action is performed, or that the justice of an institution depends on its cultural setting. A relativist, as I understand it, is someone who believes that there are or can be certain kinds of fundamental conflicts or disagreements between peoples, cultures, or epochs about whether certain specific actions are or would be right or wrong, just or unjust, and that there is no rational way of resolving such disagreements, no possible 'correct answer' to them. The Marxian concept of justice, however, involves no view of this kind. If, for example, a historical analysis of the role of slavery in the ancient world could show that this institution corresponded to, and played a necessary role in, the prevailing mode of production, then in the Marxian view the holding of slaves by the ancients would be a *just* practice; and the claim that ancient slavery was unjust, whether it is made by contemporaries of the institution or by modern men reading about it in history books, would simply be wrong. When Marx and Engels remark that men at different times and places have held diverse views about the nature of 'eternal justice', they are not espousing the relativistic position that different views are 'right' at different times and places. They are rather arguing that all glorified, ideological conceptions of justice are in some respects false and misleading, since their applicability is limited as regards time and place, and also because they often express a one-sided view even of those institutions to which they do apply.

III

I want to turn now to the question whether the appropriation of surplus value by capital is for Marx an injustice. A number of socialists in Marx's day argued that capitalism involved an unequal (and hence unjust) exchange of commodities between worker and capitalist. Their argument was based on Ricardo's principle, later adopted in a slightly modified form by Marx himself, that labour is the sole creator of exchange value and that 'the value of a commodity . . . depends on the relative quantity of labour necessary for its production'.[26] The worker, these socialists pointed out, hires himself out to the capitalist for a definite wage, and is supplied by the capitalist with tools and raw materials – what Marx calls 'means of production' (*Produktionsmittel*) – whose value is consumed by use in the process of labour. At the end of this process, however, the worker has produced a commodity of greater value than the combined values of the wages paid him and the means of production consumed. That this value, which Marx was to call surplus value (*Mehrwert*), should be appropriated by the capitalist is an injustice, according to these socialists. For, according to Ricardo's principle, the worker's labour was responsible not only for the value paid him in wages, but for the surplus value as well. Hence surplus value must have arisen because the capitalist paid the worker less in wages than what his labour was worth. If the capitalist had paid the worker the full value of his labour, no surplus value would have resulted, and the demands of strict justice would have been satisfied.[27]

Marx, however, rejected both this account of the origin of surplus value and the claim that surplus value involves an unequal exchange between worker and capitalist. He thought that this explanation of surplus value was at bottom no different from the one given by Sir James Steuart and others before the physiocrats, that surplus value originated from selling commodities above their value.[28] These socialists merely turned things around and explained surplus value by supposing that labour was purchased below its value. Both explanations made surplus value appear the result of mere accident, and were therefore inherently unsatisfactory.

The flaw in the argument that surplus value involves an unequal exchange, as Marx saw it, relates to the phrase 'the value of labour'. Human labour itself, the creative exertion of the human mind and body, is strictly speaking not a commodity at all in capitalist society. 'Labour', says Marx, 'is the substance and immanent measure of value, *but has itself no value.*'[29] In the socialists' argument, the phrase 'value of labour' is in fact used to refer to two very different things. On the one hand, it is used to refer to the value *created by* labour, the value present in the commodity over and above the value of the means of production consumed in producing it. It is in this sense that the capitalist pays the worker less than 'the value of his labour'. But, Marx points out, it is not the value created by labour which the capitalist pays for. He does not buy finished commodities from the worker, less the amount of his means of production consumed; rather, he buys, in the form of a commodity, the worker's capacity to produce commodities for him. What he purchases from the worker is not the worker's products, but rather what Marx calls his 'labour power' (*Arbeitskraft*). It is this *power* which is sold as a commodity for wages. In the capitalist labour process, the capitalist merely makes use of what he has bought antecedent to the process. 'As soon as [the worker's] labour begins,' says Marx, 'it has already ceased to belong to him; hence it is no longer a thing he can sell.'[30]

The value of labour power, Marx points out, like the value of any other commodity, depends on the quantity of labour necessary for its production (or, according to the Marxian 'law of value', the average labour time socially necessary for the production of commodities of that kind). In other words, the value of labour power depends on the quantity of labour necessary to keep the worker alive and working, or to replace him if he should die or quit. Marx does not hold, however, that this is necessarily the same as the worker's 'bare subsistence', whatever that phrase is supposed to mean in general. The value of labour power depends on what is *socially* necessary: it therefore 'contains a historical and moral element'.[31] In China, it might consist of a bowl of rice a day; in affluent America, it might include the means necessary to supply the worker with a late-model automobile, a colour television set, and similar depraving and debilitating necessities of life. The value of labour power, like the value of any other commodity, depends on the level of development of productive forces and on the concrete production relations to which they correspond. It can go up or down, but it cannot be just or unjust.

Now according to Marx, the wage worker *is* generally paid the full value of his labour power. He is paid, in other words, what is socially necessary for the reproduction of his life-activity as a worker. This is, according to the Ricardian formula and the strictest rules of commodity exchange, a *just* transaction, an exchange of equivalent for equivalent.[32] Surplus value, to be sure, is appropriated by the capitalist without an equivalent.[33] But there is nothing in the exchange requiring him to pay any equivalent for it. The exchange of wages for labour power is the *only* exchange between capitalist and worker. It is a just exchange, and it is consummated long before the question arises of selling the commodity produced and realizing its surplus value. The capitalist has bought a commodity (labour power) and paid its full value; by using, exploiting, this commodity, he now creates a greater value than he began with. This surplus belongs to him; it never belonged to anyone else, and he owes nobody a penny for it. 'This circumstance,' says Marx, 'is peculiar good fortune for the buyer [of labour power], but no injustice at all to the seller.'[34] The appropriation of surplus value by capital, therefore, involves no unequal or unjust exchange.

Nevertheless, it might still seem that Ricardo's principle could be used to argue that the appropriation of surplus value by capital is an injustice to the worker. Ricardo's principle says that labour is the sole creator and indeed the very substance of value, that the means of production do not increase in value except as they are productively consumed by labour and incorporated in its products. It would seem to follow that this entire increase ought to go to the worker, since it is through his labour alone that it comes about. 'The labour of a man's body, and the work of his hands,' as Locke put it, 'are properly his.'[35] The full value of the commodity, exclusive of the means of production consumed in producing it, seems to belong by right to the worker. In appropriating a portion of that value without equivalent, the capitalist may not be engaging in an 'unequal exchange' with the worker in the strict sense, but he is reaping the fruits of the worker's unpaid labour; he is exploiting him, taking from him what is justly his. Hence capitalism is unjust. It is really this argument, I think, that we attribute to Marx when we take his denunciations of capitalism as a system based on 'exploitation' and 'unpaid labour' to be denunciations of it for its injustice.

The argument is based on two assumptions. The first is that surplus value arises from the appropriation by capital of part of the value created by labour for which the worker receives no equivalent. The second is that each man's property rights are based on his own labour, so that every man has a right to appropriate the full value created by his labour, and anyone who deprives him of any part of this value may be said to have done him an injustice. Now Marx plainly accepts the first of these two assumptions. Does he accept the second? He recognizes, of course, that the notion that property rights are based on one's own labour is common among bourgeois ideologists, and he even sees reasons why this notion should seem plausible. 'Originally,' he says, 'property rights appeared to us to be based on one's own labour. At least this assumption must be made, since only commodity-owners with equal property rights confronted each other, and the only means of appropriating an alien commodity was by alienating one's own commodities, which could only be replaced by labour.'[36] In a mode of production in which each individual producer owns his own means of production and exchanges the commodities he produces with other individual producers, property rights would be based entirely on a man's own labour. This simple, noble, petty-bourgeois ideal of production Marx sometimes calls the system of 'individual private property'.[37] Under this system, the labourer would appropriate the full value of his product, and anyone who deprived him of part of this value (by a fraudulent exchange, say, or by robbery) would have done him an injustice. But in Marx's view, capitalist production differs from this

Allen W. Wood

idyllic *mutualité* in several important ways.[38] In capitalist production, men are engaged in cooperative labour, using jointly the same means of production (as in a factory, for example). More importantly, capitalism is predicated on the separation of labour from the means of production, on the division of society into a class which owns the means of production and a class which owns only labour power. Marx describes in *Capital* how this separation arose historically, and he argues that this class separation aids capitalist development while itself becoming more and more pronounced as a result of this development.

Now in a society based exclusively on individual private property, surplus value would not exist. But the reason for this would be simply that since every individual owns the means of production he employs, labour power would not be among the commodities traded in that society. In capitalism, however, labour power does appear as a commodity on an ever-increasing scale, owing to the form taken by the productive forces and the historical tendency towards the separation of labour from the means of production. But labour power, like any commodity, is only purchased to be *used*, and it cannot function as a commodity unless it is useful to its purchaser. If the entire value of the commodity produced by the wage labourer were expended in wages and means of production, the capitalist would have received no use from the labour power he purchased, and he would have done better simply to convert the value of his means of production into commodities he could consume. If he realized no surplus value, the capitalist would have no incentive to develop the forces of production, and no occasion to exercise that prudent abstinence for which he is rewarded by God and man alike. Hence the appearance of labour power as a commodity, according to Marx, brings about a 'dialectical reversal' of the previously assumed foundation of the right of property: under the system of *capitalist* private property, 'property turns out to be the right on the part of the capitalist to appropriate alien unpaid labour or its product, and on the part of the worker the impossibility of appropriating his own product. The separation of property from labour has become the necessary consequence of a law that apparently originated in their identity.'[39]

The justice of the transactions in capitalist production rests on the fact that they arise out of capitalist production relations, that they are adequate to, and correspond to, the capitalist mode of production as a whole. The justice of property rights based on labour in a system of individual private property arises from the fact that these rights correspond to the production relations of individual producers each owning

376

the means of production he uses. By the same token, then, the reversal of these property rights under capitalism is equally just. Capitalism is made possible by the existence of labour power as a commodity, by its use as a commodity to produce surplus value and expand capital. Labour power could not even appear as a commodity if there were no surplus value created by it for capital. Therefore, if there were no surplus value, if workers performed no unpaid labour and were not exploited, the capitalist mode of production would not be possible. Under a capitalist mode of production the appropriation of surplus value is not only just, but any attempt to deprive capital of it would be a positive injustice. Marx rejected slogans like 'a just wage' and 'a fair day's wages for a fair day's work' because in his view the worker was already receiving what these slogans were asking for. A 'just wage', simply because it is a wage, involves the purchase of labour power by capital. The worker is exploited every bit as much when he is paid just wages as when he is paid unjust ones. Thus in response to the Lassallean demand for 'a just distribution of the proceeds of labour', Marx asks: 'What is a "just" distribution? Do not the bourgeois assert that the present distribution is "just"? And isn't it in fact the only "just" distribution based on the present mode of production? Are economic relations ruled by juridical concepts [*Rechtsbegriffe*] or do not juridical relations arise on the contrary out of economic ones?'[40]

One of the reasons neoclassical economists repudiated the labour theory of value was the fact that this theory, especially in its Ricardian form, had been used by social malcontents to argue that profits on capital constitute an injustice to the worker. And on this point, at least, the neoclassical position was not merely a piece of shabby apologetics. The economists saw that the profits on invested capital were an essential part of the existing economic process, and that this process could not possibly function without them. They therefore rejected any view which made profits appear to originate merely from unjust exchanges or arbitrary practices of distribution, as a misunderstanding of the nature of the economic system and the role played in it by profits. For this and other reasons, they were content not only to repudiate much of what classical economics had accomplished but even to abdicate many of the traditional responsibilities of the science of political economy in order to free themselves from the labour theory of value. Marx's analysis of capitalism, however, shows that the notion that profits are unjust does not derive from the labour theory of value alone, but follows only when this theory is combined with the labour theory of property, a natural rights doctrine often mistakenly associated or identified with it. Marx thought, moreover, that the labour theory of value could be used to advance criticisms of capitalism which did not depend for their force on the application to capitalism of juridical principles alien to it, but derived simply from a correct understanding of the organic functioning of capitalism and the successive stages of development marked out for it by its nature as a mode of production. Those who insist on finding in Marx's critique of capitalism some 'principles of justice' analogous to the labour theory of property are therefore only shifting Marx's critique back to the level on which he found the question in the socialist writings of his own day, and from which he did his best to remove it.

We might be tempted at this point to think that whether capitalism should be called 'unjust' or not is merely a verbal issue. Marx did, after all, condemn capitalism, and he condemned it at least in part because it was a system of exploitation, involving the appropriation of the worker's unpaid labour by capital. If Marx chose to call these evils of capitalism not 'injustices' but something else, they still sound to most of us like injustices, and it seems that we should be free to apply this term to them if we like. The difference between Marx and ourselves at this point, we might suppose, is only that his application of the term 'justice' is somewhat narrower than ours.

It is extremely important to see why such an attitude would be mistaken. When Marx limits the concept of justice in the way he does, he is not by any means making a terminological stipulation. He is basing his claim on the actual role played in social life by the concept of justice, and the institutional context in which this term has its proper function. His disagreement with those who hold that capitalism is unjust is a substantive one, founded on his conception of society and having important practical consequences.

'Justice', as we have seen, is a *Rechtsbegriff*, a concept related to 'law' and 'right'. And although Marx never tries to tell us precisely what the scope of the class of *Rechtsbegriffe* is, it is clear that the central role of all these concepts has to do with political or juridical (*rechtlich*) institutions, institutions whose function is the regulation of the actions of individuals and groups through socially imposed sanctions of some kind, whether civil, criminal, or moral in nature. These institutions include those promulgating, applying, or administering laws, those in which collective political decisions are made or carried out, and those regulating the actions and practices of individuals by generally accepted norms of conduct. When something is called an 'injustice', or when it is claimed that a practice violates someone's 'rights', some sort of appeal is being made to juridical institutions, to the manner in which they regularly do act or the manner in which they should act if they are to fulfil their proper social function.

When capitalist exploitation is described as an 'injustice', the implication is that what is wrong with capitalism is its mode of *distribution*. When the appropriation by capital of the worker's unpaid labour is thought of as 'unjust', the claim being made is that the worker is being given a smaller (and the capitalist a larger) share of the collective product of society than he deserves, according to the juridical or moral rules and practices which govern distribution, or at least, which *should* govern it. It is therefore being suggested that the answer to capitalist exploitation is to be found in the proper regulation of distribution by means of the promulgation and enforcement of laws, the taking of political decisions, and the stricter adherence by individuals to correct and appropriate moral precepts.

Such a conception of what is wrong with capitalist exploitation is, however, entirely mistaken according to Marx. Distribution, he argues, is not something which exists alongside production, indifferent to it, and subject to whatever modifications individuals in their collective moral and political wisdom should choose to make in it. Any mode of distribution is determined by the mode of production of which it is a functional part.[41] The appropriation of surplus value and the exploitation of labour are not *abuses* of capitalist production, or arbitrary and unfair practices which happen accidentally to be carried on within it (like fraud, for instance, or smuggling, or protection rackets). Exploitation of the worker belongs to the essence of capitalism, and as the capitalist mode of production progresses to later and later stages of its development, this exploitation must in Marx's view grow worse and worse as a result of the laws of this development itself. It cannot be removed by the passage or enforcement of laws regulating distribution, or by any moral or political reforms which capitalist political institutions could bring about. Moreover, any 'reforms' of capitalist production which proposed to take surplus value away from capital and put an end to the exploitation of the worker would themselves be injustices of a most straightforward and unambiguous kind. They would violate in the most obvious way the fundamental property rights derived from the capitalist mode of production, and constitute the imposition on it of a system of distribution essentially incompatible with it. It is a mystery how such well-meaning reformers could expect

Allen W. Wood

to keep their scheme of 'just' distribution working once it had been set up. (One is reminded of Aristotle's remark that any system, no matter how misconceived, can be made to work for a day or two.)

But this is not all. Even if revolutionary practice should put an end to capitalist exploitation, and even if an important aspect of this practice should consist in a change in the juridical rules governing distribution, it would still be wrong to say that the end to exploitation constitutes the rectification of 'injustice'. Revolutionary politics does not consist, for Marx, in the imposition on society of whatever moral or juridical rules or 'principles of justice' the revolutionary politician should find most commendable. It consists rather in the adjustment of the political or juridical institutions of society to a new mode of production, of a determinate form and character, which has already taken shape in society. Unless a fundamental change of this kind in the mode of man's productive activity is already taking place in society of its own accord, any attempt at a truly revolutionary politics would be irrational, futile, and, to use Marx's own word, mere 'Donquichoterie'.[42] This is what Marx and Engels mean when they say in the *German Ideology* that 'Communism is for us not a *state of affairs* to be brought about, an *ideal* to which reality must somehow adjust itself. We call communism the actual movement which is transcending [*aufhebt*] the present state of affairs. The conditions of this movement result from presuppositions already existing.'[43]

Political action, therefore, is for Marx one subordinate moment of revolutionary practice. Political institutions do not and cannot create a new mode of production, but can only be brought into harmony with a mode of production that men themselves are already bringing to birth. They can only set the juridical stamp of approval, so to speak, on whatever form of productive activity historical individuals are creating and living. If revolutionary institutions mean new laws, new standards of juridical regulation, new forms of property and distribution, this is not a sign that 'justice' is at last being done where it was not done before; it is instead a sign that a new mode of production, with its own characteristic juridical forms, has been born from the old one. This new mode of production will not be 'more just' than the old, it will only be just in its own way. If the new is higher, freer, more human than the old, it would be for Marx both entirely inaccurate and woefully inadequate to reduce its superiority to juridical terms and to commend it as 'more just'. Anyone who is tempted to do this is a person still captivated by the false and inverted political or juridical conception of society, since he insists on interpreting every crucial

380

change in it as a change whose meaning is fundamentally political or juridical in character. He is treating the old mode of production as if it were merely one of the determinations of a mystical juridical structure of society, whereas in reality the actual juridical structure of society is a dependent moment of the prevailing productive mode. He is also treating the social whole as if he, in his sublime rationality, could measure this whole against some ideal of right or justice completely external to it, and could then, standing on some Archimedean point, adjust social reality to this ideal. He is removing social reality from his theory, and his social practice from reality. In Marx's view, when anyone demands an end to capitalist exploitation on the ground of its 'injustice' he is employing an argument carrying no rational conviction to urge action with no practical basis towards a goal with no historical content.

Someone might think that capitalism could be condemned as unjust by applying to it standards of justice or right which would be appropriate to some post-capitalist mode of production. No doubt capitalism could be condemned in this way, but since any such standards would not be rationally applicable to capitalism at all, any such condemnations would be mistaken, confused, and without foundation. The temptation to apply post-capitalist juridical standards (however they may be understood) to capitalist production can only derive, once again, from the vision of post-capitalist society as a kind of eternal juridical structure against which the present state of affairs is to be measured and found wanting. The Marxian conception of society and social change, as we have seen, repudiates any vision of this kind. In the *Critique of the Gotha Programme* Marx points out that post-capitalist society itself will have different stages of development, to which different standards of right will correspond. And in the long run, of course, Marx believes that the end of class society will mean the end of the social need for the state mechanism and the juridical institutions within which concepts like 'right' and 'justice' have their place. If, therefore, one insists on saying that Marx's 'real' concept of justice is the one he would deem appropriate to a fully developed communist society, one's conclusion probably should be that Marx's 'real' concept of justice is no concept of it at all.

For Marx, justice is not and cannot be a genuinely revolutionary notion. The revolutionary who is captivated by the passion for justice misunderstands, in the Marxian view, both the existing production relations and his own revolutionary aspirations. He implies, by his use of juridical conceptions, that his protest against the prevailing mode of production is a protest against evils which can and should be remedied by moral, legal, or political processes, which in fact are only dependent moments of that mode of production itself. He views his revolutionary aspirations as a kind of ideal juridical structure underlying the existing society, an ideal or hypothetical contract or set of natural rights or rational principles of right, which are being violated, concealed, or disfigured by the rampant 'abuses' and 'injustices' of the present society. He thus treats the *essence* of the actual production relations as arbitrary and inessential, as a set of mere 'abuses'; and he regards the social conflicts and antagonisms to which these relations give rise as unfortunate by-products of social abnormalities, rather than as the driving force behind his own revolutionary consciousness. His 'revolutionary' aim is therefore not really to overthrow the existing society, it is only to correct the abuses prevalent in it, to rectify its tragic and irrational injustices, and to make it live up to those ideals of right and justice which are, or ought to be, its genuine foundation. Our determined revolutionary, in other words, animated by his passion for justice, is already equipped to deliver the keynote address at the next Democratic Convention.

Marx's call to the revolutionary overthrow of capitalist production therefore is not, and cannot be, founded on the claim that capitalism is unjust. Marx in fact regarded all attempts to base revolutionary practice on juridical notions as an 'ideological shuffle', and he dismissed the use of terms like 'equal right' and 'just distribution' in the working-class movement as 'outdated verbal trivia'.[44] It is simply not the case that Marx's condemnation of capitalism rests on some conception of justice (whether explicit or implicit), and those who attempt to reconstruct a 'Marxian idea of justice' from Marx's manifold charges against capitalism are at best only translating Marx's critique of capitalism, or some aspect of it, into what Marx himself would have consistently regarded as a false, ideological, or 'mystified' form.[45]

There can be no doubt that for Marx it was of the utmost practical importance that the worker's movement not be sidetracked by a preoccupation with the attainment of 'justice' and 'equal rights'. But his insistence on the justice of capitalism was not motivated by tactical considerations. It is regarding this point that Tucker seems to me to go astray.[46] He argues persuasively that Marx did not criticize capitalism for injustice and in fact did not believe it to be unjust. But he seems to me to be mistaken as to Marx's reasons for holding that capitalism is not unjust, and to give an inadequate account of them.

Tucker says that the 'underlying issue' for Marx in his refusal to condemn capitalism for injustice was his opposition to the position, held by Proudhon and others, that the solution to the social problems posed by capitalist production must consist in striking an equitable balance between the antagonistic interests of different social agents of production. Marx, in Tucker's view, believed not in the equilibrium of antagonisms but in their abolition through the revolutionary over-throw of the capitalist mode of production. Marx sought, he says, not a balance between interests but a harmony of interests. Thus, according to Tucker, Marx rejected the view that capitalism is unjust because 'justice' and similar notions connote 'a rightful balance in a situation where two or more parties or principles conflict'. Marx believed, however, that the antagonism between capital and labour should not be compromised or turned into a harmony, but rather abolished through the revolutionary destruction of capital as a social force. Thus Tucker regards Marx's insistence that capitalism is not unjust as an expression of his fear that 'the distributive orientation ultimately pointed the way to abandonment of the revolutionary goal'.[47] Marx denied that capitalism is unjust, then, in order to persuade the workers' movement to take a revolutionary rather than a reformist direction. Following Tucker's account, Marx's critique of justice appears to be fundamentally a tactical stance, motivated by the fear that the workers' movement might abandon its revolutionary aspirations for some less radical programme of social reform.

Now I do not want to deny that Marx believed that social antagon-isms in general and the antagonism between capital and labour in particular should be abolished rather than balanced or compromised. This seems to me to have been Marx's view, and also his major reason for disagreeing with Proudhon and others like him on many points. But I do not think this view by itself accounts for Marx's insistence that capitalism is not an unjust system. In the first place, while it may seem to Tucker that the term 'justice' always connotes a rightful balance between conflicting interests, I see no particular reason to think that Marx believed this. For him, justice is the rational measure of social acts and institutions from the juridical point of view. In a class society the administration of juridical relations will normally involve some mode of dealing with the antagonistic interests generated by the contradictions inherent in the mode of production. And while justice in this regard should consist in handling these antagonisms in a way which corresponds or is adequate to the mode of production, there is no reason to think it will do so by striking a 'rightful balance' between opposing interests. Capitalist justice, for instance, which involves treating men as equals in so far as they are property owners, will presumably involve some sort of balance between the conflicting interests of two large capitalists, for example, but it can only handle conflicts between the interests of capital and labour by forcibly promoting the former and ruthlessly suppressing the latter. From a Marxian standpoint, this would be the only thing that justice as a 'rightful balance' of opposing interests could mean under capitalism, and the phrase does not sound particularly appropriate.

But secondly, even if we grant that for Marx justice connoted a rightful balance between conflicting interests, Tucker's account is still not satisfactory. What Tucker says might then explain why Marx did not dwell on the injustices of capitalism, and also why he would have criticized those who did. But it could not explain why Marx positively denied that capitalism was unjust. For if justice connotes a 'balance' between conflicting interests, Marx might very well have agreed that no such balance is being struck between capital and labour, and admitted that capitalism is unjust, but he might have urged at the same time that injustice is not the primary defect of the capitalist mode of production and insisted that the workers would be misled if they devoted all their energies to rectifying these injustices. It would have been of questionable tactical value, it seems to me, for Marx to go further than this and positively deny that capitalist exploitation is unjust, unless he thought he had good independent grounds for doing so. Marx also seems to me not to have been as worried as Tucker thinks about the danger of the distributive orientation undermining the revolutionary character of the workers' movement. At any rate he was not afraid that the long-range goals of the proletariat would be altered by such petty-bourgeois nonsense. Whether or not we think subsequent history has proven him wrong, Marx was always convinced that the situation of the proletariat could never be made tolerable to the proletarians themselves by anything short of a revolutionary transformation of production. His real worry was only that the widespread acceptance of false notions about the defects of capitalism and the conditions for their removal would delay this transformation and make it more painful. Marx's fundamental objection to the rhetoric of justice was not that it was bad propaganda, but that it presupposed a theory of society which he believed he had shown to be false. Speaking of the distributive orientation espoused by the Lassalleans, he says: 'Vulgar socialism (and from it again a part of democracy) took over from the bourgeois economists the consideration and treatment of distribution as independent of the mode of production and hence the presentation of socialism as

384

turning principally on the question of distribution. But after the real relation has long been made clear, why retrogress again?'[48]

IV

If Marx did not criticize capitalism for being unjust, the question naturally presents itself: Why *did* Marx condemn capitalism? But it would be extremely naïve to suppose that there could be any single, simple answer to such a question. The only genuine answer to it is Marx's comprehensive theory of capitalism as a concrete historical mode of production; for it was *as a whole* that Marx condemned capitalism, and his condemnation was based on what he believed was a unified and essentially complete analysis of its inner workings and its position in human history. Capitalism, in Marx's view, had performed a valuable historical task in developing social forces of production. He even speaks of this development as the historical 'justification' of capital.[49] But this development had taken place at enormous human cost. Not only had it impoverished the physical existence of the mass of workers whose labour had brought about the development of productive forces, but the intellectual and moral lives of men had been impoverished by it as well. The rapidity of social change under capitalism had created a permanent state of instability and disorder in social relationships which had taken away from human happiness perhaps more than was added by the increase in human productive capacities. But the capitalist era itself, in Marx's view, was drawing to a close. Marx argued that the capacity of capitalism further to develop the forces of production was meeting with increasing obstacles, obstacles resulting from the organic workings of the capitalist system of production itself. At the same time, and partly as a result of these same obstacles, the human cost of capitalism was growing steadily greater. The interests and needs of fewer and fewer were being served by its continuation, and its preservation was being made more and more difficult by the cumulative effects of its own essential processes.

Within Marx's account of the essential irrationality and eventual breakdown of capitalism, the concept of the 'exploitation' of labour by capital plays an important role. And since it is the Marxian charge that capitalism is essentially a system of exploitation which has done most to create the impression that Marx condemned capitalism for injustice, I would like to try briefly to explain what role I think this charge actually plays in Marx's critique of capitalism.

Human society, according to some philosophers, is founded on the harmony of human interests, the fact that social relationships are of mutual benefit to those participating in them. In the Marxian view, however, past societies have equally been founded on conflicts of interest, and on the forced labour of one class for the benefit of another. All society, Marx believes, involves an 'exchange of human activity' between agents of production;[50] but one of the essential forms of such exchanges is the social relation of dominion and servitude. This relation, in Marx's view, constitutes the foundation of class conflicts and of the historical changes wrought by them.

The essence of servitude for Marx consists in the fact that servitude is a specific form of human productive activity: it is, namely, productive activity which, by means of the loss and renunciation of its products, is itself alienated from the producer and appropriated by someone or something external to him, standing over against him as the independent aim and object of his production. Dominion, as Marx points out, involves not merely the appropriation and enjoyment of things, but 'the appropriation of another's will'.[51] When the master enjoys the slave's services or the fruits of his labour, he enjoys them as the result of the slave's productive activity, as something into which the slave has put his will and realized his purposes. The appropriation of the slave's products by the master, therefore, necessarily involves for the slave their renunciation, the alienation of the slave's own life-activity and the immediate frustration of his productive will. The labour of servitude is, as Hegel said, essentially 'inhibited desire'.[52] In its essence, such labour is, in Marx's words, 'not voluntary but coerced, it is *forced* labour, . . . a labour of self-sacrifice, of mortification'.[53]

In capitalist production, according to Marx, these relations of dominion and servitude are disguised. The capitalist and the worker appear to be independent owners of commodities, exchanging their goods as free individuals. The exchanges between them are entirely just and their equal rights as property owners are strictly respected throughout capitalist production relations, thus giving rise to the illusion that these relations themselves are entirely the result of a voluntary contract between independent persons. In fact, however, since the capitalist mode of production is founded on the sale of labour power by one class to another, capitalist production rests essentially on the appropriation by capital of a part of the worker's product in the form of surplus value. Capital, by its very nature as capital, that is, by its function in capitalist production relations, necessarily exploits the worker by appropriating and accumulating his unpaid labour. And as Marx argues in *Capital*, the end result of the wage labourer's activity is always the further accumulation of capital, of his own product in an alien and autonomous form, which becomes both the necessary condition and the independent aim of his labour, of his life-activity itself.

This exploitation of the labourer by capital is not a form of injustice, but it is a form of servitude. 'Capital obtains surplus labour,' according to Marx, 'without an equivalent, and in essence it always remains forced labour, however much it appears to result from a free contractual agreement.'[54] Capitalist exploitation is not a form of fraudulent exchange or economic injustice, but it is a form of concealed dominion over the worker. Capitalism is a system of slavery, and a slavery the more insidious because the relations of dominion and servitude are *experienced* as such without being *understood* as such. The fundamental character of the capitalist relation is even hidden from political economy, in Marx's view, so long as it fails to solve the riddle of surplus value. By solving this riddle, Marx believes he has unmasked the capitalist relation and made it possible for the workers to understand their condition of poverty, frustration, and discontent for what it is: a condition of servitude to their own product in the form of capital.

It bears repeating that although this servitude is a source of misery, degradation, and discontent to the worker, it is *not a form of injustice*. Those who believe that the notion of servitude necessarily 'connotes' injustice are the victims of prejudices which many men of less enlightened ages (Aristotle, for example) did not share. And for Marx the appearance of such prejudices in capitalist society is largely the result of the bourgeois ideology which praises capitalism for having done away with direct slavery and feudal serfdom, and for having replaced these 'injustices' and 'human indignities' with an open society of free men meeting in a free market. The actual servitude which hides behind this mask of universal liberty is, however, neither more nor less just than its predecessors in Marx's view. The servitude of the wage labourer to capital is rather an essential and indispensable part of the capitalist mode of production, which neither the passage of liberal legislation nor the sincere resolve by bourgeois society to respect the 'human rights' of all its members can do anything to remove. Nor is the mere fact that capitalism involves servitude a sufficient ground for the workers to rise against it. It is not Marx's belief that servitude as such is an unqualified wrong, an evil to be abolished at all cost with an attitude of *fiat justitia, pereat mundi*. The servitude of capitalism, according to Marx, and even the direct slavery involved in capitalist colonies, have been necessary conditions for the development of modern productive forces.[55] To condemn this servitude unqualifiedly would be to condemn all the productive advances of modern society, which Marx was not about to do. Condemning a relation of servitude when it results from historical limitations on productive forces is for Marx about as rational as condemning medical science because there are some diseases it cannot cure.

A historically potent demand, a genuine and effective *need* for emancipation arises in an oppressed class only under certain conditions. This need does not appear merely as a social ideal, but always as an actual movement within the existing production relations towards concrete historical possibilities transcending them. And it arises, according to Marx's theory, only where there is a disharmony or antagonism between the productive forces and the existing production relations. Within a given mode of production, men develop and change the forces of production. In this way they bring about new historical possibilities, and with them new human desires and needs. These new possibilities cannot be actualized, however, and these new needs satisfied, within the existing production relations. The productive forces have, so to speak, outgrown the production relations and have become antagonistic to them. It is this antagonism which, in Marx's view, supplies the conditions for an epoch of social revolution. And it is only in terms of this antagonism that an effective need for emancipation on the part of an oppressed class can take shape. 'Humanity,' says Marx, 'only sets itself tasks it can solve': 'A form of society never perishes before all the productive forces for which there is room in it have developed; and new, higher relations of production never come forth before the material conditions for their existence have taken shape in the womb of the old society itself.'[56]

Capitalism itself, Marx believed, systematically creates the forces which will eventuate in its revolutionary overthrow and historical transcendence. It is the inherent tendency of capitalist production to increase the rate of surplus value, to accumulate an ever-larger supply of social wealth in the form of capital. This historical tendency of capitalism leads, as Marx argues in *Capital*, to the mounting instability of capitalist production in a number of different but related ways. Prominent among these tendencies to instability is the increasing burden of servitude placed on the workers by capitalist accumulation. Marx does not think that as capital accumulates, the wages of the worker will necessarily decrease. Indeed, he holds that in general those conditions under which capital expands most rapidly relative to labour are likely to be the most favourable for the worker's material situation.[57] But the accumulation of capital does mean that the *dominion* of capital over the worker, and the 'golden chain' the worker forges for himself, which fetters him to capital, tend to grow heavier and heavier.[58] The slave's peculium may possibly increase, but his servitude necessarily grows more and more burdensome.[59]

According to the Marxian theory, then, capitalist production accumulates on the one side an ever-growing supply of social wealth, an ever-expanding set of productive forces; but on the other side it creates at the same time a class of restless slaves, constantly growing in numbers and in discontent. It expands the capacities for the satisfaction of human needs, while at the same time cutting men off in steadily increasing numbers from the means of appropriating and making use of these capacities. And it expands the forces of production by means of the forced labour of precisely those who are alienated from them. Thus capitalism itself produces both the need on the part of the workers to overcome and abolish capitalist production and the material forces which make the abolition of capitalism a genuine historical possibility. It produces at once an ever-growing burden of servitude and an ever-greater capacity for emancipation. In this way, the productive forces it has created become increasingly antagonistic to the production relations by means of which it has created them. This does not mean, however, that for Marx capitalism is bad or irrational *because* its downfall is inevitable. On the contrary, Marx thought that its perpetuation of a condition of unnecessary servitude, its extension of this condition to the great majority of men, and its creation of human desires and opportunities which cannot be satisfied within a capitalist framework were precisely the sorts of defects which would bring about its downfall. Capitalism, in Marx's view, was breaking down because it was irrational, and not the reverse. The irrationalities in capitalism were for Marx at once causes of its downfall and reasons for its abolition.

But if Marx viewed the workers' desire for emancipation as an important reason why capitalism should be abolished, it still seems to me almost as mistaken to say that Marx's critique of capitalism is founded on a 'principle of freedom' as it is to say that it is founded on a 'principle of justice'. I think it would be wrong, in fact, to suppose that Marx's critique of capitalism is necessarily rooted in *any* particular moral or social ideal or principle. It has sometimes been claimed that Marx was fundamentally a utilitarian, because he believed the overthrow of capitalism would bring about greater human happiness. Others have argued that Marx was really a Kantian, since the servitude and exploitation of capitalism to which he objected involve the treatment of men as means only, rather than as ends in themselves. Still others have seen in Marx's hope for an expansion of man's powers under socialism an implicit 'self-realization' theory. But of course it is quite possible for someone to value human happiness without being a utilitarian, to object to the treatment of men as mere means without being a Kantian, and to favour the development of human powers and capacities without subscribing to any particular moral philosophy. So there is no good reason, it seems to me, for the adherents of any particular position in moral philosophy to claim that Marx is one of their number. At any rate, Marx seems to me no more a subscriber to any particular moral philosophy than is the 'common man' with whose moral views nearly every moral philosopher claims to be in agreement.

Marx's own reasons for condemning capitalism are contained in his comprehensive theory of the historical genesis, the organic functioning, and the prognosis of the capitalist mode of production. And this is not itself a *moral* theory, nor does it include any particular moral principles as such. But neither is it 'merely descriptive', in the tedious philosophical sense which is supposed to make it seem problematic how anything of that sort could ever be a reason for condemning what is so 'described'. There is nothing problematic about saying that disguised exploitation, unnecessary servitude, economic instability, and declining productivity are features of a productive system which constitute good reasons for condemning it. Marx's theory of the functioning and development of capitalism does argue that capitalism possesses these features (among others), but Marx never tried to give any philosophical account of why these features would constitute good reasons for condemning a system that possesses them. He was doubtless convinced that the reasons for condemning capitalism provided by his theory were good ones, and that whatever information moral philosophers might or might not be able to give us about the nature of condemnations of social systems and the nature of reasons for them, no special appeal to philosophical principles, moral imperatives, or evaluative modes of consciousness would be needed to show that his own reasons for condemning capitalism were good and sufficient ones. That he was correct in these convictions is indicated by the fact that no serious defender of capitalism has ever disputed his critique solely on the grounds of moral philosophy. It has been argued in defence of capitalism that Marx's theory of capitalist production rests on unsound economic principles, that it distorts or misinterprets the relation between capital and labour, and that it gives an inaccurate, one-sided, or incomplete picture of capitalism. It has also been claimed that Marx's account of the genesis of capitalist production is historically inaccurate, and that his predictions about its future have been largely falsified by events which have happened since his time. But no one has ever denied that capitalism, understood as Marx's theory understands it, is a system of unnecessary servitude, replete with irrationalities and ripe for destruction. Still less has anyone defended capitalism by claiming that a system of this sort might after all be good or desirable, and it is doubtful that any moral philosophy which could support such a claim would deserve serious consideration.

Notes

1. Most recently by Robert C. Tucker, *The Marxian Revolutionary Idea* (New York, 1969), pp. 37–48. Cf. Tucker, *Philosophy and Myth in Karl Marx* (Cambridge, Eng., 1972), pp. 18–20, 222 f. (See also pp. 382–5, above.)

2. *Marx Engels Werke* (Berlin, 1959), 18: 274. Cf. Karl Marx and Friedrich Engels, *Selected Works* (Moscow, 1951), I, 562. (All translations in the text are my own.)

3. *Werke*, 18: 276. Cf. *Selected Works*, I, 564.

4. *Werke*, 13: 8. Cf. *Selected Works*, I, 328.

5. *Werke*, Ergänzungsband I, Teil 537. Cf. Karl Marx, *Early Writings*, trans. and ed. T. B. Bottomore (New York, 1964), p. 156; *Marx/Engels Gesamtausgabe* (Berlin, 1932), I/5, 25; *Writings of the Young Marx on Philosophy and Society*, trans. and ed. Loyd Easton and Kurt Guddat (Garden City, N.Y., 1967), p. 428. But for Marx the relation between civil society and the state was never something that could be reduced to simple formulas. Shlomo Avineri has argued convincingly that in Marx 'the political never appears as a mechanistic or automatic reflection of the economic' (*The Social and Political Thought of Karl Marx* [Cambridge, Eng., 1968], p. 41). The political state, Avineri notes, is not only a 'reflection' of civil society, but an alienated and distorted 'projection' of it (ibid., p. 52). Marx's transformation of the Hegelian concept of society, therefore, is not intended to provide a theory of political behaviour, but to make one possible, by removing the illusion that political and juridical institutions themselves constitute an autonomous standpoint from which social reality can be understood. Since the political state is an alienated projection of civil society, even the rationality of juridical institutions is not transparent from the juridical or political standpoint, and must be understood from the standpoint of production. This fact will be seen later on to have important implications for the notion of justice.

6. *Gesamtausgabe*, I/5, 10. Cf. *Writings of the Young Marx*, p. 409.

7. *Werke*, 20: 452. Cf. *Selected Works*, II, 82.

8. Ibid.

9. *Werke*, Erg. I, Teil 516. Cf. *Early Writings*, p. 127.

10. *Werke*, 23: 193. Cf. Karl Marx, *Capital*, trans. Samuel Moore and Edward Aveling (New York, 1968), I, 178.

11. *Werke*, 13: 8. Cf. *Selected Works*, I, 328.

12. *Werke*, 23: 192. Cf. *Capital*, I, 177.

13. *Werke*, Erg. I, Teil 574. Cf. *Early Writings*, p. 202.

14. *Gesamtausgabe*, I/5, II. Cf. *Writings of the Young Marx*, p. 409.

15. *Gesamtausgabe*, I/5, 18. Cf. *Writings of the Young Marx*, p. 420.

16. *Werke*, 13: 8 f. Cf. *Selected Works*, I, 329.

17. Hegel, *Philosophie des Rechts* (Hamburg, 1955), sec. 3, p. 22.

18. *Werke*, 13: 631. Cf. David Horowitz, *Marx and Modern Economics* (New York, 1968), p. 39.

19. *Werke*, 13: 630 f. Cf. *Marx and Modern Economics*, pp. 38 f. Compare the following passage from the *German Ideology*: 'This interpretation of history depends on setting forth the actual process of production, proceeding from the material production of life itself, and interpreting the form of interaction connected with and created by it, that is by civil society in its various stages, as the basis of all history; at the same time setting forth [civil society] in its action as state and tracing all the various theoretical products and forms of consciousness, religion, philosophy, ethics, etc., in their genesis from it. Then the matter can be presented in its totality (and thus also the reciprocal effects of these various sides on one another)' (*Gesamtausgabe*, I/5, 27; cf. *Writings of the Young Marx*, p. 431).

20. *Werke*, 13: 9. Cf. *Selected Works*, I, 329.

21. *Werke*, 23: 99: 'This juridical relation [of exchange] . . . is a relation of wills in which the economic relation is mirrored [*sich widerspiegelt*].' Here as elsewhere terms suggesting 'mirroring' or 'reflection' (such as *'sich widerspiegeln'*, *'Reflexion'*, *'reflektiren'*) have sometimes been seriously mistranslated using the English word 'reflex'. Thus Moore and Aveling translate the above as: 'This juridical relation . . . is a relation of two wills, and is but the reflex of the real economic relation between the two' (*Capital*, I, 84). This translation suggests that the juridical relation is like a knee jerk produced by an economic hammer-tap, or the mechanism of a Pavlovian dog emitting juridical saliva in response to economic stimuli. Such an impression is entirely the result of mistranslation, and has nothing to do with Marx's view of the matter. Marx's 'mirroring' terminology is of course derived from Hegel (cf. *Werke*, 25: 58; *Capital*, III, 48 and *Werke*, 23: 640; *Capital*, I, 612).

22. *Gesamtausgabe*, 1/5, 15. Cf. *Writings of the Young Marx*, p. 413.

23. *Werke*, 25: 351 f. Cf. *Capital*, III, 339 f.

24. Marx and Engels, *Kleine Ökonomische Schriften* (Berlin, 1955), p. 412.

25. This is not to deny, of course, that there has been a certain continuity in philosophical treatments of the concept of justice. The discussions of this concept in Plato's *Republic* and in Book 5 of the *Nichomachean Ethics* pose many of the same philosophical problems we meet with today. And Kant was quite correct, in the Marxian view, when he said that a universal resolution of the question *'Was ist Recht?'* is *the* perennial task of the jurist (*Gesammelte Schriften*, Akad. Ed. [Berlin, 1914], 6: 229). But in the Marxian view these facts point to the fundamental inadequacy of the tradition of social philosophy and jurisprudence based on the political or juridical conception of society. Jurisprudence, according to Engels, 'compares the legal systems of different peoples and different times, not as the expression of their respective economic relations, but as systems having their foundation in themselves. The comparison presupposes that there is something common to them all, which the jurists set forth by a comparison of legal systems under the name 'natural right'. But the standard used to measure what is and is not natural right is just the most abstract expression of right itself, namely *justice*, . . . *eternal* justice' (*Werke*, 18: 276 f.; cf. *Selected Works*, I, 564 f.). By this procedure, it is possible to ask abstract questions about the nature of social institutions from an abstract, juridical standpoint, and to provide equally abstract answers to them, seeking a single formal and universal answer to a set of questions which can only be answered in concrete circumstances. The apparent unity in their philosophical concept of justice, as Engels goes on to point out, has not prevented men from maintaining the greatest conceivable diversity in 'just' practices, and the common acceptance of universal philosophical principles of justice is even compatible with quite serious disagreement as to what sorts of actual social arrangements are just and unjust. 'The conception of eternal justice,'

he says, 'therefore belongs among those things by which . . . "everyone understands something different" ' (ibid.).

26. David Ricardo, *Principles of Political Economy*, ed. Piero Sraffa (Cambridge, Eng., 1951), I, 11. Cf. *Werke*, 21: 176 and Marx, *The Poverty of Philosophy* (New York, 1963), p. 8.

27. *Werke*, 4: 98–100. Cf. *The Poverty of Philosophy*, pp. 69–72.

28. *Werke*, 26: 1, 7–11. Cf. Marx, *Theories of Surplus Value*, trans. Emile Burns (Moscow, 1954), part I, pp. 41–3.

29. *Werke*, 23: 559. Cf. *Capital*, I, 537.

30. Ibid.

31. *Werke*, 23: 185. Cf. *Capital*, I, 171.

32. *Werke*, 23: 190. Cf. *Capital*, I, 176.

33. *Werke*, 23: 609. Cf. *Capital*, I, 583.

34. *Werke*, 23: 208. Cf. *Capital*, I, 194.

35. John Locke, *Second Treatise on Government* (Indianapolis, Ind., 1952), p. 17, par. 27.

36. *Werke*, 23: 609 f. Cf. *Capital*, I, 583 f.

37. *Werke*, 23: 791. Cf. *Capital*, I, 763.

38. Cf. P. J. Proudhon, *Système des contradictions économiques, ou la philosophie de la misère* (Paris, 1850), II, 397.

39. *Werke*, 23: 610. Cf. *Capital*, I, 584.

40. *Werke*, 19: 18. Cf. *Selected Works*, II, 20.

41. *Werke*, 13: 620–31; cf. Horowitz, *Marx and Modern Economics*, pp. 27–39. *Werke*, 25: 884–91; cf. *Capital*, III, 877–84.

42. Marx, *Grundrisse zur Kritik der Politischen Oekonomie* (Berlin, 1953), p. 77. Cf. *The Grundrisse*, trans. and ed. David McLellan (New York, 1971), p. 69.

43. *Gesamtausgabe*, I/5, 25. Cf. *Writings of the Young Marx*, p. 426.

44. *Werke*, 19: 22. Cf. *Selected Works*, II, 23.

45. A good example of this insistence on finding an idea of 'justice' implicit in the Marxian critique of capitalism is to be found in Ralf Dahrendorf, *Die Idee des Gerechten im Denken von Karl Marx* (Hanover, 1971). The same sort of misunderstanding has led Dahrendorf elsewhere to view Marx's analysis of class conflict as involving a conception of class 'based essentially on the narrow, legal conception of property' (*Class and Class-Conflict in Industrial Society* [Stanford, Cal., 1959], p. 21). If the argument of the earlier part of this paper is correct, this estimate could not be farther from the truth.

46. Tucker, *The Marxian Revolutionary Idea*, pp. 48 ff.

47. Ibid., p. 51.

48. *Werke*, 19: 22. Cf. *Selected Works*, II, 23 f.

49. *Werke*, 25: 271. Cf. *Capital*, III, 259.

50. *Werke*, Erg. 1, Teil 450. Cf. *Writings of the Young Marx*, p. 271.

51. *Grundrisse*, p. 400. Cf. *Pre-Capitalist Economic Formations*, ed. Eric Hobsbawm (New York, 1965), p. 102.

52. Hegel, *Phänomenologie des Geistes* (Hamburg, 1952), p. 149. Cf. Hegel, *Phenomenology of Mind*, trans. J. B. Baillie (New York, 1967), p. 238.

53. *Werke*, Erg. 1, Teil 514. Cf. *Early Writings*, p. 125. The concept of the alienation (*Entfremdung*) of labour is not something confined to Marx's early writings, as is sometimes believed. Marx continued to use both the term *Entfremdung* and the concept throughout his analysis of capitalist production, and he continued to compare the accumulation of social wealth in the alienated form of capital to Feuerbach's theory of religion as the alienated essence of man conceived by man as an independent object. Consider, for example, the two

following passages from *Capital*: 'The labourer, on leaving the labour process, is what he was on entering it – a personal source of wealth, but destitute of all means to actualize this wealth for himself. Since before entering the labour process his own labour is alienated [*entfremdet*] from him, and appropriated and incorporated by the capitalist, it objectifies itself during the labour process in the form of an alien [*fremdem*] product . . . The labourer therefore produces objective wealth in the form of capital, of a power alien to him [*ihm fremde*] which dominates and exploits him' (*Werke*, 23: 595 f.; cf. *Capital*, I, 570ʹ f.). 'As in religion man is dominated by a work of his own head, so in capitalistic production he is dominated by a work of his hand' (*Werke*, 23: 649; cf. *Capital*, I, 621).

54. *Werke*, 25: 827. Cf. *Capital*, III, 819.
55. *Werke*, 4: 131 f. Cf. *The Poverty of Philosophy*, pp. 111 f.
56. *Werke*, 13: 9. Cf. *Selected Works*, I, 329.
57. *Werke*, 6: 416. Cf. *Selected Works*, I, 91.
58. *Werke*, 23: 646; cf. *Capital*, I, 618. *Werke*, 6: 416; cf. *Selected Works*, I, 91.
59. *Werke*, 19: 26. Cf. *Selected Works*, II, 27.

Biographical Note

Allen Wood is Professor of Philosophy at Cornell University, where he has taught since 1968. He has also been a visiting professor at the University of Michigan, Ann Arbor. He is author of *Kant's Moral Religion* (1970), *Kant's Rational Theology* (1978), *Karl Marx* (1981) and a translation of Kant's *Lectures on Philosophical Theology* (1978).

Further Reading

Cohen, Nagel, Scanlon (eds.), *Marx, Justice and History* (Princeton University Press, 1980); Nielsen and Patten (eds.), *Marx and Morality* (Guelph: Canadian Journal of Philosophy, 1981); Allen Wood, *Karl Marx* (London: Routledge & Kegan Paul, 1981); Robert C. Tucker, *Philosophy and Myth in Karl Marx* (New York: Cambridge University Press, 1961) and *The Marxian Revolutionary Idea* (New York: W. W. Norton, 1969); William McBride, 'The Concept of Justice in Marx, Engels and Others', *Ethics* 85 (1974–5); Cheyney Ryan, 'Socialist Justice and the Right to the Labour Product', *Political Theory* 8 (1980); Richard Miller, 'Marx and Morality', *Nomos* XXVI (1982); *Marxism Today*.

Richard Schacht

Nietzsche: Art and Artists

The greatness of the great philosophers is certainly no one greatness, but of different kinds, which is one reason that those who write about them do so in different ways. Nietzsche is unique in what might be called his dramatic grandeur. Moved, perhaps overwhelmed, by what indubitably are ideas and images of great power, he gave them the fullest possible expression, and brought them to bear at different levels and on different sides of his subject-matters. There can be no puzzle about the fact that his work, although a world away from that of Frege or Mill, continues to be compelling, and often enough to be found awesome. Richard Schacht in his book *Nietzsche*, from which what follows is taken, does not attempt to reduce him to dried propositions and bare sequences of argument, neatly laid-out. It would be false and diminishing to describe Nietzsche as a merely poetic philosopher, but the nature of his thought and feeling is such that an ordinary reduction of it to propositions and arguments would be a reduction that had little use. It would have none of the resonance of the original. Schacht's way, then, is to come closer to Nietzsche's own ways. He expounds him with spirit, entering into his vision. That is not to say that he abandons the philosophical task of clarifying and ordering. Nietzsche, if not to be pinned down, is brought into clearer view.

The particular work of his in question is *The Birth of Tragedy*, in which he presents his passionate account of the nature of art and in particular of tragedy, and, no less important, his account of the place of both in human life. Never, as Schacht begins by remarking, has art been given greater significance. To mention but one aspect of the grandeur assigned to it, the artist is akin to Nietzsche's *Übermensch*, a 'higher form of being', a man who achieves a 'union of spiritual superiority

Friedrich Nietzsche, 1844–1900. Born in Prussia, lived in Switzerland and Italy. Teacher of classics, now best known for ethics and aesthetics. Friend of Wagner, praised by Freud for self-insight, died deranged.

with well-being and an excess of strength'. Nietzsche himself came to look back on *The Birth of Tragedy* as art-idolatry, and, as Schacht ends by remarking, it may with reason be taken as excessive. If it is a work of excess, however, it is also a work of creative insight, among the few classics in the philosophy of art.

Nietzsche took from Schopenhauer a very great deal of the latter's pessimistic and grim doctrine of the nature of reality. Reality is not as we experience it, or as science or religion regards it, but a blind striving, a pointless and wholly irrational profusion of processes which Schopenhauer characterized as *will*, futile will. The sum total of our own lives is that we struggle, suffer and die, with our lives having no more value or indeed sense than the rest of reality. Given this blackness, if we come to have a true view of it, how can we carry on? What is it that may be capable of 'detaining' us in life?

Nietzsche's answer is that it is what first sustained the Greeks – art – although the sustenance, despite the grandeur of art, is far from complete. That art provides even incomplete sustenance, however, in such a world, must give it the greatest of value. This is so, more particularly, since there is absolutely nothing else. The objects we immediately perceive are 'fictions', 'the soul is only a word for something about the body', and, of course, to remember Nietzsche's most famous line, God is dead.

This ultimate significance of art is set out in Sections I and II below. The latter section also introduces the principal concern of Sections III to VI. It is Nietzsche's conception of art in terms of two categories, the Dionysian and the Apollinian, and his conception of the ways in which it sustains those of us who have seen the world in its true pointless absurdity and awfulness. The sustaining nature of art, whether Dionysian or Apollinian, is in Nietzsche's terms its capability of transfiguring, transforming and overcoming.

The creation of art, works of art themselves, and the experience of art or aesthetic experience – all of these and more can be divided, despite considerable complications, and with the great exception of tragedy, into the Dionysian and the Apollinian kinds. (Indeed, Nietzsche creates a great problem for himself, given his view of art as sustaining, by characterizing nature or reality itself as 'artistic' and in terms of the two categories. This problem is noted towards the end of Section II.) Dionysian art is typified by music, has to do with an intoxication, and is of course so named for its connection with the Greek myths of Dionysian ecstasies. It gives, indeed, a 'blissful ecstasy'. It consists in symbols – where the latter are quite unlike what are usually so named.

Apollinian art is typified by sculpture, and is related to dreaming rather than intoxication. Its stuff is not symbols, but 'idealized images' – again, however, not images in any ordinary sense. If Dionysian art is a matter of ecstasy, Apollinian is a matter of delight with beauty.

Neither the symbols of Dionysian nor the images of Apollinian art *represent* reality. Their value to us is not the value of truth. Nietzsche's is no cognitive view of art. The value of these symbols and images, perhaps too plainly stated, is that they *distract* us from reality. Only art, the saving sorceress, 'knows how to turn . . . nauseous thoughts about the horror or absurdity of existence into notions with which one can live.' (p. 404) Art transfigures, which is to say that it provides for us 'a splendid illusion'. (p. 407) It transforms and overcomes the meaninglessness of existence. The sense in which art can be said, despite this, to consist in symbols and images, is difficult to grasp, but has to do with its origin in Dionysian and Apollinian states of consciousness, in particular but not only those of the artist in his creative activity. (Sections IV, V)

Sections VII to X have to do with the unique form of art which in its origin as well as its nature is both Dionysian and Apollinian. That is tragedy. The birth of tragedy in Greece has an importance greater than the fact of its unique duality, however. There is the fact that each of Dionysian and Apollinian art can fail to be sustaining. Nietzsche took the view that the modern epoch is such that both do fail. This is partly a matter of the now discredited myths of religion and the like. What is now needed is a *rebirth* of tragedy, which alone can provide us with support for our lives. It can lead to a revitalization of Western civilization.

Nietzsche's account of the effect on us of tragic works of art is in part in line with Aristotle's account of it as purging us of pity and fear. However, he goes beyond this, discerning an exhilaration in our experience. He has a confidence that tragedy can indeed enable us to meet the challenge of our existence. The confidence has to do with a conviction which pertains to tragedy in its Apollinian aspect: the Apollinian 'power of transfiguration' is the equal of whatever dread thoughts, perceptions or realizations because part of human consciousness. (pp. 422, 429)

Tragedy is unique in its direction onto the facts of individual human existence, and can alter our perception of that existence as nothing else can. It gives us 'symbols of human possibility'. In so doing, while like the rest of art a matter of illusion, it is not a matter of *mere* illusion. Nietzsche has a further idea, perhaps one whose associations are not agreeable, to the effect that tragedy can lead us to an aesthetic conception of human existence, a conception which gives a proper or somehow justified place to suffering and horror.

Be that as it may, there can be no doubt of the force of Nietzsche's account of the nature and significance of art and of tragedy in particular. It can persist, perhaps, when put in a different setting: a view of reality and life less extreme than that of Schopenhauer. That force is conveyed, as is much else, in Schacht's resolute and venturesome interpretation. He does not look over his shoulder at Nietzsche's philosophical detractors, but gets on with the job he has set himself.

The abbreviated references to Nietzsche's works are explained in the note on further reading.

Richard Schacht

Nietzsche: Art and Artists

No higher significance could be assigned to art than that which Nietzsche assigns to it in the opening section of *The Birth of Tragedy*: 'The arts generally' are said to 'make life possible and worth living' (*BT* 1). Art is never far from his mind, even when he is dealing with matters seemingly far removed from it. Thus, for example, he later characterized his 'view of the world' not only as 'anti-metaphysical' but also as 'an artistic one' (*WP* 1048), and suggested the world to be something on the order of 'a work of art which gives birth to itself' (*WP* 796). He also includes a number of artists among the 'higher men' whom he takes to stand out from the greater part of mankind hitherto, and likens to artists both the 'philosophers of the future' he envisions and the *Übermensch* he declares to be 'the meaning of the earth'. Indeed, he even aspired to art himself, investing much effort and a good deal of himself in poetic (and, in his early years, also musical) composition.

His views with respect to art (and artists) underwent a number of changes; but he never lost his concern with it, or abandoned the whole of his initial understanding and estimation of it. It would be an error to take the position set forth in *The Birth of Tragedy* to be 'Nietzsche's philosophy of art'; but it is with this book (purporting in the very first sentence to make a major contribution to 'the science of aesthetics') that his efforts along these lines began. It amply warrants extended discussion; for while it constitutes his first word about art rather than his last, it is a most remarkable one, long recognized as a classic contribution to the philosophical literature on art.

Richard Schacht, a part of 'Art and Artists', Chapter 8, *Nietzsche* (London: Routledge & Kegan Paul, 1983). Reprinted with slight excisions with the permission of the author and publisher.

I

In a foreword entitled 'Attempt at a Self-Criticism' (*BT* S–C below), written some fourteen years after the book's publication, Nietzsche shows himself to be his own best critic – both severe and insightful. He readily acknowledges that 'this questionable book' has many faults, not the least of which is that it is so obviously 'a first book'. It would be hard to imagine any fair-minded reviewer speaking more harshly of it than he does, when he writes:

today I find it an impossible book: I consider it badly written, ponderous, embarrassing, image-mad and image-confused, sentimental, in places saccharine . . ., uneven in tempo, without the will to logical cleanliness, very convinced and therefore disdainful of proof. (*BT* S–C:3)

He recognizes the seriousness of the defects resulting from his having been under both the spell of Wagner and the sway of Schopenhauer, and scornfully brands the book's author a romantic, a pessimist and an 'art-deifier' (*BT* S–C:7). Yet he also observes that the book poses a number of questions of the utmost importance, and moves at least some distance towards a proper treatment of them. 'The problem of science', 'the significance of morality', and indeed 'the value of existence' are among the 'whole cluster of grave questions with which the book burdened itself' (*BT* S–C:4). But the question in the foreground of this cluster, which guides and structures his treatment of these others, concerns the nature of art and its significance in human life – Greek art in particular, but by no means exclusively. Thus he refers to 'the task which this audacious book dared to tackle for the first time: *to look at science in the perspective of the artist, but at art in that of life*' (*BT* S–C:2).

Nietzsche's interest in art was by no means either exclusively academic or merely personal; and the urgency he felt with respect to the task to which he refers was not at all simply a function of his belief that Greek art and art generally had not previously been adequately understood by his fellow classical philologists and aestheticians. In his original preface to the book, he speaks disparagingly of readers who may 'find it offensive that an aesthetic problem should be taken so seriously', and who are unable to consider art more than a pleasant sideline, 'a readily dispensable tinkling of bells that accompanies the "seriousness of life"'. Against them, he advances the startling contention that 'art represents the highest task and the truly metaphysical activity of this life' (*BT* P). And as has been observed, he goes on to maintain that 'the arts generally' serve to 'make life possible and worth living' (*BT* 1). It remains to be seen what he has in mind in so speaking of art. But these remarks provide ample indication of the centrality of art in his consideration of the set of issues he deals with here.

Nietzsche makes no attempt to conceal the influence of Schopenhauer on both his conception of reality and his thinking about the arts in *The Birth of Tragedy*. Schopenhauer may fairly be said to have been Nietzsche's primary philosophical inspiration, in a twofold way. On the one hand, he was initially convinced of the soundness of much of what Schopenhauer had to say about the world, life and the arts. But on the other, he was deeply unsettled by Schopenhauer's grim conclusions with respect to 'the value of existence' and the worth of living. He felt obliged to grant that Schopenhauer had a *prima facie* case, and had placed the burden of proof upon anyone who would make a different assessment of them. Rather than agreeing with him to the bitter end, however, he accepted the challenge Schopenhauer had thus posed. Much of his own thought may be regarded as an attempt to meet this challenge, and to establish a viable alternative verdict. And both in *The Birth of Tragedy* and subsequently, art figures centrally in his efforts to accomplish this task. Thus it is one of his central contentions that 'it is only as an *aesthetic phenomenon* that existence and the world are eternally justified' (*BT* 5). It is to art that he turns, in discussing the comparably dangerous predicament of 'the 'profound Hellene' upon 'having looked boldly right into the terrible destructiveness of so-called world history as well as the cruelty of nature,' saying: 'Art saves him, and through art – life' (*BT* 7).

The world 'in itself' for Schopenhauer, while not in principle unknowable, is not identical with phenomena as we experience them; and it neither contains nor consists in matter in motion, irreducible mental substances, or fundamental rational structures. Rather, it has the character of a formless, aimless, turbulent principle he elected to call 'will'. He conceived the world as a profusion of processes, in which this single basic principle manifests itself in many different ways; and for him the phenomena of nature as we experience them are appearances of certain instances of it. Each form of existence (such as man), on his view, is one possible *type* (or 'grade') of manifestation of this dynamic principle, analogous to a Platonic 'Idea' – a notion taken over by Schopenhauer and employed in this connection, to designate the blueprints (as it were) followed by his demi-urgic 'will' in its concrete articulation (Schopenhauer, *WWI*, § 26).

Schopenhauer conceived the plastic arts as having to do essentially with the discernment and representation of these Ideas; while music for

Richard Schacht

him had the essentially different function of reflecting the nature of the underlying 'will' itself. To tragedy, on the other hand, he attributed yet another kind of function – to reveal the fate inexorably awaiting all specific manifestations of this 'will', and the hopelessness of the plight of even the greatest in this essentially irrational world of ceaseless strife and destruction. This recognition was for him the deepest wisdom that either art or philosophy can yield, rendering insignificant not only the concerns with which we ordinarily are preoccupied, but also all knowledge – whether consisting in the cognition of relations among phenomena attainable through scientific investigation, or in the relatively higher-order discernment of the Ideas to which all existence conforms, or in the still higher knowledge of the nature of the 'world-will'.

Schopenhauer's basic reason for taking this darkly pessimistic position was that on his view all existence and life generally are characterized by ceaseless struggle and striving, inevitably resulting in destruction, and (among sentient forms of life) involving incessant suffering of one sort or another. The whole affair, to him, is quite pointless, since nothing of any value is thereby attained (the perpetuation of life merely continuing the striving and suffering). No transcendent purposes are thereby served; no pleasures, enjoyments or satisfactions attainable can suffice to overbalance the sufferings life involves, thus excluding a hedonic justification of living; and so life stands condemned at the bar of evaluative judgement. It is, in a word, absurd. There is nothing to it but ceaseless striving, inescapable suffering, inevitable destruction – all pointless, with no meaning and no justification, no redemption or after-worldly restitution, and with the only deliverance being that of death and oblivion (cf. *WWI* § 71). Thus the pre-Christian and pre-Socratic apprehension of life attributed by Nietzsche in *The Birth of Tragedy* to the early Greeks recurs again in the modern world, as Christianity enters its death-throes.

Nietzsche does not question the soundness of this picture; and even though he later rejected the Schopenhauerian metaphysics which he here accepts, he continued to concur with this general account of the circumstances attending life in the world. To live is to struggle, suffer, and die; and while there is more to living than that, no amount of 'progress' in any field of human enterprise can succeed in altering these basic parameters of individual human existence. And even more significantly, for Nietzsche as well as for Schopenhauer and Nietzsche's Greeks, it is not possible to discern any teleological *justification* of what the individual is thus fated to undergo, either historically or supernaturally. We can look neither to a future utopia nor to a life hereafter that might serve to render endurable and meaningful 'the terror and horror of existence' (*BT* 3).

II

How can one manage to endure life in a world of the sort described by Schopenhauer, once one recognizes it for what it is – endure it, and beyond that *affirm* it as desirable and worth living *despite* the terrors and horrors that are inseparable from it? 'Suppose a human being has thus put his ear, as it were, to the heart chamber of the world will,' Nietzsche writes; 'how could he fail to *break*?' (*BT* 21). He terms this general recognition of the world's nature, and of the fate of the individual within it, 'Dionysian wisdom'; and he compares the situation of the Greek who attained it to that of Hamlet – and implicitly, to that of modern man (with a Schopenhauerian–existentialist world-view) as well:

> In this sense the Dionysian man resembles Hamlet: both have once looked truly into the essence of things, they have *gained knowledge*, and nausea inhibits action; for their action could not change anything in the external nature of things . . .
> Now no comfort avails any more . . . Conscious of the truth he has once seen, man now sees everywhere only the horror or absurdity of existence . . .: he is nauseated. (*BT* 7)

Nietzsche desperately wanted to find some sort of solution to this predicament – though he cloaked his longing in the guise of a more detached interest in the question of how it has been possible for 'life' to manage to 'detain its creatures in existence' even when the erroneous beliefs which commonly shield them are no longer in operation. For this reason his attention was drawn to a people who were already very much on his mind owing to his professional concerns, and who constituted a perfect subject for a case study along these lines: the early Greeks. They were no brute savages, mindlessly and insensitively propelled through life by blind instinctive urges; rather, they were highly intelligent, sensitive, and cognizant of the ways of the world. And what is more, they were sustained neither by anything like Judaeo-Christian religious belief nor by any myth of historical progress and human perfectibility. Yet they did not succumb to Schopenhauerian pessimism; on the contrary, they were perhaps the most vigorous, creative, life-affirming people the world has known. And thus

Nietzsche looked to them, asking of them: How did they do it? What was the secret of their liberation from the action- and affirmation-inhibiting nausea which seemingly ought to have been the result of their own Dionysian wisdom?

The answer, he believed, lay in that which was the most striking and glorious achievement of their culture: their art. Thus the passage cited above continues:

Here, where the danger to [the] will is greatest, *art* approaches as a saving sorceress, expert at healing. She alone knows how to turn these nauseous thoughts about the horror or absurdity of existence into notions with which one can live. (*BT* 7)

This is the guiding idea of Nietzsche's whole treatment of art in general, as well as of tragedy in particular. The main themes of this work are summarized in the following lines from its concluding section, which expand upon this idea by making reference to the key concepts of the 'Dionysian' and 'Apollinian', and bring to the fore the most central and crucial notions in his entire philosophy of art – the notions of *overcoming* and *transfiguration*:

Thus the Dionysian is seen to be, compared to the Apollinian, the eternal and original artistic power that first calls the whole world of phenomena into existence – and it is only in the midst of this world that a new transfiguring illusion becomes necessary in order to keep the animated world of individuation alive.

If we could imagine dissonance became man – and what else is man? – this dissonance, to be able to live, would need a splendid illusion that would cover dissonance with a veil of beauty. This is the true artistic aim of Apollo in whose name we comprehend all those countless illusions of the beauty of mere appearance that at every moment make life worth living at all and prompt the desire to live on in order to experience the next moment.

Of this foundation of all existence – the Dionysian basic ground of the world – not one whit more may enter the consciousness of the human individual than can be overcome again by this Apollinian power of transfiguration. (*BT* 25)

Before turning to a closer consideration of these notions, a fundamental ambivalence in Nietzsche's conception of the relation between art and life in *The Birth of Tragedy* must be noted. And in this connection I shall refer briefly to his thinking about art after as well as in this work. From first to last, he was deeply convinced that art requires to be understood not as a self-contained and self-enclosed sphere of activity and experience detached from the rest of life, but rather as intimately bound up with life, and as having the greatest significance in and for it. This is reflected in his later observation (in his 'Self-Criticism') that art in *The Birth of Tragedy* is viewed 'in the perspective of life' – a circumstance he regards as one of the signal merits of the work. And it is one of the most decisive and distinctive features of his general philosophical position that its development is characterized by a kind of dialectic between his understanding of life and the world and his understanding of art – each affecting the other, and bringing about changes in the other as the other worked changes upon it.

The underlying unity of the notions of art and life in Nietzsche's thinking is to be seen in *The Birth of Tragedy* in his treatment of the basic impulses operative in art – the 'Dionysian' and the 'Apollinian' – as manifestations of basic tendencies discernible in man and nature alike. And the consequences of his conviction of the existence of this unity are apparent in the subsequent development of the two notions which gradually moved to the centre of his discussions of man, life and the world in his later writings: the *Übermensch* and the 'will to power'. For the latter may be understood as an outgrowth of the dual notions of the Dionysian and Apollinian 'art impulses of nature', in which they are transmuted in a manner lending itself to a further union with Nietzsche's successor-conception to Schopenhauer's 'world will', his world of 'energy-quanta'. And the figure of the *Übermensch* may likewise be construed as a symbol of human life raised to the level of art, in which crude self-assertive struggle is sublimated into creativity that is no longer in thrall to the demands and limitations associated with the 'human, all-too-human'.

The overcoming of the initial meaningless and repugnant character of existence, through the creative transformation of the existing, cardinally characterizes both art and life as Nietzsche ultimately came to understand them. And this means for him both that life is essentially artistic, and that art is an expression of the fundamental nature of life. 'Will to power' is properly understood only if it is conceived as a disposition to effect such creatively transformative overcoming, in nature, human life generally, and art alike. And the *Übermensch* is the apotheosis of this fundamental disposition – the ultimate incarnation of the basic character of reality to which all existence, life and art are owing.

In *The Birth of Tragedy*, of course, neither 'will to power' nor *Übermensch* makes an appearance; and the relation between art and life is discussed in other terms. One of the most notable features of the discussion, however, is Nietzsche's readiness to employ the term 'art' not only to refer in a conventional manner to sculpture, music and the other standard 'art-forms', but also in a broader, extended sense. For example, he suggests that 'every man is truly an artist' to the extent that everyone engages in the 'creation' of 'the beautiful illusion' of 'dream worlds', even though no 'works of art' in the usual sense are thereby produced. Furthermore, turning his attention from such (Apollinian) 'dreaming' to the experience of what he calls 'Dionysian ecstasies', he speaks of the Dionysian throng as *being* 'works of art' themselves: here 'man . . . is no longer an artist, he has become a work of art . . . The noblest clay, the costliest marble, man, is here kneaded and cut' (*BT* 1).

Most strikingly of all, Nietzsche refers constantly to 'nature' herself as 'artistic', and terms both the 'Apollinian' and the 'Dionysian' tendencies 'art-impulses' *of nature.* Thus he initially presents them 'as artistic energies which burst forth from nature herself, without the mediation of the human artist', and goes on to say: 'With reference to these immediate art-states of nature every artist is an "imitator"' (*BT* 2). And he contends that these two 'art-states of nature' are 'the only two art-impulses' (*BT* 12). He even goes so far as to attribute the true authorship of *all* art to 'nature' rather than to human agency considered in its own right. 'One thing above all must be clear to us. The entire comedy of art is neither performed for our betterment or education, nor are we the true authors of this art world.' The human artist is said to be merely 'the medium through which the one truly existent subject celebrates his release in appearance'. Artists and the rest of us alike are 'merely images and artistic projections for the true author', which is the fundamental principle of reality – the 'world-will' – itself; and we 'have our highest dignity in our significance as works of art', as creations of this ultimate 'artist' (*BT* 5).

Yet Nietzsche also speaks of art very differently, and in a way that suggests a much less direct and even contrasting relation between it and the world. Thus, for example, he writes that 'the highest, and indeed the truly serious task of art' is 'to save the eye from gazing into the horrors of night and to deliver the subject by the healing balm of illusion from the spasms of the agitations of the will' (*BT* 19). Art spreads a 'veil of beauty' over a harsh reality – and when Nietzsche speaks of it as a 'transfiguring mirror' (*BT* 3), the emphasis belongs not on the latter term but rather on the former, which does away with any accurate reflection. Thus he writes that 'art is not merely imitation of the reality of nature but rather a metaphysical supplement of the reality of nature, placed beside it for its overcoming' (*BT* 24).

Here one should also recall the concluding passage of the entire work, in which Nietzsche returns to this theme of the necessity of overcoming whatever consciousness of the world's nature is attained by means of an art of 'transfiguration' capable of covering over what has been glimpsed with a 'splendid illusion' (*BT* 25). It was the 'terror and horror of existence' from which the Greeks needed to be saved; and 'it was in order to be able to live' that they developed their art: 'all this was again and again overcome by the Greeks with the aid of the Olympian *middle world* of art; or at any rate it was veiled and withdrawn from sight' (*BT* 3). And Nietzsche asserts that 'the tragic myth too, in so far as it belongs to art at all, participates fully in this metaphysical intention of art to transfigure' (*BT* 24).

Even while thinking along these lines, however, he supposes there to be a fundamental link between 'art' and 'life', in that the latter is held to have been the source of the Greek's salvation from the desperate situation in which it also placed him: 'Art saves him, and through art – life' (*BT* 7). 'Life' thus is cast in a dual role, with the consequence that the relation of art to it is also a dual one. It is difficult to conceive of this dual relation coherently and faithfully to Nietzsche's representations of each aspect of it, however, without the two sides of it falling irreparably apart. Can the world of art in the narrower sense be thought of as a world 'supplementing the reality of nature, placed beside it for its overcoming', and therefore distinct from it and contrasting to it – and at the same time as the creation of this very nature itself, expressing its own basic own basic 'artistic impulses', and therefore fundamentally homogeneous and identical with it? In *The Birth of Tragedy* Nietzsche tries to have it both ways; but it is far from clear that it is possible to do so.

Apollinian and Dionysian Art

III

In any event, it should by now be clear that Nietzsche thinks of what art *is* in terms of *what art does* and *how art does it*; and that for him the answers to these two questions are to be given in terms of the notions of *overcoming* (*Überwindung*) and *transfiguration* (*Verklärung*). These two notions recur repeatedly throughout the work, and figure centrally in most of his major pronouncements about art. It should further be evident that they are to be understood in relation to certain human needs which he regards as fundamental and profoundly compelling, thereby endowing art with an importance transcending that of mere enjoyment or satisfaction derived from self-expression.

His interpretation of art in terms of the second of these two notions involves him in a fundamental break with Schopenhauer and all other cognitivist philosophers of art. For if art is essentially a matter of transfiguration, its ministrations to our needs will necessarily proceed otherwise than by heightening our powers of insight and understanding. Nietzsche's frequent references to 'illusions' in this connection make this obvious; but the point holds even where he does not consider this term to apply (notably in the case of music). Otherwise put: even where some sort of 'truth' about reality is purported to come through in art, he takes it to be essential to the artistic character of the expression that a transfiguration of the 'true' content has occurred in its artistic treatment – and its artistic character and quality attaches entirely to the element of transfiguration, rather than to this content and its transmission. (On this point more shall be said below.)

It is important to bear in mind the general applicability of the notions of overcoming and transfiguration when turning to Nietzsche's discussion of the art-impulses and art-forms he is intent upon distinguishing, both in order properly to interpret what he says about them individually, and in order to avoid the error of supposing that he takes them to be entirely different phenomena. To be sure, when he introduces his idea of 'the *Apollinian* and *Dionysian* duality', he asserts that 'art' is but a 'common term' until the two are 'coupled with each other' (*BT* 1); and he does go on to analyse them along very different lines – even to the point of maintaining that these notions represent '*two* worlds of art differing in their intrinsic essence and in their highest aims' (*BT* 16). These 'art impulses' and 'worlds of art', however, while very different for Nietzsche, are none the less both '*art*-impulses' and 'worlds *of art*', with more than merely this same denomination in common – as the fact that their 'coupling' had a fruitful artistic issue (tragedy) itself suggests.

Schopenhauer had suggested that music is to be understood in terms fundamentally different from those appropriate to the plastic arts – the latter being concerned with the representation of the Ideas to which the manifestations of 'will' in the realm of appearances conform, and the former mirroring the underlying essential nature of this 'will' itself. Nietzsche believed that Schopenhauer had put his finger on an important difference here. He further accepted the suggestion that the distinction between these art-forms was linked to the distinction between the 'world-will' in itself and the world of appearances. Yet he by no means simply took over Schopenhauer's views along these lines, merely introducing the labels 'Apollinian' and 'Dionysian' in the course of restating them. He qualifies his endorsement of the idea that music 'copies' the world-will even as he gives it. For he holds that in music the nature of this ultimate reality is expressed *symbolically*, with the consequence that music neither *is* 'will' nor is a 'true' copy of it. Even here, he contends, transfiguration occurs; and it is upon the nature of this transfiguration, rather than upon the 'mirroring' relation as such, that he focuses his attention.

Even more radical is his departure from Schopenhauer with respect to the plastic arts. Gone is all reference to anything metaphysically comparable to the latter's 'Ideas', and with it, any suggestion that here too a kind of cognitive function is performed. The forms fashioned by the plastic artist are construed not as representations of types to which existing particulars do and must more or less adequately conform, but rather as *idealizing transfigurations* of experienced phenomena – 'beautiful illusions' making up a 'dream world' that departs radically from the 'real world' of ordinary experience, 'placed alongside it for its over-coming' (*BT* 24).

Thus according to Nietzsche, neither in Apollinian nor in Dionysian art do we encounter unvarnished representations of the world, either as it presents itself to us in experience, or as it is in itself (or as it might be conceived by a thinker concerned with the natures of the types to which all existing things belong). The impulses to the creation of art for him are not cognitive impulses of any sort. Rather, if they stand in any relation at all to knowledge, he holds that this relation may best be conceived as an *antidotal* one. And it is undoubtedly in part to stress the extent of his departure from any cognitively oriented interpretation of art that he introduces his discussion of the Apollinian and the Dionysian by dwelling on their connection with the phenomena of dreaming and intoxication. Each of these phenomena, he maintains, manifests a deeply rooted and profoundly important aspect of our human nature; each answers to a powerful need – and the strength of the hold art exerts upon us can be understood only if it is recognized that the different art-forms have their origins in these basic impulses, and emerge in answer to these strong needs. Nietzsche's discussion of 'the Apollinian and Dionysian duality' in *The Birth of Tragedy* is intended to bring out both the radical difference between what he thus takes to be the two basic life-serving and art-generating impulses these names designate, and also the possibility of their interpenetration – and further, the great importance (for 'life' and art alike) of the results when this occurs. Thus he asserts that in tragic art 'Dionysus speaks the language of Apollo; and Apollo finally the language of Dionysus; and so the highest goal of tragedy and of all art is attained' (*BT* 21). And again:

Where the Apollinian receives wings from the spirit of music and soars, we [find] the highest intensification of its powers, and in this fraternal union of Apollo and Dionysus we . . . recognize the apex of the Apollinian as well as the Dionysian forms of art. (*BT* 24)

IV

At the outset of his discussion of 'the Apollinian and Dionysian duality', Nietzsche singles out two art-forms as paradigms of each – 'the Apollinian art of sculpture and the non-imagistic, Dionysian art of music' (*BT* 1) – but then moves immediately to a consideration of the more fundamental experiential 'states' (also termed 'Apollinian' and 'Dionysian') to which he takes all such art-forms to be related: dreaming and intoxication. As has been observed, he contends that human beings are so constituted as to be impelled to each by deeply rooted dispositions, and to respond to each with powerful but differing positive feelings. Thus he suggests that there is something in 'our innermost being' which 'experiences dreams with profound delight and joyous necessity'; while it is likewise the case that 'paroxysms of intoxication' are accompanied by a 'blissful ecstasy that wells up from the innermost depths of man, indeed of nature' (*BT* 1).

It is these feelings of 'profound delight' on the one hand, and of 'blissful ecstasy' on the other, which are held to characterize the experience of the art-forms akin to and developing out of these two more basic forms of experience, and to render each so engaging. They touch the same deep chords in our nature, and so produce the same sort of response; and this is taken to be the key to understanding how it is that they are able to perform their life-sustaining functions (to the extent that they manage to do so). Thus Nietzsche explains his use of the name of Apollo in terms of its association with 'all those countless illusions of the beauty of mere appearances that at every moment make life worth living at all and prompt the desire to live on in order to experience the next moment' (*B T* 25) – whether in 'dreams' or in the 'imagistic' art which is a refinement and elevation to a higher plane of development of the 'creation' of the 'beautiful illusion of the dream worlds' (*BT* 1). And he likewise suggests that 'Dionysian art, too, wishes to convince us of the eternal joy of existence: only we are to seek this joy not in phenomena, but behind them', through being ecstatically transported into a state of momentary identification with 'primordial being itself, feeling its raging desire for existence and joy in existence; the struggle, the pain, the destruction of phenomena now appear necessary for us' (*BT* 17).

As Nietzsche views them, dreaming and intoxication are not merely analogues to art, or pre-forms of art, or even experiential sources of artistic activity. Rather, there is an important sense in which they themselves *are* artistic phenomena – only the 'artist' in these cases is no human being, but rather 'nature', working in the medium of human life. It is his contention that human artistic activities are to be regarded as of a piece with these more basic life-processes. They represent developments of them, to be sure, but are outgrowths sufficiently linked to them to warrant regarding 'every artist as an "imitator"' in relation to 'these immediate art-states of nature' (*BT* 2). It is in this respect alone, for Nietzsche, that art may properly be conceived as involving 'the imitation of nature'. That is, art imitates nature in that the same sort of thing goes on in the former instance as goes on (among other things) in the latter. But precisely because creative transformation is involved in the former no less than in the latter (as part of the very 'imitation' in question), true art no more involves the attempt exactly to represent nature as it confronts us, than dreaming and intoxication faithfully record it; nor yet again does true art merely give expression to the contents of experiences had while in these states.

This last point is of particular importance. It is true that Nietzsche takes these states to be the point of departure and inspiration for artistic creation, and he does consider it appropriate to speak of 'every artist' as 'either an Apollinian artist in dreams, or a Dionysian artist in ecstasies', or both at once (*BT* 2). But here the terms 'dreams' and 'ecstasies' are being used metaphorically; for it is no less central to his analysis of both types of (human) art that they involve the *further* transfiguration of what is experienced in these 'art-states of nature'. And what is more, they transfigure the already dissimilar contents of the visions associated with the two kinds of state in quite different ways.

It is with this difference in mind that Nietzsche speaks of the emergence of 'two worlds of art differing in their intrinsic essence' (*BT* 16). The basic contrast between them may be expressed in terms of the distinction between *images* and *symbols*; and the difference just mentioned bears importantly upon it. In the case of Apollinian art, the chaotic play of crude and ephemeral appearances associated with such

Richard Schacht

basic Apollinian experiential states as dreaming and imagination undergoes a transformative process, issuing in the creation of enduring, idealized images. They are 'beautiful illusions' – illusory because nothing
either in the flux of appearance or beyond it corresponds to them, and
of greater beauty than the haphazardly constituted contents of this flux.
Transfigurations of appearances, they are images akin to the stuff of
dreams, but also contrasting markedly with them.

In the case of Dionysian art, on the other hand, the transformation
from which it issues is of the experience of the inexhaustible, dynamic
'primal unity' that is 'beyond all phenomena and despite all annihilation', associated with such basic Dionysian states as intoxication and
orgiastic revelry. What *this* transformation gives rise to is 'a new world
of symbols', in which 'the essence of nature is now . . . expressed
symbolically' (*BT* 2); and it is the resulting *symbolic forms* in which
Dionysian art consists. These symbolic forms are transfigurations of
ecstatic states – expressions akin to immediate Dionysian ecstasy, but
again, differing significantly from it, no less than from the underlying
reality glimpsed in it. Thus Nietzsche holds that 'Dionysian art . . .
gives expression to the will in its omnipotence, as it were, behind the
principium individuationis', the principle of individuation (*BT* 16) – and
yet insists that even so paradigmatic a case of such art as music is not
to be thought of as identical with this 'will'. 'Music,' he writes,
'according to its essence, cannot possibly be will. To be will it would
have to be wholly banished from the realm of art' (*BT* 6). For were it
the same as 'will', it would lack the transfigured character constitutive
of all art.

It is in terms of the difference between the kinds of transfiguration
involved, rather than in terms of a division of the various art-forms
into the 'plastic arts' on the one hand and the 'musical arts' on the other,
that Nietzsche's 'Apollinian–Dionysian duality' in art is to be understood. In one sort of art the works produced have a symbolically
expressive character; while in another they do not, having instead the
character of idealized images. And it is one of the seemingly curious
but important points of his analysis that the kinds of art generally
regarded as most clearly 'representational' fall largely into the *latter*
category, while those generally thought of as primarily 'non-
representational' belong in the *former*. The idealized images of Apollinian art are not to be thought of as having the function either of
faithfully representing or of symbolically expressing *anything at all*.
They are rather to be thought of as 'beautiful illusions' to be contemplated simply for what they are in themselves, and to be enjoyed solely

on account of their intrinsic beauty. They are, as Nietzsche says, a 'supplement of the reality of nature, placed beside it for its overcoming' (*BT* 24).

If there is any significant relation between them and this 'reality', on his view, it does not consist in their linkage to the experiential phenomena of which they are transfigurations, but rather in their ability to lead us to think better of the world of ordinary experience by regarding it in the 'transfiguring mirror' they constitute, 'surrounded with a higher glory' (*BT* 3). Through Apollinian art, the world of ordinary experience is not actually transformed and its harshness eliminated. But to the extent that the idealized images created through the transformative activity of the Apollinian artist admit of association with what we encounter in this world, our attitude towards the latter benefits from this association, as our delight in these images carries over into our general disposition towards anything resembling them. Once again, however, it is not *knowledge* that we thereby attain, but rather only an altered state of mind, brought about by 'recourse to the most forceful and pleasurable illusions', and 'seducing one to a continuation of life' (*BT* 3). Those works of art he terms 'Apollinian' are creations which neither represent nor symbolize, but rather delight precisely by virtue of the transfiguration accomplished in their production.

V

In the case of Dionysian art, matters stand quite differently. The Dionysian artist too is creative, and not merely someone with insight and the ability to communicate it. It may be that there is a kind of 're-echoing' of the fundamental nature of reality in instances of Dionysian art. In terms of this metaphor, however, such art is no less a 'transfiguring echo-chamber' than Apollinian art is a 'transfiguring mirror'. For the artistic 're-echoing' does not stand in the same near-immediate relation of identity to this 'primal unity' as does the more basic Dionysian phenomenon of intoxication. It rather comes back in an altered form, the creative production of which involves 'the greatest exaltation of all [man's] symbolic faculties'. Thus, Nietzsche continues, 'the essence of nature is now to be expressed symbolically; we need a new world of symbols' (*BT* 2); and it is this 'new world of symbols' which constitutes both the language and the substance of Dionysian art.

The symbolism of which he speaks here, however, is of a rather special sort. At least in its origins, it is neither conventional nor intentional, and is far removed from the use of words to formulate and express thoughts. So, in discussing the 'Dionysian dithyramb' (which he takes to be the proto-form of Dionysian art), he writes that, in order to develop the 'new world of symbols' needed to be able to express 'the essence of nature' symbolically,

the entire symbolism of the body is called into play . . ., the whole pantomime of dancing, forcing every member into rhythmic movement. Then the other symbolic powers suddenly press forward, particularly those of music, in rhythmics, dynamics, and harmony. (*BT* 5)

Nietzsche regards the 'symbolic powers' involved in such music and dancing as sublimations of deeper and darker natural impulses, and considers the symbolism to which they give rise to be *natural* in a significant sense; even though he also conceives it to be more than *merely* natural. The latter point is important: we have to do here with a transformation in which 'nature for the first time attains her artistic jubilee', and 'days of transfiguration' supplant the nights of the 'horrible "witches' brew" of sensuality and cruelty' of pre-Dionysian savagery (*BT* 2). But the former point is no less important: the expressions in which such music and dancing consist, while symbolic, have a natural affinity with the reality they symbolize. And this reality is deeper than that of all individual thought, all social conventions and all 'appearance'; for its expression involves 'the destruction of the *principium individuationis*' (ibid.), and the 'height of self-abnegation' on the part of those through whom this expression is achieved. The Dionysian artist does not employ symbols to express some specific thought or emotion he happens to have had, or some particular feature of the cultural life and experience he shares with other members of his society. 'He has identified himself with the primal unity', in all its 'pain and contradiction' and also its inexhaustible and indestructible vitality – and, thus 'released from his individual will', he gives symbolic expression to the nature of the fundamental reality with which he identifies (*BT* 5). Some sorts and even some instances of (Dionysian) music and dance may be superior to others in terms of the adequacy with which they perform this expressive function; but it is essentially the character of these art-forms itself that accounts for their symbolic significance and their ability to perform this function.

In these arts the world's nature is expressed in a form that attracts rather than repels us – a symbolic form, the attractiveness of which is bound up with the transfiguration involved in this symbolization and made possible by the character of the 'new world of symbols' under consideration. Dionysian art does not have the character of a 'veil of illusion' radically different from the reality of nature and 'placed alongside it for its overcoming', as does Apollinian art for Nietzsche. Yet it does have a somewhat analogous character and function, in that it expresses the reality of nature in a manner enabling us to overcome our abhorrence of it and to derive 'joy in existence' from identification with it, by means of a quasi-'illusory' *medium* of transfiguring symbolic forms.

VI

Nietzsche does not take the notions of transfiguration and illusion to apply only to works of Apollinian and Dionysian art conceived as object of aesthetic experience, but rather also to the *subjects* of such experience in so far as they become absorbed in them. This point is of great importance in connection with his treatment of tragic art, as well as in his analysis of these two art-forms, and so warrants close attention. The entire significance of art is missed, for him, if one does not recognize that the consciousness of those experiencing these art-forms undergoes a transformation analogous to that occurring in their creation; and that the experiencing subject's very psychological identity thereby is in a sense transfigured, even if only temporarily and in a way that does not alter the basic reality of the subject's human nature and existence in the world. This happens in very different ways in the two general sorts of cases under consideration, however, representing what Nietzsche takes to be two fundamentally distinct stratagems by means of which 'the insatiable will' at the heart of nature conspires to 'detain its creatures in life and compel them to live on' (*BT* 18). He discusses them in terms of what occurs in the case of the 'Dionysian man' and in the case of the 'Apollinian man' (these expressions referring primarily to contrasting psychological possibilities rather than to distinct groups of human beings).

That an inward transformation occurs in the course of the kind of experience appropriate to Dionysian art is a point which has already been intimated, in Nietzsche's observation that one in the grip of the 'paroxysms of intoxication' in which the Dionysian impulse primordially manifests itself 'has become a work of art' (*BT* 1). And it has further been suggested in noting that he takes Dionysian art to mediate an identification of the individual with the reality underlying appearances. It is a common observation that art has the remarkable power

Richard Schacht

to *transport* us out of our ordinary selves and everyday lives. Nietzsche seizes upon this idea and elaborates it, in a manner influenced significantly by Schopenhauer.

Schopenhauer had contrasted our normal condition as creatures and captives of 'will', absorbed in the constant struggle for existence characterizing all life in the world, with a radically different condition purported to be temporarily attainable through aesthetic experience. 'He who is sunk in this perception is no longer individual,' Schopenhauer had written, but rather 'is pure, will-less, painless, timeless subject of knowledge' (*WWI* §34). Nietzsche modifies this suggestion, and expands it so that it applies both to the contemplation of idealized images that elevates one above the world of ordinary experience and action, and to the experience of enrapturing symbolic expressions of the reality underlying this phenomenal world that carries one beyond it. Yet in either event, he agrees with Schopenhauer that one so affected is 'no longer individual', or at any rate ceases for the moment to have the psychological identity associated with his ordinary individual existence. The transformation undergone by the Apollinian man (which is most akin to that indicated by Schopenhauer) will be considered shortly. That undergone by the Dionysian man was not envisioned by Schopenhauer, at least in connection with art; for it involves not the attainment of contemplative will-lessness, but rather the effecting of a deeper psychological union with the 'world-will'.

The Dionysian man does not exchange his physiological and socio-cultural identity and situation in the world for another, or escape them altogether in the course of the 'destruction of the *principium individuationis*' of which Nietzsche speaks. As an experiential phenomenon, however, this destruction is very real: the Dionysian man is psychologically transformed into one for whom the only reality of which he is aware – and therefore that with which he himself identifies – is that which is expressed in the movements, tonalities or other symbolic forms in which he is immersed. Thus Nietzsche contends that, through the experience of Dionysian art, 'we are really for a brief moment primordial being itself' (*BT* 16). As one in a state of intoxication may be said not to 'be himself', one immersed in the surge and flow of an instance of this type of aesthetic experience 'loses himself' in it. His consciousness is caught up in it, and his self-consciousness is altered accordingly – whether this transformation manifests itself behaviourally in an enraptured cessation of ordinary activity (outward inaction masking inward tumult), or in entrance into overt participation in the event as well. Such experience is fundamentally ecstatic, not only in the now

416

ordinary but derivative sense of being blissful, but also in the original and literal sense of the term *ekstasis*, which denotes a displacement of oneself.

To the extent that one's own existence is discovered to be a moment of the reality expressed in Dionysian art, with which one thus comes to feel at one through the mediation of the latter, this transformation may be said to have the significance of a dispelling of the illusion involved in one's ordinary consciousness of oneself as something distinct from it and to be characterized in other terms. But to the extent that such experience leads one to identify oneself so completely with this reality that one takes oneself to have even those of its features that actually characterize it only as a whole, with which one is not truly identical, this transformation may also be said to have the significance of the fostering of another, different illusion. Thus Nietzsche suggests that, here no less than in the case of Apollinian art, we are dealing with a way in which, 'by means of an illusion', life conspires 'to detain its creatures in existence' despite the harshness of the conditions it imposes upon them: in this instance, through 'the metaphysical comfort that beneath the whirl of phenomena eternal life flows on indestructibly' (*BT* 18).

The illusion in question is not that 'life flows on indestructibly' despite the ephemerality of all phenomena – for it does. We may be 'comforted' (and more) through the transformation of our psychological identity enabling us to achieve a sense of unity with this indestructible and inexhaustible underlying reality, of which we are truly manifestations. But while such comfort may be termed 'metaphysical', this transfiguration is not; for it leaves our actual status in the world unchanged, and the basic conditions of our human existence unaltered. This we discover when the moment passes, the Dionysian aesthetic experience comes to an end, and we 'return to ourselves', our psychological identities being transformed back again into their mundane non-Dionysian state. The only enduring 'comfort' is the recollection of the rapture of the Dionysian experience, and the knowledge that it remains available to us. But a profound danger attends this kind of 'overcoming', of which Nietzsche is acutely aware. For the let-down may be great, the disparity between Dionysian states and ordinary life distressing, the illusion discerned, and its recognition found disconcerting; and thus the long-term effect of such experience may be detrimental rather than conducive to life (*BT* 7). It is for this reason, more than any other, that he has reservations about Dionysian art and experience generally, despite the evident fascination they have for him.

417

Nietzsche's Apollinian man constitutes a very different case, being the product of quite another kind of psychological transformation. As has already been observed, he conceives of this type in terms rather similar to those employed by Schopenhauer. For Nietzsche, one cannot appropriately speak here of 'knowledge', since that with which we are concerned in the 'images' of Apollinian art is not representations of anything like Schopenhauer's 'Ideas', but rather 'beautiful illusions'. Yet he does conceive of the subject of Apollinian aesthetic experience as transformed (through the contemplation of these idealized images) from an individual caught in the web of the world, into something like Schopenhauer's pure subject of knowledge – transcending time and will, and his own particular individuality and circumstances along with them. As in the previous case, however, this transcendence is held to be not only merely temporary but also fundamentally illusory, and the resulting transformation only psychological rather than genuinely ontological. And here too Nietzsche sees the cunning hand of nature at work, in this instance 'detaining its creatures in life' through 'ensnaring' the Apollinian man 'by art's seductive veil of beauty fluttering before his eyes' (*BT* 18).

The realm of Apollinian art is a kind of 'dream world, an Olympian *middle world* of art' (*BT* 3). It is neither the 'everyday world' nor the underlying world of 'will', but rather a created world by means of which the latter is 'veiled and withdrawn from sight', and the former is supplanted as the focus of concern. And entrance into this world is possible, Nietzsche holds, only for a kind of dreamer, or Olympian spectator, detached from the kinds of involvements and concerns that both characterize the everyday world and endow us with our ordinary psychological identities. Indeed, it requires that one *become* such a 'pure spectator' – or rather, the images presented are such that they induce a kind of contemplative consciousness through which one's psychological identity is transformed into that of such a subject. They stand outside of time and change, need and strife; and to become absorbed in them is for Nietzsche to have one's consciousness comparably transformed. If in the experience of Dionysian art one is enraptured, one may be said here to be entranced; and in a state of such entrancement, it is as if one had become a part of this world of images – not as one of them, but as a placeless, disembodied centre of awareness, a subject fit for such objects and answering to their nature.

Schopenhauer had spoken of the occurrence of a significant release and liberation from the 'world of will' (however temporary and incomplete it might be) in aesthetic experience of this sort, as a result of which one effectively ceases to be a creature and captive of this 'will' for its duration. And for Nietzsche too, while Apollinian art involves 'the arousing of delight in beautiful forms', it serves to effect an overcoming of the distress associated with our human condition through what is felt to be a kind of redemption from it. 'Here Apollo overcomes the suffering of the individual by the radiant glorification of the *eternity of the phenomenon*; here beauty triumphs over the suffering inherent in life' (*BT* 16). For one 'is absorbed in the pure contemplation of images' (*BT* 5) and seemingly becomes nothing but the delighted awareness of them. This psychological transformation is real – even though on a more fundamental level both the objects of such consciousness and this self-consciousness are merely two aspects of the 'Apollinian illusion', which is but 'one of those illusions which nature so frequently employs to achieve her own ends' (*BT* 3).

If it is the case, however, that Apollinian art is thus 'called into being as the complement and consummation of existence' (ibid.), it follows that we have here to do with no *mere* illusion which leaves the reality of human life unaffected. It may not fundamentally alter the human condition; but if it is in some significant sense the 'consummation of existence', it may be truly said to effect a significant transformation of 'existence', or at least that portion of it which is the reality of human life. Art may be created by man, but man is also re-created or transfigured by art. This kind of experience and spirituality, which become attainable in relation to the idealized images of Apollinian art, may not constitute an elevation of those who attain to them entirely beyond the reach of the entanglements of ordinary life, and beyond the deeper harsh realities of existence in this world. Yet they do render the existence of those attaining to them qualitatively different from that of those who remain entirely immersed in the former, or who further succeed only in finding occasional respite through Dionysian experience. It is Nietzsche's appreciation of the magnitude of this qualitative difference that accounts for his celebration of the achievement of the archaic Greeks in their creation of Apollinian art.

Life cannot in the end be lived merely on the plane of Apollinian aesthetic experience, or even simply in the radiation of the reflected glory with which Apollinian art is capable of lighting the world of ordinary experience. The human condition is too recalcitrant, and the undercurrent of the 'Dionysian ground of existence' too strong, for the psychological transformation involved in the ascent into the realm of Apollinian art to prevail indefinitely. Absorbing and delightful as such experience is, it suffers from the fatal weakness of failing to come to terms with basic aspects of human life in the world that do not disappear when veiled. Yet Nietzsche is by no means disposed to conclude that what might be termed 'the Apollinian experiment' is to be regarded as a mere blind alley, to be abandoned in favour of the Dionysian alternative. There remains another, which he associates with the phenomenon of tragic art. And the kind of transfiguration Apollinian art involves – both of the objects and the subjects of experience – is of the utmost importance in the emergence alike of tragic art and of the more viable form of human existence he associates with it.

Tragic Art

VII

So, notwithstanding the full original title: *The Birth of Tragedy, Out of the Spirit of Music*, Nietzsche conceives tragic art to be no less Apollinian than Dionysian in origin and nature. At a certain point in Greek art the tendencies associated with each are said to 'appear coupled with each other, and through this coupling ultimately generate an equally Dionysian and Apollinian form of art – Attic tragedy' (*BT* 1). The burden of his entire discussion of it is that its emergence presupposed not only the prior development of the art of Dionysian transfiguration, but also the *re-transfiguration* of the latter under the influence of the likewise previously developed art of Apollinian transfiguration.

The birth of tragedy for Nietzsche was an event of the greatest significance; for it did not merely involve the appearance of a new art-form, thus opening another chapter in the development of art. It also made possible a further transformation of human life, which he conceives to have been and to be of far greater moment than is generally recognized. He does not regard tragic art as a phenomenon the significance of which is confined to but a single sphere of human experience and cultural life. Rather, he views it as the potential foundation and guiding force of an entire form of culture and human existence, which alone is capable of filling the void left by the collapse of 'optimistic' life-sustaining myths (both religious and philosophical–scientific). And he looks to it to assume anew the function of 'making life possible and worth living', which neither Apollinian nor Dionysian art as such is capable any longer of performing. The former may still entrance and delight us, and the latter enrapture and excite us; and both may continue to transport and transform us in their respective fashions. But the power of the illusions they involve to sustain us has been lost.

In light of some of Nietzsche's remarks, one could be forgiven for supposing that his understanding of the psychological effect of tragedy is not very different from Aristotle's. Aristotle had maintained that this effect is basically one of catharsis; the tragedian constructs a dramatic means of enabling us to be purged of the feelings of fear and pity arising in connection with our recognition of our own plight in this world and threatening to paralyse us, by arousing such feelings directed towards a tragic figure and discharging them upon this figure. In this way, our capacity to feel them for ourselves is held to be diminished (at least for a time), thus enabling us to return to the world of action temporarily unimpaired by them.

Nietzsche says something of a similar nature. One who 'sees everywhere only the horror or absurdity of existence' may be beyond the reach of the consolations of lesser art-forms; but art can take other forms, in which it is able to 'turn these nauseous thoughts . . . into notions with which one can live: These are the *sublime* as the artistic taming of the horrible, and the *comic* as the artistic discharge of absurdity.' And Nietzsche is close to Aristotle when he concludes that the effect of this 'saving deed of Greek art' was that 'the feelings described here exhausted themselves' (*BT* 7).

However, to say this much is not to say enough. For if one confines one's attention to this aspect of the experience of tragic art alone, one misses something of even greater significance than the discharge or exhaustion of such negative feelings: namely, the powerful *positive* feelings generated at the same time, which are akin to those associated with Dionysian aesthetic experience. In a word, what is absent from the above account is reference to the *exhilaration* tragic art serves to inspire, notwithstanding the distressing fate of the central tragic figures. This exhilaration is much more than a mere feeling of relief from the torment occasioned by the negative feelings of which one is purged. And it is also different in both magnitude and kind from the delight associated with Apollinian aesthetic experience. Thus Nietzsche contends that 'the drama . . . attains as a whole an effect that transcends *all Apollinian* effects' (*BT* 21). There may be those whom tragedy does not affect in this way (Schopenhauer would appear to have been one); but that, for him, says something about *them* rather than about the nature of tragic art. Exhilaration is on his view an essential feature of the proper effect such art should have; and this phenomenon both renders comprehensible why he attaches such great significance to tragic art, and guides his interpretation of it.

In tragedy, according to Nietzsche, we find elements of both

Apollinian and Dionysian art – not, however, merely externally combined, but rather employed in a subtle interplay. Moreover, these elements do not retain their entire original character; for here 'Dionysus speaks the language of Apollo; and Apollo, finally, the language of Dionysus' (*BT* 21). Thus Nietzsche suggests that 'in this fraternal union of Apollo and Dionysus', we find that 'an Apollinian *illusion*' is employed to admit the Dionysian 'spirit of music' into our experience, while at the same time protecting against an 'immediate unity with Dionysian music' by requiring it to be expressed 'in an Apollinian field'. And we also find that 'the Apollinian receives wings from the spirit and soars', surpassing all 'weaker degrees of Apollinian art' by being 'illuminated from the inside by music' to an extent that 'in all other Apollinian art remains unattained' (*BT* 24).

In this connection it is both crucial and illuminating to bear in mind the passage cited earlier from the last section of the book, in which Nietzsche contends – clearly with tragic art specifically in mind – that, with respect to the underlying nature and character of the world and existence in it, 'not one whit more may enter the consciousness of the human individual than can be overcome again by [the] Apollinian power of transfiguration' (*BT* 25). To be able to endure the consciousness of them of which we are capable and which cannot in the long run be prevented from emerging, and to be able further to embrace and affirm life despite the attainment of such an awareness, a transformation of this consciousness is necessary. For in its starkest, simplest and most vivid form it would be overwhelmingly horrible, 'nauseating', paralysing and unendurable.

Tragic art alone, for Nietzsche in *The Birth of Tragedy*, is truly equal to this task. It enables us to experience the terrible not as merely terrible, but rather as sublime; and it achieves something akin to a Dionysian effect upon us, which however is not identical with it. For it does not take the kind of life-endangering toll Dionysian intoxication does, rather inducing an experiential state that differs as significantly from such intoxication as it does from Apollinian dreaming. In the long run it has the character of a tonic rather than a depressant; its aftermath is held to be exhilaration, rather than either the overall exhaustion which follows upon Dionysian excitement, or the exasperation which Apollinian exaltation leaves in its train. And considered more immediately, it might be said to enthrall, rather than to entrance *or* enrapture.

Tragic art too, for him, may be said to constitute a kind of 'transfiguring mirror'. It is a mirror, however, in which we see reflected neither 'appearances' idealizingly transfigured, nor the character of the reality underlying them symbolically expressed. We are confronted instead with 'images of life' – reflections of the (and our) human condition, highlighting both the individuation it involves and the fate bound up with the latter. What we encounter, however, is not a stark and brutally 'realistic' portrayal of this condition as such. We see it in transfigured form – even though this transfiguration of it does not consist in its radical transmutation into a merely imaginary, idealized condition *contrasting* with the actual human condition on these counts. And it likewise does not involve the effective obliteration of the salient features of human life through the diversion of attention from the entire domain of individuation to the collective, the impersonal, the merely vital and the enduring aspects of life underlying it. The kind of transfiguration occurring here is rather one which pertains to our perception of individual human existence – *as* existence that is individual rather than merely a part of an inexhaustible and indestructible flow of life, and that is human rather than above and beyond the conditions to which man is subject.

This transfiguration pertains first of all to the character of the dramatic figures with which we are confronted – or rather it comes about first in the context of our confrontation with them. Yet it does not remain confined to this encounter; for it further serves to alter our apprehension of the human condition more generally. It is in this sense above all that tragic art may be said to function as a transfiguring mirror: it works a transformation upon our consciousness of the human reality that is also our own, at the same time as it reflects that reality for us to behold. The fate of the tragic figure takes on the aspect of something sublime rather than merely horrible; and thus, without being denied or glossed over, it ceases to inspire mere 'nausea' and moves us instead to fascination and awe. The life of the tragic figure is endowed with a significance that entirely alters its aspect; and what might seem from a simple recitation of the brute facts of the matter to be a merely wretched and distressing tale emerges as an enthralling and moving spectacle.

Tragic art presents us neither with an ideal to be admired and emulated, nor with an avenue by means of which to escape all thought of the hard realities of life. The latter are very much in evidence; and the tragic figure caught up in them is one with whom, as an individual, we empathize, but with whom as a character we do not identify. Yet the manner of presentation of such figures, which renders them tragic and not merely pathetic, does much more than merely purge us of our self-directed feelings of fear and pity through an empathic discharge.

It can have a powerful positive impact upon the way in which we perceive our human condition and experience the reality of our own lives, by revealing them to us in a very different light from that in which we would otherwise tend to view them. The point might be put by saying that the tragic artist, not through the persona of the tragic figure *per se* but rather in the larger structure of the tragic drama, interposes a medium between us and the reality of human existence which does more than simply give expression to this reality. For this medium further shapes and colours our consciousness of it, and is able to help us attain an affirmative attitude towards it precisely by virtue of doing so.

In short, tragic art provides us with a way of apprehending this reality that enables us to come to terms with it – and not only to endure but also to affirm what we see, as we thereby learn to see it. In this way it resembles Dionysian art; and for Nietzsche this similarity of tragic art to the Dionysian arts is by no means merely fortuitous. In tragic myth, as in music and dance, something transcending mere appearances is symbolically expressed – and in being so expressed, is transformed for our consciousness. Here, however, the symbolic forms employed are not primarily those characteristic of these Dionysian art-forms, but rather are drawn from the initially non-symbolic domain of Apollinian art.

VIII

In tragic art attention is focused upon individual figures who are no mere ordinary human beings, but rather 'great and sublime forms'. By means of them it both 'satisfies our sense of beauty' which delights in such images, and also 'incites us to comprehend in thought the core of life they contain' (*BT* 21). In the former respect it has an 'Apollinian artistic effect'; yet its effect is by no means simply Apollinian. For to the extent that it does the latter, these also have the significance of *symbols*, whose interest for us is further in part a matter of what they convey about the 'life' they symbolize, in which both they and we participate.

It is a basic feature of tragic art, according to Nietzsche, that 'at the most essential point this Apollinian illusion is broken and annihilated'. The central figures are destroyed, succumbing to forces which shatter their individual existence and give the lie to the appearance of self-contained and impervious reality of these 'great and sublime forms'. And yet the impact of tragic art upon us is by no means merely that of depression and despair, for we respond to the dramatic expression of the inexhaustible and indestructible power of the forces of life in relation to which all individual existence is merely ephemeral. What Nietzsche calls 'the spirit of music' speaks above the relation of what befalls the tragic figures, with the result that 'in the total effect of the tragedy, the Dionysian predominates once again', and we are exhilarated rather than merely mortified (*BT* 21).

This 'total effect', however, is not a purely Dionysian one. And the difference is crucial both with respect to the understanding of tragic art and where its 'value for life' is concerned. A discernment of and identification with the larger and deeper reality transcending the existence of the tragic figures and all individuals is attained – but not through an enraptured ascent into a state of consciousness in which the former alone absorbs us. Rather, this occurs in a manner which at the same time not only leaves us very much aware of individuals and the conditions of their existence, but moreover actually heightens this awareness. And the attendant exhilaration, while akin to Dionysian excitement, neither depends upon the attainment of such Dionysian transport, nor endures only as long as our consciousness remains thus transformed. On the contrary, it is wedded to a vivid recognition of the plight of particular individuals, and carries over after the event when our own lives once again come to the fore. A fundamentally Dionysian chord is sounded, and our responsiveness to it is tapped; but this is done to an importantly different effect. For what occurs, Nietzsche suggests, is not a transformation of our consciousness along lines rendering us oblivious to our individual existence, but rather a transfiguration of the character of our consciousness with respect to such existence.

Life regarded as tragic is no longer life seen as merely wretched and pathetic; and the 'displeasure' associated with 'the weight and burden of existence' is overshadowed and forgotten when the latter takes on the aspect of tragic fate rather than mere senseless suffering and annihilation. The fate of the tragic figure, when nobly met rather than basely suffered, enhances rather than detracts from his stature; and this figure serves as a symbolic medium through which individual existence more generally is dignified for us. The apparent oddity of the idea that exhilaration thus attends the attainment of a tragic sense of life disappears once it is recognized that this view of life is not a grim pessimism to which one is driven once the tenability of all forms of religious and secular 'optimism' is discerned. For it is no mere stark and unavoidable conclusion, but rather a signal accomplishment; and Nietzsche takes it to contrast in an incomparably more appealing and satisfying way with the much starker, utterly bleak conception of individual existence as the unmitigated and unadorned tale of mere ceaseless striving, senseless suffering and inevitable destruction it was proclaimed to be by Schopenhauer and ancient wisdom alike.

As has been noted, Nietzsche contends that tragic art 'participates fully in [the] metaphysical intention of art to transfigure'. He further maintains, however, that it does so differently from both Apollinian and Dionysian art. Thus he writes: 'But what does it transfigure when it presents the world of appearance in the image of the suffering hero? Least of all the "reality" of this world of appearance' (*BT* 24). It has to do with human existence in this world; and in the tragic figure we encounter a personified transfiguration of human existence, in which such existence is neither transmuted into idealized imagery purged of all conflict, pain, blemish, and vulnerability, nor reduced to the status of anonymous and individually insignificant instantiations of life. In contrast to what occurs in both of these cases, it is here ennobled within the very conditions imposed upon it. And it is by means of this transfiguration that tragic art works its distinctive transformation of our consciousness of ourselves. Thus Nietzsche goes on to contend that 'it is precisely the tragic myth that has to convince us that even the ugly and disharmonic are part of an artistic game that the will in the eternal amplitude of its pleasure plays with itself' (*BT* 24).

The unique achievement of tragic art is thus held to be that it fundamentally alters our apprehension of human existence and the circumstances associated with it, which result in the suffering and destruction of even the most extraordinary individuals. Through it these circumstances cease to stand as *objections* to human life and its worth, and emerge instead as features of it which – as part of the larger whole human lives are and can be – actually contribute to its overall significance and attractiveness. And thus, Nietzsche suggests, it serves to bring it about that 'existence' can 'seem justified' *aesthetically* – 'only as an aesthetic phenomenon' (*BT* 24). Nietzsche's use of the term 'only' here is highly important; for his general point is that it is *only* in this way, in the last analysis, that it is possible for us to find human life and our own existence endurable and worth while, without recourse to illusions which radically misrepresent the actual nature of our human reality and the world more generally.

IX

At the same time, however, Nietzsche maintains that this transfiguration of our consciousness of ourselves itself involves a kind of illusion. Thus he considers it appropriate to refer to it and the tragic art which brings it about as one of 'the stages of illusion' – albeit one 'designed . . . for the more nobly formed natures'. And given that this is so, one might well wonder why he considers it to be either superior to 'the more vulgar and almost more powerful illusions which the will always has at hand' (*BT* 18), and how he can suppose it to be any less subject in the long run than they are to the disillusionment which eventually undermines the latter and renders them ineffective.

Nietzsche contends that 'it is precisely the tragic myth that has to convince us that even the ugly and the disharmonic are part of an artistic game' (*BT* 24) in terms of which reality in general is to be conceived, and human life along with it. Dionysian art is held to convey to us a sense that things of this sort do not fatally flaw this macrocosmic 'game' as a whole, but rather contribute to its fundamentally positive 'artistic' character. But here it is suggested that tragic art goes a step further, persuading us that they likewise may be accepted and affirmed as features of our own human lives, which even on the microcosmic scale of individual existence can thus be experienced as having an 'aesthetic' justification. And, very importantly for Nietzsche, this alteration of their aspect is not achieved by means of a resort to religious or metaphysical fictions. It is instead accomplished through their artistic incorporation into an aesthetically appealing and satisfying vision of life. If this involves no resort to any such fiction, however. wherein lies the 'illusion'?

This 'illusion' has to do with the states of the 'image of life' with which Nietzsche takes us to be confronted in the tragic figure (*BT* 21). While such figures are neither simply realistically drawn, fictitious but true-to-life individuals, nor representatives of the elemental characteristics of 'Dionysian universality' (as is the chorus), they are no mere Apollinian 'beautiful illusions' either. Like Apollinian idealized images, however, they constitute something on the order of a 'supplement of the reality of nature', and of that of ordinary human existence along with it. The 'core of life they contain' is the same as our own (ibid.); but this core is artistically transformed into 'images of life' expressing possibilities which differ markedly from the commonplace, in ways moreover answering to no predetermined human essence or foreordained human ideal. They thus can in no sense be said to confront us with the 'truth' of human existence. And since what they confront us with is something other than 'truth', they may be said to present us with a kind of 'illusion'. It is in this way that Nietzsche's remarks to this effect are to be understood.

Yet this illusion is no *mere* illusion; and the transformed consciousness of ourselves which emerges, when we view our own lives in the light of the manner of those of these tragic figures, is not *merely* illusory. For the creations in which they consist are not distorted or erroneous representations of something that has a fixed and immutable character and cannot be otherwise. And they also are not simply imaginary substitutes temporarily usurping a position in our consciousness that is normally and more properly occupied by our ordinary conception of our own mundane reality. Rather, they are symbols of *human possibility*. And as such they serve to carry us beyond the mere acknowledgement of intractable aspects of the human condition, enabling us to discern ways in which the latter may be confronted and transformed into occasions for the endowment of life with grandeur and dignity.

By means of these symbols, human life thus may come to take on an aesthetic significance sufficing to overcome the distressing character of its harsh basic features. It stands revealed as a potentially aesthetic phenomenon, 'justifiable' accordingly in our estimation even in the face of its hardest circumstances. And of paramount importance for Nietzsche is the fact that tragic art does not confine this perception to the tragic figures themselves, while precluding its application to our lives. For these figures stand as symbols serving to facilitate our apprehension of the possibilities they express (together with 'the core of life they contain') *as our own* – and so to alter the aspect of our lives. To say that this is all 'illusion', as Nietzsche does, is neither to deny the reality of this alteration nor to downplay its significance. It is rather to make the point that our lives thus acquire an experiential character which is no part of their fundamental objective nature; and that this occurs through the transforming mediation of created images enabling us to discern aesthetic significance in human existence, notwithstanding that its basic circumstances as such warrant the attribution to our existence of no significance whatsoever.

X

In the attainment of a tragic sense of life the 'terror and horror of existence' are surmounted, through the remarkable alchemy of tragic art which transmutes the terrible and horrible into the sublime and magnificent. And the key to this transmutation is not the quickening of that sense of 'metaphysical comfort' that 'beneath the whirl of phenomena eternal life flows on indestructibly' – though this too occurs. It is rather the 'Apollinian power of transfiguration', which alone enables us to endure and affirm the existence that is ours as parts of this 'whirl' – not only in moments of Dionysian rapture, self-abnegation and obliviousness to the human condition, but also when we acknowledge our individuality and confront the circumstances of human life.

Nietzsche may often seem to be more concerned with what might be termed the ecstatic component of the experience of tragic art than with this companion feature of it. Yet it is the latter that he finally stresses, when he concludes his discussion by emphasizing that 'of this foundation of all existence – the Dionysian basic ground of the world – not one whit more may enter the consciousness of the human individual than can be overcome again by this Apollinian power of transfiguration' (*BT* 25). This power must be brought to bear upon our consciousness of our existence as 'human individuals', and not merely upon our awareness of 'the Dionysian basic ground of the world' as such, if we are to be able to find our lives 'endurable and worth living'. It would avail us little to regard 'the world' generally as 'justified' if no comparable 'justification' were discernible when we turned to a consideration of our own existence. And for Nietzsche in *The Birth of Tragedy* this is something which tragic myth alone can provide. It transforms what might otherwise be taken to be life at its worst into life at its best, endowing even suffering and destruction with aesthetic quality – not as such, to be sure, but as central elements of an aesthetically charged whole, into which are interwoven the tragic figure's life, circumstances, flaws, strivings, sufferings and destruction.

What is thus transformed is not tragedy; for the accomplishment of tragic art is not the transformation of tragedy into something else. Tragedy rather is the *issue* of this artistic transformation, through which existence comes to be experienced as tragic. This is indeed an artistic accomplishment, since tragedy no less than beauty may be said to exist only in the eye of the beholder, whose sensibility has been formed and cultivated by art. It is no brute fact of human existence, but rather an acquired aspect it may come to bear through the transfiguring agency of the tragic artist.

There is 'illusion' in the apprehension of existence as bearing the aspect of tragedy, since its tragic character is a matter of the imposition of significant form upon its given sundry features, rather than of the intrinsic nature of any or all of the latter. And there is a further 'illusion' involved in what Nietzsche terms the 'noble deception' generated to the effect that something more than this is encountered here. For tragic art does not merely transform our manner of regarding existence by means of its elaboration of 'a sublime parable, the myth'. It also 'deceives the listener into feeling that the music' – that is, the symbolic expression of the undercurrent of life that is manifested both in the tragic figure and in the forces to which this figure succumbs – 'is merely the highest means to bring life into the vivid world of myth' (*BT* 21).

It is in this way that the tragic myth comes to be endowed with what Nietzsche terms its 'intense and convincing metaphysical significance' (ibid.) – and also its most profoundly 'illusory' character. For it leads us to feel something to be the deepest and highest 'truth' of human existence – the tragic character it is capable of coming to bear, with all the sublimity and majesty devolving upon it therefrom – which is no part of its fundamental nature. Yet according to Nietzsche, tragic art requires ultimately to be conceived as working in the service of life. Here too, what we are said to be dealing with is simply another means (even if also the most exalted one) through which 'the insatiable will' manages to 'detain its creatures in life and compel them to live on' – in this case, by employing tragic myth to lend human existence an aspect endowing it with an aesthetic justifiability. But it does this in such a way that we are led to view life as though it were a means to the end of actualizing the aesthetic values associated with human experience as it is revealed in the transfiguring mirror of tragic myth.

In *The Birth of Tragedy* Nietzsche places his hope for a revitalization of Western civilization, in the face of the collapse of both other-worldly religiousness and rationalistic–scientific optimism, in a re-emergence of a tragic sense of life. But as he readily acknowledges, such a view of life cannot be sustained in the absence of tragic myth and an acceptance of the understanding of human existence associated with some instance of it. It is for this reason that he devotes so much discussion in this work to the importance of myth and to the need for a new and compelling form of tragic myth in the modern Western world. He ventures to hope that the ground for a 'rebirth of tragedy' and a new 'tragic culture' is being prepared by science itself, as it 'speeds irresistibly towards its limits where its optimism, concealed in the essence of logic, suffers shipwreck' (*BT* 15). But he recognizes that the 'shipwreck' of which he speaks, consisting in the collapse of the belief that scientific or other rational modes of inquiry will lead to the discovery of truths establishing the meaning and justifiability of existence, is only a negative condition of such a rebirth and renewal, and by no means suffices to accomplish it. Tragic myth alone is held to be capable of doing this, by means of tragic art. It is for this reason that he speaks of art as 'even a necessary correlative of and supplement for science' (*BT* 14).

Nietzsche obviously thought, when he wrote this book, that Wagner was well on the way to accomplishing the task he thus conceived. The details of his discussion of this and related matters, however, are of relatively little intrinsic interest – especially since he soon after both lost his enthusiasm for Wagner and abandoned his commitment to the ultimacy and indispensability of that form of art he associates here with tragic myth. He further came to be convinced that art generally has a significance in relation to life, and also a variety of features, to which his analysis of it in *The Birth of Tragedy* does not do justice. And indeed there are a number of respects in which his later thinking concerning it is clearly superior to his early treatment of it (owing both to his self-emancipation from Schopenhauer and Wagner, and to his stylistic and philosophical maturation).

Yet however unsatisfactory, questionable and excessive some of what Nietzsche says in *The Birth of Tragedy* may be, he is to be credited with a number of extremely valuable insights in this early effort, concerning such things as the relation between art and life, the transfigurative character of art, the nature of artistic creation, the distinction between imagistic and symbolically expressive art-forms, and the distinctive character and impact of tragic art. It may be that few classics in the literature of the philosophy of art are as flawed in as many particular respects as is this; but it is also the case that few so richly reward patience with their flaws and close attention to their substance.

Biographical Note

Richard Schacht is Professor of Philosophy at the University of Illinois (Urbana-Champaign). He was educated at Harvard, Princeton and Tübingen, and teaches and writes chiefly on nineteenth- and twentieth-century European philosophy. He is the author of *Alienation* (1970), *Hegel and After* (1975), *Nietzsche* (1983) and *Classical Modern Philosophers* (1984).

Richard Schacht

Further Reading

In the excerpt the following abbreviated references are employed:

BT Friedrich Nietzsche, *The Birth of Tragedy*, trans. Walter Kaufmann (New York: Vintage, 1967).

WP Friedrich Nietzsche, *The Will to Power*, trans. Walter Kaufmann and R. J. Hollingdale; ed. Walter Kaufmann (New York: Vintage, 1968).

WWI Arthur Schopenhauer, *The World as Will and Idea*, trans. R. B. Haldane and J. Kemp (London: Routledge & Kegan Paul, 1964).

All numbers used in references to these works refer to section or note (rather than page) numbers.

The best English translations of most of Nietzsche's writings have been made by Walter Kaufmann and R. J. Hollingdale (sometimes in collaboration). These include *Ecce Homo* (Harmondsworth, Penguin Books, 1979); *The Gay Science* (New York: Vintage, 1974); *Beyond Good and Evil* (New York: Vintage, 1966; Harmondsworth, Penguin Books, 1973); *On the Genealogy of Morals* (with *Ecce Homo*) (New York: Vintage, 1968); *The Will to Power* (New York: Vintage, 1968); *Thus Spoke Zarathustra* (Harmondsworth: Penguin Books, 1961); *Twilight of the Gods and The Antichrist* (Harmondsworth: Penguin Books, 1968). The last three, with *Nietzsche Contra Wagner*, are also contained in *The Portable Nietzsche* (New York: Viking, 1954). See also *A Nietzsche Reader* (Harmondsworth: Penguin Books, 1977). The definitive new German edition of Nietzsche's writings is the 30-volume *Werke: Kritische Gesamtausgabe*, ed. Giorgio Colli and Mazzino Montinari (Berlin: de Gruyter, 1967–78).

Useful English-language studies of Nietzsche's life and thought include Walter Kaufmann's *Nietzsche* (4th edition, Princeton University Press, 1974); Ronald Hayman's *Nietzsche: A Critical Life* (New York: Oxford University Press, 1980); George A. Morgan's *What Nietzsche Means* (Cambridge, Mass.: Harvard University Press, 1941); R. J. Hollingdale's *Nietzsche* (London: Routledge & Kegan Paul, 1973); Arthur Danto's *Nietzsche as Philosopher* (New York: Macmillan, 1965); John T. Wilcox's *Truth and Value in Nietzsche* (Ann Arbor: University of Michigan Press, 1974); and Richard Schacht's *Nietzsche* (London: Routledge & Kegan Paul, 1983).

Michael Dummett

Frege: Sense and Reference

Frege is celebrated as having begun modern logic, and in particular as having begun it by inventing a symbolic language or formal system capable of expressing proofs in a perspicuous way not possible before his time. This provision of an acute and powerful language was the endeavour to which Michael Dummett refers in the first paragraph of what follows, almost all of a chapter from his *Frege: Philosophy of Language*, a book perhaps more anticipated, discussed and regarded than any other book on a philosopher in recent decades. Frege was indeed a philosopher as well as a logician. He concerned himself with certain large issues which do not get or need consideration in logic and mathematics, notably the issue of meaning. He provided a theory of meaning, a philosophy of language. He provided, that is, an account of what a person knows when he understands an expression or a sentence. It in its different way is as monumental as his logic. In Dummett's view, it is a foundation for all of philosophy, a premise from which all of philosophy should start. If Frege wrote in only one other part of philosophy – that one having to do with the nature of mathematics – he attended to what needs to be attended to first.

Consider, as he did, the singular term 'the Morning Star'. What do we take to be the meaning, in an intuitive or unreflective sense, of this particular term – or, in Frege's usage, of this 'proper name'? There is the natural answer, given by more than one philosopher, that its meaning is the planet to which it refers. A related answer is that its meaning consists in its being associated or connected by us with the planet, whatever that association or connection may come to. In general, according to these natural answers, the meaning of a term is

Gottlob Frege, 1848–1925. Born in Wismar, taught at Jena. Mathematical logician and philosopher, a founder of logic and proponent of lasting philosophical distinctions. Unsettled by Russell's discovery of a contradiction in his work, recovered quickly. Died with the recognition of only a few, but including Russell.

what can be called its referent – the thing referred to – or its having a certain referent.

Frege, in his now famous article 'On Sense and Reference', makes a formidable objection. What had been called 'the Morning Star' was discovered at a certain date to be identical with what had also been called 'the Evening Star'. It was discovered that there was in fact one planet, doubly named, not two planets. But, Frege argued, if the meaning of 'the Morning Star' were the planet, and so with the meaning of 'the Evening Star', there could have been no such astronomical discovery. On this assumption about meaning, anyone who had earlier understood the two terms would have known the thing they stood for, and hence would have known that there was but one thing in question. There could have been no discovery. There is a related objection to the assumption that the meaning of an expression consists in its being associated or connected with a referent, its having a referent.

It must therefore be, Frege concluded, that meaning does not consist in a referent or the having of one. Rather, meaning has to do with something different. It has to do above all, Frege held, with the *sense* of an expression.

It has been quite common, as a result of the article 'On Sense and Reference', to regard Frege as having taken meaning to consist most importantly in both sense and reference. Meaning is at bottom that which has these two ingredients. An expression's meaning is essentially composed of reference – the fact of its being attached in some way to a referent – and in sense. It is one of Dummett's striking aims in his chapter to refute this traditional understanding of Frege. Meaning, although it has greatly to do with reference, does not itself consist in things for which expressions stand or in the connection between expressions and things.

Rather, meaning consists in three things: sense, tone and force. (pp. 437–8) Force, which is not considered below, but in another chapter of *Frege*, has to do with categories of sentences. We understand of a sentence that it is an assertion, or a question, or a command, or a wish, or of another such category. The principal distinction between sense and tone is that sense consists in those parts or features of the meaning of an expression which are relevant to the truth or falsity – the truth-value – of a sentence in which the expression occurs. (pp. 438–9). The sense of an expression is what one has to grasp in order to decide on the truth-value of a sentence containing the expression.

The expressions 'dog' and 'cur', therefore, have a common sense, but different tone. So with 'dead' and 'deceased'. So too with 'and' and 'but', as in 'She is poor and honest' and 'She is poor but honest'. Dummett dismisses Frege's own account of the nature of tone, which makes it a matter of one's mental images and hence a subjective rather than an objective fact about expressions. Meaning in all of its aspects *must* be objective. (p. 440) Tone is as objective a matter as sense – which, as Frege did rightly insist, is not a matter of mental images, not a matter of what you or I happen to conjure up in relation to an expression. (pp. 440–43) In the course of his discussion, Dummett gives a superior account of the tones of 'and' and 'but'.

Frege's idea of what exactly it is for an expression to have a referent, and hence also his idea of the relation between reference and sense, is explained in terms of the idea of interpretation. In setting up a formal system or symbolic language, there occurs a first stage in which entities are assigned to the fundamental expressions in the language, which expressions are of a number of kinds. This, which is distantly akin to the writing of a code, is to interpret the expressions. (p. 448) The idea of the interpretation of the expression can be identified with the idea of the having of a referent by an expression. Once an interpretation is assigned to an expression – although that by no means completes the construction of the language – the truth-values of certain sentences are fixed.

Given the role of referents – they fix the truth-values of sentences – it can be wondered what part can be played in meaning by the expression's sense. What more than the fact of reference is needed in an explanation or theory of meaning? (pp. 444–5) Dummett's original answer, anticipated above, is that the question presupposes a falsehood: that an expression's having a referent is part of its meaning. It is not. A person who does not know the referent of an expression may nevertheless fully understand the expression. (p. 438) Since reference is not part of meaning, there is an essential role for the sense of an expression. We need the idea of sense in explaining how language works. The sense of an expression is that part of the meaning which determines the referent of the expression and hence determines its truth-value. (pp. 445–6) The sense is that which we understand or grasp when we correctly associate a word with its referent. It is the means by which we connect a word with its referent, a route to the referent. (pp. 446–7)

There can be, for a particular thing, a number of such means or routes. There can, that is, be a number of expressions, as in the famous example mentioned above, which have the same referent but different senses. (pp. 447–51) With respect to any particular expression, further, there is no sharp line between its sense and the rest of the information we have about that thing for which the expression stands. (p. 453) There is no single feature of an object sufficient for its identification which anyone *must* know if he understands the expression which picks out the object. In the course of developing these thoughts, Dummett considers the view of a number of philosophers, notably Mill and Russell, that there are or there must somehow be expressions which lack sense: 'pure proper names' whose meaning consists only in their standing for certain objects. (p. 451)

Given the fact that the sense of an expression is not sharp and simple, do we need to concede that it is somehow subjective, despite what has been maintained? (p. 457) In giving an account of language, should we content ourselves with what is relatively simple, fixed and certainly objective – the fact of reference? One part of the answer (a secondary one, since the idea of sense is essential to characterizing meaning) is that although the sense of an expression is something whose content is far from simple, it nevertheless involves something constant, something common to all speakers. (p. 458)

The chapter ends with further reflections on the utility and importance of the notion of sense. It catches hold of and represents certain features of our linguistic practice which are of the very nature of that practice. If Frege's account of sense is an idealized one, it is none the less an account of a great part of the reality of language.

Dummett's discussion of Frege's philosophy of language is as difficult as any excerpt in this book, not only for those who are new to philosophy but to most philosophers. This difficulty is owed to the nature of the subject-matter and to the use, which is certainly necessary in connection with Frege, of many logician's conceptions, far more than could be considered in this introduction. In any case, they are not conceptions which can really be grasped by way of quick definitions. One needs an understanding of their use in formal systems. The reading of an introductory logic book can provide a good deal of that. A reader unacquainted with formal logic, however, is not debarred from acquiring a considerable awareness of Frege's achievement. Dummett's chapter, if it is also greatly more, and stands on its own as a piece of critical and innovative philosophy, is a means to such an awareness.

The marginal notes are to Frege's works and are explained in the note on further reading.

Michael Dummett

Frege: Sense and Reference

From the standpoint of *logic* as such, we need an account of the working of language only as it relates to truth, since the notion of the validity of a form of inference relates precisely to truth: a form of inference is valid just in case, in each inference of that form in which the premisses are true, the conclusion is also true. Hence, in order to fulfil his original purpose, Frege could have contented himself, as do logicians now, with an account of the structure of the sentences of his symbolic language, and with a specification of their truth-conditions as connected with that structure. The fundamental idea of his symbolic language was, of course, the recursive specification of the totality of sentences: the primitive non-logical constants will serve to construct the atomic sentences, and then the sentential operators and quantifiers provide means to generate further sentences from any given base. All that was needed, therefore, for the purposes of logic, was an account of the way in which the truth-value of an atomic sentence is determined, together with an account of the way in which the truth-value of a complex sentence is determined, given the truth-values of its constituents (the constituents of a quantified sentence being, of course, the instances). For the purposes of logic, we do not need to know what truth is, or how truth is related to meaning: whatever truth may be, and however it may be related to meaning, we know that an inference is valid if we have a guarantee that its conclusion is true, provided that its premisses are; that is enough for the logician.

It was not, therefore, qua logician, but qua philosopher, that Frege pushed his inquiry further; he was not satisfied with giving an analysis of language – or, at least, of a large part of language – adequate for the purposes of the logician: he wanted to give a general account of the

Michael Dummett, 'Sense and Reference', pp. 83–109 of Chapter 5 of *Frege: Philosophy of Language*, 2nd edition (London: Duckworth, 1981). Reprinted with slight excisions by permission of author and publisher.

workings of language, an account which did not proceed by taking any fundamental concept for granted. An account of the working of language is a theory of meaning, for to know how an expression functions, taken as part of the language, is just to know its meaning. So Frege's philosophy, so far as it is concerned with language generally, rather than specifically with mathematics, is largely constituted by his theory of meaning. It may be labelled 'philosophy of language', rather than 'theory of meaning', if one wishes: but either title is to be preferred to 'philosophy of logic' or 'philosophical logic', for the reason we have just seen; namely, if the term 'logic' is construed in its proper sense, as the study of the relation of *consequence* between statements, then Frege's philosophical concerns go a long way beyond anything that is the proper concern of the logician.

Frege drew, within the intuitive notion of meaning, a distinction between three ingredients: sense, tone and force. That is to say, he distinguished between these three things. He does not use any word to express the general notion of 'meaning', as I have here used the word, and therefore does not claim sense, tone and force as being ingredients in anything more general. Nevertheless, it is plain, from the accounts he gives of these notions, that a difference between two expressions, or two sentences, in respect of any of these three features – a difference in sense, in tone or in force – would ordinarily be accounted a difference in meaning; a mistake about the sense, tone or force intended to be understood as attached to a sentence or expression would ordinarily be accounted a misunderstanding of its meaning. Therefore, we may reasonably say that Frege discerns three ingredients within the intuitive notion of meaning: or, perhaps better, that he proposes to replace the intuitive notion of meaning by the three notions of sense, tone and force.

NS 209 (193); NS 214 (198)   What I have here called 'tone' Frege refers to as 'lighting' or 'colouring', but these are less natural metaphors in English, and we may stick to the term 'tone'. Frege also makes a celebrated distinction between the notion of sense and another notion, his term for which has come to be conventionally translated 'reference'. Frege's actual word is, of course, '*Bedeutung*', which is simply the German word for 'meaning': but one cannot render '*Bedeutung*', as it occurs in Frege, by 'meaning', without a very special warning. The word 'reference' does not, I think, belie Frege's intention, though it gives it much more explicit expression: its principal disadvantage is that it has also become customary to translate the cognate verb '*bedeuten*' by the non-cognate verbal phrase 'stand for'. The tradition is unfortunate, but it is estab-

lished, and I shall therefore for the most part follow it, giving notice
when I use some other expression for the noun '*Bedeutung*' or the verb
'*bedeuten*'.

What the customary translation of these words does correctly register
is that Frege's distinction between sense and reference could not
correctly be called a 'distinction between two ingredients in the intuitive notion of meaning'. Reference, as Frege understands it, is not an
ingredient in meaning at all: someone who does not know the reference
of an expression does not show thereby that he does not understand,
or only partially understands, the expression. Reference, for Frege, is
a notion required in the theory of meaning – in the general account of
how language functions – just as the notion of truth is so required: but
the reference of a term is no more part of what is ordinarily understood
as its meaning than the truth-value of a sentence is.

To the sense of a word or expression belong only those features of
its meaning which are relevant to the truth-value of some sentence in
which it may occur: differences in meaning which are not so relevant
are relegated to the tone of the word or expression. Thus the words
'dead' and 'deceased' do not differ in sense: the replacement of one by
the other could change neither the meaningfulness nor the truth-value
of any sentence; in so far as they differ in meaning at all, then, the
difference lies in their tone. Another celebrated example – given by
Frege in *Begriffsschrift* – is the difference in meaning between the
connectives 'and' and 'but'; the replacement of either by the other could
not alter the truth or falsity of what was said. (It could, in certain cases
– e.g. 'all but he', 'husband and wife', 'bacon and eggs' – destroy its
meaningfulness; this is not so, however, when the words connect whole
clauses.) 'Tone' has here been defined in a ragbag way, which will have
to be modified subsequently if we are to leave room for the third
ingredient in meaning, force; moreover, there is no reason to suppose
that all those variations in meaning, between expressions having the
same sense (in Frege's restricted use of 'sense'), which Frege counts as
differences in tone, are uniform in kind. Frege did apparently suppose
this. He accounts for tone as a matter of the association with a word
or expression of certain 'ideas' (*Vorstellungen*), by which he means
mental images. This is not a particularly plausible explanation of the
phenomenon: we indeed speak of words which carry the same sense
as having different associations, but we should be hard put to it to
describe the distinct mental images called up by hearing the words
'dead' and 'deceased', or 'sweat' and 'perspiration', still less by 'and'
and 'but'. Frege makes a poor explanation worse by suggesting that

BW 102
(67);
NS 152
(140)

SB 31;
Ged
63 (9)

Bs 7

NS 151–2
(139–40)

SB 30;
Huss 317 mental images are incommunicable in principle: no two people can ever know that they have the same mental image. It would follow that tone was a feature of meaning which was, in principle, subjective. This conclusion is a simple contradiction. Meaning, under any theory whatsoever, cannot be *in principle* subjective, because meaning is a matter of what is *conveyed* by language. Someone may, by mistake or design, attach a meaning to some word different from that which anyone else attaches to that word: but the meaning must be something that *could* be conveyed to another by the use of that word, and it must be such that it could be conveyed to another that the person in question was attaching that meaning to the word; if not, it would simply not be a meaning at all.

Even were Frege's explanation of tone plausible, namely that it consists in a propensity which the use of a word has to call up certain mental images, it would not follow that tone was subjective in principle, since Frege was mistaken in supposing mental images to be incommunicable in principle. Tone is not, however, in itself any more subjective than sense: the difference in meaning between 'and' and 'but' is just as objective a feature, requiring to be grasped by anyone who wishes to speak English, as is that between 'and' and 'or'. In fact, the difference in tone between 'and' and 'but' is plainly a counter-example to Frege's general account of such differences as having to do with Bs 7; Ged
64 (9) mental images: in *Begriffsschrift* he says that by using the word 'but' a speaker hints that what follows is different from what you might at first suppose. A hint is evidently not the production of a mental image. Because Frege's account of the word 'but' has since become canonical, and because large theoretical claims have been based on such examples, it is worth pausing to note its incorrectness. The claims in question are to the existence of a basic distinction between *asserting* something and merely *suggesting* (or, in a special sense, 'implying') it: if what is merely suggested by a statement does not hold, the statement will not be *false*, but only *inappropriate*. It is difficult a priori to see how there could be a place for such a distinction: how can there be two different ways in which a statement may be factually incorrect, or two different ways of conveying by means of a sentence that something is the case? This initial resistance is overcome by the production of plausible examples: for instance, the use of 'but', explained as in Frege's account, is given as a case of suggesting what is not actually stated. But, of course, Frege's account of 'but' is incorrect: the word is indeed used to hint at the presence of some contrast; but not necessarily one between what the second half of the sentence asserts, and what you would expect, knowing the

first half to be true. It has even been claimed that the function of 'but' in 'She was poor, but she was honest' is to suggest that anyone who is poor is unlikely to be honest. But the speaker may have had quite a different contrast in mind, e.g. that poverty is undesirable but honesty desirable. If a club committee is discussing what speakers to invite, and someone says, 'Robinson always draws large audiences', a reply might be, 'He always draws large audiences, but he is in America for a year'; the objector is not suggesting that a popular speaker is unlikely to go to America, but that, while Robinson's popularity as a speaker is a reason for inviting him, his being in America is a strong reason against doing so. The word 'but' is used to hint that there is some contrast, relevant to the context, between the two halves of the sentence: no more can be said, in general, about what kind of contrast is hinted at. It is the indefiniteness of the contrast, and the vagueness of the notion of relevance, that resolve the mystery of the distinction between asserting and suggesting: while we should regard a man's use of 'but' as inappropriate if he was unable to mention a contrast we considered relevant, or genuine, examples of this kind can furnish no foundation for the view that we can assign any *definite* condition as a condition for the appropriateness rather than the truth of a statement.

'But' is a very special kind of example of tone – an example for which Frege's talk of mental images is totally out of place; is there any ground for thinking that, in more typical cases, tone is subjective in a way that sense is not? It is true, indeed, that an individual may invest a word with a tone which it does not have for most speakers of the language; but, equally well, someone may attach a sense to a word different from the sense attached by others. In either case, if he discovers his divergence from other speakers, he can allow for this in interpreting the words of others; in either case, he will at first, when he has only recently discovered his mistake, have some difficulty in resisting the misinterpretation which was previously habitual with him, and in remembering to understand the word as having its intended and customary meaning. Two circumstances mislead us into thinking of tone as a more subjective feature of a word's meaning than its sense. Let us call the meaning which we are disposed to allot to a word, straight off, without reflection, our 'impression' of its meaning. Someone who has only just started to learn a language probably has no impression of the meaning of several words which he has learned, but whose meaning he can recall only by an effort: for someone who speaks a language fluently and correctly, his impression of the meaning of the words of the language will coincide with their true meaning. If someone has been habitually

Michael Dummett

disposed to misinterpret a word, his impression of its meaning will continue for some time to be the same even after he has found out that he had been understanding it incorrectly; and this applies to sense as well as tone; he has to reflect in order to bring to mind that the word does not have the sense which he is inclined straight off to attach to it. Now, in terms of this notion of an impression of meaning, we can state two differences between sense and tone. First, an incorrect impression of sense is normally gained only by having, at some time, mistakenly supposed that the word was intended to convey that sense which corresponds to the impression; e.g. the word 'incumbency' makes on me the impression of having the sense of applying to the act of lying down in bed, because in childhood I guessed at that sense for it, and for some time took it as having that sense. But an incorrect impression of tone may often be generated by experiences having nothing to do with any mistake about the tone the word is conventionally intended to carry – by, as we say, a particular association which the word has for me, which gives it a special flavour which I cannot dispel, although I have been aware throughout that that has nothing to do with the meaning which the word has for most people. Secondly, in some familiar cases, what is of importance is not a knowledge of the tone which a word or phrase has, in virtue of its commonly accepted meaning, but, precisely, the impression of tone. The most straightforward such case is the evocative – as opposed to the expressive – use of language. If a speaker selects words which serve to convey, along with the content of what he is saying, an attitude of respect on his part to the one he is addressing, his words fulfil an *expressive* function: the hearer can recognize, from the conventions governing the use of the words, that the speaker is intending to convey an attitude of respect towards him. Some languages, e.g. Javanese, possess a whole parallel vocabulary for this purpose. The expressive function is fulfilled as long as the hearer recognizes the attitude which it was the intention of the speaker to convey; it is irrelevant what feelings they evoke in the hearer. The evocative use of language is quite different: here the primary purpose is not necessarily fulfilled by the hearer's recognition of the intention underlying the selection of the words. For instance, words may be used with the intention of arousing in the hearers a sense of pathos: this is, of course, in part a matter of the content of what is said – of their *sense*, in Frege's technical use – but also in part depends on the manner of expression, i.e. on the tone of the words used. In order that the words should have the desired effect through their tone, it is necessary that the hearer's *impression* of the tone should be one of

SB 31

NS 152
(140)

pathos: if, for example, through accident the words used have, for the hearer, comic or obscene associations, the utterance will have misfired. It will not be saved by the mere fact that the hearer is aware that these associations are private to himself, that the words are ordinarily taken as having pathetic overtones, and that it was for this purpose that the speaker used them: for the primary purpose of the evocative use of language does not operate through the hearer's recognition of the speaker's intention, but through their effect in arousing in the hearer a mood or an attitude. Literary effects frequently depend upon skilled attention to the evocative power of words. The evocative use of language does, therefore, depend, in a way in which no other use of language does, upon the dispositions of the individual hearer to react in certain ways. But to conclude lightly from this that tone is always a subjective matter is wrongly to assimilate the expressive to the evocative use, and at the same time to overlook the fact that the two uses between them do not exhaust the function of tone: for instance, the use of the word 'but' rather than 'and' does not serve to convey any attitude on the part of the speaker, in the sense in which a speaker may evince, e.g., a respectful, apologetic or regretful attitude.

The carelessness of Frege's treatment of tone was due to his lack of interest in it: for him it is a very secondary feature of meaning. The NS 153 things he incorrectly says about tone serve principally to contrast with (141) his view of sense: the sense of a word has nothing to do with any propensity the word may have to call up mental images in the mind of the hearer, and is something wholly objective. It is of much more importance that Frege truly insisted on these characteristics of sense than that he incorrectly ascribed the opposite characteristics to tone.

The sense of an expression is, to repeat, that part of its meaning which is relevant to the determination of the truth-value of sentences Gg I 32 in which the expression occurs. This characterization of the notion of sense serves, indeed, to distinguish sense from other ingredients in meaning: but, for the rest, it is, in itself, purely programmatic. We can get no grasp on the sort of thing which Frege took the sense of a word or expression to consist in without scrutinizing the distinction which he drew between sense and reference.

Frege's notion of reference is best approached via the semantics which he introduced for formulas of the language of predicate logic. An interpretation of such a formula (or set of formulas) is obtained by assigning entities of suitable kinds to the primitive non-logical constants occurring in the formulas. We may assume they are of the following five kinds: individual constants; unary function symbols; binary function symbols; one-place predicates; and (two-place) relational expressions. The interpretation will assign to each individual constant an object; to each unary function symbol a unary function, defined for every object, and having an object as value for each argument; to each binary function symbol, a binary function, defined for every ordered pair of objects, and having, for every pair of arguments, an object as value; to each one-place predicate, a property, defined over every object (i.e. it is in some manner specified, for each object, that that object has, or that it lacks, that property); and, to every two-place relational expression, a binary relation, likewise defined over every ordered pair of objects. Terms are specified as expressions built up, starting with individual constants, by (possibly reiterated) application of the function symbols: each term then has some object as its denotation, under the obvious recursive stipulation that an individual constant denotes the object assigned to it under the interpretation, and that a term formed by applying a function symbol to some term or pair of terms denotes the value of the function assigned by the interpretation to that function symbol for the denotation(s) of the term(s) to which it is being applied as argument(s). Finally, an atomic sentence formed by attaching a one-place predicate to a term is stipulated as true, under the interpretation, if the object denoted by the term has the property assigned by the interpretation to the predicate, false if it lacks the property; likewise, an atomic sentence formed by attaching a two-place relational expression to a pair of terms is true if the objects denoted by the terms stand in the relation assigned by the interpretation to the relational expression, and false if they do not so stand. Complex sentences formed by means of sentential operators and quantifiers are then assigned truth-values by means of the usual inductive stipulation, starting with the assignment of truth-values to the atomic sentences as a base.

Such a semantics – such a notion of 'interpretation' as applied to sentences constructed after the pattern of Frege's symbolic language – provides us with an account of the truth-conditions of the sentences of the language that is entirely adequate for the purposes of the logician, and thus enables him to define the semantic notion of logical consequence and to frame the conceptions of soundness and completeness for a given set of formal rules of deduction. It is precisely such a notion of interpretation that Frege has in mind when he speaks of 'reference'. Indeed, this is to put the matter the wrong way round. Rather, he uses the very same notion of reference in his philosophical discussions of language – of the theory of meaning – and in his exposition of the intended interpretation of his formal system in *Grundgesetze der Arith-*

metik, that is, in the prose accompaniment to the symbolic text which sets out the semantics of the system. It is thus plain that his notion of reference coincides with the notion of an interpretation for formulas of predicate logic as currently employed in mathematical logic. Why, then, do we need a notion of sense as well as a notion of reference?

A very bad answer, sometimes given to this question, would be that the notion of sense is needed by Frege to explain operators which, in Quine's terminology, create opaque contexts – expressions like 'necessarily' and '. . . believes that . . .'. It is true enough that Frege does deploy his notion of sense in treating of such expressions: he says that, within opaque contexts, a term stands for what, in ordinary contexts, constitutes its sense. But, obviously, it would be useless to offer any such explanation unless it had first been established that there is something which, in ordinary contexts, constitutes the sense of a term: so we must be satisfied that there is a prior need for a notion of sense, as possessed by expressions occurring in ordinary contexts, before we can invoke this notion to explain opaque contexts.

The question, why there is a need for ascribing sense as well as reference to expressions, may be put in a sharper form, namely: how is there room for any notion of sense, as distinct from reference, given the way in which the notion of sense has been characterized? The notion of sense was characterized by laying down that only those features of the meaning of a word belong to its sense which are relevant to determining the truth-value of sentences containing it. But, once the reference of each word in a sentence has been determined, the truth-value of the sentence is thereby determined. It was just because of this that we were able to assign, non-effectively but determinately, a truth-value to each sentence in the language of predicate logic, relative to some interpretation which fixed the references of the non-logical constants: and in any case Frege himself is explicit, and insistent, that the replacement in any sentence of some word or expression by another having SB 33, 35 the same references leaves the truth-value of the whole unchanged. It thus appears that the sense of an expression must coincide with its reference, or, at least, that there must be a one-one correspondence between senses and references. Yet, notoriously, Frege held that many senses could correspond to the same reference. How, then, could he find room for such a notion of sense at all?

The solution to the dilemma has already been stated: reference is not an ingredient of meaning. If reference were an ingredient of meaning, then indeed the reference of a word would exhaust – or determine – its sense, since nothing more would need to be known about its meaning in order to fix the truth-value of any sentence in which it occurred (to make allowance for opaque contexts, we ought to say 'in which it occurred as having its ordinary reference'). There would then genuinely be no room for a notion of sense to be squeezed in between reference and tone. But reference is *not* an ingredient of meaning, and so sense can still be explained as constituting that part of the meaning of a word or expression which needs to be grasped in order to decide the truth-values of sentences containing it; and this means: that part of its meaning which determines its reference. Any feature of the meaning of a word which does not affect the reference that it has does not belong to its sense: it in no way follows that two words with the same reference must have the same sense.

What is meant by saying that 'reference is not an ingredient in meaning'? Meaning is an intuitive notion, and a fairly imprecise one: how can we decide the truth of a claim that something does or does not form an ingredient in it, and how can any important philosophical point hang upon the justice of such a claim? In any case, how can such a claim be a representation of Frege's views? We have seen that Frege did not employ any word to cover meaning in the generic sense of that word, in a sense in which it embraces the things which he calls tone, sense and force; moreover, the ordinary German word for 'meaning' he employs in the technical sense which we are conventionally translating 'reference': how, then, can any thesis of Frege's be expressed by the claim that tone, sense and force are ingredients of meaning, but reference is not?

These are very natural objections: but I think that if we seek to understand the claim that reference is not an ingredient of meaning, it will be seen to accord well with Frege's way of looking at the matter, although not with his way of expressing it. Many philosophers, Wittgenstein included, have inveighed against the practice of 'hypostatizing' or 'reifying' meanings – taking meanings to be entities with which words are associated. It is often a little hard to see what conception it is that they find so harmful – what would count as an instance of such illicit hypostatization: but no doubt it is a salutary practice to replace an inquiry into what meaning is by an inquiry into the application or elucidation of certain complex phrases containing the word 'meaning'; thus we may ask under what conditions we wish to say that an expression, in particular a sentence, has a meaning or lacks one; or under what conditions two expressions do or do not have the same meaning. In this way, we may substitute for an inquiry into the nature of meaning one into the nature of significance (meaningfulness) or of synonymy (sameness of meaning). Neither type of inquiry is, however, likely to lead to a satisfactory account of meaning as we intuitively apprehend this notion. Rather, the complex phrase on which attention needs to be concentrated is 'knowing the meaning of . . .': a theory of meaning is a theory of *understanding*. What we have to give an account of is what a person knows when he knows what a word or expression means, that is, when he understands it. The capacity to use a language is a highly complex ability. Our difficulty lies, not so much in explaining how human beings acquire this ability, as in giving any clear account of what the ability consists in, when acquired – an account, that is, which does not itself employ any concepts which presuppose the notion of understanding, or being able to use, language. An account of understanding language, i.e. of what it is to know the meanings of words and expressions in the language, is thus at the same time an account of how language functions, that is, not only of how it does what it does, but of what it is that it does. No doubt, once we have a workable account of what it is, in general, to know the meaning of a word or expression, we shall derive, as a by-product, an account of what it is for two expressions to have the same meaning, or for an expression to have a meaning at all. Even if we do not, it is no great matter: it is knowing the meaning – understanding – which remains the important concept.

Thus what we are going to understand as a possible ingredient in meaning will be something which it is plausible to say constitutes part of what someone who understands the word or expression implicitly grasps, and in his grasp of which his understanding in part consists. The possession of reference by a word or expression consists in an association between it and something in the world – something of an appropriate logical type, according to the logical category to which the word belongs. To claim that reference is not an ingredient in meaning is, therefore, to claim that our understanding a word or expression never consists, even in part, merely in our associating something in the world with that word or expression.

The claim does not mean any more than this. It does not mean that reference has nothing to do with meaning. On the contrary, on Frege's view, it is precisely via the reference of the words in a sentence that its truth-value is determined. The sense of a word – as opposed to any other ingredient its meaning may have – constitutes the contribution which it makes to determining the truth-conditions of sentences in which it occurs precisely by associating a certain reference with it. The semantic account, formulated entirely in terms of reference, thus quite correctly displays the way in which the truth-value of a sentence is determined from the constituent words of the sentence and the manner in which they are put together. Where the semantic account is lacking is that it does not go far enough back: it postulates an association between each primitive symbol and an appropriate referent, but it does not tell us how this association is established. For the purposes of logic, this is unnecessary: for the purposes of a theory of meaning, it is essential.

The sense of a word thus consists in some means by which a reference of an appropriate kind is determined for that word. To say that reference is not an ingredient in meaning is not to deny that reference is a consequence of meaning, or that the notion of reference has a vital role to play in the general theory of meaning: it is only to say that the understanding which a speaker of a language has of a word in that language – even just that part of his understanding of it which is relevant to his recognition of sentences containing it as true or as false – can never consist merely in his associating a certain thing with it as its referent; there must be some particular *means* by which this association is effected, the knowledge of which constitutes his grasp of its sense. It follows that, upon occasion, the same thing can be associated with two different words or expressions as their referent, the association being effected by different means in the two cases, and the two words or expressions thus having different senses in spite of having the same reference.

A terminological note is needed at this point. Frege almost always uses the noun '*Bedeutung*' to apply to the actual thing for which a word stands, though the verb '*bedeuten*' signifies the relation between them. It is nevertheless desirable to be able to draw the distinction between the relation and the thing to which the word is so related; for the latter we may employ the word 'referent'. We shall therefore henceforth use the abstract noun 'reference' only as applying to the relation between the word and the thing, or to the property of standing for something, or, again, to the property of standing for some particular given thing – context should resolve ambiguities between these three uses; but we shall use the word 'referent' as applying to the thing for which the word stands.

It should now be clear that the thesis which we expressed in such unFregean language, that reference is not an ingredient in meaning, not only has a clear sense, but is in complete consonance with Frege's views. These views were set out for the first time in the celebrated article 'Über Sinn und Bedeutung', in which the distinction between the two notions was for the first time explicitly drawn. In that article, Frege approaches the matter in the first place in connection with singular terms ('proper names'). The referent of a proper name is an object: in the standard semantics for the language of predicate logic, each individual constant (i.e. simple or primitive proper name) is assigned an object, or, as we should now say, an element of the domain that has been specified as the range of the individual variables, and each function-symbol is assigned a function of appropriate degree from objects to objects (from the domain into the domain); in terms of these assignments, it is then possible to define inductively a mapping of each term on to an object (an element of the domain), called its denotation. The notion of reference, for proper names, thus coincides with that of denotation, as used in the standard semantics. If the language contains any higher-order term-forming operators, for instance a class abstraction operator or a description operator, operators, namely, which form a term when attached to a first-order predicate, thus binding the variable in the argument-place of the predicate, then to each such operator must be made to correspond a mapping of first-order properties on to objects, so as to confer a reference (denotation) on the terms formed by means of it. Thus, for instance, the description operator 'the x such that . . . x . . .' must be understood as satisfying the condition that, when a is the one and only object satisfying the predicate 'A(x)', then 'the x such that A(x)' must stand for the object a.

Frege now argues that the sense of a proper name cannot merely consist in its having the reference that it has. His argument is set out in terms of the notion of 'cognitive value', that is, information content. Frege asks how, if the sense of a proper name consisted just in its having the reference that it does have, any true statement of identity could be informative. The notion of 'information' being appealed to here does not require any elaborate explication: I acquire information when I learn something which I did not previously know, and Frege is asking how it is possible that I may be in a position to know the sense of an identity-statement, i.e. to understand it, and yet learn something that I did not know before by being told that that statement is true. On the theory that the sense of a proper name consists just in its having the reference that it has, this cannot be explained: for then my understanding of the two names connected by the sign of identity would consist just in my associating with each the object that was its referent, and I can surely not be said to understand the sign of identity if I do not know that an identity-statement is true provided the two names connected by the sign of identity have the same referent. I should thus be unable to understand an identity-statement without immediately recognizing it as true or as false.

In invoking the notion of information to support his contention that the sense of a name cannot consist merely in its having the reference which it does have, Frege is tacitly connecting the notion of sense with that of knowledge; and this is the justification for our representing Frege's views by saying that sense is an ingredient in meaning, where meaning is that which a man knows when he understands a word. For the argument, spelled out in full, runs thus: If the sense of a name consisted just in its having a certain reference, then anyone who understood the name would thereby know what object it stood for, and one who understood two names which had the same reference would know that they stood for the same object, and hence would know the truth of the statement of identity connecting them, which could therefore not be informative for him. The underlying assumption is the compelling principle that, if someone knows the senses of two words, and the two words have the same sense, he must know that they have the same sense: hence, if the sense of a name consists merely in its reference, anyone who understands two names having the same referent must know that they have the same referent.

In grasping the sense of a proper name, we are not merely aware that the name is associated with a particular object as its referent, but we connect the name with a particular way of identifying an object as the referent of the name. Hence two names may have the same referent but different senses: with the two names are associated different methods of identifying some object as the referent of either name, although it happens that it is the same object which satisfies the two pairs of conditions of such identification. Such an account can hardly be doubted when complex 'proper names' (singular terms) are in question; when, for example, one of the two terms presents its referent as the value of a certain function for a certain argument, and the other presents it as the value of a different function for a different argument; or when we have two definite descriptions, formed by attaching the description operator (represented in natural language by the definite article) to NS 95 (85) different predicates. Frege uses the metaphor of a route from the name to the referent: names with different senses but the same referent correspond to different routes leading to the same destination. In the case of complex proper names, the difference of route is sign-posted by the structure of the proper names themselves: we could not do justice to their complexity – the way they are compounded out of their constituent expressions – without acknowledging this difference in the way in which we recognize an object as being referent of one name and of the other. Many philosophers have, however, felt drawn to a conception of a category of expressions which are *pure* proper names: names used to refer to objects, for which it would be true that the whole of their meaning consisted in their standing for just those objects which they named. Since complex singular terms obviously do not satisfy this requirement, these philosophers have sought to apply this account to proper names that are logically simple – words which are proper names in the usual, restricted, sense of the expression. Such a view was expressed by Mill; a more sophisticated version of it by Russell. For Mill, the account held good for those words in natural language which we ordinarily call 'proper names' – singular terms which are simple in the sense of not being explicitly compounded out of two or more words, in such a way that their meaning could be determined from the meanings of the constituent words. Russell perceived that such proper names could have been introduced, tacitly or explicitly, as the equivalents of some complex singular terms – definite descriptions, for example – and was therefore prepared to allow that the ordinary proper names of natural language might – in Frege's terminology – have a sense going beyond their mere possession of a certain reference; indeed, he became convinced that they all actually did. But he was still convinced that there must be a category of 'logically simple' names – names which could not even be analysed as the equivalents of complex terms, and which therefore had no more to their sense than just their possession of a particular reference.

The example which Frege gives in 'On Sense and Reference' of a pair of simple proper names having the same reference but manifestly different senses has been endlessly repeated – the example of the terms 'the Morning Star' and 'the Evening Star'. These expressions, though typographically complex, may be claimed as logically simple, for we cannot be expected to determine their sense just from knowing the senses of the constituents: for one thing, they both refer to a planet, not to a star at all. Granted the principle that whoever knows the senses of two expressions must know that they have the same sense, if they do, it is also evident that the two expressions have different senses, since the truth of the identity-statement 'The Morning Star is the same (heavenly body) as the Evening Star' was an astronomical *discovery*. All the same, the expressions are verbally too close to definite descriptions to have convinced everyone of Frege's thesis that even ordinary simple proper names have a sense to which there is more than their just having a certain referent. It might therefore be helpful to cite another example

NS 213 (197); FB 14; BW 196 (127); BW 234 (152)

which Frege gives in correspondence, a hypothetical example very similar to one later used by Quine. Frege imagines a traveller going into an unexplored region, descrying a mountain on the northern horizon and adopting for it the name 'Afla' used by the local people. Another explorer spots a mountain on his southern horizon, and adopts for it the name 'Ateb'. The stories of both travellers receive considerable publicity, and both mountain-names pass into common use: but it is many years until these regions are more systematically explored and mapped, and, when this is done, it is discovered, to the surprise of all, that the two explorers had been viewing the same mountain from different angles; owing to errors on their part in estimating distances, plotting their positions, etc., this had never been envisaged as a possibility. It is thus a geographical discovery that Afla and Ateb are one and the same mountain. Of course, once the discovery is made, either one name will be dropped, or both will be used as in effect synonymous. But, before the discovery was made, they provide an example of two perfectly ordinary proper names used with different senses.

BW 128
(80)

NS 242
(224–5)

Such an example would have no force against the view subsequently to be taken up by Russell, for whom all ordinary proper names are disguised definite descriptions (i.e. tacitly understood as the equivalents of definite descriptions): Frege could hardly have been expected to foresee the possibility of anyone's combining such a concession with the thesis that there nevertheless exist 'logically proper names' for which sense shrinks down to reference. Examples of this kind are meant by Frege to controvert only the kind of position taken up by Mill. They have led many to suppose that Frege conceives of the sense of an ordinary, that is, a non-compound, proper name as being that of some definite description; e.g. of the sense of 'Afla' as being the sense of some description of the form 'The mountain seen by traveller A on such-and-such a day on the southern horizon'. Of course, in trying to *say* what the senses of different names may be, Frege is naturally driven to citing such definite descriptions: but there is nothing in what he says to warrant the conclusion that the sense of a proper name is always the sense of some complex description. All that is necessary, in order that the senses of two names which have the same referent should differ, is that we should have a different way of recognizing an object as the referent of each of the two names: there is no reason to suppose that the means by which we effect such a recognition should be expressible by means of a definite description or any other complex singular term. Other writers may perhaps have maintained this: but there is no ground to impute any such thesis to Frege.

Frege's examples of proper names differing in sense but not in reference – both the Morning Star/Evening Star and the Afla/Ateb one – are carefully chosen. They are chosen, namely, so that we do not have much difficulty in giving an account of the criterion for identifying an object as the referent of the name, as employed before it was discovered that both names had the same referent. In the Afla/Ateb example, the identification of the mountain for which each name stands is clearly tied to the reports given and maps drawn by one of the travellers; in the astronomical example, we are concerned with bodies of which all human beings have the same view (at least before the age of space travel). It is different for names of geographical features familiar to many – e.g. 'the Thames' – and, still more, with personal proper names. In such cases, we know a great deal about the object for which the name stands, and we may appeal to any part of this knowledge in determining whether or not an object presented to us is to be identified with the bearer of the name. If, for example, on a walk I come across a small stream, and I wish to know whether or not it is the Thames that I have encountered, there is not just *one* form that my investigation has to take. It is not merely that there are different ways to find an answer to the question – this is usually true: it is that there are many different questions, the answer to any one of which will settle the identity of the river – for instance, many questions of the kind, 'Is this the river which flows through Clifton Hampden?', or, '. . . through Radcot Bridge?', or, '. . . through Henley?'

Here it is not merely that the sense is over-determined, that it carries far more criteria for identification than are required for the sense of the name to determine an object as referent for it. Rather, it is that we can draw no sharp line between the sense of the name and information that we possess about its bearer. What one person may use in identifying an object as the referent of the name may be, for another whom we should ordinarily take as understanding the name, information about the object: one person may settle that a certain stream is the Thames by tracing it to Radcot Bridge, while another may be informatively told, 'The Thames flows through Radcot Bridge.' Of course, this is in itself unproblematic: there is no reason why one should not use collateral knowledge in making an identification. Rather, the point is that there is no one condition, sufficient for an identification, which holds good of the Thames just in virtue of the sense of the name, that is, such that ignorance of it would count as showing that a person did not understand the name. One person might be unaware that the Thames flowed through Oxford, and still be said to understand the name 'the

Thames'; another might be ignorant that it flowed through Reading, and yet another might even not realize that it flowed through London, and still be capable of using the name correctly. This does not mean, indeed, that there is nothing which is true of the Thames in virtue of the sense of its name – for instance, someone who thought that the Thames was in Russia, or even in Wales, would not be using the name as it is normally used. Moreover, any one person, if he is to be said to understand the name, must be in command of *some* correct means of identifying the river: if he knows only that 'the Thames' is used as the name of a river, and cannot in any way tell which river it is the name of, he is in the same position as one who knows that 'beige' is a colour-word, but does not know which colour it applies to; he has only a partial understanding of its sense. The person who thought that the Thames was in Russia might be in this situation: he knows that the expression 'the Thames' is commonly used as the name of a river, and has the false impression that, when so used, it names a river in Russia; in this case, he also does not profess to know more than part of the sense of the name. If, on the other hand, he uses the name 'the Thames' with a definite criterion of identification in mind, one involving the river's being in Russia, then, whether or not he believes that he is using the name in the same way as others, he attaches a determinate but incorrect sense to the name. It remains, however, that there is no one condition *sufficient for identification* which anybody must know the Thames to satisfy if he is to be said to have a complete and correct understanding of the phrase 'the Thames'.

It is in view of considerations of this kind that philosophers (Ryle, for example) have been disposed to maintain such theses as that proper names 'are not part of the language', or that what fixes their reference is not any part of their meaning: such contentions are frequently backed up by quite false assertions about dictionaries, such as that they do not contain proper names, or that they explain them only by saying flatly 'proper name'. (Dictionaries contain few or no personal proper names, but they frequently contain place-names, adequately defined: and names like 'Florence', 'Germany', etc. require transformation even in translating from one European language to another, let alone when translating into, say, Chinese.) It is true enough that, in everyday discourse, the term 'meaning' is often applied to proper names as referring to their etymology ('Did you know that "Susanna" means "a lily"?'): but to legislate that everyday idiom has to be slavishly followed in this respect has nothing to do with the thesis of Mill that Frege was controverting. If someone is to be able to employ a proper name in sentences, or to understand its use in the utterances of others so as to be able to judge of their truth and falsity, he must know more about the expression than just that it is a proper name: he must know some correct means for recognizing an object as the bearer of that name. Mill held equally strongly that someone able to use the name in sentences had to be able to pick out the object which it named: his difference from Frege was that he thought that there was no question of any 'means' of recognizing this object, which might differ from one name to another although the object named by both was the same, but that there was, as it were, a direct mental association between the name and the object. Whether or not that which serves to fix for us the reference of a name is to be counted as part of its sense, or its meaning, has nothing whatever to do with the dispute between Mill and Frege: it is a point which could be raised whichever of them one agreed with, and it is a pretty trivial point at that. Since an understanding of that which is necessary to determine the reference of a name is essential to a capacity to use the name within sentences, in which it occurs as a word along with other words, it seems smoother and more natural to allow this understanding as constituting part of the knowledge of the meaning of the name.

There appears even less reason to extrude all but the fact that a word is a proper name from its meaning when we realize that the phenomenon which prompted this response is not confined to proper names, although it is most striking in their case. It has, for instance, frequently been remarked that the identification of chemical substances may resemble that of geographical objects in that a range of distinct criteria may be used in practice without its being possible for us to single out any one of them as that which anyone who understands the sense of the word for that substance must be aware of. The point can equally be made for animal and plant species, for diseases, and the like. It has nothing especially to do with the fact that in all these cases we may speak of names of chemical substances, species or diseases, that we use collective or abstract nouns and a vocabulary for predicating things of what such nouns stand for, as in such sentences as 'Neon is an inert gas', 'The gorilla is rapidly becoming extinct', 'Measles is infectious': the point would remain the same if we used words for substances, species and diseases only as predicates or parts of predicates. It is likely to hold good whenever we have a word for some complex character, condition or process which lends itself to identification by different criteria. In fact, what brings this situation about is precisely the same state of affairs as that which makes it possible for two expressions to have different senses but the same reference. If the same object – or the same state, process or relationship – can be identified by different criteria, corresponding to two expressions with different senses, the two expressions are likely to retain distinct senses only so long as we do not realize that their reference is the same. As soon as we do realize this, we are unlikely to continue to tie the two criteria to the two expressions: we shall almost certainly come to use either criterion indifferently for the application of either expression. And, when we are unconcerned about the possibility that the criteria may diverge, and uninterested in any systematic display of the interrelation between the propositions we hold to be true, that is, in the development of a rigorous theory, we shall frequently be content that different people may come to acquire a mastery of the application of an expression in different ways, so long as they all apply it correctly. For language to function, it is essential that there be agreement among its speakers about the application of the expressions of the language: it is not necessary that there be a uniform foundation for the principles governing this application.

A closely related point is dealt with by Wittgenstein in his discussion PI 79 of the name 'Moses' in the *Philosophical Investigations*. In a case where the information which we have about the bearer of the name is uncertain or conjectural, we may be prepared to find ourselves forced to acknowledge the falsity of any single statement about the referent of the name, even when, as things stand at present, we should now regard that statement as an acceptable characterization of the use of the name. Thus, for instance, the question, 'Who was Moses?', or, 'Whom do you mean by "Moses"?', could be answered by saying, 'Moses was the man who led the Israelites out of Egypt', or in a number of other ways, such as 'Moses was the man who gave the Israelites their law in the desert of Sinai', etc. But if it turned out that the man who initiated the Exodus was not the same as the one through whom the law was given, who was in command between the departure from Egypt and the entry into Canaan, who was the brother of the first High Priest, etc., then we might well say that, after all, Moses did not lead the Israelites out of Egypt. We should now restrict the range of acceptable answers to the question, 'Who was Moses?'; but we should not have lost the use of the name 'Moses'. We should lose the use of the name – be forced to say that there was no such person as Moses – only if it ceased to seem probable that there was some one man to whom most of the characterizations which we should now regard as acceptable answers to the question applied: but there is no one such answer which, so long as we retain the use of the name at all, we must regard as a true statement.

Such a situation, as we have seen, does not arise only for proper names, but for other categories of expression as well, although, doubtless, it is more common and more striking in the case of proper names. The occurrence of such situations should not, therefore, be taken as a ground for singling out proper names as functioning in any markedly different way from words of other kinds. Rather, the problem which it raises is of a much more general kind: is sense after all something subjective, and therefore without significance for the theory of meaning as an objective feature of linguistic expressions? The sense of an expression was supposed to consist in the way in which we determined its reference: but now it appears that, often, there is no one favoured way to determine the reference of an expression, but that different people may determine it in different ways, and even that what is taken at one time as an acceptable means of determining it may later be dropped as not agreeing with the others. If so, then what is objective about the employment of an expression, what is shared by all the speakers of the language, is after all its reference. It may be that, for any one speaker at any given time, there are certain means by which he would recognize something as the referent of the expression: but this is a subjective, transitory feature, of no great significance in the general theory of meaning. As we have seen, this conclusion, if it is to be drawn at all, would not be confined to proper names: just as, on this account, the only permanent, objective feature of the use of a proper name would be its reference, so the only permanent, objective feature of the use of a general term would be its application.

This conclusion has been, in effect, embraced by Quine. Those who would not wish to draw so radical a consequence have for the most part followed the bad example of Frege, by noting, by way of concession, the facts from which it is drawn, and then setting them aside as if they constituted minor irregularities, without facing the threat which they pose to the whole notion of sense, taken as distinct from reference.

It is conceded, by those who raise this objection to Frege's distinction, that, for any one individual at any one time, it makes no sense to suppose that he attaches the reference directly to the expression: there must be some route that he uses for reaching the referent from the expression, for instance, in the case of a proper name, some criterion he has for recognizing an object as being or not being the bearer of the name. The contention is, however, that the sense, taken as the particular manner in which someone associates a reference with an expression, is neither permanent nor common to all speakers of the language, so that what determines the use of the expression, considered merely as an expression of that language to which it belongs, is simply its reference.

This contention is evidently as far removed from actuality as would be the belief that every expression of our language has a single, unalterable and ideally sharp sense. It is difficult to say whether anyone has ever held this latter belief: certainly not Frege, who was perfectly well aware of the variations in sense attached by different individuals or at different times to the same expression, and of the haziness of the senses so attached. Frege can, perhaps, be criticized for tending to view this feature of natural language as one of its many defects, whereas it is probably unavoidable and certainly highly convenient. But the thesis that there is nothing held constant, or shared between the speakers of the language, save the reference is equally far from giving an accurate picture of what in fact happens. Only what is known about the referent of an expression, and is taken by the individual to be reliable information about it, can enter into the sense attached by that individual to the expression; and only what is more or less common knowledge will normally be taken as part of that sense. That by means of which an individual determines the reference of an expression cannot, after all, by the nature of things, rest upon some knowledge possessed by him alone, at least, if the sense he attaches to the expression is to any extent determined by the way in which he first acquired an understanding of its use; for this understanding must have been acquired either by his having been expressly given an explanation of the expression by some other person, or by his having picked up a grasp of its use by hearing examples of that use in the mouths of others. This will, indeed, leave a great deal of play – a wide range of equally acceptable ways of explaining the expression to another who does not know it, or of equally legitimate ways of determining the application of the expression, say in the course of deciding the truth-value of a sentence in which it occurs. It remains, however, that it is very far from being the case that only the commonly agreed reference of the expression fixes the extent of this range. When sentences of natural language are concerned, the notion of a tautology shades into that of a truism: there is often no determinate answer to the question whether a given statement merely conveys the definition (or part of the definition) of a word, or whether it states a truth known to all. But, although of course the notion

of a truism is not a completely sharp one, there is a clear difference between a truism and a genuinely informative statement, still more a highly
contentious one. Any form of words which can be regarded as a legitimate explanation of one of the words contained in it must express
what, for anyone who already understands the word, is at best a truism.

One might acknowledge all this, but still feel that the concessions
that have had to be made to this objection against the whole notion of
sense rob the notion of its utility, or, at least, of its importance. If we
are not, at this stage, to lose the whole point of the introduction of the
notion of sense, we must go back to the connection which Frege made
at the outset, when first introducing the distinction between sense and
reference: the link between sense and informative content ('cognitive
value'). In order to determine whether or not a sentence is true, it is
enough to know the reference of the various constituent expressions;
but, in order to know what information it conveys, we must know
their sense. If we simply amassed knowledge in a linear, cumulative
manner, no attention to sense would be necessary: a sentence would
be informative for a given individual just in case it was not already in
the stock of sentences he had already expressly acknowledged as true
(or perhaps also of those he was not already disposed at once to recognize as true), and there would be no need to inquire at any later date
just what its informative content had been when it was first added to
that stock, nor to ascribe any particular such content to it at the later
time. But, of course, such a picture of our progress in acquiring information is a travesty. What in fact takes place is a process of continual
revision. Sometimes we are led to reject decisively as false what we had
previously, tentatively or with equal decision, accepted as true. But just
as often we find ourselves in a state of uncertainty, unable to reconcile
the claims to truth of new statements inconsistent with some of those
we had formerly accepted, and with no clear means before us to achieve
a resolution of the conflict. In such circumstances, and in others in
which there is no particular opposition to be resolved, but in which a
doubt has arisen about whether we may not earlier have accepted
certain statements too hastily, we are forced to inquire into the *justification* of statements we had formerly accepted as true. Such an inquiry –
which, according to the nature of the statements involved and the
character of the doubt that has arisen, may be straightforwardly empirical, or philosophical, or mathematical, or a mixture of these –
requires us to determine, wholly or partially, the senses of the
statements into whose justification we are inquiring. Precisely
because just what it is that we can claim to know has been called into

459

question, we cannot allow that the references of the expressions contained in the statements after whose justification we are asking may be determined by appeal to just anything we may happen to know. What is of interest to us is not, indeed, a historical question – by what means we thought of the references of those expressions as being determined when we originally accepted the disputed statements as true; nor is it a sociological question – how most people would regard the references of those expressions as determined. What we are called on to provide is a reconstruction and systematization of part of our language: we seek to *fix* definite senses for the relevant expressions in order to confer a clear content on the question whether we are justified in accepting the disputed statements as true, and, if so, on what grounds. A familiar, fully-fledged, example of this process occurs whenever a mathematical or scientific theory is subjected to the procedure of axiomatization, or when an inquiry, which may be partly mathematical or scientific, partly philosophical, is made into the foundations of a theory already axiomatized. But the same process, in a less penetrating and more partial manner, occurs in everyday contexts, when no highly articulated theory is involved: it frequently happens, for instance, that we are not disposed either to accept or to reject outright some proposition that has been advanced by another, but wish to inquire into his grounds for holding it, and, in the process, require him to fix more precisely the senses of the expressions he is using in stating it. Of course, while we are aware, in making such stipulations of the senses of expressions, that we are doing more than merely recording generally accepted practice, we are also in part responsible to that practice: we seek to avoid making stipulations which would correspond to statements that would not be generally accepted, or to ones which would be regarded as contentious.

The notion of sense is thus of importance, not so much in giving an account of our linguistic practice, but as a means of systematizing it. The picture of language which Frege employs in discussing sense is that of one in which each logically simple expression of the language is introduced or explained, whether by means of definition or (since it is impossible that every expression be defined) by some other means, in a unique manner, without room for variation, to each person when he first becomes familiar with its use: thereafter, the manner in which it was introduced determines the favoured manner in which he may determine its reference, so that, while of course he may use short-cuts rendered possible by further knowledge he has acquired, he will always bear in mind that sense, that manner of determining its reference, which is proper to the expression, and will appeal to that whenever any question arises as to the justification of or grounds for a statement in which it occurs. The objection we have been considering arises from the fact, as obvious to Frege as to anyone else, that this is a highly idealized picture, which is far from corresponding closely to our actual practice in the use of language. Frege's response to this gap between idealization and reality was a false one: to declare that our actual practice is, so far as it falls short of the idealization, defective, and ought to be purified so as to correspond to the ideal. But the response of the objectors, to repudiate the notion of sense altogether as spurious or at best useless, is in greater error. The ideal picture is of importance, not because we ought to purge our language so as to correspond completely to it, but because, in particular problematic situations, we need to impose a new practice, which approximates to the ideal picture, on the employment of some or other fragment of our language, in order to resolve the problems with which we are faced. It is, however, unreal to maintain a sharp distinction between the practice of speaking a language and the construction of a theory of its working. For theoretical purposes it is often convenient to adopt a picture of one language – the object-language – of whose working we desire to construct a theory, and another language – the metalanguage – in which the theory of meaning or semantics for the object-language is expressed. The theoretical ground for employing such a picture is twofold. First, we are aware, from the studies that have been carried out in the essentially simpler case when the object-language is not a natural language but a formalized one for the expression of some mathematical theory, that it is strictly impossible to construct a complete semantics for a language within that same language, provided we demand a consistent semantic theory. Secondly, by separating object-language and metalanguage in thought, we are able to determine, as seems best suited to the purposes for which the semantics or theory of meaning is being constructed, the application of certain crucial terms – for instance, 'true' and 'false' – without the intrusive necessity of being responsible to the way such terms are commonly applied *within* the language (i.e. the object-language) under consideration. But, when the language in question is our natural language, such a separation of object-language and metalanguage is only a picture. In practice, we cannot effect it, for the simple reason that we do not have any alternative language, richer than natural language, to employ as metalanguage: any new linguistic device, of superior expressive power, or with richer conceptual or ontological content, which we may introduce automatically becomes part of our own language, that is, of the natural language which we happen to speak, and, in view of the intercommunication between speakers of different natural languages, corresponding expressions rapidly become part of every natural language. This means, of course, that we can never succeed in constructing a complete theory of meaning or semantics for any natural language: but that is of no importance. It is of no importance, partly because many of the philosophical problems which most tantalize us, and which would be resolved by the successful construction of a theory of meaning for our language, are resolved when we have shown the general lines along which such a theory of meaning is to be constructed, without the necessity of actually constructing it in detail; and partly because other problems that arise, which may be philosophical or may be quite unphilosophical in character, can be dealt with by the detailed construction of only a fragment of a theory of meaning, since what is in question is the manner of functioning of only a particular fragment of our language. Such problems can be tackled piecemeal, and so the continual growth and enrichment of our language is no obstacle to their solution. But the artificiality of the separation between object-language and metalanguage does not lie only in the impossibility of our constructing any language which could serve as metalanguage: it arises also out of the fact that theorizing about our language and its working, theorizing which is carried out within that language itself, the only language that we have, is not an activity confined to philosophers, linguists and other specialists. It is, rather, an activity in which all speakers of the language constantly engage, however inchoately or inexplicitly, and which consequently affects our actual linguistic practice all the time. We do not merely employ the words of our language according to certain patterns, which a theorist could observe from our practice and encapsulate in his theory: we carry with us pictures, often vague but for all that exceedingly compelling, of the kind of pattern which we are observing in our employment of them, that is, of the kind of meaning which they have. Such impressions of meaning frequently have a decisive influence upon our employment of these words. When, as in the sort of case we have been considering, the justification of certain statements is called in question, we are forced to scrutinize these patterns of use, and perhaps to revise them or make them precise, with the intention of abiding, in our future use, by the new precise patterns. The practice of speaking a language and the theory of meaning which gives an account of that practice can thus not be separated, except in thought: they constantly interact with one another. The notion of sense is, therefore, not a mere theoretical tool to be used in giving an account of a language; it is one which, in an inchoate fashion, we constantly appeal to or make use of in our actual practice (as, for instance, when we challenge someone to make precise the sense in which he is using some expression).

Perhaps one or two disparate examples may help here to make more palatable the thesis I have been maintaining that a great deal of half-explicit theorizing about our use of language influences that use. (This thesis has no resemblance to anything Frege maintained: I have put it forward here solely in defence of Frege's notion of sense against an objection he could perfectly well have formulated, but never concerned himself to develop any explicit answer to.) As a first example, consider the long recognized futility of the positivist objection to scientific and metaphysical paradoxes such as Eddington's statement that physics has discovered that none of the material objects we ordinarily encounter is really solid. The positivist answer is to say that the meaning of the word 'solid' is constituted by the application we learn for it when we first become acquainted with the word, so that it simply is not open to discovery that objects like knives and tables are not solid (the 'paradigm-case' argument). But, of course, the fact is that, in one sense (note the expression, which is one *in use* in ordinary discourse, and not just a technical term of linguistic theory), if physicists have shown such objects to be composed of small particles separated by distances many times their own diameters, then they have shown that these objects are not, after all, solid. (Objections on the score that physicists have not shown that these objects are 'really' any such thing are quite a different matter.) For, as well as following the customary application of the word 'solid', the application according to those criteria we were taught to apply when we first acquired the use of the word, we also have a picture of the content of applying it to some object, namely as involving that the volume of space occupied by the object is continuously filled by matter. Exactly similar remarks apply to the positivist attempt to provide an easy solution of the free-will problem, and many other applications of the paradigm-case argument.

A quite different example concerns our use of the words 'true' and 'false'. These words are likely to figure as important basic notions of a theory of meaning for a language; and, as already noted, the application of them which is made in that theory of meaning has no need to correspond in detail with that application of the corresponding words of the object-language (if it does contain such words). Yet it is impossible to understand the dispositions which we have to apply or refuse

Michael Dummett

to apply the English words 'true' and 'false' to statements made in English if we do not grasp that such dispositions reflect an inchoate theory for the explanation of certain sentential operators in terms of truth and falsity. It is commonly observed that our intuitive application of the term 'false' is largely governed by the principle that a statement is false if and only if its negation is true, supplemented by a general disposition on our part to construe as the negation of a statement the simplest plausible candidate for that role. It is much less commonly remarked that our application of the term 'true' to a statement is almost equally tightly bound up with our use of that statement as the antecedent in indicative conditionals. Our ordinary dispositions concerning the employment of the words 'true' and 'false' are governed in considerable part by a half-formed *theory* about an account of the use of negation and of the indicative conditional to be framed in terms of the truth-conditions of the constituent statements.

As a third example, let us consider the attitude we adopt to philosophical revisionists, such as, for instance, the intuitionists in mathematics. By 'revisionists' I mean those who, on the basis of considerations, sound or unsound, concerning meaning, propose an alteration in the established use of certain expressions or forms of statement: thus the intuitionists propose (among other things) to alter our assessment of the validity of forms of argument employed within mathematical proofs. If we considered any established practice unassailable, just in virtue of being established, such revisionists would have no title to advance their claims: they would be reformists in an area where reform was not to be contemplated. The very test of a theory of meaning would be, on this account, its harmony with observable practice: the revisionists would be self-condemned, because their theory of meaning confessedly entailed consequences inconsistent with that practice. But we do not take such a short way with revisionists of this kind: even when we reject their account, we do not suppose that it is a priori impossible for any account calling for a change of practice to be correct. The revisionist claims that he has arrived at his position by an analysis of the actual meanings of the statements with which he is concerned, as we derive these meanings from the training we receive in employing them. But, according to him, we form, by means of false analogies, a misleading picture of the kind of meanings which we attach to these statements, and, as a result, are seduced into certain particular practices in using them which are abuses precisely because irreconcilable with a correct picture of the meanings which those statements have, and which we have not altered but only misconceived. We do not have to

464

accept any of these revisionist accounts in order to concede the truth of the thesis that our employment of our own language is not merely the phenomenon to be explained by a theory of meaning for that language, but already bears the imprint of our own only half-explicit theorizing about it: it is enough that we treat such accounts as at least conceivably correct.

Biographical Note

Michael Dummett has been Wykeham Professor of Logic in the University of Oxford, and Fellow of New College, since 1979. Before then he was a Fellow of All Souls College, Reader in the Philosophy of Mathematics, and a Senior Research Fellow at All Souls. He has been a visiting professor at a number of American universities, and was William James Lecturer at Harvard in 1976. He has been a member of the executive committee of the Campaign Against Racial Discrimination, and was a founder of the Joint Council for the Welfare of Immigrants, and the chairman of an inquiry into disturbances in Southall in London in 1979. His books, in addition to *Frege: Philosophy of Language*, include *The Justification of Induction* (1973), *Elements of Intuitionism* (1977), *Truth and Other Enigmas* (1978), *Catholicism and the World Order* (1979), *The Game of Tarot* (1980), *Twelve Tarot Games* (1980) and *The Interpretation of Frege's Philosophy* (1981). He is a Fellow of the British Academy.

Further Reading

Translations of Frege's works: *Translations from the Philosophical Writings of Gottlob Frege*, ed. and trans. P. Geach and M. Black, 2nd revised edition (Oxford: Blackwell, and New York, 1960); 'Begriffsschrift, a formula language, modelled upon that of Arithmetic, for pure thought', trans. S. Bauer-Mengelberg, in J. van Heijenoort (ed.), *From Frege to Gödel, a Source-Book in Mathematical Logic, 1879–1931* (Cambridge, Mass.: Harvard University Press, 1967); *The Foundations of Arithmetic*, trans. J. L. Austin (New York: Harper, 1960); *Posthumous Writings*, trans. R. White and P. Long (Oxford: Blackwell, 1979); *Philosophical and Mathematical Correspondence*, ed. B. McGuinness, trans. H. Kaal (Oxford: Blackwell, 1980); *Logical Investigations*, trans. P. Geach and R. Stoothoff (Oxford: Blackwell, 1977); *The Basic Laws of Arithmetic*, trans. M. Furth (Berkeley and Los Angeles: University of California, 1964).

See also Jane Bridge, *Beginning Model Theory* (Oxford University Press, 1977).

The abbreviations in the margins of the text, followed by page numbers, refer to the following works by Frege.

Bs *Begriffsschrift* (Halle a. S., 1879).

BW *Wissenschaftlicher Briefwechsel*, ed. G. Gabriel et al. (Hamburg, 1976).

FB *Function und Begriff* (Jena, 1891).

Ged 'Der Gedanke', *Beiträge zur Philosophie des deutschen Idealismus*, 1918.

Gg *Die Grundgesetze der Arithmetik*, 2 vols. (Jena, 1893, 1903).

Huss Frege's review of E. Husserl, *Philosophie der Arithmetik*, in *Zeitschrift für Philosophie und philosophische Kritik*, 1894.

NS *Nachgelassene Schriften*, ed. H. Hermes et al. (Hamburg, 1969).

SB 'Über Sinn und Bedeutung', *Zeitschrift für Philosophie und philosophische Kritik*, 1892.

465

FB, Ged, Huss and SB are included in Frege, *Kleine Schriften*, ed. I. Angelelli (Darmstadt and Hildesheim, 1967).

In the case of BW, the page reference in brackets is to the translation in *Philosophical and Mathematical Correspondence*; in the case of Ged, the page reference in brackets is to the translation in *Logical Investigations*; in the case of NS, the page reference in brackets is to the translation in *Posthumous Writings*. (See the translations listed above.)

A. J. Ayer

Russell: The Theory of Descriptions, Names, and Reality

In Ayer's persuasive and corrective view, Russell's aim in philosophy was to arrive at secure truths about what there is, rather than truths about language. He would not properly be described, certainly, as a linguistic philosopher. His aim, differently expressed, was to assess our beliefs about reality, to examine their justification. This enterprise, however, somehow requires a general understanding of the expression of our beliefs, our statements about the world. This is not a certain kind of analysis for its own sake – getting clear about just what we do in fact mean, and with the question of the truth of the statements left unquestioned – but the pursuit of a particular analysis or understanding such that the statements so analysed or understood can be regarded as true and in no way excessive.

If a metaphor is helpful, our beliefs constitute a mirror or image of reality, and the nature and details of the mirror or image are to be examined not for themselves but in order to arrive at a true account of what it is that is mirrored or imaged. To come to a different view of the mirror or image is to come to a different view of reality. As Ayer would allow, there is both obscurity and promise in Russell's large and imaginative endeavour.

In considering our beliefs, Russell was one with other philosophers and indeed all inquirers in beginning from certain assumptions which embody premises taken for granted rather than conclusions arrived at by argument. Russell began importantly from the assumption that our beliefs about the world must somehow rest, at bottom, on what he called atomic propositions, and that these involve what he called names.

Bertrand Arthur William Russell, third Earl Russell, 1872–1970. Godson of John Stuart Mill, educated at Trinity College, Cambridge. Subsequently taught there and elsewhere. Prolific writer, the propounder of several philosophical theories of lasting significance. Imprisoned for pacifism, and leader of an enlightened campaign against nuclear arms. Married five times.

Such a fundamental name has as its meaning the object for which it stands. His idea, perhaps, was that such names and their meanings must constitute the fundamental connection between language and the world. For something to be such a name – for something to have meaning in the way supposed – it is necessary that a certain object exists. If the object were missing, so would be the meaning, and hence also the name.

In his early philosophy, Russell proceeded from this to the conclusion that there *somehow* do exist entities which in the ordinary way do not exist. That is, there exist entities which are the meanings of such obviously meaningful expressions – which he took to be names of the given kind – as 'the present King of France' or 'the Golden Mountain' or 'the Cyclops'.

Russell was soon overcome, as other philosophers were not, by the want of realism of all this. Furthermore, he became aware of difficulties that do not have to do with expressions for mythological entities and the like, but expressions that do have ordinary things for which they stand. The initial assumption about names of a certain kind and their meanings, if conjoined with the idea that 'Scott' and 'the author of *Waverley*' are such names, and also the truth that Scott was indeed the author of *Waverley*, gives us the mistake that to say Scott was the author of *Waverley* is just to say that Scott was Scott, or that the author of *Waverley* was the author of *Waverley*. This follows from the idea that the meaning of 'Scott', being a certain man, is identical with the meaning of 'the author of *Waverley*'. Russell also took the initial assumption to issue in other difficulties.

His way of dealing with all the problems was in effect to suppose that a very great many expressions which might be supposed to be fundamental names in his sense are in fact not such. That is, they are not expressions whose meanings are the things for which they stand. These expressions contribute to the meaning of sentences which include them, but they do not do so by themselves having meanings which are denoted objects. What account is then to be given of such expressions? The Theory of Descriptions gives what Russell took to be the correct account.

Consider the assertion 'Some man has walked on the moon', and in particular the initial expression 'some man'. That indefinite description does not have as its meaning an entity for which it stands. Rather, it itself, as distinct from the whole assertion, is to be understood in terms of a certain assertion: something exists, or there is something, such that it is human. In place of the idea that 'some man' is a name of the given kind, we have the idea that what it comes to, roughly, is that there is something, at least one thing, which has a certain general property. A general property is assigned to an otherwise unspecified something. (To speak generally, and in the way of logicians, such expressions involve the assertion that a property is assigned to something, x.) In place of 'some man' being a fundamental name, we have the idea that its sense consists in the affixing of a predicate, 'is human', to what is called a variable.

The most familiar illustration of the theory of descriptions in Russell's writing is given by way of the sentence 'The present King of France is bald'. The initial expression is not an indefinite but a definite description, which is to say that no more than one thing is in question. This idea can be captured in a way consistent with the general idea of the Theory of Descriptions, the idea of reducing expressions to assertions.

What we get as an analysis of the meaning of the sentence 'The present King of France is bald' and its contained definite description, is that the sentence comes roughly to this: 'There is something that is now King of France; there is only one thing that has that general property; and the thing also has the property of being bald.' (There is an x such that x has the general property of being King of France, and such that if y has the property of being King of France then y is identical with x, and such that x is bald.) There is the upshot that the sentence – which might well be taken as neither true nor false, since there is no present King of France – is definitely false. It is false in virtue of being taken as asserting that there is now something that is King of France.

It was Russell's idea that if ordinary names such as 'Scott' and many other expressions are not names in his sense, such names must none the less turn up in the final analysis of our beliefs. If they do not turn up in such an analysis as has just been given of 'The present King of France is bald', then they must turn up in some further analysis of that analysis. In Section 4 below, Ayer gives a further characterization of Russell's names – they are pure demonstratives, related to the demonstrative use of 'this' in ordinary language, as when we say 'This is the man.' However, they are different in being absolutely devoid of any descriptive meaning, of any suggestion as to the general properties of what they denote.

The question arises of what sort of objects could be denoted by these fundamental names. Ayer holds that for Russell, if such a name is to be meaningful in the given way, the object denoted by it must exist, be such that its existence is guaranteed by the use of the name. However, on any tenable theory of our perceptual experience, physical objects do not satisfy that strong condition. The only objects that do satisfy the condition are those which are parts of our indubitable private experience: our sense-data or percepts. The upshot of the doctrine of fundamental names, then, is a view of what can be said fundamentally to exist. We arrive at a view of reality as somehow founded on or constructed out of our private experience.

It is at this point that Ayer in his discussion goes beyond Russell, and indeed in a direction which leads him to reject Russell's supposition that names of the given kind are fundamental to our beliefs. He argues that two roles which Russell assigns to his names, each of them having to do with private experience, can be performed by the use of a variable *x* and its attached predicates, or by more ordinary demonstrative signs that do not have the special feature of Russell's names – that there must exist objects which the names denote. Russell himself, it is noted, eventually came to allow that there was no need to suppose that anything plays the first of the two roles assigned to names – picking out a supposed bare substratum or substance in which properties inhere.

Thus, while Ayer is sympathetic to Russell's inclination to take our beliefs as somehow founded on private experience – and reality somehow to be conceived in terms of private experience – he does not suppose that Russellian names are essential to its description. He does not suppose, as Russell appears to, that an analysis of our beliefs requires the supposition that they involve names of the chosen kind, and hence certain atomic propositions, and that it is this that leads us to the given view of reality. Rather, we can characterize our beliefs in a way which does not depend on Russell's names. What we need are predicates or descriptive signs – whose meanings *can* be identified with general qualities – along with pointers or demonstratives signs, and such logical terms as those which enter into the use of variables. Given this, we do not have anything that pushes us in the direction of taking reality somehow to be a matter of sense-data or the like, whatever other reasons there may be for this.

Russell's philosophy is audacious, speculative and often enough elusive, despite his use of logic and his aversion to kinds of philosophical spirituality and mystery. Ayer's account of it given here, which is elaborated in various ways in the book from which the excerpt comes, does not conceal its difficulty, and directs us to its foundations. In this account of Russell, and in others of his many writings, Ayer carries forward a philosophical tradition of clarity, judgement, explicit argument, and clear-sighted concern with fundamental questions. Like Russell, Ayer has a place in the philosophy of our century.

A. J. Ayer

Russell: The Theory of Descriptions, Names, and Reality

1. His Conception of Philosophy

For all that contemporary philosophers owe to him, Russell's own conception of philosophy is old-fashioned. He stands much closer to the classical British empiricists, to Locke and Berkeley and Hume and John Stuart Mill, than he does to the followers of Moore or Wittgenstein or Carnap. The main reason for this is that he makes the now unfashionable assumption that every belief that we hold stands in need of philosophical justification. Of course he does not think that any philosophical argument is sufficient to settle such empirical questions as the date of the Battle of Waterloo, or even such formal questions as the validity of Pythagoras's theorem, but he takes it to be necessary. The reason why he takes it to be necessary is that we cannot have reason to believe that the propositions in question are true unless we have reason to believe that certain types of entity exist. There cannot be battles unless there are men who fight them and places and times at which they are fought: unless there are right-angled Euclidean triangles, there cannot be any relation between the squares of their hypotenuses and the squares of their other two sides. But whether we are justified in believing that there are men whose bodies are located in space and time, whether we can rationally believe in the occurrence of events which we situate so far in the past as the Battle of Waterloo, whether and in what sense we are entitled to assume the existence of Euclidean triangles, are all, in Russell's view, questions for philosophy. Not only that, but all the questions which legitimately arise for philosophy are questions of this type or connected with them.

The central part which this ontological question plays in Russell's treatment of philosophy has not, I think, been at all widely recognized.

A. J. Ayer, *Russell and Moore: The Analytic Heritage* (London: Macmillan, 1971), pp. 10–17 and 28–47, with excisions. With the permission of author and publisher.

One reason for this may be that ontology is traditionally associated with speculative metaphysics; and, after his early Hegelian period, Russell's attitude to speculative metaphysics of any kind was predominantly hostile. Another possible reason may be found in the impetus which his work has undoubtedly given to the practice of forms of philosophical analysis in which questions of ontology are at least not explicitly raised. Thus there are many who would agree with the view expressed by Morris Weitz, in his contribution to *The Philosophy of Bertrand Russell*, that the method of analysis, conceived as a method of arriving at real or contextual definitions, is the fundamental element in Russell's philosophy.[1] It is true that Russell himself, in his rather perfunctory reply to his critics, does not demur to this assessment of his work, but I am nevertheless sure that it is mistaken. Russell certainly practised the method of analysis, in the various ways that Weitz records, but I can find no evidence that he ever practised it for its own sake. On the contrary, I think it can be shown that he always used it as a method of justification. We shall find that the motive for his search for definitions is that successful definitions reduce ontological commitments. If it can be shown that one type of entity can be defined in terms of another, then we have only one ontological problem on our hands in place of two: in short, we are giving one less hostage to fortune.

This interpretation of Russell's aims is borne out by his approach to the theory of knowledge, in contrast, say, with Moore's. For Moore, the fact that there are physical objects, of the sort that common sense believes in, is not in question. The function of the theory of knowledge, so far as it relates to our knowledge of the external world, is simply to tell us what we mean by such propositions as that there is a lectern in this room: it has nothing to say with regard to their truth. For Russell, on the other hand, the point of analysing such propositions is to try to find an interpretation of them which will give some of them a fair chance of being true: there is no reason to believe that the interpretation which satisfies this condition will be one that accords with common sense: it can, indeed, be argued that the analysis tells us what we ordinarily mean by talking about physical objects, without knowing it, but Russell is much more inclined to say that it proves the common-sense conception of the physical world to be simply false: finally, even if we are able to formulate a set of propositions of which it can legitimately be said both that they imply the existence of physical objects and that we have good reasons for believing some of them to be true, we are asking too much if we expect these reasons to be conclusive; if we can be said to know for certain only what is not problematic, then we do not know for certain that physical objects exist.

I have said that Russell's conception of philosophy is old-fashioned, but this is not to say that it is misguided. The main objection which is likely to be brought against it is that he brings philosophy into a domain where it has no jurisdiction. There are recognized procedures for deciding the existential questions which he raises, and if these procedures are carried out correctly, the questions are settled one way or the other: except in the way of clarification, there is nothing left for philosophy to do. It is an argument of this kind that underlies Moore's defence of common sense; and I believe that a generalization of Moore's argument occupies a key position in the later philosophy of Wittgenstein. I try to show elsewhere that the argument is not cogent, either in its generalized or in its more restricted form. Here, all that I propose is that we suspend judgement. Setting aside, at least for the time being, the question whether there are *a priori* objections to Russell's approach, let us see how he actually conducts it and what are the results which he achieves.

Every philosopher, even a sceptic, starts with certain assumptions. At the very least he must subscribe to some standards of evidence and operate with some criteria of meaning and truth. In Russell's case I think it is possible to distinguish ten main assumptions from which all his characteristic doctrines are derived. In cases where he changed his views, it was nearly always because he put a different construction upon one or other of them.

Seven of these assumptions, of particular relevance to his famous theory of descriptions, are as follows:

(1) There is a special class of propositions which serve as premisses for all the beliefs that we hold concerning empirical matters of fact. Our knowledge of the truth of these propositions is practically, even if not theoretically, certain, in that there are no other premisses from which we could legitimately infer that they were false.

(2) These propositions are atomic both in the sense that they are not compounded out of other propositions and in the sense that any pair of true propositions of this class are logically independent of one another.

(3) The sentences which express atomic propositions are composed of names and predicates. A name may be distinguished from a predicate by the fact that it can occur in an atomic sentence of any form, whereas a predicate can occur in an atomic sentence of only one form: for

example, a three-termed relational predicate can occur only in an atomic sentence containing three names.

(4) The meaning of a name is to be identified with the object which it denotes. Consequently a name which fails to denote anything is meaningless.

(5) The only things which one is in a position to name are one's own percepts and one's own mental states. These things are said to be known to us by acquaintance. At one time Russell talked of our being acquainted with sense-data, rather than with percepts, but he gave up this locution when he ceased to believe that there were acts of sensing of which sense-data could be the objects. Like sense-data, percepts are taken by Russell to be private entities. In fact the only way in which percepts appear to differ from sense-data is that they are not correlative to acts of sensing, as sense-data, for Russell, necessarily would be.

When he wrote *The Problems of Philosophy* Russell was also disposed to include one's self among the objects of acquaintance. He gave up this view when he became convinced, by the time that he wrote *The Analysis of Mind*, that the self could be defined in terms of its experiences.

(6) It is also possible to be acquainted with abstract entities of the sort which Russell calls universals. It is not very clear, in Russell's earlier writings, how widely our acquaintance with universals is supposed to extend, but at least in his later work it is made a necessary condition for any universal to be an object of acquaintance that it be exemplified in one's experience. This goes with the principle that a predicate is intelligible only if it stands for a universal which satisfies this condition, or is analysable in terms of predicates which do so stand.

(7) Things which are not known to us by acquaintance may be known to us by description. It is, however, necessary that the descriptions be such as eventually to relate the things in question to things with which one is acquainted.

Not all these assumptions would now pass unquestioned. In particular, it has become fashionable to reject the concept of sense-data, on grounds which would also rule out the part that Russell assigns to percepts, and it is also, thanks mainly to the later work of Wittgenstein, now generally thought to be a mistake to identify the meaning of any sign, even a name, with the object which it denotes. On the issue of percepts I shall, with a reservation about the question of their privacy, take sides with Russell. I claim to have shown that the arguments, stemming mainly from Austin, Ryle and Wittgenstein, which are believed to discredit any form of sense-datum theory, are not at all cogent.[2] On the other hand, I agree with the Wittgensteinians that it is a mistake to identify the meaning of names with their denotation, and I shall even go further to the point of arguing that there is no good reason why the non-existence of the object which a given sign is understood to denote should necessarily disqualify the sign from being counted as a name. Since it was the problem of explaining how expressions which were apparently nominative, but failed to denote anything, could nevertheless be meaningful that led Russell to his theory of descriptions, it might be thought that this was a serious point of disagreement. In fact, I believe it to be of very minor importance. I shall try to show that, from a logical point of view, the theory of descriptions is largely independent of the decisions which we take about the assignment of meaning to names and the extension which the concept of a name is to be allowed to have. We shall see that the question which the theory of descriptions poses has little directly to do with any problem that there may be about the relation of names to the objects which they may or may not denote. It is rather the question whether names, as opposed to predicates, have any necessary function to perform at all.

2. On Denotation

I have said that one of Russell's basic assumptions is that the meaning of a name is to be identified with the object which the name denotes. This makes it a necessary, though not a sufficient condition for anything to be named that it be capable of being denoted. At the time that he wrote *The Principles of Mathematics*, Russell interpreted this condition very liberally. Anything that could be mentioned was said to be a term; any term could be the logical subject of a proposition; and anything that could be the logical subject of a proposition could be named. It followed that one could in principle use names to refer not only to any particular thing that existed at any place and time, but to abstract entities of all sorts, to non-existent things like the present Tsar of Russia, to mythological entities like the Cyclops, even to logically impossible entities like the greatest prime number. Not only that, but Russell also held that expressions like 'all men', 'every man', 'any man', 'a man', 'some man', all denoted separate objects. 'All men' was supposed to denote the members of the class of men, taken collectively, 'every man' the members of the same class, taken severally, 'any man' a variable member of the class, and so forth. Neither any man, a man, or some man was identical with any particular man, and none of the objects denoted by any of these expressions was identical with the abstract object which was denoted by the word 'humanity'.[3]

Very soon afterwards, however, Russell came to think that this picture of the world was intolerably overcrowded. He ceased to find it credible that to speak of the members of a class collectively and to speak of them all severally was to speak of different single objects, or that any man could be an object distinct from any man in particular. He also found himself unable any longer to believe in the being of logically impossible entities or even in that of possible things which were known not to exist. His comment on his earlier theory was that it showed 'a failure of that feeling for reality which ought to be preserved even in the most abstract studies'. 'Logic', he continued, 'must no more admit a unicorn than zoology can; for logic is concerned with the real world just as truly as zoology, though with its more abstract and general features.'[4]

It was, however, not only the growth in his feeling for reality that led Russell to look for a different account of denotation. He found that the position which he had adopted in *The Principles of Mathematics* raised problems to which it could not supply an answer. Some of these problems are set out in an article 'On Denoting' which first appeared in *Mind* in 1905 and is reprinted in *Logic and Knowledge*. For example, if 'the author of *Waverley*' is a denoting phrase, it has, on Russell's original theory, to function as a name. But on the assumption, to which Russell still adheres, that the meaning of a name is identical with the object which the name denotes, it would follow that what was meant by saying that Scott was the author of *Waverley* was simply that Scott was Scott. Yet it is surely obvious, as Russell remarks, that when George IV wished to know whether Scott was the author of *Waverley*, he was not expressing an interest in the law of identity. Again, if the phrase 'the present King of France' denotes a term, and if the law of excluded middle holds, one or other of the two propositions 'The present King of France is bald' and 'The present King of France is not bald' must be true. Yet if one were to enumerate all the things that are bald and all the things that are not bald, one would not find the present King of France on either list. Russell remarks characteristically that 'Hegelians, who love a synthesis, will probably conclude that he wears a wig'.[5] Indeed, we run into trouble even in saying that the present King of France does not exist. We are required to attribute being to the term as a condition of denying its existence. The same difficulty can arise even in the case of abstract entities. If A and B differ, it can be said, rather pedantically, that the difference between *A* and *B* subsists. If *A* and *B* do not differ, this difference does not subsist. But if the difference does not subsist, how can we significantly speak about it? 'How can a non-entity be the subject of a proposition?'[6]

Russell does not think that any of these difficulties can be met by having recourse to Frege's well-known distinction between sense and reference. On this view, when we say that Scott was the author of *Waverley*, we are, indeed, saying no more than that Scott was Scott, but the way in which we express this trivial statement implicitly conveys the non-trivial semantic information that the senses of the two names 'Scott' and 'the author of *Waverley*' have the same reference. It might be thought that we should do better to construe the utterance as explicitly making the implied statement which gives it its point, but this would not yield the desired result, because in saying only that the senses of 'Scott' and 'the author of *Waverley*' had the same reference, we should not be saying what reference they had. This difficulty could, indeed, be met by adopting the construe: 'The sense of "the author of *Waverley*" refers to Scott', but then we are exposed to the objection that in saying that Scott is the author of *Waverley*, we are surely not talking about the English words 'the author of *Waverley*', as indeed becomes obvious if we translate our statement into French. There is also the more fundamental difficulty that we do not know what senses are, or how they, as opposed to the expressions which have them, can be said to refer. Another odd feature of the theory is that whereas, according to it, the question which George IV actually asked, in saying 'Is Scott the author of *Waverley*?', was whether Scott was Scott, the question which we report him as having asked, when we say 'George IV wanted to know whether Scott was the author of *Waverley*', is the quite different question whether the senses of 'Scott' and 'the author of *Waverley*' had the same reference. This follows from Frege's assumption that when an expression occurs in *oratio recta* it refers to its denotation, but when it occurs in *oratio obliqua* it refers to its sense. It is to be observed that neither of these questions is equivalent to the question whether Scott wrote *Waverley*, which is, after all, what George IV wanted to know.

3. Russell's Analysis of Descriptions

It appears, then, that the main source of the difficulties which Russell has brought to light is the assumption that all the expressions which he earlier classified as denoting phrases have the properties which he attributed to names. This being so, there are two courses that he could take: he could look for a different theory of the use of names, or he could drop the troublesome assumption. It is the second course that he chooses. His theory of descriptions is designed to show that expressions like 'every man', 'some man', 'an English author', 'the author of *Waverley*', 'the present King of France', that is, expressions classifiable either as indefinite or as definite descriptions, are not used as names, in as much as it is not necessary for them to denote anything in order to have a meaning. Or rather, since he concludes that expressions of this kind have no meaning in isolation, we should say that it is not necessary for them to denote anything in order that they should contribute in the way that they do to the meaning of the sentences into which they enter. Such expressions are said by Russell to be 'incomplete symbols', and what he means by saying of an expression that it is an incomplete symbol, apart from its not needing to have a denotation, is that the meaning of any sentence in which it occurs can be spelled out in such a way that the resulting sentence no longer contains the expression or any synonym for it. Accordingly, what is required of the theory of descriptions is that it should provide the machinery for handling descriptions in such a way that they are shown to be incompletes symbols in this sense.

In the earliest version of the theory, which is set out in the article 'On Denoting', and repeated, anachronistically, in the *Introduction to Mathematical Philosophy*, this machinery is rather complicated. Russell takes as primitive the concept of a propositional function's being always true, that is to say, its being true for all the values of the variable. Let us suppose that the function has the form ϕx. Then the sentence 'everything has the property ϕ' is taken to mean just that ϕx is always true. 'Nothing has ϕ' is taken to mean that 'ϕx is false' is always true. 'Something has ϕ' is taken to mean that it is false that 'ϕx is false' is always true, a definition for which 'ϕx is sometimes true' can be used as an abbreviation. Having got so far, we can clearly see how to deal with indefinite descriptions. To say, for example, that some man has walked on the moon is to say that the propositional function 'x is human and has walked on the moon' is sometimes true, or in other words, true for at least one value of x. When it comes to definite descriptions, there is the further complication that we have to stipulate that the function is true for only one value of the variable. This is achieved by adding the rider that it is always true of any object y that if y satisfies the function in question y is identical with x. So the translation of 'Scott is the author of *Waverley*' is 'It is sometimes true of x that x wrote *Waverley*, that it is always true of y that if y wrote *Waverley* y is identical with x, and that x is identical with Scott'.

In *Principia Mathematica*, this whole procedure is very much simplified by the use of quantifiers. Instead of 'ϕx is always true' we can say 'for all x, ϕx'. Instead of '"ϕx is false" is always true' we can say 'for all x, not ϕx'. Instead of 'ϕx is sometimes true' we can say 'for some x, ϕx' or 'There is an x such that ϕx'. Then 'Some man has walked on the moon' becomes 'There is an x such that x is human and has walked on the moon', and 'The author of *Waverley* was Scott' becomes 'There is an x such that x wrote *Waverley*, such that for all y, if y wrote *Waverley*, y is identical with x, and such that x is identical with Scott'. The use of quantifiers not only simplifies the translation, but also avoids the undesirable implication of Russell's earlier formulae that whenever we use a descriptive phrase we are speaking in metalinguistic fashion *about* propositional functions and the extent to which they are satisfied.

With the introduction of quantifiers, it also becomes clear that the theory itself is very simple. It rests on the premiss that in all cases in which a predicate is attributed to a subject, or two or more subjects are said to stand in some relation, that is to say, in all cases except those in which the existence of a subject is simply asserted or denied, the use of a description carries the covert assertion that there exists an object which answers to it. The procedure then is simply to make this covert assertion explicit. The elimination of descriptive phrases, their representation as incomplete symbols, is achieved by expanding them into existential statements and construing these existential statements as asserting that some thing, or in the case of definite descriptive phrases, just one thing, has the property which is contained in the description. So 'The present King of France exists' explicitly asserts that just one thing has the property of being King of France at the present time; 'The present King of France does not exist' explicitly asserts that no one thing has this property; 'The present King of France is bald' covertly asserts that just one thing has this property and explicitly asserts that whatever has this property also has the property of being bald.

The case of 'The present King of France is not bald' is slightly more complicated, because the sentence can be interpreted in two ways, according as we assign a wider or narrower scope to the word 'not'. If we take it as only negating the adjoining predicate, so that what is being asserted is that there is a present King of France and that he is not bald, the proposition will again be false: if we take it as negating the whole sentence, so that what is being asserted is that it is not the case that the present King of France is bald, the proposition will be

A. J. Ayer

true. On the first interpretation, the descriptive phrase 'the present King of France' is said by Russell to have primary occurrence: on the second interpretation, it is said to have secondary occurrence. This distinction comes out more clearly in symbolic notation, a descriptive phrase having primary occurrence if and only if the quantifier which governs the existential statement into which it is expanded also governs the whole statement in which this statement occurs. It is a distinction which is mainly important in the interpretation of indirect discourse. Suppose, for example, that I say that it is not known whether Stalin was Lenin's murderer. If the expression 'Lenin's murderer' is contrued as having primary occurrence, I shall be understood to be committing myself to the assertion that Lenin was murdered, but leaving it undecided whether Stalin was responsible: if it is construed as having secondary occurrence, I shall be understood to be admitting the possibility not only that Stalin was innocent of the murder but that Lenin was not murdered at all.

4. Names and Sense-Data

Russell thinks that there are two ways in which we can refer to an object. We can say of it that it is the one and only object which has such and such properties, or we can simply *point* to it by the use of a demonstrative symbol. In the first case, the object is identified by description, in the second case by name. It is true that even in the second case what we are pointing to, strictly speaking, is still a set of properties, but our being actually confronted with the complex of properties is held to constitute acquaintance with the object which has them. In short, naming for Russell in the end simply consists in a process of demonstrative identification; and the only objects which can be demonstratively identified are those which are directly presented to us through our observation of their properties. Genuine names, therefore, are pure demonstratives, from which all connotation has been taken away. Everything that we are capable of saying is built into propositional functions and then the names do not describe but indicate the particular objects by which the functions are satisfied.

It can now be seen why this theory of names, when its implications are fully developed, requires that the objects which are denoted by names should be of the order of sense-data. It is not enough, for anything to be a name, that it should in fact refer to an existent object, since this can also be achieved by a description. The name has to guarantee the existence of its object, in the sense that the failure of the object to exist deprives the name of any significant use. But this entails that the object which a name denotes cannot be physical, since, on any tenable theory of perception, it is at least conceivable that the physical object which we suppose our demonstrative symbol to be indicating should not exist. If the use of the demonstrative is to guarantee the existence of its object, it must be a sufficient condition for the object to exist that it makes its appearance on just this occasion; what happens at other times or what appears to other observers must be irrelevant. But this condition is satisfied only by what Russell calls sense-data or, at a later stage, percepts, and indeed only by present percepts. If at one period Russell allowed the possibility of our being acquainted with, and so being able to name, past sense-data, it was because he held the view that, in the most favourable conditions, remembering could be assimilated to sensing. In memory, we had, or could have, direct acquaintance with the past, so that an object which figured in our act of memory could be ostensively symbolized in the same way as a present sense-datum. When, in *The Analysis of Mind*, Russell discards the conception of such mental acts, he also, very properly, gives up this view of memory. The knowledge obtained through memory now becomes indirect, being based on the content of present experience. Russell does not himself relate this change of view to the theory of descriptions but the consequence clearly is that any percept which lies outside the confines of the specious present cannot be named but only described.

It appears, then, that the part played by names in Russell's system is extremely limited: so much so that one again begins to wonder whether he needs them at all. A point which he does not bring out clearly, and perhaps only saw much later when, as we shall find, he revised his theory of names, is that while he permits names to work only very short hours, he overworks them while they are working. They are made to perform a double duty. They refer to the substances in which the sensory properties that we perceive inhere, and they also do the work of orientation: in the second capacity the demonstrative shows us where to look for what is being talked about. But the task of referring to substances, whatever their properties may be taken to be, is perfectly well performed, in the case of anything but present percepts, by the signs for quantified variables, and even in the case of present percepts the names achieve nothing more: they do not extract the substances from their covering of properties; they have no penetrative power that signs for quantified variables lack. If names are essential, it must therefore be for the work of orientation. But here we see at once that they are not needed either. It is obvious that demonstrative signs can do the work of indicating the area in which we are to look for the fulfilment of a description, without our having to suppose that there are objects which they infallibly denote. In fact, on Russell's principles, the assumption that demonstrative signs are names makes it very much more difficult for them to do the work of orientation. After all, the main use of demonstratives is to make it easier for other people to take up one's references, and there is going at least to be a difficulty in explaining how they achieve this, if we start with the assumption that each of us uses them to name objects which are not perceptible to anyone else. If we cease to conceive of them as names, we are no longer obliged to relate them to percepts: we can give an account of their employment which would be neutral with respect to theories of perception; so far as this goes, our only ontological commitment will be to the existence of some sorts of context in which they are produced. This is not to say that the question how communication is possible will not still present a problem, or that we are entitled to leave percepts altogether out of account: on the contrary, I have no doubt that Russell was quite right in taking them to be epistemologically primitive. The point that I am now making is that he would have done better not to bring them into his account of reference. Thus, while I think that I have succeeded in showing that the conclusion that names denote percepts does follow logically from Russell's ideas about names, I agree with his critics that it is an excrescence on the theory of descriptions, not because it represents an intrusion into the philosophy of logic of Russell's theory of knowledge, but rather because we improve the theory of descriptions by detaching it from this particular theory of names.

An interesting fact is that Russell himself came to think that this part of the function which I have shown that he assigned to names was not really called for. In *An Inquiry into Meaning and Truth*, he argues that it is possible, at least at the lowest logical level, to dispense with substances. Sensory properties do not need a *substratum* to support them, and the work of holding them together can be done, he now thinks, by a relation of compresence. Unfortunately, instead of drawing the conclusion that names become otiose, he thinks of them as denoting the complexes of properties which he supposes that we perceive. Since this gives names a connotation, there is no longer any difficulty in holding that they can refer to past as well as to present percepts. The complexes of qualities which names denote include spatial and temporal qualia, conceived as constituents of private sense-fields.

But now if the particulars which names denote are to be no more than complexes of qualities, then, so far as their denotation is concerned, there is no longer any reason to distinguish names from descriptions. It can no longer be maintained that the use of the name guarantees the existence of its object, since it is clearly conceivable that the qualities of which the complex in question is meant to be composed should not in fact be found in that combination; consequently, the name will retain its meaning even though the object which it purports to denote does not exist: and from this it will also follow that, just like a description, a name can be significantly coupled with an assertion or denial of existence. It may be objected that the possibility of the name's failing to denote anything is still excluded by the fact that it can refer only to an object with which one is acquainted. But the point is that this is now an arbitrary stipulation: it is not logically connected with the meaning of the name, which would remain the same even if we were mistaken in thinking that we had been acquainted with the object which we took it to denote. We can, of course, decide to use the *word* 'name' only for those descriptive signs that denote existent objects with which we are acquainted, but this division of descriptive signs would not correspond to any semantic differences between them. It follows that we can dispense with names altogether in this employment.

But if we can dispense with names in this employment, then Russell would himself agree that we do not need them at all. For, in *An Inquiry into Meaning and Truth*, he divides names into two classes, those that designate spatio-temporal and other perceptible qualities, and those that have, as he puts it, 'an egocentric definition'.[7] This second class consists of demonstrative signs like 'I', 'you', 'this', and 'that'. And while he still speaks of such demonstratives as names which denote what he calls egocentric particulars, the account which he gives of them reveals that he really no longer thinks of them as names, in any sense which he had previously given to the term. He shows that they can all be defined in terms of the one demonstrative 'this', and then explains the meaning of this demonstrative in terms of the causal conditions of its use rather than in terms of the objects which it may denote. In particular, he now represents the word 'this' as 'having, in some sense, a constant meaning',[8] whereas if he were still treating it as a proper name, he would have to say that it had a different meaning on every occasion on which it denoted a different object.

This completes my argument that the logical development of Russell's theory of descriptions leads to the elimination of names. We are left with descriptive signs, which stand for properties or groups of properties at various logical levels; with demonstrative signs, which are neither names nor predicates but signals, which simply do the work of orientation; and of course with connectives which may or may not be limited to the logical constants of *Principia Mathematica*.

I have included demonstrative signs in the list of materials with which the theory of descriptions leaves us because Russell never thought that one could do without them. It can, however, be argued that they too are dispensable.

Notes

1. M. Weitz, 'Analysis and the Unity of Russell's Philosophy', in *The Philosophy of Bertrand Russell*, pp. 87 ff.

2. See my *Metaphysics and Common Sense*, pp. 126–48; *The Problem of Knowledge*, pp. 104–25; and *The Concept of a Person*, pp. 39–51.

3. See *The Principles of Mathematics*, pp. 55–62.

4. *Introduction to Mathematical Philosophy*, p. 169.

5. *Logic and Knowledge*, p. 48.

6. ibid.

7. *An Inquiry into Meaning and Truth*, p. 96.

8. ibid., p. 109.

Biographical Note

Professor Sir Alfred Ayer was Wykeham Professor of Logic in the University of Oxford from 1959 to 1978, before which he was Grote Professor of Mind and Logic at University College London, Fellow of Wadham College, and Lecturer and Student in Philosophy at Christ Church. His books, other than *Russell and Moore: The Analytical Heritage*, include *Language, Truth and Logic* (1936), *Foundations of Empirical Knowledge* (1940), *Philosophical Essays* (1954), *The Problem of Knowledge* (1956), *The Concept of a Person and other Essays* (1963), *The Origins of Pragmatism* (1968), *Metaphysics and Common Sense* (1969), *Probability and Evidence* (1972), *The Central Questions of Philosophy* (1973) and *Philosophy in the Twentieth Century* (1982). He is a Fellow of the British Academy.

Further Reading

Works by Russell: *The Principles of Mathematics* (1903); *Principia Mathematica*, with A. N. Whitehead (1910); *The Problems of Philosophy* (1912); *Our Knowledge of the External World* (1914); *Mysticism and Logic* (1918); *Introduction to Mathematical Philosophy* (1919); *The Analysis of Mind* (1921); *The Analysis of Matter* (1927); *Inquiry into Meaning and Truth* (1940); *Logic and Knowledge: Essays 1901–1950*, ed. Robert C. Marsh (1956).

Peter Winch

Wittgenstein: His Treatment of the Will

It is no unkindness to say that the future standing of Wittgenstein's work must remain uncertain, given the ups and downs of philosophical reputation over the long run, but it would be rash to suppose that it will not be accorded a major place in the philosophy of the twentieth century. It is safe to say that it is unique, and certainly it has engrossed many philosophers of the century. Some it has captured. A small part of the explanation of these several facts is that it is really two philosophies, not merely different but even opposed in character. Inevitably there are continuities in commitment, but it is very nearly as if the two parts of Wittgenstein's work had come from two philosophers.

This is true of the entire philosophical outlooks of the *Tractatus Logico-Philosophicus* and Wittgenstein's later writings, most notably the *Philosophical Investigations*. It is as true, as a consequence, of his views of particular subject-matters. One of these is that of the will, once conceived as a faculty of the mind, more recently conceived somewhat less grandly as a kind of cause or instrument of one's actions. Wittgenstein's struggle with the notion of the will, certainly a baffling one, and the solution to which he came, is the subject of Peter Winch's paper, reprinted from his book, *Ethics and Action*. It is a paper that illustrates Winch's careful command of Wittgenstein's thought. If it is written from within certain assumptions of that thought, and from a conviction of its profundity and fertility, it is also a paper of intellectual independence. It is not true, to refer to its first line, that it is *only* an exegetical paper.

The *Tractatus* contains a number of reflections on the will. Proposition 5.631 seems in part to assert that certain parts of my body are

Ludwig Josef Johann Wittgenstein, 1889–1951. Born in Vienna of Jewish descent, studied engineering in Manchester, taught philosophy in Cambridge. With Russell, proponent of Logical Atomism. Subsequently developed second philosophy, unlike anything else. Of considerable influence in late twentieth-century philosophy. Gave away inherited wealth.

indeed subject to my will, and some are not, but conjoins this paradoxically with a denial of the existence of something to do the willing,
a willing subject. The ordinary fact of my actions being subject to my
will, and such things as my perspiring not being so, seems also to
conflict with what appears to be a flat denial of the freedom of the will
as we ordinarily think of it. According to proposition 5.1362, what our
freedom of the will comes to is no more than our in a sense not
knowing what our future actions will be, for which contention
Wittgenstein has particular reasons. Furthermore, the mentioned ordinary fact conflicts with the greatly puzzling proposition 6.373 that 'The
world is independent of my will' – *everything* in the world, as it seems.

Winch throws light on these conflicts (p. 491) mainly by way of
Wittgenstein's distinction between two concepts of will, and indeed
what one is tempted to call, perhaps mistakenly, two wills. One is 'the
will as a phenomenon', which is 'of interest only to psychology', and
is a matter of at least some kind of determinism. It is a caused cause
of actions. The other is 'the will in so far as it is the subject of ethical
attributes', or the transcendental or ethical will. The distinction is close
to one of Kant's, between the phenomenal and the noumenal self.
Winch gives an account of the ethical will in terms of a man's having
a certain attitude to the world, or being of a certain spirit. However,
there remains a great problem. The ethical will must somehow actually
issue in actions, presumably by way of the phenomenal will. One large
difficulty about that is the deterministic nature of the phenomenal will,
which is itself an effect of other things within the natural world. This
stage of Wittgenstein's thought, in Winch's view, 'leaves things in a bit
of a mess'. (p. 496)

It is a puzzling fact, for the reason that in this early period,
Wittgenstein did also have on hand at least the rudiments of a wholly
different account of the will, an account later developed in the *Philosophical Investigations*. The rudiments are given in an entry in his notebooks, which includes the following lines. '. . . willing is acting.' 'The
fact that I will an action consists in my performing the action, not in
my doing something else which causes the action.' 'The wish precedes
the event, the will accompanies it.' (p. 497) It is a principal aim of
Winch's paper to explain why this wholly different picture of the will,
making it identical with the action, was not espoused by the
Wittgenstein of the *Tractatus* in order to attempt to deal with the evident
difficulties he encountered.

The explanation rests on the fundamental doctrine of the *Tractatus*
concerning our relationship with the world, including events of our

own bodies. That relationship is made wholly a matter of propositions, which in a certain sense picture states of affairs. The picturing relation is the only one that connects me with the world. Put most plainly, there is no room, in this constricted view of the world and our place in it, for the fact of our *acting on the world*. The outlook of Wittgenstein's later philosophy is dramatically different. In place of propositions, picturing and states of affairs, our existence is perceived in terms, above all, of 'forms of life'. These are human activities or practices which encompass particular actions, standards and principles, and much else. *Action on the world*, it might be said, is a fundamental part of this later view of the world and our part in it. In this picture, it is therefore possible to take up the idea of will as action. The distinction between 'the will as phenomenon' and the ethical will, as it seems, is abandoned.

Wittgenstein was a philosopher driven by his own thoughts, and not one whose first imperative was to communicate them. It seems true, too, that they are thoughts of an individuality which does not allow for kinds of straightforward expression. It is a striking virtue of Winch's overview of Wittgenstein's thoughts on the will that their location and importance in his two philosophies becomes greatly clearer, and that their nature becomes more accessible to us.

Peter Winch

Wittgenstein: His Treatment of the Will

This is an exegetical paper. Wittgenstein said in the 'Preface' to the *Philosophical Investigations* that his 'new thoughts' 'could be seen in the right light only by contrast with and against the background of my old way of thinking'. It has been argued that we are not bound to accept this. And of course Wittgenstein could have been wrong about it – it could be that the thought of the *Philosophical Investigations* is obscured when seen against the background of the *Tractatus*.

However, I do not believe that this is so: and I am going to try here to see what the *Tractatus* background *is* as far as concerns the *Investigations* treatment of the will. I believe this can be illuminating – both as concerns our understanding of Wittgenstein's thought and as concerns our understanding of all sorts of questions in philosophy.

In the *Tractatus* the discussion of the will begins at 6.373:

> The world is independent of my will.

This discussion comes immediately after a prolonged treatment of the nature of causality and of 'laws of nature' in science. It turns into some reflections on ethics and value, which in their turn are linked with the final remarks on '*das Mystische*'. What Wittgenstein says about the will in the *Tractatus* is the tip of an iceberg, some of the underside of which is revealed in various entries in the *Notebooks, 1914–16*. These entries reveal the enormous difficulties which the concept of the will gave Wittgenstein. They also reveal something else and very curious. In a long entry dated 4 November 1916, Wittgenstein clearly achieves a major breakthrough. He suddenly introduces some ideas which are entirely new as compared with his previous entries on the subject and sketches an account which (as Miss Anscombe remarks in her *An Introduction to Wittgenstein's Tractatus*) appears to contain many of the essen-

Peter Winch, 'Wittgenstein's Treatment of the Will', *Ratio* Vol. X, 1968, reprinted in his *Ethics and Action* (London: Routledge, 1972). Reprinted with permission of author, editor, and publisher. Correction of quotations and minor consequential alterations.

tials of the views developed in the *Philosophical Investigations*. Yet none of these new ideas appears in the *Tractatus*. Now two questions which I find interesting and which I want to raise in this essay are:

(1) What is the relation between this new approach and the earlier one?

(2) Why is it not introduced into the *Tractatus* treatment of the will?

I believe that some quite large issues concerning Wittgenstein's philosophy as a whole are bound up with the answers to these questions. But I have quite a long way to go before I can elucidate this.

Let me start by drawing attention to certain apparent contradictions between different things Wittgenstein says about the will in the *Tractatus*. I believe that many of these really are contradictions, but that the difficulties which give rise to them lie beneath the surface and that the contradictions themselves are not quite what they appear to be at first sight.

5.631 There is no such thing as the subject that thinks or entertains ideas.

> If I wrote a book called *The World as I Found It*, I should have to include a report on my body, and should have to say which parts were subordinate to my will, which were not, etc., this being a method of isolating the subject, or rather of showing that in an important sense there is no subject for it alone could *not* be mentioned in that book.

Now there are already internal difficulties involved in understanding this passage. How is one to combine the view that my book, *The World as I Found It*, will have to distinguish between different kinds of event in the world according as their occurrence is or is not dependent on my will, with the view that I, the subject – that is, surely, the *willing* subject – can*not* receive any mention? How then, one asks, is the distinction in question between different kinds of event to be expressed? It looks as though whatever would show that 'in an important sense there is no subject' would *also* show that the distinction referred to is an illusory one.

It might be argued that this difficulty merely rests on a mistaken interpretation: that of identifying the 'subject' here alluded to with the *willing* subject. For in the *Notebooks* (p. 80) Wittgenstein distinguishes between the willing subject and the thinking subject, as follows: 'The thinking subject is surely merely illusion. But the willing subject exists.' Now it is not easy to reconcile this with the view that, in distinguishing between those parts of my body which are, and those which are not, subject to my will, I am 'isolating the subject' *and showing that it does not exist.* Moreover, at other points in the *Notebooks*, Wittgenstein shows himself to be attracted by the idea that thinking itself is an activity of the will and that it is impossible to conceive of a being capable of Idea, but not Will – in which case I suppose that the distinction between the real willing subject and the illusory thinking subject would have to go by the board. Interestingly he also wonders in the *Notebooks* (p. 77) whether this idea of thinking as an activity of the will is not precisely the mistake which is getting him into difficulties. But this is an issue I must shelve till later.

Tractatus 5.631 does seem to say unequivocally that there *is* a distinction between parts of my body which are, and parts which are not, 'subordinate to my will'. Indeed, how could this be denied? I can raise my arm at will, but not change the functioning of my liver – at least not directly, though I can of course do other things, like eating certain kinds and quantities of food, which will result in a change in the functioning of my liver. Any philosophy which ignores these obvious facts would seem to have little prospect of carrying conviction.

But in closely adjacent passages of the *Tractatus* Wittgenstein says other things which are hard to reconcile with this admission.

> 6.373 The world is independent of my will.

And again:

> 5.1362 The freedom of the will consists in the impossibility of knowing actions that still lie in the future. We could know them only if causality were an *inner* necessity like that of logical inference. – The connection between knowledge and what is known is that of logical necessity.

I shall consider this passage more closely in a moment. But it seems clear that in both passages Wittgenstein wants to place human actions on the same level as all other events. And indeed, it is clear that he thought it essential to do this, as appears in an extremely revealing passage in the *Notebooks* (p. 88), which will be very important to what I want to say later:

> The consideration of willing makes it look as if one part of the world were closer to me than another (which would be intolerable).

> But, of course, it is undeniable that in a popular sense there are things that I do, and other things not done by me.

> In this way then the will would not confront the world as its equivalent, which must be impossible.

Now the following points emerge from this passage at the present stage. First, that there are general philosophical considerations which make Wittgenstein reject what a consideration of the 'popular sense' in which I am said to do some things and not others *seems* to imply. Second, there *is some* sense to the popular way of speaking, which remains to be accounted for. Third, when this has been done, there will nevertheless remain something to be said about the will which goes beyond this 'popular sense'.

It will be best to postpone fuller examination of the first point – the general philosophical considerations which lie behind the difficulty – until I am in a position to consider the relevance of this topic to the general relations between the philosophy of the *Tractatus* and the philosophy of the *Philosophical Investigations*. But something must now be said about the second two points; and this means that a hitherto unmentioned, but vital, distinction of Wittgenstein's must now be introduced. In the *Tractatus* (6.423) he distinguishes between 'the will as a phenomenon' (which he says 'is of interest only to psychology') and 'the will in so far as it is the bearer of the ethical' (of which, he says, 'it is impossible to speak'). Now the notion of 'the will as a phenomenon' belongs to Wittgenstein's account of acting in the popular sense, of the difference between those parts of my body which are 'subordinate to my will' and those which are not. It is apparent, e.g. from *Tractatus* 5.136 to 5.1362, that Wittgenstein wants to elucidate this distinction in terms of causality. Exposition of this point is made difficult by the fact that he claims that prediction justified by reference to causal relations can *never* amount to knowledge, on the grounds that belief in 'the causal nexus' is in general 'superstition', so that 'we *cannot* infer the events of the future from those of the present' since 'there is no causal nexus to justify such an inference'. But I do not think that this doctrine needs to be engaged at the present point. When Wittgenstein says that the freedom of the will consists in 'the impossibility of knowing actions that still lie in the future', his point is that our predictions of our own future actions have no different basis from our predictions about anything else. The relation between the will *qua* phenomenon and the phenomenon of the willed action is like the relation between any other pair of phenomena which stand as cause to effect. This is supported by a remark in the *Notebooks* (p. 77), made at a time when Wittgenstein still conflated willing with wanting (which he later came to think of as radically distinct): 'it is a fact of logic that wanting does not stand in any logical connection with its own fulfil-ment'. That is, whether or not what is wanted actually happens depends on conditions other than the condition merely of being wanted. So (construing willing as a form of wanting) I have to discover by experience what events are causally connected with my willing and what are not. I cannot will that anything should be connected with my will; and in *this* sense 'the world is independent of my will'. This is amplified in the *Tractatus*, 6.374:

Even if all we wish for were to happen, still this would only be a favour granted by fate, so to speak: for there is no *logical* connection between the will and the world, which would guarantee it, and the supposed physical connection itself is surely not something that we could will.

But, for just the same reasons, my will *qua* phenomenon is *itself* dependent on conditions outside my control: on other phenomena. Wittgenstein makes this point in the *Philosophical Investigations* (I, § 611) where, obviously restating his *Tractatus* view for criticism, he says:

'Willing too is merely an experience', one would like to say (the 'will' too only 'idea'). It comes when it comes, and I cannot bring it about.

If the world is independent of my will, this does not mean that I am independent of the world. On the contrary, so far as I am to be considered simply in terms of the phenomenal will, I am entirely dependent on the world.

I cannot bend the happenings of the world to my will: I am completely powerless. (*Notebooks*, p. 73)

The world is *given* me, i.e. my will enters into the world completely from outside as into something that is already there . . . That is why we have the feeling of being dependent on an alien will. *However this may be*, at any rate we *are* in a certain sense dependent, and what we are dependent on we can call God. In this sense God would simply be fate, or, what is the same thing: the world, – which is independent of our will. (*Notebooks*, p. 74)

So it is an illusion to suppose that I can exert my will – my phenomenal will – and so make myself even relatively independent of the course of events. Now strictly this is all there is to say; for all that is left for us in any attempt to show that there is any sense in which we are *in*dependent of the world is the 'will as the bearer of the ethical' and of this, Wittgenstein has said, 'nothing can be said'. The reason why nothing can be said of the will as the bearer of the ethical – which I will sometimes call the 'transcendental will', both because it is shorter and also to note the Kantian analogies to what is going on here – are closely connected with the reasons why the notion of the phenomenal will cannot do what is needed and, through them, with the general philosophy of language from which all these difficulties stem. The transcendental will cannot involve us in any relation with particular phenomena – otherwise it itself at once becomes a phenomenon – and so, if it *does* bring us into any relation with the world, it can only be the world as a whole; and about *this* 'nothing can be said'.

If good or bad willing does alter the world, it can alter only the limits of the world, not the facts – not what can be expressed by means of language.

In short the effect must be that it becomes an altogether different world. It must, so to speak, wax and wane as a whole.

The world of the happy man is a different one from that of the unhappy man. (*Tractatus*, 6.43)

Now, whatever exactly this means, it is obviously connected with Wittgenstein's view of ethics as 'transcendental', which is hinted at in the *Tractatus* and the *Notebooks* and developed more fully later in the *Lecture on Ethics*. This view of ethics is also of course connected with his doctrine that the existence of the will *qua* phenomenon does *not* really mean that anything in the world is under my control – his doctrine that the 'willed' movements of my body have exactly the same status as all other happenings. He says (*Notebooks*, p. 84):

A stone, the body of a beast, the body of a man, my body, all stand on the same level.

That is why what happens, whether it comes from a stone or from my body is neither good nor bad.

But as far as concerns the transcendental will, the position seems to be this: values are not to be found in the world; they constitute its limits; they are, we might perhaps say, a feature of how I regard the world; and this notion of 'how I regard the world' involves the notion of an exercise of the will – in the transcendental sense. What I now want to ask is: what sense are we to make of *this* notion of an 'exercise of the will' and how is it related to the notion of the will *qua* phenomenon? (The question is, of course, closely analogous to that with which Kant was concerned in his account of freedom as attaching to the noumenal rather than to the phenomenal self and his attempt to show that one and the same action could consistently be regarded as both free *and* determined.)

In the *Notebooks* Wittgenstein seems to me to suggest two accounts of what might be involved in such an act of will which are quite different and which answer to contrary pulls in his thought. The first account is in some ways strongly reminiscent of Spinoza. It comes at page 81 of the *Notebooks*:

Suppose that man could not exercise his will, but had to suffer all the misery of this world, then what could make him happy?

How can man be happy at all since he cannot ward off the misery of this world?

Through the life of knowledge.

Good conscience is the happiness that the life of knowledge preserves.

The life of knowledge is the life that is happy in spite of the misery of the world.

The only life that is happy is the life that can renounce the amenities of the world.

To it the amenities of the world are so many graces of fate.

When Wittgenstein says, at the beginning of this passage, 'Suppose that man could not exercise his will', he is clearly speaking of the will *qua* phenomenon. He is asking us to imagine that human experience did not include the 'phenomenon of willing' which actual human experience is supposed to contain. But, of course, it is clear from Wittgenstein's discussion of the phenomenal will, that whether man has such an experience or not makes no difference to his power to escape the misery of the world. We *are* all 'powerless'. The supposition here is a rhetorical device to ensure that we do not succumb to the illusion of having some power over the course of events.

But Wittgenstein still asks how man nevertheless he *can* be happy – as if there is some choice that is open to him. I think we must clearly regard this choice as an exercise of the ethical (transcendental) will, which is *not* a phenomenon. And this exercise consists in taking up a certain attitude to the world. Later, on page 87 of the *Notebooks*, Wittgenstein explicitly talks of the will as 'an attitude of the subject to the world'. The attitude of a happy man will be one based on the recognition that the appearance of power created by the existence of the will *qua* phenomenon is an illusion. It seems to me that it must come very close to that 'patience' which Kierkegaard describes in *Purity of Heart* as the state of mind of a man who 'wills the Good', a notion which I discuss in 'Can a Good Man be Harmed?'[1]

The point to emphasize about *this* account of the ethical will is that it is in terms not of a man's deciding to do this rather than that, but in terms of what one might call the 'spirit in which' he does, or suffers, anything at all. The emphasis is on what has sometimes been called the 'inwardness' of the agent rather than on his external acts. It might look, then, as if one could speak of an exercise of the ethical will without running into the difficulties involved in attaching any sense to the idea that human action is the exercise by human beings of power over events: the difficulties, that is, stemming from Wittgenstein's attempt to treat this idea in terms of the concept of the will *qua* phenomenon.

Attractive as it would be for this to be the case, however, it is unfortunately *not* entirely the case. For though the distinction between the man who (to use Kierkegaard's language) 'wills the good' and other 'double-minded men' is not as such a distinction between men who do *these* actions and men who do *those*, it is nevertheless the case that such a man *will* sometimes act differently from other men. Or, if this were to be denied, we should still be left with the problem of giving an account of the difference in attitude between a good and a double-minded man and this would surely involve some reference – as it does in Kierkegaard – to differences in the ways one and the same action may be performed by different men. And such differences, being as 'phenomenal' as differences between actions themselves, do not escape the difficulties arising from the account of action in terms of the phenomenal will.[2] In other words, it looks as though the ethical will must be related to the phenomenal will after all; and some account of this relation is required.

This problem crops up in the *Notebooks* in the following way. On page 75 he writes:

In order to live happily I must be in agreement with the world. And that is what 'being happy' *means*.

I am then, so to speak, in agreement with that alien will on which I appear dependent. That is to say: 'I am doing the will of God'.

Fear in face of death is the best sign of a false, i.e. a bad, life.

Now 'being in agreement with the world' is a matter of one's attitude to the world, rather than of the particular things one does in the world *as such*. Nevertheless, there is an internal connection between the possibility of such an attitude and the particular things one does and has done. This appears from the continuation of the entry I started to quote.

When my conscience upsets my equilibrium, then I am not in agreement with Something. But what is this? Is it *the world*?

Certainly it is correct to say: Conscience is the voice of God.

For example: it makes me unhappy to think that I have offended such and such a man. Is that my conscience?

Can one say: 'Act according to your conscience whatever it may be'?

Live happily!

If one *can* say, 'Act according to your conscience', and if this is connected with the ethical will in terms of which the worlds of the happy man and of the unhappy man are described, then it seems that *a* condition of having the attitude of a happy man is deciding to do certain things rather than others: and, failing an alternative account of action, *this* seems to reintroduce the will *qua* phenomenon.

Wittgenstein faces this problem directly on pages 76–7 of the *Notebooks*.

What really is the situation of the human will? I will call 'will' first and foremost the bearer of good and evil.

Let us imagine a man who could use none of his limbs and hence could, in the ordinary sense, not exercise his *will*. He could, however, think and *wish* and communicate his thoughts to someone else. Could therefore do good or evil through the other man. Then it is clear that ethics would have a validity for him, too, and that he in the *ethical sense* is the bearer of a *will*.

Now is there a difference in principle between this will and that which sets the human body in motion?

Or is the mistake here this: even *wishing* (thinking) is an activity of the will? (And in this sense, indeed, a man *without* will would not be alive.)

But can we conceive a being that isn't capable of Will at all, but only of Idea (of seeing for example)? In some sense this seems impossible. But if it were possible then there could also be a world without ethics.

What Wittgenstein is presumably trying to do with this example is to think of a situation in which a man could be said to have an ethical will, without having a will in the ordinary sense. It is noteworthy, though, that in the example too there is reference to *doing* good and evil: hence, presumably, doing one thing rather than another. And it seems that the notion of the will 'in the ordinary sense' is involved after all: in the decision of the man, for instance, to communicate or not to communicate, his thoughts to another. What sort of 'communication' is in question is not explained. If it is by *talking*, then this seems to involve at least some movement of the body. But even if it is conceived as a sort of immediate thought-transference – telepathy – it seems to me that nothing in principle is changed. For it is clearly being regarded as possible for the man to choose between thus transferring and not transferring his thoughts. And the outcome of this decision is being held to affect what *happens*.

On the evidence of the *Notebooks* it seems to me that this is the extreme limit to which Wittgenstein was able to take the problem, as conceived from within the *Tractatus* position. And obviously it leaves things in a bit of a mess. Now towards the end of the *Notebooks* (pp. 86–8) there occurs a long entry (dated 4 November 1916), which clearly represents a major breakthrough. In it a conception of the will is developed which contains many of the essentials of the sort of view Wittgenstein puts forward in the *Philosophical Investigations*, §§ 611 ff. Here Wittgenstein raises the question: what is the 'foothold for the will in the world'. He rejects the idea (involved in his previous talk about the will 'as a phenomenon') that this foothold consists in any 'feelings by which I ascertain that an act of the will takes place', since these do not have 'any particular characteristic which distinguishes them from other ideas' (cf. the discussion of kinaesthetic sensations in relation to the will in the *Philosophical Investigations*, II, viii). He abandons the idea that the will is the cause of the action and replaces it with the idea that it is 'the action itself'; and, as a corollary, he for the first time makes a clear distinction between *willing* and *wishing*.

Does not the willed movement of the body happen just like any unwilled movement in the world, but that it is accompanied by the will?

Yet it is not accompanied just by a *wish*! But by will.

We feel, so to speak, responsible for the movement.

Wishing is not acting. But willing is acting.

The fact that I will a process consists in my carrying out the process, not in my doing something else which causes the process.

The wish precedes the event, the will accompanies it.

Suppose that a process were to accompany my wish. Should I have willed the process?

Would not this accompanying appear accidental in contrast to the compelled accompanying of the will?

Wittgenstein also seems flatly to contradict the view which appears in the *Tractatus* that I cannot know my own future actions. He says:

Then is the situation that I merely accompany my actions with my will?

But in that case how can I predict – as in some sense I surely can – that I shall raise my arm in five minutes' time? That I shall will this?

Now it is at first sight extremely puzzling that none of these ideas appears in the *Tractatus*, and I want to raise the question why this is so.

The answer, I think, lies in the fact that this new account is quite flatly and fundamentally at variance with the whole conception of the relation between language, thought and the world, which the *Tractatus* expresses. And that Wittgenstein was well aware of this is shown by the remarks which I alluded to earlier and left unexplained:

For the consideration of willing makes it look as if one part of the world were closer to me than another (which would be intolerable).

But, of course, it is undeniable that in a popular sense there are things that I do, and other things not done by me.

In this way then the will would not confront the world as its equivalent, which must be impossible. (*Notebooks*, p. 88)

Why are these things 'intolerable' or 'impossible'?

The reason is surely this. In the *Tractatus* my relation to the world is mediated through, and only through, the proposition. The proposition is a picture of a state of affairs and the relation between a proposition and a state of affairs is always of the same sort. I discover whether a proposition is true by comparing it with a state of affairs – by seeing whether things are in reality as the proposition says they are. But the consideration of willing seems to imply that I can be related to reality in quite a different way: that I can formulate a proposition and then not discover whether it is true by comparing it with the facts, but *make* it true by tinkering with the facts. The point is the one that Miss G. E. M. Anscombe and A. J. Kenny have both talked about in terms of 'practical knowledge', distinguished from theoretical knowledge, according as, given a discrepancy between proposition and fact, what is wrong is located in the fact or in the proposition. Kenny compares, e.g., one and the same plan considered first as appearing in a guide book (theoretical knowledge) and second as appearing as an architect's blueprint (practical knowledge).[3] But to allow anything like this is to allow a role for the proposition totally different from anything that could be accommodated within the general *Tractatus* position. Or, to put the same point differently, it presupposes quite a different conception of 'the world'.

I want now to raise the question: what, with regard to the will, is the nature of the change from the *Tractatus* to the *Philosophical Investigations* account of the way language enters into the relation of men to the world? Two points have emerged concerning the treatment of the will in the *Tractatus* which are important here: (1) will 'in the ordinary sense', 'as a phenomenon', i.e. as involving the idea that there are some happenings in the world which I can control and some which I cannot control, is for the *Tractatus* an anomaly to be explained away; (2) nevertheless, Wittgenstein was strongly inclined to say that the idea of a being capable of Idea but not of Will was an impossibility. Whether 'will' in this context is to be taken 'in the ordinary sense' or 'as the subject of ethical attributes' is not absolutely clear, though some of the passages from the *Notebooks* that I have discussed suggest the latter. I think the point really is that the thinking through of this idea is impossible if the will is thought of in terms of this distinction. The reason for (2) is not made entirely clear; but it seems to rest on the idea that thinking itself is somehow an exercise of the will. Connected with this may be the idea that the correlations between names and objects necessary for language, as conceived in the *Tractatus*, involve an exercise of will. This consideration also counts in favour of saying that it is not the *phenomenal* will that can be in question here, since these correlations are at the *limits* of the world and are not facts *in* the world.

Now, one way of seeing the big difference between the *Tractatus* and the *Philosophical Investigations* is this: in the latter, correlations between words and objects no longer have to be conceived as lying at the limits of the world in any sense which would prevent us from saying anything specific about them. Instead, 'forms of life' are treated as what is 'given' (rather than the 'objects' themselves and their correlations with names). It is argued, indeed, that it is only in the context of forms of life that we can make any sense of the idea of there being objects of a particular category, and *in* making sense of such an idea, we *also* grasp the sort of 'correlation' with a 'name' that goes along with the idea of such an object. But forms of life are, or involve, human activities, things that men do; or better, they provide a context within which we can make sense of the idea of men doing things, in that they enable us to speak of standards and criteria by reference to which human choices are made and understood: by reference to which, that is, we can see what it is for a man to have an alternative before him and to do one thing rather than another. So we can say that the human will is placed much more firmly and explicitly at the centre of the whole account of the relation between thought and the world than it was in the *Tractatus*: the 'human will', that is, in the sense in which it is involved in the 'popular' idea of a human action. It is now no longer a question of building up the concept of human action from the more primitive concept of the will (something which the *Tractatus* attempted and failed to do); rather, the concept of a human action is taken as what is primitive and the notion of the will is explained in terms of it.

In so far as, in making use of the concept of forms of life, we are concerned with actual things that people do and refrain from doing, we are concerned with what the *Tractatus* concept of the will as a phenomenon was introduced to account for. But the new centre of gravity makes it impossible to draw the sort of distinction between the will as a phenomenon and the will as the subject of ethical attributes which was characteristic of the earlier position. For it is now no longer possible for Wittgenstein to speak as he had done about the world as 'the totality of facts' and of the 'limits' to that totality. The argument of the *Philosophical Investigations* shows that it is only from within a given form of life that we can make the distinction between what is and what is not a phenomenon. The role which the concept of an action plays in our various forms of life does *not* allow for the concept of willing as a phenomenon. But to say 'willing is not a phenomenon' is not to say that willing lies outside the realm of phenomena, at its limits, for there *is no* 'realm of phenomena'; and so, in rejecting the notion of the will *qua* phenomenon, we are not forced back on to the notion of the transcendental will as the subject of ethical attributes. If the ethical dimension of human life does involve a conception of the will which differs from that involved in the ordinary concept of acting, then this too will have to be accounted for by reference to the particular features of certain forms of life, language games, and not by reference to any all-embracing distinction between what lies in the world and what lies at its limits. It may indeed be the case that certain language games (e.g. certain religious language games) do make *a* distinction between the world and what lies beyond the world, but, if so, that distinction will have to be understood as it is in fact made in such language games not as a distinction which underlies the whole possibility of language. Regrettably though, this line of thought is not followed up in the *Philosophical Investigations*, and the range of questions which exercised Wittgenstein in the *Notebooks*, which I have alluded to in this essay, is not given any further treatment. I think it is quite certain, though, that many of these questions remain and are not automatically dissolved along with the dissolution of the distinction between the will *qua* phenomenon and the will as the subject of ethical attributes as it had been made earlier.

Let me amplify the point I made a little way back about the way in which, in the *Philosophical Investigations*, the human will is given a central place in the discussion of the nature of language and its relation to reality, instead of being regarded, as it seems to be in the *Tractatus*, as an anomaly which has to be dealt with after the main outlines of the picture have been drawn. There is a very strong analogy between the *Investigations* account of intentional action on the one hand and of following a rule on the other: the latter notion, of course, being a dominant component in the conception of a form of life and in the account of language. This analogy is noticed by Wittgenstein himself:

The grammar of the expression 'I was then going to say . . .' is related to that of the expression 'I could have gone on'. In the one case I remember an intention, in the other I remember having understood. (*Philosophical Investigations*, I, § 660)

And in the cases both of intending and of following a rule Wittgenstein insists on a point which he had equally insistently denied in the *Tractatus* – that when it is a question of my own actions I can *know* what is going to happen (what I am going to do) in a sense which does not imply that my knowledge is based on inductive evidence (or indeed on any evidence at all).

A point I feel inclined to make in this connection – one that Wittgenstein himself does not, I believe, make and which might be regarded as contrary to the spirit of the way he does speak in the *Philosophical Investigations* – is this: whereas in the *Tractatus*, the idea that I can know my own future actions in a way in which I cannot know of other events in the future is regarded as anomalous; the *only* way in which I can make predictions (not amounting to knowledge in any case) is by inductive methods; in the *Investigations* such knowledge is in a way *more* fundamental than inductive knowledge. For the possibility of inductive knowledge itself depends on the existence of forms of life in the context of which certain kinds of investigation are carried on and certain kinds of inference made – and those involve the idea (or something like the idea) of acting in accordance with established rules and standards; and the elucidation of what is involved in acting in accordance with such rules and standards *always* involves the conception 'now I can go on', i.e. the conception of *knowing* what my actions in certain future circumstances will be, in a way which is not itself based on inductive evidence.

However, talk about one thing being 'more fundamental' than another is dangerous and, in general, it is quite contrary to the spirit of the *Investigations* to attempt to find any one conception in terms of which everything else has to be understood. Certainly, from Wittgenstein's new point of view there is no difficulty in the idea that 'one part of the world should be closer to me than another'; he insists, indeed (II, x), that 'My own relation to my words is wholly different from other people's' – and it is a corollary, I think, that my relation to my own actions is wholly different from my relation to anything else. This 'different relation' will have to be explained in terms of different language games, or forms of life; and this is what Wittgenstein does (cf. I, §§ 630–31).

Here, the relation between the will and action is no longer seen as the relation between a mental process and a bodily movement. Instead, the concept of an action, in its context in certain sorts of language game, is taken as primary and then Wittgenstein asks what role the notion of the will, in relation to that of an action, plays in that language game.

'Willing, if it is not to be a sort of wishing, must be the action itself. It cannot be allowed to stop anywhere short of the action.' If it is the action, then it is so in the ordinary sense of the word; so it is speaking, writing, walking, lifting a thing, imagining something. But it is also trying, making an effort, – to speak, to write, to lift a thing, to imagine something, etc. (ibid., I, § 615)

It is because, besides doing a thing, our talk about action also includes reference to trying, choosing, deciding, intending, etc., to do a thing, that it is possible to drive a wedge between acting and willing. Or, more generally, this possibility arises because the concept of acting requires that agents should have a concept of what they are doing, that there should be such a thing as talking about and discussing one's actions. But the possibility of such a wedge in some cases does *not* mean that it can *always* be driven. There are cases, many and standard cases, where no distinction at all can be drawn between willing and acting.

When I raise my arm I do not usually try to raise it.

'At all costs I will get to that house.' – But if there is no difficulty about it – *can* I try at all costs to get to the house? (ibid., I, §§ 622–3)

The fact that we have both these sorts of case (where doing is and where it is not distinct from 'willing') reinforces certain more general tendencies in our language, and the result is the idea, which we have seen to give so much trouble in the *Tractatus*, of the will as both in and not in the world.

Doing itself seems not to have any volume of experience. It seems like an extensionless point, the point of a needle. This point seems to be the real agent. And the phenomenal happenings only to be consequences of this acting. 'I *do* . . .' seems to have a definite sense, separate from all experience. (ibid., I, § 620)

But of course this seeming is a transcendental illusion.★

★ This essay is a great deal better than it otherwise would have been owing to comments made by Miss H. Ishiguro on an earlier draft. I also want to thank Miss M. Barabas for pointing out misquotations. I have occasionally modified official translations where they seemed misleading.

Notes

1. See *Proceedings of the Aristotelian Society*, 1965–6; reprinted as Ch. 10 of *Ethics and Action*.

2. It ought to be said, perhaps, that this remark of mine is more in the spirit of the *Philosophical Investigations* than of the *Tractatus*. I think that, on the *Tractatus* view, it would be misconceived to suppose such an account possible: this is one aspect of the view that one 'cannot speak' of the ethical will. But of course one has got to try to speak of it if one is to make any sense of the notion, and the *Notebooks* provide the spectacle of Wittgenstein trying to speak in a way which his presuppositions rule out as impossible.

3. A. J. Kenny, 'Practical Inference', in *Analysis*, January 1966. Cf. G. E. M. Anscombe, *Intention*.

Biographical Note

Peter Winch studied philosophy at St Edmund Hall, Oxford. He lectured at Swansea in the University of Wales from 1951 to 1964 when he went to Birkbeck College, London, as Reader in Philosophy. Since 1969 he has been Professor of Philosophy in the University of London at King's College. He has held visiting professorships at Rochester, Arizona, Brooklyn, and Konstanz. He edited the journal *Analysis* from 1965 to 1971. He is the author of *The Idea of a Social Science* (1958) and *Ethics and Action* (1972). His other writings on Wittgenstein include 'The Unity of Wittgenstein's Philosophy' in *Studies in the Philosophy of Wittgenstein*, ed. Winch (1969); 'Eine Einstellung zur Seele' in *Proceedings of the Aristotelian Society*, 1980–81; 'Im Anfang war die Tat' in *Perspectives on the Philosophy of Wittgenstein*, ed. I. Block (Blackwell, 1981). (Both these last two essays are in English.)

Further Reading

Main works of Wittgenstein: *Tractatus Logico-Philosophicus*, trans. D. F. Pears and B. F. McGuinness (London: Routledge & Kegan Paul, 1961); *Philosophical Investigations*, trans. G. E. M. Anscombe (Oxford: Blackwell, 1973); *On Certainty*, trans. Denis Paul and G. E. M. Anscombe (Oxford: Blackwell, 1975); *Remarks on the Foundations of Mathematics*, trans. G. E. M. Anscombe (Oxford: Blackwell, 1978); *Philosophical Grammar*, trans. A. Kenny (Oxford: Blackwell, 1974); *Philosophical Remarks*, trans. R. Hargreaves and R. White (Oxford: Blackwell, 1975); *Culture and Value*, trans. Peter Winch (Oxford: Blackwell, 1980).

Arthur Danto

Sartre: Shame, or, The Problem of Other Minds

To sit alone in a room, aware of a lamp, books, a bed, a cypress hill out the window, is to be the centre of a world, and thus to be something wholly different in kind from the other items in it. These other items of my world, objects, are faced to me, grouped around this one point of view, meanings for me. When someone comes into the room, there occurs a transformation, one that is most sharply affected by my seeing a look, the other person's look at me. What is true now is that I also perceive the various objects as within another structure, their reality for him, which is forever impenetrable to me. They have fled from me. Above all, I cease to be the unique centre of a world and become, to myself, an object in another's world. In that I do become this, I have an identity forced upon me, one that is not of my choosing, and hence I lose a certain freedom. I resist this, and seek to reduce the other person from a consciousness to an object. It is as true, of course, that his situation and desire are as mine. I am not, to him, just another object in his world, but another consciousness, the possessor of a private awareness, and hence the imposer of a perception or definition upon him. There is therefore a struggle between us for centrality, and for self-determined identity. It is a struggle which neither of us can either win or give up.

This vignette, derived closely from several given by Arthur Danto in what follows (pp. 515–18), is not an attempt to catch the feelings of a curious moment, the passing experience of two oddly self-willed individuals. It serves, rather, as a model for *all* of our ongoing relations with others, of whatever kinds and in whatever settings, as they are perceived by Sartre. Our relations with others, the subject of that part

---

Jean-Paul Sartre, 1905–81. Born and worked in France, as philosopher, playwright, novelist. Best-known Existentialist. Political activist, of Marxist sympathies. Proponent of a doctrine of absolute individual freedom and responsibility for most of his life, until near the end.

of Sartre's work through which Danto works so meticulous a passage, somehow consist in mutual futile attempts to be master, somehow to exist only in that way in which one perceives oneself. Danto's perspicuous and often startling account, a chapter from his *Jean-Paul Sartre*, is not derivative in the way of my vignette, but is none the less written from within, and takes us into, Sartre's envisioning of our lives. It is the nature of this envisioning that it could not survive an attempt to translate it into other terms, to put it into some shared or standard mode of philosophical discourse, or to divest it of metaphor. In part this is the result of its having not only a philosophical but also a literary expression in Sartre's work, the latter being as essential as the former. If its structure is set out as part of the book *Being and Nothingness*, its creative enrichment is given by such writings as the play *No Exit*, in which there occurs the deceptive but summative line that hell is other people.

Sartre's view of the nature of our personal relations needs distinguishing from a number of things, and, on the other hand, is bound up with certain philosophical propositions, doctrines and positions. Sartre's problem, or rather our common problem in his view, can indeed be described as the problem of other minds, but is certainly to be separated from what philosophers have generally understood by those words. (p. 511) Our problem is not that of explaining the rationality of believing in the existence of consciousnesses other than one's own, those of other people, but in characterizing one's connection with them. Again, he speaks of shame in setting out our experience of being deprived of mastery of our situations, and deprived of our chosen identities, but what is in question has nothing to do with moral or spiritual failing in any ordinary or traditional sense. The shame in question has to do with the given kind of subjugation by another person, and the inevitable failure in struggling to escape it. (p. 518).

This view of our existence with others is bound up with the intensionality of most mental states, including the most important of them, the fact that they are *directed*, that they are *of* things. (pp. 509–11) The view of our existence with others is also bound up with a fact which gives further intractableness to that existence. If my chosen individuality is destroyed by others, I also depend precisely on them for my sense of individual existence. (pp. 512–14)

The struggle to have only a chosen individuality, as remarked above, is one which is the nature of, or enters into, all of the ways in which we are related to other persons, but it is a struggle which takes on different characters. The case of love between two persons involves the attempt on the part of each to become the whole world of the other, to possess the other's freedom, and to do so by the subterfuge of concealing one's own freedom. It is foredoomed, inevitably a matter of mutual dissatisfaction. (pp. 520–21) The relation of a torturer or sadist to his victim involves the desire to concentrate the victim's consciousness upon his body, to limit his consciousness to what is within the mastery of the torturer. There are further respects in which torture and sadism are consonant with Sartre's picture of human relations. (pp. 521–3) For all of that, and despite all that has been said so far, the given picture is somehow consistent with more agreeable parts of human life, such as comradeship and cooperation, and in a way it involves as a necessity the treating of others as ends and not merely as means. (p. 523)

After a consideration of Sartre's view of groups and of such things as shared ideals, and his social psychology having to do with scarcity, Danto takes up again the question of human freedom. It was Sartre's conviction that while our actions do proceed from causes, it is we who determine that these causes shall be such. We constitute them as causes. A universal determinism of a kind is in a way consistent with freedom, although not at all in the way maintained by Hume and the other empiricist philosophers. We do have an absolute freedom which is partly a matter of how we view our own lives. It is a matter, too, of an ultimate project which forms an individual's life. This freedom is not a blessing but a burden, something to which we are condemned.

There can be no doubt that Sartre's account of our lives is in several fundamental ways elusive, and that it runs against firm convictions. The two matters are connected. We may not at all recognize ourselves or others in his account of our existence as a kind of war of all against all. At this point, however, what was noted above needs to be remembered. The given war of all against all is somehow consistent with comradeship and the like, and something of which a certain morality is a precondition. It is therefore not easy to catch hold of the way in which his picture of human relations is intended. Do these relations in fact *consist in* the given war, or is it that they have the war as a deep foundation, which foundation does not much determine what it carries? No doubt there are other possibilities. There is the question, too, of the extent to which Sartre's philosophy is not only supplemented by imaginative literature, but itself moves in that direction. To think that it does is not necessarily to suppose that it is less than wholly philosophical in intent.

It is not Danto's first purpose to press such inquiries, but rather to do what must come first, which is to bring Sartre's response to life, as he expressed it, into an acute focus. This he does with a rare subtlety, and in a style which is the effective means to that end.

Arthur Danto

Sartre: Shame, or, The Problem of Other Minds

Towards the end of *No Exit*, Sartre's most original if not his finest play, when the situation in which they are locked has become rudely clear to the three occupants of a room in hell, the male character, Garcin, voices what must be Sartre's most famous phrase: '*L'enfer c'est les autres.*' Hell is 'other people' in the respect that each of these personages is trapped eternally in moral and erotic impasses from which none is able to allow any of the others to escape. The basis of their spiritual torment lies deeper, however, than their diabolically mismatched psyches imply (mismatched save for the purposes of inflicting agony upon one another, that is: for *that* purpose they are fiendishly matched). Each demands that he or she be taken at the value he or she would want to be taken, that others perceive him as they would want to perceive themselves; because there is a mutual refusal, indeed incapacity to do this, each is forced to see himself through the eyes of the others, and none can escape an identity imposed from without. Each sees the acts of the others in the harshest possible light, and since these acts sum up their several lives, and since each is dead, none can by any further act redeem his life from these chill and fatal assessments; the lives are all played out. And so, by a cruel cunning, the stalemated fellowship in this banal and so all-the-more-hideous chamber – so different from what the mythology of hell has taught those who fear it to expect – is composed of persons who are exactly suited to be one another's psychic torturer; instead of a pit of flames and pincers, hell is a hopeless conversation in which the soul of each is ruthlessly exposed and the identity of each is hostage to his spiritual captors – none breaks free from a circular dialogue turning forever about the same dead centre.

But *No Exit*, which is perhaps the most remarkable literary embodi-

Arthur Danto, 'Shame: or, The Problem of Other Minds', Chapter 4, *Jean-Paul Sartre* (London: Fontana Modern Masters Series, 1975). Reprinted with slight alterations by permission of author and publisher.

ment of a philosophical idea ever written, is meant to have a universal application, and the architectures of cruelty so vividly exhibited by the rather despicable inmates – each of whom in his life had betrayed others and certainly caused suffering enough to merit a moral penalty in hell, each of whom was morally weak and deeply selfish – are precisely meant to exemplify the human condition everywhere and always, even as lived by saints and moral heroes, certainly by you and me. Hell is other people just because they are people and other, and the saying does not have reference only to the commonplace recognition that people vex and frustrate one another, drag one another down as in bad marriages or unhappy families or thwarted enterprises where the needed cooperations are not forthcoming. For there are happy marriages and happy families too, as well as successful common under-takings in which individuals function marvellously as members of a team. Even in these, however, 'Hell is other people' is applicable and applies; the structures it is meant to epitomize are just the structures in which we are related to others, however benignly. From these struc-tures there is no exit, and the dividing line between hell and ordinary daily life is not there to be drawn; other people are hell in and out of any specific inferno. The practices and feelings which might commonly be believed to provide avenues of escape – love, trust, charity, friend-ship, and the like – are, in Sartre's corrosive and deflationist argument, examples of the disease it is an illusion to suppose instead they might cure, examples rather than counter-examples, all the more cruel because they seem to be counter-examples to the general case they in fact illus-trate. Like all of Sartre's slogans, this one condenses philosophical theories of the most extraordinary scope and subtlety, and illustrates in the darkest colours a thesis in ontology and epistemology, a concept which can be framed and phrased in the tight thin idiom of pure philosophy. It would, of course, not be Sartre were there not this double vocabulary and dual mode of presentation: the art gives life to the philosophy, and the philosophy structure to the art. But nowhere more than in this topic must the reader keep his philosophical bearings, for only so can he judge the suitability of the illustrations. I shall accord-ingly here be concerned with the subject of our relations with others, analysed in Part Three of *Being and Nothingness*, where Sartre introduces an ontologically primitive kind of being to complete his inventory of the posits of consciousness: *être-pour-autrui*, or being-for-others.

Let us recall a basic logical feature of those propositions by means of which we describe mental states, or ascribe mental states to persons.

These are irreducibly intensional, in the respect that fear, for example, or desire or belief or hope or whatever, have objects: Garcin fears death, Inez desires Estelle and believes that Garcin is a coward, Estelle hopes that she is attractive to Garcin, and so on. There may be exceptions. There may be states of anxiety having no specific objects which, because of this, will be contrasted with specialized anxieties (over one's job, one's sexual abilities, or the like): their object, if any, is life itself, or the world at large. Or again, in contrast with happiness *that*, or depression *over*, there may be objectless states of euphoria or dejection. But let us stick with the clearly intensional cases. If a man fears something, say a snake, he also believes that what he fears exists – for what otherwise is there to be afraid of? – and that it is threatening. (I shall disregard cases in which a drug might induce phobic states in which a man is caused to fear things he has enough cognitive sobriety left to recognize are not really threatening at all.) Someone like Descartes who held serious doubts about the external world would have to regard all such fears as logically groundless, since he also must believe that nothing answers to their purported objects – though his vagabond mind might persist in fearing what his philosophically instructed intelligence dismisses as epistemological fantasies. But this sort of disparity can exist only because the mind is insufficiently disciplined by reason. Again, to believe that *p*, is not *just* to be in a certain state, it is to believe that the world itself is in a certain state if the belief is about the world: namely, the state that makes the belief a true one. For to believe that *p*, is to believe that *p* is true or at least to be committed to this; and again a Cartesian who had what he regarded as rational grounds for doubting the reality of the world would have to give up any lower-order beliefs he might have about it – though once more there might be problems in disciplining his mind to bring his propensities for believing into conformity with his philosophical intuition. But the point is in any case quite general: that mental states refer those who are in them to objects which exist, or which at least they are committed to believe exist, externally to those states: and the mental states then cannot rationally survive recognition that no such objects are there. Moreover, certain sorts of objects are such that if I did not believe in their existence, I could not be in the mental states which presuppose them. Consider, in this light, the state of *shame*. Some sort of objectless shame may exist, but commonly the structure of shame is this: one feels shame *before* someone because of something one is or one has done – before God, or one's parents, or someone whose moral perceptions one respects and whose good opinion somehow matters. Of course there may be no such person. One may really be alone in the universe. An ashamed solipsist would be an odd case. Still, to feel shame is to be committed to the belief that one is not alone, the existence of others as a structure of one's consciousness being built into the very concept. The feeling of shame before God, for example, could hardly survive, save as a mental aberration and a conceptual impurity, the conversion to atheism. Discounting the special case of shame before oneself, say because one has not lived up to one's expectations or ideals, the structure of shame is such that one who had no concept of other persons could not sensibly be supposed to feel shame; the feeling simply cannot arise except with reference to other persons. The question before us is how the concept of another person, an alien consciousness, gets introduced into our conceptual scheme. (Shame, of course, is only one example of a mental state whose content requires the person to have this conceptual structure: jealousy, gratitude, condescension are others, and there are many, many more.) Reference to others arises from *within*.

Since Descartes at least, the existence of other minds has been a treacherous topic in epistemology. Passers-by, he proposed, might for all one knew be intricately engineered robots, mere ambulating machines. He might have gone further: minute examination of the behaviour or structure of these cloaked and hatted beings might leave me as uncertain of their personhood as my first glance at them from my window; I *judge* that they are persons but do not observe that they are, for my observations might be true and the judgement false, and how am I to know whether it is false or true? It is always, then, a sceptical possibility undetermined by external scrutiny that they have no *interiors*, which is to say, no awareness or consciousness at all. Of the fact that *I* am conscious my consciousness assures me at every instant because I am prereflectively conscious of it. But the consciousness of which I am in this way conscious is always in the nature of the case my own. So neither by this avenue nor by that of observation can the doubt once planted be removed. And even if the problem of the external world is solved, so that I can say with surety that there are things, the solution does not entail that some among these things are conscious. A whole extra apparatus is required for this, and what can its logic be?

These are questions for knowledge, it may be said, not for understanding. And one can argue this way: I must at least have the concept of an other consciousness if the doubt regarding the existence of other consciousnesses can intelligibly be raised. The question then concerns the provenance of this concept. The *pour-soi*, situated in and giving by his presence a situational structure to his world, need not ever have situationalized it to take others into account. He may be utterly alone, a kind of Crusoe insularly stranded in existence. Still, he hardly can conceive of himself as alone without the concept of company, and perhaps he could not so much as rise to a concept of *himself as himself* if he did not have this further notion. After all, he might merely have been conscious of the world and of himself after the manner of the teaching in the *Transcendence of the Ego* – as an object amongst objects having no specially intimate relationship to the one who is conscious of all this; that he is conscious might never have been raised to the levels of reflective awareness. My connection through consciousness with these various objects is not a further object, so it need never intrude upon the outwardly directed consciousness filled to logical satiety with the objects of the world. I could give a complete enumeration of the objects of my world without including, as a further entry, this fact of being conscious of them. And the way in which consciousness is self-aware, on Sartre's account, cannot turn the trick. So a person might live his whole life out in this way, never once thinking that it was a *person, himself,* that was doing all this, and so of an ontologically distinct order with reference to the furnishings of his world.

Nietzsche, in a marvellously speculative passage, asks what might be the origin of consciousness,[1] not as a matter of physiology but as something which is present to itself as consciousness, however it becomes that; and he asks what in the end could be the function of this further datum for consciousness, which is itself. He raises the question of its use deliberately, asking in a way what might be lost if it were lost. And the answer he gives is that in a way nothing would be lost: coming to an awareness of awareness adds no new objects, any more than learning that one sees adds special visibilia to the perceptual field, since one does not *see* that one sees. Yet something is after all added, since Nietzsche believed that consciousness has social, not to say linguistic, origins: I am thrust into position to refer to myself only through recognizing that I am the one to which others refer when they refer to me. And the advent of all this is a matter not so much of mastering some special vocabulary as of mastering a complex referential system through which a vocabulary is applied to the world, myself as a self included. There are, after all, languages without pronouns and perhaps even languages whose verbs do not conjugate into first- and third-person cases or do not conjugate in any way. But the 'I', or whatever its referential equivalent might be, is co-implicated with the 'you' and indeed with 'he' – I master the ability to describe myself, knowing it is myself that is being described, *just* when I recognize concurrently that I am the object of description for others. This interreferential structure is needed, for after all a person could master a language of sorts without getting the notion of himself: there would just be objects (including the object which was him but which he did not specially recognize to be him), that emitted signals to one another and by so doing modified one another's behaviour in a manner not remarkably different from the way they modify it by contact; even his feelings would be 'out there'. But, as we have seen in connection with the example of shame, shame could not under the circumstances be amongst them.

Sartre's thought on these matters is not utterly different from the following. My consciousness of myself is interlocked with my consciousness of others, and specifically with their consciousness of me: to be seriously aware of myself as subject presupposes an awareness of others' awareness of me as an object. Or better: *I exist for myself* at the level of self-consciousness just and only just when I become aware of existing for others. I wish to stress the *for myself* in this phrase: it is not the respect in which consciousness is *pour-soi* at the level of prereflectivity. For it might have existed for itself in *that* way without ever attaining to this fresh perspective on its being. These remarks help, too, in explaining Sartre's notion that my body, so far as I *live* it, is unknown and unknowable to me. Since I am my body, I arrive at bodily self-consciousness only when I have the concept of my body as it is for others. 'To study the way in which my body appears to the Other or the way in which the Other's body appears to me amounts to the same thing . . . The structures of my being-for-the-Other are identical to those of the Other's being-for-me.'[2] So I acquire the status of a person only when others do. Once more, I must emphasize that there may not be other persons: I may be the only consciousness there is. Still, the concept of myself, having being as a person for myself, entails an understanding of my existing for others, as the concept of an exterior presupposes the concept of an interior, so that I cannot speak of others as having only exteriors without making room in the very description for their having an interior as well. As a conceptual truth, inside and outside function as conjugate notions, but equally, I think, there is no concept of myself as interior without a concept of myself as exterior, and to attain this sort of conceptual awareness in my own case immediately extends to others. Before I was conscious of others and so of myself in this internally complicated manner, I could not have described the objects in the phenomenal field as *merely* having exteriors. Though in one sense no new things may be added, to respond to the query I raised in considering Nietzsche, the things already there enter into very different relationships and acquire under this new mode of description remarkably different structures than any I would believe them to have had without this insight.

I have made a great deal here of the distinction between understanding and knowledge, between conceptual entailment and epistemic truth. For it is one thing to insist that the concept of an other consciousness is required by the application of certain descriptions to myself, and quite another matter to say that this in any way entails that others exist. It may very well be true that a man might have no sense of sin if he were innocent of the concept of God and of human disobedience, for these are interrelated notions. But we cannot argue from the fact that there are men who live with a sense of sin that God exists or that Adam disobeyed him – or we should find a proof of God's existence in any Baptist sanctuary. Sartre's altogether brilliant analysis of the self as having a being-for-others as a precondition for having consciousness of being-for-himself and others as being-for-him, does not deliver him from 'the reef of solipsism'. So far as solipsism demands that the existence of others be demonstrated as a condition for vanishing away, solipsism is with us for the duration, for no such demonstration is to be had. Sartre's thought can give us a demonstration at best only if taken in conjunction with a certain theory of how concepts *must* be acquired: that is, with a certain theory of learning.

There are theories, of course, and classical empiricism is an example, according to which my *basic* concepts at least are caused by some immediate sense-experience, so that if my history lacks the requisite encounter with experience, my repertoire of basic concepts is correspondingly limited. But in the first place it is questionable whether I experience individuals as conscious in anything like the way I experience apples as red – if I did, the Problem of Other Minds would be solved at a stroke. And in the second place all such theories of learning are empirical and contingent, and so cannot furnish a demonstrative support for any conceptual truth. Conceptual analysis yields only truths about concepts, not truths about the world unless the world corresponds to our concepts; and something more than conceptual analysis is required to establish such a correspondence. If there is a truth in philosophy at all, it is this: that one cannot deduce from concepts alone anything about how the world in fact is; one can only deduce how it *must* be, given certain conditions, which cannot be deduced from concepts alone. It is this which in the end renders the Ontological Argument untenable. Sartre admires certain audacious attempts by philosophers like Husserl to find 'at the very heart of consciousness a fundamental, transcending connection with the other which would be constitutive of each consciousness in its upsurge',[3] and Sartre's is just that sort of attempt. But all such endeavours are based on a quite mistaken belief that conceptual analysis can furnish factual truths, and that bare understanding alone can be cashed in for knowledge. So in the end his enterprise is intended less to solve than to bypass the epistemological problem of other minds by insisting that the problem really is an ontological one: that one could not exist as a consciousness reflectively aware of itself unless one also existed for others. But I am insisting that one could exist 'for others' in the required way – which is to say, have an exterior and perceive oneself as from without – even if there were not (and certainly without its following that there are) others for whom in fact one exists. Still, the essential and quite brilliant point remains that the emergence of a consciousness of others is of a logically different order than a consciousness of mere objects, entailing as it does a transformation of consciousness of self; entailing a loss of naïveté and of un-self-aware aloneness.

Let us now return to the structures of 'my world'. The *pour-soi* is, we may recall, the centre of reference for the complex system of *meaningful* objects which compose it. The centre, we may also recall, is not part of the field whose structure refers back to it. Or better, the body is my point of view on the world, but points of view are themselves not perceived: 'The body is, in fact, the point of view on which I can take no point of view.'[4] Now I am in a park, that scene of so many Sartrian discoveries. There are benches to sit on if I wish to use them, flower beds to avoid, trees to shade me, and the rest. A man sits on one of the benches. Now is he just another item in 'my world', the way, say, the ornamental statue of Neptune spewing water in the fountain before me? Then, Sartre writes, 'his relationship with the other objects would be of the purely additive type',[5] one more thing. But in fact to perceive him *as a man* is to perceive the whole field in a quite different way: things organize about *him* in a manner structurally like the way in which they so far have organized themselves about me. So, in a way, I get the concept of 'my world' only when I get the concept of 'his world'. Obviously, this is not in any sense a physical change: the objects have all the same physical properties as before and sustain between themselves all the same geometrical relationships – and all of this invariant to this total transformation of the field's organization. But in recognizing him as a consciousness, 'instead of a grouping *towards me* of the objects, there is now an orientation *which flees from me*'.[6] It is as though the man had stolen my world by making it his. Of course, were I to discover that it was not a man there after all but merely a dummy or some sort of quirky shadow, the world would once more revert to having me as its only centre, and he would be just another additive object in it. As it stands, however, another centre has appeared, with the effect of negating my centre – or me – by drawing me into the world as an object for him. Or so Sartre says. My world, of which I as its centre am not a proper part, is taken from me and I am reduced to an object become a proper part of the world of another. Of course, it should follow that the same thing happens when he perceives *me* as a consciousness rather than a stolid entity like a statue. At this point, accordingly, a kind of logical drama begins, in which there is a spontaneous struggle for centrality and for ownership of worlds: as though I could get my world back as mine only if I can reduce him to an object in it, and he likewise with me, as though there could not be room for two foci in a single world. When the park exists for him, it immediately acquires an aspect it cannot have for me and at the same time acquires an aspect I would not otherwise know about. Something always escapes me – namely, that aspect which things have for him.

The concept of reality in Sartre is that of things having aspects not immediately given to consciousness of them: one is aware of their having aspects beyond what one perceives. But here a new *sort* of aspect altogether is revealed, one which cannot in principle be given to me, namely, the world as it is for an other will always be logically hidden to me. But of course these are not physical aspects but, rather, meanings: things have for him the meanings he gives them, and these will differ from mine just from the fact that they are given by him. The drama, then, is one in which I seek to reclaim the world as mine by reducing him to an object, a somewhat hopeless project in view of the fact that it presupposes that what I seek to objectivize is a consciousness and not an object. So the world is never going to be the same again. In any case, this recognition of another consciousness, and its recognition of me, is the conceptual translation of the literary *mot* 'Hell is other people', and it is the basis, in Sartre's curiously morbid psychology, of *all* my relations with others: I shall always seek to make objects of them and they of me. And all of us shall fail.

Let us note before anatomizing these relations further that even if I should have discovered that it was not a man but a dummy – a scarecrow, say – the game is already lost. This is because the very possibility of an other consciousness is an absolute boundary on my world and thus a limitation on me. For in a way, one might say, until I had the concept of a world-for-an-other, I did not have really the concept of a world-for-me. What I now see to have been my world had heretofore been regarded by me as *the* world. Moreover, until now I did not perceive myself as having a location in a world at all, being logically outside it looking in. I was not an object for myself. But I have become just that by recognizing that I am, or at least can be, an object for an other. This is achieved through the concept of the look.

Sartre's discussion of looks is stunningly original. To see someone as looking at me is not just to see his eyes. For eyes as eyes are but further objects in the field, like the dead eyes in the *têtes de veau* at the butcher, things I might study and learn the physiology of without ever understanding from within that eyes can see. But in perceiving an eye as looking, I perceive myself as a possible object for that look: I lose my transparency, as it were, and become opaque even for myself. The transformation in perception in which an eye becomes a thing that looks goes together with a transformation in self-perception as well. But the point is quite general, and to perceive a look need not entail seeing someone's eyes. Walking through a village or a deserted landscape, I can get the sense that someone is looking at me though I see no one, and so no one who is seeing: and this is quite enough for me to achieve a sense of my objecthood. Sartre gives an example, now quite famous, of a voyeur peering through a keyhole. He is aware only of the keyhole and what is to be seen through it, when the sudden sound of footsteps in the corridor precipitates him into objectivity; instead of just observing a forbidden scene through a secret aperture, he is abruptly made conscious of a man, himself, peering at a forbidden scene through a keyhole – his world has expanded to include himself. Sartre restates the matter in his own terms: '. . . I have my foundation outside myself. I am for myself only as I am a pure reference to the Other.'[7]

Needless to say, the voyeur will feel shame, having been caught in a compromising posture. At least he will if he is a voyeur, having internalized the conventions of privacy and the institutionalization of rights to privacy which he is violating – someone from another planet or even another culture would not necessarily be ashamed of looking through a keyhole, which is just a convenient opening. Sartre is curiously insensitive here, as elsewhere, to what we might term institutional facts, though he makes an effort, later, in the *Critique de la raison dialectique*, to introduce social concepts into the structure of consciousness. It is a failing to which he is oblivious here and, more damagingly, in his discussion of values. But shame, for Sartre, has a technical meaning considerably wider than the moral sentiment that passes under that name, and that the voyeur feels or should feel. This is one of those cases where the philosophical structure takes on a misleading colouration from the example used to illustrate it, for in the end what shame comes to is a metaphysical rather than a moral feeling. 'I can be ashamed only as my freedom escapes me in order to become a given object,' he writes. 'The Other's look makes me be beyond my being in this world and puts me in the midst of the world which is at once *this* world and beyond this world.'[8] But this would be a true philosophical characterization, if it is true at all, whatever act I were observed to perform: helping a child, saving a drowning man, battling to save the city – or eating plums, reading *Le Monde*, walking the dog: largely neutral acts all.

So we must divest shame of the moral overtones lent it by the example of the voyeur if we are to understand how its concept really functions in Sartre's philosophy. And how it functions is as follows: the content of shame is that I am an *object* and constituted as such by the other. I exist for him and even for myself as I exist for others, rather than as a pure spontaneity who 'is not what it is'. And as an object I depend in an ontological way upon a consciousness other than my own. The same, in effect, concerns my solidification as an object of consciousness, and a loss or seeming loss of freedom. 'I am somebody rather than nobody. I have acquired an identity I have not given myself.' In the end, it is not just the way in which I might be for another consciousness that induces shame: it is, rather, the fact that I have the kind of existence that can appear to another consciousness, however it may do so.

It should be clear from this that the discovery of bad faith itself presupposes the discovery of my exteriority. I can take myself to be a waiter only in so far as I exist or can exist for others as a waiter. But to the degree that I exist as a waiter *for them* (or even for myself, in taking an external viewpoint), my freedom and identity are captive to the freedom and identity of the other. What each of us aims at – what it is our nature as humans to aim at always – is to be the 'foundation' of our own being; and here we discover that our foundation lies in the freedom of another. The degradation, if it is that, is, accordingly, metaphysical rather than moral. '*I am no longer master of the situation*,' as Sartre says,[9] giving a banal phrase a remarkable philosophical weight. One may, then, describe this as shame. But it is shame which is shared by everyone who has the concept of the other, and has nothing to do with any special act we perform or way we happen to be, and indeed it need not be felt as shame at all. It could even be felt as pride, the feeling one has when one believes one is seen at one's best, doing some marvellous, noble deed. To be sure, I can never guarantee that others will perceive me as I would want to be perceived, but shame in this generalized sense concerns the fact that they can perceive me at all. And in any case if there is a *feeling* of shame which exactly should correspond to the way Sartre has characterized it, this will be had only by someone who has internalized Sartre's philosophy. It is moot whether anyone who is merely conscious of others will spontaneously exemplify the Sartrian structures.

Sartre has arrived at a sort of dualism, only weakly parallel to the familiar dualism of mind and body associated with Descartes. For mind and body are logically distinct and perhaps causally independent entities, whereas the structure of consciousness and objecthood – Sartre's dualism – is much more complex. I am an object for my own consciousness only through my having become conscious of others' consciousness of me. Others cannot then be *merely* objects for my consciousness or I would not become an object for myself. The structure of self-consciousness, then, is logically social, but since I finally am an object for myself only through the provenance of other's perception of me, what I am (as an object) depends upon others and not upon myself. And this is why they are hell: my identity, even for myself, depends finally upon them. And so, as Sartre assesses the situation, I can only achieve the autonomy I seek by dominating them (and conversely, of course). And I cannot achieve this, since at least the concept of the other always intervenes between my consciousness of myself and myself.

We are in any case now in a position to describe what are in general our concrete relationships with others, hence ultimately the interpenetrating desperations of the *dramatis personae* of *No Exit*, which have as their common logical core the structures we have just described, however morbidly embellished. They are all, and there can be no exception in any human relationship, doomed attempts to escape from structures we can neither endure nor overcome. The pages in which these relations are exhibited through a series of dramatic and depressing scenarios, are among the most powerful and psychologically rich pages to be found in Sartre's or anyone's writing. The insight into human practices, apart from the ontological armatures which they simultaneously illustrate, are saddening and deep. They have at every point the ring of human truth, even if the philosophical analyses behind them are haywire and perverse. Sartre's discussion bears comparison with Spinoza's deduction of the modalities of passion in Book Four of the *Ethics*, where the logical derivation is a kind of *tour de force* but where the penetration into the hopelessness of the human psyche is independent of that, even if an extra appreciation is attained if it indeed can be shown that our private flaps and failings are part of the cosmic order, and inevitable. In each case Sartre takes up, whether of love or brutalization, the attempt is to capture the consciousness of an other by making the other an object. When he is an object, I get my freedom back because I am not an object for him any longer, since nothing is an object for an object. I thus disarm that consciousness from a reciprocal disarming of mine. 'While I attempt to free myself from the hold of the Other, the Other is trying to free himself from mine; while I seek to enslave the Other, the Other seeks to enslave me.' I am never successful in this, and I cannot be. But there is no resting place and no shrugging off the effort to repeat the effort. It is, to pre-empt a phrase of Hobbes, a restless striving for power after power which ceaseth only in death. 'Conflict,' Sartre goes on, 'is the original meaning of being-for-others.'[10] Let us show how this works in love, and the circle of attitudes it generates. 'Love must always end in sorrow,' runs the song in *O Lucky Man*, 'and everyone must play the game.'

The paradigm of love in Sartre's vision of it is Marcel's unhappy pursuit of Albertine in Proust's novel, though it could as easily be Swann's unhappy pursuit of Odette. Jealousy is its spring and motive, and Marcel seeks virtually to enslave Albertine, making her as absolutely dependent upon him as is possible and in every possible way. What he cannot capture is her consciousness or, hence, her freedom: 'Through her consciousness Albertine escapes Marcel even when he is at her side.'[11] Marcel, to be sure, is concerned to own her not as a thing but as a consciousness: 'He wants to possess a freedom.' And the strategy into which he falls is this: to become in a way the beloved's *whole world*, the sole object of her consciousness. So he consents in a way to being an object for her, anchoring in this way the fickle awareness of the beloved towards him, fastening it down. I must in a certain way conceal my freedom, enslave myself, as it were, in order to enslave her; I cannot treat her as an object, for when I do so her subjectivity or freedom disappears, and since it is just this that I want, the enterprise would fail. Speaking figuratively, I must avoid looking at her.

And now suppose this strategy succeeds, and the beloved becomes a lover in her own right, in love with me. Surely this is what I thought I wanted. But what now happens is that, like me before, she seeks to become *my* whole world, enslaving herself in order to enslave me, and so to possess my freedom as I sought to possess hers, by *concealing* her freedom. If I succeed, I fail, since her freedom escapes me; there is no balance point in the affair. 'To love,' Sartre writes, 'is to want to be loved.' This is reciprocal and foredoomed, in as much as the love on the other side is also the desire to be loved. We have a kind of unedifying comedy, in which both unhappy erotic athletes lose the main thing each wants, namely, the other's freedom. Until she loves me she is free, when she loves me her freedom is dissipated, and in neither case can I have it neat. 'Hence the lover's perpetual dissatisfaction.'[12] In seeking to throw off my freedom by flattening myself into an object for purposes of netting the freedom of the other, my freedom is returned to me when the purpose is fulfilled, but when it is I have lost the freedom of the other as well. One has a sense that Sartre and Simone de Beauvoir, in their remarkable and even monumental love for one another, sought to escape the metaphysics of erotic disillusionment by pursuing an ideal this analysis ought to render impossible: a mutual fidelity to freedom. Perhaps it is an escape: certainly it is one of the admirable liaisons of modern times. But if it is an escape, it is remarkable, for *Being and Nothingness* leaves no room for escape, either in masochism, in which the lover seeks to become an object *in his own eyes* in a futile endeavour to alienate a freedom which must be presupposed in the very act, or in indifference and hate, or again in sadism – which might be singled out for comment here, since it smokes of Sartrian themes and is the inverse of love, and thus may show love's structure by a kind of indirection.

If love gets its wish, the other becomes an object but, in a way, through the other's own choice, and so the other's choice is an exercise of freedom rather than an enslavement. The sadist then tries to take matters into his own hands and acts upon the other's body in order to incarnate that freedom. When that freedom is coincident with the other's body, in being master over that body I am master over that freedom. Now I have her in bonds or chains. Now I can 'do with her what I will'. In touching her body I touch *her*. And pain is a marvellous instrument for purposes of incarnation. For pain is an insistent thing: 'In pain, facticity invades consciousness.'[13] And by applying pain, I aim to embody the other's consciousness by making it nothing but consciousness of her body: what I am after is a collapse of consciousness onto the object, namely the body, which I am perfect master of in the den of torture.

Sartre has in his discussion of sadism a very powerful concept of obscenity, which he contrasts with grace. In the grace of a dancer, for example, the body literally disappears behind its movements, so that even if the dancer in fact is nude, the grace disguises by spiritualizing the flesh. As spectators, we are aware then of movement, and the graced body cannot simultaneously answer to lust: 'the nudity of the flesh is wholly present, but it cannot be seen'.[14] Obscenity is grace's antonym, and consists exactly in the rendering of flesh visible as flesh. It is achieved by putting the occupant of that flesh in a position from which he cannot act with the flesh and is helpless to control its movements, which are subject then to external forces rather than control from within. Jiggling, for instance, is obscene in this sense: 'The *obscene* appears when the body adopts postures which . . . reveal the inertia of its flesh.'[15] Sartre's analysis of obscenity is a pornographic transform of Bergson's concept of the comic, it having been Bergson's view, roughly, that the basic source of ridiculousness consists in an otherwise autonomous individual becoming subject to mechanical forces acting from without, as classically exemplified in slipping on a banana peel: the sort of thing, Russell archly put it, which 'makes M. Bergson laugh'. Sadism, then, is the effort to destroy grace, incarnating the other by dispossessing him of freedom over his own body, making his body, hence him, a mere manipulable thing. Of course, *he* must be there to be thus dispossessed: killing him destroys freedom, rather than ensnaring it. And it is after all the freedom of the other which the sadist wants and needs. But where there is a show of freedom on the victim's part, his pleasure is frustrated. In the end, the victim must be brought to humiliate *himself: he* must freely identify with his flesh. But then it is *his* choice to do so. Hence failure on the sadist's side.

The question of how long one can endure torture was not an academic question for the captured member of the Resistance during the war. He always had to ask whether he could endure systematic pain in order not to betray his comrades. This issue figures in Sartre's stories as a moral crux, it haunts his play *Morts sans sépulture* (*The Victors*), it obsessed Malraux, it worried Camus. In the end, however – and Sartre reverts to this in any number of contexts – one chooses the moment at which one yields, when the body is rendered wholly flesh and the heretofore resisting self an incarnated agony: 'this distorted and heaving body is the very image of a broken and enslaved freedom'.[16] Lack of control over one's body, at least those parts of one's body over which one normally does have control, is indeed deeply humiliating, as in incontinence. The Nazis, Hannah Arendt tells us, ingeniously exploited the excretory functions of prisoners in order to force regressions and crack their wills. And this is the sadist's project as well. But, Sartre argues, the moment of the sadist's success is the moment of his failure. The sadist has to see the body as an instrument to catch the will, but when the end is achieved, the body loses its status as a means and there is nothing to *do* with it any longer – 'It is there and it is there for nothing': a disconcerting mass of flesh. Sartre is not especially convincing here. Anything leads to satiation, any tool collapses into a thing when I have no use for it or it loses any use by falling out of the *Zeugganzes* it belonged to. True, he attempts a firm analysis, suggesting that when the victim looks at the sadist, the sadist realizes that his very practice depends upon its acceptance as such by the victim: he is dependent in a kind of hideous symbiosis upon the one over whom he seeks final, total control – like the master by the slave in Hegel. He must therefore turn to something else, sadism ending in a dry defeat. But everything else must end that way too. The motivations of the sadist are, of course, complex, far more so than the torturer who is simply concerned to do his job, pull out a bit of information or a confession from the secret knowledge of the victim, and go about his business: *he* hasn't failed. Even so, for all its luridness and incidental truth, Sartre's analysis of sadism only lamely serves its philosophical purposes. And so did the analysis of love.

The claim that conflict is the essence of human relationships must not mislead us. If there is an unremitting war of all against all, it is a special metaphysical sort of war where the stakes are freedom in some special metaphysical sense, which has nothing much to do with political freedom or economic enslavement. And it leaves room for all sorts of cooperative enterprises – like working together with pals to bring out *Les Temps modernes*, to choose a Parisian instance. Sartre would have been as aware of this as anyone, and it cannot have been his intention to deny plain facts. The outcome of all those futile projects catalogued under Concrete Relations with Others merely underscores the metaphysically inalienable freedom of others and ourselves. One cannot but treat men as ends and not as means the moment one is aware of one's own freedom and collaterally of the freedom of the other: by the very advent of self-consciousness one realizes the Categorical Imperative, and it is presupposed in all these attempts to violate it. So all of these relations are exercises in bad faith in the sense that one condition of morality as construed by Kant is implicit. They are, indeed, moral postures all, in as much as they are assumed in the full recognition that the other is an agent and a free being. Sartre's personages are not tyrants who see men *merely* as means. (The tyrant in this sense is not even indifferent – so far as indifference is a moral attitude in which one must know the facts in order to disregard them – he is just blandly unaware of other men as *men*; *his* world is *the* world, because he has not attained to a consciousness of other consciousnesses.) If they did not first recognize other freedoms, there could not be conflicts of the sort their enterprises exemplify. The existence of other consciousnesses penetrates the structure of their own, and if they did not acknowledge those freedoms, they would have nothing to try to capture.

Meanwhile, we might note that conflict remains the original relationship to one another in the *Critique de la raison dialectique* – a work devoted less to ontology than to the social psychological possibilities of group life. Here the focus and occasions of conflict are material and economic, rather than consequences of moral pathology, as in *Being and Nothingness*; they are due to material scarcity and metabolic requirements, rather than to the spiritual ambition to reclaim the world for oneself, a matter of eating rather than moral domination. 'Our history . . . emerged and developed in the permanent context of a field of tension engendered by scarcity.'[17] And this defines the relationship in which we stand to one another, as competing consumers: to recognize oneself as having material requirements simultaneously discloses the other as 'the simple possibility of consuming an object one needs'. Each, in short, discovers in each 'the material possibility of his own annihilation through the annihilation of a material object of primary necessity'.[18] This does not, of course, entail that men are inherently oppressors – the view remains in the *Critique* that man has no permanent nature, so that men could be humane as well as swine – 'and yet, as long as the sway of scarcity is not yet ended, there will be in each man and in everyone an inert structure of inhumanity which is, in short, nothing but the material negation in so far as it is interiorized'.[19] This internalized structure of inhumanity is externalized as violence, perceived always as counter-violence in the respect that I am violent towards those whom I am required by the structure of my praxis to believe violently disposed towards me, as we compete for the same scarce goods. Violence as counter-violence is a reflection in a dark mirror of love as the desire to be loved. But since anyone can compete with me and I with anyone, the object of violence is men, not just this or that particular man: 'It is man *qua* man . . . whom I am attacking; it is man, and nothing else, that I hate in the enemy, that is myself as Other, and it is certainly I whom I wish to destroy in him in order to prevent him from destroying me, actually, in my body.'[20] As with the fields of sophisticated tension in *Being and Nothingness*, which simultaneously unite and divide us as hostile freedoms, scarcity here, at this more primitive material level, unites and divides us: 'We are united by the fact that we all inhabit a world defined by scarcity.'[21] I, others, and the material world are melded together in a field of praxis by our several needs, by the niggardliness of nature in furnishing enough for our satisfaction, and so the structural competition in which this thrusts us with one another is inevitable. But since scarcity is contingent, this analysis permits a more hopeful attitude, at least in principle – unless the conflicts painted in *Being and Nothingness* await us when we enter the material paradise of each according to his needs, others being hell even in the classless society.

Being and Nothingness denies the possibility of a structure of a *we*, my consciousness always being *mine* – even if, perhaps necessarily if, penetrated by awareness of others. True, I can experience a *feeling* of 'we', but this alone cannot 'constitute an ontological structure of human-reality', since it is psychological rather than ontological. The 'we' is always experienced, as anything else must be, by an individual consciousness, and it is not required that those with whom I feel it should feel it in their turn, and even if they do so, even if we all feel as one and as part of a community, the feeling is distributed through our several consciousnesses and so is just a sum of individual feelings, rather than 'an inter-subjective consciousness [or] a new being which surpasses and encircles its parts as a synthetic whole'.[22] So 'being-with' – what Heidegger spoke of as *Mitsein* – is only a specialization of the structure of being-for-others. It is so whether we approach the matter from the perspective of subject or object, for Sartre recognizes a possibility that my relationship with another may acquire a certain status as an object upon the appearance of a Third who perceives us as part of the same structure, as fighters, say, or lovers: the Third sees *two* people fighting or fucking *one another*, constituting them as an 'us'. But this presupposes, Sartre says, still an individual consciousness, namely that of the Third, with whom a conflict of much the same sort as we have been discussing arises, partly based on the insistence that *us* is not a single entity but two individuals in the end sundered from one another and from the Third. So there is in Sartre a scepticism regarding the possible primacy of any kind of group life, any life that resists collapse into a constellation of individual consciousnesses in which it exists as an object – though why the consciousness of sociality does not become the sociality of consciousness never gets worked out. In any case, this becomes a matter of considerable concern to Sartre in the *Critique*, which discusses among other things the morphology of groups.

The typical group is the serial one, whose example is that of a sundry collection of persons waiting for a bus. The bus is a common object which may be said to unite them as a group, but then they perceive one another only as competitors for seats and otherwise are in a relationship of characterless indifference. Most social groups are of this order, but Sartre does speak at a certain point of *groups-in-fusion*, and supposes the mob at the storming of the Bastille might have been one. The case is exceedingly complex as analysed. The individuals are, through a common threat, fused into a common freedom. 'It is not that I am myself in the other, it is that within this praxis there is no other, there are only myself [*il y a des moi-même*].'[23] 'It is impossible to deny that it posits itself for itself . . . or, if you prefer, a new structure must be taken into account – the *group consciousness*.'[24] This is quite another matter, obviously, from the 'we-consciousness' of *Being and Nothingness*, as though the group here were the *pour-soi* writ large, existing, Sartre thinks, for itself as a group. His analysis of how the individual consciousnesses can be overcome by a group consciousness in which it nevertheless participates is exceedingly intricate, but under any circumstances the new entity is ephemeral, degenerating rapidly, and the attempt to will it into existence, or legislate it, say by the members of the group declaring through some form of oath that the group exists as a group, is futile: 'the group has not and cannot have the ontological status that it claims in its praxis'.[25]

There may be such sublime moments of togetherness, in which our apartnesses appear obliterated and transcended. Georges Sorel imagined they might be achieved through a general strike given the status of a myth. But, to paraphrase Sartre, we are dealing with something sociological rather than ontological here, and the possibility along with its rareness merely heightens a deep pessimism concerning the possibility of a genuinely moral, not to say altruistic mode of conduct towards one another. If our radical selfishness can be overcome only in moments of moral sublimity, there is very little hope indeed. But in compensation it may be said that the actual structures of ethics can hardly depend upon such unpredictable and essentially transitory phrases of trans-individuality. Morality, as Aristotle said, is made for men, and so must have application in the most ordinary circumstances of human intercourse: to base an ethics on them would be like basing our concept of cognition on experiences which happen rarely if at all.

I should like now to take up a point touched upon *en passant* in connection with abjuration under torture, for that issue connects with an extraordinary feature of Sartre's philosophy which integrates a great deal of what he has said about freedom and the responsibility one has for one's life, one's choices, and one's world. The moment of surrender, of yielding to one's body, of becoming one with the suffering it is being made to undergo, can always be postponed. I might always have held out another second, and then another. So the question of why I yielded when I did, or at all, cannot be shirked. Each of my actions could have been otherwise or forborne, and this must follow from my utter freedom. But in one respect it is correct to say that though in a deep sense I *could* have held out, I *would* not have done so. I would not because of the sort of person I am. And the sort of person I am, whether one who endures torture until death or one who confesses at the mere threat of it, thinking my skin more worth saving than that of my fellows, is altogether a matter of my having chosen to be it. This Sartre speaks of as my original choice, which is the notion I want now to describe.

Analytical philosophers concerned with the topic of human action have laid down a distinction between the causes and the reasons for an action. At times they have stated the concept of action in these terms: a piece of behaviour is not an action if it is caused; it is one only if performed for a reason, or only if it is at least relevant to ask what the person's reason was for his performance. Naturally, something can be done 'for no reason', but if this is true in a given case, the person who denies that there was a reason at least accepts the legitimacy of the question. For merely mechanical behaviour, say the breakdown of protein molecules, the question has no application: there is no reason because there could have been none, since the behaviour in question was not 'done'. In such cases, the question of why, for what reason, is conceptually ruled out. There can then be only causes. Reasons, again, can be regarded as a species of cause, and an action thought of as a performance which, if caused at all, is caused by a reason, but the connection between a reason and an action involves more than is thought to be required by ordinary causes in relation to their effects: for one thing, the reason is formulated in terms of the action it explains, where it is a mark of ordinary causes that they may be formulated without reference to their effects. This was why Hume was able to argue that causes and effects are logically independent of one another, whereas modern philosophers have been tempted to say, with some justification, though it must be carefully stated, that reasons and actions are not in this sense logically independent.

Sartre exploits something like this distinction intuitively in his discussion of freedom and action, and his argument is more or less as follows: a reason specifies what it is in the world that I mean to change by means of my action. But that objective state of affairs does not and cannot all by itself cause the action; it does so only if constituted a reason by the agent. The agent, as it were, transforms these states of affairs into causes by regarding them as reasons for action. Briefly, I determine which circumstances and events are going to explain my actions. Thus I may close the window because the noise outside is intolerable. But its being intolerable explains the action only because I found it so. And this is generally the case. The very having of reasons implies a stand outside the causal order, and involves a 'double nihilation', as Sartre says: the agent posits an ideal state of affairs which the world at this point is *not* and which itself is *not* a present reality. But the critical point is that 'no factual state . . . is capable by itself of motivating any act whatsoever . . . [and] no factual state can determine consciousness to apprehend it as a *négatité* or as a lack'.[26] So if, in the end, my actions have causes, these are such only through having been constituted causes by my mode of apprehending them, and all explanations of human action have to be filtered through the agent's way of reading the world, and not with reference to the world alone. In fact this may be supported by considering that a man may wholly misperceive the world, so that there is no objective state of affairs to explain his action. He may recoil before what he takes to be a snake but is only a serpentine stick. Still, his reason was 'to avoid getting bit', and his situation was determined by his perception of it.

So, there may be no action without a case.[27] But this, instead of supporting a universal determinism, is precisely what is required by the fact of freedom: I *make* the world such that my actions can be explained through my apprehension of it. 'There is freedom only in situation, and there is a situation only through freedom.' Consciousness lays down the conditions of its bearer's conduct.

Sartre calls this the Paradox of Freedom, but there is, if my account is correct, nothing paradoxical in it at all. The thesis combines the Principle of Sufficient Reason with the constitutive character of consciousness: each of us is free only to the extent that we determine what are to be causes of our acts. The constitution of causes is what makes choosing sensible and even logically unavoidable, but of course I have no choice as to whether, only how, to choose: I am, as Sartre characteristically puts it, condemned to be free. I am so because there is no consciousness without a world of which it is conscious, but then the way the world reveals itself to me has to be referred back to the structures of my consciousness. Or, to use another of his phrases, *I* am never the foundation of my freedom. If actions are explained with reference to the structures of freedom, freedom itself cannot be explained that way. It is the brute, primitive, given fact of my existence. I cannot choose not to choose, except within the framework of choices, where not-choosing is a kind of choice, as when I choose no one for my wife. The moment I exist I am already, and cannot escape having to be, a maker of choices. To be the foundation of my freedom would mean being able to choose to be free. And this makes no sense.

Sartre's analysis of motivation, whatever may be the consequences he draws from it, seems to me largely impeccable. We may not wish to endorse his vocabulary, e.g., that 'contingency and facticity are really one'. Or again, 'Human-reality everywhere encounters resistance and obstacles which it has not created, but these resistances and obstacles have meaning only in and through the free choice which human-reality is.'[28] But the thought behind these formulations is clear and, I believe, philosophically defensible. In terms of what he says, it follows that my place in society, my biology, and my past are not sheer determinants of my conduct, but attain an explanatory role only with reference to the interpretation I give of them. It is only verbally paradoxical of Sartre to say that we choose to be born and that we choose to die: what he means is that we choose what meaning our births and deaths happen to have for us. So it is a fair conclusion that 'I am responsible for everything, in fact, except for my very responsibility, for I am not the foundation of my being.'[29] I am, that is, responsible for all the interpreted facts. But for consciousness there are no other facts.

It must follow that no causes of actions lie outside consciousness, are *unconscious* causes. For this reason a wholly different sort of psychoanalysis is required than the sort we have learned about from Freud and his followers, who may disagree with their master in various ways and yet share with him the theory that there are hidden causes of human behaviour. Sartre proposes in its place what he calls existentialist psychoanalysis, which has choice as its core, and is one of his most fascinating innovations.

Given that something is a cause of my action only if I constitute it as such, is there no further explanation of why I constitute *it* as a cause and in just the way I do constitute it? Could I not have constituted other things as causes of my actions, structured the world differently, live quite different possibilities out? To be sure, we have invoked the idea that freedom is freedom, and has no 'foundation'. Still, one's schedule of choices is not chaotic and utterly unpredictable. We know about one another and often a man knows about himself the sorts of choices he will make, that *given* a choice he will go one way rather than another. How are we to account for this? It has always been an obsession of Sartre's to have an answer to this sort of question. A favourite case of his has been Flaubert: 'Why,' he asks, 'does Flaubert turn to writing rather than to painting or music for . . . symbolic satisfaction?'[30] The question is posed over and over again in Sartre's writings, and it gets a massive concrete answer in his last study of Flaubert, whose life, he feels, like every life, is a permeating order. 'This book,' he writes in the preface to *L'Idiot de la famille*, 'seeks to prove that . . . each bit of information put in its place becomes the portion of a whole which does not cease to work itself out and, at the same time, reveals a deep homogeneity with every other one.'[31] But our concern is less with specific answers to such specific questions than with the philosophical principle that underlies the legitimacy of all such questions. Sartre's objection to Freud and to Marx is that they fail in principle to enable us to understand why just *this* man or woman responded in just *this* way to the supposedly common Oedipal situation or class condition, the individual being swamped by the general theory. Unless a theory of human beings allows for this utter degree of individualization, it is incomplete or even inconsistent with the basic structures of its basic subjects – individual persons. We need, then, specific answers to specific questions, and a kind of 'veritable irreducible'. But more than just a very detailed description is needed: we want to understand why he is who he is and his world what *it* is; the form of answer to this, and that which gives a unity to someone's entire life, is what Sartre speaks of as the *ultimate project* of the individual in question.

The concept of the ultimate project has a complex metaphysical task to perform, which goes far beyond the theoretical enfranchisement of the sorts of biographies Sartre has devoted himself to in one dimension of his literary life: it plays something like the role the soul plays in traditional schemes, accounting for the unity of a person from stage to stage of his life. Sartre, of course, would repudiate the notion of a soul as an underlying and inalterable substrate on which biographical events are hung like laundry on a line. But still, a person is a totality, the bits of his life belong together, penetrating one another the way we saw the qualities of a thing to do, and the original project is the principle of this unity, as the *thing* is the principle of the series of it interbleeding appearances, in each of which it is wholly manifest. He is not just a series of discrete episodes, as Hume came close to believing: 'in each inclination, in each tendency the person expresses himself completely'.[32] So each act and gesture holds, if we can read it, the key to all the others. But this, even if true, represents the position of the outsider to a life, that of the biographer or historian, and the question we must consider has instead to do with the *lived* unity which is externally presented as a totality. In invoking the notion of an original project here, we are invoking something which, however different in many ways, is after all not so remarkably different from a soul.

Let us work this out, using one of Sartre's best examples. A man is out hiking with friends. At a certain point, he throws himself on the ground from exhaustion: he can walk no farther. None of his comrades do this, though they have about the same physical shape and muscular endowment as he, and they have hiked just as far. Why should he have chosen just now to find his fatigue unbearable? They have chosen it as something to be borne and want to press ahead to the camp. These diverging choices, Sartre argues, have to be explained 'within the perspective of a larger choice in which [they] would be integrated as a secondary structure'. Their choice, like that of their comrade on the ground, is emblematic of the way they have chosen to live their lives. A man who abandons himself to fatigue is going to be a self-indulgent person, treating himself 'to a thousand little passing gluttonies, to a thousand little desires, a thousand little weaknesses'.[33] The point is perfectly general: there are no isolated symptoms, even in psychoanalysis, only signs of a 'free and global project' which the analyst has to bring to the surface, as it were, before he can tell what anything means. 'I choose myself as a whole in a world which is a whole.'[34]

In *Morts sans sépulture*, a group of captured *maquisards* are questioned one by one, and each ponders whether he will be able to endure the torture he knows awaits him. In the end, not talking becomes more important than keeping their secret, winning out against their captors more important than not betraying their comrades. One of them wonders how he will hold up, feeling he does not know *himself* as a self until he sees how he comes through this extreme trial. He cries out, he would tell anything he knew: 'And now I know myself,' he says. His friends remonstrate with him. 'We are not made to live always at the limits of ourselves,' one of them says, wisely enough. Most of us would agree. Most of us would say that what we know is just that we would break under torture: and why should this be the *real* us? But if Sartre is right, this is too reassuring. The episode is never so extreme that we could not have known it would happen as it did happen, that it is one with the whole of life as we have lived it. To be sure, some men are lucky and die in their beds – 'Cowards like me without ever knowing they are.' Extremity reveals a pattern that was always there to be seen, probably even in the way and order in which a man tied his shoes.

Our basic freedom, then, lies less in our power to choose than to *choose* to choose, in the respect that the primal and original choice determines a *style* of choosing, and the style is the man himself, as Buffon said. Choosing to choose does *not* mean that each act of will requires a separate act of will to get it moving; for that would lead to an infinite regression. But still, there is no freedom, Sartre feels, unless we are free in this higher-order mode, choosing in such a way as to define our lives. This concept, needless to say, raises a large class of difficult questions. The past, for example, was exactly to have no constraint upon the present – unless I choose my past, making (consistent with the analysis just worked out) certain episodes of my past causally relevant to my present and future. So how can an original choice as a datable historical episode continue to determine my choices *now*? And does 'original' mean 'earlier in time' or merely 'more basic than' some present choice? Sartre seems to have supposed the first as well as the second, seeking out that *moment* in the life of Baudelaire or Genet or Flaubert when the die was cast, the mould formed for everything that followed. That is what existential analysis comes to. But there may be another answer, though I offer it diffidently. It is that in each choice I do more than choose a specific course of action; rather, I choose a style of choosing. So the original choice is made in every choice. For choosings, let us remember, are not serially ordered isolated episodes. With each choice I am integrating all previous choices into a totality. I am, then, not just choosing to take the bus instead of walking: I am choosing the sort of man I am and the sort of life I have and the sort of world I live in. My responsibilities are *enormous*. As much so as God's. If every choice is an original choice, there are no gratuitous or meaningless acts. And since at each instant I am choosing a world, the world that is mine is up to me.

This view requires immense philosophical elaboration, which it goes beyond the limits of these reflections to pursue. But it plainly has an implication for moral conduct: namely, that we are not to evaluate an action in its own right and alone but only as an ingredient in a tapestry of choices that total up to an entire life – as though there were an implicit, almost categorical imperative binding upon us at every moment, to so choose that the form of life the choice implies is one we would be willing to live always. The question always before us is what sort of person we are making of ourselves.

Notes

1. Friedrich Nietzsche, *The Gay Science*, V.
2. *Being and Nothingness*, p. 339.
3. ibid., p. 233.
4. ibid., p. 340.
5. ibid., p. 254.
6. ibid.
7. ibid., p. 260.
8. ibid., p. 261.
9. ibid., p. 265.
10. ibid., p. 364.
11. ibid., p. 366.
12. ibid., pp. 376–7.
13. ibid., p. 399.
14. ibid., p. 400.
15. ibid., p. 401.
16. ibid., p. 404.
17. R. D. Cumming, *The Philosophy of Jean-Paul Sartre*, p. 436. As the *Critique de la raison dialectique* has not been completely translated, I refer to the translations in Cumming's anthology, except for the item in note 23, which he has not included.
18. ibid.
19. ibid., p. 438.
20. ibid., p. 442.
21. ibid., p. 445.
22. *Being and Nothingness*, p. 414.
23. *Critique de la raison dialectique*, p. 420.
24. Cumming, op. cit., p. 473.
25. ibid., p. 445.
26. *Being and Nothingness*, pp. 435–6.
27. ibid., p. 489.
28. ibid., pp. 486, 489.
29. ibid., p. 555.
30. ibid., p. 559.
31. *L'Idiot de la famille*, p. 1.
32. *Being and Nothingness*, p. 563.
33. ibid., pp. 455, 456.
34. ibid., p. 461.

Biographical Note

Arthur Danto is Johnsonian Professor of Philosophy at Columbia University and chairman of the philosophy department. He has taught at Columbia since 1951 and been a visiting professor at Princeton, Pennsylvania, San Diego, the Catholic University and elsewhere. He was Fullbright Distinguished Professor in Yugoslavia in 1976. His books, as well as *Jean-Paul Sartre*, include *Analytical Philosophy of History* (1965), *Nietzsche as Philosopher* (1965, 1980), *What Philosophy Is* (1968), *Analytical Philosophy of Knowledge* (1968), *Mysticism and Morality* (1972), *Analytical Philosophy of Action* (1973) and *The Transfiguration of the Commonplace* (1981). He is a Fellow of the American Academy of Arts and Sciences.

Further Reading

Translations: *Being and Nothingness*, trans. Hazel Barnes (New York: Philosophical Library, 1956); *Nausea*, trans. Lloyd Alexander (Norfolk, Conn.: New Directions, no date); *Critique of Dialectical Reason*, trans. Alan Sheridan-Smith (London: New Left Books, 1976); *No Exit*, trans. Stuart Gilbert (New York: Knopf, 1946).

Critical works: Peter Caws, *Sartre* (London: Routledge & Kegan Paul, 1979); Robert Cumming, *The Philosophy of Jean-Paul Sartre* (New York: Random House, 1965).

MORE ABOUT PENGUINS, PELICANS
AND PUFFINS

A companion volume, published in Pelicans

PHILOSOPHY AS IT IS

Edited by Ted Honderich and Myles Burnyeat

Ted Honderich and Myles Burnyeat set out to fulfil four aims: to represent philosophy as it is; to represent it through clear, non-technical essays; to represent recent developments in philosophy; to give the reader in an introduction to each essay an admirably lucid resumé of its arguments. Where the essays become difficult the editors say so, but in most cases the general reader will find that, among others, Bernard Williams on Utilitarianism and moral integrity, Richard Wollheim on art as a form of life, A. J. Ayer on perception and the physical world, Donald Davidson on mental events, Saul Kripke on identity and necessity and Alvin Plantinga on God, freedom and evil, offer a welcome, but not insuperable, challenge.

Contributors to this volume are:

A. J. AYER

DONALD DAVIDSON

PHILIPPA FOOT

STUART HAMPSHIRE

TED HONDERICH

SAUL KRIPKE

J. L. MACKIE

ROBERT NOZICK

DEREK PARFIT

ALVIN PLANTINGA

HILARY PUTNAM

JOHN RAWLS

ROBERT STALNAKER

P. F. STRAWSON

GABRIELE TAYLOR

BERNARD WILLIAMS

RICHARD WOLLHEIM

VIOLENCE FOR EQUALITY
Inquiries into Political Philosophy

Ted Honderich

Is political violence justifiable?

With force and elegant reasoning, Ted Honderich questions the morality of political violence and challenges the presuppositions, inconsistencies and prejudices of liberal-democratic thinking.

For this volume, the author has revised and greatly enlarged his highly praised *Three Essays on Political Violence*. The five essays which go to make up *Violence for Equality*, given as political philosophy lectures in Britain, Ireland, the United States, Canada, France, Africa and Holland, in fact comprise a completed treatise on the subject.

Reviewers' comments on *Three Essays on Political Violence*:

'Very good, very original . . . enormous merit . . . should be examined and re-examined by anyone interested not only in philosophy, but in the ordinary discourse of politics' – *Listener*

'Clear, rational and continuously interesting' – *New Statesman*

'Inherent interest and importance' – *The Times Higher Education Supplement*

'Masterful argument' – *The Times Literary Supplement*

THE PROBLEM OF KNOWLEDGE

A. J. Ayer

What is knowledge, and how do we *know* things? Moreover, how do we know that we know them, in view of the doubts that the philosophic sceptic casts on our grasp of facts? The presentation of the sceptic's arguments leads here to a general discussion of the topic of scepticism and certainty. This is followed by a detailed examination of the philosophical problems of perception, memory, and our knowledge of other minds, which occupies the greater part of the book. In the course of the discussion Professor A. J. Ayer has also attempted to throw light upon the nature of the philosophical method and upon some of the problems connected with time, causality, and personal identity.

AQUINAS

F. C. Copleston

Aquinas (1224/5–1274) lived at a time when the Christian West had recently become acquainted with a wealth of Greek and Islamic philosophical analysis and speculation. To some minds Greek philosophy, particularly Aristotelianism, appeared to constitute a naturalistic menace to the integrity of the Christian faith. But Aquinas is remarkable for the way in which he used and developed the legacy of ancient thought, which made his contemporaries regard him as an advanced thinker. He embodies the thirteenth-century ideal to have a unified interpretation of reality, in which philosophy and theology play their distinct parts in harmony and not in opposition. Whether this is an outmoded ideal or the form taken at a particular time by an ideal which possesses lasting value is one of the questions discussed by Father Copleston.

Aquinas' thought is of more than historical interest. There is a large group of contemporary philosophers, the Thomists, who draw inspiration from his writings. Indeed, strange as it may sound, his influence is greater today than it was during the Middle Ages. This book attempts to explain Aquinas' philosophical ideas in a way which can be understood by those who are unacquainted with medieval thought. And where possible, it relates these ideas to problems as discussed today. In a final chapter something is said about the development of Thomism in modern times.

DESCARTES: THE PROJECT OF PURE ENQUIRY

Bernard Williams

'Excellent' – *The Times Educational Supplement*

'His biographical digest is as succinct as his philosophical analysis is thorough' – *Sunday Times*

Descartes has often been called the 'father of modern philosophy', and justly so. His attempts to find foundations for knowledge, and to reconcile the existence of the soul with the new physical science, are among the most famous and influential examples of philosophical thought.

One of the most distinguished of modern philosophers, Bernard Williams, has written this important and comprehensive study of Descartes's thought (published here for the first time), couched in accessible and modern terms. He has tried not only to analyse Descartes's project of founding knowledge on certainty, but also to uncover the philosophical motives for this search. The project itself, the basic motives for it, and many of the ideas that Descartes used in his unsuccessful pursuit of it, are shown in a sustained argument to be fundamental to the definition of many problems in modern philosophy.

KANT

S. Körner

Immanuel Kant, who was born in 1724 and died in 1804, is by universal consent one of the greatest philosophical thinkers of the modern Western world. He combined the rare gifts of analytical acumen and constructive imagination with the still rarer gift of keeping the balance between the two. Perhaps no thinker ever influenced his successors more. Even the writings of those among them who opposed or oppose him, or who have never properly studied his work, abound in thoughts which he was the first to formulate.

This introduction offers an outline of Kant's system, one of its chief aims being to show that his problems and solutions are not merely of historical interest, but that they concern everybody who makes statements of fact and judgements of value.

'An admirable addition to a successful series. It provides what has long been needed, a clear and reliable guide to the convolutions of the Critical Philosophy in its main outlines' – *Mind*

SPINOZA

Stuart Hampshire

Spinoza is probably the most difficult of all the great philosophers to understand at first reading and without some general introduction to his methods and purposes. He is also supremely worth understanding, as one of the greatest of the metaphysicians who have tried to construct a coherent account of the universe and of man's place within it. His system embraces the whole range of the traditional problems of philosophy including the problems of a creator and his creation, the relation of mind and body, the freedom of the will, the nature and limits of human knowledge, and also the problems of moral and political philosophy of the main themes of philosophical speculation can be found in his work. This book is designed as a general introduction which explains the connections between the various aspects of Spinoza's philosophy, between his logic and his metaphysics, and again between his metaphysics and his moral and political doctrines.

'This book is a model of its kind ... Mr Hampshire's critical summary of the system is admirable: it is full, clear – or as clear as the subject allows – agreeably written, wastes no words and shirks no difficulties' – *The Times Literary Supplement*

WITTGENSTEIN

Anthony Kenny

A clear and concise account of the whole range of Wittgenstein's work in the philosophy of language and the philosophy of mind.

'Dr Kenny lays out the main elements, exposing apparent conflicts and misfits, and then, by dint of some deft shuffling of the pieces, suddenly reveals an interpretation of Wittgenstein's work that reconciles its apparently disparate elements. His achievement is an account of Wittgenstein's philosophical development which yields a persuasive picture, with minimum force, maximum ingenuity and admirable clarity' – *The Times Literary Supplement*

'A welcome appearance in paperback ... the only commentary that surveys the whole of Wittgenstein's currently available work' – *Modern Language Review*